Kiowa, Apache, and Comanche Military Societies

Enduring

Veterans,

1800 to # KIOWA,

The Present # APACHE, AND

COMANCHE

MILITARY

SOCIETIES

William C. Meadows

 University of Texas Press
Austin

Requests for permission to reproduce material from this work
should be sent to Permissions, University of Texas Press,
Box 7819, Austin, TX 78713-7819.

⊚ The paper used in this book meets the minimum requirements of
ANSI/NISO Z39.48-1992 (R1997) (Permanence of Paper for Printed
Library Materials).

Library of Congress Cataloging-in-Publication Data

Meadows, William C., 1966–
    Kiowa, Apache, and Comanche military societies : enduring
veterans, 1800 to the present / William C. Meadows. — 1st ed.
        p.   cm.
    Includes bibliographical references and index.
    ISBN 0-292-75212-1 (cloth : alk. paper)
        1. Kiowa Indians—Societies, etc.   2. Apache Indians—Societies,
etc.   3. Comanche Indians—Societies, etc.   4. Secret societies—
Great Plains.   5. Indians of North America—Great Plains—Ethnic
identity.   I. Title.
E99.K5M43   1999
305.897—dc21   98-49958

For my matrilineal *Aniyunwiya* kin: my mother, Judith A. Meadows Chandler; my grandmother, Virginia Walls Fisher; my grandfather, William E. Fisher Jr. (1916–1993); and my great-grandfather, John David Walls (1880–1976), whose knowledge, wisdom, love, and support guided me toward my destiny. And for my Kiowa mother, Vanessa Paukeigope (Struck the Enemy In the River) Jennings, without whom this work could not have been accomplished.

Photo credits: Apache Sam Klinekole holding Manatidie staff, *photo by Gilbert McAllister, courtesy of Mike Davis; Gonkoncheyhastayyah* or Apache John holding Manatidie staff, *photo courtesy of William Hammond Mathers Museum, Indiana University, Wanamaker Collection, #W1658;* Chebatah, Comanche Big Horse Society whipman, *photo courtesy of Phillip Narcomey;* Comanche World War I veterans being honored, *photo courtesy of Phillip Narcomey;* Rolling Pony and wife, *photo courtesy of Western History Collections, University of Oklahoma;* all other photos are the author's. Material from *The Indians of Texas in 1830* by Jean Louis Berlandier, edited by John C. Ewers, published by the Smithsonian Institution Press, Washington, D.C.

CONTENTS

ILLUSTRATIONS (following p. xx)

Kiowa women's Scalp Dance, Black Legs Society Dance, Anadarko, Oklahoma, 1994.

Kiowa Black Legs Society parading in Anadarko, Oklahoma, 1994.

Kiowa Black Legs Soceity parading in Anadarko, Oklahoma, 1993.

Kiowa Black Legs Society Turn-around or Reverse Dance, Anadarko, Oklahoma, 1994.

Kiowa Ohoma Lodge Pipe Dance, Anadarko, Oklahoma, 1995.

Kiowa naming ceremony, Kiowa Black Legs Society Dance, 1992.

Apache Sam Klinekole holding Archilta's Manatidie staff, 1934.

Gonkoncheyhastayyah (Man Over His Camp or Man Guarding His Camp) or Apache John, holding wooden Manatidie Society whip in 1909.

Redbone Society Honor Dance, Apache Tribal Dance Grounds, Fort Cobb, Oklahoma, 1993.

Apache Tribe Veteran Association Marker.

Apache Tribe of Oklahoma tribal license plate depicting Manatidie staffs and dancers.

Four Manatidie Society dancers, 1993.

Chebatah (Lipan Apache), a Comanche Big Horse Society whipman, ca. 1930.

Comanche World War I veterans being honored by Comanche elders, ca. 1919.

Food baskets about to be given away, Comanche War Dance Society, Cache, Oklahoma.

Rolling Pony (Manatidie whipman and Kiowa Agency policeman) and wife, 1900.

TABLES

PREFACE

When I began working with the Kiowa in 1989, I was interested in traditional dance and music, particularly in the origins of the modern powwow. This led me into the world of Plains Indian military societies. I was introduced to the Kiowa Black Legs Society, on which I eventually wrote my master's thesis (Meadows 1991). As I began to comprehend the vast historical and symbolic importance which this society holds for the Kiowa people, I began to look at other Kiowa and, later, Comanche, Apache, and Cheyenne societies. Though they are qualitatively different, I found great general and temporal similarity in the structure, functions, and continuing symbolic importance of veterans within these communities. Even more importantly, however, I began to comprehend the extent to which traditional sociocultural forms were being associated with traditional ways of honoring veterans through public dance, song, and ceremony to commemorate the past and present martial heritage, ideology, and ethos. While some prereservation cultural elements had been lost and new ones adapted, much had survived, and other forms had even been revived through the social arena of martial-based cultural events. As other social institutions in these cultures declined in their enculturative roles, Southern Plains Indian military society events continued to provide arenas for enculturation and even increased in complexity.

This study of Southern Plains military societies delineates comparatively and ethnohistorically the martial values embraced by the Kiowa, Comanche, and Apache (KCA) since circa 1800, describing how military society structure, functions, and ritual symbols connect past and present. In contrast to most ethnographic religious studies, I combine ethnohistorical documentation and oral traditions with symbolic analysis to elucidate the temporal evolution and role of these more secular sodalities and their symbols, focusing upon the continuity and change, meaning, and functions of martial symbols. While Plains Indian sodalities were not homogenous, they are central to understanding past and present Plains social organization, law, politics, warfare, and religion. Individual tribal histories cover four periods: preservation (pre-1875), reservation (1875–1900), postreservation (1901–1945), and post–World War II or contemporary (1945 to the present).

Larger patterns of social change and development applicable to other external populations are also discussed. Despite change and cultural syncretism, traditional views and concepts regarding veterans remain largely intact. These cultures had strong warrior traditions and a strong martial ethos in which military societies were the largest form of prereservation sodalities. Because they never relinquished the ideology surrounding the role of the warrior, these groups were able to regain status in their own terms as warriors with widespread participation in World War II. The traditional roles, symbols, and warrior ethos of these military society systems continue via military societies. While these societies and their associated ideology were formerly adaptive in fostering social order, integration, defense, and competitiveness, they continue to serve as an important vehicle for traditional enculturation today, as demonstrated by their adaptive significance for the preservation and maintenance of ethnic identity in a larger socioeconomic and politically encapsulating society.

This study demonstrates the extent and variety of relationships between Plains military societies and their tribal-level social organization, which have been inadequately documented and investigated. I hope that it will fill a gap in the ethnological picture, while demonstrating that a critical revaluation of these societies is necessary to understand their role in Plains Indian social organization. This study also develops a set of more clearly defined military society characteristics which can be used to describe Southern Plains societies and compare others cross-culturally. While some functions and material culture have been examined (Wissler 1916b), this study looks at other organizational and social features.

Furthermore, I want this work to be useful for the Native American communities which participated in its making, as well as for the anthropological community. Many ethnographies today present only data which are needed to support the larger theoretical points of the scholar and offer little for the native community. During my fieldwork, members of several tribes often stated that many recent works on their respective tribes were "of no value to us," "had no practical use," were "too technical and too scientific to understand," and "included hardly any of the material which we worked so hard and long to provide them." One of the ethnohistorian's strongest commitments is to publish primary data. There is a growing interest in cultural awareness among many native peoples who are actively trying to research, document, preserve, and revive elements of their culture. During my fieldwork, many military society leaders and elders expressed concerns that these data be published as completely as possible to help them document and preserve their military societies. I am seeking a middle ground between the ethnography of old and the academic theoretical concerns of today, by providing solid descriptive accounts for each group, while also addressing anthropological concerns. To have deleted much of this material would have eliminated crucial elements such as regalia, song texts, and dance choreography, which describe and convey many of the ongoing symbols and ideology of these groups. A sound ethnographic description can make the results accessible to the native communities involved, better support their claims, and allow the reader to examine and critique the material on which my arguments are based. Raising the issue of practicality in current ethnohistory, many native peoples ask, "What's in it for us?" If scholars wish to continue to work in various communities they need to make the published results more rewarding for the individuals upon whom such work depends—the native community—for without their hospitality research opportunities become limited and more archival in nature. Part of this involves making the consultants active participants in the research process.

This study is primarily aimed at defining military societies on a regional level and then comparatively analyzing their interactions concerning various levels of symbolic and social organization and integration. Throughout the immense changes Plains Indian communities have experienced over the last two centuries, a large part of their social structure and fabric has remained. Much of the ideology and ethos associated with traditional veterans in these communities has also remained. As we shall see, these veterans have indeed endured.

ACKNOWLEDGMENTS

I would like to offer my extreme gratitude to many individuals for helping contribute to this text, which is the culmination of nearly eight years' work. Foremost, I offer my appreciation to all those individuals in the Kiowa, Comanche, Apache Tribe of Oklahoma and Southern Cheyenne Indian communities discussed in this work, who have all contributed in some fashion. Their knowledge, insights, patience, and willingness to contribute, to teach, and to preserve have allowed me to complete this undertaking. *Kiowas:* Gus Palmer Sr., Dr. Parker P. McKenzie, Mac Whitehorse, Oscar Tsoodle, Atwater Onco, David Paddlety, Bill Koomsa Jr., Billy Evans Horse, Dixon Palmer, Rueban Topaum, Gabe and Seth Morgan, Blas Preciado, Alice Littleman, Grace Tsonetokoy, Gertrude Yeahquo Hines, Vanessa Santos Jennings, Martha Poolaw, Anne Yeahquo, and others. I offer special thanks to those who died prior to the completion of this work: Harding Big Bow, Harry Domebo, Victor Paddlety, the Reverend George Saumpty, Laura Sankadota Tahlo, Weiser Tongkeamha, Francis Tsonetokoy, John Emhoola Sr., Ernest Chanate Sr., Hattie Tsoodle, and Joyce Auchiah Daingkau. A special thank you to the Kiowa Black Legs Society, the Kiowa Ohoma Lodge, the Kiowa Gourd Clan, the Kiowa Tia-Piah Society, and the Kiowa Warriors Descendants. *Apaches:* Alfred Chalepah Sr., the late Houston Klinekole Sr., Alonzo Chalepah, Irene Chalepah Poolaw, Wallace Redbone, and the Chalepah and Redbone Blackfeet Societies. *Comanches:* Carney Saupitty Sr., Charles Chibitty, the late Roderick Redelk, June Sovo, Hammond Motah, Jack Codopony, Vann Codynah, Melvin Kerchee Sr., the late Forrest Kassanavoid, and the late Ed Yellowfish. Special thanks to the Comanche Little Ponies, the Comanche *Tuhwi* Society, the Comanche Indian Veterans Association (CIVA) and the Comanche War Dance Society. *Cheyennes:* Eugene Black Bear Jr., Roy Dean Bull Coming, Catharine Bull Coming, and Lance Allrunner.

I am very grateful to Hammond Motah and Sherry Tofpi, who provided me with a residence in 1990, and to Vanessa Santos Jennings, who has provided me with a periodic residence from 1990 to the present, which has allowed me to interact with the KCA communities for several years. A special thank you to my uncle Parker McKenzie for help and insights concerning Kiowa language, names, songs, and military society terminology, Àhô Sègî. I would also like to thank Gus Palmer Sr., Alfred Chalepah, and the late Forrest Kassanavoid for sharing their time and extensive knowledge and the late Ed Yellowfish for sharing vital cultural knowledge and for inducting me into the Comanche Little Ponies Society. Many elders expressed the wish that this work would help them preserve portions of their culture for future generations. I hope that I have succeeded in this endeavor. Many other individuals extended various forms of aid and courtesy during my research, and I offer my heartfelt appreciation. I would also like to thank the Kiowa, Comanche, and Apache elders and society leaders who read and commented on drafts of this work.

I offer a sincere thank you to Ray DeMallie, Tom Kavanagh, Jerrold Levy, William Bittle, and the late Demitri Shimkin and Gilbert J. McAllister. Ben Kracht graciously shared his copy of the 1935 Santa Fe Kiowa fieldnotes and Kiowa Agency Papers. Mike Davis, Dan Gelo, Ross Hassig, Thomas Kavanagh, and Eric Lassiter provided valuable comments upon drafts of this manuscript. Maurice Boyd shared his experiences in compiling the two volumes of *Kiowa Voices*. I would also like to thank Towana Spivey and Judy Crowder of the Fort Sill Museum Archives, John Lovitt of the Western History Collection at the University of Oklahoma, Candace Greene of the Smithsonian Institution, and the staffs of the National Anthropological Archives (Smithsonian Institution), Chicago Field Museum, University of Oklahoma Western History Collections, Norman, and Oklahoma State Historical Archives. I express my thanks to my dissertation committee and am especially grateful for the academic guidance and encouragement from John H. Moore and Ross Hassig. A one-week fellowship from the Smithsonian Institution (1991) and field research grants from the American Philosophical Society (1993) and the Jacobs Research Fund of the Whatcom Museum Society (1995) provided essential research aid. Finally, I am most grateful to Theresa May, Kathy Lewis, and Jean Lee Cole at the University of Texas Press.

PRONUNCIATION GUIDE
The Parker McKenzie Kiowa Language Orthography

Having been developed over ninety years of formation and standardization, the McKenzie orthography is the most accurate and exacting orthography for pronouncing and writing Kiowa to date. Parker McKenzie's comprehensive linguistic contributions rival those of Seqyoyah, being the second known orthography devised by a tribal member for his own language. Combining the skills of a linguist with the insights of a native speaker who learned English as a second language, McKenzie has been able to incorporate numerous insights from both native speaker and academic perspectives.

In the McKenzie orthography, there are twenty-two consonants, one more than in English. Fourteen of these consonants are relatively the same when voiced with vocals as their English counterparts: *B, D, G, H, K, L, M, N, P, S, T, W, Y, Z*. The remaining seven English consonants—*C, F, J, Q, R, V, X*—do not resemble any of the Kiowa consonants. The consonants *K, P, S*, and *T* each have two related variants in Kiowa for which English has no counterparts. To fulfill the void, digraphs were devised for each of the first variants and trigraphs for each of the second variants, with English symbols that somewhat match the Kiowa consonants: *GK* and *KCH*, respectively, for the first variant and for the second variant of *K*; *DT* and *THD*, respectively, for *T*, etc.

McKenzie realized that because the English consonants *C, F, J, Q, R, V*, and *X* do not occur in Kiowa they could feasibly replace his multiple symbols, rather than letting these English letters go unused. Consequently, *C* and *Q* became the respective Kiowa variants of *K; F* and *V* of *P;* digraph *CH* and *X* of *S;* and *J* and digraph *TH* of *T*. Since no other English symbol remains for adaptation, the digraph *TH* was devised to represent the second variant of *T*.

KIOWA CONSONANTS

B, D, G, H, K, C, Q, L, M, N, P, F, V, S, CH, X, T, J, TH, W, Y, Z

Kiowa Consonantal Variations

Kiowa	K			P			S			T		
1. McKenzie	K	C	Q	P	F	V	S	CH	X	T	J	TH
2. Watkins (1984)	Kh	K	K'	Ph	P	P'	S	C	C'	Th	T	T'
3. S.I.L.	Kh	K	K'	PH	P	P'	S	TS	TS'	TH	T	T'
4. Harrington (1928)	K'	K	K	P'	P	P	S	TS	TS	T'	T	T
5. Mooney (1898)	K	*	K'	P	*	P'	S	*	TS	T	*	T'

The first and second variants of each of the four consonants *K, P, S,* and *T* are respectively "soft" and "plosive," or like a regular English *P*, a soft English *P*, and an explosive English *P*. Thus, the three variants of the consonant *P* would be páu (male bison bull), a regular *P*; fáulkàu (drums), a soft *P*; and vǎu (moon), an explosive *P*. The regular, soft, and explosive pronunciations are likewise added to *K, C,* and *Q*; *S, CH,* and *X*; and *T, J,* and *TH*, respectively.

KIOWA VOWELS AND ENGLISH PRONUNCIATION COUNTERPARTS IN PARENTHESES

E (ay), *A* (ah), *AU* (aw), *I* (ee), *O* (oh), *U* (woo)

The Kiowa vowel system was developed along with the consonantal system without difficulty because the six Kiowa vowels sound relatively like their English counterparts, except that the Kiowa vowel *A* (ah) falls midway in sound between the *A* in the words "act" and "are." The vowels are *E* (ay), *A* (ah), *AU* (aw), *I* (ee), *O* (oh), *U* (woo), with their appropriate English sounds shown in parentheses.

KIOWA DIPHTHONGS

AI (ah-ee), *AUI* (aw-ee), *OI* (oh-ee), *UI* (woo-ee)

The four Kiowa diphthongs are *AI* (ah-ee), *AUI* (aw-ee), *OI* (oh-ee), and *UI* (woo-ee), with the vowel *I* (ee) serving as the second element and the elements being rendered in the same voice impulse.

The vowel *U* occurs in Kiowa syllables *only* after the consonants *G, K, C,*

Q; in every instance of its occurrence, the *W*-sound *always* falls before it when the syllables are voiced, but it is arbitrarily omitted when the syllables are written: e.g., *GU* (gwoo), *GUI* (gwoo-ee), *KU* (kwoo), *KUI* (kwoo-ee), *CU* (cwoo), *CUI* (cwoo-ee), *QU* (qwoo), *QUI* (qwoo-ee). The consonants *L*, *M, N, P,* and *T* are the only syllable-ending elements of the twenty-two Kiowa consonants, with *S* occurring as such in only two exclamatory terms: a-jos and wis-je. The consonant *K* also occurs occasionally with some speakers as a substitute syllable-ending terminal for *P* or *T,* but since the usage is considered nonbasic, it is relegated to faulty speech. Within syllables, the six Kiowa vowels may properly terminate with any of the five basic terminating consonants, but the four Kiowa diphthongs cannot. No double consonants occur within syllables (as in the English "call," "glass," etc.).

Somewhat analogous to the *W*-containing syllables are ones which also open with consonants *G, K, C, Q,* but are followed with vowel elements *A* (ah) and *AI* (ah-ee) where *Y* falls between, as *W* does, to form syllables *GYAH, GYAH-EE, KYAH, KYAH-EE, CHAH, CHAH-EE, QUAH, QUAH-EE.* The *Y*-sound is retained (like *W*) when the syllables are voiced, but it is omitted in written Kiowa, just as *W* is omitted. In this instance, however, there are very few exclamatory terms, a number of words from foreign sources, and an infrequent occurrence of Kiowa contractions that equate to "isn't," "don't," "here's," etc., that occur *without* the *Y*-sound. The absence of *Y* in such cases is indicated with the apostrophe; e.g., ac'a (not *ah-cyah*), and C'aiwau (not *Cyah-ee-wau*), the Comanche rendering of "Kiowa." Incidentally, *W* is very rare as an independent consonant in Kiowa, whereas *Y* is quite prevalent.

The three English *As* (ā, ă, ä) are rendered in Kiowa with the specific vowels *E* (ah), *A* (ah), *AU* (aw). The English *I* is assigned to Kiowa *I* (ee); *O* to Kiowa *O* (oh), and *U* to Kiowa *U* (woo). Therefore, there is only one basic sound for each of the six Kiowa vowels: *E* is always *AY; A,* always *AH; AU,* always *AW; I,* always *EE; O,* always *OH;* and *U,* always *WOO.* These as well as their kindred diphthongs are affected in varying frequency by nasalization, vowel quantity or length, and pitch accent or accentuation without veering from their respective basic sounds.

Pitch

Because Kiowa is a tonal language, pronunciation pitch is involved and is essential in conveying meaning. Nasalization is indicated with the underscore (a̠); vowel quantity or length with the overscore or macron (ā); pitch accent is indicated with the grave mark (à) and acute mark (á), which are otherwise referred to as "low" and "high" pitch, respectively, and the rising-falling voice effect is indicated with the conventional circumflex mark (â). All of the ten tonal effects are shown below for vowel *A* (ah) and diphthong *OI* (oh-ee) with various diacritical marks to make clear how they are applied for exact pronunciation of words, because a word form bearing the same spelling may have as many as five, six, or even seven different definitions according to the pronouncing pattern of each. Since there are ten vowel elements in Kiowa and each syllable bears ten different pronouncing patterns, the Kiowa language has one hundred tonal effects (pronouncing patterns) that occur with varying frequency for every two-syllable word and so on.

TEN KIOWA PRONUNCIATION PATTERNS FOR MONOSYLLABLES

à á à̲ á̲ â a̲ á̲ à̲ á̲ â̲

SPELLING

One does not need to learn the spelling of Kiowa words as one has to in English because Kiowa is almost totally phonetic (as in the McKenzie orthography), but one must learn the pronunciation of syllables, a task that is as arduous as spelling is in English. The same pronunciation of an English word often carries several definitions (as with a homonym), whereas in Kiowa a word form spelled the same way may have four, five, or as many as seven different definitions according to the pronouncing pattern. Accordingly, English spelling of words letter by letter is tantamount to Kiowa "spelling" (learning the pronunciation of syllables that derive from the same word form).

When compared with earlier works involving the Kiowa language, the McKenzie system is the most comprehensive, accurate, easily read, and easily written system.

Kiowa women's Scalp Dance, Black Legs Society Dance, Anadarko, Oklahoma, 1994. Vanessa Jennings in front.

Kiowa Black Legs Society parading in Anadarko, Oklahoma, 1994.

Kiowa Black Legs Society parading in Anadarko, Oklahoma, 1993.

Kiowa Black Legs Society turn-around or reverse dance, Anadarko, Oklahoma, 1994.

Kiowa Ohoma Lodge Pipe Dance, Anadarko, Oklahoma, 1995.

Kiowa naming ceremony, Kiowa Black Legs Society Dance, 1992.

Apache Sam Klinekole holding Archilta's Manatidie staff, 1934.

Gonkoncheyhastayyah (Man Over His Camp or Man Guarding His Camp) or Apache John, holding wooden Manatidie Society whip in 1909.

Redbone Society Honor Dance, Apache Tribal Dance Grounds, Fort Cobb, Oklahoma, 1993.

APACHE TRIBE VETERAN ASSOCIATION
MEMBERS
DEDICATED NOV. 11, 1992

ALVIN ARCHILTA
CLIFFORD ARCHILTA
HAROLD ARCHILTA
LOUIS ARCHILTA
RICHARD BANDERAS
ANTHONY BITSEEDY
NATHANIEL BITSEEDY
OPHELIA BITSEEDY
THOMAS BITSEEDY JR
THOMAS BITSEEDY SR
BIZARRALTA
GLEN ALLEN BOYD
RAFAEL BOVIDDLE
SILAS BOVIDDLE
STANLEY BOVIDDLE
ALFRED CHALEPAH JR
ANTHONY NEAL CHALEPAH
CLARENCE CHALEPAH SR
DAVID LEE CHALEPAH
FRANCES LEE CHALEPAH SR
LEONARD R. CHALEPAH
MICHAEL CHALEPAH
RAYMOND CHALEPAH III
RAYMOND CHALEPAH JR
RICHARD CHALEPAH
RICHIE DEAN CHALEPAH
DAVID CHARCOAL
ALLEN FLUTE
DAVID FLUTE
GENE FLUTE
HOMER FLUTE
TOM FLUTE JR
ROGER FLUTE
JERRY HIGH
WEBSTER HIGH
ELMER R. JAY
BOBBY JAY
MOSES JAY
BRUCE KAUDLEKAULE
HARRY KAUDLEKAULE
SAM KAUDLEKAULE
AUSTIN KLINEKOLE
BRUCE KLINEKOLE
GEORGE KLINEKOLE
GLENDAL KLINEKOLE
HOUSTON KLINEKOLE
HOUSTON KLINEKOLE SR
WILLIAM KLINEKOLE
CARTER KOMARDLEY
GEORGE KOMARDLEY
HENRY KOSTZUTA

KENNY LOOKINGGLASS
LUCIEN J. LOOKINGGLASS
RICHARD MAYNAHONAH
BILL NESTELL
BRUCE NESTELL
CURTIS NESTELL
DON NESTELL SR.
PAUL NESTELL
STRATFORD NESTELL
TIMOTHY NESTELL
CORY NIMSEY
GEARY NIMSEY
GERALD NIMSEY
GERALD NIMSEY JR.
JAMES NIMSEY JR
LEROY NIMSEY
ROCKY PACE JR.
AMOS R. PEWENOFKIT
JEROME PEWENOFKIT
DONALD R POOLAW
LESTER GENE POOLAW
LINDY WAYNE POOLAW
PASCAL CLEATUS POOLAW JR.
GEORGE QUETONE
DENNIS REDBONE (TSELEE)
FRANK REDBONE (TSELEE)
HERBERT REDBONE (TSELEE)
HUGH REDBONE (TSELEE)
NATHAN REDBONE (TSELEE)
NATHAN W. REDBONE (TSELEE)
WALLACE REDBONE (TSELEE)
MARVIN SADDLEBLANKET
FLOY MARIA SHINGULT
HOWARD SOONTAY JR
HOWARD SOONTAY SR
RICHARD SOONTAY
ROBERT SOONTAY
RALPH SPOTTEDCROW
GEORGE D. STARR
ELTON STUMBLINGBEAR
RICHARD SUNRISE
PHILEMON TSELEE
PATRICK TOAHTIGH
TIMOTHY TOAHTICH
ARNOLD WETSELLINE
BARRY A. WETSELLINE
KENNETH B WETSELLINE
PHILLIP M WETSELLINE
TERRY L. WETSELLINE
JANET WILLIAMS
MARKIE WILLIAMS
PHILIP KILSFIRST SR.

Apache Tribe Veteran Association Marker. Apache Tribe of Oklahoma Tribal Complex, Anadarko, Oklahoma.

Apache Tribe of Oklahoma tribal license plate depicting Manatidie staffs and dancers.

Four Manatidie Society dancers, 1993.

Chebatah (Lipan Apache), a Comanche Big Horse Society whipman, ca. 1930.

Comanche World War I veterans being honored by Comanche elders, ca. 1919.

Food baskets about to be given away, Comanche War Dance Society, Cache, Oklahoma.

Rolling Pony (Manatidie whipman and Kiowa Agency policeman) and wife, 1900.

Kiowa, Apache, and Comanche Military Societies

1 SODALITIES AND PLAINS INDIAN MILITARY SOCIETIES

In the anthropological literature, Plains Indian military societies have often been labeled voluntary associations (social groups based on voluntary membership) that assumed preparatory functions for communal ceremonies such as the Sun Dance and policed communal hunts and the camp. In addition to these functions, the societies are largely described as men's social dance associations differing primarily in songs, dances, and regalia. Virtually all studies of Plains military societies focus on functional explanations, concentrating on ecological aspects, such as their role in policing communal buffalo hunts, while giving little attention to their organizational roles. Economic aspects perhaps have been functionally overemphasized by scholars such as Symmes Oliver (1962). Beyond brief ethnographic descriptions and limited use of ecological data (Wissler 1916b), there has been little analysis of ethnographic or historical data to assess these organizations and the extent of their relationship to the larger levels of social organization, interpersonal relations, tribal integration, and economics. Archival and field research among Southern Plains populations indicates that military societies (1) often were much more structured than previously noted, (2) shared many general similarities yet varied significantly in detail from one population to another, (3) functioned in a variety of social and political contexts, and (4) differed in their individual roles within their respective communities and that (5) current societies often exhibit a high degree of cultural continuity from their antecedents. These data can be further explored to gain insights concerning not only past and present military societies, but their impact upon other components of past and present Plains Indian cultures. Moreover, a comparative analysis permits the temporal exploration of larger patterns of social behavior for the North American Plains cultures.

SODALITIES

In anthropology, "military societies" are categorized as sodalities, from the Latin word *sodalis*, referring to voluntary associations in contrast to kinship and residence groups (Lowie 1948:14). As Elman Service (1962:21) describes, a sodality is a "nonresidential association that has some corporate functions or purposes." Such a definition resembles the German term *Gesellschaft* or "special purpose group," yet does not imply voluntary membership or a mandatory single special purpose. Sodality is therefore a broader concept that is explicitly defined as nonresidential, whereas other forms such as clan, nonlocal clan, various residence groups, corporations, and societies are less clearly defined in terms of residence and purpose and are nonresidential only by implication or expectation. Service (1962:116) distinguishes between kinship-based sodalities (clans, kindred, and segmentary lineages) and non-kinship-based sodalities (associations, age-grades, and warrior and ceremonial societies). Unlike residential groups, sodalities are usually not directly demographic and do not respond in the same way to population increases and greater densities of residential groups. Because they are nonlocal, sodalities acquire political functions by crosscutting, and thus integrating, various residential units. Sodalities integrate residential units and configure society and therefore are important in social structure (Service 1962:22).

All sodalities have latent and manifest functions and contain sociologically integrative (latent) functions simply by being nonresidential, because they crosscut some segment of the residential groups, however small. Because a sodality's manifest functions are related to its structure, sodalities can vary greatly. They normally have one or more manifest functions, which are usually related to their structure. They are in a sense, then, special-purpose groups, with their structures dictated by their functions and with integration as a by-product. Service (1962:23) differentiates residential groups from sodalities because the structure of the family is more varied and complex in form and because nearly any form of family structure can still accomplish its manifest functions.

Sodalities vary worldwide, but are most common in the anthropological literature of Africa, Melanesia, Taiwan, and North and South America (Ritter 1980). Cross-culturally, sodalities occur in numerous forms, with specialization in various areas, such as police, warfare, status, religion, recreation, and medicine or curing (Lowie 1927; Service 1962:118). Although the distinguishing features categorizing sodalities are more functional than organizational or ideological, all societies perform overlapping functions in numerous social spheres. Men's sodalities typically occur in greater frequency, are more highly organized, and are more secretive than female sodalities (Hunter and Whitten 1976:362). Sodalities are generally secondary groups or associations in which membership is voluntary in most cultures.

Some cultures require sodality membership as a prerequisite to all major life events, such as marriage (Lowie 1920:80, 276). Membership can be by ascription, inheritance, achievement, purchase, and/or performance. Sodalities may also serve as special-purpose political associations organized on the basis of sex, age, economic status, and personal interests and are found in both public and secret spheres of action (Hunter and Whitten 1976:362).

Service (1962:113) defines pantribal sodalities as "the means of solidarity that are specifically tribal additions to the persisting band-like means," the addition of an encompassing integrative structure to an existing form of social organization. He suggests that all sodalities are formed from preexisting ingredients found in band society that were transformed by two primary adaptive circumstances, the natural (organic and inorganic) environment and the superorganic environment (presence of competing societies). Clans, segmentary lineages, and kindreds are modeled after vertically formed family units, while warrior societies and age-grades follow the horizontal forms of brothers, old men, and cooperative hunting and ceremonial groups (Service 1962:113, 116). Thus, he attributes the development of pantribal societies to competition between societies in the neolithic phase of cultural development and suggests that complete tribal integration would not occur without foreign political problems (Service 1962:113–114). By adapting the way in which groups maintain a nonlocal base, pantribal sodalities unite bands beyond the limitations of intermarriage. Service (1962:115–116) asserts that "pan-tribal sodalities are the emergent features which made bands over into a new level of socio-cultural integration and thus a new cultural type." According to Service (1962:115, 181), pantribal sodalities, as one of five basic types of human integration, were prerequisite to tribal formation.

While most theoretical contributions concerning sodalities have come from Service (1962), his assertions are still undocumented, unqualified, and largely unproven. More recently James Boon (1982:97–111) has reanalyzed Robert Lowie's and Franz Boas's earlier rejection of Lewis Henry Morgan's theoretical view that nonliterate cultures were centered exclusively on kinship. As Boon notes, Lowie suggested that state organization arose when the androcentric "voluntarist component" came to dominate in the absence of other social structures. More importantly for this study, Boon (1982:102) points out Lowie's observation that sodalities "reveal a tribe's capacity to sample alternate social forms, without necessarily adopting them as the central components of the social machine." He also shows that a tribal group commonly experiments with patterns of social organization "that are fundamental to its neighbors." These points are essential in comparing Southern Plains military societies.

PLAINS MILITARY SOCIETIES

In the anthropological and historical literature, the term "military" or "war-rior society" most commonly refers to the martial-oriented sodalities of the North American Plains and Africa. The exact origins of the term, however, are unknown. For purposes of clarity, in this study the terms "military so-ciety," "society," and "sodality" are used synonymously. Thus Kiowa soci-ety (culture) and Kiowa societies (sodalities) are distinguishable by context.

Perhaps the earliest mention of an organization resembling a North American military society is Louis Hennepin's (1698:280; Abel 1939:187) 1680 description of a group near present-day St. Paul, Minnesota, who served as police by seizing the goods of individuals who had broken com-munal hunting laws as punishment. In 1803 Pierre Antoine Tabeau noted the temporary authority of appointed Brulé Lakota police to kill horses and dogs, to destroy lodges, to break weapons, and to confiscate or destroy goods to enforce civil decisions as well as bison hunting laws. Resistance generally brought a beating, while penitence resulted in restoration of one's lodge and goods, often in an increased amount, reflecting patterns of military society policing in many Plains communities. Although Tabeau, like most writers, was most impressed with the coercive powers associated with the collective hunt, he also mentioned public functions of Brulé societies, including initia-tions, feasts, and naming ceremonies (Abel 1939:116, 245).[1] Indeed, Clark Wissler's (1912) and Lowie's (1916a:908–910) findings indicate that the policed bison hunt and the association of police duties with Plains soci-eties originated among the Western Dakota (Lakota). On August 30, 1804, Meriwether Lewis and William Clark describe a Teton Sioux military so-ciety with obligatory battle behavior and fraternal characteristics of sitting, camping, and dancing together, reportedly in imitation of one of several Crow military societies (Thwaites 1904:1:130). Their references further demonstrate the widespread temporal presence of Northern Plains Indian military societies, from which later scholars infer their diffusion to other tribes (Lowie 1916a).

Wissler (1914:12, 18) asserts that such "typical" Plains traits as the Sun Dance and military societies were well distributed among Plains populations prior to the diffusion of the horse and its subsequent role in diffusing other traits. William Christie MacLeod (1937:199) states that Plains military so-cieties derived from some form of Woodlands culture police prior to adapt-ing to the Plains, which seems likely because several of the later Plains tribes with strong military society traditions such as the Cheyenne, Lakota, and Crow (formerly Hidatsa) were previously agriculturalists or, like the Omaha and Pawnee, continued semisedentary, agricultural pursuits. Francis Haines (1976:171–194) suggests that Plains Indian men's societies became extremely important with the increase in warfare, which is also likely in light of Bernard Mishkin's (1940) and Jane Richardson's (1940) Kiowa data. Thomas Biolsi (1984) has demonstrated that resource competition and large-scale warfare on the Great Plains, to which military societies were related, resulted from the simultaneous effects of ecological and cultural causes.

By the mid-1800s Plains dream, police, dance, and military societies were known to Euro-Americans, but remained undefined and undifferentiated.[2] Military societies continued to be poorly understood because of widespread similarities in society obligations, names, regalia, functions, and associations with warfare. Despite individual tribal variations, these components served to strengthen societal solidarity. Many early writers automatically assumed the historical and psychological unity of all Plains organizations under discussion and grouped them under the name of "military" or "warrior" societies (Lowie 1916a:883). Because of frequent associations with Plains warfare, the term "Dog Soldiers" was often used to refer to all Plains Indian military societies, from an imperfect rendering of one of the Plains' most prominent and widespread forms of military societies (Mooney 1898:229; 1912d:862).

Hugh Lennox Scott and W. P. Clark (1982:354–365) both used the terms "soldier," "soldier bands," and "societies" when discussing several Plains military societies in their works on Plains Indian sign language.[3] Several consultants interviewed during this work frequently used terms such as "group," "band," "clan," "society," and "lodge" in describing tribal military societies. The first to attempt to provide an ethnological definition for the term "military societies" appears to be James Mooney, who writes:

Throughout the plains from N. to S. there existed a military organization so similar among the various tribes as to suggest a common origin, although with patriotic pride each tribe claimed it as its own. . . . In each tribe the organization consisted of 4 to 12 societies of varying rank and prominence ranging from boys or untried warriors up to old men who had earned retirement by long years of service on the warpath and thenceforth confined themselves to the supervision of the tribal ceremonies. The name of each society had reference to some mystic animal protector or to some costume, duty, or peculiarity connected with the membership. . . . Each society had its own dance, songs, ceremonial costume, and insignia, besides special taboos and obligations. The ceremonial dance of one society in each tribe was usually characterized by some species of clown play, most frequently taking the form of speech and action the reverse of what the spectators were expecting. . . . At all tribal assemblies, ceremonial hunts, and on great war expeditions, the various societies took charge of the routine details and acted both as performers and police (Mooney 1912d:863).

More recently there has been some question whether the term "military society" accurately categorizes such Plains organizations. Because most Plains military societies were non-kin-based and pantribally organized, they are not believed to have fought as units during any given battle. Thus, it has been suggested that the term "military societies" is not accurate.[4] E. Adamson Hoebel (1978:40) supports this point:

> The societies are not organized companies on the order of colonial militia in the early days of American settlement. They are, in their way, somewhat more comparable to local American Legion or V.F.W. Posts— social and civic organizations mainly centered on the common experience of the members as warriors, with rituals glorifying and enhancing that experience, and with duties and services performed on behalf of the community at large.

Hoebel maintains that Plains military societies are similar to American veterans' groups: members perhaps did not fight together in the same units and battles, but, upon returning home, entered the same veteran fraternity of their local residence area. New Plains data indicate that Hoebel's characterization is valid only in later (ca. post-1850) historical periods. The presence of a common and collectively shared ideology, ethos, and associated symbols significantly counters this assertion.

PRERESERVATION PLAINS MILITARY SOCIETIES, SODALITIES, AND VOLUNTARY ASSOCIATIONS

In this study I wish to distinguish between a voluntary association or sodality and a Plains Indian military sodality. A voluntary association or sodality includes a wide range of social forms; thus, any voluntary organization can take practically any form (poetic, athletic, theatrical, hunting, medical) and can function for various purposes (education, entertainment, exercise, common interest, economic, curing). A major problem arises in how to classify sodalities, with emphasis generally being given to elements of social structure or functional attributes. Service (1962:23) asserts that a sodality is often organized so that it can perform specific "manifest function"(s). However, a sodality can accomplish a variety of personal, group, and communal goals. Boon (1982) discusses Lowie's assessment of voluntary associations as a springboard for a sense of solidarity exceeding the family level, which holds true, as nearly every sodality provides integration, socialization, and benefits to a segment of the larger society. In addition to being based upon common interests and providing varied communal services, however, several elements more narrowly distinguish Plains military societies from other North American sodality forms and from regional patterns within the Plains.

Numerous Plains societies of several different types existed among both sexes. Alfred R. Kroeber (1907:63) associates three spheres of action with men's societies: civil, military, and religious. He notes that a men's society may include elements of one or all three spheres of action and that the difficulty in classification lay in differentiating the primary function of a society from its secondary functions, which were subsequent or subsidiary developments. Pointing out the high degree of variation in Plains societies, Lowie (1963:113) observes that some organizations had virtually no religious aspects, while others, such as the Pawnee and Arapaho societies, were religiously structured. However, as N. D. Humphrey (1941:431) contends, attempts to classify Plains societies must include not only factors of social organization, but their functional roles: "the organization typifying the nature or character of these societies cannot be determined by denoting mere structural elements. Rather the character of societies is a reflection of their functional role in Plains culture, and in order to characterize these societies it is necessary first to formulate and understand their functional roles."

Several criteria distinguish the prereservation military societies of mobile Plains hunting and gathering groups from those of the Prairie and other areas and from other types of Plains Indian sodalities or voluntary associations. One of the most visible and perhaps overemphasized roles is policing large communal hunts. On the Plains, such duties were generally performed in one of four ways: (1) by a particular society or clan (the Mandan Black Mouths Society or the Iowa Elk Clan), (2) by a temporarily appointed portion of an individual society (Ponca), (3) by various societies in turn (Kiowa and Cheyenne), or (4) by a group of temporarily appointed distinguished men without associational affiliations (Pawnee, Kansa, Osage). Like many semisedentary Siouan and Caddoan populations, other Southern Plains tribes such as the Caddo, Lipan Apache, Osage, Tonkawa, and Wichita had more temporarily organized social organizations that similarly performed the functions provided by Plains military societies. However, these social units were often kinship and not sodality based.[5] As Lowie (1943:70–71) states, "Where military societies are lacking, such activities quite as naturally devolve on other preexisting units, such as clans or a general honorary class of braves." Many Prairie tribes lacked a form of military sodality which functioned collectively beyond temporary policing duties.

Ecologically the Plains area differs from other geographic areas and thus provided opportunities for different social organization duties and roles than in other ecological zones. More importantly, Plains military societies are not (1) regulated by a priesthood as among some Puebloan groups, (2) organized in military moietylike war and peace divisions as among the Sac and Fox, (3) clan or town oriented as among the Creek and some sedentary Prairie-Plains groups, or (4) temporary appointments of members not of the same sodality as among some Prairie-Plains groups. Plains military societies (1) tend to be based upon voluntary membership with the exception of some contrary societies, (2) contain cross-band membership, (3) are either age-graded or coordinately organized, (4) contain a group name which is generally associated with some aspect of their dress, dance, duty, or associated group ideology, (5) conduct meetings in conjunction with tribal aggregations, (6) may (but not always) engage in warfare as a collective unit (prior to circa 1850), and (7) contain a central focus on warfare and individual deeds, including coup recitations and performances celebrating and enhancing martial activities, as opposed to doctoring and shield societies focusing upon specific forms of war power and healing.

While some military societies contained items associated with war power, they differ from shield societies. In contrast to the pantribal, non-kin-based membership of most military societies, shield societies were much smaller sodalities, generally composed of limited units of bilateral kin, with a focus on shield and warfare power, were generally more secretive, had fewer public social events than the larger military societies, and were largely residential units according to Service's criteria (1962).[6] Thus, there are several basic differences between Plains and Prairie sodalities in terms of social structure, functions, interpersonal relations, and economic and ecological roles. In view of such variations, Plains and Prairie societies should not be classified as a single homogeneous topic, but perhaps as subsets of a larger social form.

While all of these criteria are significant and are addressed in this study, it is the last criterion which plays a dominant part in the history of these organizations. Plains men's military societies visibly promote the common central theme of a warrior tradition—a warrior ideology, which at specific times can be argued to be an ethos. Much of the work of Margaret Mead, Gregory Bateson, and Ruth Benedict (Harris 1968:393–448) involved attempts to define ethos and national character in studies of culture and personality. Roger Pearson (1985:78) defines ethos as "the distinctive quality of any individual culture or society." Charles Winick (1968:193) defines it as "the totality of the distinctive ways of living that separate one group from another, especially its values. Ethos also denotes the emotional quality possessed by socially patterned behavior." Benedict (Harris 1968:398–403; Winick 1968:193; Pearson 1985:78) suggests that the ethos of a society might be classified as "Apollonian" or "Dionysian"; however, most theorists believe that she oversimplifies the concept of ethos, which is rooted in the complex totality of a society's mores, customs, and cultural traits.

For this study, I define "ideology" as the opinions and doctrines of a particular group and the associated expressive means (symbols, words, songs, etc.) that reflect them and "ethos" as the deeper-seated, more pervasive, core cultural principles that characterize a particular group. Any culture can of course have more than one type of ethos, and transition to and from an ideology to an ethos also occurs. That is, an ethos is flexible: it can expand and contract or increase and decrease in intensity, depending upon appropriate circumstances that overlap, enhance, or supersede existing ideology. Thus, while a military and patriotic ideology could be argued to exist in American society, nationalism is more reflective of its ethos. However, during the recent Persian Gulf War, the American ethos could be argued to have become more martially focused, yet still nationalistic. Likewise, a martial ideology can be argued to exist throughout the annual cycle of many prereservation Plains Indian military societies, which was periodically enhanced to an ethos during times of intensified group integration such as society meetings, communal aggregations, and horse and revenge raids. Boon's (1982) discussion of voluntary associations as a source of solidarity exceeding the family level suggests the flexibility of Plains military sodalities in periodically providing such solidarity in a martial context for various larger socially integrative purposes.

A martial ethos is only one type of ethos common to many Plains communities. On a general level, I contend that there is a similar shared martial ideology (and at times ethos) for the groups discussed in this work, which has continued through time and has remained an important part of ethnic identity. These sodalities have performed a number of enculturative functions that, though varying among individual military societies and among tribes through time, are of a generally similar pattern. As an adaptive form of social organization, these societies have changed through time (membership requirements, frequency of contact), yet have retained a number of organizational and functional forms (ceremony, organization, community services, cultural preservation). As they have changed, these societies have assumed new and adaptive strategies (integration of U.S. military participation, incorporation of other tribal traditions, etc.) in becoming new integrative social forms. In doing so, these groups exhibit a generally shared pattern of martial-based ideology and ethos, conveyed through rituals and symbols. Like an actual arena used to hold Plains society dances and powwows, military societies serve as a cultural foundation through which various enculturative forms (language, belief, cultural heritage, ethnicity, values, ethos) are maintained and into which changes (adaptation, syncretism) are introduced—arenas of enculturation. Thus, traditional cultural forms are maintained while adapting to new sociopolitical and economic circumstances. Although individual societies differ on a number of levels, many of their larger core functions, the types, content, and uses of symbols, and adaptations follow a general temporal pattern.

In addition to these criteria, prereservation Plains military societies (1) were voluntary associations focusing upon shared interests, (2) provided various forms of social services (such as aid to the needy) to the larger community, and (3) collectively fostered military spirit, ideology, and ethos while recalling and enhancing the military accomplishments of members individually and as a sodality. In view of the widespread traditional Plains emphasis on veterans, it is this third criterion which most visibly characterizes and defines Southern (and possibly all) Plains Indian military societies as a distinct type of sodality. Thus, an understanding of the associated ideology and ethos, and not solely the functions, of a sodality is necessary to differentiate types of sodalities. Prereservation Southern Plains Indian men's military societies were comprised of members of varying veteran status, who periodically and collectively met for social or semisacred purposes, including the representation of individual and collective war-related performances, provided social and economic services to the larger community, and enhanced tribal integration. Military societies also performed other socioeconomic functions such as camp security and alignment, charity, preparation for communal ceremonies, and regulation of the communal hunt, which was enforced by confiscating illegally seized game, destroying property, and inflicting public shaming and corporal punishment (Wissler 1916b). Although Plains women's societies have largely been overlooked, their spheres of action included religious, military, and craft guilds (Lowie 1954:105–114). Like Plains men's societies, women's organizations also frequently contained overlapping functions in more than one sphere of action. Similarly, Plains Indian women's military societies participated in and promoted a shared martial ideology and ethos. They resembled men's military societies by being (1) voluntary organizations whose members performed (2) social and or semisacred activities (sometimes including prayer, blessings, supplication, and the use of supernatural power) to support and ensure the success of the military activities of their male counterparts, while (3) providing various community services.[7]

Among prereservation Plains groups, this martial ideology was often maintained and promoted through a series of collective social and semisacred gatherings at both divisional and pantribal levels, focusing upon rituals, dancing and singing, feasts, and public validation of individual accomplishments and status via coup recitations and the redistribution or giving-away of property, while social and public services to the larger community were performed. These ceremonies validated individual and collective (societal) accomplishments while reinforcing individual (member), collective (societal), and communal (divisional or tribal) recognition of warrior status.

As this work covers a lengthy period (ca. 1800–1999) it includes significant changes in many aspects (dress, songs, membership requirements, functions). This baseline definition of military societies works well for the prereservation era, but subsequent periods and adaptations necessitate changes in definition. While an emphasis on a martial ideology and ethos can be seen as an Anglo romanticization of Plains life (such as Mails 1973), which neglects the varied socioeconomic functions of military societies, or as a retrospective ideology that twentieth-century Plains communities have used to establish their own sense of history and continuity (perhaps in response to external stereotypes and expectations), I demonstrate that such a martial ideology has continued to the present, through strategic adaptation, and still exists.[8] Much of the core ideology (emphasis on veteran status, means of honoring veterans, community functions, ethnic identity, social integration, and incorporation of other cultural elements) associated with prereservation military societies remains in successor organizations today, though not in the romantic form portrayed by popular writers and in movies. Although the specific social functions of a martial ideology have varied over time, important elements of a tribal heritage stemming from earlier martial traditions remain a prominent aspect of contemporary Southern Plains Indian communities.

FORMS OF SOCIETY GRADING AND DE FACTO AGE-GRADING

Nineteenth-century sodalities, including Plains Indian military society complexes, have traditionally been categorized in two major forms of organization: age-graded and nongraded or coordinate. An age grade is a category of persons who fall within a culturally distinguished age range. Members typically enter age-graded systems by age and purchase (Lowie 1916a:884). In age-grade societies young men of a relatively similar age or age-set (a set of persons of similar age and sex who move through some or all of life's stages together as a group) joined the lowest or first society at an age deemed sufficient by the respective culture. Each age-set progressed upward through a hierarchy of societies as a collective unit, by periodically purchasing the ceremonies, songs, regalia, ritual knowledge, and position of the next higher group (Lowie 1963:107). Thus, advancement was heavily linked to ritual knowledge and age. The process continued, with the oldest age-set normally retiring with every series of upward purchases and movements.

Age-grading was limited to five Plains groups: the Arapaho, Blackfeet, Gros Ventre or Atsina, Hidatsa, and Mandan. W. F. Whyte (1944:68) defines age-grading as "a system of differential distribution of rights and obligations, of prohibited, permissible, and required activities, according to different (socially recognized) periods of life and according to the social distinctions established between the sexes." In general aspects, Plains Indian age-sets are similar to those of Africa, Melanesia, and elsewhere, consisting of age-sets of ranked, relatively homogeneous age-groups. The sequential passage of age-sets through a number of grades required a formalized right of passage for each new level. Lowie (1916a) determined that Plains societies (1) originated among the Northern Plains village tribes (especially the Mandan and Hidatsa), (2) developed from a series of previously ungraded societies, (3) represent a special and late development, and (4) were transmitted by the Hidatsa to the Arapaho and later to the Blackfeet and that (5) in some instances even the same society varied in order, age affiliation, and content between tribes.

Contrasted with age-graded systems were the non-age-graded or coordinate systems, in which a man of appropriate age would join a society through invitation, choice, or some sort of qualification, and, depending upon the individual tribe, could either remain in that society for his entire life or shift membership among other societies, also based on personal choice or invitation (Lowie 1963:110–111). Nongraded military societies were more common than age-graded societies on the Plains and were found among the Kiowa, Cheyenne, Lakota, Crow, and others. Except among the Arikara and Sarsi, no Plains nongraded military societies required age qualification or entrance fees (Lowie 1916a:884). Other variations existed, however: the Comanche developed divisionally specific societies at a relatively late date (Meadows 1995), while the Plains Cree had one warrior society per tribal band, but occasionally purchased new societies and dances from other bands or tribes (Lowie 1963:110). Comanche and Cree military societies were based largely upon factors of proximity and dependent upon the territorial range of residence bands that exploited a common area.

This work focuses on Southern Plains tribes exhibiting nongraded military sodalities that exclude membership based on clan, moiety, or phratry functions. As previously defined, these groups all contained what could be called "classic" or "typical" military societies when speaking generally of nineteenth-century mobile hunting and gathering Plains cultures. Although descendants' organizations characterized by annual gatherings and traditional dances are common among the Kiowa, Comanche, and Apache (KCA), I have excluded them because of their kinship-based descent structure (usually from an apical ancestor) and their qualitative difference as a lineage-based structure and not a sodality.

New data on Southern Plains military society systems and a review of Wissler's (1916b) *Societies of the Plains Indians* suggest that the traditional classification of age-graded and nongraded societies needs revision, as the age-grade factor is not the sole determining factor for both variations. Lowie (1916a:883) states: "Although systems of societies graded by age are confined to five of the Plains tribes . . . many other tribes of this area have societies so closely resembling the age-organizations in name, regalia, and functions that a hard-and-fast line cannot be drawn with the age factor as the basis for classification." Several "ungraded" Plains societies exhibited numerous patterns of differential membership, status, ritual knowledge, economics, and functions associated with age; thus, characterizing them as "non-age-graded" is not totally accurate. Therefore, I suggest that it is perhaps more accurate to view the two types as variations of a single form of social organization (age-graded and de facto graded) rather than as polar opposites (age-graded versus nongraded). Kiowa, Apache, and other Plains data point to the existence of a widespread form of de facto age-grading or at least a sodality-based clustering of largely (but not totally) similar aged cohorts in many Plains populations previously considered to have ungraded or coordinate societies. Widespread characteristics involving differentially defined membership and a series of specific and socially ranked or de facto graded societies combined with children's societies, varied forms of intra-tribal intersocietal rivalry, differential ritual knowledge and assignment of duties, association of general age cohorts, individual war rank, and wealth and social status all point toward this conclusion.

Background

Most literature on sodalities exists in tribal ethnographies and varies enormously according to the individual ethnographers' assessments of the primary functions of various sodalities. The recorded foci of Plains Indian sodalities range widely, including religion, politics, recreation, warfare, property owning, wife owning, cooperative aid, and so on, making generalizations difficult (Stewart 1977:2–3, 7). Most works dealing with sodalities emphasize age-graded forms, with theories largely derived from Africa and Taiwan, where the most highly developed, numerically largest, and most widespread forms of age-group sodalities occur. The enormous literature on age-groups depicts sodalities as the central institution in many tribal societies and has generated larger theoretical questions following comparison with sodalities elsewhere (Stewart 1977).

Aside from ethnographic descriptions, little discussion of North American military sodalities exists. Theoretical works largely discuss origins and development (Schurtz 1902; Lowie 1920, 1927; Whyte 1944; Eisenstadt 1954; Oliver 1962; Hanson 1988), although Frank Henderson Stewart (1977) attempts a more comparative survey of the fundamentals underlying age-group systems. Most later works are concerned with determining their development, importance, and effectiveness as a means of coercive power in social control (MacLeod 1937; Provinse 1937; Lowie 1943; Hoebel 1954; Bailey 1980) or their role as germinal instruments in the process of state formation (Hoebel 1936; Llewellyn and Hoebel 1941). The largest concentration of anthropological work involving Plains military societies is volume 11 of the American Museum of Natural History publications (Wissler 1916b). This survey involved a detailed ethnographic investigation of Plains military societies and the Sun Dance, concentrating on tribal groups which had not yet received ethnographic attention. These works focused primarily upon trait distribution and clusters to reconstruct the historical development and diffusion of these complexes within and among various Plains tribes.

However, as Fred Eggan (1966) and Oliver (1962:6) discuss, these publications do not address how societies functioned. While they described society regalia, little emphasis was given to the more functional or organizational relationships of military societies to tribal integration, religion, kinship, or social, political, and economic organization. Moreover, those tribes which had already been studied were not revisited and Southern Plains populations were almost totally ignored. Lowie (1915a, 1916b) published a total of seventeen pages for the Kiowa and Comanche (visiting both only briefly), the Plains Apache were not included, and further Cheyenne and Arapaho research was precluded because of the brief society descriptions in Mooney (1907), Dorsey (1905), and Kroeber (1983). This paucity of material resulted from a lack of research time in the respective areas and not from the absence of such organizations.

Because many scholars considered Plains Indian military societies (especially nongraded forms) to have been adequately explained, they were largely dismissed. It was not until the mid-1930s that further data on Southern Plains military societies were collected in general ethnological field schools, by the Santa Fe Laboratory of Anthropology among the Comanche in 1933 and the Kiowa in 1935 and by scholars such as J. Gilbert McAllister for the Plains Apache in 1933–1934 and E. Adamson Hoebel for the Northern Cheyenne in 1935. Yet few of these data concerning military societies have been published (McAllister 1935, 1937; Hoebel 1936, 1940; Llewellyn and Hoebel 1941). These data are invaluable primary sources and counter the acculturationist attempts to document what was believed to be the last of the pristine and rapidly disappearing prereservation Indian cultures.

METHODOLOGY, THEORY, AND APPROACH

This study of Southern Plains Indian military societies is based on five major areas of focus: (1) a controlled regional and temporal comparison of three distinct ethnic populations (Kiowa, Comanche, and Apache, frequently referred to within these communities and in this work as KCA); (2) a multifield ethnohistoric approach combining personal fieldwork, critical examination, and use of extensive archival and oral history sources; (3) an approach countering the weaknesses of acculturation studies and using the strength of New Indian History to emphasize indigenous meaning, to document the active role of native communities in their own processes of culture change and to show cultural innovation, change, and continuity, rather than cultural loss; (4) a concern for the temporal processes of change, syncretism, and cultural revival; and (5) a focus on the cultural role of martial symbols through time.

This study combines extensive ethnographic fieldwork, archival research, and analysis of symbols to (1) reconstruct the history of KCA military sodalities and demonstrate how they reflect past and present tribal values, particularly through military society rituals; (2) determine the significance of these societies for their respective tribal forms of social organization; (3) show how these groups serve as enculturative and adaptive forms of social organization for the maintenance of a distinct tribal ethos and ethnicity and, later, for identity in a larger, encapsulating society; and (4) delineate ethnohistorically and diachronically the military society symbols embraced by the KCA and how these functioned in social integration and enculturation through time. Traditional military society social structures have an enduring reality and in being periodically reinvigorated have been adapted to modern circumstances.

Research Selection

The Southern Plains was chosen as a research area for three reasons: (1) Southern Plains military societies have received little ethnographic attention in comparison with the Northern Plains (Wissler 1916b); (2) ironically, the largest percentage of surviving ancestral-based military societies are on the Southern Plains; and (3) the KCA have shared a generally similar history throughout much of the nineteenth and twentieth centuries.[9] I was also able to work with the last elders with direct information concerning older society activities. An ethnohistorical approach offers a broader view of the process of repetitious and changing structures and order.[10]

A comparative regional approach is necessary to elicit both individual tribal data and broader regional patterns. This approach facilitates the comprehension of the social and cultural dynamics of each group as a whole in the context of its own relations and interactions, as well as those with the neighboring groups with which it continues to share a generally similar historical experience. Like distinct ethnic communities, individual sodalities react to those within its own population as well as to those in neighboring communities, especially to sodalities possessing similar cultural forms. To discuss the societies of one tribe without comparing and contrasting the others distorts the cultural dynamics of their historical experiences, which include change, borrowing, diffusion, perception, readjustment, innovation, and creativity.[11] In many respects the Kiowa, Comanche, and Apache define and reinforce their identity in reference to one another, much as Loretta Fowler (1987) describes for the Gros Ventre and Assiniboine. In addition, they all contained what could be called "classic" or "typical" military societies for nineteenth-century mobile hunting and gathering Plains cultures. Numerous KCA similarities allow an in-depth comparison of military societies in the social structure of several ethnic units existing within a generally similar cultural and ecological region—the boundaries for an excellent controlled regional analysis and comparison.[12]

Sources and Research Methods

While ethnohistorians generally emphasize archival or documentary sources over oral sources, both are necessary, when available, to achieve the most thorough assessment of any phenomenon. They must be used critically and in different ways. I have emphasized written (archival) and contemporary "oral history" sources over many other forms of archival sources due to concerns about quantity and relevance and because many sources are either inferential (contain limited, but sufficient data to infer a connection) or substantive (contain a great quantity of data). The difference often lies in the purposes of the recorders and their familiarity with the culture and topic being described. For military societies, most early European sources are inferential regarding time and location and often lack further content. Archival sources are not always sufficient in quantity or quality for historical reconstruction. The Kiowa Agency records contain a plethora of data concerning attempts to prohibit the Sun Dance, Ghost Dance, and intertribal powwows, but virtually no references to men's societies. The combined use of oral and archival sources is necessary to supplement and confirm one another.

The alleged invalidism of oral history is no longer credible (as shown by the works of DeLaguna 1960:205; Vansina 1965, 1985; Miller 1980; Brown and Roberts 1980; Wedel and DeMallie 1980; Keesing 1986; Moore 1987:5; Kracht 1989; Krech 1991:360; and others). I have relied heavily on "archival" oral histories in the form of ethnographic fieldnotes for several reasons. In contrast with many sources of archival data, ethnographers are trained for ethnographic work, have linguistic and cultural insights, follow a formulated research agenda and a more holistic approach, and appreciate cultural relativity, which often makes their data more accurate than other external accounts. As primary sources, ethnographic and ethnological materials (1) were obtained with an organized and planned approach, (2) generally contain more detailed data than other sources, (3) include a more sensitive line of inquiry, and, most importantly, (4) were often obtained firsthand from the last generation of actual participants in these preservation systems. My reliance on fieldwork, ethnographic fieldnotes, and oral historical accounts for early portions of this work is stressed, yet they are used cautiously, to complement, supplement, and cross-check the archival record.

Ethnographic Fieldwork

This study would not have been possible without long-term, intensive fieldwork, which is crucial for gaining an understanding of another people's culture. Fieldwork is necessary in order to reveal a people's ideology and ethos—their characteristics and habits, motivations, styles, and their viewpoint and manner of solving problems (Lurie 1961:87; Keesing 1986:290). Without fieldwork one can never truly have an accurate feeling for a culture, and it is from the small and intricate details that the larger patterns evolve. Personal and family histories, knowledge of the language, songs, genealogies, oral history, anecdotes, and previously undocumented ceremonial accounts provided the insights that led to new questions and directions of inquiry in this work. These produce a more complete and dynamic depiction of a culture. As Richard Perry (1991:9) has shown for the San Carlos Apache, traces of a people's heritage remain despite numerous social and ecological changes and continue to serve as important clues to understanding a culture's past.

The importance of contemporary fieldwork cannot be overemphasized. To reiterate Moore (1987:317): "any historian or ethnohistorian who raises issues that are within the experience of modern informants simply *cannot* be excused from the necessity of doing fieldwork." No archival study or brief anthropological fieldwork stay would have yielded the data or results included here. Only extensive, long-term, and frequent interaction permitted the elicitation of integral information and connections between various segments of these three cultural systems. The comparative approach allowed a constant cross-checking and inquiry, which in turn produced better methods of inquiry and more thorough results. This work demonstrates the possibilities for those interested in combining published ethnography, modern practice, and early documents (Moore 1987), as one documentary source or an elder in one community often prompted questions and led to answers in another.

Observations of society activities and interviews with tribal members were conducted from October 1989 to the present. Residence in Oklahoma allowed me to conduct lengthy summer visits as well as year-round fieldwork for six years. Reputable and knowledgeable society leaders and male and female tribal members ranging in age from sixteen to ninety-nine were consulted. Younger tribal and nonsociety members provided valuable internal (tribal) yet "external" (nonsociety member) voices.

Acculturation Studies

The great variety in responses to contact by native peoples in North America suggests numerous factors behind the maintenance of distinct cultural communities. Acculturation studies often examine differences between earlier and contemporary social forms, while ignoring the meaning of those forms to native peoples themselves. These works thereby frequently proclaim cultural loss where there is in fact continuity and adaptation and thus are based on what the ethnographer rather than the people themselves deem important. While promoting the stereotype of inevitable culture loss and further assimilation, these approaches distort the process through which native communities change and disregard the perception, interpretation, reaction, and adaptation of native peoples. Subsequently, acculturationist approaches have been largely revised (Redfield, Linton, and Herskovits 1936; Linton 1940; Bruner 1957; Herskovits 1958; Spicer 1961, 1971; Fowler 1987, Garbarino 1983:72–73, Trigger 1986:265). As Fowler (1987:7–8) discusses, cultural continuity results from both persistence of certain ideas or customs and resistance to change, as well as from the emergence of new concepts and values as groups adapt to a changing social world. As borrowed ideas, objects, and customs are given new meanings which make them acceptable as innovations, they become, in time, traditions.

This study seeks to counter the weaknesses of acculturation and ethnicity studies, first, by examining the adaptation and cultural growth of Southern Plains military societies as an ongoing and adaptive social institution which maintains valuable and conscious enculturative forms for these groups and, second, by examining the temporal use of military society symbols for ethnic maintenance.

Old and New Indian History

Ethnohistorians refer to many historical studies (such as Berthrong 1976; Hoxie 1984; and Hagan 1990, 1993) focusing on Indian-white relations as "Old Indian History," because they emphasize an Anglo viewpoint and often rely solely on archival sources. Such works are largely theoretical and documentary and focus on the detrimental effects of national policies on local populations, attributing cultural change to Anglo exploitation, which is seen as the seminal cause of contemporary situations. While sympathetic to the problems of native peoples, these works generally ignore native peoples' ability to perceive, to interpret, to form strategies, and to set goals, portraying them merely as passive recipients of new sociocultural forms dictated by a dominant society. Many current ethnohistorians emphasize Indian-Indian relations in what is known as "New Indian History" (Fowler 1982, 1987; Moore 1987; Kehoe 1989; Foster 1991; White 1991; Dowd 1992). Using a multifield approach, these works place native peoples at the center and seek to understand the reasons for their actions. Native peoples are seen as conscious actors and participants in the larger historical picture and no longer as simply the passive recipients of external and eventually dominating policies. Scholars are now concerned with recognizing and demonstrating a number of features, including ethnogenesis of social forms, exploring relationships involving change and continuity, demonstrating process or how the present evolved from the past, and recognizing that all cultures undergo multiple and varying adaptations in their evolution.

Culture Change and Syncretism

Several works emphasize syncretism (Ryan 1969; Jules-Rosette 1979; Kracht 1989). Although most syncretic studies focus on the fusion of religious symbols and "cultural and religious admixtures" (Jules-Rosette 1979: 18), "syncretic fusions can occur in the integration of nearly any range of ideas and social structures such as art styles, kinship systems, languages" (Ryan 1969: 283). In emphasizing syncretism, Kracht (1989) has shown that contemporary Kiowa religious belief systems change, yet maintain a sense of continuity, while being infused with symbols from various historical periods. Military societies offer an excellent opportunity to examine secular change and continuity.

Several recent Plains Indian studies have used an ethnohistorical approach to examine sociocultural change and continuity. Loretta Fowler (1982, 1987) examined changing Arapaho and Gros Ventre patterns of social interaction as the result of external changes in social conditions and found that old symbols and structures are reinterpreted and adapted to new circumstances through time. John Hartwell Moore (1987, 1996) demonstrated that prereservation Cheyenne social structures have an enduring reality, continuing to the present. Morris Wade Foster (1991) examined the Comanche maintenance of social face through adaptations to changing social contexts that have limited physical proximity to one another, resulting in alteration and innovation in the means of intracommunity interaction and in the means which the Comanche have used to interact. These innovative approaches have examined largely individual social systems.

Cultural Revivals

While past acculturation studies have contained several weaknesses (Fowler 1982, 1987:4–9; Garbarino 1983), a more useful approach involves a temporal perspective on a people's participation in the processes of change and their views regarding the meaning of cultural forms, demonstrating the historical processes leading to change, including both adaptation and continuity. In examining cultural change and religious syncretism in Ndembu rituals, Victor Turner (1968:22) found that the introduction of "Western Individualism" frequently caused tribal religions to "wilt and perish in a surprisingly short time, and with them vanish the ritual symbols." While the establishment of a new social order brought new symbols, social cohesion, and instability, Turner discovered that traditional rituals infused with new symbols were revived once the initially rapid social change slowed and stabilized. The ritual symbols associated with the revival were a "hybridization between old and new," causing difficulty in distinguishing between the two (Kracht 1989:9–11).

Bruce Ryan (1969) discussed the concept of "syncretic integration" or "pattern of adjustment," which occurs during a union of alternative systems, such as native and Anglo religions. "Traditional" and "innovative" patterns or symbols fuse during coalescence and appear as individual entities. Upon the syncretic blending of such vastly different religions, "social conflict" and "ideological competition" generally occur, such as the spread of Christianity through conquest and colonization throughout the world. Examining the effects of Euro-American conquest and acculturation for native peoples of Australia, New Zealand, and North America, Wilbur Jacobs (1987) distinguished three acculturative stages that occurred when aboriginal territories "were overrun by advancing white frontiers": (1) congenial relations reinforced by gift exchange and trade, which give way to overt hostility and warfare following white encroachment on aboriginal lands and warfare resulting in native defeat, bewilderment, and a loss of respect for their culture; (2) an "era of depopulation and despondence" beset with diseases, alcoholism, and loss of land and leadership, during which native peoples often develop scorn for many of their own customs; and (3) the "contra-acculturation" stage in which natives tend to revive their culture in modified form with renewed appreciation of their own arts, crafts, and rituals (Jacobs 1987:134). Jacobs's model illustrates that the "revival" of modified traditional practices served as an adaptive counterstrategy to cultural and religious extinction (Kracht 1989:13–14).

James Slotkin's (1975) model of how "nationalistic" movements form when a dominant society exerts acculturative pressures on smaller cultures is similar. Social conflict and competition generally occur when the subordinate group is expected to abandon indigenous customs in favor of those of the dominant group, resulting in discrimination by the dominant group, which often leads to a breakup or decline of indigenous social organization. Members of the subordinate group revert to a "marginal" status in the new social order, and prolonged discrimination eventually produces "group unity and solidarity" among the "marginal persons" who resent their subordinate status. A group that rejects and attempts to change its status relative to the dominant group is a "nationalistic" action group (Slotkin 1975:1–5; Kracht 1989:14–17). James Boon's (1982:103) discussion of how modern forms of state organization arise as a voluntarist component assumes domination in the absence of social structures reflects the importance of sodalities as precursors to state formation.

Defined as such, "nationalism" is a movement to "overthrow the dominant to subordinate relation socially by means of militant nationalism" or
"nativistic nationalism." While militant movements use military, political,
economic, and/or supernatural means to foster "distinct societies," nativistic nationalism attempts to achieve change through cultural means, often in
the form of cultural symbols "created" in opposition to the dominant group.
Such symbols display syncretism because acculturation brings about irre-
versible culture change, making it "impossible to revive the traditional culture" completely. As Slotkin (1975:5–6) states, "In addition to this changed
culture pattern, some persisting traditional customs are continued, others
previously discarded are revived, and innovations are adopted which seem
symbolic of that ethnic group. Customs forced upon it by the dominant
ethnic group . . . are discarded, as well as other customs which seem symbolic of the dominant group." Both types of nationalism in Slotkin's model
(Kracht 1989:16) attempt to counter or stabilize externally forced changes
or "reverse the acculturative cycle"; one uses physical or "social" means
such as warfare, while the other uses a more passive cultural means to establish syncretic symbols which represent the ethos of the oppressed "culture."
Nativistic nationalism is in accord with Fowler's (1982, 1987) assertions that
much assumed acculturation has in fact been accommodative adaptation.
"Thus nativistic nationalistic movements can give rise to cultural and/or religious syncretism" (Kracht 1989:16).

The third dimension or "revival" stage of Jacobs's model resembles Slotkin's "opposition to accommodation" stage, as cultural revivals and nativistic
movements are oppressed peoples' responses to externally induced acculturative pressures. Such social movements frequently give rise to syncretic religious institutions, with associated symbols reflecting the group's values,
goals, ethos, and world view. That religious symbols establish order out of
chaos is substantiated by the fact that people often turn to various forms
of religious expression in periods of stress (Geertz 1973:99–100; Kracht
1989:16). Syncretic religions that arise during nativistic movements are
often called "cults of despair," from their rapid appearance during crisis periods of acculturation (Slotkin 1975:17; Jacobs 1987:135; Kracht 1989:16).
The introduction of new cult institutions with syncretic features characterizes "revitalization" movements—nativistic social movements featuring
prophecy and a coming utopian state (Wallace 1956:264; Ryan 1969:188–
189; Kracht 1989:17).

Revitalization or "transformative" movements are social movements
through which a culturally stressed group attempts to improve its subordinate position in the larger sociocultural structure during the members' life-

time (Jorgensen 1972:6–7; Aberle 1982:318–320; Kracht 1989:17). As Ryan (1969:186) discusses, "[there is] in a pre-existing group, or sub-group, frequently an ethnic or religious body in which individuals are feeling severe stress and anxiety at the apparent loss of meaningful life in the existing socio-cultural structure. In the depths of the collective helplessness, the anxious and apathetic group is awakened, united, and enthused by a prophetic destiny which is to be theirs." Symbols projecting "a glorious future state" based on the "legends of the past" and the associated doctrine promising that everything associated with the subordinating population will be destroyed upon the "rebirth" of the oppressed people are frequently found in prophecies which culturally motivate people toward "revivals" (Nash 1955:377; Ryan 1969:186). Philleo Nash (1955:377) describes rituals in revitalization movements as extremely "elaborate" and often founded in "aboriginal ceremonialism." The ritual symbols in revitalization movement ceremonies frequently reveal the deprivation and destitution experienced by the participants while reflecting the general attitudes of the populace and their chosen course of action (Nash 1955:442; Kracht 1989:18).

Anthony Wallace (1956) first defined revitalization movements, identifying six cross-cultural forms or behavioral patterns (Kracht 1989:18). The second form, revitalization movements, which attempt to revive past or currently threatened cultural traditions, is most closely associated with military societies. However, because these categories are nonexclusive, a number of patterns can be manifested in one form (Wallace 1956:267; Ryan 1969:186). Most major religions throughout the world started as revitalization movements, later taking on millenarian and messianic characteristics (Ryan 1969:188; Kracht 1989:18).

Another type of revitalization that appears during the "revival" stage of acculturation is known as an "expressive" or "redemptive" movement, which serves in the "reformation of soul and mind rather than of society and culture" (Jorgensen 1972:6–7; Aberle 1982:318–320; Kracht 1989:19). Expressive movements attempt to change individuals, and not the larger social order, and are "inward" movements which "arise in circumstances wherein disturbed and upset people are unable to act overtly in reference to their frustrations" (Ryan 1969:184). Such movements occur when people in a disintegrating culture are "overwhelmed by an unacceptable social order," so that the movement offers "individual gratification by virtue of participation" (Ryan 1969:184). These movements can result in social change, but usually as a latent function of the "collective actions" of the group, as members are not actively seeking change in sociocultural status, but merely attempting to cope with a new social order (Kracht 1989:20).

Most scholars maintain that revitalistic and expressive movements are adaptive responses to externally induced acculturative pressures on indigenous peoples (Kracht 1989:21). While these models imply acculturation, a viewpoint emphasizing resistance, accommodation, and change better acknowledges the conscious role of encapsulated peoples. Syncretic cults or institutions usually emerge during cultural revivals, with the associated symbol systems reflecting the ethos and values of the subordinate population. To comprehend syncretic religious symbolism it is necessary to determine the origin and development of syncretic traits in relation to the larger sociocultural conditions which caused them. Ryan (1969) also suggests that late-nineteenth-century acculturative pressures often resulted in revitalization movements which produced religious cults that syncretized old and new religious symbols. The resultant coalescent religions were a response to a loss of aboriginal religions and the arrival and enforced acculturation of Christianity (Kracht 1989:21–22). Establishing these factors permits the ethnohistorical analysis of the growth and decline of revitalistic religions over time through the examination of historic documents and ethnographic data (Kracht 1989:21).

Several works (see Kracht 1989:19) have focused on native North American religious revitalizations, such as the Ghost Dance of 1890 (Mooney 1896; Lesser 1978; Miller 1985; Barney 1986), the Plains Grass Dance and Hand Game (Lesser 1978), the Native American Church (Slotkin 1975; Stewart 1987; La Barre 1989), the Klamath Earth Lodge Ceremony and Dream Dance (Nash 1955:420–435), and the Shakers of Puget Sound (Mooney 1896:708–763). Few studies have focused on more secular topics. Only William Bittle (1962) and James Howard (1976) focus on military society revivals, which continue as vital contemporary Native American cultural events. William Powers (1980:225, 1990:86–110) has challenged the use of the terms "revival," "nativism," and "revitalization," asserting that the term "revival" is only appropriate if applied to reestablished traditions which were previously given up voluntarily. For reestablished cultural patterns which were formerly coerced into cessation, Powers suggests that "vitalization" of temporarily suppressed forms is more appropriate. Eric Lassiter (1992, 1993, 1995) asserts that the Kiowa Gourd Dance is not a revitalization movement in part because some of the songs, the basis for the dance and sodality, were never totally lost. Yet some Southern Plains military societies ceased prior to Anglo disruption, while others changed, became inactive, totally ceased, or were reactivated during later periods of governmental coercion. Songs of defunct societies which have never been reactivated also still exist. More is involved in reestablishing cultural patterns than partial cultural retention. A close examination of Southern Plains military societies demonstrates varied and changing sociocultural structural forms which reflect elements of revitalizing, transformative, expressive, and nativistic nationalistic movements. While the KCA have undergone various periods of cultural stress, and periodically revived some of their military societies, they exhibit significant elements of continuity over some two hundred years. This study is concerned primarily with reestablished movements which attempt to revive past or currently threatened military society traditions.

Symbols and Culture Change

Recent ethnographies frequently reiterate Geertz's interpretation that "culture" is a system of symbols created and used by humans (Geertz 1973:5; Fowler 1982, 1987; Kracht 1989). Geertz suggests that symbol systems are mental constructs of "meaning" which allow individuals to orient themselves and to interpret their position in both natural and supernatural realms of daily existence. In this context, symbols motivate behavior or "social action." As Fowler (1982:4) states, "Symbols express conceptual frameworks and at the same time impel belief and motivate action." That is, symbols "both express the world's climate and shape it" (Geertz 1973:95). Some scholars have criticized symbol-inspired studies for their lack of a temporal dimension.[13] Only recently have scholars combined an ethnohistorical method, a temporal perspective, and symbolic analysis (Fowler 1982, 1987; Kracht 1989) to clarify the contexts and underlying causes that explain contemporary situations. The addition of a diachronic dimension to symbolic studies is necessary to acknowledge "the fact that people change their behavior and develop new interests and concerns in response to new opportunities and challenges" (Fowler 1987:6–9).

Fowler's (1982, 1987) works on the Arapaho and Gros Ventre are the most recent and theoretically stimulating works combining the ethnohistorical method with the symbolic interpretation of Native American culture. Fowler (1982) has shown how traditional Arapaho age-graded military society and political structures and values have continued in modified form since the mid-1800s. Fowler (1987) explores differences between Gros Ventre and Assiniboine explanations for shared history and shared political, sacred, and ritual symbols. Through examination of symbols Fowler (1987:6) demonstrates that these two groups have remained somewhat independent by creating culturally acceptable innovations that they can control and that progress in the dominant society's view does not inevitably lead to cultural loss for the other society, but to distinct cultural adaptation.[14] Symbols are invented, discarded, and reinterpreted as they are adapted to new social circumstances. While both tribes shared a number of cultural similarities, each community adjusted to its changed social conditions differently in the reservation period. Such is the case with the Kiowa, Comanche, and Apache.

Fowler's works (1982, 1987) demonstrate how current sociopolitical and socioreligious symbol systems operate within these tribes today. Each tribe has maintained a traditional sense of community by attaching meaning to "traditional" and adaptive forms of contemporary life while adapting to changing constraints on social interaction within and beyond each respective tribal community. The Arapaho maintenance of age-graded based authority and the Gros Ventre reliance on a shared community in which they have redefined and reused shared cultural symbols are, in actuality, innovations based on earlier and ongoing cultural traditions. As such, they are continuations of traditions and not simply products of Native American/ Euro-American interaction. As Fowler (1987:9) notes, "An approach that emphasizes the powerlessness of Indian people—the political economy of Indian-White relationships—and overlooks the way the exploited population interprets and reacts to those relations distorts the process by which Native American societies change." What is involved is the interpretation of new social realities that are culturally acceptable to the peoples themselves, as well as being adaptive to the larger sociopolitical circumstances of Anglo political encapsulation. As Fowler (1982 : 5) describes:

> The Arapahoes resolved problems of legitimation of authority and advocacy of tribal interests by interpreting new social realities in ways that were culturally acceptable as well as adaptive. Symbols emerged that worked to revitalize or reassert traditional values and relationships, yet at the same time reassured Whites that the Arapahoes were neither dangerous nor uncooperative. At the same time, old symbols took on new meanings that both reinforced traditional understandings and motivations and made innovation culturally acceptable.

Changes in the social conditions of native communities have necessitated changes in the construction of their social relationships, cultural beliefs, and symbols. Because these adaptations are primarily derived from existing traditional forms and not from Anglo-imposed forms, they allow native peoples to construct communities in terms that are sensible to them so that the members' interactions continue to be organized and facilitated through their own cultural forms.

Symbols, Ritual, and World View

Geertz (1973:91) defines a "symbol" as "any object, act, event, quality, or relation which serves as a vehicle for a conception—the conception is the symbol's 'meaning,'" indicating that there are both verbal and visual symbols which convey meaning and are communicable (Kracht 1989:6). Geertz (1973:89) maintains that culture is "an historically transmitted pattern of meanings embodied in symbols" and that individuals continuously construct personal or explanatory models which aid them in explaining and orienting themselves to their own world. Sherry B. Ortner (1978:5) states that symbolically religion "is first and foremost a system of meaning—goals, values, concerns, visions, [and] world constructions." If symbols function as vehicles for meaning which motivate human behavior or social action, then religion, as a cultural system, is "articulated through symbolic forms and activities" (Fowler 1982:4). To understand a culturally particular religion or phenomenon, an observer must develop familiarity with the associated symbols, observable in cultural activities contained in social events (Geertz 1973:91).[15] Ortner (1978:1) contends that most societies contain some major ritual or ceremonial form which they see "as embodying in some way the essence of their culture, as dramatizing the basic myths and visions of reality, the basic values and moral truths, upon which they feel their world rests." Geertz (1973) maintains that sacred and secular rituals are cultural acts where motivation and the general world view or conception come together. Religious, and I contend secular, symbols become manifest in cultural performances.

Victor Turner (1967, 1968, 1977:184; Kracht 1989:9) developed the concept of "ritual symbols" as "the smallest unit of ritual which still retains the specific properties of ritual behavior . . . the ultimate unit of specific structure in a ritual context." Turner (1968:2) conceived of ritual as aggregations of visual and verbal symbols, with the ritually associated symbols as "storage units" of traditional knowledge; rituals convey "messages from or about the gods" and reflect information concerning the "crucial values of the believing community." Ritual symbols can be observed through fieldwork. Turner (1967:19) noted such symbols as "empirically, objects, activities, relationships, events, gestures, and spatial units in a ritual situation," while Fowler (1982:4) found "many symbolic vehicles" in the form of Arapaho political symbols that could be observed in the field, such as ritual objects, personal names, clothing, body decoration, language, and ceremonies. The public nature of Southern Plains military society activities provides the opportunity for observing a plethora of ritual symbols and data (meetings, dances, singing practices, song texts, regalia, painted tipis, war trophies, naming ceremonies, giveaways, language, cedarings or incensed prayer blessings, combat recitations, oral history, archival sources).

Every culture contains a meaningful set of symbols or cultural patterns that are historically transmitted, convey information, and aid in interpreting the world. Symbols thus express cultural ethos and world view, and a diachronic focus allows a temporal examination of that ethos and world view. Symbolic anthropologists assert that religion, as a belief system, contains a meaningful system of symbols which motivates and compels believers to adhere to sanctioned group values (although nonbelievers exist in every society). Rituals as group activities or cultural acts containing symbols can be observed, and learning the ritual symbols of a particular culture facilitates insight into world view and ethos. Because every culture has undergone some degree of change or syncretism with contact with the other cultures it is necessary to understand a group's sociocultural system and associated ritual symbols prior to external influence. Culture contact situations characterized by varying interaction, forced acculturation, and change often produce cultural revivals or syncretic forms. Both native to native and Anglo to native influences regarding social structures must be addressed, as well as the conditions underlying culture change.

RESEARCH FORMAT

While emphasizing a strong ethnohistorical approach combining extensive ethnographic fieldwork and archival research, my approach differs from other ethnohistorical and religious-based symbolic studies in three ways: (1) I temporally examine the functional role and adaptations of a single form of social-secular institution (military sodalities); on a larger, comparative basis, (2) I apply elements of interpretive anthropology, which have been used primarily to examine religious and political systems, to a more secular form, to show that social structures and their associated symbols have an enduring reality; and (3) I emphasize the use and identification of varied sources.

I propose that military societies have been and continue to be major institutions of cultural adaptation, social organization, and enculturation for the Kiowa, Comanche, and Apache (KCA) to the present day. Through time, these cultures have been exposed to a series of crises or cultural stress periods. One form of cultural continuity has been facilitated through a continually adapting ideology and symbols associated with traditions concerning warfare, veteran status, and world view as demonstrated through their military societies. While these sodalities have not functioned continuously, they have been periodically revived during times of cultural stress and have served as adaptive strategies or arenas of enculturation that have facilitated and prolonged the survival of numerous cultural forms (contained in song, dance, ritual, language, kinship, economics, naming and semireligious ceremonies) for their respective tribal communities.

Like the Plains Indian powwow, which serves as a public social arena, Southern Plains military societies and many other Native American traditions serve as public forums or "arenas of enculturation" through which contemporary Native American cultures maintain, integrate, and even introduce new cultural forms. Like powwows, contemporary military society functions and associated activities are large and varied. They serve as major forms of enculturation for cultures that are encapsulated in the larger United States political and economic system. These revivals achieve this through the continuity, reformation, and innovation of their traditional social structures and their numerous associated functions and enculturative symbols associated with military sodality activities, the hallmark of which has been the maintenance of a warrior ethos.

Although the means of acquiring veteran status have changed significantly over the last two hundred years, this status remains an important social and integrative feature of Southern Plains Indian communities. While the maintenance of a martial ethos should not in any way be construed as militancy, a continuing martial ethos has served as a means of integrating society on a number of social, cultural, political, and economic levels. These systems may be examined by reconstructing their origins, structural organization, and functions and by gaining an understanding of the relationship between traditional military ideology, ethos, world view, and associated symbols and the social organization and cultural continuity in larger individual social units. Central to Fowler's (1982, 1987) works is the theory that an age-graded tradition helps legitimize centralized tribal government and intermediary leadership. The maintenance of a warrior ideology or ethos among non-age-graded and/or de facto graded society structures similarly serves to centralize social structure and traditions through cultural continuity.

Most symbolic studies have focused upon religion. Geertz (1973:90–108, 123–125) and others have shown that symbol systems, mental dispositions, and relationships between self and other exist in religious structures. I contend that they also exist in more secular structures and systems, including Plains military societies. Thus, I focus primarily on examining martial symbols on a group rather than individual level and on a temporal basis.

Although examples of what symbols mean for individuals are included and reflect larger community patterns, I emphasize the use of sodality and community military society symbols, how these symbols function in the continuation of a martial ideology and ethos, and their role in providing social integration and enculturation in respective tribal communities.

This study differs from past studies of North American military sodalities. In contrast to Stewart (1977:7), this study considers the relationship between military societies and other structural elements (in this case, the larger units of social organization) and the various functions (e.g., political, economic, religious, and recreational) of military societies in Plains communities. As the KCA contained nongraded or coordinate societies (although some exhibit de facto age-graded elements), the results here differ from Stewart's (1977) model for age-group societies, but provide a clearer view of Plains military societies than previously achieved.

Despite similarities, Plains Indian military societies were in no way homogeneous units of social organization as they have been presented in previous works. As units of social organization, these sodalities were part of larger tribal structures. I focus upon their functional and organizational basis and on the use of symbols in social organization and integration. These sodalities were not a set of static organizations, but, in some ways similar to tribes, underwent their own evolution, adaptation, and change. As Alice Beck Kehoe (1989:126) discusses, cultural reformations occur repeatedly in every culture, as societies modify customary patterns of behavior to account for changes in resources, population, and interaction with other societies. Natural and social circumstances are not indefinitely stable and require responses to their changes. A temporal examination reveals a series of cultural reformations and multiple ongoing adaptations. As broadly similar units of social organization, these sodalities functioned differently in their social communities.

Format and Presentation

Throughout periodic cessation and revival, the maintenance of similar functions and symbols and their uses as enculturative tools can be divided into four distinct political-economic periods: prehorse and posthorse preservation (pre-1875); reservation (1875–1900); postallotment (1900–1941); and post–World War II or contemporary (post-1941). Each chapter includes historical information on military societies from the early ethnographic period to the present. The prereservation data are largely based on ethnohistorical reconstructions of earlier archival sources which focused on documenting prereservation cultures, supplemented by my own fieldwork and later sources. Beyond data concerning dances, songs, and some ceremonial traditions, elders could provide only brief descriptions of the organization and functions of societies for this period; yet archival data were often independently confirmed by elders and were thus complementary. For the reservation era, archival data on military societies were limited; however, some data were obtained from elders who had firsthand accounts from their parents or grandparents, who experienced these events. Postallotment data were the least documented, but were easily obtained from elder eyewitness participants, family genealogies, photographs, tape recordings, and various handwritten accounts. Most twentieth-century data are based on my own fieldwork and interviews, corroborated and supplemented by independent interviews and archival materials.

Each Southern Plains community is discussed individually, establishing the origins, organization, functions, and historical development of each respective tribe's military society system. A historical reconstruction of the earliest known organizational and functional aspects of each group's military societies and the relations between societies and with the larger tribal community during the prereservation period (ca. 1830–1875) serves as a baseline for examining development and change. This is followed by discussion of the processes causing prereservation systems to be altered along with other changing cultural forms, resulting in ongoing secular and religious factions. Descriptive ethnographic reconstructions of each group's respective military societies and their historical developments to the present are presented through use of archival data, interviewing, and examination of current rituals. Reconstructing the evolution of these societies through time reveals the causes of change, continuity, and adaptation and establishes similarities between traditional and current structures and functions.

To understand the processes of change and the relationships of symbols between 1800 and 1997, I identify, compare, and contrast these symbols, combining elements of (1) Geertz's (1973) and Ortner's (1978) symbolic interpretation and framework for investigating religion; (2) Turner's (1977) emphasis on ethnographic interviewing, participant-observation, and contextual analysis of ritual symbols; (3) a multifield ethnohistorical research method; and (4) analysis in light of explanatory models employed by Fowler (1982, 1987), Clifford (1986b), and Kracht (1989). This provides a sound ethnographic approach, eliciting the way in which a people perceive themselves in a constantly changing world.

Each tribal community is addressed in an individual chapter to reduce confusion and constant cross-referencing for the numerous tribes, their respective military societies, and organizational and functional characteristics. This format enables a clearer presentation of each individual tribal sodality system and its historical developments and establishes similarities and differences.

A concluding chapter brings into perspective an ethnographic and comparative overview of these societies temporally, for each of the four periods discussed. Comparisons and contrasts are elicited in light of the larger social, cultural, and historical changes encountered by these groups. Particular attention is given to the associated symbols of each tribe, the role of military societies in respective units of social organization and enculturation, and the underlying causes of change for each group. The maintenance and revival of warrior activities and concepts are reconstructed for each tribal population. My results are discussed in light of larger Plains ethnology and current theories relevant to Plains scholars.

My goal, then, is to determine the role of Southern Plains military societies to the present day, through an ethnohistorical reconstruction focusing upon function, social organization, integration, and associated symbols. I wish to explicate how beliefs associated with warfare and military sodalities relate to the individual and collective Southern Plains tribal ethos and sense of reality and how these sodalities relate to their larger social communities. These integral and adaptive forms of social organization have facilitated the preservation and maintenance of distinct sodality and tribal identities among neighboring Native American communities, as well as in the context of the larger socioeconomically and politically encapsulating American society. The revival of military societies and their ritual symbols following World War II reflects a reversal of the lengthy denial of access to warrior status—the primary traditional means of acquiring male honor and status for many Plains Indians.

2 YÀPFÀHÊGÀU: KIOWA MILITARY SOCIETIES TO 1875

This chapter reconstructs Kiowa military societies from their known origins to circa 1890.[1] Because of greater ethnographic material and the seminal role played by the Kiowa in the revival of Southern Plains military societies in the late 1950s, the Kiowa material is considerably longer than the Apache and Comanche material and thus serves as a model for comparison. While the Kiowa data are primarily of post-1840 origin, they allow the most thorough, in-depth reconstruction and examination of a set of Plains military societies to date.

THE KIOWA

The Kiowa refer to themselves as Cáuigú, probably from qócáuigú (the tri-plural form for elks), from which the Anglo pronunciation of Kiowa is derived. In the past they have also referred to themselves as Kòmfàubîdàu (Big Tipi Flaps), Kútjáu (Coming Out or Emerging [rapidly implied]), Tépjáu (Coming Out or Emerging [slowly implied]), and less frequently Tépkîgàu (Blossomed Out Ones). Following a dispute over an animal killed on a hunt while still in the northland, a portion of the tribe separated and went away to the north never to be heard from again; they are referred to as the Aùzáthàuhòp (Those Who Went Away Disgruntled Because of/on Account of the Udder). Of the remaining Kiowa who continued southward, the northernmost Kiowa bands were known within the tribe as Thóqàhyòp or Thóqàhyòi (Northerners [literally Cold People]), while the southern bands were known as the Sálqáhyóp or Sálqáhyói (Southerners [literally Hot People]). Some of the southern bands which formed in the 1850s and frequented the Staked Plains were also known as Gúhàlècàuigù (Wild Mustang Kiowa), from the Kiowa enunciation of the Comanche word gúhàlè and the proximity of segments of both tribes to the wild horse herds. Recorded tribal traditions (Mooney 1898; Parsons 1929) place the Kiowa around the headwaters of the Yellowstone region of western Montana before 1700.

After allying and associating with the Crow for a period, the Kiowa migrated southeastward onto the Plains. The Kiowa belong to the Kiowa-Tanoan family, with the only close linguistic relative being Taos Pueblo in New Mexico. Migrations onto the Southern Plains began by at least the late 1700s, as the Kiowa formally made peace with the Comanche around 1790 (Mooney 1898:162–164; Northcutt 1973) or 1806 according to Elizabeth John (1985). Debate continues over whether the Kiowa were hunter-gatherers originating from the Northwest or were of southwestern descent, migrating north, perhaps prior to the advent of intensive southwestern agriculture. My own fieldwork has recorded historical information indicating that the Kiowa did indeed originate from the Southwest prior to migrating northward and later southeastward from Montana onto the Plains.

By the time the Kiowa had settled on the Southern Plains they possessed many of the sociocultural forms considered typical of nineteenth-century Plains Indians and were well adapted to a mobile hunting-and-raiding economy which emphasized the horse, tipi, and bison. The Sun Dance, sweat lodge, tribal medicine bundles, and vision quest all played prominent roles in Kiowa religion, which focused upon the acquisition of individual dáudáu (supernatural power) for success in warfare and life.

Supernatural Power, Bison, and Warfare

The concept of dáudáu was central to the Kiowa universe, a spirit force which was present in all things, including the earth, sun, moon, mountains, air, water, plants, and animals (Kracht 1989:80). The Kiowa believed that these natural entities possessed souls or spirits which manifested themselves through natural phenomena such as thunder, lightning, and the four (cardinal) directional winds or through more animate forms such as animals and birds.[2] All spirits had dáudáu; however, some were more powerful than others, as demonstrated by one animal dominating another in a natural setting. In addition, powers derived from above were stronger than those from the earth and animals, as sun power was stronger than bison power, and there were both good and bad powers (Kracht 1989:80–81).[3]

The Kiowa supplicated numerous spiritual forces for longevity and success, including the sun, moon, stars, plants, animals, and birds. Dáudáu could be acquired through vision quests in which power seekers (usually men) entreated certain spiritual forces; however, unsuccessful attempts were common since many spirits were not always willing to give their powers away. Yet some individuals received dáudáu, and others acquired several forms of power throughout their lives (Kracht 1989:80–81).[4] Because the nineteenth-century Kiowa economy was integrally based on hunting and raiding, skilled hunters and brave warriors had the utmost status in Kiowa society. The strongest form of dáudáu—sun power—was closely associated with warfare, and sun motifs were common on men's body painting and shield patterns in warfare for invulnerability. Proof that power was legitimate generally came from repeated success in warfare. Similar sun symbols permeated the Sun Dance, which was closely affiliated with the sun and war power (Kracht 1989:81–83).[5]

Also closely linked to war power was the strongest form of animal power, bison power, which was believed to come directly from the sun (Kracht 1989:89–90). Bison were seen as intermediaries between the sun and the Kiowa, bestowing their power on individuals in the form of their "cud" or round ball of hair contained within their stomachs, which made the bison and thus owners of such medicine difficult to kill.[6] Because the sun helped the bison grow (through grass), and the Kiowa in turn used the bison as a food source, sun, bison, and Kiowa were integrally connected, and hunters often sacrificed pieces of freshly butchered bison meat to the sun. Bison were also closely associated with warfare: killing a bison symbolized killing an enemy, and bison hearts were used to divine whether a man's son would grow up to become a successful warrior. From observations of seasonal changes in herd composition (winter divisions into male and female herds and summer rut aggregations), the Kiowa viewed bison herds as warrior societies, and bulls were recognized as "chiefs," just as among the Kiowa (Kracht 1989:90). Finally, the Kiowa recognized that the bison had special medicine powers related to great resuscitative strength; the Páuiyòi (Sons or Offspring of the Bison Bull), often known as Buffalo Doctors, contained this strength and thus specialized in war-related wounds involving bleeding.[7]

Social Organization

Kiowa tribal social organization was divided into six recognized and formally named autonomous divisional bands: the Cáuigú (Kiowa); the Kîèt (Big Shield [or Big Shields, Kíbìdàu]), also known as the Káugàbîdàu (Big Hides/Robes); the Kòtályóp or Kòtályôi (Black Boys), also known as Séndèiyòi (Sainday's Children); the Qáutjáu (Biters [literally Arikara]); the Qógûi (Elks); and the Kútjáu (Emerging/Coming Out [Rapidly]), who were exterminated by the Sioux around 1780. The Plains or Naishan Dene Apache (Kiowa-Apache) tribe (called by the Kiowa Tàugûi, Sitting on the Outside, and Sémhát, Thieves, from the Apache name for themselves, *Naishan Dene* meaning Those Who Carry Things About or Stealers) was a bandlike, but autonomous component which often formed a segment of the Kiowa Sun Dance or Qáujó, Lying House (probably shortened from Páuqáujó, Bison Bull [Robe] Lying House, or Qáujéjó, Meeting House), with ceremonies focusing upon the Táimé (Alone or Lonesome) Bundle. Each named band generally had a ranking leader and a single head tribal leader was recognized until 1866, when Jóhâusàn (Little Bluff Recess or Concavity), the last pre-reservation Kiowa tribal chief, died.

Each tribal band or division was composed of multiple jòfàujógàu or jódáu (camp or residence bands) composed of smaller families and individuals formed around one or more core extended families, generally containing the jòfàujóqì (camp or band leader). Band size fluctuated considerably by season and by wealth, prestige, and family size of the jòfàujóqì. Bilateral descent permitted close kin relationships on both sides of an individual's family. As in Hawaiian kinship terminology, the Kiowa lumped all children of parents' siblings (cousins) as siblings, while parents' siblings included bifurcate merging, with one term for mother and mother's sister and another for father and father's brother. Separate terms were used for father's sister and mother's brother. Grandmothers were differentiated, but grandfathers were not. Sororal polygyny, the levirate, and arranged marriages extended and strengthened sibling bonds. Postmarital locality varied; patrilocality predominated, but a significant portion chose short-term matrilocality.

Kiowa Sodalities

In the nineteenth century the Kiowa had two women's societies and several types of men's religious, doctoring, shield, and military sodalities. The Bear Old Women Society (Sétchôhyòp) was a women's auxiliary to the Ten Medicine Keepers. These ten women held great power and had secret meetings upon the requests of individuals who sought power for war ventures or who had made vows in extremely dangerous circumstances.[8] The Calf Old Women's Society (Xálìchôhyòp) had greater war power than the Bear Society and was associated with the Sun Dance. Similarly, men sought out this society to acquire war power or because of vows made in return for recovery from illness. This society also blessed the ill, newborn, and recently married.[9] The Pehodlma (Very Soft Hide Women) are often cited as a women's society in the 1935 Santa Fe fieldnotes, but were actually an informally organized number of the older and most experienced craftswomen. These women were the tribal elite in tipi making, midwifery, hide tanning, warbonnet making, and other domestic skills. The group apparently functioned on an informal level, with no known association with war power.[10]

There were also men's shield societies associated with medicine and curing such as the Buffalo Medicine Men and the Owl Prophets. The Buffalo Medicine Men or Páuiyòi (Offspring of a Bison Bull), commonly called Buffalo Doctors, were the only shield society that was a formally organized group of curers. They accompanied war parties and specialized in healing war wounds, particularly those involving bleeding. Other smaller doctoring sodalities included men specializing in owl power for prophecy, such as those who studied under *Mamanti* (Cáumâmájè or Goose Flying Overhead), and those specializing in power associated with underwater animals, such as those who apprenticed under Tónàuqàut (Rough Tailed Turtle or Snapping Turtle), are little known today.

The Ten Medicine keepers formed a sodality of priests that was both religious and civil in nature and cared for the ten Tàlyópcàu (Paternal Grandmother Bundles), also known as Tàlyîdàui (Paternal Grandmother Medicines), Dáuigú (Medicines), Dàuqígáu (Gods), and Áulbéáuihyà (Ones of Many Scalps). Following James Mooney (1898:239), many people confuse Tàlyîdàui (Paternal Grandmother Medicines) with Tàlyîdáui (Boy Medicines). Although Alice Marriott's (1945) translation of "grandmothers" was correct, the confusion concerning the name for these bundles results from (1) her failure to distinguish between the pronunciation of tàlyí (singular) and tàlyóp (triplural) for boy and tàlyî (singular/dual) tàlyôi (triplural) for paternal grandmother (hence Tàlyópcàu), disregarding differences in Kiowa terms for address, possessional, and reference for these two kin categories, and (2) her failure to recognize that only two of the ten bundles are referred to as the Záidètàlyî (Split or Half Boys). These priests received individuals coming to pray and leave offerings at one of the ten bundles, renewed them at the Sun Dance, served as civic role models for the tribe, and mediated civil and criminal disputes. Associated with the Sun Dance were a series of dream shield societies including the Démgùtqò (Yellow Breasts or Tàimé Shields), the Télgùdàu (Gypsum Painted or Hótòyài, Traveled By [Hotoyia] Shields), and the *Kowde* Shields, which were inspired by Poor Buffalo (Kracht 1989:210–218).

Nineteenth-century Kiowa placed great emphasis upon social status, which was directly linked to one's individual war record (Mooney 1898; 1935 Santa Fe Laboratory of Anthropology Fieldschool Notes; Nye 1937; Mishkin 1940). The concept of dáudáu (supernatural power), which permeated traditional Kiowa culture, encompassed Kiowa cosmology and belief. Much of a man's youth was spent undertaking activities which served as training for adult martial-related activities and the acquisition of supernatural power, often for success in warfare. A number of war-related sodalities, known as shield societies, were associated with war power, including the Eagle and Bird (Fish Hawk) Shields. Numerous other individual doctors and shield owners with small groups of understudies existed within the Kiowa tribe.

Before the Kiowa entered the reservation in 1874–1875, the band system was considerably rearranged, resulting in the formation of several reservation communities extending from Verden to Hobart, Oklahoma, bordered by the Washita River to the north and the Wichita Mountains to the south. These Kiowa communities included Verden, Anadarko, Hog Creek, Stecker, Meers, Red Stone, Carnegie, Zodletone (Zólt̞ǫ) or Stinking Creek, Mountain View, Saddle Mountain, Hobart, and Lone Wolf; individuals later took allotments around these communities. Estimates for the Kiowa population are suspect prior to 1875, when 1,070 Kiowa were enumerated. The Kiowa probably never exceeded 3,500–4,000 before being struck by several epidemics during the early to mid-1800s. Population continued to decline overall, reaching 1,000 in 1920. The Kiowa numbered 2,692 by 1940 and numbered 4,337 in 1970, with 2,081 residing in their allotted areas. As of October 1994 the Kiowa Tribe contained 10,049 enrolled members (*Kiowa Indian News*, 1994). Most of them reside within the previously described area, centering around Carnegie, which is considered by many to be the heart of Cáuidàumg̀a (Kiowa country) and contains the majority of tribal facilities. Smaller yet significant groups of Kiowa have relocated to urban areas such as Oklahoma City, Tulsa, Dallas, and San Francisco. Throughout the twentieth century the Kiowa have been extremely influential in art, music, dance, the Native American Church, and Native American legal issues.

YÀPFÀHÊGÀU: THE KIOWA MILITARY SOCIETIES

The Kiowa name for their military societies is Yàpfàhêgàu, which is frequently translated "soldier" or "warrior societies." The name actually refers to the temporary authority of these organizations to serve as police and thus means "temporary police or guards." Frances Densmore (1992:313) provides a similar translation for the term for Lakota military societies: "The word *aki'ćita* is commonly translated 'soldier,' but its meaning is akin to 'guard' or 'police,' the proper word for 'warrior' being *iki'ćize*." Today the term Yàpfàhêgàu is occasionally heard among the eldest generation. The term Sólègàu, from the Kiowa corruption of the English word "soldier" plus the plural Kiowa suffixal form gàu for people or collective group (in this case, society), gained frequency sometime in the late 1800s and is still used in speech and songs today.[11]

Although data concerning the origins of the Kiowa societies are scanty, it is likely that at least some of the known Kiowa societies were in existence by the late 1700s or very early 1800s. Accounts of the Qóichęgàu around 1790–1806 and Hugh L. Scott's reference to the Tǫ́kǫ́gàut as a fully developed society policing tribal aggregations in 1834 suggest a lengthy existence for Kiowa military societies.[12] By the third quarter of the eighteenth century the Kiowa maintained six active military societies. A seventh society, the Cáuitémgòp, was known to have sung and danced in place after choosing a position to remain until the battle ended. The Cáuitémgòp were annihilated in battle after refusing to retreat, and the society was not resuscitated because of the danger that this incident represented to the tribe. An eighth society, the Óhǫ̀mò, which was introduced to the Kiowa in 1884, represented the late-nineteenth-century diffusion of the Plains Grass-War-Omaha Dance. One Kiowa account collected by Scott in the 1890s indicates that there had previously been more prereservation societies: "There are five soldier bands for the men. . . . We used to have a great many other soldier bands when we had more men, but when we got fewer in no. [number] we put those ceremonies aside when they sun dance, until we only had five left. Now we have but thrown all away."[13]

According to Jerrold Levy (n.d.a: 13, n.d.b), who has not used the 1935 Santa Fe data, the Jáifègàu Society was believed by Marriott's informants to be the oldest Kiowa society, but was eventually outranked by the Qóichęgàu, which was founded later. However, these statements prove inaccurate. Most sources (e.g., Boyd 1981: 114; Tsonetokoy 1988: 30) associate the formation of the Jáifègàu Society with the noted historic battle between the combined Kiowa, Comanche, and Apache and forty-eight Cheyenne Bow String Society members in 1837. Silverhorn's 1935 account of the sole survivor of the Qóichęgàu in a battle against the Comanche prior to the Kiowa-Comanche peace around 1790 (1806) argues for an earlier existence. Levy (n.d.b: 13–14) states that the Tǫ́kǫ́gàut and Chęjánmàu societies developed later and suggests that the younger ages of members in these two societies indicate that the social ranking of the societies represents an expansion of the larger society system which brought together men of the same social and economic levels.

Kiowa military society ethnonyms have been recorded in various fashion by W. P. Clark (1982 [1885]), James Mooney (1898), Robert H. Lowie (1916b), Mildred Mayhall (1962), Hugh L. Scott, and the 1935 Santa Fe Laboratory of Anthropology Fieldschool notes.[14] Despite numerous versions and spellings of society names through the years, these societies have usually been listed in the same order and are easily correlated.

Military Society Division

Kiowa military societies were roughly divided by age, social status, and achievement. Complete age sets did not progress as a unit as in the graded Plains societies. However, the Kiowa had de facto age-grading based upon war and socioeconomic status in their prereservation societies. The Pòlą́hyòp (Rabbits) consisted of all the boys from those who were old enough to walk up to the ages of twelve to fourteen. This society trained the boys in skills that they would need in adult life. The Rabbits met, feasted, and danced like the other societies, were supervised by adult leaders, and learned by emulating the adult societies.[15] The Áljóyìgàu was comprised of teens and younger adult men. The members of the next three societies, the Chèjánmàu, Tòkǫ́gàut, and Jáifègàu, were primarily young to older adult men, the majority of the adult male fighting force. The Qóichègàu consisted of ten men (or sash owners), ten apprenticelike assistants, a number of retired members, and a group of young apprentice members or colts. The Qóichègàu were structured like the previous four societies except that they had more rituals, strenuous initiation practices, and more dangerous battle obligations. The ten sash owners were considered the greatest and bravest warriors in the tribe, as the society was reputedly the first into battle and the last to retreat. Using contrary speech, these members were required to stake themselves down in battle by shooting an arrow through their sashes, unless someone yelled *twgiaw'kw* and released them from this requirement, to which they replied àhô, àhô (thank you, thank you). As exemplary leaders in battle, these men assumed the most dangerous warfare responsibilities.[16] Unlike the other societies, the Qóichègàu reportedly policed the Sun Dance only once.[17]

Military Society Rank and Social Status

Lowie (1916b:841–842), Donald Collier (1938), and Elsie Clews Parsons (1929) viewed Kiowa societies as equally ranked, while Mooney (1898), Alice Marriott (1945, 1968), and Bernard Mishkin (1940) viewed the four adult societies (excluding the Pòlą́hyòp and Áljóyìgàu) as ranked in social status (Levy n.d.a:13). The Kiowa are the only Plains tribe to have developed a system of formally named social ranks and socially ranked warrior societies (Levy n.d.a, n.d.b). Kiowa military societies were ranked in terms of status, but this was not completely fixed and varied with changes in membership, leaders, and popular consensus at any given time. Popular consensus often swayed, dependent upon the charisma of a society's membership,

TABLE 1   Kiowa Military Society Synonymy

Men's Societies			
Mooney 1898	Lowie 1916	Clark 1885	Meadows 1995
1. Polanyup or Tsalnyui (Rabbits)	Fulanyu (Rabbits)	—	Pòláhyòp (Rabbits)
2. Adaltoyui/Tenbeyui (Young Wild Sheep)	Altoyuhe (Shepherds)	Adaltoyui (Sheep)	Áljóyìgàu (Wild Mountain Sheep)
3. Tsentanmo (Horse Headdresses)	Tsetanma (Rulers?–of Horses)	Tsentanmo (Feather Head)	Chèjánmàu or Chètánmàu (Horse Headdresses)
4. Tonkonko (Black Legs)	Tunkunqot (Black Feet-Leggings)	Tonkonko (Raven Soldiers)	Tòkógàut (Black Legs)
5. Tanpeko (Skunkberry People) or Tsen-a-dalka-i (Crazy Horses)	Taipeko (Berries)	Tanpeko (War Club)	Jáifègàu (Unafraid of Death) (Skunkberries) Chèàulkàuigù (Crazy Horses)
6. Ka-itsenkop (Real/Principal Dogs)	Qoitsenko (Horses?)	Ka-itsenko (Horse)	Qóichégàu (Sentinel Horses)
7. —	—	—	Cáuitèmgòp (Kiowa Bone Strikers)
8. —	—	—	Óhòmògàu (Omaha or War Dance)
Women's Societies			
1. —	tsalietsu 'nyu'p Old Women Society		Xálìchôhyòp Calf Old Women
2. —	onna'atema Bear Society		Àunhádèmàimàu Bear Women aka Sétchôhyòp Bear Women

the status of its officers as war chiefs, and the recent achievements of its warriors. While a generally fixed pattern of progression into the higher societies correlated with an increase in age, increased warfare status, and wealth, some exceptions occurred; youths of fifteen to twenty-five years of age were occasionally inducted into the Qóichégàu as colt members, while a few adult men remained in the Áljóyìgàu throughout their lives.

Interviews collected by the 1935 Santa Fe party and by Alice Marriott in 1935–1936 agree that the Pòlą́hyòp Society was the beginning level in the Yàpfàhêgàu system while the Qóichę̀gàu was the highest level. Likewise, most past and present consultants consider the Áljóyî̀gàu a transitional stage from the Pòlą́hyòp into the adult societies.[18] The Áljóyî̀gàu Society was composed of teen and largely unmarried adult males. Members concentrated on acquiring war honors to raise their individual social status and candidacy for membership in other societies; they had a reputation for recklessness in battle, being good-looking, being great lovers and good hunters, and having dashing costumes that "created a flutter in the hearts of all the young ladies."[19]

The Áljóyî̀gàu Society was rather large, with fifty to seventy-five members, but was depleted after each Sun Dance through heavy recruitment of prominent members by other societies or recruitment to replace a recently deceased relative in another society. Thus, the Áljóyî̀gàu were continually left with a group of unwanted young men. The Áljóyî̀gàu were never known to have recruited from the other societies except for officers or to have deterred other societies from recruiting their own members. Only the leaders were qájâi (literally brave men, but frequently translated as chiefs), men who had distinguished themselves in battle. Being a qájáqî̀ was required for membership in at least some and perhaps all upper-level societies and may have been required for socially nonprominent members to reach the upper-level societies.[20]

Although the relative ranking of the Chè̀jánmàu, Tọ̀kọ́gàut, and Ją́ifè̀gàu is certain, the exact criteria for membership in the three is unclear, although they may relate to individual military, social, and economic rank. The Chè̀jánmàu were generally considered by Kiowa elders in 1935 to have been slightly lower in status than the other societies and reportedly lacked hereditary positions. The Tọ̀kọ́gàut and Ją́ifè̀gàu often competed for status. Many members of these two societies were older, more established warriors, and other societies frequently recruited leaders from the Ją́ifè̀gàu.[21]

Individual Rank

An individual's status and potential for membership in a society depended largely on the quantity and quality of war honors and on his social class. As in most Plains groups, military society leaders included many of the top-ranking warriors of the tribe. Exclusive of the Sun Dance gathering, all Kiowa military society leaders were reportedly jò̀fàujóqî̀ (camp chiefs or headsmen) or leaders of residence bands.[22] According to Mishkin (1940:36), all camp chiefs and society chiefs belonged to the ǫ̀dè, the top social class. A 1935 survey of the twenty-five most famous Kiowa men included the leaders of all five adult men's societies (Mishkin 1940:54). All society officers (fàujóqì and áljóqì) were required to be qájâi, someone who distinguished himself in battle. In the Áljóyìgàu, only the leaders were said to be qájâi, as the younger members had not yet proved themselves in battle. A man's first achievement in war usually resulted in a change in his society membership (Mishkin 1940:38), as indicated by the descriptions of large annual recruitment from the Áljóyìgàu Society and of the desire to acquire such war honors quickly and move into a higher-ranking adult society.[23]

A minimum of four such war deeds brought the rank of qájáisàupàn (literally big brave man, often translated as big chief or brave, great warrior) and eligibility for Qóichę̀gàu membership (Mishkin 1940:38–39). Only the Qóichę̀gàu and Tǫ̀kǫ́gàut Societies are known to have required war honors for membership. Regular Qóichę̀gàu membership generally exceeded the minimum of four war honors, while the ten "assistant" members were also required to have four war honors. Whether war honors were required for membership in the other societies remains unclear. According to Levy (n.d.a:13) and Marriott, the Tǫ̀kǫ́gàut required war honors; however, the exact number is unknown. While recording Kiowa descriptions of warfare bravery by society sash and staff owners in the 1890s, H. L. Scott also noted the societies' differential martial status: "That Elk Skin [Qóichę̀gàu] have the hardest road, the Black Leggings [Tǫ̀kǫ́gàut] next, and the other bands [societies] behind."[24] Tso'odl (Packing Stones) stated that a man did not have to have a big war record and that some men had never gone on a war journey before joining a society, suggesting that only some societies required war honors for membership or that the qualifications had changed by the time of his entrance into the men's societies circa 1880. Obviously ą́udé (favored or aristocratic) youth who were inducted had no war qualifications. It is likely that a war record may not have been required for entrance into most of the societies below the Qóichę̀gàu. Nevertheless, it made a man more desirable as a potential recruit.

There was a correlation between increasing individual social status and progression to membership in the higher-level societies. The Kiowa social system during the mid-1800s consisted of four loosely defined social ranks or classes (Mishkin 1940:35; Richardson 1940:15): ǫ̀dè, ǫ̀gòp, or ǫ̀dèǫ̀gòp; ǫ̀dègùfà; káuàun; and dàufǫ̀. The ǫ̀dè or ǫ̀dèǫ̀gòp were affluent, had war honors, were generous, courteous, the headsmen of the tribe, etc. The ą́udé were the favored and usually oldest male or female children of an ǫ̀dè family, received the best clothes, food, and often their own tipi, and were not required to work as youths. The ǫ̀dègùfà were the second best, largely the same as ǫ̀gòp except lacking in war honors and thereby being less wealthy; they included many specialists in religion, doctoring, art, and upcoming war leaders. The káuàun (pitiable) were common people, hard working but poor, including many captives. The dàufǫ̀ (no good, worthless) were a very small minority of unmotivated, lazy, and dishonest individuals.

Levy and Marriott's research also indicated a correlation between Kiowa social status and the social ranking of military societies. While male youths generally progressed through the Pòlą́hyòp (Rabbits) and Áljóyìgàu (Herders or Young Sheep) before advancing to other societies, this was not always mandatory; in some instances, children of high-status families were recruited directly from the Rabbits into the upper-level societies, usually to serve as an errand boy or servant (áujòqì) for that society. These youths became regular members of their society upon reaching adulthood. Thus, the system was not truly age-graded, but resembled de facto age-grading: membership in the five adult societies was clearly linked to individual increases in social status, wealth, and war rank. While presents were formally made to members of a society upon induction, there was nothing approaching the concept of an entrance purchase, as found in graded societies. Above the Pòlą́hyòp and the Áljóyìgàu, certain social statuses as defined by Mishkin (1940) were correlated with membership in particular societies. The Chèjánmàu (Horse Headdresses) Society contained mainly káuàun and ǫ̀dègùfà members. The Tǫ̀kǫ́gàut Society contained mostly ǫ̀dègùfà members, while the Jáifègàu Society contained ǫ̀dè and ǫ̀dègùfà members, and the Qóichégàu all ǫ̀dè members. It is not clear whether the societies had a formal, absolute ranking or could periodically change in prestige with the composition of their membership (Levy n.d.a: 13–14), but the latter is likely, as Mooney notes (1912d:861–862). Levy has suggested that individuals of dàufǫ̀ status were excluded from society membership; however, several consultants in 1935 and my own consultants born around 1900 indicate that nearly all adult males belonged to a society. It is likely that individuals of dàufǫ̀ status remained in the Áljóyìgàu. In any event, the proportion of people of this social status in the entire tribal population was relatively small.

That Kiowa societies were roughly ranked is given credence by the fact that youths were taken directly from the Pòlą́hyòp only into the upper societies, reflecting the higher social position of the family and the hereditary replacements in the upper societies. Other youths had to work their way up the social and societal ladder by gaining war honors and wealth and increas-

TABLE 2 Kiowa Military Society Membership and Social Class Correlations

Pòlą̂hyòp: all male children.
Áljóyìgàu: largely teens and young men.
Chèjánmàu: mostly ộdègừfà and ką́uàun.
Tòkǫ́gàut: largely ộdègừfà, some ộdè; *war honors required.
Jáifègàu: mostly ộdè and ộdègừfà.
Qóichę́gàu: all ộdè: *war honors required.
Óhòmògàu: ộdè and ộdègừfà members initially.
Cáuitémgòp: Unknown, but probably ộdè.

ing their social position. Likewise, the age of membership increased in the higher-status societies. At the time of initiation, wealth was generally required to validate war honors and to provide feasts and gifts for spectators. As a man's age and war record increased, so did his progression into the higher-status societies, which required war deeds to recite and validate and the goods necessary for such giveaways.

SOCIETY PARTNERS

The institution of cóm (friend) or châ (friend or partner), the pairing of men within the same society as "society brothers," permeated Kiowa military societies. Of all the Southern Plains tribes, detailed data on society partners are greatest for the Kiowa. The formation of society partners involved the formal establishment of society brotherhood, involving two men of similar age and social and economic status. This arrangement was generally made by the head society leader and not by the paired individuals themselves. Members could be new recruits, but were often "stolen" from another society and inducted into a society as a replacement. Kiowa military societies were non-kin-based sodalities, so the institution of society partners becomes significant because it formed an important bonding mechanism, promoting horizontal integration on a family, sodality, and tribal level. As partners were not allowed to be consanguineal or affinal relatives, these friendship pairings (known in anthropology as fictive kinship) crosscut band affiliation and kinship classifications to cement the tribe on a wider level.[25] There were a variety of types of society partners, including childhood friends, intertribal friends, intertribal trading partners, and intertribal friends through, for example, the marriage of two unrelated men to sisters. The term komto (exact etymology unknown, but probably a combination of cą́u-jàu, to shop, trade, or buy; and cóm, friend, and thus cómjậu or trading friend) was used for intertribal friends or trading partners. With the exception of the society princesses, no formal relations as society partners existed in religious activities or for women. Within the military societies the institution of cóm flourished and held the most social impact.[26]

A member addressed all other members of their society as cóm (single/dual = friend) or cǫ́bàu (triplural = friends), while addressing specific individuals as châ (friend or partner). The term cóm was commonly used to refer to the institutionalized friendship itself and was only occasionally used to refer to one's partner. Society partners usually addressed each other as châ (friend) or fǎbí (brother, including male first cousins, etc.). A man might also refer to his partner as a member of a society, such as Tǫ̀kǫ́gàcòm (Black Legs Society friend) or Áljóyìcòm (Young Wild Sheep Society friend). The reciprocal terms between two partners also extended to their families, who assumed consanguineal kin behavior although related fictively. The ascending and descending relatives of both partners addressed each other as if they were actual relatives, through the two "brothers." Thus, the sons of two society partners also addressed each other as brother (an English "cousin" is classified as a brother or sister in the Kiowa kinship system). Likewise the daughter of your partner became your daughter, you her father (father's brother), and so on. Due to death and replacement, a partnership could frequently be formed late in life, even after the age of fifty. No matter how late in life the relationship was established, the two men began addressing their partner's relatives by the appropriate consanguineal kinship terms. The relationship between a man and the wife of his society partner was a joking one, like that of a biological brother's wife. Although partners generally fought and raided together, one partner might provide for the wife of a partner who was away on a war party; however, there were no marital rights sanctioned by this practice.[27] If a man was killed, his partner might marry his widow and the children would continue to call him father, just as in the normal use of the levirate. A man could not marry a sister of his society partner even after the partnership had ended, as she was considered his sister as well.[28] A biological brother was said never to have been allowed to replace a deceased brother in a society pairing, although some families made this request in order to keep a member of their family in a particular society. One example is cited for the Qóichégàu, when Yellow Bison Bull (Páugútqójè) took the place of his brother Killed One with His Hands (Máunjòfáhóljè) upon the latter's death. The formation of society partners could be used to join two families in a stronger alliance, as it was with Luther

Samonte (Cocklebur) and Blue Necklace (Qólpásàuhèqî) of the Black Legs Society.[29] Theoretically, a friendship was broken only by death. As long as the two men remained in the same society they could not take another partner if the friendship was genuine and of duration. When one man left the society to join another, the relationship ceased, although the two appear to have interacted amicably even after ending the partnership. As Jimmy Quoetone stated in 1935, "Once a kom [cóm], always a kom."[30]

In forming partners, the society leaders tried to match up congenial pairs of men. Although a man usually conceded to the selection of his partner by the society leaders, this was not required. Áljóyîgàu and Chèjánmàu Society members are said to have frequently picked their partners, which often led to later problems in staying together as members switched to other societies. When society partners insisted on staying together, the societies sometimes realized that to get one member they had to take the other, which was referred to as "carrying along his friend." Kiowa and Apache men could become society partners because this was the only other tribe that was allowed to have regular members in some of the Kiowa societies, perhaps due to their close and lengthy political association.[31]

Following the ritual head bumping and exchange of horses between the two men at the establishment of cóm relations, a ritual which at least ideally symbolized their lifelong friendship, a continual exchange of merchandise between the two partners began. When Belo Cozad left the Áljóyîgàu to join the Óhòmò Society, his Áljóyîcòm, Henry Tso'odl, was paired up with Dadlate'. They continually visited each other. Tso'odl gave his partner an "irongrey horse"; his partner reciprocated with a bay. Later Tso'odl gave him a bay racing horse, and Dadlate' returned a buckskin mount. The continual exchange of gifts was common between two partners of equal or nearly equal economic status.

This continual exchange and mutual economic aid were the source of the most important social impact of the institution of society brothers. A member could always rely on his partner for social and economic aid and cooperation at times throughout the year when the members could not be in collective proximity as a society. Society partners between áudé (favored children) are said never to have been broken except by death, induction into the Qóichégàu Society, or the replacing of one's relative in another society. After the ritual head bumping the two men were responsible for each other in warfare and in life in general. If one was killed, the remaining man might name his deceased partner's replacement or fellow society members might suggest a replacement. The remaining man, however, occasionally held out,

honoring his deceased partner's memory by refusing to accept a replacement. It was not uncommon for a number of older men to be without partners, having lost them through death and thereafter honoring their memory
by not accepting a replacement. If several men in a society had lost their
partners, the society leader might pair them up. Pairs of partners from other
societies were sometimes taken in to increase the society's size, but usually
only single members were needed to fill vacancies created by recent deaths
or retirement. There may once have been a fixed number of membership
positions in some of the upper-level societies.[32]

Whenever possible, equality of social status and in particular age was almost always desired in forming society partners. Partners could be on different economic levels, and there seems to have been some competition to
become partners with a favored boy (ą́udétàlyî), who was known to be
wealthy. Lone Bear, for example, was partners with Pulw (Poolaw), a boy
who was much poorer at that time. Unlike adult pairings, if ill feelings existed between pairings of favored children they simply did not visit one another; while the arrangement was not considered a "good friendship," the
two remained institutional friends. If an older man retired for reasons of
age, his partner often retired too, to prevent competition for recognition
from a younger replacement who sought to achieve a level of prestige equal
to the older man's. In some cases the remaining older man might adopt the
younger man as his partner, which is said to have alleviated the differences
in status; however, this form of adoption was not common and it is unclear
just how this raised the younger man's social status. If one partner retired in
favor of his son, the other might also retire, resulting in their sons becoming
partners. This type of practice appears to have been appointed and not inherited, as it was not common and contradicted the rule of prior nonconsanguineal or affinal relations between society partners. These sons might address each other as friend or partner (châ) and brother (fấbî).[33] If one of the
two older men retired, the son of the other usually would not become the
partner of the remaining older man because he had already been calling him
father for some time. The society would thus find the son a society partner,
reflecting the usual practice of taking in individuals who were not related
and not inducting pairs.[34] Offspring of two society partners reportedly could
not intermarry into the third generation. Grandsons of two partners addressed each other as brother, but never as friend or partner (châ), because
the relationship of partners is said never to have been inherited.[35]

Society partners collected and gave property for the marriage of a partner's daughter and received part of the total amount of property that was
reciprocally collected. In disputes concerning his partner a man often at-

tempted to mediate the matter for his partner. If a man's partner smoked on the matter, he was obligated to settle it, just as if biological brothers had smoked on the matter.[36]

Partners often lived in different camps but frequently visited each other, continually exchanging gifts. In some instances one moved to live with the other, and they were reportedly closer to each other than to their own biological relatives. The wives of two partners (fictive sisters-in-law) treated each other as sisters.[37] In addition to exchanging horses after the head bumping, partners often received their own song and were required to dance whenever it was played. Today this practice has continued in only a very few families, mostly in the Óhòmò Society. Thus, partners always sat and danced together during society activities. At death, a partner gave more gifts to his partner's family than did ordinary society members. On war parties partners stayed together and generally looked out for each other's welfare. Families often did not like this, because if one man was wounded or killed his partner would probably also die, trying to rescue him or making a final stand together.[38]

One such incident involved two young men, Tanwte and K'opa, who were partners and both in love with the same woman. When they were leaving on a war party, she gave them a blanket and said not to return until it was worn out. After raiding with the Comanche for two to three years, they got into a battle with some whites. The Comanche retreated, and the two Kiowa were forced to hide in a creek bed. After holding their adversaries off with rifles, one of the men was finally killed. His partner could have escaped but remained by his side until he too was killed. The Comanche buried the two together. The seriousness of the institution among the Kiowa is perhaps best expressed by Frizzlehead, who stated, "Kom [cóm] in any society were required to fight and die together." [39]

The institution of cóm was most active in the military societies and necessitated the stealing of members as vacancies occurred. This institution became more formalized with a progression into the upper societies. The Áljóyìgàu Society was seen as the place for those who were not taken directly from the Pòlá̖hyòp into other societies to start their careers. Membership in the Chèjánmàu Society was a higher progression but not as prestigious as the Tòkógàut and Jáifègàu. These two societies seemed to have a more or less set number of partnerships within certain families. However, warriors who achieved distinction were also taken in. The Qóichégàu had no direct hereditary positions, but members' sons sometimes became colts, who could later become regular members. Here the relationship of society partners was highly ritualized, as demonstrated ceremonially by the use of a sash or rope between the regular Qóichégàu members or sash owners and their partners who served as assistants.[40]

SOCIETY LEADERSHIP

Except for the Óhòmò Society and the Cáuitémgòp, whose organization is unknown, each of the societies above the Pòlą́hyòp contained the same leadership offices. Each society had two fàujóqì (keepers or leaders), one of whom was the tháumjóqì (first or head leader or head society chief). Elected for life, the leaders were replaced only upon voluntary retirement or death. The head leader generally carried the standard of the society, which was often a form of no-retreat staff (Parsons 1929:91). With the exception of Big Bow in the Áljóyìgàu, society leaders were reportedly always older men (around age fifty or more), and a man usually became a society chief before he became a camp chief (jòfàujóqì). Case histories suggest that this age estimate is probably high, as some noted warriors were society leaders in their mid-thirties and early forties.[41]

Society leaders generally held top authority within their society and controlled all activities and decisions. Second only to the fàujóqì were the two whipmen known as áljóqì (drivers) or less frequently as qîàlqì or qîàljòqì (men drivers or men driver keepers). Serving as sergeants at arms, and commonly referred to as whipmen, these two men sat on each side of the lodge door during society meetings, were in charge of recruiting new members, kept order in meetings, forced members to rise and dance, and were frequently chosen to succeed as society leaders. The two whipmen carried insignia of office for their society such as quirts, swords, tomahawks or in the case of both Tòkǫ́gàut and one of the Áljóyìgàu whipmen a flat, serrated club known as a qópcúgàut. Although qópcúgàut was translated as "mountain striker" by Kiowa consultants in 1935, the origin of the etymology is presently unknown. It appears that in earlier times the whipmen of all Kiowa societies carried these serrated quirts as badges of office, which gave way as newer items captured in warfare such as swords and tomahawks came into fashion. The popular name "whipmen" is derived from the use of these whips as insignia of their office. The wooden serrated whips or mountain strikers (qópcúgàut) were also known as chętàóttàgàu (fox pelt handles), from the use of fox hides as quirt handles; the two whipmen were also referred to as chętàjóqì (fox pelt keepers). Although used by many societies as the insignia of whipmen, serrated quirts were not limited to this position and reportedly could be made by anyone (presumably male) in the tribe. Several such whips are in the Smithsonian collections; although differences between society and individual whips are presently unknown, riding quirts and whips were generally smaller than society whips or clubs.[42]

As exemplary leaders in warfare, society leaders frequently assumed the most conspicuous and thus most dangerous positions in battle. The society chiefs frequently changed due to deaths in battle and recruitment into the Qóichégàu. Each society also contained between five to eight elder fáuljògàu (drum keepers, society singers and drummers) who provided music during society functions. The position as a society singer (fáuljòqì) was a rather informal one and changed more frequently than the other leadership positions. Each singer used a small, hand-held rawhide drum (fáulkàu), which were later replaced by large rawhide single-base drums copied from Anglo military bands in the reservation period. As the Kiowa were highly mobile prior to the reservation period, large bass drums would have been more of a hindrance than a benefit. Some groups adopted Anglo commercial band base drums for use in their dances as early as the 1880s, although traditional rawhide base drums continue to be made and used today.[43]

Military Society Youth Members

Each of the societies between the Pòlá̖hyòp and Qóichégàu contained two áujòqì (literally those who keep things handy) or íjéqì (distributors or rationers, in reference to serving food during feasts), young male assistants to the áljóqì. Collectively known as tályì̖yîgàu (boy members), these two youths were á̖udétàlyì (favored boys) and were inducted around the age of seven or eight. These youths were usually the oldest sons of wealthy ô̖dè parents and were lavished with the best clothing, their own tipi, and feasts (Levy n.d.b: 15). Around the age of seventeen they became regular society members and were replaced by two new youths. The male youth members were adopted as little brothers by the whole society, after which both boy members and every regular society member used reciprocal kin terms for each other's relatives, in accordance with the fictive kin relationship extended to these youths. Lonebear stated that these reciprocal kin terms died out when he was about twenty years old (ca. 1883). These boys maintained the fire, served food, heated the dancing drums, ran messages, did chores, and in general assisted the whipmen.[44]

There were also two girl members known as mátàunyì̖gàu (girl members) or á̖udémátàun (favored or special girls) in the Tò̖kó̖gàut, Áljóyì̖gàu, Chè̖jánmàu, and later Óhò̖mò Societies.[45] For many Plains tribes, the position of female youths in men's military societies is the original form of "princesses," preceding those selected in twentieth-century Indian Fairs by at least a century. These girls were taken in around the age of seven or eight and were from wealthy, aristocratic (ǫ̀dè or ǫ̀gòp) families. They were frequently the daughters of society leaders, who were always of ǫ̀dè status, and the position was commonly maintained within particular families, being inherited from one female to another. In such father and daughter cases, society leader and kin terms were used reciprocally (Richardson n.d.).[46] Reciprocal use of kin terms by the male society members and the female youth members for each other's fictive relatives probably occurred.

The female society members were beautifully dressed and cherished by their families and society. These girls wore none of the paint or items of insignia that the men did, but donned their best clothes, wore rouge, and painted the parts in their hair yellow. They attended all society meetings and dances and often led the society parades. Kintadl (Kį́tàl, Moth), a Black Legs Society ą̨udémátàun during the 1850s, stated that female society members were not allowed to dance (Richardson n.d.). Tso'odl's account to Marriott, however, states that although their dance steps differed from the men's, their attendance and participation in dancing were mandatory. This discrepancy may represent changes in their participatory roles between the 1850s, when Kintadl held such a position, and the 1880s, when Tso'odl entered into the men's societies. These girls were considered members (yîqàu) of the society and were society partners (cóm) to each other. Relationships as partners for female society members were particularly close, as such formal pairings for women did not exist outside of military societies. Although they did not bump heads as a part of their initiation, they continued this special relationship for life. All favored girl members addressed their own family in a regular manner, but were addressed as jájé (the possessional form of sister) by the society and as vî (the address form of sister) by the other favored girl.[47]

A society-favored girl retained her position within the society until she married, whereupon the position was passed on to another, who was frequently a female relative; thus, the position appears to have been maintained among particular lineages. Regarded as "sisters" by all of the male members of the society they belonged to, they were prohibited from marrying any of their "brothers." These nonblood kin relations also prohibited a male member from marrying the sister of a favored girl of his own society, even after she had left the society, as she was likewise a sister. When a marriage occurred, her society gave horses and goods to the girl's father (to be given later to the groom) as compensation for the many feasts he had sponsored in honor of his daughter's position in the society.[48] These girls were cherished and protected and were never taken on war parties.[49]

TABLE 3 Kiowa Military Society Organizational Positions

	Fàujóqî	Áljóqî	Áujoqî-íjèqî (ą́udétàlyî)	Mátàunyîgàu (ą́udémátàun)
1. Pòlą́hyòp	1	1 (temp.)	0	0
2. Áljóyîgàu	2	2	2	2
3. Chèjánmàu	2	2	2	2
4. Tòkǫ́gàut	2	2	2	2
5. Ją́ifègàu	2	2	2	0
6. Qóichégàu	2	2	0	0
7. Cáuitémgòp	?	?	?	?
8. Óhòmò	—	—	—	2

Due to the prestige and the feasts which their families would provide, societies realized the economic value of having favored (ą́udé) youth members. Families of favored children taken into the men's societies regularly provided feasts and gave-away to the society to honor and recognize their children's position. When a favored boy (ą́udétàlyî) danced for the first time with a society, a female relative placed a shawl on the ground in front of him. The boy danced across it and then a female spectator picked it up and kept it. Likewise, the boy's father had a prominent society member call designated people to receive horses in the boy's honor.[50]

Military Society Membership

Interviews with Kiowa in both the 1935 Santa Fe notes and Alice Marriott's fieldnotes indicate the existence of a formal set of social ranked military societies in regard to age and social status. With a man's increase in age, rank, and wealth came a general increase in the society to which he belonged. Thus, as an individual's social and war status increased so did his membership in the higher-status societies.[51] Membership in Kiowa military societies was truly pantribal, in that membership was open to and usually included members of all the formally named tribal bands. Society membership was not localized solely to any particular Kiowa residence or tribal bands. Silverhorn, for example, recalled living in a residence band of nine tipis which contained members of all military societies except the Qóichę́gàu. However, society membership was often dominated by the larger northern Kiowa bands due to their population size. Most of the later Ją́ifègàu members were of the Qógûi Band, while the majority of the Áljóyîgàu and approximately thirty of the fifty

Chèjánmàu were from the northern groups.[52] Most 1935 consultants stated that all men in the tribe belonged to a society, even those of dàufô status. Society membership was regarded as fairly equally distributed except for the Qóichégàu.[53] Most estimates of society membership are from twenty-five to sixty members, changing constantly due to death, disease, the recruitment of members, and retirement.[54] The 1935 consultants gave membership estimates for the Kiowa military societies: Pòláhyòp, all male children; Áljóyìgàu, fifty to seventy-five; Chèjánmàu, forty or more; Tòkógàut, forty-five to sixty; Jáifègàu, fifty or more; Qóichégàu, thirty to thirty-five.[55]

While the acquisition of dáudáu (supernatural power) was more common among individuals of ôdè and ôdègùfà status, nearly every Kiowa male is believed to have belonged to a warrior society, as no-accounts (dàufô), captives (cóbòp), and even some non-Kiowa were members (yîqàu). Levy (n.d.b: 14) estimates that approximately one-third or more of all adult Kiowa males were unable to join a society due to inability to acquire war honors and thus the wealth to validate such honors. Practically every male went into the Áljóyìgàu, except for some favored youths who were adopted into the higher societies. His assessment seems unlikely except when considering membership in the Tòkógàut and Qóichégàu, which are known to have required war honors, and Jáifègàu, whose members were considered to be of high status. Some young men such as Yellow Wolf, however, were already raiding at the age of about twenty, but were not yet in a society, while others were taken into a society prior to any warfare experience. Thus, supernatural power and military prowess were not required for joining at least the lower-level warrior societies.[56]

Another factor distorting the accuracy of these estimates may be the exclusion of retired members in the upper societies who attended meetings but did not dance. While a few individuals remained in the same society all of their life, the majority of individuals belonged to two or three different societies during their lifetime. Frank Givens, for example, belonged to all of the Kiowa societies except the Qóichégàu during his lifetime. While a man could change his membership or be "captured" by another society, he could only maintain membership in one organization at a time.[57]

Unless they were disabled or considered lazy or unworthy, most male captives were also taken into societies. In the reservation period even one Kiowa boy who was paralyzed from the waist down belonged to the Jáifègàu. Some captives were taken into societies even if they had not been formally adopted by families.[58] Captives sometimes remained in their first society for life unless they rose quickly through the acquisition of war honors or another society desired their membership. There was no set pattern for captives in joining the society of their captor-father, and no captive was ever known to have risen to the level of Qóichégàu. Genealogies I have recorded demonstrate captive membership in all societies below the Qóichégàu.[59]

Chapter Organizations

As in other tribes, Kiowa Sun Dances and associated warrior society dances frequently attracted intertribal visitors. Mooney (1898) lists numerous tribal delegations including Dakota (1844), Osage (1849, 1854), Crow (1854), Southern Cheyenne (1854, 1867–1868, 1873), Arapaho (1854, 1868, 1873), and Nez Perce (1883). The Naishan Dene Apache frequently attended the Kiowa Sun Dance, maintaining a bandlike position in the encampment. Other tribes including the Southern Cheyenne and Arapaho, and in particular the Comanche, also frequently visited Kiowa Sun Dances. The Naishan Dene Apache and Comanche were the only other tribes known to have participated in the Kiowa Sun Dance proper. Visitors were said to have come both for the visual aspects of the dance and for the lavish gifts.[60]

Interviews in the 1935 Santa Fe notes indicate that certain societies of other tribes were regarded as equivalents of the Kiowa organizations. This is significant in that it demonstrates the similarity among many of the types of military societies found across the Plains. Frizzlehead indicated that the Apache had equivalents of three of the Kiowa men's societies: "The Apaches had a rabbit dance and two warrior societies which were called *twgui ko-itsenko* [Tàugûiqòichègàu] and *twgui tonkongia* [Tàugûitǫ̀kǫ̀gàut]." Tàugûi is the Kiowa name for the Naishan Dene Apache tribe, meaning "Sitting on the Outside": the Kiowa viewed them as a sociopolitical unit of the Kiowa tribal circle, yet recognized them as a distinct tribe and as distinct in language, origins, and some cultural aspects. The Apache thus had the equivalents of the Kiowa Rabbits (Pòlą́hyòp), Black Legs (Tǫ̀kǫ́gàut), and Qóichégàu, which are clearly reflected in the descriptions of the Katsowe, Manatidie, and Klintidie Societies by McAllister (1937). During Kiowa Sun Dances, Apache Manatidie members are known to have participated with the Tǫ̀kǫ́gàut and Klintidie members with the Qóichégàu in the Kiowa society meetings and dances. Similar participation by the Kiowa Pòlą́hyòp and the Apache Katsowe is also likely. They also joined the analogous Kiowa societies in obtaining the center pole and brush dragging for the Sun Dance lodge. These ethnonyms for Apache military societies are important because they indicate that the Kiowa recognized the similarity of Apache societies to their own. Similar intertribal societal associations existed among the Mandan, Hidatsa, and Arikara (Bowers 1992 : 185).[61]

According to the Kiowa consultants in 1935, the Cheyenne and Arapaho were considered to have equivalents of the top five Kiowa societies, while the Pawnee were considered to have equivalents of the Qóichégàu and Jáifègàu Societies. When members from these tribes attended a Kiowa Sun Dance, they also participated in their associated society's activities, including the sham battle, nightly dances, and the brush dragging. The Quaker missionary and schoolteacher Thomas Battey (1968:125–126) observed Kiowa in 1873 performing what he called an "Osage war dance"; the Kiowa had been at peace with the Osage since 1834 (Mooney 1898:262–263). The Ananthy (Cáulánàundáumà, Standing in the Tracks of Bison) Odlepaugh ledgerbook records such a visit in 1883. A picture showing men constructing a brush Sun Dance arbor has the caption: "The above picture records a sun dance in the summer time at which time a band of friendly Ponca came to the same and made everything ready for the ceremonies."[62] Whether the visitors were actually Ponca, a contingent of Nez Perce, whose visit instigated the naming of the 1883 Sun Dance (Mooney 1898:351), or both, the continuation of the intertribal participation into the reservation era is important; it is likely that both participated with the Kiowa societies in the preparatory aspects of the 1883 Sun Dance. Jimmy Quoetone stated that the Nez Perce were welcomed by the two Chèjánmàu leaders and took part in the Sun Dance.[63] In contrast to Hazel Hertzberg (1971) and Sally McBeth (1983), all of these accounts demonstrate that intertribal social dances developed prior to the reservation period (ca. 1875–1900) as argued by Nancy Oestrich Lurie (1971:449), Gloria Young (1981:166), and William Powers (1990:50).

Some Naishan Dene Apache were initiated into Kiowa societies; most were inducted to the Tòkögàut, with others in the Chèjánmàu and the later Óhòmò Society, and only a few in the Jáifègàu. Only one Comanche was known to have been formally taken into a Kiowa society, the Chèjánmàu. Aside from the Apache and a few Comanche, it was normal for visiting men of another tribe to dance with a Kiowa society that was considered analogous to theirs, but they generally were not inducted as regular members.[64]

Except for the Pòláhyòp, there was no set pattern in joining any society. A man might join a society due to family membership, inheritance, or invitation, to fill a broken cóm relationship, or because of a friend's membership.[65] If a member joined the upper societies directly from the Pòláhyòp, this indicated that his family was of first rank, as these memberships were generally limited to favored boys. The majority of Kiowa men joined the Áljóyìgàu when they outgrew the Pòláhyòp. Males joined an adult society at about age twenty or after puberty (seventeen to eighteen years old according to one individual). Some men were known to be past the age of twenty before ever joining a society above the Pòlą́hyòp. Most men of nonprominent families were therefore members of the Áljóyîgàu at one time.[66]

Advancement to the Chę̀jánmàu was based on an increase in prestige, while in the Tò̩kó̩gàut and Jáifègàu there is a definite pattern of replacing members, as they retired or were killed, by the oldest sons, some of whom were taken directly from the Pòlą́hyòp, reflecting their high social status. In the Tò̩kó̩gàut and Jáifègàu Societies there appear to have been a set number of places within the society, reflected by the replacement policies. In the Áljóyîgàu and Chę̀jánmàu Societies there apparently was no father-son replacement; thus, retirement was not necessary for a man's son to enter.[67]

New Members and Initiations

After the ride-around camp and during preparation for the Sun Dance, names of prospective individuals were discussed at society meetings. The whipmen often suggested potential candidates, who were decided upon by the society leaders. Few names were ever rejected, especially if they were suggested by a close relative of the prospect, such as a potential member's uncle.[68] Final decisions were made by the two society leaders, whereupon the two whipmen usually brought the individuals back to a society meeting. In some cases, two regular members were sent in place of the two whipmen. These men surprised the initiate and, if necessary, took him by force to the society feast or nightly meeting, where the leaders discussed and chose his society partner (cóm) as quickly as possible.[69] Ritual forced recruitment was practiced by all of the Kiowa societies including the Qóichę̀gàu, in which men reportedly avoided membership due to the dangerous requirements in warfare and lengthy initiations. In reality, avoidance was apparently the appropriate form of modesty when being selected into a society (Parsons 1929:93). In 1935 White Fox elaborated on the consideration of potential candidates:

> Adltok'i . . . they go get new members and initiate them. Will kidnap them. If they refuse they may drag them by force as with [the] other societies. This is because initiates are ashamed to be brought up before [the] people, where they will have to dance (ie. they really want to join but are bashful). And their resistance is usually little; some go without [a] struggle. A man who wanted to join another society would actually run away from the adltok'i or have a suspicion that he might be recruited and therefore stay away from the group of spectators.[70]

A man already belonging to a society could refuse an invitation to join another society if he wished, which reportedly occurred frequently if the recruiting society was not the same as his father's society (Parsons 1929:90).[71]

Initiations were held the first time a man danced with a society, and war deeds were usually recited by the society chiefs. Most accounts indicate that a man was brought in by the two whipmen, who requested four songs for the man to dance to; after this he was considered a member. Following the initiatory dancing, a giveaway was generally sponsored by the candidates' relatives in his honor. If a man's family was unable to make such gifts the initiate was disgraced. Accounts vary as to whether initiates held giveaways at the time of their initiation or at a later date. The differences represent variations in the type of induction being performed and the social and thus financial status of the individual inductee and his family. If the initiate was surprised and "forcefully" inducted, there was little warning to prepare for a giveaway; thus, the family might perform this at a later meeting or social event. As Tso'odl stated in 1936,

> After they get him in, he has to dance. If he doesn't know how he must make the effort anyway. Then the leaders tell their brave deeds. Then he's a member, after he has once danced. There isn't any give-away then. They have that later when he really dances. His relatives give-away to anyone they wish. If an outside tribe is there, the gifts are usually given to the visitors.[72]

If the induction involved a succession or retirement, the likelihood that a giveaway accompanied the actual induction was greater. An individual from an affluent (ǫ̂dè) or large family was able to produce a large giveaway more readily than someone of pitiable (kä́uàun) status. At least one giveaway was held for each new member, lest he be disgraced by a lack of family support.

The goods to be given away were collected from various family members to demonstrate their respect for the honoring of their family member. The initiate led a horse loaded with gifts into the middle of a ring formed by the other society members. Individuals were then called by the family to receive a gift. While gifts were frequently made to members of the initiate's new society, gifts could be given to anyone, with visiting tribes generally receiving preference. The initiate's family usually feasted the entire society and gave away their best possessions, especially horses. The man's father and paternal uncles were obligated to organize the giveaway. Any relative could give-away extravagantly to show respect for a favorite relative, particularly a paternal uncle; however, goods given at the induction of a new member were in no way viewed as purchase, as with age-graded Plains societies. Initiates could be taken in during the dáucâum ("instruct how to sing" or closed) meetings or might be caught during any of the society dances or parades. Once inducted, a man could remain in the same society for his entire life. This, however, appears to have been uncommon, as most Kiowa men belonged to more than one society in their lifetime, excluding the Pòlą́hyòp. A man might leave for a number of reasons, such as the invitation of another society, to inherit a family position in another society, to fill a broken society pairing, or by being captured by another society (the whipmen of another society might catch a man's horse by the bridle and force him to join another society).[73]

The practice of stealing society members is illustrated in the following incident, which was recorded by Jane Richardson from Jimmy Quoetone (Kuito) in 1935. "On the last stop before the entry to the Sun Dance circle, Kuito was all dressed up, and ready to ride with the Adltoyui, when the Tsetanmw [Chę̀jánmàu] came up and told him to come and ride with them, which he did. When the Adltoyui [Áljóyî̀gàu] asked him what he was doing, he said he had joined another society."[74] Another initiation method that seems to have been common and continued into the 1900s was for the initiate to be awakened from his sleep and taken to the society meeting, whereupon he was made to dance and became a member. This method was described by Andele to J. J. Methvin (1927:165–168) and by Andele and others to Lowie (1916b:845).

Officer Replacement

Upon the death of a society leader a man of equal rank (war record) and distinction (social status) was sought as a replacement. If no candidate could be found among the existing society membership, a replacement from another society was sought, being chosen from the Tǫ̀kǫ́gàut or even more frequently from the Ją́ifègàu. As there were always plenty of chiefs (qájâi) in other societies who were not officers, substitutes were plentiful. One individual stated that the replacement position went to a son or nearest male relative; this would probably have depended upon his own personal rank as a warrior and does not appear to have occurred frequently. However, there is a feeling of some degree of hereditary rights regarding succession. While a general consensus was sought from the members prior to choosing a replacement, members appear to have gone along with the endorsements of the remaining leaders. Regular members reportedly had no voice in the ultimate decision, and the society leaders' decision was final. To be a leader of any society was considered more of an honor than to be a regular member of any society except the Qóichégàu, in which even regular membership surpassed the status of any other society's leaders.[75]

In many instances a whipman replaced a deceased society leader; although he was eligible, he was not automatically chosen. When the position of society leader was filled from outside of the society's membership, the remaining leader chose another to be his partner. This man was then brought by the two whipmen or by the remaining whipman and a temporary replacement. The process was reversed if one of the whipmen positions was being filled from outside of the society, in which instance the two society leaders brought the replacement back. The remaining leader of either position had the choice of his former partner's replacement, albeit subject to the approval of the society assembly. The approval of the remaining society leader and whipmen was obtained, and then the society member's approval was obtained. By 1935 there are indications that the final decisionmaking by the head society leader had shifted to seeking society consensus; as White Fox stated, "Leaders chosen after discussion and voting, general agreement necessary. No factions, all must agree or choose another."[76]

For such a replacement, the retrieving members went to the society dance of their selected replacement and danced that society's dance, after which they recited a deed and stated the purpose of their visit. The promotion to either position for any society, especially that of a society leader, was so important that it was said never to be turned down, as only a Qóichégàu position was higher. Officer positions in the other societies did not entail the dangers that Qóichégàu membership did.[77]

The status of the deceased and, if possible, his age were matched in seeking a replacement. If possible, society partners were not broken up to fill this vacancy; however, this situation did sometimes create such a division. In some instances a distant relative of the remaining member was chosen; since a partnership could not exist between two men of any consanguineal or affinal relations, the two leaders fulfilled the obligations of the office, but functioned without the typical society partner relationship.[78] A Black Legs whipman who was too old retired. The remaining whipman named his choice, Sun Appearing (Fáibáudài or Báudài, aka Háunèmídàu, Unafraid Of Danger), a Jáifègàu, to replace his retiring partner as whipman. Two Tòkógàut members went to the Jáifègàu dance and danced with their society. The two Jáifègàu whipmen, Bird-Eagle Running (Thènéhâljè) and Bushy Head or Frizzlehead (Áulpépjè), knew their reason for coming, but asked anyway. The two stated that they had come for Sun Appearing. The two Jáifègàu leaders, then Sun Appearing, then the society consented, and the Tòkógàut members took him back to their society. If the replacement was already a leader or was considered "useful," his society might object to the other society's request to recruit him.[79]

If a man was called upon to fill a place in another society, his son generally remained in his father's previous society. If he was not yet in a society, he might join the group of his father's previous affiliation. A society leader could take in his own son and train him to take his place as the society leader. When a society leader (fàujóqî) retired, he could then appoint his son as successor. While a society leader could not retire and give the position to his own son outright, a leader's son could be chosen by the society as the successor if he was distinguished, which reflects the society's respect for the former leader and his family. These data suggest hereditary lineages in society offices; although some father-son replacements occurred, membership rosters do not extend far enough back in time to fully document this practice.[80]

Regular Membership, Inheritance, and Replacement

A man usually wished to retire from his society due to old age or his inability to continue strenuous activities. He often wanted his son or his sister's son to replace him in his society, at which time he dressed up his son and took him to his society's meeting. During the singing, the father entered, leaving the son outside. While dancing, the father would announce, "I am too old, I want my boy to take my place." The father then recited a war deed (qóitáujétjàu), and the boy was called in. The head society leader told the son, "Your father was a strong and brave man," then ordered a fast song for the boy to dance to. The retired father retained honorary membership and could attend regular society functions, having merely been relieved of the more strenuous activities. Retired members were known as tál.[81]

If the father had been deceased for some time and his position had not been filled, the society frequently chose an eligible son to fill his position. In the event the deceased had no living son, another male relative or heir was selected as a replacement. When a man left a society to replace a deceased relative in another, the man could not appoint a successor in his old society—the former society decided this. When a man came to replace his relative, the head society leader confirmed the induction by reciting war deeds and announcing the succession.[82] Often these sons were members of other societies; if the societies argued over the individual, it was up to him to decide. In cases involving a death, a society leader had the right to come to another society meeting, ask for, and take a member if he was to fill his father's position in another society. If a man was not sought for a father-son replacement the man's society might argue strenuously over him, especially if he was a promising member. In this case the membership was an invitation and was again left to the individual to decide.[83]

SOCIETY MEETINGS AND FEASTS

No society meetings or dances occurred throughout most of the year. Because members of the same society were regarded as brothers, it is likely that men of the same society residing in the same band acted cooperatively in various economic functions such as hunting, trading, and perhaps raiding. Meetings of an entire society occurred only at the Sun Dance encampment. Various-sized residence bands often met en route to the encampment and traveled together. Some members away on extended journeys or war parties were not present at the Sun Dance. Big Bow was once on a war journey for three years, but returned singing the song of his society (Nye 1962:83). Upon noting that the upcoming Sun Dance had been vowed, small groups of members in the same camp occasionally gathered to practice society songs. However, there was no special dressing or dancing at these informal meetings.[84]

Prior to the Sun Dance, a meeting with at least two members of each society was held to choose the "announcing society" for next year. Later that winter, when the time and location of the upcoming Sun Dance had been chosen, the appointed society was responsible for informing the rest of the tribe. The appointment was made in an informal manner, usually to the first society that suggested it; the members enjoyed the traveling and visiting involved. This appointment was considered a privilege, and a society could not perform the duty in successive years.[85] Visiting and raiding parties also helped to spread the news concerning the ceremony.[86]

During the preparatory period of the Sun Dance, each society held meetings in the lodges of an officer or member. There was no set position inside the camp circle for a society to meet. Tipis used for society meetings had no fixed position in the encampment and were changed several times, depending upon who was sponsoring the next feast. The tipis were moved inside the encampment circle, but well outside the actual Sun Dance lodge. Dances were often announced several days in advance. Societies maintained no special painted tipi as a group, but used the tipi of any member, usually whoever had pledged that evening's events. Meetings were also held in the lodges of the society leaders; the Jáifègàu, for example, often met at the red tipi of White Bear. According to Frank Givens, each society had an assigned part in the Sun Dance and was more or less segregated from the others prior to the actual Sun Dance, by which time the military society meetings had concluded. Each society might dance on different days or simultaneously and was visible throughout the tribal encampment. Individuals often circulated through the camp, visiting multiple society performances.[87]

Collectively society dances were known as Yàpfàhêcùngà (Temporary Police-Soldier Dances) and in later years as Sólègàucùngà (Soldier Dances), from the Kiowa pronunciation of the English word "soldier" and the similarity of their meetings to soldier formations. Individual society dances were designated by reference to a particular society, such as a Black Legs Society Dance (Tǫ̀kǫ́gàcùngà).[88] Society activities were clearly differentiated on the basis of their functions and the time during which they were held. Eight types of Kiowa military society meetings, feasts, and parades associated with the Sun Dance encampment are known: 1. tháumkúgà, the "first feast"; 2. dǎucâum (instruct how to sing), listed in the fieldnotes as "dw.kom" or "adw.kom," or closed meetings; 3. gíkúgà, night feasts; 4. kúqàlfìgà, invited to eat feasts; 5. kífákùgà, daytime invited to eat feasts; 6. ǫ̀tǎ̀kúgà or ǫ̀tǎ̀kúqàl, vowed feasts; 7. jòthàukúgà, camp setting up feasts (literally camp [to pound or drive] feast), listed as "do.t'wiku.gya," or new camp feasts; 8. kátgà, parades.

The tháumkúgà (first feast) was given while the bands were still gathering and provided a reintroduction and organizational meeting for the societies. This meeting was held just after the encampment known as the Qǎ̀ujójòcài (Gathering for the Sun Dance or "ride-around camp"), referring to the Sun Dance priest's ride around the camp to make several announcements. The main function at this time was to solicit members to volunteer feasts for the following ten days of the Sun Dance preparation. The leaders asked for volunteers; after ten men had volunteered, spirits were high, as this meant they would have a feast every day after the camp circle was set up while everyone worked on the Sun Dance lodge. If more than ten feasts were volunteered, these were given before the final camp circle was set up, so that there would still be ten feasts as originally planned.[89]

The first night of singing after the ride-around camp was devoted to visiting the families of society members who had died in the last year. Members met at the tipi of their head society leader and began to sing. The society then proceeded through camp, singing and wailing at the tipi of any deceased member's wife or parents for approximately one-half hour. If a man had more than one wife and they did not live together, multiple visits and mourning sessions were made. Longer pilgrimages were made if a society had lost many men in the preceding year. After comforting the relatives, the family granted the society members permission to dance, telling them to enjoy themselves and thanking them for their respect. After the mourning, it was said that the society leader had "wiped the tears away." Throughout the Sun Dance, those in mourning could attend society functions and eat, but were not required to participate unless they felt like it. A head society leader, however, was required to subordinate his personal grief to his society's duties and was required to attend.[90]

The second type of activity was called the "dw.kom" or "adw.kom" (closed meetings), which occurred on the first three nights of the camp circle. The name recorded by the Santa Fe party indicates dáucâum (instruct how to sing), which may refer to the use of these meetings for singing instruction and practice. All-night meetings were held by all Kiowa societies except the Rabbits and were characterized by closing the society lodge door and taking roll call. A society's members went through the camp singing, stopped at a member's tipi, and asked if they could stay, even though this tipi might not yet be in the camp circle or have food prepared. Each night the societies sang, danced, played games, and socialized until around 5:00 A.M. or daybreak.

These meetings were limited solely to members, and attendance was mandatory. Women tested their lovers at this time by demanding that they visit them on such a night, fully knowing of their predicament because of their societal obligation. Men were thus forced to make excuses concerning going to relieve themselves, during which they hurriedly visited their lovers then returned to their society meeting before being absent for too long. At a certain point in the meeting, the lodge door was formally closed and laced shut, locking out any absent members. Roll call was taken; those missing, who were usually out courting, checking on their wives, or stealing another's wife, were accused the next day of "ado.momo" (having slept with their mother-in-law). This form of social admonishment was practiced by the Chêjánmàu, Tǫ̀kǫ́gàut, Jáifègàu, and probably the other adult men's societies as well. The next day societies often sung the following song (naming the individual) to shame any absent members:

> He married his mother-in-law
> Her husband ran after them
> So jealous that he was crying.

Another song sung for such absences told of how the absent individual had married his mother-in-law and her sisters were his second wives; they all ran after him, jealous because he had chosen their sister over them. This was such a great disgrace that an embarrassed man often remained inside his tipi during the entire day following an absence, resolving not to repeat his offense a second time. The society would not sing the song again unless another absence occurred.[91]

Members who fell asleep were doused with water to awaken them. Tardy members often had their blankets and or clothes torn up and in one instance were whipped with stinging nettles. Punishment generally involved forcing the tardy member to perform some form of clowning entertainment before being allowed to enter. This usually involved a Turkey Dance (Fêcùngà). Once when Sangko was tardy, his society forced him to enter dressed in black paint with a red rag on his throat and a bell on his forehead, gobbling and dancing like a turkey. Occasionally, in humorous fashion, an old man or woman at a daytime meeting of the Tòḱó̱gàut or Jáifègàu Societies arose and danced awkwardly or crazily to make the people laugh. Having worked on the Sun Dance arbor all day and socialized with their society all night, members hurried home to sleep, as there would be another feast at noon. These were the only closed meetings, and new initiates were frequently discussed.[92]

The gíkúgà (night invitation or feasts) were regular nightly meetings held every night before the Sun Dance proper began. Societies not participating in the dáucâum meetings (type 2) had this type of meeting at the same time. A small group went around singing and was soon joined by more and more members. Eventually they decided to go to the tipi of a member who had pledged a feast. This man was expected to provide food and lodging at a moment's notice; his wife quickly cleared out the tipi and prepared food. If the man's tipi was not in the camp circle, the society might move it inside the circle. Tipis used for these meetings, which occurred every night from the ride-around camp onward, were taken down early each morning and removed from the inner camp circle.

The fourth and fifth type of activities were called kúqàlf̱ị̀gà (invitational meals or invited to eat feasts), held in tipis moved into the compound, and kífákùgà (daytime invitational or daytime feasts), given during the day in a tipi which had its sides rolled up and a shade built around it. These meetings were usually held from noon to sundown, were open to the public, and might be sponsored by a member, his father, or an ą́udé child. Up to three daytime feasts might be given by one ą́udé during one Sun Dance.[93]

The camp crier (ǫ̀èljò̱qì, big voiced talker [man]) announced the feasts to all society members, who came dressed in their best clothes for dancing and singing, while women donned their finest clothing. Food was brought to the middle of the tipi and served by the two íjéqì (rationers or distributors); the leftovers were later removed by the women. It was not uncommon to see the four middle societies all having a feast, meeting, or dance simultaneously inside the camp circle. The meeting lodges were later removed by the feast sponsor.[94]

The ǫ́tą̄kúgà or ǫ́tą̄kúqàl (felt good so pledged a feast or vowed feast) was a feast given because of a vow made by a sister or a mother for the safety of a brother or son during the year. In the event of death, a woman sometimes gave this feast anyway. A society leader or whipman might make a similar vow, provided the society did not lose a member during the year. A man might also make this kind of vow for his society partner. Nonmembers did not vow these feasts except for the father of a favored (ą́udé) youth member. The ą́udé-sponsored feasts had no specific name and did not have to be vowed a year in advance. This kind of feast applied to all six societies, and all were held in the camp circle.[95] The "do.t'wiku.gya" (new camp feast) as recorded by the 1935 Santa Fe party is most likely jòthàukúgà (camp setting up feast; literally camp [to pound or drive in] feast), referring to a feast held shortly after arriving in a new camp and erecting tipis. This feast was given for the Jáifègàu Society alone by the Lone Bear family after he became the favored boy for that society. The members were hot and hungry after their regular arrival at the final Sun Dance encampment on foot.[96]

Parades (kátgà) were held once per Sun Dance by each society. These were announced by society leaders at nightly feasts or meetings for the next day. The next morning horses were elaborately painted in red, white, and yellow paint, with special decoration for horses which had been shot in battle. Men were dressed in full regalia but did not use red paint unless instructed to, probably because of the taboo against red objects associated with the Sun Dance. Led by their leaders, the societies gathered outside the encampment entrance and lined up two by two, reflecting the institution of society partners.

Society members who had saved their partner after being left behind in battle were frequently seen riding double on a horse, with the man who was saved riding behind as he did on the battlefield. The societies paraded in order of rank, being led by the Qóichégàu and concluding with the Pòlą́hyòp. After riding around the inside of the encampment, each society exited and completed a circle around the outside of the entire camp, after which all went home (Nye 1962:62). The Pòlą́hyòp relished these parades but were impossible to keep together in an orderly group. Parades were a good time to steal members from other societies, although they were also stolen while they were dancing. Societies paraded as groups when attending councils or other important political meetings, as the Kiowa societies lined up as groups when going to meet a contingent of visiting Pawnee at a Wichita village near present-day Verden, Oklahoma, in 1869.[97]

The eighth type of society activity was the jòbyôidǫ́bècùngà (inside camp circle dance), a special dance performed by one society per day. This form of dancing allowed societies to "show off" their dress and dancing skills to the general public while providing another choice opportunity to steal members, who could not easily get away. After feasting inside a tipi, the members dressed in their distinct society dress and were led two abreast by the two society leaders (fàujóqî) followed by the whipmen (áljóqî) on horseback, the drummers, and women. If the society leaders were on horses they remained outside the circle; if on foot they remained on the inside. The dancers formed a ring inside the camp circle, with the women and spectators on the outside. After dancing awhile, the two whipmen, wearing bonnets, rode in and recited four coups. The dancing resumed, and this process was repeated six times.[98] Although women often attended society meetings, the sexes ate separately. Women could dance outside of the meeting lodges during daytime dances or join in a procession around the camp circle during parades. At night dances the men danced in place while the women danced behind them, usually outside of the society meeting lodge, encouraging them with their sáuàuljò̀gà (ululations).[99]

Military Society Songs

Each society maintained a large inventory of songs of various types, including (1) individual society songs such as Tǫ̀kǫ́gàdàugà (Black Legs Society Songs) sung at meetings and while going to war; (2) Gúdáugá (Stirring Up [Emotions] Songs) or Going to War Songs, popularly called War Journey Songs, the ancestral form of today's 49 Songs, sung the night before departing on a war journey and used to announce an outgoing party (any man who wished to join would come to sing) and while en route to a war journey; (3) Gómdàugà (Wind Songs), sung while traveling on war journeys and by relatives at home; and (4) Câifègàudàugà (War Dead or Memorial Songs). Each society also had (5) Áuldáucúndàugà (Scalp and Victory Dance Songs), sung upon a victorious party's return; (6) Ákùidàugà (Brush Dragging Songs), sung during the brush dragging at the Sun Dance; and (7) informal Wife Stealing (Tásèmdàugà) and Courting Songs sung during the preparatory period for the Sun Dance. There were also numerous individual (8) Qóitáujéldàugà (War Deed Reciting Songs) for its members, sung at meetings and by families. In addition, numerous specialty songs for various parts of an individual society's ceremonial were sung during society performances.

While society songs were common knowledge to most people and might be sung by a nonmember or members of other societies for pleasure, only the songs of an individual society were sung at its functions. Only members of a society were allowed to dance at their own functions, and dancers did not sing. According to HeapoBears, old songs were passed on to new members and thus became part of a common stock of songs. Occasionally, after the tribe began to congregate for the Sun Dance, two societies would "song fight" (dáuvâidè), competing to see which was the better group of singers. Jáifègàu songs were popularly used as hand game victory songs. The intertribal exchange of society songs undoubtedly increased until the end of Sun Dancing, when the societies of most tribes began to decline. As a reflection of intersocietal rivalries, societies often mocked, and thus knew, the songs of other societies in their own meetings. Thus, it seems likely that Apache and analogous Kiowa society songs were exchanged, because of the high amount of interaction between the two tribes. In recognizing the existence of "chapter organizations" in Plains military societies, it becomes apparent why so many regional similarities exist between men's and women's songs, dances, and regalia. Such is the case among many of the current Kiowa, Apache, Comanche, and Cheyenne societies in Oklahoma, where origins and traditions continue to be vehemently disputed. A prime example of this is between the contemporary Kiowa Black Legs (Tǫ̀kɔ́gàut), Apache Black Feet (*Manatidie*), and Comanche Black Knives (*Tuhwi*) Societies, who all claim that the other organizations stole "their" songs and dances.[100] Of these organizations, only the Kiowa maintain songs with texts in them today, which lends greater credence to their claims.

Besides serving as the main focus of dancing, society meetings were the principal arena for warriors to advertise and enhance their individual social status, through the recitation of war deeds and coups to the accompaniment of social approval through drumming, yelling, and the redistribution of goods to validate one's status. Elders in 1935 reported that in ancient times war deeds were sung and not spoken in the Sun Dance or at society meetings and that grandmothers sometimes sang such songs to their grandchildren as an example for them to follow. Because society meetings were used for the public announcement of martial deeds, numerous individual war-related songs were sung and thus became associated with particular societies through the membership of prominent warriors. Several War Deed Reciting Songs (Qóitạujéldàugà) recorded in 1935 and by the author are included in the sections describing individual societies. These songs often combine historical renditions of actual war accomplishments with eloquent figures of speech, as illustrated in the following song:

1. Jé-àu-qò-bè câi-gù á áui
   There are many enemies surrounding us.

2. Kâun nắu-chò báu câi-dầu-qùl
   You do not have a pile of enemy dead as I do.

3. Át-fá-chàt ę̇ câi-dầu-qàu
   On the tip of a tree lies an enemy I killed.

4. Mầu-sáu-iyòi dé bót-hòt-jàu
   Little Crows I have stuffed [with the flesh of enemy dead].

1. Jé-àu-qò-bè câi-gù á áui
   There are many enemies surrounding us.

2. Kâun nắu-chò báu câi-dầu-qùl
   You do not have a pile of enemy dead as I do.

3. Tọ̇-kó-vạui-gà ę̇ câi-dầu-qầu
   In the middle of the river lies an enemy I killed.

4. Mầu-kàui-iyôi dé bót-hòt-jàu
   Little flat-nosed perches I have stuffed [with the flesh of enemy dead].

At such meetings a man could publicly display his martial prowess without being viewed as boastful, by broadcasting perhaps the most essential element required to increase his social status, his war honors. As Mishkin (1940:40) describes, "The Tonkonga, one of the more important men's societies, gave those men who had turned back from a retreat to charge the enemy an opportunity to narrate their experience." At this time witnesses to a man's accomplishment were publicly asked to affirm or deny any coup that was being claimed. Wealth was required to be given away by a man's family in order to validate his status following the recitation of such coups and songs, enabling not only the public acceptance of his martial claims, but the increase of his social status, as well as demonstrating his generosity and ability as a provider, which attracted and maintained a following for his headsmanship.[101]

MILITARY SOCIETY FUNCTIONS

As the largest type of prereservation sodality, Kiowa military societies performed numerous social, religious, military, economic, and legal functions. Although most of these activities centered around ensuring the success of the tribal aggregation and the Sun Dance, others occurred throughout the year. This section outlines society functions and demonstrates their importance in tribal integration and everyday life.

Sun Dance Activities

As was typical of most Plains military societies, Kiowa societies functioned primarily in the preparatory aspects of the Sun Dance, the only annual tribal aggregation. While the Kiowa Sun Dance itself requires a lengthy discussion, I will focus only on those activities involving military society participation. After the keeper of the Ṭ̣aimé (the central bundle in the Kiowa Sun Dance, Qǻujó) had decided and announced the location for the Sun Dance, residence bands began to aggregate in late spring and early summer. Up to two weeks of hunting could follow the ride-around camp. In addition, there were ten days of camp and lodge preparation, and three and a half days of the actual Sun Dance ceremony. The period during which residence bands were in contact with each other during the Sun Dance varied from three weeks to more than two months, depending upon the time of their arrival and dispersion following the ceremony.[102] Those activities involving Kiowa military societies are presented here in their order of occurrence in the Sun Dance.

Prior to the aggregation of residence groups, members of the announcing society had traveled to announce the time and location of the Sun Dance. As numerous local residence bands congregated they were patrolled by the societies. Hunting occurred frequently en route to the Sun Dance as families needed to secure adequate food for the duration of the ceremonial encampment and for the many feasts accompanying the tribal gathering. When the various bands had congregated in one general area, the Ṭ̣aimé Keeper (Ṭ̣aiméqì) or Sun Dance Man (Qǻujóqì), the head priest of the Sun Dance, announced that a single camp known as the ride-around camp or Qǻujójòcaì (gathering for the Sun Dance) would be set up the following evening. The Qǻujóqì announced the appointment of one of the warrior societies to serve as camp police. Known as qíthádàu (men stoppers), the appointed society prevented all individuals from hunting or departing on war parties. Hunting regulations were only in effect from the time of leaving the ride-around camp until reaching the actual Sun Dance location. By ensuring that herds were not scared away by individual hunters, hunting regulations guaranteed that an adequate food supply would be secured by all. Unrestricted hunting by individuals was allowed before the ride-around camp and after reaching the final Sun Dance location.[103]

With the continually arriving bands dispersed along a water course, this assemblage was the first real gathering of the Kiowa as a single encampment, although a camp circle did not form until they reached their final location. The next morning the Ṭ̣aimé Keeper rode around the entire camp with the Tą́imé. On this day the Tą́imé Keeper or Tą́iméqì̀ became known as the Qą́ujóqì̀ (Sun Dance Man), signifying the formal progression toward the final location for the Sun Dance. After the ride-around camp, between three and thirteen encampments were made en route to the final Sun Dance location. While the average was five or six, the number of encampments depended largely upon the availability of bison. The slow progression of encampments facilitated acquisition of enough meat for the entire Sun Dance encampment while providing a socialization period during the leisurely approach. The appointment of the policing society (qí̀thá̀dàu or men stoppers) marked the beginning of the nightly society meetings, singing practices, and regulated hunting. Some 1935 informants stated that the two society leaders of each of the four middle societies held a meeting and decided which society would serve as police. The appointed society's authority formally lasted until the buffalo skin was tied on the center pole in preparation for the actual Sun Dance ceremony; however, the Qą́ujóqì̀ could call upon them at any later time to enforce regulations if needed. Because of their positions as the older and more mature warriors, the Tǫ̀kǫ́gàut and Já̀ifègàu were most frequently chosen as police.[104]

Proceeding in a leisurely pace toward the Sun Dance location, the policing society fanned out two to three miles ahead of the main body, scouting for bison. Any stray bison found behind or to the side of the main body was fair game and could be killed by anyone. When a scout located a herd, equal access was ensured by the patrolling society, which rode back and forth in front of the waiting hunters. When all were ready and had an equal starting point, the policing society broke to each side and all of the hunters rushed toward the herd. The number of policed hunts depended upon the number of bison encountered and killed. Often only one policed hunt was required. After each policed hunt, two to three days were spent there in order to process and dry the meat before continuing. If no large herds were found, no policed hunt occurred; this was typical of nearly all later Kiowa Sun Dances, as bison neared extinction on the Southern Plains.[105]

On the third camp following the ride-around camp, the Sun Dance Priest and his assistants scouted for and selected a center pole for the Sun Dance Lodge (Qą́ujó). Lowie (1916b:843) states that two chosen society members performed this duty. These men refrained from drinking until they found a suitable center pole and tied a rag around it (Spier 1921a:438). Apparently the societies were meeting and singing since consultants indicate that the Já̀ifègàu met on the north side of the camp, while the Tǫ̀kǫ́gàut met on the south; the latter sent two members who held war honors or were qá̀jâi to scout for the center pole. After locating a suitable tree for the center pole, the two scouts returned to the waiting camp, recited a deed involving actually meeting the enemy, and were thus called scout bringing in the news (qǫ́qíjèhòpbȁu). The policing society also prevented anyone else from leaving camp to practice dancing at this time, as some men would reportedly sneak off to the woods to practice their dance steps. When someone caught them they would call out, "Hey you're a pretty good dancer," to embarrass them.[106] The next morning the entire camp followed the Sun Dance Priest to the actual Sun Dance location, except the Jáifègàu Society, who always walked to the final camp, symbolizing the prehorse culture tradition of departing for war on foot.[107]

On this day the tribal procession made four stops in approaching the final location. At each stop the Sun Dance Priest and Ten Medicine Keepers smoked, while the societies, dressed in their finery and riding their best horses for the tipi race, sang and danced. The societies then held the people back; at the signal of the Sun Dance Priest, everyone raced the remaining one-quarter to one-half mile to the final Sun Dance location marked by a miniature tipi made of sticks. The first individual to reach the spot was given a first coup, which honored his society.[108]

Camp Alignment

Upon arriving, the Tǫ̀kǫ́gàut, Áljóyìgàu, and Chèjánmàu Societies aligned the inner camp circle. The society leaders stood in the center of the camp and directed the other men to form a perfect circle by sighting through a centrally positioned man.[109] Each society patrolled a portion of the circular area and held the people back, while the leaders arranged the inner row of tipis. Four or five members of each of these three societies might be chosen by the leaders for this job; these varied annually.[110]

Each band and family had designated spots in which to camp, which were enforced by the aligning societies. The societies had both the authority and the power to order the owners to move tipis. If the order was disobeyed, the society members could tear down a lodge and instruct an individual to leave or place one man on each pole and physically move the lodge themselves. In 1873 Wolf Appeared (Cȕibáudài), a Ten Medicine Keeper who was generally mean and a bully, refused to camp in the designated location of his band and had his tipi moved by the Jáifègàu. Upon threatening the society and raising his weapons, he was knocked down by the society chief. Still refusing to move, he was struck by every society member, finally returning to his proper band and area (Richardson 1940:22).[111] In the evening on the day of arrival, the Jáifègàu arrived on foot and were joined by the Qóichégàu as they made four approaches to the camp. Then they went to a Jáifègàu member's tipi (after 1860 to the tipi of Lonebear's family) for feasting and dancing.[112]

The Sham Battle

The next morning the men's societies painted and dressed near the tree chosen for the center pole. The Jáifègàu and Qóichégàu, having earlier built a brush and stick structure around the tree, prepared to defend it. After two Tòkógàut members confirmed this structure, the three remaining societies attacked the tree. This sham battle was called the Timber Fight (Ácàijàu or Ácàijàugà). The attackers struck the defenders with brush switches, while the defenders hit them with mudballs slung from the end of dogwood sticks, which was known as Mud Flinging (Chènqààdàu). The "battle" continued until the fortification was knocked down. The sham battle was often a rough affair, and numerous cases are reported where one man took the opportunity to deal a healthy blow to an adversary. In some cases fights broke out, necessitating mediation by a Ten Medicine Keeper. Generally these injuries resulted from one man being suspicious or jealous about a rival's relations with his wife.[113] After a specially selected woman (usually a captive) cut down the chosen tree, it was ritually prepared. One society which volunteered or was appointed by the Sun Dance priest was responsible for carrying it in four processions to the camp, where all five men's societies placed it upright in a hole dug by the Calf Old Woman's Society.[114]

The Brush Dragging

All of the societies except the Pòlǫ́hyòp participated in the brush dragging and the construction of the Sun Dance Lodge. The Qóichégàu and Jáifègàu Societies were in charge of getting the pole and brush materials for the north side of the Sun Dance Lodge, while the Áljóyìgàu, Chèjánmàu, and Tòkógàut provided materials for the south side.[115] These arrangements may have varied; one 1935 consultant reversed the sides, stating that the north side belonged to the Áljóyìgàu, Tòkógàut, and all non-Kiowa visitors, while the south side belonged to the Qóichégàu, Jáifègàu, and Chèjánmàu.[116] Unlike the center pole, the seventeen side poles, supports, and brush were obtained in a secular atmosphere.[117]

In each society two leaders, probably the whipmen, acted as police in directing the work. Individual society Brush Dragging Songs were sung to accompany the work. Each society took four drums and carried dance paraphernalia to keep time while marching and working. The Qóichégàu wore their eagle bone whistles around their necks and carried hoof rattles; the Jáifègàu and Chèjánmàu carried gourd rattles; and the Tòkógàut and Áljóyìgàu wore dancing bells and were painted. All the societies sang and danced as they worked, making frequent stops to dance. The brush dragging was marked with much joking and flirtation, as society members, dressed in their best clothes, rode double, with their admirers behind them. Whenever two Sun Dances were held in the same year, the societies repeated the process, acquiring a fresh supply of brush.[118] During the brush dragging, wives of society members were supposed to stay with their husbands' society, where all worked cooperatively. Societies were not supposed to leave any of their wives behind, as the potential for wife stealing or affairs during this period was considered high. Once society members were out searching for poles when they saw a Jáifègàu member's wife with another man. The society tore up the clothes of both individuals, and the husband of the woman could not defend her in any way without loosing face.[119]

Although wife stealing was not a sanctioned function of the societies, it flourished during military society activities throughout the Sun Dance period. Despite the announcement by the head priest that the Sun Dance was the time for love affairs and that all should refrain from jealousy or anger, problems arose because men often pursued the wife of a fellow society member. During the brush dragging, individuals frequently wore visors of leaves to conceal their identity while riding. If a man caught his wife with another he might pull him off, beat him, and take his wife home to beat her. If the husband caught the two *in delicto* he would beat the other man; often the other would interject, "Let me go now, I will give you a good horse," which usually ended the matter. If the husband tried to kill the other man or to cut off his wife's nose, the societies frequently intervened and mediated the dispute. If caught, a man was generally beaten by the husband, but any further aggression led to intervention by the leader of the offended husband's society. Because of the high level of respect for the head society leader the matter was usually settled quickly.[120]

During the brush dragging and associated general period of sexual license, songs were often sung aloud to taunt other men. The following examples demonstrate the directness of these society songs, informally known as Tásèmdàugà (Wife Stealing Songs).

1. Áljóyìgàu: "This is what I want you to know. You have a pretty girl. I have made up my mind to have her."

2. Chẹjánmàu: "In peace time people are not expecting trouble but sometimes it shows up. If you find out and hit us both it will be all right."

3. Tọ̀kọ́gàut: "When you hear of this [an affair] you can come and strike us both."

4. Jáifègàu: "You awful people. It is terrible how crazy you young people are. As crazy as you are, we are going to have another Sun Dance [meaning another chance to get the other man's wife]."

5. Óhọ̀mȯgàu: "Her husband was jealous when he followed us. We didn't know he was so jealous when he followed us." [121]

During the entire Sun Dance period promiscuity flourished, especially during society meetings. Although wives often attended some of their husbands' society meetings, sitting outside the society lodge, they sometimes left to watch another society as a change of entertainment, occasionally resulting in problems. As some society meetings lasted all night long, members were prohibited from leaving. Leaving to check on one's wife brought ridicule, and failure to attend a meeting brought joking accusations of "having slept with one's mother-in-law"; the sisters of the mother-in-law often ran after the husband to humiliate him more by "showing their jealousy" at not having been chosen. Men were not supposed to show jealousy toward their wife; complaining about one's wife's behavior resulted in further teasing by the society, who then sang songs about the disgruntled fellow member. Society members frequently ran by another society's meeting tipi, with taunts about how they were going to visit a certain individual's wife. Members did periodically slip out to check on their wives or to visit another man's wife, as the husband was of course occupied in his own society meeting. Upon returning to his society's meeting a man often had to wait outside, beg, or perform some labor or humorous dance before reentering. Occasionally a father-in-law would harass his son-in-law for checking on his wife, which also greatly embarrassed him.[122]

Societies frequently came to the aid of a cuckolded society brother, often demanding property from the society of the man who had offended their brother member, just as a family did when a man absconded with their daughter. According to Sangko, a Tọ̀kọ́gàut member once stole the wife of a Chẹjánmàu member. The Chẹjánmàu Society was angered and raided the Tọ̀kọ́gàut man and his family; Sangko himself had to give a horse as part of the restoration. The two society chiefs later scolded the members to restore order. A man whose wife had left him was mocked by his fellow society members, as was a woman by her sisters when her husband left her.[123] In addition to having policing authority, societies also used public shaming to moderate behavior. If a member of a society frequently beat his wife, the society chief could make him cut his sleeve, producing a fringe and publicly marking a habitual wife-beater, which proved a source of great embarrassment (Nye 1962:62). If a society came to ask for a woman's aid in their meetings and she had been forbidden to go by her husband, the society would cut her sleeve into fringes, reflecting her husband's behavior. Beyond cases of personal interest, societies also tried to restore peace upon the eruption of any similar problem. Four Jáifègàu men, for example, once broke up a fight between a man and his son over an Arapaho girl following a Sun Dance.[124]

The Kick-Fight

Following the brush dragging was the Kick-Fight (Aùnmáijàu or Foot Upward Fight), which took place in the actual Sun Dance Lodge after it was completed prior to being cleaned for the ceremonies. If the work was finished too late at night, the societies might remain in the Sun Dance Lodge all night and begin the fight in the morning. This event was held on the first day of the Sun Dance proper. One consultant stated that the Jáifègàu and Qóichégàu were paired against all other societies, while another placed these two societies plus the Chèjánmàu against the Tòkógàut, Áljóyìgàu, and Óhòmò. This is a relatively late description (post-1884), as indicated by the presence of the Óhòmò. Other tribes reportedly did not participate in the Kick-Fight.[125]

Each side lined up from east to west, facing the other, from the lodge entrance toward the center pole, with one man from each side going against another. When one man was thrown to the ground, the "fight" was on and a general melee continued until one side was pushed out of the lodge. Old water-soaked moccasins were worn; this made them stiffer and rougher and, as with the sham battle, provided men with the opportunity to deal a healthy blow to an adversary.[126] A Scalp Dance was then held by the victors. Thomas C. Battey (1968:169) describes the Kick-Fight during the 1873 Sun Dance; "The soldiers of the tribe then had a frolic in and about it [the Sun Dance Lodge], running and jumping, striking and kicking, throwing one another down, stripping and tearing the clothes off each other."

Following the Kick-Fight, the majority of the military societies' functions for the Sun Dance were completed, with the exception of policing duties. Once the actual Sun Dance ceremonies began, the regular meetings of the societies ceased for that year, as the Sun Dance ceremonies were the focus of attention for the remainder of the annual encampment. On the second day of the Sun Dance proper, the Pòlą́hyòp helped the Old Woman's Society place white sand on the Sun Dance lodge floor. Upon completion of the Sun Dance the camp began to break up. Occasionally the policing of additional tribal or intertribal hunts followed the Sun Dance; large segments of the tribe(s) remained together for extended hunts and to visit as they traveled prior to dispersing for fall hunting and the selection of winter camps.[127]

OTHER SOCIETY FUNCTIONS

Although the period of greatest social integration and functioning of the men's military societies coincided with the Sun Dance, societies or portions of them played numerous other social roles throughout the year.

Warfare

Using the root word dàumbánmà (literally land-going to go) the Kiowa collectively referred to warfare under the generic term dàumbánmà (land journeying). They further differentiated between the two major types of Plains warfare activities: economically oriented horse raiding journeys, known as chę̀dàumbànmà (horse land journeying) and martially oriented revenge raids or qájáidàumbánmà (bravery land journeying) (Mishkin 1940:28). Collective military society efforts in warfare and raiding were formally practiced by some Plains societies who were known to have gone to battle as a society, but later ceased as some societies were severely defeated or completely exterminated in battle. Evidence from songs supports the contention that societies previously went to war as units. As exemplified by the following Black Legs Society war song, White Horse and Charley Apekaum stated in 1935 that "a slow *tokogia* [Tǫ̀kó̧gàut] war song might be sung by a group of society members going out to war together . . . it might be sung around the rawhide the night before [departing]. They sing that they are all going to die, that they are not coming back."

Tǫ̀-kó̧-gáut jé á hêm.
(Legs-Black-members/all/they/died)
Black Legs members have all died.

Several Kiowa society songs contain similar references to warfare and dying in reference to their own society's name and the role of a warrior. By the mid-nineteenth century Kiowa societies rarely went to war as composite units. While Plains revenge parties were larger and were a tribal effort involving nearly all able-bodied men, a raiding party was generally smaller and composed of relatives and supporters of the man who formed the party. Tso'odl (born in 1860) stated in 1935 that "all the members of a society did not go to war together. The raiding parties were mixed." While members of one's own society might be recruited for raiding and revenge parties, both were open in membership. Raiding parties were also formed for more economically based reasons. It is plausible to assume that some members of the same society raided together, as they would be closely associated through the presence of their society partner, kin ties, and mutual "brotherhood" through society membership.[128] It can therefore be suggested that military society membership as exhibited in raiding and warfare activities formed a significant social and economic bond throughout the year.

During society meetings held just prior to the Sun Dance leaders of a revenge raid carried a pipe to the chief of each society to solicit membership for their cause. If the society leaders approved of the cause, they smoked the pipe and often served as adjutants of the party leader. The society chiefs then presented the pipe to the other members, who signified their willingness to join in the raid by smoking (Mishkin 1940:29). One such solicitation for a revenge party was initiated by Young Sitting Bear, who asked the Jáifègàu Society to join him as a unit, while at a meeting inside the society tipi. The group left as soon as the Sun Dance was over; according to Marriott (1968:77–87), Young Sitting Bear and Young Lone Wolf were both killed. While carrying a pipe to the different societies is a well-known method of soliciting support for such ventures, this account conflates two separate incidents. Young Sitting Bear (the son of Sitting Bear I) was killed in Texas in the spring of 1870, while Tàuágài (Sitting in the Saddle or Sitting Astride) and Cûitèndè (Wolf Heart), the sons of Lone Wolf and Red Otter, were both killed in Mexico in 1873 (Mooney 1898:327, 337–338). Nevertheless, the documentation of such solicitation is significant in clarifying the earlier role of the men's societies in warfare.

One factor that prevented a society from raiding or fighting as an entire unit was the fact that, except during the Sun Dance and surrounding activities, society members were widely dispersed throughout many bands and camps and thus difficult to gather. A second and perhaps stronger factor may have been the extermination of the Cáuitémgòp Society, who sang upon approaching an enemy, choosing a position of no retreat to stand and fight until either victory or defeat. According to Silverhorn, the Cáuitémgòp was wiped out because it would not retreat and was not resuscitated because of the danger to the tribe.[129] Similarly, the Cheyenne Crooked Lance (aka Hoof-Rattler or Elk) Society was severely defeated by the Crow in 1819, and a war party of forty-eight Bowstring Society men was exterminated by the Kiowa, Comanche, and Apache in 1837 (Mooney 1898:271–272; Hoebel 1978:40; Grinnell 1983:25, 45–62).

Several statements indicate that members of the same sodality were distinguishable by various forms of society insignia. Members of the same society might be in the same raiding, war, or revenge party, but not necessarily because of society membership. Most visible of the insignia would have been the special sashes, lances, and whips of the various officers. Kintadl's husband, Chiefs Call Him (Qájáiácàumą̀), a Tǫ́kǫ́gàut Society whipman, once used a society whip to kill an enemy in a battle. Jái̜fègàu members reportedly wore mescal bean bandoleers (káuhòl), signifying society membership. Similarly, Qóichę́gàu members were known to have worn their sashes, red paint, and owl feather headdresses just as they did during society dances. According to Sangko, members of the same society tended to camp and sleep around the same fire, while the party leader stayed with members of his own society, which is likely because of the high level of camaraderie and fictive kinship among fellow society members. Frizzlehead, however, claimed that there was no special behavior or relationship between society members while on a war party.[130] Unlike shield societies, members of the same military society did not stay particularly close to each other, and individual engagement of an enemy was the norm. Society partners were known to have remained close together, protecting each other. Parents did not want partners to go on the same war party, for if one was injured or killed the other was often killed trying to rescue him or refusing to leave him.[131]

Death and Burial

Elders in 1935 differed greatly regarding the societies' role in death and burial. Some stated that when a member of a war party was killed the society was responsible for the return of the body. If burial occurred before the war party returned, all contributed to the preparation of the deceased and the family did not owe for this service. Another elder specifically stated that societies had nothing to do with burial of their members, while another stated that the burial was the duty of the war party leader (tǫ̀yópjòqì̜). This may have occurred in cases where few or no members of the deceased's society were present or may have depended upon the time available for such arrangements while on a raid or war party.[132]

In contrast to one 1935 consultant, others stated that a main function of a society, upon the death of a member from old age or in war, consisted of helping with the burial preparation, dress, and payment for and digging of the grave, regardless of the number of relatives a deceased man had. A society had authority over even the family in this instance. At least two cases of burials performed by the Áljóyìgàu are known. In the first case a processional and burial of a captive, who was probably a member, was led by the Áljóyìgàu leader Big Bow and included many society members. In a second case, the society performed a burial for a woman who was killed by her enraged husband, Saddleblanket (Tàukàuidè), a Ten Medicine Keeper, after she had been courting Kitawdla, a member of the Áljóyìgàu. The Áljóyìgàu went after Saddleblanket; being outfaced, he ran away and reportedly became poor after the incident. Society members threw their finger rings into the grave and sang a war song over the interment as an indication of their readiness to fight and die over the matter; this was prevented by the headsmen, who persuaded Saddleblanket to smoke a pipe, thus resolving the matter.[133] This event is unique in that it demonstrates that the society was ready to come to the aid of a member regarding even an adulterous love affair. When a camp or band leader (jòfàujóqì) died, his society and the family worked together to make the burial a great event to honor such an important leader. The degree to which a society could aid the deceased also depended upon the number of members in a camp at the time. Therefore, the society played the most significant role when it was together as a unit during the Sun Dance.[134]

One funeral practice common to all the Kiowa societies was official society mourning, held after the ride-around camp. After a society met at the head leader's lodge, the society members proceeded to visit the wife or the parents of any member who had died since the last Sun Dance. If a man had two wives who were not camped together, they made separate visits. If there had been several deaths within a single society, a long pilgrimage was made. The society came singing to the relatives at their camp, where a wail was held for about half an hour. After this a surviving relative gave the society permission to hold a dance. This practice was still in use by all the surviving Kiowa societies in the 1930s. Kiowa and other Southern Plains tribes still observe this custom in modified form today.[135]

Whether differences existed in the mortuary practices of various Kiowa military societies is unknown. There was no clear consensus in 1935 regarding the role of the societies in death and burial, which seems to have varied due to several factors, including the season in which the death occurred, the status of the individual, the number of members or relatives present, available time, and presence or absence of a society partner. Since most burials on war parties were hastily performed because of factors of time and danger, later war or revenge parties generally returned to the bodies, which were collected, dressed, reinterred, and covered with rocks. These secondary burials were organized by fellow society members of the deceased and were done out of respect for the individual, having nothing to do with the journey of the soul, which had already departed at the moment of death. As military societies in several Plains populations such as the Ponca (Dorsey 1893–1894:148; Skinner 1915b:785; Howard 1965:140, 155), Iowa (Skinner 1915c:691), Crow (Lowie 1983:177–179), and currently the Cheyenne Bow Strings, Apache Manatidie Society, and Kiowa Black Legs Society are known to have performed funerary duties for deceased members, it is likely that most Kiowa societies performed some funerary functions in the mid-1800s.[136]

Mutual Aid

A society provided some mutual aid to its members, but more often a man turned to his society partner (cóm) for the most support; this remained the closest relationship through the annual cycle when the societies were dispersed. Societies sometimes helped pay doctoring fees for wounded members or for an ordinary illness of a member. The society generally did not intervene in personal matters, which were considered to be between the individuals involved and their families. A man's society partner frequently came to his aid, but from modesty they would never ask their own society for aid.[137] Levy (n.d.a:12) states that the society membership system provided a number of fictive brothers in other camps who were obliged to help a fellow society member in need. Viewed as credit unions in which fictive brothers loaned one another capital and financed raiding ventures, Kiowa military societies functioned like the economic aid provided by clan relatives in a clan system. As a catastrophe would normally affect an entire camp, the kin brothers were frequently unable to help one another extensively; thus, the military society's more dispersed distribution countered such emergencies by providing fictive brothers who could provide aid across a wider geographical, social, and economic network. Because the societies were not kin based, such mutual aid promoted horizontal social stability and tribal solidarity that functioned somewhat like extended relatives in a clan system. By economically extending ties of brotherhood, the societies, whose members were of similar socioeconomic status, thus provided aid to fellow members in times of need, as well as financing activities to maintain and increase their future socioeconomic status.

Societies frequently provided support to either male or female plaintiffs in cases involving adultery. If a man stole a fellow society member's wife, the society might come to the aid of the offended member, but it was more likely to do so in cases involving two societies. Several such cases are recorded for the Áljóyìgàu. If the adultery involved members of different societies, the cuckold's society had the right to punish the offender, whose society could not interfere. The family of the offended man would also search for the wife to cut the tip of her nose off and cut her hair, marking her unfaithfulness. The society of the offender might take up a collection of goods and horses to present to the offended man or to his brother through the services of a Ten Medicine Keeper, who delivered the society's request on behalf of the member and asked the brother of the offended man to smoke on the matter. If the man or his relative smoked on it and accepted the gifts, the matter was settled, and no revenge was sought. To refuse a Ten Medicine Keeper's request was itself a serious matter, which would bring ill-fortune in the future. The use of a Tòkɔ̀gàut Society club, and thus a whipman, to settle a social dispute was also recorded.[138] One elder in 1935 stated that if a member suffered misfortune in his camp, such as from an enemy attack, the society did not provide any aid; this duty apparently fell upon his relatives and residence band. If a member was in potentially serious trouble the society collected property and the society leaders paid a Ten Medicine Keeper to help him and to distribute the collected goods.[139]

Society partners continually exchanged gifts after their relationship was established. If a collection was taken up for a man, his society partner was expected to give more than the nonrelatives. Societies did not give-away for their members, as this was done by the member's family or by a warrior's older brother. A giveaway could take place at any time and did not necessarily have to be for a favored child (ą́udé) or because the person being honored had performed a special deed, but was simply a reflection of the family's love for relatives.[140]

Although data concerning mutual aid within a society are scarce, it seems that the society intervened only when a situation became economically or judicially serious. When it became apparent that a personal dispute could not be resolved between parties and might escalate or that the support of a member's society partner was not enough, the society supported a member to save him from potential danger.

Youth Member Functions

The parents of society ą́udé (favored youth) members frequently sponsored feasts for their children's society, often having giveaways for the society in their honor. Their chief economic function consisted of contributing to the collection of property or helping to fulfill the personal needs of any tribal member. Thus, other than the feasts provided to their society by their families, the youth members' services were not specifically limited to a society, but to the tribe.[141]

Society Functions for Youth Members

A society-favored girl (áudémátàun) relinquished her position upon marriage. As all the male members of her society were classificatory, and thus regarded as actual brothers, she was required to marry a man from outside the society. The two societies did not arrange the marriage; but upon the marriage of a society-favored girl, who was thus their "sister," her "brothers" in the society exchanged gifts with the groom's society. The couple received nothing. There was no societal exchange for regular marriages, even for the daughter of the society leader, unless she was a society áudémátàun.[142]

Society Leader Authority

During the policing period and second only to the Táimé Keeper, the head leader of the appointed society was in charge of the tribal aggregation. The Táimé Keeper and Ten Medicine Keepers could be and in some recorded instances were punished by the policing society for breaking laws. Within the society, the authority of the head society leader was quite strong; he was not required to consult the regular members on matters of importance, although he often consulted with the other three society leaders. During meetings society leaders stopped any disputes that arose. The head society leader generally did not intervene in intrasocietal wife-stealing disputes unless one man was endangering another. In intersocietal wife-stealing disputes, the offended man's society and often his family took property from the offender or his relatives, and the offender's society could not interfere.[143]

Outside the period of appointed authority, the head fàujóqì could not use martial power to enforce his decisions; but as society leaders were generally camp chiefs (jòfàujóqì), they used influence, persuasion, logic, reasoning, and mediation—methods typical of Plains civil chiefs. The society fàujóqì frequently used cajolery and public opinion to correct an individual's behavior, demonstrating that conformity for the public welfare was preferable to individual punishment. A head society leader could also remove the support of the society, which would greatly reduce the support available to an individual in a crisis.[144]

The great respect for a society leader is illustrated by the following incident. A Jáifègàu man stole the wife of a member of another society and refused to return her at the direction of his society fàujóqì. Later that summer he scared a buffalo herd away while hunting alone. The society met him, and he and the society leader drew guns on each other and fired, each killing the other's horse. When both got up, the society chief aimed his gun at the man and said, "I am aiming at you. I'm going to kill you. I'll give you a chance to shoot me too. Go ahead and aim." Losing courage, the man refused to fight. The fàujóqì clubbed the man over the head, knocking him unconscious, then ordered all to strike him or else receive the same punishment. All the society members walked by and said, "Here uncle, grandfather, brother, etc.," as they struck him, leaving him a bloody pulp.[145] It is unclear whether this society was the appointed police at the time; but as all societies had the power and authority to police, they were simply enforcing the normal sanction for a crime that affected the entire tribe on an individual who had previously proven to be a renegade. Other incidents list more than one society punishing an offender for breaking hunting laws.[146] This illustrates that all societies had the authority to punish such crimes, but that the temporarily chosen society served as the "official" police with the utmost power.

Societies as Police

The four middle societies all had the right to serve as police during the Sun Dance. The duties of policing the hunt were alternated, and rarely did the same society perform them two years in a row. The Tòkǫ́gàut and Jáifègàu Societies were usually chosen as camp police because of their higher social seniority and degree of maturity in relation to the Áljóyìgàu and Chèjánmàu. Hugh L. Scott notes that the Tòkǫ́gàut served as hunt police in 1834. The appointed society could delegate other societies to help keep peace or accomplish tasks for the good of the whole. During the policing period members were admonished to be on good behavior to set an example for others.[147] The Táimé Keeper alone had the right to appoint the society for policing duties. In one instance, before the societies had met at the camp circle, the Táimé Keeper appointed two men to supervise some Jáifègàu members to ensure a successful hunt.[148]

In 1935 one elder had never heard of the Chèjánmàu policing the hunt. The Qóichègàu had policed it once, but before this informant's time. The Cáuitèmgòp policed the hunt prior to their demise. When a policed hunt became necessary in a large camp, a society leader might call the members together and organize the hunt without even consulting the camp or band leader (jòfàujóqì), with the head society chief as the hunt leader. However, society leaders were reportedly always camp or band leaders. In regular camps, a man who had found a herd returned to notify his camp. The camp or band leader (jòfàujóqì), having authority over other visitors or higher-ranking jòfàujóqì, then designated a location for all to meet before proceeding as a group.[149]

Policed hunts after the Sun Dance occasionally occurred if the majority of the tribe had remained together or when portions of several tribes had camped together. In such cases the Táimé Keeper appointed a society to perform this function. One such hunt included the Kiowa, Comanche, Cheyenne, and probably the Naishan Dene Apache, who were camped together after the 1873 Sun Dance. Likewise, the Kiowa, Comanche, and Apache were camped together after the 1869 Sun Dance. In 1879 there were no policed hunts due to diminished buffalo herds.[150]

Law during the Kiowa Sun Dance period was generally decided by the Táimé Keeper, while the Ten Medicine Keepers frequently decided domestic cases throughout the year. These decisions were then enforced by the soldier societies. When necessary, the societies backed up the authority and decisions of the Táimé Keeper with military power. Cases of domestic disputes involving the enforcement of legal decisions by military societies are numerous in the Plains literature (Provinse 1937:344–362; Mishkin 1940; Richardson 1940; Llewellyn and Hoebel 1941). During the march to the Sun Dance and on the hunt, the policing societies could punish disobedient persons by confiscating their weapons and horses and destroying their property. During the Kiowa Sun Dance all people including the Ten Medicine Keepers, the Apache, and all visitors were under the authority of the policing society. Any Kiowa who broke the law rarely left the tribe to hide or to run away; this was unthinkable, since the soldier societies would soon apprehend the offender anyway.[151]

The key point in the enforcement of law by the policing society was whether the offender fought back or, swallowing his pride and admitting guilt, took his punishment. If he resisted and fought back when the police came to punish him then he could be physically beaten; if he continued to resist he could legally be killed by the police, with public sanction. Offenders were hit with wooden bows or war clubs. If the person was caught sneaking off to hunt buffalo and thus endangering the entire group with possible famine, the police would generally break his bow and arrows, shoot his horse, and beat him and could confiscate and destroy additional property if this was deemed necessary. Some consultants indicate that punishment was by all societies and not just the acting policing society. However, it appears that most judicial measures were the focus of only one society at a time or those present at the crime; otherwise, practically every man in the tribe would be punishing a single offender. If a relative in the policing society was present, he also had to punish the lawbreaker, regardless of how closely they were related, or else be punished himself with the offender.[152]

If a man submitted to his punishment without resisting, the society reimbursed him later; this was the only time the society owed economic obligations to an individual. If a man willingly met the police as they came and said, "Here is my property," they did not beat him but went off to discuss the matter.[153] If he resisted them, they could destroy his property and did not have to replace it. It becomes clear that the goal was conformity to ensure the welfare of the whole group and not the desire to mete out physical punishment to someone for an infraction. Thus, it was really up to the individual to decide whether he wanted a beating or a temporary loss of his property and public embarrassment. The difficult aspect of accepting the confiscation and destruction of his property was the public admission of his guilt, which brought shame. Submission required swallowing one's pride and in most cases was sufficient punishment to prevent future infractions.

The following cases show the seriousness with which this law was enforced. In one instance a Kiowa chief named Many Wives (Táauiqî), who was reportedly arrogant and always had his way because people were afraid of him, decided to separate from the group after being told not to. The Qóichégàu, who were then policing, delivered an ultimatum: "If you cross that creek, you are a dead man." Realizing their sincerity, he turned back.[154]

In another instance a Ten Medicine Keeper, Wolf Appeared (Cûibáudài), and two of his male relatives tried to obtain fresh meat for his sick sister, who was Kicking Bird's wife. This violated the no-hunting rules then in effect. The Jáifègàu were called and sang their song, thus vowing to do their duty. Lacking courage, the other two offenders ran away, but Wolf Appeared remained and received his punishment for sneaking out to hunt buffalo from the Tòkógàut and Jáifègàu. He was struck with bows, his horse was killed, and his bow and arrows were broken. The Jáifègàu chief Black Bear and Wolf Appeared shot each other's horses, then Black Bear clubbed him over the head with his bow and ordered all to do likewise. Thereafter, Wolf Appeared was notorious for mistreating Jáifègàu members on war parties that he led. Unlike a regular member, a Ten Medicine Keeper could only be struck after a man announced that he would strike him and recited a coup, for fear of future supernatural repercussions.[155]

Although individual disputes were generally left to the individuals involved and their relatives to settle, societies intervened in extreme cases. At the 1873 Sun Dance Páukǫ̀gái (Black Bison Bull), a Chę̀jánmàu member, stole the wife of Cûibáudài (Wolf Appeared), an Áljóyìgàu member. Wolf Appeared killed several of Black Bison Bull's horses and took several others, which was customary for the offense involved. He threatened to kill Black Bison Bull, refusing all settlement offers, including those of several Ten Medicine Keepers. Wolf Appeared heard that the Tą̀imé Keeper had ordered the societies to prevent this. White Bear (Sétthą̀idé), of the Ją̀ifègàu, served as spokesman and offered two horses from Black Bison Bull's father as a settlement. When Wolf Appeared refused to answer, White Bear, supported by the Ją̀ifègàu, offered him one more chance to change his intentions and then raised his lance to kill him. Wolf Appeared finally consented, upon the condition of doing with his wife as he pleased.

White Bear warned him about not submitting completely, referring to the threat concerning his wife. Wolf Appeared was left alone until the end of the Sun Dance, when he was again confronted. He refused to depart and was about to be killed by White Bear when Sàu̧ǫ̀détòn (Squirrel Tail, a Tǫ̀kǫ́gàut leader who had recently outfaced Wolf Appeared on his own war party) stepped in and saved his life, thus publicly as well as individually shaming him. He had the Tǫ̀kǫ́gàut forcibly move his tipi and mount him on his horse. The Black Legs Society escorted Wolf Appeared to the next encampment and instructed him where to set up there, with the society authority being extended after the normal term (Mooney 1898:337).[156]

Societies also guarded against raiding parties' setting out at undesirable times. In the summer of 1873 the Tą̀imé Keeper appointed the Áljóyìgàu and Chę̀jánmàu to guard against outgoing raids because White Bear and Big Tree were being held as prisoners in Texas. Appointing the younger societies to perform this duty strategically prevented their members from leaving on a raid; younger members, overanxious to make a name for themselves, were usually the ones to make premature decisions regarding raids and warfare. Wolf Appeared, who again disobeyed consensus policy and set out on a raiding party, was forced by the guards to return to camp. After the prisoners returned that fall, raiding resumed (Mooney 1898:336–338). War party leaders (tǫ̀yópjòqì or tǫ̀yópqì) were also occasionally persuaded to cancel or to postpone raids against other tribes depending upon political and economic circumstances involving relations, location, and the size of a leader's following.[157]

Societies also kept order and enforced appropriate behavior on all levels, serious as well as humorous, during the Sun Dance encampment. Sangko, who was always into some mischief, was once going through the camp sing-

ing with a group of friends, when one of the party was pushed into the
Tòkóǧàut Society tipi. The Tòkóǧàut members caught them, hobbled
them, and tied their hands behind them. The miscreants were all laid face
down until the leader of their own society ransomed them by giving presents
to the Tòkóǧàut. Announcing their capture to the whole camp provided a
good laugh for all.[158]

Naming Ceremonies

Although there were no names owned by a military society, prominent society leaders, who were always among the most successful warriors, were
often chosen to name individuals. When a prominent chief decided to name
a young man of proven worth or to bestow his own name upon the young
man, a great celebration was held. While a regular naming could be held for
a youth of any age, those receiving a distinguished chief's name usually did
not receive such an honor before they were thirty years old. The chief informed the individual that he would name him then rode around for up to
eight days announcing this and inviting people from nearby camps. The
female relatives of the man to be named set up a large tipi in the center of
camp. The chief rode around the camp on three consecutive days, inviting
everyone to come to the event. On the fourth day the military society of the
chief who was to name the youth and the female relatives of the chief and
youth performed War and Scalp Dances, respectively. The young man and
the chief danced together with the society, and the women were invited to
dance with and/or to sing for the man. The man's family had a giveaway; the
recipients would reply, "Thank you" (àhô) and bow with outstretched arms.
The name was then bestowed upon the man by the chief, prayers were said
for the man, and his family provided a feast. This practice was rare and one
of the few social functions that a society held outside of the preparatory
period for the Sun Dance.[159]

There is some indication from Kintadl that a man could only name children of fellow society members and that the society that danced prior to the
naming was the namer's society. This also suggests the presence of hereditary membership in the higher-level military societies. Whether this was
merely a preference or a social norm is not known.[160] Lowie (1956:133)
reports that several years after an honored warrior's death his son's society
might decide to reinstate the deceased's name by conferring it on his son
(their fellow member) by having an elder ride around the camp announcing
the change. I have recorded one such reinstatement in the Óhòmò Society
around 1950.[161]

SUMMARY

The Kiowa ethnography demonstrates how a large seasonally dispersed sociopolitical entity was linked together through a widely extended bilateral kinship system and a series of horizontally linking military sodalities. Other social links such as band leaders, religious bundles, shield and doctoring societies, and heraldic tipis provided vertical integration to extended family groupings within the tribe, while supporting the larger horizontal ties. These societies were ranked based on individual progress in wealth, war honors, age, and social class. Societies were permeated by the institution of cóm, the pairing of "society brothers" who were neither consanguineally nor affinally related. While some social and economic support could be obtained from one's society in case of need, depending upon the time of year and proximity to fellow society members, a man was most closely associated with his individual society partner in nearly all social and economic interests. Leadership included two leaders and two subleaders or whipmen. Youth members included two young boys and, in some societies, two girls. Membership in most societies included captives and in some societies members of other tribes. The replacement process relied largely on recruitment from the Áljóyìgàu and the stealing of members from other societies. The high frequency of father-son replacement in the Tǫ́kǫ́gàut and Jáifègàu Societies suggests that these societies had a relatively stable number of hereditary positions.

Preparation for the Sun Dance was the period of most society activities, including announcing the time and location of the Sun Dance as well as policing the camp after the ride-around camp and the communal hunt until reaching the Sun Dance location. For the Sun Dance proper, the societies played major parts in the search for the center pole, the camp alignment, the sham battle, the carrying and erection of the center pole, the brush dragging and lodge building, the Kick-Fight, and a whole series of day and nighttime feasts, dances, and parades. Societies also performed functions concerning warfare, death, mutual aid, naming, and serving as police.

Martially speaking, it was the individual and the individual war party that functioned for the benefit of the tribe. The Cáuitémgòp were known to have fought as units; however, later societies rarely did so as war parties had a mixture of societies represented in their membership. At the Sun Dance the societies fostered and represented military spirit while serving social and economic functions, validating war deeds and social status, redistributing wealth, and providing a period of socialization. Excluding leaders, members of the same society were largely men of the same rank in terms of age, social class, and military achievement. Forming societies on this basis provided mutual aid and cooperation across band lines, while promoting horizontal social stability and tribal solidarity. Although data concerning society activities outside of the Sun Dance period are scarce, it is likely that members of the same society, especially those within the same band or camp, maintained relations throughout the year. Through familiarity and kinship ties as society brothers, members most likely hunted, raided, and met in small social groups, though not as an official society activity.

Possibilities of De Facto Age-Grading

Plains scholars have traditionally viewed Plains military societies in terms of polarities, as either age-graded or coordinate. However, one of the most theoretically important points that still requires investigation is at what point and to what degree any of the Plains tribes were shifting toward a more age-graded structure. While this is difficult to reconstruct at this late date, we cannot assume that this dichotomy always existed. Lowie (1916a:954) concludes that "the graded system is not the original form from which ungraded military organizations have developed, but arose through the grading of originally ungraded societies"; this is supported by the greater numerical presence and wider distribution of nongraded forms.

Based upon Lowie's (1916a) findings, Kiowa societies have been regarded as age-graded or coordinate in membership. Yet Mishkin (1940:38) recognized but did not explore the fact that "Kiowa societies were roughly graded according to age and achievement." Did Kiowa (and other Plains) societies have features that represented de facto age-grading or were the Kiowa on their way to acquiring many of the traits of age-grading, if not gradually becoming age-graded? I contend that prereservation Kiowa military societies possessed clear elements of de facto age-grading and that they, along with many other Plains populations, were germinating the seeds of age-grading. This reflects the larger socioeconomic Plains development as described by Mishkin (1940) and Foster (1992:vii–x). Due to the wealth of detailed documentation on men's societies, the Kiowa provide the best opportunity to examine this possibility; while documentation on the men's societies of neighboring tribes is scarcer, reasonable inferences from several other Plains populations offer support. It is first necessary to review Mishkin's (1940) assessment concerning the evolution of the role of warfare and property in Kiowa rank and social status before demonstrating the relationship of Kiowa military societies to this process.

Mishkin (1940:8) argues that the individual pursuit of social status through military activities was linked to Plains communal economics primarily through the horse, which greatly transformed native social organizations and cultural values. He contends that the horse was both a means and an end in the postcontact transformation of Plains communities; it increased mobility and intercommunity interaction, which in turn led to increased trade and warfare opportunities. Increased interaction led to a wider cultural pattern, including the development of relatively uniform military behavior. Warfare was largely on an individual basis, by parties formed without the sanction of any larger social unit; although coordinated efforts occurred, individual acts of heroism were valued above collective actions. Later redistribution of wealth and public recitations of individual acts at Kiowa community gatherings served as claims for individual social advancement. Thus, the individual achievement of social status became an important by-product of warfare, in addition to acquiring community territory and wealth.

As Mishkin (1940) reconstructs, an elaborate system of etiquette regarding military activities developed which subjected warriors to communal regulation largely through socially sanctioned forms of appropriate behavior aimed toward the benefit of the larger community. Covering a retreating war party, countercharging an enemy, and rescuing a comrade were among the most highly valued military acts and channeled individual behavior toward the benefit of others, and thus the group, often forcing an individual to choose between acquiring wealth (horses, etc.) or status (war honors). Legitimization of military deeds through public narration provided the community with the opportunity to evaluate and screen claims for higher rank and upward social and political mobility. Upward social movement brought social expectations of generosity and furthered forms of community regulation. Increased social rank was linked to economic success, yet required a high maintenance price through the redistribution of goods to demonstrate generosity and validate deeds, thus limiting individual accumulation of status and wealth. Acquisition of status in warfare frequently involved acquiring horses, entangling status and wealth with individual action and thus causing problems for social organization. In addition to the individual achievement of social status, differential wealth among individuals, families, and extrafamilial social units also posed difficulties for maintaining social order and solidarity. The increased flow of economic goods necessitated new conventions to regulate their value, distribution, and exchange in relation to other material and social values (Mishkin 1940; Foster 1992 : vii–x).

Because most prereservation Plains horses were acquired through raiding, their status as economic goods accelerated warfare and, despite the redistributive mechanisms mentioned above, Kiowa society was not totally

egalitarian (Mishkin 1940). Advantages or disadvantages of wealth and social status became hereditary as an individual inherited the economic and
social status of his family's rank. Those born into affluent families were not
under the daily pressures to acquire horses and goods through raiding for
normal subsistence and thus could afford to engage in military activities
focusing primarily on rank. In contrast, a poorer man, who was dependent
upon wealthier individuals for mounts to use in military activities and had
to share a portion of his spoils, focused upon martial activities emphasizing
wealth over status. The Kiowa social stratification and public etiquette of
rank produced a carefully balanced economic and socially productive form
of warfare which served to maintain the Kiowa community while adapting
to the larger regional political economy (Mishkin 1940; Foster 1992 : vii–x).
Before demonstrating how Kiowa military societies mirror the shift toward
this larger process of political economy which developed on the Plains, it is
necessary to review those aspects which demonstrate elements of de facto
age-grading.

For the Kiowa there are several indicators that a de facto age-graded
stratification possibly existed based on the relationship between political
economy and individual social status, in relation to military society hierarchy, and that social status existed prior to additional external cultural in-
terruptions which ended the historic Plains economy and indigenous autonomy, forcing the Kiowa to enter a reservation. Ethnohistorical accounts
by Kiowa (1935 Santa Fe Notes) and Apache (McAllister 1935, 1937) elders
who were the last actual members of these societies prior to their cessation
suggest the establishment of an increasing hierarchy of personal and war-
related social status that was closely linked to social class and economic levels. These patterns are reflected by membership level and age in the Kiowa
societies of the third quarter of the nineteenth century. Increased war deeds
enabled membership in the higher-ranking men's societies. References indicating that individual social status increased with progression in membership in the higher-level societies are numerous and in some instances are
even linked to the categories of Kiowa social status as defined by Mishkin
(1940) and Richardson (1940). While the leaders of all the societies were all
decorated veterans holding multiple war honors, this discussion is concerned with the regular membership.

Through emulation, the children's Pòlą̃hyòp Society taught the skills and
behavior (feasts, dancing, giving-away, group cooperation, coup recitations,
acknowledgment and maintenance of authority positions) needed as an
adult in a warrior-based culture. The Áljóyĩgàu Society was essentially
viewed as a finishing school for young warriors, who were frequently re-

cruited after acquiring a warfare deed. The Chè jánmàu was seen as a movement upward, but centered around members of ordinary status with few war honors and wealth, while societies such as the Tò̜kó̜gàut, which originally required combat experience, and the Jáifègàu were considered to include older, more mature, and socially higher-ranking war veterans. Membership in the Qóichę́gàu was of course the highest level, requiring several honors and representing the best and bravest in terms of war record and social status. Often war honors, and thus increased social rank and wealth, were required to move into the higher-level men's societies, as demonstrated among the Tò̜kó̜gàut and Qóichę́gàu. Thus, war rank was directly linked to status and wealth and in turn was both linked to and reflected in society membership and advancement.

Wealth and family status (descent and inheritance) were also factors; nearly every male youth (except the wealthiest and highest-social-ranking, who were often inducted as an ą́udétàlyì into one of the higher-level societies) was at one time an Áljóyìgàu member and had to work his way up the military society social ladder. Otherwise, men had to work their way up the ranks into the other societies by increasing their war record and wealth. Although one's socioeconomic status was inherited, it still required maintenance, and a wealthy and high-status family had more economic resources to do so than a person of less wealth and lower social class. While membership did not involve complete grades or cohorts of men collectively purchasing membership as a group, wealth was required to be given away by a new initiate's family and during coup recitations and increased in amount with progression into the higher societies. A fixed number of hereditary positions in the Tò̜kó̜gàut and Jáifègàu were facilitated and maintained by association with the more affluent ǫ́dè and ǫ́dègùfà social classes. The correlation between wealth and high-status families is again reflected in social status and society membership. As Mishkin has argued, it was the wealthy who would have been able to support such societal positions economically through giveaways and through having the capital to further the war and raiding interests of their kindred. The status of Kiowa societies was also reflected in the parades held at the Sun Dance, which began with the Qóichę́gàu and concluded with the Pòlą́hyò̜p (Nye 1962:62), and in the assignment of increasingly more important functions to the higher-level men's societies.

While comparably detailed accounts for the Apache are lacking in some aspects (especially regarding their exact level of participation in Kiowa societies) there are sufficient data to suggest that their societies were experiencing a similar development. Estimates of the relation between age and membership in societies, requirements of war honors for membership in the Manatidie and Klintidie, generalized references (in non-class-specific terms) to individual social status, the assignment of particular functions to respective societies, intersocietal rivalry, and a demonstrable correlation between increased war experience, wealth, and social status and society membership imply that the Apache military society system contained at least many general similarities with the Kiowa system. The Comanche, due to their later acquisition of military societies and their distinct divisional distributions in the prereservation era, had not yet developed the numbers of societies per division or any recognizable characteristics resembling de facto age-grading.

The numerous similarities between particular Kiowa societies may reflect an expansion of the number of societies, intrasocietal rivalries, and a de facto age-graded system. Similarities occur in the dance style and lack of female youth members of the Chệjánmàu and Jáifègàu societies; the similarities of dress, dances, and presence of female youth members in the Áljóyìgàu and Tọkógàut; and similar divisional groupings between societies in the sham battle, in the Kick-Fight, and in the playing of the Cáumáuqàu-dàl (Aiming Circle/Wheel) Game.[162] Lowie (1916a:887) reports that intersocietal rivalry in the form of acquisition of warfare deeds, athletic competitions, and in some cases wife stealing and other antagonistic forms was one of the most widely distributed and presumably oldest characteristics of Plains societies.

Several of these characteristics are found in other Plains communities, suggesting a wide distribution of de facto age-grading among "ungraded" Plains societies. Intersocietal rivalries are described for a number of Plains populations such as the Crow, Iowa, Ponca, Lakota, Cheyenne, Apache, and others (Wissler 1916b; Lowie 1916a:887; McAllister 1935; Lowie 1983) and could reflect historical relationships or possible fission representing an expansion of the system. Mooney's (1912d) statement regarding the periodic rise and fall of an individual society's popularity, size, importance, and influence suggests that periodic fluctuation in individual systems occurred. Such fluctuation is still present in contemporary Kiowa, Comanche, and Southern Cheyenne societies.[163] The presence of general age differences between societies is reported for the Lakota and Apache and in some Crow societies (Wissler 1912:18, 44; Lowie 1916a:888, 904). The presence of male youth societies among the Kiowa, Apache, Crow, and Lakota (Lowie 1916a:915) and the differential assignment of duties to specific Kiowa, Apache, and Lakota societies and thus approximate cohorts (Wissler 1912; Lowie 1916a:908) provide other indicators of widespread de facto grading.

While these inferences are plausible, insufficient data on pre-1840 society organization, individual and societal social status, and society origins preclude a full conclusion; however, widespread evidence of de facto age-grading is clear.

Although we lack many detailed data regarding pre-nineteenth-century Plains military society organization and functions to compare with later data, military societies appear to have adapted to the larger sociopolitical-economic process or hierarchy that was developing in the Plains region. The factors created by the introduction of the horse as outlined by Mishkin (1940) led to a unique political economy which furthered, if not initiated, a sort of de facto age-grading by social class and wealth which correlated with, but was not solely dependent upon, loose age cohorts. Social status, age, wealth, war status, political position, and economic status became entangled in a growing system containing numerous checks and balances. The effects of this system on social and economic levels were further reflected in the organization, functions and activities, increasing social status, and economic levels of members and societies, each of which contained a unique set of associated symbols. Thus, Kiowa military societies reflect what Mishkin (1940; also Foster 1992 : vii–x) argues concerning the evolution of the role of warfare and property in Kiowa rank and social status.

3 THE DECLINE AND REVIVAL OF KIOWA MILITARY SOCIETIES, 1875 TO THE PRESENT

This chapter addresses the general processes that affected the vitality of Kiowa military societies temporally, from 1875, when the Kiowa entered a final reservation, to the present day. This material serves as the model for comparing and contrasting the Apache and Comanche military society histories presented in Chapters 4 and 5.

Decline of the Kiowa Societies

Government agencies and Christian missionaries continued their general assault upon American Indian cultural institutions of all forms in the late nineteenth century when Plains groups entered reservations. Many of these efforts emphasized the eradication of traditional religious institutions. As in most Plains tribes which had some form of the Sun Dance and men's societies, Kiowa societies were the primary foci of a prereservation martial ethos, dancing, and served as primary public arenas for individual and collective martial enhancement through coup recitations and giveaways. These were occasions in which individual status was raised through public acclamation. As auxiliaries to the Sun Dance, military societies performed many preparatory activities for the annual event.

The Kiowa encountered enormous social, political, economic, and demographic changes from nineteenth-century Anglo encroachment, Anglo-removed eastern Indian populations, disease epidemics, economic competition, and warfare with various groups (Mooney 1898; Levy n.d.a). Yet Kiowa military societies continued to function actively after taking up permanent residence on a reservation in 1875.[1] The decline of access to three activities would rapidly alter their vitality: (1) active warfare and war-related power, (2) bison hunting, and (3) participation in communal Sun Dances.

Warfare

Throughout much of the nineteenth century, the Kiowa were one of the most important Southern Plains tribes in regard to raiding and horse acquisition and distribution in Texas and Mexico. As demographic pressures from eastern tribes and Anglos increased, the Kiowa became a major impediment to Southern Plains expansion during the 1860s and 1870s. Although the Kiowa came from a much longer warrior tradition, it was during the 1860s and 1870s that they were in direct competition with Anglos and gained the reputation among Anglos as one of the fiercest Plains tribes. The reservation period (1875–1901) ended many nineteenth-century Kiowa rituals associated with warfare as rapidly changing sociopolitical conditions resulted in the cessation of raiding and warfare, which were vitally important to pre-reservation Kiowa economics and social status. In 1874–1875 only two of the major Kiowa leaders were at peace with the United States—Kicking Bird (Thȩnéàungópjè, Eagle Striking with Talons) and Stumbling Bear (Sétèmqî̧à, Bear That Runs Them Over)—confirming the contemporary Kiowa belief that they maintained a strong warrior tradition prior to being defeated and forced onto the reservation late in 1875 (Levy 1958).

The cessation of warfare resulted in several problems for the Kiowa. In addition to the inability to acquire war honors, there was also an end to obtaining, using, validating, and passing on forms of dáudáu (supernatural power) associated with warfare, as well as a rapid decline in the acquisition of new forms of power through vision quests. Only a relatively limited number of men possessed dáudáu which protected them from bullets and arrows. They demonstrated that their claim to possessing dáudáu was genuine by using it successfully in warfare. Thus, those men with the strongest dáudáu and the strongest war records frequently served as leaders of war and raiding parties. War power was often signified by possession of a dream shield containing symbols acquired through a vision. Those possessing proven power often attracted followers who lacked or were unable to acquire their own dáudáu, who accompanied them on raiding ventures. As dáudáu could be purchased, individuals who obtained the same form of power often belonged to shield societies, with shields containing the same protective power and symbols. With the cessation of warfare, there was little need for dream-sanctioned shields containing war power, and most were either discarded or not passed on to male heirs. Many were confiscated by the U.S. Army at Fort Sill during the Kiowa's surrender in the winter of 1874. Similarly, many of the Páuiyòi (Offspring or Sons of the Bison, known as Buffalo Doctors), who specialized in doctoring war-related wounds, especially those involving bleeding, also became inactive. Members continued to doctor into the early 1920s, but their dáudáu was often not passed on and soon faded away.

Although membership in some Kiowa military societies required war deeds, none required ownership of personal war power. For those lacking dáudáu, membership in military societies offered a form of social status that was otherwise unavailable without dáudáu. Kiowa warfare was strongly associated with belief systems involving the concept of dáudáu, as success in warfare was usually attributed to supernatural intervention. Because proof of dáudáu was often demonstrated through success in warfare, the decline of active warfare when the Kiowa entered the reservation soon removed the context for war power as well.[2]

Older warriors were prevented from gaining additional war rank and their war status became frozen as of 1875 (as exhibited by the rapid end of the Qóichégàu). Younger men were being indoctrinated in boarding schools and forced education programs and were completely unable to achieve war honors until World War I. Performances of ceremonial song and dance, which signified the importance of warfare in prereservation Kiowa culture, became problematical with the cessation of active warfare, which also caused a collapse in the prereservation political economy. No longer could successful warriors acquire goods to redistribute in validation of their deeds or as gestures of generosity by headsmen to members of their bands. Kiowa societies appear to have continued largely unaffected during the first few years on the reservation, as there were still many veterans with deeds to recount; however, they began to change significantly by the mid-1880s. As J. Gilbert McAllister (1935:14) found with reservation-era Apache societies, Kiowa societies continued as honorary groups, no longer able to engage in or actively promote war-related activities. Some societies died out, while others ceased requiring military deeds for membership.[3]

Scouting

Scouting and agency police roles offered some remnant of earlier warrior roles, but were lacking in comparison with the past (Dunlay 1982). While some Kiowa served as scouts in 1874–1875, their roles involved no combat and ended for the most part with the aggregation of their peoples onto the reservation. Although the Kiowa represented the majority of the Fort Sill Troop L of the Seventh Cavalry (mustered from June 30, 1892, to May 31, 1897), there was no combat action and their roles were limited to patrolling, hunting, and menial labor.[4]

Similarly, a number of Kiowa men served on the tribal police force (post-1880), which sometimes involved little if any actual police work and often provided labor for the construction and maintenance of agency buildings and schools (Nye 1937).[5] The beginning of forced education interrupted the traditional maturing processes for children and youths for lengthy periods. Disruptions in participation in the Pòlą́hyòp and Áljóyĩgàu Societies, the foundation for the upper-level men's societies, produced generational and social breaks throughout the links of the entire Yàpfàhêgàu system. With the generational replacement process interrupted, the older societies found themselves with fewer and fewer members as older warriors died off. This in turn resulted in the retention of society ritual knowledge by a decreasing number of individuals in an "inactive" period (Goldstein 1972).

Bison

The decline of Southern Plains bison herds, which were scarce by 1879 and extinct by 1884, resulted in great socioeconomic changes for the Kiowa. Because bison were symbolically linked to warfare (killing a bison was analogous to killing an enemy), bison were considered to have great dáudáu, which held great resuscitative healing powers (Kracht 1989:89). Bison were also believed to have had warrior societies due to the seasonal shifts in group membership and herding, reflecting the seasonal aggregations and dispersals of men's societies (Kracht 1989:90). Bison were considered to have the strongest power of all animals, and their decline was symbolically and psychologically detrimental to Kiowa concepts of power and warfare. The shift to an annuity-based subsistence involving government commodities and longhorn cattle removed the necessity for policed communal hunts, ended the traditional association of bison with dáudáu, and inhibited the performance of the Sun Dance, in which bison were an integral part of Kiowa religious belief and ceremony (Scott 1911; Spier 1921a).[6]

The transition from eating bison to eating cattle produced significant changes in Kiowa sociopolitical organization, undermining the traditional authority of former band chiefs in several ways. Traditional leaders were now referred to as "beef chiefs," who were relegated to overseeing the distribution of cattle on ration days to local reservation groups known as "beef bands." Even this practice was terminated when the slaughtering of issue cattle was prohibited during the term of Indian Commissioner Thomas J. Morgan (1889–1893). Changes in residence from nomadic camps to extended family households on individual allotments changed traditional band and leadership structures. Indian agents also began to back "Progressives" or those Indians making visible efforts toward Anglo concepts of civilization, including many Indian judges in the Court of Indian Offenses and later officers on the KCA Business Committee.

The Sun Dance

The cessation of warfare, the extinction of the Southern Plains bison herds, and the reservation economy and experiences all led to the end of the Sun Dance. Missionaries and Indian-defense groups opposed indigenous religious forms and spent considerable time and energy attempting to eradicate such "anti-Christian" practices. The most sudden and dramatic force leading to the end of the men's societies was clearly the loss of the Sun Dance, due to Anglo efforts to eradicate indigenous cultural forms through the Court of Indian Offenses established in 1882. The actual prohibition of Kiowa dances did not begin until the term of Commissioner Morgan, whose Bureau of Indian Affairs policies aimed at abolishing tribal customs lasted until 1934, when Commissioner John Collier issued Indian Office Circular 2970, entitled "Indian Religious Freedom and Indian Culture" (Young 1981:284–285; Prucha 1984:951–952).

While the Sun Dance was periodically not held annually due to warfare, recent deaths, pledges, and climate (Mooney 1898), several factors from 1870 to 1890 hastened its decline. Aùnsójèqàptàu (Old Man Feet) or Aùnsócínyíjè (Long Feet), the Táimé Keeper for over thirty years, last conducted the ceremony in 1870. He died in 1871, and no dances were held in 1871 or 1872. He was succeeded by Jòhéjè (Without Moccasins), who conducted the Sun Dance between 1873 and 1875 and died in 1876. Without Moccasins was replaced by Sétjáuáuidè (Many Bears aka HeapoBears), who led five dances before his death in 1883, when his cousin Táiméjè (One Who Is Táimé) assumed the position and served as Táimé Keeper (hence his name) until his death in 1894. During his tenure only three Sun Dances were held, and the 1890 dance was prevented by fear of military sanctions (Mooney 1898). After his death and the last attempted Sun Dance in 1890, the Táimé bundle was passed on to Émàà (Being Provided with Food [Continuatively]), who cared for it until her death in 1934 (Mooney 1898:241).[7]

Before a Sun Dance could be held, an individual had to pledge to sponsor the event, which could result from pledges by individuals in relation to warfare or recovery from illness or by the Táimé Keeper himself. In addition to the rapid series of deaths of Táimé Keepers, the end of warfare in the mid-1870s resulted in an absence of warfare-related pledges to sponsor the dance and less frequent Sun dances. The 1874 Sun Dance was the last Kiowa Sun Dance held prior to confinement on the reservation. Subsequent Sun Dances were frequently accompanied by cavalry troops from Fort Sill, who escorted the Kiowa on their communal bison hunts and monitored their ceremonies in 1875, 1877, and 1878 (Mooney 1898:339–343). Troops dispatched by Agent P. B. Hunt in 1878 and 1879 reported that the Kiowa encountered great difficulty in procuring enough meat to sustain themselves during the ceremonies.[8] Periods of starvation during this time resulted in the name of the 1879 "Horse Eating Sun Dance" (Mooney 1898:344–345) and the name of Prairie Dog Eating Creek between Mountain View and Gotebo, Oklahoma.[9] The lack of bison created difficulties in reenacting portions of the Sun Dance ceremonies such as the ritual hunt, the acquisition of a bull's skin for the center pole, and the numerous feasts associated with the ceremony's preparation. One Kiowa elder stated in 1935 that the 1879 Sun Dance did not include a policed hunt because of the scarcity of bison; while the ceremony was not delayed because the Kiowa found a bison bull, a general lack of meat and limited government rations restricted the number of feasts.[10] Another 1935 consultant stated that the scarcity of bison during this time increased the number of camps held between the ride-around camp and the actual ceremony yearly, and the hunting prohibition following the ride-around camp was discarded after 1875.[11]

Hot weather, droughts, and lack of bison prevented Kiowa Sun Dances from being held in 1880, 1882, 1884, and 1886. In 1881 it took until August to find a bison bull; hence the name "Hot Sun Dance" for that year's ceremony. The bulls for the final two ceremonies in 1885 and 1887 were provided by Texas ranchers (Mooney 1898:346–355). The Sun Dance was not held in 1888 or 1889 because of opposition from Agent W. D. Myers, who threatened military intervention if the Kiowa attempted to hold their ceremony.[12] In 1890 several Kiowa leaders sought permission from Agent C. E. Adams to sponsor one last Sun Dance. After first consenting to their requests, he received notification from Commissioner Morgan to prohibit the dance. Meanwhile, the Kiowa were constructing the Sun Dance lodge near present-day Carnegie, Oklahoma, where a great camp circle had been pitched and an old bison hide for the center pole had been acquired by Little Bluff or Daunpai (Dáunfài, Humped Shoulder Blade Area) (Mooney 1898: 356–359; Methvin n.d.:73).

According to Mooney (1898:359), Adams informed the commander at Fort Sill on July 19, 1890, of the Kiowa's intention to hold their Sun Dance despite his warnings. The next day three troops of cavalry were dispatched toward Anadarko to stop the proceedings. Learning of the troops' intentions, Quanah Parker informed Stumbling Bear (who had stayed away from the activities because of the recent death of his son) that troops were coming from Fort Sill to stop the dance and might kill the Kiowa and their horses. Stumbling Bear sent two messengers to the encampment to warn the Kiowa to break their camps and go home; after heated discussion, they did so, leaving the unfinished Sun Dance Lodge standing. Thus, the last attempted Sun Dance in 1890 became known as the "Sun Dance Where the Forked Poles Were Left Standing" (Mooney 1898:359). The Reverend J. J. Methvin (n.d.:73) reports that some of the Kiowa, led by Big Tree, were willing and ready to fight; but after preparations and messengers asking him to come to the agency, he consented and came after a few days. When word of the Kiowa's dispersal reached the agency in Anadarko, the troops returned to Fort Sill, having never reached the encampment near Carnegie. The Kiowa made no further attempts to revive their Sun Dance until 1927–1931.

In reviewing the Kiowa Agency Records for the late 1800s, I found hardly any reference to military societies; the most frequent correspondence focused on the "medicine dance" (Sun Dance) and agency efforts to end it. It is clear that these efforts ended the Kiowa Sun Dance. Following the prevention of the last attempted Kiowa Sun Dance in 1890, Indian Commissioner T. J. Morgan expressed his approval and sent the authorization of section 496 of "Regulation of the Indian Department," outlawing the Sun Dance, to Agent C. E. Adams: "I am glad to learn from your letter that the "medicine dance" has not taken place. . . . Other dances, while less debasing, are injurious to the Indians in keeping alive old superstitions and in taking away their time and thought from agriculture and other civilized pursuits. And should be discouraged by all possible means instead of encouraged."[13]

Anglo concerns about the Sun Dance took precedence over other matters such as military societies, as the Sun Dance was the primary cultural institution to be suppressed. Therefore, efforts were directed toward its termination, which in turn disrupted all associated religious, military society, and social components. Following the last attempted Sun Dance in 1890, efforts soon turned toward eradicating any vestige of social, cultural, and religious institutions. In 1896 the following rule concerning Kiowa dancing was authorized: "Rule 4 of Section 580 of the Rules & Regulations of the Indian Office, governing the Court of Indian Offenses, provides that the 'sun dance,' the 'war dance' and all other so-called feasts assimilating thereto shall be considered 'Indian offenses' and any Indian found guilty of being a participant in any one or more of these offenses shall be punished in the manner therein provided."[14] The persecution of dancing, social gatherings, giveaways, and any other social form involving large aggregations was accelerated.

With the end of warfare in 1875, depletion of the Southern Plains bison herds by 1879, and the end of the Sun Dance in 1890, few functional contexts for Kiowa men's military societies remained. According to Henry Tsoodle Sr., both of the societies to which he belonged (the Tòkógàut and Áljóyìgàu) ceased functioning at the last attempted Sun Dance in 1890, having no further purpose.[15] The Qóichégàu ceased meeting in 1882, five years before the last completed Sun Dance in 1887 (Mooney 1898:358–359).[16] As Kiowa women's societies were directly linked to assuring male martial success in warfare, they also rapidly declined following the end of warfare, but occasionally performed other social and healing functions until circa 1905. The 1935 Santa Fe Field School notes contain several cases of men changing society memberships during the 1880s as they left one declining society to join another which was still functioning. As Richardson described, "Frizzle-head was first a member of the Qóichégàu, then joined the Chèjánmàu, then the Tòkógàut. Each one was on the verge of going out of business at the time, hence his joining so many."[17]

All Kiowa societies experienced these circumstances, as many men left the older societies for membership in the burgeoning Óhòmò Society acquired from the Cheyenne in 1884. Some societies amended their veteran requirements to continue as active organizations; the membership rosters for the Tòkógàut and Jáifègàu Societies in the late 1800s included many men in their late teens and early twenties who were born too late to gain veteran status; members normally would have been in their forties in prereservation times. Lowie (1916a:971) found similar changes throughout the series of Arapaho age-graded societies as the ages for membership dropped drastically from the prereservation to reservation period. Nevertheless, the acquisition of the Óhòmò Society and other, albeit short-lived, religious-based sodalities such as the Fáiiyòi (Sons of the Sun) indicates that men's sodalities were still useful for the Kiowa in the reservation era.[18]

Other Influences

Several other factors also contributed to the cessation of society dances and meetings. These came from both native and Anglo sources. The formation of ten reservation-period communities, and later allotments in severalty, increased the fragmentation of traditional bands, which had already begun to fragment and reorganize prior to entering the reservation in 1875. This, in turn, further weakened society ties and restructured new levels of group interaction. Elders indicate that this dispersion of people led to decreases in all dances, religious ceremonies, hand games, and other communal social forms.[19]

Religion

The establishment of various post-1887 missionizing interests led to fervent proselytization against dancing. While Methodists were somewhat more lenient toward dancing, Baptists often blackballed those who "digressed" to participation in dancing: several Kiowa members of the Red Stone and Saddle Mountain Churches were expelled for attending and participating in dances.[20] The rise of Kiowa Peyotism after 1885 also detracted from military society participation. In some cases individuals gave up dancing after joining Peyotism (and the later Native American Church). However, the growth of Peyotism had less direct impact than did Christianity, as numerous individual family histories demonstrate that the Peyotist segments of several Kiowa communities have been among the staunchest supporters of dancing from at least circa 1890 to the present.[21] Although the introduction and growth of Peyotism (though by no means the sole factor) decreased the frequency of dancing in some cases, it did not directly proselytize against dancing. Between 1890 and 1930, many members of the Tòkóǵàut, Jáifègàu, and Óhòmò Societies whose annuity payments were withheld by the agency for participation in social and war dancing, the Ghost Dance, and giveaways were devout Peyotists.[22] Peyotists also represented the majority of individuals involved in the later initial revival of military society and social dances in the 1950s.[23] As Kiowa Christian converts were taught to adhere to Anglo Christian teachings, which included opposition to dancing and Peyotism, this created some factionalism within the tribe which has continued in some forms to the present; however, many Kiowa have learned to tolerate or participate in both Kiowa and Christian value systems.

The Ghost Dance (1890 to 1917) replaced the annual Sun Dance gathering as the annual summer gathering for most non-Christian Kiowa. Kiowa Ghost Dance adherents were closely allied with and participated in other non-Christian activities, particularly Peyotism. Frizzlehead's comment that no men's societies met during the Ghost Dance underlines the intrinsic association between the societies and the Sun Dance, bison, and warfare complex.[24] Two eyewitnesses indicated that the only dancing involved at the Ghost Dances they witnessed between 1908 to 1917 involved the Feather Dance (Àmácùngà) of the actual ceremony itself and that no war, military society, Óhọ̀mò, or social dancing of any kind occurred at the Ghost Dance. These individuals observed no role for the men's societies in the preparatory aspects of the Ghost Dance, as had previously existed in the Sun Dance.[25] Although the newly acquired Óhọ̀mò Society met during these years, it conducted its ceremonies at separate gatherings. Those who adhered to more traditional activities, such as dancing and hand games, were often labeled the "Ghost Dance crowd" or followers of the "Dance Road," in opposition to Christian Kiowa following the "Jesus Road."[26]

KIOWA MILITARY SOCIETY ACTIVITIES, 1890–1941

With the exception of the Óhọ̀mò Society, the dormancy of Kiowa military societies increased after the last attempted Sun Dance in 1890. In discussing the Ghost Dance, Frizzlehead stated in 1935: "At that time, none of these war [i.e., military] societies were going on at all."[27] According to Jimmy Quoetone, the Black Legs had ceased to function as an organization before it was revived in 1912, but some individuals occasionally gathered to dance for recreational purposes.[28] Although it is possible that groups of society members met intermittently after 1890, whole societies apparently did not. By 1912 the Tọ̀kọ́gàut and the Jáifègàu had been revived and were holding at least intermittent dances, while the Óhọ̀mò society continued to gain in popularity.[29] During this time men's societies with the majority of members and support centered around specific communities were formed: (1) the Tọ̀kọ́gàut centered around the Stecker community, (2) the Óhọ̀mò in the Red Stone community, and (3) the Jáifègàu around the Carnegie area (particularly in the southeast portion).[30] Brief descriptions of these revived societies' activities during the early 1900s illustrate a continuation of the earlier Kiowa military society patterns and martial ethos through World War II.

The Óhọ̀mò Society

Óhọ̀mò Society dances continued to flourish during the 1884–1935 era. Although dances were held during the years of the Ghost Dance (1890–1917), Óhọ̀mò Society members and tribal elders report that the Óhọ̀mò Society never danced at the Ghost Dances, in contrast to Kracht's (1989, 1992, 1994) contentions that they did. Francis Tsonetokoy and Parker McKenzie, both of whom attended several Ghost Dances, stated that no Óhọ̀mò dances or powwow dancing of any kind occurred at the encampments they attended.[31] By combining archival records with interviews of society and tribal elders, a general picture of the society's activities during this period can be reconstructed. During the 1920s visiting contingents of Cheyenne continued to come south and participate in Óhǫmò dances with Kiowa.[32] The Óhǫmò Society was a principal target of agency efforts to stop Indian dancing due to the frequent practice of giving-away (Kracht 1989), a standard part of the larger Plains War–Omaha Dance tradition. As the society was known to have a Give-Away Song, agents applied pressures to teach Kiowa to become materialistic, property-owning, conservative Christian farmers. Yet the Óhǫmò Society refused to cease meeting or to give up its traditions.

Later generations of Kiowa who grew up hearing of the government's attempts to suppress their ancestors' cultural freedom have continued their commitment to preserving the society and its associated ideology. One individual described the association between Óhǫmò songs and images of her grandfather:

> When I hear those songs I can see my grandpa dancing. Oh my grandpa was handsome, my grandpa was fancy. He was wonderful to look at and then when I was growing up, I grew up on stories about how they were deprived because they were heathens, they were not Christians. . . . I grew up on stories about my grandpa and them . . . my great grandfather. You know my great-grandfather was one of the ones who said, "If you want me to give up Óhǫmò, if you want me to give up my Óhǫmò ways you'll have to kill me. Death is the only thing that will keep me from Óhǫmò," and so it's this kind of thinking you know, that we were here, we never quit, you know as "heathens" we are the ones that saved something. . . .
>
> Óhǫmò is the one society that never had to be revived, we never quit. . . .
>
> My grandfather said, "I'm Óhǫmò, I could belong to anything I wanted to. I could join the JC's. I could join anything that I wanted to but I'm Óhǫmò," he said. "And I'll be Óhǫmò until the day I die." And so it's that kind of respect for that society. That's something that I try to tell my sons about. You know because that's important, because that man provided something for them to take care of them, so it's only right that they take care of it and get it ready for the next generation coming after.
>
> But for myself, it's important for my family to take part and be a part of and be supportive, simply because if my grandfather were here, that's what my grandfather would have done. So for me it's important to live my life just as if my grandmother and grandfather were here beside me.

Everything that I have was provided by them and so it's important that I carry on the things that were important to them.[33]

One of the greatest changes in the society came when the Fancy Dance style of "War Dancing" was adopted by the Kiowa. Although dancing contests in the KCA area are known as early as 1894 (Brant 1969:83, 101), another elder Kiowa remembers that dancing contests started in 1918, which coincides with the introduction of the "Fancy Dance" among the Kiowa in 1917.[34]

The location for the annual Óhòmò Society encampment varied from year to year, as different members sponsored four-day dances on their private allotments. One of the earlier dances was held at Rainey Mountain during a Kiowa grass payment encampment.[35] Between 1915 and 1923 dances were held at Kiowa Jim Tongkeamha's allotment, thirteen miles south of Carnegie. At the 1915 dance, Agent C. V. Stinchecum came and asked for the dance to be stopped; however, the Kiowa would not relent and continued their activities.[36] Several Fourth of July Óhòmò encampments were held at Konad's between Washita and Redstone from 1910 to 1925. The flourishing intertribal friendships, visiting, and growing enthusiasm for War Dancing are illustrated in this case, as Cheyenne, Arapaho, Ponca, Otoe, Osage, Pawnee, Comanche, Apache, and even Taos Pueblo attended these dances. Like the societies of surrounding tribes, the Óhòmò Society also performed at the Dietrich's Lake Fair in 1923. Most society dances were held at the homes of members of the Redstone and Anadarko Kiowa communities, and the Redstone community came to dominate most of the Óhòmò activities and membership from the 1920s to the present.[37]

According to Parsons (1929:92–94) and tribal elders, significant changes in organizational offices occurred with the decreasing number of surviving Kiowa with warrior status. As a result of the lack of available veterans, an emphasis on ancestral integrity developed: often a younger nonveteran descendant of an earlier veteran member was inducted "instead of his ancestor" (Boyd 1981:65).[38] Even prior to 1900, many new Óhòmò initiates were from "good families," which were considered to be socially "prominent." Reflecting a continuation of the loosely ranked traditional social statuses, the majority of initiates were favored boys (áudétàlyòp) from high-status (ǫ̀dè and ǫ̀dègùfà) families. As Weiser Tongkeamha explained, "First time was near Hobart. They mostly took in áudétàlyì, first-born boys, favored boys, and those from respected families. These were the ones they wanted in Óhòmò."[39] These procedures continued from the late 1880s until the 1930s. Óhòmò Society dances maintained several rituals characteristic of nineteenth-century Kiowa military societies, including all-night meetings and dances, brush dragging, society partners, martially oriented dances such as the Sit Down or Squat Dance and the Charging Dance, and initiation by eating boiled dog, a widespread Plains War or Omaha Dance tradition.[40]

The Tǫkǫ́gàut

Descriptions of the Black Legs between Mooney's work starting in the 1890s and the 1935 Santa Fe notes are few and lacking in depth. Like other Kiowa societies the Black Legs ceased to meet formally in 1890 with the end of the Sun Dance and the beginning of the Ghost Dance, but the society formally revived in 1912. In addition to the better-known and publicized Kiowa calendars (Mooney 1898) of Dohausen (Jòhâusàn, Little Bluff Recess/Concavity), Setta'n (Séttàun, Little Bear), Anko (Àunkóvàuigàdédè, Standing in the Middle of Many Tracks), and Polan Yi Katon (Pòlą́hįkàutǫ̀, Rabbit Shoulder), many less-known family and individual calendars also exist. In contrast to earlier "tribal" calendars, which varied somewhat, but included most of the important events known throughout the tribe, later calendars often included more local or community-specific events and thus had greater variation. One such postreservation calendar, drawn by Andy Domebo (Jǫ́bâu, Whistle or Bugle) and listed as the Alice Soontay Domebo calendar in the Doris Duke Oral History Collections, contains drawings from the summer of 1905 to the winter of 1912–1913.[41] The season of each drawing is indicated by a tree with leaves for summer and a tree without leaves for winter. As in most Kiowa calendars, there are two entries per year. The drawings have no dates, but each entry has a name or description and a number written in English below it.[42]

One summer entry, #105, depicts a man with blackened legs, followed by the description "Ton-Kon-Gah Organize." Known historical events on the calendar support a date of 1912. These supporting events are drawing #94 (the beginning of John P. Blackman's term as agent, October 10, 1907), drawing #96 (the beginning of Ernest Stecker's term as agent, January 1, 1908), and drawing #102 (the death of Quanah Parker, February 11, 1911). This places the date of drawing #105, the year in which the Tǫkǫ́gàut reorganized, as the summer of 1912.[43] The date of this revival is further supported by the induction of two ą́udémátàun by the society in 1912 (Bantista n.d.: 13), by the Quoetone interviews in the Duke collection, and by Robert Lowie (1916b:847), who recorded a dance and feast held by the Tǫkǫ́gàut in the spring of 1914.[44]

Society organization at this time remained largely intact from the past, with two fãujóqî (society leaders), two áljóqî (whipmen), and two ąudémá-tàun (favored girls). There is no reference to áujòqî or boy members in the society in this later period. Induction methods at this time resembled those of earlier descriptions and society partnerships continued.[45] Society dress including yellow and black body paint was initially maintained; however, the society later ceased dressing as a unit.[46] Annual dances were held during four- or five-day encampments, including afternoon Black Legs Society dances and evening War Dances and social dances. All-night meetings included smoking, storytelling, singing, dancing, feasting, and giveaways. After a meeting started the tipi door was closed with a piece of stiff rawhide, representing the dáucâum meetings of earlier times. Late-coming members were often made to pay fines and/or perform the comical "Turkey Trot Dance" as punishment.[47] Evidence of continued society-based coercive police functions also exists. In 1916 a large contingent of the tribe had gathered at the invitation of Charley Oheltoint to repaint the historic Battle Tipi, including many prominent combat veterans of the prereservation era who were invited to record their deeds. On this occasion a portion of the Black Legs Society gathered and publicly admonished Belo Cozad for allegedly beating his wife, continuing the role of societies in publicly sanctioning this behavior.[48]

Elders indicated that all of the society's dances during this period were held on various members' allotments in the Stecker, Oklahoma, area.[49] Approximately twenty members participated in society dances in the early 1920s. Weiser Tongkeamha, whose father, Kiowa Jim Tongkeamha, frequently sang for the Black Legs at this time, attended several dances during this period. The men danced inside a tipi with the sides rolled up. Mr. Tongkeamha saw the society perform the Reverse or Turn Around Dance (Xãkói-gácùngà); the men paraded out of the tipi when beginning this dance, which was concluded by the recitation of a war deed by an elder. The Óhòmò Society attended these Black Legs gatherings and held war dances in the evenings.[50]

Although new members were inducted during these years, anyone who wanted to take part was allowed to do so. Membership in the society at this time was based on being financially well-off, well respected, generous, and of outstanding social status.[51] These qualities are usually associated with traditional affluent (ǫdè) status. Individuals descended from Kiowa families of ǫdè and other prereservation social classes were members at this time, reflecting the continuation of the society as an honorary organization. This change occurred because men could no longer achieve war honors as in the past. There was a logical connection between affluence and military deeds:

many prereservation Black Legs Society members were older, in the upper social ranks, and could afford the resources for giveaways. A review of the ages of members during this period confirms that almost all were born too late to have had prereservation combat. Parsons (1929:90) states that "members were chosen from the point of view of the help they and their families could give to the society, at its feast or celebration," which reflects these changes in membership criteria during this period. The last Tòkógàut dance during this period occurred approximately three miles northwest of Stecker, Oklahoma, on the allotments of Jack Sankadota and Sam Ahboah in 1927.[52]

Although many of the activities associated with the Sun Dance, the hunt, and warfare had ceased, the society continued to maintain several prior functions. It is clear that the society at this time was sponsoring social gatherings, feasts, social recognition through honoring, and economic redistribution through giveaways. Community welfare was maintained through the efforts of the haves on behalf of the have-nots in the larger Kiowa community. The society still provided a place for its members to smoke, feast, sing, dance, recite coups, and reminisce about past individual or ancestral warrior achievements. It therefore celebrated and enhanced the past experience of warriors, while performing services and duties on behalf of the Kiowa community as a whole. Despite changes in certain ceremonial characteristics after the last Sun Dance, the general role of the Black Legs in the 1912–1927 period remained largely intact from prereservation times.

The Jáifègàu Society

The activities of the Jáifègàu Society are vaguely known from 1890 to 1912. Clyde Ellis (1990:21) writes: "The practice of the Gourd Dance [Jáifègàu Society] became culturally vital to the Kiowas in the last decade of the nineteenth century when it began to be used as a substitute for the annual Sun Dance"; Eric Lassiter (1992) makes similar remarks.[53] Again, Frizzlehead's statement that no military societies (except the Óhòmò) met during the time of the Ghost Dance (1890–1917) and accounts which suggest that the annual Ghost Dance encampment functioned more as a substitute for the Sun Dance (Kracht 1989, 1992) contradict this.[54] Like the Tòkógàut, the Jáifègàu were revived in the summer of 1912. Again an ethnohistorical approach using Kiowa calendars and oral history clarifies the picture. The Domebo calendar contains a revival entry for the Tòkógàut in the summer of 1912, and a similar entry for the Jáifègàu occurs in the Ananthy Odlepaugh calendar.[55] The summer entry for 1912 reads, "The first big dance was held at Stinking Creek," and is accompanied by a picture of a gourd dance rattle and a multitipi encampment. Parker McKenzie (born in 1897) stated that he knew of no Gourd Dances during his youth prior to the "one which was held on Tsoodle's allotment on Zóltǫ [Vomit (Stinking) Creek] in 1912, which was attended by several wagon loads of Cheyenne who came to visit." Francis Tsonetokoy, born in 1899, also confirmed the lack of Gourd Dances during this period prior to "the one at Tsoodle's place in 1912."[56] With the general revival of dancing in the early 1900s, Jáifègàu dances, like other dances, began to be held in association with the Fourth of July holiday. Dances between 1912 and 1928 were held on the allotments of Ned Brace, Eagle Heart, Jack Bointy, Henry Tsoodle, and Lone Bear around Carnegie and at Kiowa Bill Maunkee's (Máunhę̀dè or No Hand) near Hobart, but had shifted to the Kiowa community around Carnegie by circa 1920. Kiowa elders report the attendance and participation of significant contingents of Cheyenne at the dances held on the allotments of Tsoodle and Kiowa Bill.[57] The sponsoring of dance encampments by a number of men reflects the earlier practice of society members sponsoring meetings each day of the Sun Dance. With the cessation of the Sun Dance in 1890 and the taking of allotments after 1901, this practice had shifted to individual allotments.

Throughout the 1920s the Jáifègàu continued to have summer dance encampments on Lone Bear's allotment, southeast of Carnegie, Oklahoma. A photograph of a Gourd Dance held at the Lone Bear grounds on July 4, 1921, depicts sixteen men seated under a brush arbor on the west side of the arena and twenty-six women, some wearing feathered bonnets and carrying lances, standing on the north side of the arena. Five singers are seated around a drum in the middle of the arena and a large American flag hangs from atop a log flagpole. The camp consists of a variety of canvas shades and tents, horse-drawn buggies, a covered wagon, and automobiles. Witnesses of these dances report that brush dances continued to be held.[58] The Ananthy Odlepaugh calendar contains an entry for another Gourd Dance (a gourd dancer underneath a brush arbor) in the summer of 1926 held on Jack Bointy's allotment, during which a large contingent of visiting Otoe were given gifts.[59]

Dances continued to be held at the Lone Bear dance grounds in July 1928. On April 19, 1929, at approximately 8:00 P.M., a tornado struck the Carnegie area and killed Lone Bear's wife, Tòiémdè (To-em-ty or Standing Ready to Strike), injured five other members of the Lone Bear family, and destroyed over sixty houses. After the loss of his wife, Lone Bear declared that there would be no more Gourd Dancing at that location because to do so would lead to failure; after this Gourd Dancing among the Kiowa practically ceased, with only much smaller and very infrequent gatherings.[60] According to the data collected by the Santa Fe Laboratory, the Jáifègàu and the Óhò̀mò̀ were the only Kiowa societies still meeting in 1935. Although listing thirty-one members, White Fox (1870–1959) reported only twenty active members in 1935, who were all elderly men, with the oldest member being eighty-four.[61] As Tso'odl stated in 1936, "None of the old societies are going on now. There are some men who call themselves tampeigo [Jáifègàu] but they are not the real members. They are just boys."[62]

Nearly all elders report having seen Jáifègàu dances until 1928, although some report having seen smaller, occasional dances until 1938. Alice Marriott attended and documented a large dance at George Tsoodle's home near Carnegie on July 14–18, 1937. A large Otoe contingent was invited to this dance, having visited the Kiowa ten or eleven years before on Jack Bointy's allotment. Pawnee, Ponca, and Osage visitors also attended. While the encampment focused primarily on Fancy War Dancing, hand games, and other social dances, some of the older society dances were also held. As Marriott writes:

> Such members of the old soldier societies as are still living took part in the dancing and served as camp police. The few members of the Gourd Society, for instance, danced on the first day, as was their privilege during the Sun Dance. The camp caller was a member of the Horse Society, the principal host was a member of the Herders. He was assisted in his hospitality not only by his sons, but by other members of his society.[63]

Participation by members of several societies and intrasocietal support for the sponsoring member were recorded. While Brush Dances were held each afternoon, differences in the types of dances and times that they were performed by different age groups were clearly present: "The afternoon dances were primarily for the older people, few of the younger ones taking part. . . . The dances in the evening were largely for the younger people, but a few of the older men and women took part. Most of the dancers were men."[64] These later dances are reported to have been very small and were composed mostly of elderly men. As was occurring in neighboring tribes, participation in the older traditional tribal dances such as military society dances was limited primarily to middle-aged or elderly men, while younger generations were attracted to and participated in newer, more social forms of dancing. After this, Kiowa Gourd Dancing ceased until after World War II.

Rabbit Society Dances

Following the end of the Kiowa Sun Dance in 1890 Pòláhyòp meetings and dances declined along with the older men's societies. However, occasional meetings and dances continued to be held on occasions for communal dances, which tended to focus upon Independence Day and Armistice Day celebrations. Rabbit Society dances also occurred in conjunction with dances of the Tǫ́kǫ́gàut and Jáifègàu Societies (revived in 1912) and the burgeoning Óhǫ̀mò Society during the 1930s. The regularity of Rabbit dances in 1927 was unknown (Parsons 1929:111). While the frequency of Rabbit Society functions undoubtedly decreased together with the decline in men's societies and tribal-level integrative ceremonies, so did the society's importance as a unifying agent that introduced and prepared children for many of the social activities they would be exposed to as adults.[65] The emergence and growth of the Óhǫ̀mò Society and the later development of the powwow and Fancy Dancing furthered the decline of the older societies, as younger men were attracted to the newer style of dress and dance.

THE ASSAULT ON DANCING, 1890–1934

Between 1890 and 1934 there were many agency and federal efforts to end Indian religious, linguistic, and sociocultural activities, including dancing. The Kiowa Agency records contain the most thorough documentation of the events of the period. Based on these records, which provide a sound archival review, Benjamin Kracht (1989:820–875, 1992, 1994) has written a more lengthy account of this period focusing on the suppression of nearly all native cultural and religious forms and the changes encountered. Dr. Kracht graciously gave me copies of the original Kiowa Agency records from the National Anthropological Archives concerning dancing. The following section is based on these records supplemented by my own cultural and linguistic fieldwork. Although the majority of the Kiowa Agency documents focus on the Kiowa, the efforts to suppress native sociocultural and religious forms also affected the neighboring Apache and Comanche, who were under the same agency. While the Kiowa were perhaps the most active in dances during this period because of their emphasis on the Sun and Ghost Dances, all three groups danced actively and frequently. Therefore, this period is discussed most fully here and is only briefly mentioned in the Apache and Comanche chapters.

Agency efforts to suppress Kiowa religion and dancing focused primarily on (1) the Ghost Dance led by Afraid-of-Bears, (2) attempts to revive the Sun Dance by Edgar Keahbone and others in 1927–1931, (3) the Peyote religion, (4) a dance the agents refer to as the "Gift Dance" (giveaways), (5) "49" Dances, and (6) later dancing at fairs and exhibitions (Kracht 1989). I will focus only on those events affecting dancing and military societies. The Bureau of Indian Affairs began to outlaw some native ceremonies and rituals during the term of Commissioner Morgan (1889–1993), which set the standard for Indian policy until John Collier's appointment in 1934. Agency efforts against Kiowa religious and dancing groups were strongest between 1909 to 1921, culminating in 1917, during the terms of agents Ernest Stecker (January 1, 1908, to March 31, 1915) and C. V. Stinchecum (April 1, 1915, to March 31, 1922). Although most current elders I interviewed remembered these events only in generalities, all specifically cited the terms of Stecker and Stinchecum.

Indian agents were concerned that Indians frequently left their homes and farms unattended to go on lengthy visits and encampments to other communities or tribes. These visits were alleged to result in disease and loose morality. Agents continually misunderstood and condemned the practices of intertribal visiting, friendship, and giveaways. In their eyes the Indians were simply giving away their possessions as soon as they accumulated them and could never gain ground in the materialistic Anglo world. The goal of the agents was to keep Kiowa families at home and productive on their farms by preventing these activities (Kracht 1989:823–829).

Superintendent Stecker became disgruntled when a large contingent of over two thousand Kiowa, Comanche, Cheyenne, and other tribes attended a camp meeting sponsored by the Baptist Mission Association in July 1909 at Red Rock Mission (Redstone Baptist Church), where prolonged visitation and gift giving occurred. To the chagrin of the agents, many Kiowa and Comanche afterward traveled to visit the Cheyenne and Arapaho. During the next per capita payment, many Cheyenne again came to visit and dance with the Kiowa. Stecker instructed the Kiowa that they must cease such activities and delayed their payments until the Cheyenne had returned home, which caused much discontent among the Kiowa. In attempting to counter the growing visits and social activities, he subsequently requested permission from the Bureau of Indian Affairs (BIA) to withhold payments due to any Indian who visited any other reservation without his permission.[66]

BIA officials responded that Stecker should find ways to interest the Indians in their homes and to support the field matrons in their efforts to prevent communal encampments.[67] Stecker replied that the last time the Indians came to receive their annuity payment (January 1910) he reproached them for leaving their homes and threatened that their annuities would be withheld unless they increased their crop yields that year (Kracht 1989:823).

This was done to impress upon them the importance of individual effort towards their support, and to discourage visiting other reservations, and leaving their homes, stock, etc., without the proper care and attention. The only means whereby they may be compelled to remain at home and attend to their stock and farms is . . . to withhold their moneys or a portion of it until they show the proper interest in their homes.[68]

Despite being informed in February 1910 that there were no laws allowing him to withhold Kiowa annuity payments (per capita payments from the sale of surplus lands during the allotment period), Stecker continued to make frequent threats to decrease tribal visiting and gift giving.[69]

Stecker recruited Ahpeahtone (Apiatan or Áfìt̬u, Wooden Lance or Spear), a Kiowa progressive and member of the anti–Ghost Dance faction, to help end intertribal visiting and gift giving, which were an integral part of maintaining and building intertribal relations. Stecker wrote to newly appointed Indian Commissioner Cato Sells in July 1913 that Ahpeahtone had named the leaders of three factions of "Give-away dances" (Kracht 1989: 824). These leaders and their residential communities were (1) Kau-ti-ke-ah (Cáuáuthágài, Good or Handsome Crow, aka Big Joe) and San-ka-do-ta (Xógàdáudè, Medicine Plume) from Stecker; and Charley Oheltoint (Áutthǫ̣ui, High Forehead aka Charley Buffalo) from Redstone; (2) James Waldo (Qócáuitául, Lean Elk, a Carlisle graduate) and Ko-nad (Qâunᶏ, Always Frowning, aka Páuthǫ̣idé, White Bison Bull, aka White Buffalo) from Redstone; and Tane-tone (Thè̬nétón, Eagle Tail) from Hog Creek; and (3) Maun-kee (Máunqî or Máunhé̬dè, No Hand [Fingers], aka Kiowa Bill) from Hobart; Au-kaunt (Áqǫ̀udèápᶏ̣dè, Chimney Swift Tied on His Head, aka Frank Givens) from near Rainey Mountain Church southwest of Mountain View; Ah-dong-ky (Áɖǫ̣gài, Among the Timber, aka Páuthǫ̣idé, White Bison Bull or White Buffalo) from Carnegie; and Tong-ke-ah-bo (Tǫ̣càbáudài, Appeared from the Water) from near Carnegie. Stecker recommended that a *"strong* letter be written to each, all those who participate in the 'Give-away dance' or any other detrimental dance, will be punished by forfeiting their right to share in the annuity payment following such dance—and that all other funds due them shall be deposited in banks and be expended under approved authorities only."[70]

At this time permission from the agent had to be obtained before a dance could even be held, and many agency letters of this period record visits by dance leaders requesting permission to hold dances. Agents still monitored many of the larger dances, and memories of military subjugation were still fresh in many people's minds. KCA members frequently conducted Fourth of July dances under the guise of holding "picnics." Stecker reported that "a class of cheap lawyers" continued to inform the Kiowa of their rights to dance as long as no state laws were broken, frustrating agency attempts to end dancing.[71] He also singled out the Ghost Dance as a catalyst for auxiliary dances.[72] The Ghost Dance did promote a general continuity in dancing in other locales, but not at actual Ghost Dance gatherings.

Using his authoritative position, Stecker continued to intimidate the Indians by threatening to take away their annuity payments, the only source of income for many of them, especially the aged. Because the agency controlled the dispersal of five percent payments from the sales of reservation land and four percent payments from tribal pastures, the Kiowa were subjected to the dictatorial whims of their agents. Stecker received instructions from the Office of Indian Affairs to gather more data before implementing any further charges or sanctions against leaders of the "Give-away Dance" and was asked to gather further information on the Ghost Dance (Kracht 1989:825–826). However, at this time Indian dances were not prohibited,

> . . . except for the sun dance or dances under other names which partake of its characteristics. The office recognizes the strong desire of the older Indians to indulge occasionally in these dances and while it does not sanction them it has not taken any positive steps to prohibit them where they have not been indulged in more than once or twice a year. However, no dance should be permitted which materially interferes with the industrial work of the Indians.[73]

Afraid of Bears visited Stecker in June 1914 requesting permission to hold a Ghost Dance in July. Denied permission, he accused Stecker of acting against official policy and, having sought out legal counsel who advised the Kiowa of their legal rights as citizens to dance, continued preparations for the dance. Stecker asked Commissioner Sells to write to Afraid of Bears regarding official Indian Office policy against the Ghost and Gift Dances. Supporting Stecker, Ahpeahtone wrote to the commissioner denouncing the Ghost Dance and Give-Away (Kracht 1989:826).[74] Stecker in turn collected letters of support from missionaries H. H. Clouse, B. F. Gasaway, and Harry H. Treat, who purported to be familiar with the dances, and from Andrés Martínez, a Hispanic Kiowa captive.[75] While most misunderstood the reasons behind the dances, gift giving, and intertribal visiting, both agents and missionaries denounced the Ghost Dance and give-away because of governmental and religious interests. In support of the termination of these activities the Ghost Dance was described as (1) a rudimentary religious development ("a crude form of Spiritualism"); (2) revering the "Indian medicine man or woman"; (3) "recounting old war times and telling ghost stories"; and being a place of (4) disease, (5) loose morals, (6) sexual liaisons (a tradition of past Sun Dances, which missionaries claimed did not occur at church camp meetings); (7) a bad influence for Indian youths returning from off-reservation boarding schools; and (8) a gathering of generally filthy, immoral, backward Indians, as opposed to communities of legally married Christian Indians living in clean homes.[76] Thus, allegorical comparisons were made between those Indians viewed as progressive and those who were viewed as pagan or indolent for maintaining older customs (Kracht 1989: 830). This dichotomy would subsequently be used to attack other ceremonies and dances which the agency found unacceptable.

These events prompted Sells to write one letter to Afraid of Bears denouncing the Ghost Dance and asking for his assistance in ending the dance, which Stecker read to him, and another to Stecker himself supporting the superintendent's opposition to the dance: "you are therefore requested to continue your refusal of permission for the dance and discourage in every reasonable way indulgence therein at points outside your jurisdiction."[77] Several months later Assistant Commissioner E. B. Meritt sent Stecker the following proclamation: "The Office desires that the Indians shall not be permitted under any circumstances . . . to indulge in dances in connection with which it is the custom to give valuable presents. You should give this matter your close attention with a view to seeing that your instructions are complied with."[78]

Resistance to the agency had grown to include even some of the "progressives" formerly allied with the agency. Meritt stated that Ahpeahtone reported that none of the KCA Business Committee members except D. K. Lonewolf and Otto Wells would "assist him in keeping the Indians from indulging in the Gift Dance and other harmful practices" and recommended calling for an election of a new committee if Ahpeahtone received no further cooperation.[79] Prior to leaving as superintendent in March 1915, Stecker informed Sells of two Kiowa political factions: (1) Ahpeahtone (of Carnegie) and the anti–Ghost Dance faction, which was described as the "more law-abiding element in the tribe," and (2) Kiowa Bill (a KCA Business Committee member from Hobart) and Jim Waldo (of Redstone) and the "dance crowd," which was portrayed as "that class who seize upon every effort made toward their uplift" (Kracht 1989:831–832). Aware of Kiowa Bill's political aspirations to usurp Ahpeahtone as recognized tribal chief and that his efforts outside business meetings to gather political support for his aspirations created problems for the progressives, Stecker recommended that the honorary position of head chief not be retained after Ahpeahtone (Kracht 1989:832–833).[80]

C. V. Stinchecum, Stecker's replacement, took office on April 1, 1915, and inherited the task of stopping the Ghost Dance. Approximately five hundred Indians planned a week-long Fourth of July Ghost Dance armed with a letter from lawyer J. S. Rinefort to Red Buffalo, advising them to proceed despite Stinchecum's prohibitions. Stinchecum immediately inquired as to whether he was authorized to withhold annuity payments from some twenty-five dance leaders.[81] After several days with no reply, he wrote to the Indian Office on July 1, reminding the BIA that Stecker had not terminated the Ghost Dance, that the Kiowa held it in 1914 against Stecker's orders, and that he was powerless to prevent the upcoming dance (Kracht 1989:833–834).[82]

As the Kiowa prepared for their dance, the commissioner's office proposed action. Assistant Commissioner E. B. Meritt wrote to Assistant Secretary Bo Sweeney about Stinchecum's telegraph and the situation at the Kiowa Agency.[83] Meritt supported Stinchecum's idea of withholding payments of four and five percent funds from dance participants. According to Meritt, the five percent fund was a mandatory annual payment, whereas the four percent fund was paid at the discretion of the secretary of the interior. Thus, Meritt believed that the four percent fund could be frozen to force the Ghost Dance to stop (Kracht 1989:834).[84] The day after Meritt's letter, the Department of the Interior sent a memorandum stating that the monies were not really annuities, but were distributed by the secretary for the maintenance of Indian homes; thus, this anonymous document supported Stinchecum's desire to withhold these funds: "The Indian Office goes upon the theory that the authority to prescribe regulations supports the proposed action. We are justified in going a long ways and probably stretching our authority if thereby we may put a stop to celebrations of this sort."[85]

An undated telegraph message from the Department of the Interior to Stinchecum granted him permission to withhold shares of the four and five percent funds from all who participated in the Ghost Dance, but was never sent to the Kiowa Agency (Kracht 1989:835).[86] After reporting on the subsequent gathering and receiving no reply, Stinchecum "took matters into his own hands" when he threatened visiting Ghost Dance leaders with withholding their four percent annuities if they held their dance (Kracht 1989:835). Already encamped, the Kiowa compromised by holding a two day picnic on July 4 and 5, with no dancing, and broke camp on July 6, 1915.[87]

Although stating that he meant no irreverence toward the dance and religion, Stinchecum proudly boasted of his success to Sells. It becomes obvious that Stinchecum "opposed all types of Indian dances" (Kracht 1989: 836): "I have no objection whatever to the Indians getting together and holding a picnic in a decent manner. I do not even wish to discountenance the proper kind of social dances, but similar dances of such nature as the ghost dance and give away dance must, if possible, be relegated to the dim past."[88] To Stinchecum "proper dances were not Indian dances" (Kracht 1989:836), as giveaways formed a part of all social, war, and society dances. Continuing to use one of the Kiowa's biggest foes, misinformation, Stinchecum used secondhand information to describe, evaluate, and ridicule some of the alleged activities involved in Ghost Dances (Kracht 1989:837).[89] The Indian Office informed him that the legality of withholding annuities for any possible future Ghost Dances would be investigated.[90] Ahpeahtone wrote to Stinchecum in August 1915 expressing his allegiance, describing the two Kiowa factions, and fully supporting Stinchecum's plan to freeze the annuity funds of "the Indians who stand for the dances and the Payote [peyote] worship."[91] Meritt responded by thanking Ahpeahtone for his support and "efforts to dissuade Kiowas from dancing" (Kracht 1989:838).[92] In opposition to false reports that were circulating, Afraid of Bears wrote to Meritt to explain the Ghost Dance religion and its harmless nature, noting the incorporation of various Christian elements into the ceremony, which was accompanied by a supportive letter from I-see-o (Áisêàuidè, Many Camp Smokes [Fires]).[93]

Swayed by the missionaries' reports, Meritt was unsympathetic to the Kiowa's cause; he stated that "the [Indian] Office feels that it understands better than some of these old people what is best for the Indian as a whole" and proclaimed: "The Ghost Dance, as practiced by the Kiowas, has been the subject of much correspondence and investigation and the facts thus gathered are such as to convince the [Indian] Office that it ought to be discontinued" (Kracht 1989:839).[94] Ghost Dance advocates, including Big Tree, campaigned throughout the winter and spring of 1915–1916 to explain the religious nature of the dance, that all prayed to the same God, and that no alcohol was involved as had been alleged, citing exemplary records of children in schools and adults in neighboring communities, but to no avail. Meritt finally responded, stating that the "old dances are inconsistent with the civilization and industrial and moral development of the Indians." The BIA would no longer condone such activities (Kracht 1989:841).[95]

In April 1916 Stinchecum sought permission from Commissioner Sells "to withhold the four percent annuity payments from those involved in any dancing that summer" (Kracht 1989:841).[96] Sells replied:

You are hereby directed to use every practical means to prevent a repetition of it this or any subsequent year, and as a means of enforcing this order you are hereby further directed to withhold, until further advised, the share in the annual appropriation of $250,000 of Kiowa, Comanche, and Apache 4% funds of any Indian who shall participate in said dance at or near your reservation. . . . The ghost dance is vicious, and extreme measures to put an end to it are justifiable.[97]

In light of these changes, members of the dance faction sought to hold other dances throughout the summer. James Ahtone wrote to Meritt for permission to hold dances on his allotment near Stecker; Meritt responded that the decision was up to Stinchecum, as the Indian Office did not condone dances and customs "regarded as detrimental to the progress and civilization of the Indian" (Kracht 1989:841–842).[98] Upon receiving Meritt's reply, Ahtone wrote to Commissioner Sells, requesting permission to hold a picnic, stating that no Ghost Dance, gambling, or consumption of alcohol would take place and asking if there was any law against holding picnics.[99] Meritt admonished Ahtone for attempting to overstep the superintendent's authority and said that he must obtain permission from Stinchecum. Thus, Stinchecum was given absolute authority over all Indian gatherings and authorized none during the summer of 1916.[100] However, dances did continue on remote allotments; Stinchecum was beside himself in July as he reported that a "large number of Cheyenne and Arapaho" visited and participated in Gift Dances with the Kiowa (Kracht 1989:843).[101] Elders indicate that several dances were held during this period.

Dancing "within the KCA jurisdiction prompted the Indian Office to enforce its policy forbidding the Ghost Dance and Gift Dance," and Meritt instructed Stinchecum to punish all offenders by withholding their four percent payments (Kracht 1989:843).[102] Tennyson Berry, an Apache member of the KCA Business Committee, wired Congressman Scott Ferris to report Stinchecum's plan to withhold their monies for dancing that summer, which prompted an investigation lasting several months.[103] Although an upcoming Apache dance was canceled in August 1916 when the sponsor heard of the threat to withhold annuity payments, the Kiowa held their dance. A list of ninety individuals, mostly men, was compiled from reports by district farmers, and their annuities were withheld.[104] Stecker also frequently used Jasper Saunkeah, a Kiowa and United States marshal, to blacklist individuals and leaders participating in dances.[105]

Berry, who was reported attending the dance as a spectator, was informed by Meritt that the listed members would receive their annuity shares after reassuring the superintendent that they would not engage in any more Ghost or Gift Dances, even if these dances were "called by another name."[106] By December 1916 Stinchecum had decided that if the ninety individuals signed an affidavit "that they will not in the future attend or participate in either the Gift or Ghost dance, the shares of such Indians shall then be paid to them" (Kracht 1989:844).[107] Although approving of Stinchecum's intimidating tactics, the Indian Office requested further information on the listed individuals and when they signed the affidavits (Kracht 1989:844).[108]

In January 1917 a list of 109 individuals (mostly Kiowa, with a few Apache and Comanche) was compiled and their monies were withheld. This list contained many well-known Kiowa who were prominent military society members, including White Horse, Charley Buffalo, Silverhorn, White Buffalo, Henry Poolaw, George Mopope, Pauquodle (Red Buffalo), and Walter Kokoom of the Óhòmò Society; Big Joe (Kau-te-ke-ah), Little Joe (Hah-to-go), Bert Geikaunmah, Guy Quoetone, Conklin Hummingbird, Charlie Domebo, and Kiowa Jim Tongkeamha of the Tòkògàut Society; Frank Givens, Lynn Brace, and Kiowa Bill of the Jáifègàu Society; and Max Frizzlehead and Hummingbird.[109] By May 1917 sixty-five of the blacklisted dancers had consented and signed the affidavit; however, a review of this list shows that many of the older pro-dance military society members refused. In July Stinchecum resubmitted a revised list of seventy-nine dance offenders, of whom only forty-four had signed.[110]

Kiowa elders and Óhòmò Society members indicate that society members were steadfastly resisting such coercive agency attempts to impede their cultural freedom. The lyrics of one Óhòmò Society song composed during this time imperatively demonstrate the society's attitude regarding these attempts to suppress dancing:

1. Fòi bé aú-gá-kàu-jàu
   (Do not/you all/be hesitating [imperative])
   Do not hesitate (to dance)!

2. Dá bà tó-pá-bà-hò
   (You must/you all/legs-tied-go-ahead [imperative])
   Go ahead and be arrested/jailed![111]

The result of these share withholding policies was that, despite having their civil rights abused, KCA members persevered and continued dancing in more remote locales or in neighboring Indian communities where there was less pressure. Francis Tsonetokoy, who was blacklisted by the agency for attending, but not participating in, dances, and Parker McKenzie, who retired as head of the finance department at the Anadarko agency, stated that many of the Kiowa who signed affidavits simply collected their money and, getting the best of the agents, headed in "high spirits" for dances in "Cheyenne country, where the heat was off at the time."[112] While the Ghost Dance ended in 1917, occasional gatherings continued until the end of World War I and Ghost Dance songs are still occasionally sung today. Although many individuals separately belonged to the Óhòmò Society and participated in the Ghost Dance, both groups were associated with the "dance crowd." The Óhòmò Society absorbed much of the traditional "Ghost Dance crowd" after it ended in 1917 and continued to grow and prosper.

Several Tòkógàut, Jáifègàu, and Óhòmò Society members appear on the agency blacklists. However, whether they were blacklisted due to participation in specific society events, general powwows, or other group activities is unknown. Yet despite specific references to blacklisting of individual military society activities during this period, these groups continued to meet and agents assuredly knew of their activities. It is thus very likely that some of the agents' frustrations were derived from society dances.

One concerted effort of the agents during this period concerned abolishing native practices of giving-away and what was labeled the Gift Dance. Although the Óhòmò Society had a "Gift" song and dance (Qíkódàugà, Give-Away Song) and Kracht (1989) suggests that the "Gift Dance" was a strictly Óhòmò Society practice, Kiowa elders indicate that giveaways occurred at all society, Scalp, and social dances of this period. The elders indicate that the agency was concerned with any dance that contained giving-away, period.[113] For the agent's purposes this would have covered all Kiowa social and religious activities, which all contained various elements of property redistribution through sacrificial donations of food and goods to tribal religious bundles and giveaways at dances.

World War I

Involvement in World War I gave the Kiowa new veterans to honor (fourteen veterans; with six overseas and eight stateside, three of whom saw active combat) and opportunities to celebrate their bravery and military service. Gilbert Kauley was wounded and highly decorated. New veterans necessitated traditional forms of honoring and were accordingly honored at dances held in several Kiowa communities (Anadarko, Mount Scott, Red Stone, Carnegie) in the summer of 1919.[114]

Charley Apekaum, a stateside World War I Navy veteran, stated that many Scalp Dances were held after Kiowa soldiers returned home safely. Apekaum had several songs dedicated to him at a Scalp Dance near Meers, Oklahoma, and was asked to name several children based on his experiences.

Continuing the past tradition of warriors naming individuals on the basis of their war experiences, some of the names he gave included Watching Out for the Enemy (Qóǫ́gài, Sitting Scouting aka Scott Tonemah) and Crossing the Ocean (Dàumáuntǫ̀cáutjàudè). In the past a warrior had to swear to the truth of his war deeds and frequently called upon witnesses to verify his claims. War-based names were traditionally thought to help children grow up to be healthy.[115] New songs were composed by community members while their relatives were overseas and about their war experiences after they returned. The Kiowa Flag Song was also composed at this time in honor of the war dead and returning veterans.[116]

Although the veterans' return fostered a brief series of celebratory dances including Scalp and Victory Dances, there is no indication that any direct association with the older men's societies continued beyond this short-lived period. Participation in World War I was significant in that it preserved older forms of dances and songs. More importantly, veterans were honored according to traditional cultural forms during what would be a lengthy period with limited opportunities for military service between 1875 and 1941. Although Superintendent Stinchecum's antidancing campaign had eradicated the Ghost Dance by the end of World War I, he was never able to abolish the "Gift Dance" and other forms of War Dancing. War Dancing and newer forms of social dances were rapidly becoming the primary dance and social events in community gatherings, especially for younger generations. Despite a temporary reprieve in World War I, the Kiowa were still struggling through a lengthy period of cultural suppression and declining military opportunity.

War Dancing continued with a plethora of dancing following World War I. The impact of the war and the traditional protocol necessitating the honoring of returning veterans was simply too much for even the agency to suppress. Even progressives such as Ahpeahtone, who had supported agents Stecker and Stinchecum in their antidance and giveaway campaign, who had denounced Kiowa pro-dance leaders, and who wrote in opposition to dancing, apparently acquiesced; Ahpeahtone sponsored a large homecoming celebration on his allotment west of Carnegie for his son, veteran Lon Ahpeahtone, in 1919. Parker McKenzie, who attended the celebration, reported several days of Scalp, Victory, and War Dances.[117] In 1919 Warren K. Moorehead, a member of the Board of Indian Commissioners, visited the KCA jurisdiction and informed the Indians that Stinchecum could no longer legally withhold money from individuals participating in dancing. Frustrated, Stinchecum complained to the new Indian commissioner, Charles H. Burke:

During the season following his [Moorehead's] visit here the Indians' dances probably quadrupled in number. . . . After more than four years hard work my entire influence was destroyed by what I consider the ill-advised statements of Mr. Moorehead. . . . It is almost impossible to prevent every dance, because the Indians are more and more realizing that they are citizens and that they have the right to do things which are not in violation of the State and Federal laws. . . . The chief difficulty is that the worst offenders usually are those Indians who have received the patents in fee. They realize that we have no hold upon them whatever, and flagrantly violate the known wishes of this and your Office.[118]

In reference to Circular 1665, which Commissioner Burke distributed soon after taking office in 1921, this letter allowed superintendents to suppress Indian dances that they deemed immoral and against the best interests of the Indian communities. Supported by the Indian Rights Association and the Board of Indian Commissioners, Burke proposed a House bill in 1926 that would empower the Courts of Indian Offenses to levy fines and jail sentences on anyone in violation of Circular 1665. The Leavitt Bill did not pass, however, largely due to the efforts of John Collier, a journalist and pro-Indian reformer who was rapidly rising in influence and would later serve as commissioner of Indian Affairs (Olson and Wilson 1984:97; Prucha 1984: 2:803–805; Kracht 1989). However, as the KCA Indians had been subjected to strong antidancing policies since 1915, this did little to change their circumstances. Prior to July 4, 1921, Stinchecum met with local leaders who were planning dances and read Burke's circular, which allowed them to hold war dances, but no "gift" or "Forty-niner's" dances.[119] To some degree, Stinchecum had acquiesced.

The "49," as it had come to be known, was an evolved version of the old War Journey or Gúdáugá Songs (Stirring Up [to Emotions]) sung by men and women as social songs the night before a war party left. By the 1920s, when Indian fairs (previously outlawed under Stinchecum's tenure) were increasing, the 49 Dance, an all-night event featuring socializing, dancing, and drinking, had become popular throughout western Oklahoma (Young 1981: 239, 279; McBeth 1983:140). Morris Doyeto, a Christian Kiowa who wrote in opposition to 49 Dances and attributed many loose morals to the events, stated that the dance began in 1917 or 1918 at the Comanche County Fair held in Lawton and was taught to the Cheyenne in 1919 (Kracht 1989: 489).[120] Attached to his letter was a list of Indian gatherings which included 49 Dances: the Arapaho Sun Dance at Watonga; a Kiowa dance gathering seven or eight miles west of Anadarko (probably in conjunction with

Óhòmò Society Dances of the Redstone Community); the Comanche Rabbit Dance; and county fairs, especially the Caddo County Fair in Anadarko. The 49 Dance was soon added to Circular 1665 as a prohibited dance.[121]

In mid-1921 Stinchecum cited nine individuals for "the reckless giving away of property" at a dance held near Washita, probably at Konad's (aka White Buffalo). Stinchecum suggested withholding their four percent annuity payments until they signed an affidavit and asked Commissioner Burke to admonish each individual by letter. Although he assured Burke that "the withholding of funds will not be carried to such an extent as to actually cause suffering," he was in no objective position to make this determination.[122] Burke approved the action and sent two letters to the individuals involved stating that they would not escape the penalty of Stinchecum's administrative decisions. Nevertheless, by November only three of the nine men involved had come to the agency (Kracht 1989:850–851).[123]

The Kiowa persevered in their endeavor to keep dancing and giveaways alive even though they lost much of their income with the agency freezing their four percent funds for seven years. County fairs and exhibitions run by local Anglo entrepreneurs profiting from tourism encouraged Indian "contest" dancing and became the medium through which War Dancing survived (Young 1981:279–284). Stinchecum could not prevent Indians from camping and dancing at the Comanche and Caddo County fairs. In 1923, Frank Rush sponsored an Indian fair at Medicine Park which continued throughout the 1920s and featured a performance of a Ghost Dance for spectators in 1929 (Young 1981:281–282).

A Kiowa ledger book entry for 1922 depicts the performance of several military society dances held at Craterville. This entry contains pictures of a man with his lower legs painted black (Tòkógàut Society), a rattle made from a metal can with black and white eagle feathers attached (Jáifègàu Society), a man wearing a crow belt dancing (Óhòmò Society), and depictions of women dancing. Despite agency efforts to end dancing, all three of the active Kiowa men's societies participated at this event. Ironically referring to Agent Stinchecum, the entry states, "At Dietrich's Lake. Every tribe dances, Kiowas, Comanches, Cheyennes, etc. Stinchecum Agent." Accounts from elders participating in these dances suggest that all active Kiowa, Apache, Comanche, Cheyenne, and Arapaho military societies performed at Dietrich's Lake in 1922.[124] The all-Indian Craterville Fair, sixteen miles west of Lawton, was held from 1924 to 1932. In 1933 the Frank Rush fairs were replaced with what became known as the American Indian Exposition, which continues to the present during the third week of August (Wright 1946:159–161).

Despite continued agency efforts, War Dances, 49 Dances; and give-aways continued throughout the 1920s. Similar attempts to suppress Peyote ceremonies and the later Native American Church were also undertaken by Indian agents between 1886 and 1941 (Kracht 1989:58–75). Many individuals blacklisted for dancing are listed in my military society membership records and were also some of the strongest Peyotists and later Native American Church members (see also Kracht 1989:869). Attempts to stop dances which were called "picnics" were reinvigorated in May 1931, but ended soon after John Collier took office as commissioner of Indian Affairs in 1934. The passage of the Indian Reorganization Act reversed the previous cultural genocide by permitting and encouraging traditional cultural, religious, and linguistic practices.[125]

Neither the Sun Dance (despite attempts by Edgar Keahbone and others to revive it between 1927 and 1930) nor the Ghost Dance survived (Kracht 1989:778–819, 854–856). By 1935 only the Óhòmò and the Jáifègàu Societies remained active (the former having never formally ceased to function, and the latter maintaining twenty to thirty elder members). After 1927 for the Tòkógàut and 1937 and 1946 for the Jáifègàu, the older men's societies ceased to actively function until the revival of the Kiowa Gourd Clan in 1957 and the Black Legs in 1958. Only the Óhòmò Society and increasing summer and holiday intertribal powwows with War Dancing and social dancing remained as the primary forms of Kiowa dancing up to World War II.[126]

After the Kiowa were confined to a reservation, the role of military societies in providing large-scale tribal integration and a collective sense of community centering upon the celebration and demonstration of shared martial themes and ritual symbols decreased but by no means ceased. Although these opportunities were temporarily dormant or "inactive" on a large public scale (Goldstein 1972), they continued in more "active" family and local community contexts (oral history, song, and material culture), preserving ritual knowledge in a manner sufficient to permit later revival. Despite this inactivity, the Kiowa never forgot their history as a warrior society or the traditional views and practices associated with the Kiowa veteran ideology and ethos.

WORLD WAR II AND AFTER

More than three hundred Kiowa men and women served in the United States forces during World War II. Kiowa participation in this war and in the Korean conflict produced a large segment of the population who were now veterans and were once again regarded as warriors by the tribal elders. Veteran the Reverend David Paddlety described the Kiowa elders' views of returning World War II veterans: "They held them in high esteem, just as they did way back then. Whether or not you faced actual battle or warfare, they still put you in the same place as those that faced enemy fire, that you were doing them a service by protecting them, so they said."[127] Having regained status as warriors by the traditional Kiowa means, through warfare, veterans needed to be honored and recognized in traditional ways in public contexts. Coinciding with this, increased economic opportunities fostered by the war improved the general economic standard for many Indian communities.

Kiowa Women's Societies

In the nineteenth century the Kiowa had two women's societies closely related to warfare and war power: the Xálìchǫ̀hòp (Calf Old Women) or Xálìchǫ̀hì̀ (Calf Old Woman) and the Ằunhádèmàimàu or Sétchǫ̀hyòp (Bear Women). Both societies were said to have been founded by men who dreamed of them while seeking power, but they had ceased after 1905, largely because of lack of warfare opportunities.[128] The large-scale participation of Kiowa servicemen in World War II led to the formation of three Kiowa women's organizations: the Kiowa War Mothers, the Carnegie Victory Club, and the Purple Heart Club. These organizations reinvigorated traditional Kiowa women's martial roles in recognizing and honoring warriors.[129]

These Kiowa women's organizations are attributable to two primary factors: (1) their origins in prereservation women's societies which were integrally linked to the assurance of success in warfare and the honoring of returning warriors; and (2) the revival of opportunities for Kiowa men to participate in warfare through military service and thus the cultural necessity to honor these veterans according to tribal tradition. Although the Kiowa women's societies were formally revived during World War II and functioned prior to the men's societies in 1957 and 1958, it was their prereservation origins and auxiliary functions which led to their revival and integral role in contemporary veterans' affairs and society dances. Since their revival, these organizations have largely been based around particular Kiowa communities. The Purple Heart Club has centered around Stecker, the Victory Club around Carnegie and Mountain View, and the Kiowa War

Mothers around Carnegie. The Kiowa Veterans Auxiliary (associated with the Kiowa Black Legs Society or the Kiowa Veterans Association after 1958) is more pan-Kiowa based.[130]

Continuing traditional women's martial roles, all of the women's organizations generally hold the same traditional women's dances for servicemen, including women's Scalp and Victory (Áuldáucúngà), Round (Aúqóbêcùngà), Shuffle (Tǫ́sódêcùngà), and, since World War II, War Mothers' Songs (Câijàuchàudàugà, literally Fight or War Mothers' Songs) and dances (Câijàuchàucùngà), which were traditionally performed for successful returning war parties. While some songs and dances are used by all women's groups, each organization has its own genre of society or "club" songs and regular singers. There is a tendency for men who have been honored at one of these organizations to attend the dances of that club, as this organization usually includes the majority of his female relatives. Clubs in which a member has a relative in service normally put on a celebration for that serviceperson and are thus often community based. Other families which do not have female members belonging to any of the women's service organizations frequently solicit a club to sponsor a dance in honor of their relative. The women's organizations frequently co-host or co-sponsor each other's events, and often there are kin connections between the various organizations. Although the level of activity of the women's societies fluctuates in accordance with the prevalence of military service and participation of community and tribal members, the functions and dances sponsored by the Kiowa women's service organizations have continued since World War II through Operation Desert Storm.[131]

As revivals of earlier cultural forms, these organizations have combined elements and functions of traditional prereservation women's roles in supporting men's martial activities with forms of organization, procedure, and regalia from both Kiowa and Anglo women's service organizations. The continuity of these organizations is culturally significant because they serve as the primary enculturative arena that belongs to and focuses upon women and continues to enculturate younger generations in traditional Kiowa women's roles. Direct participation in these activities, as an integral part of most Kiowa community celebrations, assures the survival of traditional dances, martial ideology, and the use of the Kiowa language in songs. Participation further serves as a traditional form of maintaining and enhancing women's roles. It also preserves a distinctly Kiowa ethnicity, as reflected through differences from other tribal and intertribal women's veterans' auxiliaries, but more importantly through songs which explicitly describe and address the experiences of Kiowa veterans and the Kiowa community. While these organizations continue earlier women's traditions, they also function as integrative sociocultural forms which adapt to meet contemporary needs.

A large genre of War Mothers' Songs (Câijàuchàudàugà) were composed during World War II. During my fieldwork I collected recordings and translations of over fifty War Mothers' Songs, and many others exist. Many of the original War Mothers' Songs were composed by Louis Toyebo, a remarkably gifted composer. As Bill Koomsa described, these songs reflect the continuity of traditional veteran ideologies to contemporary military service: "There's a lot of songs you know that have words in them, the words have good meanings, good meanings. A lot of them are used during the veterans' dances and they have good words in them about boys that have served in the service. They have words pertaining to the deeds that they did and coming back home and stuff like that."[132]

Examination of translations of War Mothers' Song texts reveals several constant themes: the high esteem in which young Kiowa men are regarded as warriors, their willingness to travel far away, the prominence of the United States flag throughout the world, the joyous feeling of the Kiowa community meeting their young men returning from the war, and the courageous deeds, fearlessness, and bravery displayed by Kiowa warriors in battle. The following War Mothers' Song texts demonstrate these themes and the continued emphasis the Kiowa place on honoring their veterans.

Song 1

1. Cáui-jò-gù-dàu è jái-dàum, è qá-jái-dàu
(Kiowa–young men/they/brave/they [are] heroes)
Young Kiowa men they are brave, they are heroes.

2. Cáui-jò-gù-dàu è jái-dàum, è qá-jái-dàu

3. Cáui-jò-gù-dàu è jái-dàum, è qá-jái-dàu, è qá-jái-dàu, è qá-jái-dàu

4. Táup-càu è dàum-tó-yà-dò
(Far away/they/land/travel/because or was)
That's why they have traveled/been far away.[133]

Song 2

1. Áu-gáu-dàum-gà ǫ́-dé-jó-gúl bá àui-qàu-jè
(Our own-land/joyous, good or nice-young man/we/again-met)
In our own land, we met a joyous young man again.

2. Háun-dé-ǫ́-dé !
   (It is–nice or good)
   It is good/nice.

Song 3

Many prereservation Kiowa songs were composed about war-related experiences. This practice was significantly revived with Kiowa participation in
World War II. The following song composed by Louis Toyebo is the Kiowa
D-Day Invasion song. The text describes the mass movement of troops and
their acquisition of the Normandy beachhead on June 6, 1944, followed by
the offensive advance of the Allied forces against the attacking German
defenses.

1. Cáui-jò-gù-dàu è jái-dàum-hèl è jái-dàum-hèl è tǎu-jé-bàu-dà
   (Young Kiowa men/they/brave-reportedly/they/brave-reportedly/
   they/news-appeared).
   Young Kiowa men, they are reportedly brave, they are reportedly
   brave, news about/of them appears.

2. Hé-gàu gà ái-qǎu-jě-jó-àum-dè-hèl-nàu
   (And then/it is/smoky-together-into the midst/and)
   And then, they reportedly came together, (established a base) in the
   midst of the smoke and

3. Cǐ-dè ét kóp-fé-hâ-fè-hèl-nàu
   (Toward something moving toward you/they/in a run-charged-
   reportedly/and)
   They reportedly charged at the approaching, charging enemy, and

4. Hàun ét í-dàu-hèl-nàu
   (Not or without/they/afraid-reportedly-and)
   They were reportedly unafraid (without hesitation) and

5. Gà sǎu-mí
   (It is/noteworthy, interesting, etc.)
   It is noteworthy.[134]

The Response of the Kiowa Community

Kiowa involvement in World War II immediately reinvigorated the Kiowa
martial ethos as it had in prereservation times and during World War I.

With more than three hundred Kiowa servicemen and women, this was now on such a large level that it affected nearly every family in the tribe. In addition, the large number of Kiowa involved in the stateside wartime economy further focused community participation in the war effort. Daily reports from newspapers, radio, letters, and incoming veterans drew tribal attention to the war. Nearly every serviceman had some form of "send-off" or farewell celebration, including dances, feasts, and prayers, sponsored by the family and one of the women's organizations.[135] The prereservation use of dáudáu (supernatural power) in warfare was continued, although qualitatively different, in Native American Church and Christian church prayer meetings held for veterans preparing to go overseas. Many men went through "send-off" NAC meetings and were given protective medicine in the form of small peyote buttons in decorated buckskin bags to carry with them for protection and strength overseas. Several veterans I interviewed carried and used such medicine in combat.[136] With the focus of the Kiowa community centered upon the war, the Kiowa ethos during World War II was clearly martially oriented.

The surrender of the Japanese in August 1945 signaled the end of the war and produced an instantaneous and tumultuous series of celebrations throughout Indian communities. For many KCA peoples, the announcement of Japan's surrender came during the 1945 American Indian Exposition in Anadarko, Oklahoma. As the Reverend David Paddlety recalled:

> When the Japanese capitulated, I mean you never saw such a celebration in your life. . . . There was a great celebration through the community and all of the state, as far as the Indians were concerned I mean, along with everybody else I guess that had people in the war. But here, whenever that happened, they announced that to the audience and it was bedlam. People began to sing and dance, and lulu, and holler of victory, victory yells, and they sang victory songs, they also sang war party songs. It was literally bedlam at that time. Of course, the rest of the day and the rest of the week it was nothing but celebrations and giveaways, and prayers of thanksgiving, and I guess everything that happened to the nation . . . here [at the exposition] happened to us. Twenty-three tribes and thousands of Indians celebrated into the night.[137]

The return of World War II veterans fostered an enormous series of homecoming dances and celebrations sponsored by family and women's societies lasting into 1946. Most returning veterans received some form of welcoming, often in the form of a feast and dance, including Scalp and Victory Dances. Many individuals had personal veterans' songs composed for them and were now viewed by the elders as warriors. During the war the only active Kiowa society, the Óhǫ̀mò, continued to foster martial-related ideology through songs, dances, and honorings of returning veterans, as evidenced by numerous accounts of family-sponsored Óhǫ̀mò dances held for returning veterans who were Óhǫ̀mò Society members. The society Bustle Keeper, Charley Whitehorse, kept a patriotic banner containing a star for every society member in service. During my fieldwork I collected several personal Óhǫ̀mò Society songs composed by elder relatives of society members upon their return from military service. A large percentage of these songs refer to the veterans' bravery, to thankfulness for their return, and to "feeling good" upon hearing the songs or other references to the society— all prereservation martial themes found in traditional Kiowa military society songs.[138]

The following two songs composed for veterans' returns from World War II demonstrate these themes. The first song was composed by Jeanette Berry Mopope for her nephew Gus Palmer Sr. and was presented during his homecoming celebration.

1. Mái-fâu-qì jó-cà dáu áui-chàn
   (The enemy bounces as they are hit/home/we-he for us/again-came)
   Mái-fâu-qì came home (back) for us again.

2. Nàu è ǫ́-dáu, nàu è ǫ́-tá̧, nàu è ǫ́-dáu
   (And/we/felt elated or very happy; and/we/good-felt; and/we/were-felt elated or very happy)
   And we were elated, and we felt good, and we were elated.[139]

The following song was composed by Martha Doyeto to honor the return of her younger brother Roland Whitehorse from the war.

1. Háun-èm-í-dâu-qì á qá-jái-dàu
   (Not-he-danger-male/he/chief-state of)
   Unafraid of Danger, he is a chief.

2. Háun-èm-í-dâu-qì á qá-jái-dàu

3. Háun-èm-í-dâu-qì á qá-jái-dàu

4. Háun-èm-í-dâu-qì á qá-jái-dàu

1. Tén-á-zél-bé-dò á qá-jái-dàu
   (Heart-he-strong-because [he is]/he/chief-state of)
   Because he is strong-hearted, he is a chief.

2. Háun-èm-í-dâu-qî á qá-jái-dàu.
   Unafraid of Danger, he is a chief.[140]

Traditional forms of honoring veterans were also employed by the then in-active Jáifègàu Society, which held a Gourd Dance on White Fox's allot-ment, west of Carnegie, Oklahoma, in 1946. The Kiowa women's societies sponsored a general tribal celebration in the summer of 1946 for all World War II veterans in the Carnegie, Oklahoma, city park.

Upon returning, some Kiowa joined local Anglo veterans' associations such as the American Legion and VFW (Veterans of Foreign Wars). In the late 1950s Jerrold Levy (n.d.b) discovered that many Kiowa veterans found Anglo veterans' associations unsatisfactory, and many members of these vet-erans' groups I interviewed voiced similar mixed feelings. Several veterans stated that while Anglo veterans' associations undertake many beneficial projects and are more assertive in pushing veterans' issues, the social atmo-sphere of these associations was lacking for Native American servicemen. One Kiowa veteran of World War II and Korea expressed his views con-cerning American Legion and VFW posts: "The only way they can have fun is in drinking [alcohol] and partying" and they "drink alcohol at all func-tions." The sanctioned use of alcohol was a main difference cited between Anglo and Indian organizations that discouraged Kiowa membership and participation.[141]

Some members perceived discrimination in legion or post activities and, even when they were included, were treated as minorities. As one member described, "You kind of feel out of place, like you don't belong there. It's run on a social level, Anglos' way."[142] Several Kiowa VFW and American Legion members indicated that some participated more for access to a dinner club than for the social integration afforded by a veterans' sodality. Thus, the social opportunities, integrative functions, and social and martial recogni-tion provided by Anglo veterans' associations were largely lacking for re-cently returned Kiowa veterans. Having recently regained warrior status within their own tribe, Kiowa veterans were largely without a traditional means to display and integrate their shared veteran status following the ces-sation of homecoming celebrations.[143]

The Korean War

The response of the Kiowa community to the Korean War reinforced the recently revived traditions of "send-offs" and "homecomings" and empha-sized the ongoing lack of traditional veterans' associations. These revivals in turn led to the formal revival of Kiowa military societies: the Kiowa Gourd

Clan in 1957 and the Kiowa Black Legs Society in 1958. Prior to World War II the majority of Jáifègàu Society membership was focused around the Carnegie community, while that of the Tòkógàut was focused around Redstone and Stecker. Because the Gourd Clan revival included more of the western Kiowa communities, the more eastern Kiowa communities may have been induced to revive the Black Legs. Thus, each society was revived by the particular community which was most familiar with and active in maintaining its traditions.

Adding to the economic decline following the end of much of the urban migration and wartime industry and the lack of traditional cultural forms for returning veterans, governmental policies also influenced postwar tribal sociocultural and political movements. Southern Plains military society revivals and factions developed at a time when there was a considerable amount of uncertainty about the continuation of the KCA government as a result of the Termination Act movement, the Relocation program, and a series of attempts to break up the joint KCA government into three separate tribal units. Several elders and veterans I spoke with stated that, although the Kiowa were never formally recommended for termination, the possibility weighed heavily on their minds. As one individual stated in discussing termination, "We have to show that we were still Indians. . . . We're still Kiowas. . . . So that's one reason why I think that this culture and dancing all came back."[144] The return to veteran status, a renewed confidence in espousing Indian pride as a result of the experiences and highly praised service in World War II, and fear of the political arena of termination lay at the core of the post–World War II cultural revivals that were to follow.

KIOWA MILITARY SOCIETY REVIVALS AND INCREASING POWWOWS

The revival of Kiowa military societies in the late 1950s and the restrengthening of War Dancing at powwows must be viewed in light of the postwar sociopolitical arena. Several factors including internal Kiowa tribal factionalism, KCA intertribal governmental factionalism, the need to honor large numbers of returning World War II and Korean War veterans, concern about potential termination legislation, and rising ethnic awareness all contributed to society revivals. The Ghost Dance crowd, which contained many Peyotists and tribal bundle keepers, reemerged as Levy's (1959) "conservative" faction in the 1950s. Levy (1959:54–58) describes two major Kiowa factions that emerged during this time: (1) the "conservative" or "G" faction, which centered around the Kiowa community of Carnegie and included many Peyotists and medicine bundle keepers and (2) the "progressives," a recent mixture of Peyotist and Christian Kiowa associated with the Mount Scott and later Anadarko communities. Although some scholars consider this factionalism to have been brief, it continues in various forms to this day. These two factions were probably outgrowths and reinvigorations of the earlier Ahpeahtone (anti–dance/giveaway) versus Kiowa Bill and James Waldo (pro–dance/giveaway) political and cultural factions, although shifts in power concerning respective Kiowa communities and specific lineages had occurred.

Some factionalism between Kiowa Christian and Peyotist communities has existed since the late 1800s. The underlying cause of this factionalism resulted from sudden changes in the tribal leadership and business committee, which had been controlled by the ǫ̀dè class prior to 1940, but had shifted to the lower káuàun class through new methods of obtaining political power (electioneering techniques and democratic elections), more equalizing social factors (education, use of English, non-Indian interaction), and the increasing political power of the lower class. According to Levy (1959:38–54), the conservatives were considered to be grass-roots people who perceived the progressives to be anti-Peyotist and antitraditional, particularly concerning the then pressing issue of termination policies. Only a small number of people, rallying primarily around kin interests, were directly involved in these factions. The leader of the G faction was a prominent member of the KCA business committee (1945–1960) and chair of the annual American Indian Exposition who used his influence with the exposition to gain support from the grass-roots people in the Carnegie community. This was perceived by the progressives as conservative or traditionalist and non-cooperative behavior. Yet mergers between Christians and Peyotists and mergers of both with groups centered around tribal medicine bundles increased during this period. According to Levy (1959:54–56, 96–98), the progressives were involved in the revival of the Gourd Clan in 1957 and Black Legs in 1958 and in the subsequent extension of warrior society, Peyote, and Christian alliances to other tribes. There are also indications that this was part of the progressives' strategy to counter the influence of the G faction in the annual American Indian Exposition. Coinciding with the internal Kiowa community factionalism was a growing fission of the KCA tribal government and business committee.

Between the late 1880s and World War II many Kiowa families converted to Christianity (mostly Baptist and Methodist sects) and were taught that dancing was both sinful and useless. Later generations growing up in strict Christian households, many of which contained elders who had become

Christian ministers and deacons, were raised for the most part "detached" from dancing and its associated traditions. Although most elders agree that conversion to Christianity resulted in the loss of the active practice of many traditions, it did not entirely result in a loss of knowledge associated with such traditions. One elder who attended the Baptist church in Hobart as a boy recalled that elders often told traditions in the Kiowa language on Sunday afternoons after services. These accounts, which dealt with military societies, warfare, travels, how Sétthą́idé (White Bear) was placed in jail, general history, and community news, showed that, despite missionary attempts, some cultural knowledge was passed down. In addition, elders were known for rising early in the morning and singing a variety of society, Ghost Dance, War Journey, War Dance, and other songs, which produced memories of earlier times and were learned by some of the younger generation. Despite somewhat divergent Christian and traditionalist lifestyles, the dividing lines began to ebb and flow following World War II, as more and more Christian Kiowa began to participate in society and social dances. Examination of initial society revival membership rosters demonstrates that while the initial revival of the Gourd Clan and Black Legs included many more Peyotists than Christian Kiowa, members of both sides were involved. Participation of Christian Kiowa in military society activities and powwows continued to increase during the late 1950s and early 1960s (Levy 1959).

Although some families still feel that attendance at society dances or powwows is inappropriate unless required to support a relative who is being honored on a special occasion, there are fewer and fewer Christians who do not at least periodically attend some dance functions. Because powwows and church services are generally held at different times, they do not overlap and thus are not in direct competition with one another. Some individuals participate in both the "Christian" or "Jesus Road" and the "Dance Road." As Christian church attendance, picnics, baseball games, and Christmas and camp meetings began to decline following World War II, powwows increasingly attracted greater attendance. Even though dancing and religion were not directly competitive, powwows became the primary community event. Subsequently, as the attendance at Kiowa Christian churches has decreased, attendance at weekend powwows, benefit dances, Indian fairs, military society dances, and family reunions has increased.

The Revival of Kiowa Gourd Dancing: The Kiowa Gourd Clan

In August 1955 current Kiowa tribal director for the American Indian Exposition Fred Tsoodle called together several Kiowa elders who were knowledgeable about the Gourd Dance for a special presentation to be given at that year's exposition. This presentation was reportedly so emotionally moving that it produced tears and soft crying among the elder spectators, which rekindled a flame leading to the revival of the Gourd Dance among the Kiowa (Kiowa Gourd Clan 1976:22). By 1956 plans to revive the Jáifègàu were underway among the Kiowa, many of whom were descendants of White Bear (Séttháidé), the prominent Jáifègàu Society leader of the early 1870s, and still knew some of the society songs.[145]

On January 30, 1957, at a meeting held at the home of Taft Hainta, a Gourd Dance association was formally organized, voted on, and adopted under the name of the Kiowa Gourd Clan. Several tribal elders, including former Jáifègàu Society members, selected the new officers for the organization (Kiowa Gourd Clan 1976:22; Poolaw 1981:2). Some Kiowa state that the elders initially advised the men not to elect officers but simply to keep the dance open to all Kiowa, as leadership positions would lead to factionalism and fission in the society. Many indicate that the installation of officers for life terms caused immediate factions within the newly revived society and its later breakup. After one year, Bill Koomsa Sr. resigned his position as vice-president and was replaced by Oscar Tsoodle, who retained that office until retiring around 1985. Taft Hainta remained leader of the Gourd Clan until his death in September 1990; Glen Hamilton was installed as the new leader in July 1991.[146] There are indications that earlier attempts to revive the dance between the 1946 Armistice Day Dance and the 1957 revival were prevented due to a personal rivalry between Taft Hainta and Bill Koomsa Sr., both of whom were descendants of White Bear, which undoubtedly strengthened their respective claims as society leaders.[147]

Although no form of official recruiting was undertaken at this time, participation increased as more and more Kiowa, many with ancestors who were Jáifègàu members, began to take part. The first celebration of the revived society was held at Carnegie Park over the Fourth of July weekend in 1957. The purpose of the society at the time of its revival was clearly the promotion of Kiowa cultural heritage through a conscious effort to maintain and strengthen both Kiowa culture and Jáifègàu Society traditions in the arena of the Kiowa Gourd Clan. The Kiowa Gourd Clan Ceremonials Booklet (1976:22) states: "The purpose and function of this organization was to perpetuate our Indian Heritage and to revive the Kiowa dance as near as possible from the past original ceremonies." Symbolizing the martial ethos of earlier days, many well-known society war trophies including feathered lances, a bugle, and a lariat were incorporated into the current ceremonial (Kiowa Gourd Clan 1976:22). Members' families pledged "beeves" to support the next year's celebration and money for the Kiowa Native American Church Chapter.

The attention to preserving Kiowa cultural heritage, the Gourd Dance, and the memory of ancestors are all prominently visible in the contemporary Gourd Dance. Numerous Kiowa have stated to me that great emphasis is placed on remembering elders and Kiowa heritage through Gourd Dance songs, dancing, camping together in the old fashion, "taking care" of visitors (hospitality), and general fellowship. When asked the purpose of the Kiowa Gourd Clan, one individual stated:

> The Kiowa Gourd Clan, they're thinking of their ancestors and we try to carry on what they left us, what they showed and what they left us . . . people always say, "We're trying the best we can." There's nobody to look up to anymore, they're all gone, so we're going to do the best we can, how we're doing it, that's the best we can do. We don't have anybody to tell us anymore, they're all gone, which is true you know, there's even a song that says that. We got a certain song that says, "Where have all the Kiowas gone? Where are they? The only thing they left us was these songs." [148]

Although many members are veterans, military service was not mandatory for membership in the Kiowa Gourd Clan, as it was in the Black Legs Society revival in 1958. While non-Indian participation in singing, dancing, and membership is prohibited, the Gourd Clan has inducted members from various other tribes, many married to Kiowa. Despite intertribal membership, the Kiowa Gourd Clan is undeniably a Kiowa-based organization which frequently and publicly espouses the maintenance of Kiowa traditions. Elders regularly indicate the need to show respect for the dance, by maintaining an all-Kiowa drum during Gourd Dance sessions and prohibiting non-Indian participation.

Contemporary Kiowa Gourd Dance clothing is a blend of Kiowa, Jáifègàu Society, Native American Church, and pan-Indian dress styles, which vary with the individual dancers' funds and resources.[149] While appropriate dress is essential and traditional dance clothes are highly valued, the Kiowa place more emphasis on participation, community, meaning, and especially the "Spirit" of the songs and dance than on how fancy an individual's set of clothing is—a distinction that many Anglos fail to understand.

Several items of post-1957 Gourd Dance dress have been borrowed from the Native American Church. In old pictures of Kiowa Gourd Dances prior to 1920 there is a notable absence of the red and blue blankets which became a standard part of Gourd Dance dress following the 1957 revival. Red and blue blankets can be traced back to the 1850s as a high-status luxury trade item acquired and made by prominent Southern Plains families. With the later introduction and growth of the Native American Church (post-1885 for the Kiowa), these blankets became a regular part of church dress.

Upon reviving the Gourd Dance, many members who were also Native American Church members brought red and blue blankets into the Gourd Dance arena, where they have since remained. Several elders have expressed disapproval of this. As one man stated, "It has no place in the Gourd Dance, it belongs to the [Native American] church." Some people similarly stated that such blankets are worn by "priests" or "roadmen" in the Native American Church. Others, however, have argued that because the Gourd Dance and the use of various types of sheets and blankets preceded the beginning of the Peyote religion and later formation of the Native American Church in 1918 such blankets are appropriate for use in the Gourd Dance. Some contemporary Kiowa describe the red portion of the blanket and the wearing of red mescal bean bandoliers as symbolic of blood spilled by past Kiowa warriors. These and other items of dress have been placed in a whole host of new social and ritual contexts, including everyday wear, and are now standards of Kiowa Gourd Dance apparel.[150] Similarly, the use of gourd versus metal rattles in the contemporary Gourd Dance is disputed by some, who feel that gourd rattles are for use solely in the Native American Church, while the use of metal salt shaker rattles should be restricted to the Gourd Dance.

The Revival of the Kiowa Black Legs Society

In 1957 a short performance of the Kiowa Tòkógàut or Black Legs Society songs and dances was given at the American Indian Exposition. The performance was well received and prompted further interest. On November 23, 1958, Gus Palmer Sr., a World War II veteran, called a meeting of all Kiowa veterans at the VFW hall in Carnegie, Oklahoma. Approximately fifty veterans attended that afternoon and the Kiowa Veterans Association (KVA) was formed. After organizing the KVA, Palmer, with the support of his brothers George and Dixon Palmer, incorporated the revival of the Kiowa Black Legs Society into the KVA. According to Palmer, the goal at this time was to organize the men who had served their tribe and country and to explain the importance of maintaining their identity as veterans. Although the name Tòkógàut actually means "Black Legs," in reference to the painting of the lower legs with black paint, the society since 1958 has been commonly known as the "Black Leggings" or "Black Leggins Warrior Society" as the majority of members no longer paint their legs black but wear black leggings or stockings. However, society and tribal elders encouraged use of the correct translation "Black Legs" here. Requirements for membership since 1958 include being an enrolled Kiowa tribal member, being a veteran, and dressing as a uniform group for society ceremonials.[151]

Reflecting recent postwar membership in Anglo veterans' associations, the leadership structure of the society since 1958 has closely modeled VFW and American Legion Posts. Following the initial afternoon meeting a social and war dance was held in the Carnegie VFW building to recognize the newly elected officers. Gus Palmer Sr. was elected commander and still maintains that position (Bantista n.d.: 5).[152] The new officers were introduced one week later at a powwow held in the Carnegie VFW building, where the society was reintroduced to the Kiowa people. The first formal Black Legs Society dance following this revival was held in June 1959 at a Kiowa princess contest powwow. In 1959 and 1960 Veterans' Day dances were held by the society at the Carnegie city park; the newly formed Kiowa Veterans Auxiliary held a processional (Bantista n.d.: 7). They were soon joined by the Kiowa War Mothers and Victory Club, and all three organizations continue to participate in the society's processionals today. Although the initial number of active participants following the revival remained small, the persistence and strength of a few core members resulted in the growth of the society, which is now one of the major Kiowa tribal ceremonies.

In 1958 there were still several tribal elders who had been active society members when the group ceased to function in 1927. When approached for knowledge about the society, the older members were pleased and encouraged Palmer's interest in reviving the society. According to Palmer, "These elders felt that it would be only right if they (the younger veterans) would revive the society and keep it up, keep it going," and that "they had the right to do so, since they were the veterans of the tribe."[153] The older members taught the society songs, dances, and ceremony to the younger veterans. Palmer decided to revive the Tòkǫ́gàut in dedication to his brother Lyndreth Palmer, who was killed in France during World War II, and in honor of all Kiowa veterans. He did not want his brother's name to die out, and he says that he has always gained strength from this desire and has never gotten discouraged through the years.[154]

Reflecting a syncretization of both nineteenth-century Kiowa military societies and recent service in the U.S. military, the Black Legs decided to adopt a uniform dress code and to keep the society dress as nearly authentic as possible. In keeping with the society's name, the legs from the knee down were to be kept black by paint, knee-length stockings, or buckskin leggings. A fur-covered curved staff or fàubôn would continue to be the societal insignia, and each man could carry a straight lance, containing individual decorations of his military service. Society leader Gus Palmer, for example, has twenty-one eagle feathers on his lance to represent the twenty-one bombing missions he made in World War II.[155] In memory of their great-grandfather Gúlhèî, who captured a cape from a Mexican officer he killed in battle and donned it in celebration, the Palmer family gave the right to all society members to wear similar individual red capes in society dances. Continuing the traditional emphasis on veteran's status, members commonly wear modern U.S. military insignia and medals on their capes.[156] Women may wear an auxiliary shawl containing the name and symbol of their organization and the name and rank of a veteran relative or older forms of cloth, velvet, or buckskin dresses. Another dress style associated with the Black Legs is the "Red Sleeve Dress" (Màunkàugúlhòldà), a cloth or wool dress consisting of a black or navy-blue body and red sleeves and sides. These dresses, which date back to at least 1857, were common among several Southern Plains tribes and were worn by Kiowa women of affluent (ǫ̀dè) status to show their support and love for their warrior relatives.[157]

Continuing the tradition of holding military society meetings in tipis, the society (since 1973) uses a tipi derived from the famous Jòqígácút (Return from Battle Marks Tipi) or "Battle Tipi" of Jòhâusàn (Little Bluff Recess/Concavity). The yellow stripes on the south side of the tipi were already present when it was given to Jòhâusàn by the Cheyenne leader Sleeping Bear in 1840 and are believed to have represented successful war expeditions he had led. Jòhâusàn then added black stripes to represent successful war expeditions that he had personally led on which he had brought back scalps with no loss of members. The other side was filled with depictions of battle scenes by noted Kiowa warriors who were invited to display their personal war deeds and periodically changed with the acquisition of higher-ranking battle deeds (Ewers 1978:14–15).[158]

The tipi used today by the Black Legs combines portions of the Jòhâusàn model with symbols of modern military service. The choice to use the Jòhâusàn design was made for several reasons. First, Jòhâusàn was the last Kiowa tribal chief (1833–1866) to have relatively undisputed authority through tribal consensus, and his tipi design is not only known by nearly every Kiowa, but remains an important symbol of Kiowa military and political tradition. For the Kiowa, the tipi of Jòhâusàn is perhaps analogous to the Liberty Bell for Anglo Americans—a symbol of freedom and tribal autonomy. Although Jòhâusàn is better known as the leader of the Qóichégàu, he is believed to have belonged to the Tǫ̀kǫ́gàut and, according to some, to have once been that society's leader.

The left half of the current society tipi consists of yellow and black stripes or "war trails" taken from the "Battle Tipi" of Jòhâusàn. The right side of the tipi was decorated to commemorate Kiowa participation in the era of modern warfare. The right half consists of a red painted upper portion, said to symbolize the blood of Kiowa killed in action serving in the United States military, and a white lower portion, separated by a thin blue stripe. On the first society tipi made in 1974 by George and Dixon Palmer, this portion depicted modern-day battles in which the Black Legs Society members had actually participated, including scenes of tanks, B-17 airplanes dropping bombs, paratroopers, and infantry. This tipi was never completely painted and was later replaced by a larger one. The current tipi was built and painted in 1986. The battle scenes, however, have not been included on it. On the right side below the upper blue stripe, extending from the front of the tipi to the middle of the back and then running downward, are military insignia and divisional crests of Kiowa veterans. The Kiowa have had veterans in every major conflict from World War I to Operation Desert Storm. Near the top of the tipi in the center of the back is a figure of an eaglelike bird centered on a light blue circular background. This figure has the head and wings of an eagle attached to a red, yellow, and blue shield, which forms the body of the figure. On the front of the right side is a list of those Kiowa who are specially recognized, having made the supreme sacrifice for their country.

Today the Black Legs Society tipi is used for members to meet and to purify themselves prior to dancing. Cedar sprigs are placed on hot coals brought in by the two society boy members, to produce smoke. Prayers are offered for society members and any families who have recently lost a member as they are fanned and incensed with the smoke. The society members pray in honor of a recently deceased family member and ask to receive strength to carry on in life.

Additional Revivals

With the revival of the Kiowa Gourd Clan in 1957, the Black Legs in 1958, a renewed interest in the Óhòmò Society, and the formation of various other Gourd and War Dance and women's societies, the Kiowa continued to honor and induct servicemen. Throughout the 1960s and 1970s Kiowa societies grew and influenced the revival of similar societies among the Apache in 1959–1960 (Bittle 1962) and the Comanche in 1972–1976 as well as the general spread of the Gourd Dance (Howard 1976; Ellis 1990; Lassiter 1992) throughout Oklahoma and later the United States. Some Apache and Comanche I interviewed acknowledged the influence of Kiowa organizations in their causes to revive their own organizations, in some cases citing participation in Kiowa Gourd Dances prior to reviving their own societies. With the post–World War II revival of dancing, increasing Indian identity, and pan-Indian influences (Howard 1955), the Kiowa continued to influence other groups through their dominant role in dance and music. The rise of ethnic awareness in the 1960s and subsequent Indian Awareness Movement was facilitated by the regrowth of dancing and cultural forms which were strengthened by the rise and reinvigoration of veteran status and Indian ethnicity.

CONTEMPORARY SOCIETIES AND MARTIAL SYMBOLS

Contemporary Kiowa military society dances are replete with martial-based ideology and symbols that reinforce traditional concepts of recognizing and honoring veterans and distinct elements of Kiowa ethnicity and heritage. The current ceremonials of all three societies contain varying elements of nineteenth-century Kiowa military society structure, social integration, and martial ethos.

The Kiowa Gourd Clan

The annual July Gourd Clan encampment is held in the Carnegie City Park, on a low plain along the Washita River that is well shaded by large cottonwood trees, and lasts for three or four days. Many members set up camp several days in advance and often remain to visit for one or two days after the dancing ends. The encampment is not associated with the celebration of American independence, but the Fourth of July holiday is used as an occasion for gathering for practical reasons. As the emcee stated on July 4, 1991, "This is not a Fourth of July celebration. The occurrence is due to free time from jobs. We are in no way promoting or celebrating the American Fourth of July."[159]

In many ways, the annual celebration is replete with symbols of the old Sun Dance and Jáifègàu Military Society ceremonies. The dance is held at approximately the same time of year as the Sun Dance and continues the use of a large circular shade arbor, similar to the building of a Sun Dance arbor by the societies in the past. Many Kiowa set up tipis or wall tents around the circular dance arena in the center. In addition, Brush, Gourd, Rabbit, War, and social dances all relate back to activities which originally focused on the socialization period prior to the annual Sun Dance. While communal hunts are a thing of the past, daily rations are distributed during the encampment by society members. Pledges of money and beef provide resources for meals during the encampment, just as individuals pledged and sponsored feasts in the past.

Activities generally begin around 6:00 A.M. with a devotional and a flag-raising ceremony. At around 9:00 A.M. rations are distributed to the entire encampment. At 10:00 Gus Palmer, the leader of the Pòlą́hyòp (Rabbit Society) and known as Grandpa Rabbit, calls the children to organize for the Rabbit dances. The Rabbits are given trash bags with which they rapidly clean the dance grounds of debris. After performing this public service, songs are played for them to dance to and they are rewarded with treats such as candy or cake. Around 11:00 A.M. a session of Brush Dragging Songs (Ákùidàugà) are sung which last for approximately thirty minutes, during which women hold up cottonwood branches, shaking them in time to the music as they dance. A processional led by several gourd dancers and singers holding a drum and playing Brush Dragging Songs, and followed by women accompanying the singing, dances the Brush Dragging Dance (Ákùicùngà), slowly proceeding through the entrance and into the middle of the arena. After the last Brush Dragging Song, the women walk over to the edge of the arena and place the crowns and small branches of cottonwood trees on top of the circular shade arbor, reminiscent of past brush dragging in the construction of the Sun Dance arbor. About 1:00 P.M. several Kiowa men enter the center of the arena and plant four solidly red painted forked poles into the ground from south to north. On these poles the Kiowa Gourd Clan displays the symbolic war accouterments obtained by the Jáifègàu members in the nineteenth and twentieth centuries, most of which are said to relate to the society leader White Bear.[160]

The afternoon program consists of Gourd Dancing, initiations, giveaways, and speeches. Current Kiowa Gourd Dance music is a blend of Jáifègàu, Áljóyìgàu, and Chèjánmàu Society songs and Brush Dance, sweat lodge, Sun Dance, and individual family songs. Several old Jáifègàu Society songs, which contained only vocables, have had words added to them, while other entirely new songs have been composed as well. Several Mountain Sheep and Horse Headdress Society Songs, which are very similar in composition, have been adopted or changed since the 1957 revival and serve to keep alive the memory of that society. As one elder singer described, "Them clans [military societies], you know they're all about forgotten and some songs that sound very similar, they change them and put them into the Gourd Dance now."[161]

Following an evening prayer, which is usually given by a Kiowa minister, everyone returns to the camps for supper. Continuing the tradition of hospitality, visitors are invited to break bread at various Kiowa camps. Dancing resumes around 7:00. Beginning with the Kiowa Flag Song, a single-file processional parades in from the east side of the arena. This processional is led by the Gourd Dancers, followed by the male Fancy, Straight, and Traditional Dancers, then by the women and younger girls who will later participate in the program.[162]

The Role and Impact of the Kiowa Gourd Dance

Following the revival of the Kiowa Gourd Clan, three other independent Kiowa Gourd Dance groups have emerged through factionalism and differing interests, the Tia-Piah Society of Oklahoma, the Tia-Piah Society of Carnegie, and the Kiowa Warrior Descendants. These fissions are significant in that they demonstrate that while sodalities contain essential integrative qualities for social organization, they are not immune to kin, family, and communal political factionalism. Over time the general and specific functions and uses of the Jáifègàu and its dance and music began to broaden. Before 1890 the dance was performed prior to the Sun Dance by a select sodality of men who were generally all warriors, but later, during the reservation and postreservation periods, the society inducted nonveteran members of high-status families. The Jáifègàu changed dramatically as many of its roles, such as policing the communal bison hunt and emphasis on fostering martial spirit for warfare, were no longer available. By 1912 the dance had been revived but was performed mainly by elderly men, who were increasingly lacking in veteran status, but who had been raised with a continued emphasis on martial and society traditions. In 1935 White Fox described the purpose of the Jáifègàu as "part social [and] part honorary."[163] His comments suggest that in the early 1900s the society still had several functions in commemorating particular lineages through membership of their descendants and commemorating the Kiowa heritage, in which the Jáifègàu fulfilled significant social, political, economic, military, and cultural roles.

By the time of the society's revival in 1957, the Gourd Dance had undergone major transformations and had expanded its functions or "consolidated" a range of new functions that constitute a significant part of the contemporary form of the dance. Perhaps foremost in the society's goals is the perpetuation of Kiowa heritage. As proclaimed by the Kiowa Gourd Clan in 1976, this emphasis demonstrates the importance placed on the historical persistence of Kiowa culture, maintenance of ethnicity, and Jáifègàu martial traditions and heritage:

The purpose and function of this organization was to perpetuate our Indian Heritage and to revive the Kiowa dance as near as possible from the
past original ceremonies. . . . It was also decided to display early day trophies taken from enemies during frontier encounters. The Army bugle
taken at one of the Frontier Posts, a lariat rope captured from the Texas
Rangers; also feather staffs and lances owned by the past members. These
trophies are regarded as mark and symbol of courage and bravery of the
Kiowa tribe. (Kiowa Gourd Clan 1976:22)

In essence, "the Gourd Clan became a rallying point for continuing the
unique heritage that had unfolded among the Kiowa. As a performance, the
Gourd Dance was now a conscious symbol of what it meant to be Kiowa"
(Lassiter 1992:30). Several Kiowa of various ages have made statements to
this same effect. One Gourd Clan elder recently reinforced the continuity
of this ideology at the 1993 annual dance, stating that "the Kiowa Gourd
Clan will be used to revive and strengthen several Kiowa traditions" (there
was concern that they were becoming obsolete).[164]

Following the conscious emphasis and promotion of Kiowa culture and
identity through the Gourd Dance, a variety of revived and newly interrelated uses for the Gourd Dance developed. The performance of the dance
to honor war veterans is a continuation of past society practices. The use of
the Fourth of July weekend as an annual encampment, in many aspects resembling the former Sun Dance, and the ability of all Kiowa men (and not
just former Jáifègàu members) and, after the mid-1960s, women and children to participate in Gourd Dance activities can be seen as adaptations
of great integrational significance for the Kiowa tribe. Economically, the
Gourd Dance has become a major portion of nearly every Kiowa and neighboring Southern Plains social dance or powwow and serves as an arena
for various forms of fundraising. While the Kiowa's understanding of the
dance's significance has evolved and adapted, so have the ways in which the
dance is now used. It is frequently performed in afternoon and early evening sessions prior to evening non-society-focused powwows and in benefit
dances in which the dance itself is not the primary reason for gathering as it
is during annual society celebrations (Lassiter 1992:33). This in turn has led
to some divisiveness among the Kiowa; many people have expressed the
opinion that the current manner and frequency of the dancing have led to
the loss of respect for the essence and the "Spirit" of the dance. Many individuals have similarly echoed one elder's sentiments: "They're not upholding it like they should. They don't do it like it is supposed to be done, the
way it used to be done."[165] The growing interest and participation in the

dance by many non-Kiowa (both non-Kiowa tribes and non-Indians) have resulted in other problems.

The Spread of the Kiowa Gourd Dance

The revival of the Kiowa Gourd Clan in 1957 undeniably heralded a general cultural revival of military societies and dancing among many Southern Plains tribes that continues to the present. The Gourd Dance revival grew in popularity among not only Kiowa, but among other Native Americans in Oklahoma and among non-Indians (Howard 1976, 1983; Kracht 1989; Ellis 1990; Lassiter 1992, 1993, 1995). James Howard (1976:249) attributes the Gourd Dance's rapid growth in popularity and diffusion to the increasing Oklahoma-centered "Pan-Indian powwow complex," which he character-izes as including a Plains culture base, with its musical appeal, simple and affordable attire, and a heightened level of tribal and Pan-Indian group identity and awareness. When asked why they thought the dance was so popular with others, the Kiowa gave several reasons, including the rhythm of the dance, the relatively simple dress, the bonding process involved in creating new friendships, the spiritual significance which "makes you feel like something," and the strength of the songs.[166] The Kiowa played a semi-nal role in the dance's diffusion across the country to other Indian and non-Indian groups. Much of the Anglo interest has been spurred by Kiowa who have relocated to urban areas, where they then started their own Gourd Dance societies, which later took in non-Indians (Anglo hobbyists who have adopted the Gourd Dance through Boy Scout organizations or various hobbyist Indian dance clubs) as full or auxiliary members. I have observed non-Indian hobbyists performing a Kiowa-styled Gourd Dance and singing Kiowa Gourd Dance songs in numerous states across the nation.

Over the years the increasing inclusion of non-Indian participants and especially the use of the Kiowa "Tia-Piah" name have produced some hard feelings between various Kiowa Gourd dancing groups. Many Kiowa in the home community are outraged and feel that no one has the right to give the dance away and that it is "owned" only in a tribally collective sense. They have expressed the feeling that the name is a Kiowa name and should there-fore remain so. As one elder put it, "It's O.K. if those other groups gonna dance. I know a lot of other Indians and non-Indians, they like to dance. But Jáifè that's our name, our society. It's a *Kiowa* name. It shouldn't be used by any other groups, Indian or non-Indian. They got no right to it and no one got the right to give it away either." [167] As the predominantly Kiowa version of the Gourd Dance continues to grow in popularity among other tribes and non-Indians from coast to coast, significant relationships and attitudes, both at home and abroad, will arise from this influential dance form.

The revival of the Kiowa Gourd Dance not only served as a catalyst for other tribes which once practiced a form of the dance, but stimulated further revivals of other types of military and formal War Dance societies among many tribes as well, during a time (1955–1976) when a tremendous revitalization of Indian awareness, dancing, and culture was occurring. Although the dance was formerly practiced by a number of Plains tribes, the contemporary Gourd Dance revival is undeniably heavily Kiowa influenced, as demonstrated by the heavy utilization of Kiowa dance style, dress, and music. The singing of Kiowa songs with Kiowa lyrics is commonly found among current Gourd Dances of Plains, Eastern Woodlands, Great Lakes, and Southeastern tribes, as well as Anglos. The Kiowa helped to disseminate the dance by performing it throughout the country, as demonstrated by its popularity among Anglo hobbyists and its adoption by the Alabama-Coushatta near Livingston, Texas. The Alabama-Coushatta, a southeastern tribe who originally never performed the dance, continue to be assisted by Kiowa, who often serve as head staff, singers, and dancers, at their annual tribal powwow in June, at which the Gourd Dance constitutes the principal dance. The Otoe, who have maintained a lengthy friendship with the Kiowa since the late 1800s and attended Kiowa Gourd Dances in the 1920s and 1930s, also formed a Gourd Clan modeled after the Kiowa Gourd Clan. Several Otoe have been inducted into the Kiowa Gourd Clan, and contingents of the two tribes attend each other's annual Gourd Dances. Similarly, there is an Osage Gourd Clan, and the Gourd Dance was brought to the Omaha reservation in Nebraska in April 1970 by two Omaha men who had been inducted into the Kiowa "Tia-Piah Society" (Liberty 1973). Finally, several intertribal Gourd Dance organizations influenced by the Kiowa have been started in urban communities such as Oklahoma City, Tulsa, Wichita, Dallas–Fort Worth, and San Francisco that contain high numbers of transplanted Native Americans as a result of the Relocation Program of the 1950s and subsequent urban migrations necessitated by the lack of employment opportunities in tribal communities. In addition, the presence of these groups has further attracted and influenced non-Indian hobbyist organizations, some of which have adopted the Kiowa name "Tia-Piah."

Clyde Ellis (1990, 1993) provides a good summary of the role of the revival of the Kiowa Gourd Dance in light of national native policies and trends.[168] Eric Lassiter's research (1992, 1993, 1995) and ongoing fieldwork focusing on a symbolic analysis of the Kiowa Gourd Dance and its music offer fresh and original insights into the various social and symbolic roles of the Gourd Dance, particularly the relationship between Kiowa Gourd Dance music and Kiowa ethnicity. My fieldwork and participation in Kiowa Gourd dances from 1989 to 1997 focus on a more in-depth ethnohistorical perspective on the society's and dance's history, but generally correlate with and support Lassiter's (1992, 1993, 1995) more symbolic and ethnomusicological published and unpublished findings, which he generously shared during my work.

While military societies among several tribes were revived after 1957, the revival, enormous popularity, and diffusion of a Kiowa-style Gourd Dance produced a pan-Indian phenomenon similar to the role of the Kiowa and Comanche in the spread of the Native American Church in the late 1800s. While the Gourd Dance initially spread after 1957 to include the majority of Plains and Prairie tribes (Howard 1976), it has continued to grow in popularity and can now be found from coast to coast in the United States. While elements of this diffusion, particularly the use of the Kiowa name by other tribes and non-Indians, bother some Kiowa, others encourage interested outsiders. The impact of the post-1957 diffusion of the Kiowa Gourd Dance remains a significant part of the contemporary Plains-style powwow throughout much of Indian and hobbyist country, where a Gourd Dance can be found on nearly every program and Kiowa are found serving as head staff for powwows and Gourd Dances throughout much of Oklahoma and hobbyists' dances across the country.

Howard (1976:243) classifies the Gourd Dance as a "revitalization movement" and compares the dance to Nancy Oestreich Lurie's (1971:418) "articulatory movement" based on the absence of "identifiable leadership and spokesmen." However, as Lassiter (1992:66; 1995:206–207) points out, the dance "is probably not best understood as a revitalization movement (or even an articulatory one) as Anthony Wallace [1956:265–68] first defined it," for two reasons: (1) "a *distinct* belief system connected with the dance's historical development" exists in the Kiowa community, and (2) no standardized body of belief associated with and leading to the rapid diffusion of the dance to other populations exists, as was associated with the Ghost Dance and Native American Church. Therefore it is not a "true" revitalization movement (cf. Lassiter 1992, 1995).

Howard (1976) discusses several nineteenth-century Plains and Prairie military societies with similar Gourd Dance choreography, including the Cheyenne, Arapaho, Comanche, Ponca, Omaha, and Iowa, who all attest to their own claims to the revived dance. Southern Cheyenne and Bow String Society members I have spoken with maintain that the dance was "stolen" from them by the Kiowa in the 1830s.[169] Some Kiowa also report hearing these claims from Cheyenne. As Lassiter (1992:66) notes, whether these claims are true or not is not really the question. What is most relevant today is that "the Kiowa unquestionably revived their distinct form of the Gourd Dance" and "produced the popular expansion to other groups in Oklahoma," some of which historically had similar society dances. The Kiowa revival of the Gourd Dance also provided the Comanche, Cheyenne, Arapaho, Omaha, Ponca, and others with a historical connection to the modern (revived) dance. As Lassiter's (1992:66) discussion of other non-Kiowa Gourd Dancing groups and my own fieldwork and participation in Kiowa, Comanche, and Cheyenne Gourd Dances indicate, the dance has been conceptually changed to be tribally specific in each respective community.[170] "Because the dance and music styles were similar, the Gourd Dance underwent what William K. Powers (1980:217) has called 'homostylic diffusion.' Even within the geographical proximity of Oklahoma, the selective traditions of the revival had their origins with the Kiowa, which gave them a specific relationship with the songs in a modern context" (Lassiter 1992:66). While several tribes had prereservation Gourd Dancing societies, the contemporary version found among numerous tribes is heavily influenced by the post-1957 revived Kiowa form. The large quantity of Kiowa Gourd Dance songs, especially those containing texts, supports the Kiowa claims to the songs, which have in some cases been lost in neighboring tribes. The prevalence of Kiowa-dominated Gourd Dance music is reflected in the commercial cassette tapes and compact discs of Gourd Dance music, which are predominantly by Kiowa singers.

With the increasing popularity of the Gourd Dance and spread of the pan-Indian movement, "it came to symbolize what it meant to be Indian, rather than what it meant to be Kiowa," because "the conceptualization around the dance is not generally homogeneous outside of Kiowa country." Powers (1980:217) has called this process [of spreading dance and musical forms] "transcultural diffusion," which "occurs when the songs and dances retain their original structure but either most of their functions are lost or new functions added" (Lassiter 1992:66–67). Lassiter (1992:67) refers to the Gourd Dance revival among the Kiowa as a "popular revival," because it originated within the context of the Kiowa community and has become popular outside of this center. Classification as a "revitalization movement" does not reflect the nature of the Gourd Dance's diffusion, which is instead characterized by an "activation of selective traditions—in this case Kiowa ones" that "have taken on new meanings and connotations—in most cases, Indian identity in terms of Pan-Indianism," once outside of the Kiowa community and Oklahoma (Lassiter 1992:67). Because the Gourd Dance has a tribally specific, known history and meaning for the Kiowa, they perform the dance as the original 1957 revivers, and not as a result of pan-Indianism (Howard 1976; Lassiter 1992:67).

The Role of the Gourd Dance and Music in Kiowa Ethnic Continuity

Anyone who has witnessed, let alone participated in, a Kiowa Gourd Dance can attest to the intensity and "Spirit" of the emotion, concentration, music, and dance. Pleasing music that often leads to tapping of the foot is known as fáultàgà. Many Kiowa intellectual processes are personified in the masculine gender. "Spirit" of the type which emanates from Kiowa song and dance is best translated with the term fégàqì. Kiowa become fégàòtàmà when they become overjoyed from singing, praying, and talking. Participation is essential to gain a feeling for and understanding of music and dance (or any cultural form) and spirit; there is simply no other means to learn. From my perspective, sufficient linguistic knowledge to permit an understanding of the song texts is also necessary.

Lassiter (1992, 1995) has shown that while the processes of Westernization caused drastic changes in many aspects of life, the reaction to enormous cultural transformations may have been in favor of cultural retention, by producing a unique ethnic continuity for the Kiowa Gourd Dance. Despite the impacts of colonial development and Westernization, many populations around the world have preserved and maintained their traditional musical repertoires (Nettl 1985; Lassiter 1992:67). The Kiowa have successfully maintained the Gourd Dance and music in new ways that, while undergoing changes, have adapted to continue the vitality and intactness of the performance aspects of the dance and Kiowa ethnic identity. Performances of traditional dance, song, and speeches are the result of unique individual Native American community histories and "maintain and preserve a specific ethnic continuity in American society" (Lassiter 1992:2). While some performances such as the Plains style powwow are more "pan-Indian" oriented, other performances continue to address and maintain more specific ethnic distinctions such as the Kiowa Gourd Dance (Lassiter 1992:2), the Kiowa Black Legs Society (Meadows 1991), the Cibecue Apache Gan Dance, the Creek Green Corn Dance, or the Cherokee Booger Dance.

The Kiowa Gourd Dance continues to connect ethnic identity with performance (Lassiter 1992). It maintains such specific distinctions by providing the Kiowa with a unique cultural identity by reinforcing uniquely Kiowa concepts and values. As with each Kiowa military society, dance, and specific society history, the Gourd Dance contributes "to the continuation of Kiowa culture"; as "an embodiment of seasoned traditions, it exemplifies how Kiowas have forged their singular identity in modern America while still being true to their Kiowa heritage" (Lassiter 1992 : 3).

In conversation and in singing, the Kiowa display deep feelings for their music, and Gourd Dance music perhaps plays the most dominant role in the maintenance of ethnic continuity. As in many Native American communities, music is extremely meaningful for participants and serves as the drawing card for events (Nettl 1989; Lassiter 1992 : 8). Central to this relationship is the "Spirit" of the Gourd Dance music, which many elders state is the most important and most difficult aspect to understand. Based on his research and participation in the Kiowa Gourd Dance and singing, Lassiter (1992 : 8–9) writes:

> For most Kiowas, Gourd Dance songs have a special power of their own, a power beyond the comprehension of many untrained outsiders. "I may sing these songs for ten hours, and if the Spirit hits me for five seconds, it's all worth it," one singer told me. Each Gourd Dance must ideally invoke the "Spirit of the Dance," and this begins with the songs. . . .
>
> No matter how one might define it, this Spirit is apparent when one attends a Gourd Dance and hears the music about which the Kiowas feel so strongly. . . . the Gourd Dance songs invoke a Spirit that is a multifaceted relationship entailing a dialogue between God, the natural and cultural environment, and human beings. An important part of this dialogue is the retention of Kiowa language—the songs now an important container of tradition. In addition, the Spirit ultimately involves a link to both the historical and mythological past through song. These combinations are the circumstances that allow for the expression of a unique ethnic continuity of a Kiowa-specific life. Seen in this light, the songs are the soul of the Gourd Dance. They embody and preserve precious and vital knowledge that define [sic] the Kiowa people. Gourd Dance songs are not merely a reflection of Kiowa traditions; they are an embodiment of their religion, their connection to God. As a potent symbol, both of the Kiowa struggle with the U.S. government and the Kiowas' persistence, the songs are about Kiowa people, by them, and for them.

When properly performed, "the songs themselves" have "the power to invoke the Spirit of the Dance" (Lassiter 1992 : 17).

In each Kiowa military society I worked with, the Kiowa have in part sustained their ethnic and military society identity through songs while undergoing tremendous sociocultural, economic, demographic, and political changes. As the functions of the music changed through time, it took on new roles for Kiowa people, and this "broader cultural significance" of the music has become "a new rallying point for ethnic continuity" (Lassiter 1992:10).

The relationship between song texts and language is also important in maintaining Kiowa ethnic identity. Presently there are less than 400 fluent Kiowa speakers in a total Kiowa population of nearly 10,000 and clear indications that the younger generations are not learning the language, which produces a change in how songs are understood, sung, and composed and in what it means to be Kiowa.[171] "How some Kiowas understand the Kiowa language is shaped by their participation in the Gourd Dance and not by directly speaking the language; they know the language through the songs they sing" (Lassiter 1992:52). Most current linguistically fluent and knowledgeable singers are over the age of fifty.[172] The religious significance of the Gourd Dance varies tremendously among individual Kiowa and different generations, but the meanings of song texts are more precise and easily observed (Lassiter 1992:51). While younger singers often cannot speak the Kiowa language fluently, many understand the basic meanings and translations associated with certain songs. For nonspeakers, "songs and their texts have now become a container and preserver of language," and songs with Kiowa lyrics clearly reinforce Kiowa history, ethnicity, cultural continuity, and survival (Lassiter 1992:50–51). In some ways, song texts, like prayers, which are nearly always in native languages, have come to possess sacred qualities by reinforcing the unique relationship between the Kiowa and God, the environment, and their history. Linguistic retention represents the maintenance of distinct heritage and ethnicity in any culture.

Based on my participation in three semesters of Kiowa language classes and linguistic fieldwork which has included the translation of nearly two hundred Kiowa song texts of various genres, rarely can an individual under the age of forty speak fluent conversational Kiowa. Thus, the retention of song texts has begun to absorb the role of intensifying the maintenance and reinforcement of a distinct Kiowa ethnicity, even for nonspeakers (Lassiter 1992:52). The debate about whether the retention of language is necessary in retaining culture affects most tribes, including the Kiowa. The retention of the Gourd Dance, as well as the dances of other societies, figures prominently in the retention of Kiowa language and culture, as reflected in the use of song texts as extremely meaningful ritual symbols in Gourd Dance performances (Lassiter 1992:53).

Ownership of music is important among the Kiowa. While some songs are "open" or "let go" and can be sung by everyone, others are "owned," often by individuals or families. The ownership of a particular song and question of who has the "right" to use it are variously defined and often visibly contested in private conversations as well as in public arenas. Some songs are sung in two versions, with and without lyrics; those with lyrics are more precisely defined as owned by a specific family. In instances in which a song text explicitly and openly expresses personal names and elements of Kiowa or family history, ownership is more specifically implied and the "Spirit" of the dance is more specific (Lassiter 1992 : 50). This applies to Gourd Dance, Black Legs, and Óhòmà songs as well as other types of non-society songs. As such, songs, and especially song texts, unify the Kiowa as a distinct group by clearly telling and reinforcing their story of struggle, continuity, and cultural survival. "The survival of the songs" alone is often used to "justify the Kiowa's historical struggle" (Lassiter 1992 : 50). Because song texts are sometimes reserved for and sung at "special times," they "help to invoke a unique relationship, they authorize a special distinction, giving them a 'sacred' quality" (Lassiter 1992 : 53).[173]

The Ethnic-Religious Significance of the Kiowa Gourd Dance

For many Kiowa the Gourd Clan celebration has in some ways come to replace the Sun Dance. It is the largest annual Kiowa summer encampment that focuses on a ceremony of tribal-level integration. As stated by the Kiowa Gourd Clan (1976:22), "The present day Kiowa Gourd Clan celebration comes at the time of the Sun Dance and has replaced the Sun Dance." Many Kiowa stress the religious character of the dance and music, often in reference to the Sun Dance of the past. One of my elder consultants echoed this analogy:

> The songs mean so much. A lot of them have a Kiowa interpretation. The Kiowas know and can't help but feel about our deceased relatives that are gone, the elders. A lot of songs have words in them about our elder people that are all gone. A lot of things, I belong to the Jáife and I'm gonna enjoy myself. It's just the Kiowa words in them. That's why I say it's pretty much like the, it's not the Sun Dance, but what I'm saying, it pretty much functions like it, the social gatherings and all that—tie in with the Sun Dance that was stopped years ago.[174]

Some younger Kiowa find religious connotations in the importance of the dance, while the elders I have interviewed state that it is spiritual and has spirituality, but is not religious; this indicates that the Gourd Dance has been elevated in socioreligious importance as a Kiowa tribal ceremony.

There is no doubt that the dance is highly respected and venerated among the Kiowa. As the 1976 Kiowa Gourd Clan (1976:23) booklet says: "There are several other gourd clans that have branched off from the original clan and the dance itself has spread to the other tribes over the United States. BUT ONLY THE KIOWAS venerate, in other words, look upon with feelings of deep respect, THIS, OUR DANCE, OUR SONGS, AND OUR HERITAGE."

The importance and the meaning of the dance vary greatly among the Kiowa I spoke with. Personal opinions ranged from "purely social," to "highly respected and dignified," to "spiritual—but not religious" in the sense of other tribal religious forms such as the Sun Dance, Native American Church, and Ten Medicines. Most elders over the age of seventy spoke of the dance in terms of being "dignified," "serious," "spiritual," "highly respected," "traditional," and "cherished," but in no way a form of worship in a "religious" sense. The range of the various interconnected socioreligious aspects of the dance, including martial overtones, and its meaning for contemporary Kiowa were expressed by one of my consultants:

> It's an organization that is highly respected. It's a traditional Kiowa chieftain dance and I look at it that way. When a person dances that, you're saying that I'm not afraid to die. And a lot of people are dancing that don't know what it is all about, especially non-Indians.
>
> I can't help but think that this is a sacred dance and it should be carried on that way. It shouldn't be taken lightly.
>
> It's a dignified sacred dance. It's not a social dance. When I get involved in Jáifè dancing, when I really get involved, there's spirit involved in there. When you're really at a Kiowa dance you feel like you're the only one out there dancing. You don't know if there is anyone dancing out there. That's what I get out of it when I dance the Jáifè dance. I don't care if there's a hundred there, I feel like I'm the only one there. There is spirit involved, spirituality involved. You can't help but think of your ancestors that carried this on, no telling how many years back there and it's still here today. I look at that and it's not a social dance. It's a ceremony.[175]

This degree of respect and reverence again suggests that the elevation of the dance is perhaps a result of the loss of the Sun and Ghost Dances as the central tribal-level integrative ceremonies. Among the Southern Cheyenne, where the dance is performed in both societal (Bow String Society) and nonsocietal (powwow) contexts, the Gourd Dance has not been elevated to the same levels as among the Kiowa and Comanche. Among the Southern Cheyenne, the Gourd Dance of the Bow String Society remains integrally connected to ensuring that the preparations necessary for the Sun Dance are completed. Cheyenne military society functions continue to be formal, yet non-public-oriented tribal events focused upon serving a larger cause, the Sun Dance. Unlike contemporary Kiowa, Comanche, and Apache military societies, Cheyenne societies do not perform large-scale dances with elaborate society dress that are, for the most part, open to the public. For the Kiowa the cessation of the Sun Dance has led to the elevation of events associated with revivals of earlier military societies or transformed manifestations of these earlier societies such as the contemporary powwow to fill the various roles of tribal-level social integration and ethnic, social, cultural, spiritual, and political community fulfilled by earlier tribal-level ceremonies.

As the popularity of the Gourd Dance continues to spread throughout the United States, some Indian and non-Indian participants have begun to "identify with the dance to the point of religious or spiritual fervor"; however, this is usually limited to the popular ideas of the dance associated with being "Indian" (Lassiter 1992:32; see also Howard 1976:255; Ellis 1990: 25–28). While the accounts of nearly forty Kiowa elders contained in the 1935 Santa Fe Laboratory notes indicate that the relationship of the military societies to the dance during their lifetime was limited to its preparational and later largely symbolic phases, the current religious characterization is increasing among many Kiowa today. As with other societies, the contemporary Kiowa Gourd Dance and songs reflect the emphasis placed upon the "importance of belief and faith in Kiowa life" (Lassiter 1992:41). By no means do all Kiowa associate this significance with the dance; the various traditions, functions, and uses of the dance produce varied meanings for individual participants. Thus, the unique relationship involved in reviving and helping to disseminate the dance has resulted in its ambiguous religious and spiritual character; its personal meaning may appear to be homogeneous but is actually heterogeneous (Lassiter 1992:42).

Much of this relationship is integrally linked and symbolized through song. The Kiowa are widely known throughout Indian country for their abilities as singers and dancers, and song and dance remain one of their primary tribal markers today. From the Kiowa viewpoint, the songs have an association and continuity that is distinctly Kiowa and cannot be claimed by others; while some form of the Gourd Dance was common to many Plains groups (Howard 1976), the twentieth-century revival of the dance and more importantly the songs was Kiowa. Although other tribes make claims to the Gourd Dance, the Kiowa openly contend with pride that Gourd Dance songs are distinctly Kiowa.[176] From the Kiowa perspective, songs are the determining factor in distinguishing cultural boundaries, which are readily pointed out when Comanche or Cheyenne sing Gourd Dance songs containing Kiowa lyrics (Lassiter 1992:44). As the twenty-fourth annual Kiowa Tia-Piah Society (1990) program points out, "Cheyennes say this is their dance, but all of the old Gourd Dance songs are Kiowa. Of course, alot [*sic*] of songs were recently composed and some by different tribes besides the Kiowas, but even today most of the Gourd Dance songs are Kiowa. The older Kiowas say that this is a Kiowa dance."

Lassiter (1992:44–45) writes: "More critical to understanding the importance of the Gourd Dance is comprehending how Kiowa people maintain a connection to their larger group of traditions through this musical repertoire." The significance of the musical origins is demonstrated by the "wolf cry" at the end of each song (also once standard in Kiowa Black Legs and Cheyenne Bow String Society songs), recognizing the gift of the dance and songs from Red Wolf (Lassiter 1992:45–46). Lassiter (1992:46) demonstrates that "through this musical enactment of traditional Kiowa mythology, Gourd Dance songs establish a link between the performers, the natural environment (the wolves), the mythological past (the Red Wolf Legend), and God" (Kiowa religion); this "creates yet another factor of what it means to be Kiowa. The enactment of the Gourd Dance songs . . . personifies the songs as seen in Spirit," which can be invoked with the appropriate singing and which is more personified in the collective performance (Lassiter 1992:46).

Songs also unite Kiowa people with their past. Memories of elders, family ancestors, and Kiowa history permeate individual and collective Gourd Dance experiences which individuals shared with me and serve as a primary foundation and function of contemporary Gourd Dances. Nearly all the individuals who discussed Gourd Dance songs with me spoke of reflecting about their elders who had performed the dance before them, of the history of the dance, of spirituality, and of having a good feeling from the "energy" and "Spirit" derived from the dance. When asked what he felt while singing Gourd Dance songs, one elder singer stated:

> There's certain songs that makes [*sic*] me feel of certain people that sang them at one time. You know, and that gives you a good feeling to really sing it hard. You know these people sang them or you heard them sing them at one time or whatever. That's the way I look at it. . . . Certain times you feel good. Well, in this arena when you see some of our older people take part it makes you feel good. You picture their fathers and mothers that were actual members, that took part all the time. You think of them and it makes you feel good sometimes when you sing some of

these songs and there's a lot of spirituality in it. You get going and it makes you feel good. On certain songs you think of some of these older people.[177]

Another elder singer stated: "To me it's a spiritual, I have a spiritual feeling. . . . The song and the spiritual aspect of it is based on their prayers and what they believe in, in their existence. It's the same in the Bible all over the world, 'make a joyful noise unto the Lord.'"[178]

Memory of Kiowa ancestors and history is an integral part of the overarching ideology and "Spirit" associated with the Gourd Dance which can be conveyed through music (Lassiter 1992:47). In a larger view, Kiowa Gourd Dance music functions as "a reminder of Kiowa perseverance [and cultural survival] throughout history" (Lassiter 1992:47). Together, the Gourd Dance music and shared heritage produce a "Spirit" that is distinctly Kiowa and forms a cultural boundary between Kiowa and non-Kiowa (Lassiter 1992:47). Song texts "affirm and transmit Kiowa identity" by specifically addressing Kiowa people and "their unique ethnic heritage" (Lassiter 1992:48).

These connotations are not limited to songs with texts. The majority of Kiowa songs sung today do not have texts.[179] Although most Kiowa do not formally distinguish between songs with and songs without texts, vocable songs (those containing no lyrics) also have histories and individual significance, which are likewise conveyed in speech and in performance. As one elder stressed, "To completely understand a song you've got to know its history in addition to the meaning of the words" (i.e., in addition to the melody and/or lyrics).[180] Vocable songs can invoke strong emotional feelings or "Spirit" just as songs with texts do. Songs sung with lyrics generally provide a more intense experience for fluent speakers, which is observable in the numbers of dancers, the intensity and duration of the singing and dancing, and sometimes the amount of honoring and giving-away in dance arenas. Thus, an understanding of the history and meaning of songs as reflected in actual behavior is stressed. As Lassiter (1992:48) states, "Understanding the texts of the songs no doubt brings individuals closer to what it means to be Kiowa" (cf. Lassiter 1995:243–334).

Lassiter (1992:48–49) also notes that "these song texts do not merely reflect about the past; they invoke several layers of belief. They open a dialogue with history and heritage; and in so doing, link past, present, and future." References to these topics in song and in the previous quotations reflect the prevalence of this interlinked ideology, which in turn reflects the lengthy persistence and not resistance of the Kiowa people. Once associated with a select men's military society, the Gourd Dance has taken on "new functions and uses" through time; the songs have played a major role in the transformation (Lassiter 1992:55). The cultural, religious, and symbolic character of the dance and music, with its associated song texts, reinforces a unique Kiowa heritage; Lassiter (1992:56) asserts that Kiowa people stress that this is integral "in what it means to be Kiowa in modern America."

Diachronically, the Gourd Dance reflects Ortner's (1973) "summarizing and "elaborating" symbols (Lassiter 1992:56). Symbolically, the dance exemplifies the ethnic and cultural evolution and persistence of the Kiowa. "The Gourd Dance is clearly a powerful symbol of the Kiowa struggle to be Kiowa in American society" (Lassiter 1992:56). Beyond serving as socio-cultural-religious symbols of Kiowa history, the songs remain an active, growing, and adapting cultural form which links past and present and are not merely a symbolic relic of the past. As a performance in the participation of "Spirit," the Gourd Dance gives meaning to contemporary Kiowa life and serves as one form of rejuvenating Kiowa Spirit (Lassiter 1992:56–57), similar to the Sun Dance.

However, a complex combination of circumstances and a procedure which Lassiter (1992:57) refers to as "dialogue" must be reached in order for Spirit to form completely.

Through the Gourd Dance, Spirit invokes a dialogue between song, dance, and the Kiowa people. From the musical center, the songs increase this multi-layered dialogue to encompass the mythological past, the natural and cultural environment, and God. Furthermore, in the core of the music itself, we find that the song texts, as a set-apart and sacred entity, augment the dialogue further to include, through language, the incarnation of a selected group of traditions that express a vital history important to the Kiowas. That is, being a symbol of Kiowa cultural survival and continuity, song texts explicitly and precisely affirm and transmit Kiowa traditions and heritage. Yet, while song texts make a unique ethnic heritage specific, as a contemporary container of language, the Gourd Dance transforms to become a forum for negotiation in an ever-changing dialogue about the retention of Kiowa language and culture within the Kiowa community. Thus, the Spirit of the Dance is a complex dialogue between all aspects of the Gourd Dance: past (historical and mythological), and future, human and environment (natural and cultural), human and God, dance and song, song and text.

The continual role of Gourd Dance songs in maintaining Kiowa identity has also been transplanted by Kiowa who have relocated to urban contexts.

I was able to attend Gourd Dances sponsored by the Colorado Tia-Piah Society in Denver, Colorado (1995–1997). While the society's leaders, and often many of the singers, are Kiowa, the majority of members are non-Kiowa tribes and non-Indians. Yet the continued emphasis on the history of the society, remembrance of elders, and the importance of the dance and songs from a Kiowa perspective and of having a good time were all visible. Every dance I attended contained a portion where one of the society Kiowa leaders addressed all in attendance, discussing the martial origins of the society, the society trophies, that "the dance was not a powwow but a ceremonial dance originating from the Tia-Piah warrior society," Kiowa military societies and their functions, that "the dance commemorated a fight the Kiowas were in" and that "even though the dance was given by Red Wolf, it is still a God-given thing," and the importance of the dance and songs for Kiowa people. Although these dances are qualitatively different from Gourd Dances in the Kiowa home community, they still emanate distinctly Kiowa qualities of ethnicity and "Spirit" for Kiowa in Colorado.

Many non-Indian Gourd Dances lack this dialogue, which must be in its fullest form for the "Spirit" to be present. The Fourth of July Kiowa Gourd Dances remain the occasions where this dialogue and "Spirit," in its most complete form, can occur naturally and easily. Dances outside of the Kiowa community are complicated by the problems created by a lack of understanding of the full significance of the dance and fluency in the Kiowa language. However, even when performed elsewhere, the contemporary Gourd Dance emanates a uniquely Kiowa quality or Spirit (Lassiter 1992:58–63).[181]

The Gourd Dance is only one arena in a larger Kiowa and Plains Indian lifestyle involving what it means to be Kiowa. Participation in activities including other society dances, powwows, sweatlodges, handgames, the Native American Church, Christian churches, softball leagues, and bingo constitutes the core of cultural life for various segments of the Kiowa population. The Gourd Dance is a significant arena because it addresses the ideology integral to the maintenance of earlier Kiowa ethnic identity as described by Kracht (1989) and Lassiter (1992, 1995). The dialogue between culture and belief in the dance becomes more and more ambiguous and heterogeneous in modern Kiowa society the further one gets from the associated song texts and the people who understand them (Lassiter 1992:63). As such, songs serve as a "reference point" which allows the specificity of Kiowa identity despite diffusion and participation by others (Lassiter 1992:63). Direct participation in Kiowa community celebrations, including the Gourd Dance, and in the "Spirit" of the dance (with an emphasis on maintaining tradition and the appreciative commemoration of what earlier generations of Kiowa provided) is a major part of how people defined to me what it means to be Kiowa. As Anne Yeahquo, a young Kiowa woman who dances every Fourth of July at the Kiowa Gourd Clan celebrations, stated: "During that last song [the last Gourd Dance song], when all the men are dancing hard, everyone is dancing so hard, and the women's shawls are swinging, and all that money is being put on the ground [given-away]. Then I can imagine the past and what it was like for the old people way back there in the buffalo days. That's what it means to be Kiowa." [182]

The Kiowa Black Legs

Although the Kiowa Gourd Clan still contains many martial themes associated with the earlier Jáifègàu Society, those of the Kiowa Black Legs Society are more visible. While the Gourd Clan initially emphasized honoring and recognizing veterans, which it continues to this day, there is a greater emphasis on Jáifègàu traditions and on promoting and maintaining Kiowa ethnicity and culture as a whole. This is largely because the revival of the Black Legs, with their explicit veteran status, Kiowa tribal enrolled membership requirement, and ceremonial emphasis on martial ideologies, absorbed most of the martial expression for the Kiowa tribe. The Gourd Clan and other Kiowa Gourd Dance societies do not require veteran status for membership and permit varying degrees of intertribal and non-Indian participation. Due to their rigid membership requirements and martial focus, the Kiowa Black Legs have remained a smaller, but distinct cultural entity.

As the most visible post–World War II arena of Kiowa martial ethos, the Kiowa Black Legs Society activities are replete with martial themes.[183] The Black Legs ceremony contains numerous sociocultural forms which reflect the continued emphasis upon recognizing and honoring veterans, as well as the ability of military sodalities to serve as enculturative arenas for a variety of sociocultural forms. Continuing prereservation mourning practices, the society sponsors a feast for the families of recently deceased members prior to their twice annual ceremonials. Society members and their families are prayed for and "cedared" (incensed with burning cedar) before eating and socializing.

Each afternoon of the twice annual weekend ceremonials begins with an invocational prayer followed by the Kiowa Flag Song (Tháikáuóltádàugà). Next the two society processional songs are sung. During these songs a processional of Black Legs Society color guards carrying the flags of the United States, the Kiowa Tribe, and the four United States military branches is followed by the society princesses, women wearing the Màunkàugúlhòldà (Red

Sleeve Dress) or "Victory Dress," followed by the Kiowa women's auxiliary societies, the Kiowa Veterans Auxiliary, the Kiowa War Mothers, the Kiowa Warrior Descendants, and the Carnegie Victory Club. Serving as a theme song for the society, the first processional song reflects on the community's elation at the return of their servicemen:

1. Jó-gú-dáu thá-gà yán tén-xò-dàu-dò
   (Young men/good/you/permitted or allowed-because)
   Because you are privileged to be fine young men.

2. Thá-gài dáut âui-chàn-dò
   (Good/you all plural [for us embodied]/again-returned-because)
   Because they all returned [to us] in good condition.[184]

The second song instructs the veterans to enjoy their day and to dance in happiness:

1. Jó-gúl-ǫ-gòp á dáu-dò,
   (Young men/highly regarded/they/are-because)
   Because they are highly regarded young men.

   Ám-kì-dà báu dáu-dò
   (*You*/day/you all/is-are) [Ám denotes emphasis]
   Because it is *your* day.

2. Jó-gúl-ǫ-gòp á dáu-dò, Ám-kì-dà báu dáu-dò

3. Jó-gúl-ǫ-gòp á dáu-dò, Ám-kì-dà báu dáu-dò

4. Jó-gúl-ǫ-gòp á dáu-dò, Bé ǫ-tá-gùn
   (You and we all/feel good/dance)
   Dance in joy-happiness (appreciation).

5. Ám-kì-dà báu dáu-dò, Bé ǫ-tá-gùn

6. Jó-gúl-ǫ-gòp á dáu-dò, Ám-kì-dà báu dáu-dò

1. Jó-gúl-ǫ-gòp á dáu-dò, Bé ǫ-tá-gùn

2. Ám-kì-dà báu dáu-dò, Bé ǫ-tá-gùn

3. Jó-gúl-ǫ-gòp á dáu-dò, Ám-kì-dà báu dáu-dò.[185]

Color guards proceed to the center of the arena, while the remaining processional continues around the arena.

Two Memorial Songs (Câifègàudằugà or War Dead Songs) are sung next, during which all remain standing. At the start of the first song, the names of all Kiowa killed in action in the twentieth century, beginning with World War II and concluding with Vietnam, are read over the public address system. The second Memorial Song, which is used by both the Kiowa War Mothers and the Black Legs Society, was composed by Louis Toyebo in memory of Lyndreth Palmer, the first Kiowa killed in modern warfare on December 5, 1944, and tells the parents of the recently deceased soldier to be proud of their son's contribution.

1. Dấu-gá èm thâu-yì-thầu
   (Song/you/hear-shall continuatively)
   When you shall hear this song.

2. Ém ọ̀-tạ́-yì-thầu nàu
   (You/good feeling/shall be/and)
   You shall be feeling good.

3. Á-í câi-hèm nàu gà sấu-mí
   (Your-son/fighting-died/and/it is/noteworthy, amazing, or prominent)
   Your son died fighting and it's noteworthy.

4. Dấu-gá èm thâu-yì-thầu

5. Ém ọ̀-tạ́-yì-thầu nàu

6. Jó-gúl câi-hèm nàu gà sấu-mí.
   (Young man/fighting-died/and/it is/noteworthy, amazing, or prominent)
   A young man died fighting and it's noteworthy.[186]

After posting the colors the men exit the arena and enter the society tipi, while the women's part of the program begins with clockwise Round Dances to the War Mothers' songs. Inside the tipi the men offer prayers and are "cedared" before dancing. Commander Gus Palmer Sr. addresses the society, emphasizing the importance of retaining its unity and the need to "keep it up." He stresses that the unity demonstrated in military service should be continued upon returning to their homes and tribe by teaching others to work together and stay together as they did while serving in the military. These dances are clearly linked to past warrior ideology as well as to contemporary aspects of maintaining tribal and individual Kiowa ethnicity. As

Palmer emphasized to me, "As veterans they fought for their land and their people, and therefore each dance is like a homecoming for veterans. Therefore they should work together and stay together. Then they can feel good about coming out to celebrate and enjoy the songs and dances that were performed before this part of the country was opened up."[187]

As in many Plains populations, Kiowa women danced Scalp and Victory Dances upon the safe return of all members of a war party to honor their returning warriors, and this tradition continues today. As in the past, the women always dance before the men on such occasions. Before entering the society lodge, the men stick their lances upright into the ground beside the lodge. A set of War Mothers' Songs is sung, to which the women Round-Dance. Following this, a set of Áuldáucúndàugà (Scalp Dance Songs) begins; women take the lances of one of their relatives and begin to perform the Scalp Dance (Áuldáucúngà). Each man's lance is decorated with the individual accomplishments and style of the owner. In memory of her brother killed in battle, one woman dances with a staff containing several long feathers suspended along the shaft to represent the battles in which he fought, while a cluster of several shorter feathers at the top represent the number of enemy he personally killed in battle. During the fall dance, women may wear the four society bonnets to dance in honor of relative society members. Today women frequently wear military insignia, listings of their relatives' names and honors, and even relatives' medals displayed on the backs of their shawls. Next the women line up with the men's lances for the Victory Dance.

It is during these dances that the women's most integral role in the traditional military complex—honoring and recognizing warriors—is performed. During the Scalp and Victory Dances the arena belongs to the women, and men are not allowed to enter. During these dances and throughout the remainder of the afternoon women frequently wear the Màunkàugúlhòldà (Red Sleeve Dress), red and blue or red and black cloth dresses which are frequently referred to as "Victory Dresses." One Kiowa woman poignantly described the importance of these dresses and of the women's role in recognizing and honoring the veterans' sacrifice and maintaining the tradition of Kiowa warriors:

When you go and dance at Black Legs there's a reason for you to be there. I mean it isn't anything to play with. It is a sincere heartfelt emotion, that's what brings me to Black Legs. You know this country that we live in, the way of life that we have here, to me it's important. It's important because there were so many of our men who were willing to leave. You know they were like those old Kiowas, they were willing to leave their camp, they were willing to leave the safety of their homes. Some of them died, some of them were disfigured, some of them maybe a physical disfigurement, some of them maybe an emotional disfigurement. There was a large price of blood paid for our freedom. So when you go to Black Legs you're honoring those men and their sacrifice and that's why it's important when you go that you understand why. It isn't something [the time] to go, "Oh gee whiz, don't I look keen," you know, that has no place at Black Legs. So when you go and you take part there is a way for you to dress if you really feel strongly about Black Legs and that's where you dress a certain way. To me that's where you dress in that Màunkàugúl, that battle dress. To me that's the time for the coup marks on the leggings, that's the time for the woman to carry out that lance and dance with it because it honors that veteran. That's the one place where no man can come into that arena. You know that's the time for that woman and it's her responsibility to take care of things in a certain way.

With Kiowas there are certain things that men only can take care of and over here there are certain obligations and responsibilities—those are just for women, a man can't come in and take care of them. And so for me personally I see it as a woman's responsibility to take care of things the right way. You get everything ready. . . . If you're not going to have a dance for him you have a singing for him, you know, because these men are willing to go off and they are willing to fight for your right to enjoy liberty and to enjoy the pleasures that you have here. These are like those old-time warriors that were willing to leave their camp while you're here and you're safe, they're trying to preserve a way of life for you. Maybe it's not the ponies and the buffalo and the hunting era, but it's the, in a sense it's like that because you can sit here and enjoy ESPN, you can enjoy the basketball game, you can enjoy whatever you want, you can go to a movie, I mean you don't have to worry about your liberties being taken away from you. Which for me is why I take part in Black Legs, you know, because I never knew what it was like to face enemy fire. I never knew what it was like to crawl over my dead buddy's body. I never knew what it was like to jump off the back of a boat on some beach that was land-mined. You know there's so many of my uncles that had that. You know I've got a grandfather who survived the Bataan Death March. I have another grandfather who was at Bataan and he lost an arm. I have an uncle Lyndreth who was killed and he's buried in France you know . . . and these men never had a chance, well maybe they had a chance, but they chose to go instead of staying home. . . .

My great-grandma had a Màunkàugúl and it was made from a captured flag and it had bullet holes in the flag and so when they [the veter-
ans] brought it back to my great-grandma, it was a battle trophy, and how
else could a woman honor that battle deed, you know a man can't—it's
not proper for a man to brag on himself so as a woman that was something that was important to my great-grandma. . . . It was like World
War I . . . in this century which is interesting you know because it's still a
carryover, a holdover of an attitude of the free days. You know they've
just updated it and brought it into this century. It still fits with that idea
of Kiowas being warriors.[188]

Upon the conclusion of the women's Victory Dances, the men, having
finished their prayer and purification inside the tipi, exit and gather their
lances in preparation for their processional or parade-in (kátgà). Today there
are several kinds of dances performed by the society. Led by the society
leaders and princesses, the society starts the two Chátqâutèldàugà (literally
Door Cut Open Songs or Opening-Dedication Songs), which the society
members sing together as they parade in. The second song ends with a
group yell and then the members plant their lances in front of them and are
seated. These Opening Songs represent the opening of the ceremony, similar to the opening of a tipi without a door by taking a knife and cutting open
a door from within. This song is directly related to the practice of the q̓ajái-
sàupàn (top warriors), who sang four Chátqâutèldàugà, danced, and then
recited war deeds at the beginning of the Sun Dance, before placing a stone
at the entrance of the Sun Dance Lodge.[189]

The next two songs, called Yáuldáudàugà (Excite or Stirring Emotions
to Action Songs), represent the overwhelming joy and enthusiasm felt upon
the warriors' return. The name of these two songs and dances is derived
from the imperative verb yául-àum, to excite or stir to action, and the verb
yául-jàu, to carry on with wild behavior, and denotes the fervent display of
emotions at their return. The dancers are seated following these two songs,
then they arise and continue with the Émhâcùn (Arise and Dance [in Place])
dances, dancing in place in front of their planted lances, with their hands
closed and held near chest level while keeping time with the music. This
dance resembles the practice of some warriors who danced in front of their
enemies prior to battle, showing their willingness to stand their ground and
to fight without weapons if necessary. The choreography consists of bouncing in place interspersed with small forward steps and is similar to Gourd
Dancing (Richardson n.d.).[190] Throughout the afternoon women frequently
dance in place along the outer edge of the arena, entering the arena only

to honor an individual or to take part in a family song. At this time the society leader, Gus Palmer Sr., addresses the crowd, welcoming all in attendance and relating various aspects of Kiowa military history. In particular he stresses the sacrifice that veterans have made to ensure the freedoms enjoyed today and the need to honor, uphold, and recognize veterans. He also regularly names all of the prereservation Kiowa military societies, briefly discussing their functions and relationship to one another.

During the next type of songs and dance, society members pick up their lances and begin to dance with their lances held point down, while keeping time with the music. The momentum of the music and dancing increases as the dancing continues throughout the afternoon. The following song describing how the community looks upon the society veterans in honor as they dance is a favorite during this part of the ceremony.

1. Tǫ̀-kǫ́-gáut jɛ́ bé-hâ gàu
   (Legs-Black-members/all/you-arise/and)
   Black Legs members arise—get up and

2. Hét bé gûn-jàu
   (Let/us/dance-shall)
   Let us dance.

3. Nàu báu sáum-bǫ̀-jàu
   (And/they-us/look upon-shall)
   And they shall look upon us.

4. Jó-gúl-ǫ̀-gòp á dáu
   (Young men-outstanding/they/in a state of)
   They are outstanding young men.[191]

This may be followed by induction of new members, historical accounts, giveaways, or naming ceremonies. On October 6, 1990, an "Empty Saddle" ceremony was held in which a saddled horse was paraded around the arena, without a rider, symbolizing those warriors who were killed in combat and did not return. Memorial Songs (Câîfègàudàugà, War Dead Songs) were sung, speeches by the deceased veteran's relatives and friends were made, and horses were given away. Induction of new members begins with citation of their military records; then they are taken out to dance with the entire society to the society induction song. Members lend the initiates their lances to dance with, while relatives give-away for the initiates by placing shawls and blankets on their backs. Other forms of "honoring" veterans such as

giving away cash, blankets, shawls, or other goods at the feet of a dancer also
occur during regular society songs.[192]

Continuing an emphasis on traditional forms of honoring veterans, a set
of Tǫ́sódêcùngà (Feet Crossing Over or Shuffle Dance), which was performed by returning warriors and reportedly belonged only to the Black
Legs Society, is performed. The United States flag is retired during the latter portions of the afternoon dancing, with different Kiowa veterans selected to perform the flag retreat.[193] Many songs have been composed describing Kiowa military service and the various battles in which the United
States flag has been carried. The society has at least two Flag Songs which
are used when lowering the colors, which convey the great respect for the
United States flag and its role in military actions.

1. Thǎi-káu-ól-tâ-gàu thá-gài mài bét hâ-fî-gǜ
   (Flag/good-careful/upward/you all/be raising)
   Be raising the flag carefully [with respect].

2. Jé-dàum-tái è câi-jàu-tǒ-yà
   (All over the world/it/been involved in fighting-all over)
   It has been involved in wars all over the world.

3. Jé-dàum-tái ét câi-bà-jàu-dò
   (All over the world/it is/to be respecting-because or for)
   Because it is respected all over the world.

4. Ấu-gàu-tâu vấu + qấu-chȩ̀-àl è só-lè-dè
   (Up yonder/moon/is positioned also/it/soldier-standing).
   Even on the moon it is standing at attention like a soldier.[194]

The most martially visual type of dance, the Xàkóigácùngà (Turn Around
or Reverse Dance) is performed only as the last dance on the second day of
the fall ceremonial. It represents a series of reversals and counterattacks or
charges back into battle and reportedly originated from a battle in Texas in
the 1830s, in which a group of Tǫ̀kǫ́gàut were outnumbered (Bantista n.d.:
33). In the past, this dance was performed only by the Tǫ̀kǫ́gàut and Ál-
jóyî̀gàu Societies. During the first song members dance in place just in front
of the benches and adjust and secure their dress as if prior to entering a
battle. At this time, the leaders take off their roaches and put on the four
eagle-feather war bonnets; the society leader wears the only bonnet with a
long trailer. The leaders carry carbine rifles, while some younger members
carry automatic rifles.

There is no pause between the first and second songs, only a change in the music, at which time the society forms a single-file line on the south and west sides of the circular arena facing north or clockwise. There are four positions of importance during the Xàkóigácùngà, which were traditionally filled by the four society leaders. The society commander Gus Palmer heads the line, while a second leader is chosen to take the end position. On the outside of this line is a third leader, while the fourth leader is situated on the inside of the line of men. The choreography of the Xàkóigácùngà is very simple; the line of men begins to dance in a clockwise direction on the west side of the arena. The outside man likewise proceeds clockwise around the arena, while the inside man proceeds counterclockwise. The direction of these two men does not change during the dance. When the inside and outside men meet, the society members (as a line) raise their lances, shoot off guns, give war hoops, and reverse their direction. This process is repeated every time the two men complete their circuit around the arena and meet, thus causing the line to reverse its direction, while the inside and outside men both continue in their original directions. Upon the firing of the guns, the members are traditionally supposed to howl like a wolf. The music progressively increases to an incredibly rapid pace and the guns are fired more frequently as the dance progresses.[195]

This dance cannot stop until a combat veteran stops the drum by placing his lance across it. He is then required to recite a personal war deed or combat experience (qóit̮áujétjàu). This veteran stops the drum because he "feels sorry for the men" (dancers). One such recitation of a war deed was performed in 1991 by Rueben Topaum, a sniper in Darby's Rangers in World War II and a recipient of two Purple Hearts, who still carries a German bullet near his heart. He recited how an enemy sniper held his unit under fire and killed two of his fellow soldiers. In the snipers' duel which followed, Topaum was severely wounded; thinking he had his third confirmed kill, the German sniper concentrated his efforts elsewhere. Though wounded, Topaum managed to pull himself back up on the line and sight in on the sniper's fire, whereupon he shot the German sniper out of a tree, killing him. Upon completing the recitation of the combat action, the singers struck the drum hard several times, with everyone shouting words of encouragement in Kiowa while the women ululated (sáuàuljò̱gà). Another recitation, given in the fall of 1990 by Larry Kaulaity, a Vietnam War veteran, told how he and his unit threw grenades to clear out an enemy bunker, while pinned down under fire.[196] After the recitation of a war deed is completed, the afternoon concludes around 6:00 P.M. with an evening prayer, followed by a dinner break as groups congregate throughout the various campsites surrounding the dance grounds. Following dinner, a session of Gourd Dancing, followed by a session of social and War Dancing, is sponsored by the Kiowa Gourd Clan and the Kiowa Ohoma Lodge respectively, who serve as co-host organizations.

Current Functions

The functions and martial ethos of the current Tǫ́kǫ́gàut closely resemble those of earlier days. Since its revival in 1958, the organization is undeniably a veterans' organization which continues to enhance the past military exploits of its members in song and dance, while performing duties on behalf of the Kiowa community as a whole. The society recognizes and celebrates all past and present Kiowa veterans who have served their country, tribe, and family.

In Kiowa tradition, the Black Legs society provides rations for each camp within the encampment and feasts for all in attendance. When a member dies, the society sends flowers and groceries to the family's home. A contingent of society members attends the funeral of every society brother and performs the graveside singing of the Black Legs Society Honor and War Dead (Câifègàudàugà) or Funeral Songs, which clearly illustrates that many of the traditional values associated with the role of the warrior-veteran in Kiowa culture continue to the present.

1. Cáui-jò-gù-dàu è qá-jái-dàu-gàu
   (Kiowa/young men/they [are]/warriors/and)
   Kiowa young men, they are warriors [have been to battle] and

2. Bé qá̰-hí-tà̰u-jè-báu-dà
   (You/manlike [he-man]/news/appears–comes about)
   You hear news [literally he-man stories] about them.

3. Á qá-jái-dàu-gàu chól-hằu á ó-báui-hè-mà.
   (They/warriors/and/that's the way/they/really do die)
   They are warriors and that's the way they really die.[197]

The Black Legs Society also holds an annual Christmas fellowship meeting in December, which includes the singing of Kiowa hymns and the viewing of videotaped society dances. The society also frequently provides a color guard for various events across the state such as the Red Earth festival, religious and sovereignty conferences, and Indian educational events.[198]

Despite numerous changes and adaptations, the Black Legs have continued many of their former traditions. Changes in leadership positions have occurred, yet the functions and symbols associated with these officers continue to reflect Kiowa and Tòk̓ógàut cultural traditions. The society still provides an opportunity for Kiowa veterans to come together, dance, sing, and celebrate their individual and collective military service and accomplishments, while performing duties on behalf of the community as a whole. The society continues to sponsor feasts for all in attendance. Giveaways still honor and recognize individuals, while redistributing goods to individuals. The society has retained many of the prereservation symbols (staff, whips, leadership positions, oral history, dances, songs), which, despite limited modernizations and adaptations, function in traditional ways. With the decline of other prereservation Kiowa societies, the Black Legs Society symbolizes and defines what it means to be a warrior or veteran for many Kiowa. The society holds a number of weekly preparatory meetings for each dance, similar to the series of society organizational meetings during the Sun Dance. Likewise, traditional mourning practices are continued before each dance, with cedaring and food for the families who have recently lost members.

The requirement of war honors for Black Legs Society membership in the 1800s (Levy n.d.a) has been revived, although veteran status was unavailable and apparently waived from 1912 to 1927. While various types of modernization have been adapted by the society under social and cultural pressures, they are generally in the peripheral structure. The core elements and ideology on which the society and Plains warrior societies in general were based have remained largely the same or in some instances have been revived.

The Black Legs society exemplifies the spirit of Kiowa military ideology and the cultural forms associated with this genre. The society has continued to function as an adaptive form of social organization and as a vehicle for Kiowa enculturation by integrating various Kiowa traditions into a single sodality's functions (veterans' ceremonies and recognition, community service, naming ceremonies, mourning and purification rituals, song and dance, camping, feasting, social dances, socializing, language, oral history, and kinship retention). Although many current Kiowa Gourd Dance and Black Legs Society songs are new forms of older songs (changed melodies or new texts added to old melodies) or newly composed songs (postrevival), they are similar to ancestral themes and forms. While many of these cultural forms could be conducted in other types of social gatherings, they are not found in such variety or quantity there, which reflects the role of Kiowa sodalities in integrating these varied forms. A sodality facilitates social integration on

a level larger than that permitted by kin-based groups. Because military societies continue to be the largest form of Kiowa sodality, they are in the
position to integrate varied social forms and to adapt temporally. The continued Kiowa emphasis on recognizing their martial ideology and history
and on honoring past and present veterans provides a primary arena for
cultural continuity. Based upon traditional concepts and focusing upon society symbols, the military society maintains tribal traditions. As a sodality-
based structure, it functions as an adaptive social form, acting as an enculturative tool through which other cultural forms are integrated and thereby
continued.

THE ROLE OF CURRENT KIOWA SOCIETIES
Integration

Contemporary Kiowa sodalities are truly pan-Kiowa, pantribal, and in
some cases, intertribal; although the majority of the political power within
a society may be held by one or more core families, Kiowa from all local
communities and abroad participate. Thus, societies perform integrative
functions on a number of levels. Because Kiowa societies cross-cut family
and descendants' groups, they provide a further-reaching and greater degree
of social, kin, economic, and cultural integration than other cultural forms
can. Today Kiowa military societies and their outgrowths in the forms of
dance or powwow clubs are the largest sodalities within the tribe. Although
there is no official single Kiowa tribal gathering, these societies provide the
largest tribal-level ceremonies and aggregations at their respective annual
encampments.

Although multiple Kiowa Gourd and War Dance groups exist, they are
beneficial because they integrate significant segments of the tribal community, which in turn are frequently integrated through the continual co-
hosting of societies. Because the dates of most society preparational meetings and ceremonials do not overlap (Black Legs in May and October,
Gourd Clan on July 4, and Óhòmò in late July), they provide large-scale
integrative cultural events throughout much of the year. This promotes further socioeconomic cooperation with competition for limited resources and
followers, while promoting Kiowa enculturation.

Military societies and their outgrowths constitute nearly all Kiowa dance
activities. All Kiowa dances center around some military society function or
dances which originated from these men's and women's societies (Gourd,
War, Round, or War Mothers' Dances). These dances constitute the ma-

jority of the program of nearly every annual society ceremonial and club, memorial, family, descendants' group, and benefit dance, with Gourd, War, and Round Dancing the most prevalent. Dances thus provide socio-cultural integration for all Kiowa interested in participating in society and non-society-oriented dances.

Contemporary Kiowa military society dances of the Black Legs, Gourd Clan, Óhòmò, and Rabbits are replete with martially based ideology and symbols which reinforce traditional Kiowa concepts of honoring veterans and their heritage. Songs, dances, staffs, whips, women's Victory Dresses, and distinct ritual and ideology all provide forms of prereservation Kiowa emphasis on a warrior ideology. Most Kiowa I spoke with, even members of other societies, agreed that, while all societies honor veterans to some extent, the Black Legs Society honors contemporary veterans the most. As one Kiowa woman described the role of the Black Legs:

> I think it is Black Leggins. The reason why I say this is because the societies from way back were, you know how it was, the little boys were prepared because eventually they were going to be teenagers and they're going to be young men and probably way back in the old days they went out on the raiding parties very young you know, so they had to have that teaching and that experience and I feel like because the Black Leggins is really a warrior society, and it's all, you know, you have to qualify by being a veteran and then the other qualification is that you have to be enrolled Kiowa, you know with Kiowa descendancy. So when you go out there just every one of them out there are veterans and they're the only ones that are just right there in the heart of the circle. . . .[199]

While this ideology is most viable in the contemporary Black Legs Society, it is nonetheless present in the other Kiowa societies. Despite numerous innovations, traditional Kiowa ways of honoring veterans and the views associated with their lengthy prereservation military history, later veterans, and contemporary military service continue in a syncretic form similar to earlier traditional forms.

During Operation Desert Storm I was able to observe the daily responses to the war of the Kiowa and neighboring tribal communities: prayer meetings, decoration of towns and highways with patriotic banners, parades, numerous dances for outgoing and returning servicemen and women, and daily conversation centered around the most recent events in the war.[200] On January 22, 1991, the Black Legs Society took part in a rally supporting Operation Desert Shield and the United States participation in the Persian Gulf War. The Chief's Song (Qájáidàugà) was played at the 1991 July ceremonial for the induction of four returning veterans of Operation Desert Storm, reflecting the martial ideologies on which the Óhọ̀mò Society was originally based. Wearing their uniforms and eagle-feather bonnets, these veterans were led in a processional around the arena. Numerous shawls and blankets were placed at their feet to be given away, after which each veteran was asked to speak about his tour of service in the war. Led by these four veterans, another processional followed as a Victory Song was sung. Similarly, returning veterans were honored, asked to speak of their experiences overseas, and inducted into the Black Legs Society on October 13, 1991. As reflected in these societies, the response of the Kiowa community was an observable shift from regular activities to those focused upon the war—a shift from a martial-based ideology to an elevated level of martial ethos.

Numerous send-offs, powwows, and rallies were held for incoming and outgoing servicemen and women during Operation Desert Storm. New songs were composed for returning veterans on both an individual and collective basis. The "Desert Storm Song," composed by Leonard Cozad Sr., reflects the Kiowa community's rejoicing at the return of their veterans:

1. Háun-dé-ọ́-dé jọ́-fè dàut aûi-chàn; jó-gú̄-ọ́-góp
   (How wonderful/to home/they/again-returned/young men-outstanding)
   How wonderful [it is], the outstanding young men returned home again.

2. Jé gà thá̄-gà
   (All or everything/it is/good or all right)
   Everything is good.[201]

Cozad composed another Desert Storm song when the war ended. The words to this song, known as the "Appreciation Song," concisely describe the Kiowa community's appreciation for the end of the war and the men's return:

1. Jé gà thá̄-gà; jé gà ọ́
   (All/it is/good or of good quality or all right; all or everyone/it is/happy or feeling good about).
   Everything is good, all right; everyone is happy [feeling good].[202]

Tribal and societal identification and maintenance of ethnicity are fostered through culturally distinct dance societies which exhibit unique symbol systems of Kiowa and individual society identification through song, dance, dress, insignia, and rituals, many with historical connections to nineteenth-century warrior-based themes. Each society contains various levels of symbols and meaning that, while distinct from one another, follow earlier Kiowa military society patterns. The increasing visibility of tribal, martial, and societal pride is conveyed by numerous recent symbolic forms such as the Kiowa tribal logo depicting an armed warrior on horseback donning a cape (perhaps symbolic of the current Black Legs Society), which is printed on various T-shirts, jackets, official tribal stationery, and many other items.

Enculturation

Many Kiowa describe the Kiowa Black Legs, the Kiowa Gourd Clan, and the Ohoma Lodge as conservatives, which is reflected by the families involved in their revivals and the societies' continuation of Kiowa cultural traditions. Military societies provide a significant arena for furthering Kiowa culture and history, by providing opportunities for the maintenance of language, song, dance, ceremony, history, kinship, ethnicity, economic redistribution, and socialization. Many of these features are conveyed through use of traditional martial symbols associated with Kiowa societies. The societies now often include more modern cultural features such as cedaring (since the 1960s), which used to be performed on a more family-based level, sign language performances of the Lord's Prayer and various songs, and a color guard for various Indian and non-Indian events.

Almost all large-scale Kiowa events held today involve participation of at least a segment of one of the current societies. As cultural leaders, officers and prominent members of military societies generally have high status and are frequently sought to serve in other tribal capacities such as tribal governmental offices, to conduct Peyote meetings and naming ceremonies, to cedar and pray for people, or to provide invocational prayers, blessings, or historical or memorial speeches at cultural events. A program for a recent traveling exhibit of drawings by Silverhorn (1860–1940) at the Kiowa Tribal Complex, for example, included the prayer by the commander of the Black Legs Society, Gus Palmer Sr., Gourd Dance Songs sung by the "Tia-peah-ga," and a Rabbit Dance held for the children—three of the four major current Kiowa societies.[203]

As the origin of the post–World War II Southern Plains military society revivals, Kiowa societies have established and maintained a dominant position in the Southern Plains military society and powwow community, as demonstrated by the revival and spread of the Gourd Dance, the significant influence of Kiowa dances upon the larger powwow circuit, and the frequent use of Kiowa singers, songs, dances, and head staff at various tribal and intertribal events. An exhibit at the Oklahoma Museum of Natural History in 1989–1990 featuring Kiowa dance clothing made during Works Progress Administration projects in 1939 to 1942 was entitled "Dancing to Remember." The extent of Kiowa influences upon other tribes has even been noticed by anthropologists conducting fieldwork among neighboring tribes, who acknowledged that the Kiowa dominate the Southern Plains powwow circuit (Gelo 1986:186). As large organizations, Kiowa military societies are well known throughout Indian country and have attracted a lot of attention, recognition, and, in some instances, disdain and jealousy from other tribes. Kiowa frequently state that they were "born to dance," and song and dance are clearly one of their strongest markers in the Indian and non-Indian community today, as demonstrated by the number of Kiowa serving as head staff at various Indian and non-Indian powwows and the number of successful Kiowa singers and dancers in contests, cultural demonstrations, and Indian recordings. Powwows continue to reflect Kiowa pride in their heritage and provide a strong link with their past.

The consciousness of the earlier Kiowa warrior tradition and associated symbols (songs, dances, dress, societal kinship, respect, honoring of veterans, cedaring, sense of community, cooperation) attached to these values remain a vital and adaptive part of contemporary Kiowa culture. Many of these cultural elements are promoted through the enculturative features of contemporary Kiowa military and dance societies. Each society contains a number of distinct but generally similar symbols and functions as a larger symbol in itself. Thus, Kiowa societies continue to serve as visible cultural manifestations fostering a martial tradition which serve as enculturative agents for the continuation of numerous Kiowa cultural forms.

4 PLAINS APACHE NAISHAN MILITARY SOCIETIES

Throughout Southern Plains history, the Naishan or Naishan Dene (commonly known in historical literature as the Kiowa-Apache and officially known now as the Apache Tribe of Oklahoma) have been historically and ethnographically overshadowed by their larger neighbors the Kiowa and Comanche. This chapter establishes the development, functions, organization, and integrative roles of nineteenth- and twentieth-century Apache military societies in comparison with surrounding Plains tribes.

THE APACHE

The use of the name "Kiowa-Apache" to refer to the Naishan developed in the late nineteenth century. W. P. Clark (1982:230) first mentioned the Apache position in the Kiowa camp circle as the "Apache Kiowa band" in 1885 and later (1982:355) referred to the "Kiowa Apache," in listing their military societies. Use of the ethnonym "Kiowa-Apache" for the Plains Apache became common after the works of Mooney (1898, 1907). The people known to Anglos as the "Kiowa-Apache" refer to themselves as *Naishan* or *Naishan Dene*, roughly translated to mean "Our People" (Mooney 1898:245–246, 1912c; Swanton 1952:296). Some Apache elders I interviewed translated this name as "Those Who Carry or Transport Things About" or "Stealers" in reference to widespread Plains raiding activities. The Apache also refer to themselves as *Khat-tleen-deh* (Cedar People) and *Bay-cah-yeh* (Whetstone People). In the nineteenth century the Apache were most commonly known to other tribes in name and sign language as Whetstone People (Mooney 1898:245–246, 1912c; Swanton 1952:296; Clark 1982:33).[1] The Naishan are also frequently referred to in the literature as the "Plains Apache" to distinguish them from other southwestern United States Apachean groups. Today the officially recognized political and governmental name for this group is the Apache Tribe of Oklahoma; with the exception of quoted materials, they are referred to here as Naishan or simply as Apache, as my consultants stated they prefer.[2]

ORIGINS, LANGUAGE, ETHNONYMS, AND EARLY HISTORY
Origins and Language

The origins of the Apache remain obscure. Representing the easternmost extension of the Southern Athabascan–speaking peoples, the Apache were the only Athabascan group who inhabited a true Plains environment in historical times (Bittle 1962:152). The Apache belong to the Apachean branch of the Athabascan language family along with the Navajo, Western Apache, Mescalero, Chiricahua, Jicarilla, and Lipan Apachean peoples (Hoijer 1938 and Young 1983, cited in Foster and McCollough; Davis 1988:79) and developed within the context of Southern Athabascan prehistory. The Jicarilla, Mescalero, and Lipan demonstrate more similarities to Plains populations than do the more western Athabascans (Davis 1988:72). Harry Hoijer (1938, 1962) first classified Plains Apache as an Eastern Apachean language, along with Jicarilla and Lipan, but more distant from those two languages, which were more closely related to one another (cited in Foster and McCollough n.d.:3). William E. Bittle (1956) later supported this; however, Hoijer (1971; Davis 1988:79, 1996) "later concluded that the Apache language should be in a category of its own, equidistant from the other six [Apachean] languages which make up a more homogeneous dialect cluster" (Foster and McCollough n.d.:4). Subsequent works (Hale and Harris 1979 and Young 1983, cited in Foster and McCollough n.d.:4) support Hoijer's later views.

Ethnonyms and Early History

The most developed discussion of Apache ethnonyms and origins is provided by John Swanton (1952:296), James Gunnerson and Dolores Gunnerson (1971), William Bittle (1971), Michael Davis (1988:67–74, 1996:49–55), and Morris Wade Foster and Martha McCollough (n.d.:3, 5–15), who demonstrate the importance of nomenclature in the ethnohistorical interpretation of the Apache. References to the Naishan occur most frequently in the early Apachean literature as Plains Apache. Southern Plains Apachean peoples were first encountered by Spanish explorers in 1541, who referred to them as Vaqueros. Little is known concerning their internal organization. Francisco Coronado, Juan de Onate, Alonso de Benavides, and Alonso de Posada describe a "relatively homogeneous sociocultural organizational pattern" (Foster and McCollough n.d.:5–6, citing Ray 1974, Schroeder 1974, and Posada 1982; Davis 1988:67). Posada (1982:41–42) suggests small, politically autonomous Plains Apache bands or *rancherías* with headsmen leading through informal influence. Due to sparse accounts, their linguistic and cultural boundaries and sociopolitical interaction are presently impossible to discern (Gunnerson and Gunnerson 1971; Foster and McCollough n.d.:6). A lack of agriculture, frequent nomadism, hide tipis, and use of dogs as pack animals distinguished Plains Apache from other Apachean peoples residing along the front (eastern) range of the Rocky Mountains (Schroeder 1974: 235, 253; Davis 1988:67–68). These semisedentary agricultural and bison-hunting Eastern Apache (Carlana, Cuartelejo, Faraone, Jicarilla, Llanero, Paloma, Natage, and Sierra Blanco) became intermediary traders between New Mexican Spanish and western and northern Plains communities. Oral and archival sources suggest that competition existed between semisedentary and bison-hunting and exclusively bison-hunting Apachean groups (Smith 1959; Brant 1951; Davis 1988:68–69; Foster and McCollough n.d.:7), possibly due to competition for Puebloan and Spanish trade sources.

Several scholars have suggested connections between the western Plains Apache and the Dismal River archaeological complex (Gunnerson and Gunnerson 1960, 1968, 1979; Davis 1988, 1996). However, as Davis (1988:70) points out, because of "the lacunae in our archaeological knowledge, solutions to the problems of the historical and cultural background of the Kiowa Apache must be sought in the historical and ethnographic literatures." The Plains Apache adaptation to a full-time nomadic hunting economy with surplus bison products for trade allowed them to engage in trade in the southern markets. The availability of horses on the Southern Plains by 1660 undoubtedly provided another motivation (Schroeder 1974:113). René Robert Cavalier de La Salle noted in 1682 that the Pawnee and Wichita obtained horses from the Gattacka (a nineteenth-century name for a Kiowa-Apache band) and the Manrhroet, who resided to the south and traded with the New Mexican Spanish (Margry 1879:201). Gattacka is a corruption of the Pawnee name for the Naishan Apache, "tska-taka" meaning "face-white" (Gunnerson and Gunnerson 1971:15). In 1686 Posada (1982:41) described the emphasis Plains Apache placed on maintaining amicable relations with the Spanish to ensure access to Spanish goods and horses. Visiting the Wichita in 1719, Bernard de La Harpe noted the role of the Cancy and Padouca in acquiring Spanish horses and trading them to Southern Plains peoples and to Northern Plains Arikara villages (Smith 1959:379; Davis 1988:69, 157; Foster and McCollough n.d.:8). According to La Harpe's account, the names "Cancy" or "Cannecy" and "Padouca" were sometimes used for Eastern and Plains Apache, which suggests Apachean and not Comanche peoples (John 1975; Davis 1988:69). La Harpe's (Smith 1959: 529–530) mention of Cancy and Padouca warfare with Pawnee, Ute, and Comanche suggests continued Eastern and Plains Apachean competition to control the southern Plains-Puebloan horse trade (Davis 1988:69; Foster and McCollough n.d.:8).

Eastern and Plains Apache trade intermediaries between the supply of horses in New Mexico and the Southern Plains village markets had been displaced by Comanche bands by 1720 (Thomas 1932:57–58, 1940:20). Meanwhile, French traders increased the demand for horses, while providing an alternative supply of European goods by establishing contacts with the Caddo, Wichita, Pawnee, and Arikara. Most Eastern Apache moved closer to Spanish and Puebloan settlements to obtain protection from Comanche raids, and Plains Apache may have moved southward into eastern New Mexico to join the Lipan (Davis 1988:69; Foster and McCollough n.d.:9). Other Plains Apache moved north in response to Comanche incursion. While this movement facilitated a continued mobile bison hunting and trading subsistence that was closer to their Arikara trading associates, whose sedentary villages were a major Plains trading market, it was further from Spanish horse sources. Carl Wheat's (1957:1:map no. 98) 1717 French map shows ten identifiable Padouca villages north of the Panis or Pawnee villages. Earlier maps had recorded the Gattacka or Padouca as south of the Pawnee (Foster and McCollough n.d.:9). These peoples are henceforth referred to as the Plains or Naishan Apache.

Although archival references for the Naishan Apache are sparse until the late eighteenth century, it is likely that they allied with several Northern Plains groups who were likewise venturing into Plains hunting and trading opportunities during this period. James Mooney's fieldnotes report numerous Apache intermarriages with Sarsi, Kiowa, and Crow, all of whom were allied, well into the middle to late 1700s.[3] Many later intermarriages between Apache and Arapaho and Cheyenne are also known. Apache oral history maintains that they and the Sarsi were once the same tribe, who later divided, and my eldest Apache consultant, Alfred Chalepah Sr., who visited the Sarsi in the 1930s, reported largely communicable dialects.[4] It is also likely that the Apache acquired some of the more typical Plains sociocultural features that distinguish them from other Apachean peoples, such as tribal bundles, military societies, and participation in the Sun Dance, all of which diffused from the Northern Plains. Apache oral history states that the three original tribal medicine bundles were found on the banks of *Kutizze* (Medicine Water [Lake]) in the Black Hills (McAllister 1965:215), which implies that the Apache began using such bundles after 1720. Foster and McCollough (n.d.:10) suggest that the Apache adopted tribal bundles from Northern Plains "peoples which used such items to articulate membership in a social unit with religious beliefs and practices."

Davis (1988:69–72, 1996) and Foster and McCollough (n.d.:10–13) have outlined the problems associated with early Plains Apache encounters and their numerous, sometimes multiple ethnonyms, as these have been discussed in past scholarship. (The following summary in general follows Foster and McCollough, pp. 10–14.) The first probable Spanish reference to the Naishan Apache comes from a 1785 report (Nasatir 1930:531, 1952: 1:127), which notes significant population decline of the Pado or Toguibaco to include only four small wandering groups totaling approximately 350 men. The first part of the latter name (*Togui-*) closely resembles the primary Kiowa (who were already allied and intermarried with the Apache) politically based name for the Naishan Dene Apache, Tàugûi (Sitting [on the] Outside). Due to confusion in the use of the early ethnonym Padouca, which is sometimes used for the Comanche, this may not refer to the Plains Apache. Apache oral history reports that one of the three original tribal bundles was divided into two "when the band to which it belonged became too large" to remain together (McAllister 1965). If this "reference to four bands is correct," then the bundle division may have occurred before 1785 (Foster and McCollough n.d.: 10–11).

In 1796 the Tokiwako or Tokiouako were reportedly allied with the Arapaho, Cheyenne, and Kiowa on the Cherry River while the Padou resided on the nearby southwest branch of the Platte River (Nasatir 1952:1: 379, 384); Truteau describes the Catarka (an arguable variation of Gattacka), Datami, and Padouca as allies of the Arapaho, Cheyenne, and Kiowa (Foster and McCollough n.d.: 11, citing Nasatir 1952). By 1800–1801 the "Apaches del Norte" or Apache of the North were associated with Kiowa bands and other tribal populations which had moved into Comanche-held territory in the Southern Plains and were repeatedly attempting to establish trade relations with Spanish populations in Texas and New Mexico (Perrin du Lac 1807:63; Morse 1822:366; Abel 1939:239; Gunnerson and Gunnerson 1971; Moulton 1987:423–425, 438–439; Cortés 1989:95; Foster and McCollough n.d.: 11–12, citing John 1985:382–383).

These accounts suggest an established political and economic association of Apache bands with the larger Kiowa, Arapaho, and Cheyenne groups, most of which appear directed toward acquiring access to Euro-American trade or protection from larger hostile Plains groups such as the Comanche, Pawnee, and Lakota (Foster and McCollough, 12). The Apache primarily allied with nomadic peoples possessing amicable relationships with Euro-Americans, while avoiding relationships with populations involved in "hostilities with Euro-Americans" (Foster and McCollough, 12). The numerous references to alliances with the Kiowa, Arapaho, Cheyenne and, after 1806, Comanche serve as a diachronic marker for Apache activities (Foster and McCollough n.d.: 12–13); Apache ethnonyms may also include the "Cuampe," whose trade activities are recorded in the Taos and Santa Fe areas, in alliances with the Kiowa, Cheyenne, Arapaho, and Comanche against the Pawnee (Twitchell 1914, cited in Foster and McCollough, 13), and in descriptions as one of the hostile peoples (along with the Kiowa and what may possibly be the Arapaho) occasionally raiding New Mexico in 1774 and visiting the Arikara in 1794 (O'Crouley 1972:56, drawn from a larger almost verbatim section from Pedro de Rivera in 1728; Rivera 1946). Members of the Long Expedition (1819–1820) used the name "Kaskaia" or "Kaskaya" to refer to allies of the Arapaho, Cheyenne, and Kiowa (James 1823:vol. 2, 176, 184). *Kaskaia* (Bad Heart) is recorded in 1853 (Marcy 1853:3), and Paul Wilhelm, duke of Wurttemberg, described the "Apache," apparently identifying the same people he visited in 1822 (Wilhelm 1973:313). José Francisco Ruiz (1972:8) in 1828 and Jean Louis Berlandier (1969:134–135) in 1830 used the name "Plains Lipan" or "Lipans of the Plains" to refer to a Naishan Apache band associated with the Charitica or Arapaho (Bittle 1971:2; Davis 1996:76; Foster and McCollough n.d.:14). Bittle (1971:2) also reports use of the ethnonyms "Tejas" and "Kantsis."

The Apache are first clearly referred to in Anglo-American sources in 1835 by Henry Dodge, who states that the "Appachees" of the Plains shared the same residential area of the west-central Plains with the Kiowa (Dodge 1836:25). In 1837 the Kataka, Kiowa, and Wichita signed a treaty with the United States (Kappler 1973:489–491). "Most subsequent pre-reservation references to the Kiowa-Apache are as 'Apache'" (Foster and McCollough n.d.:14). Verne Ray (1974:79) reports Apache associations with the Mescalero Apache in 1846 and the Arapaho and Cheyenne in 1848.[5] From 1850 to 1855 the Apache associated primarily with the Kiowa and Comanche, signing a joint treaty with these groups and the United States in 1853 (Kappler 1973:600–602). From 1858 to 1867 the Apache were closely associated with the Arapaho and Cheyenne, but joined in an unratified treaty with the Kiowa and Comanche in 1863 (DeMallie 1977). A second unratified treaty in 1865 would have placed them on a reservation shared with the Arapaho and Cheyenne (Kappler 1973:891–892; Foster and McCollough n.d.:14).

Raiding, Warfare, and the Reservation Period

Like their Kiowa and Comanche neighbors, the Apache maintained an equestrian, nomadic hunting and raiding economy well into the third quarter of the nineteenth century (Bittle 1979; McAllister 1937:120–121). They frequently participated in raiding activities into Texas and portions of Mexico for horses and other goods (McAllister 1935:15–16; Nye 1937; Brant

1969:2–3). As Bittle (1979:34) notes, "Warfare among these people, as among the other tribes of the Plains, was of compelling economic and social import. Perhaps for no other area of Kiowa Apache activity are stories and recollections preserved in such profusion."

Like neighboring tribes, the Apache actively promoted and recognized martial bravery, which played the most significant role in an adult man's social status and acquisition of leadership positions. All men were expected to be fearless or brave (*ah-teh-klooth-gjee*) in battle. Warriors (*klath-ti-di-eh*), scouts (*dah-klo-ehth*) or men who had been to war (*dah-klo-ehth-jho-ay*, fighters) were all viewed with honor, resulting in a higher martially based social status. To be a chief (*nah-yeh-klah'*), a war party leader (*dah-klo-ehth-jho-yeh-nah-yeh-klah'*, fighter or warrior chief), and to touch an enemy in battle (*dah-klah-eh-dah-veh-yeht-tah-glez-mah*, touch the enemy) were the standards for Apache martial behavior.[6] In addition to his ability, bravery, and performance in battle, positive characteristics such as wisdom, ability in decisionmaking, persuasiveness, leadership, and all-around good qualities enabled a man to become a leader.[7] Such positions were tenuous, however, as people depended upon the decisions and abilities of their leaders for survival. Thus, such positions had to be maintained through good decision-making, generosity, and the ability to provide for and protect the people, lest they lose their faith in a leader's ability and switch their support to another leader.

Physical and psychological training were employed throughout a youth's life to prepare him for warfare, which centered around revenge and acquisition of horses (Bittle 1979). Apache participation in raiding and warfare resembles that of neighboring tribes in terms of resistance against displaced and encroaching eastern tribes and continuing intermittent raiding and warfare following the signing of treaties with the United States in 1837 and 1853 (Brant 1969:11–12). These activities correlate with membership and participation in nineteenth-century Apache military societies. With increasing population and military pressures, the Apache signed the Treaty of the Little Arkansas on October 17, 1865, detaching them from the Kiowa and Comanche and relocating them with the Cheyenne and Arapaho on lands reserved in Kansas and Indian Territory.

Legislative efforts to cease raiding and warfare, which inhibited Anglo settlement and railroad development, resulted in the Treaty of Medicine Lodge in 1867. After careful evaluation, the Apache signed the treaty and, at their own request, were reunited with the Kiowa and Comanche, choosing to share a reservation with these groups on increasingly reduced lands in southwestern Indian Territory (Kappler 1973:982–984). Apache bands were again associated with the Arapaho and Cheyenne from 1868 to 1875, when most Plains peoples in Indian Territory began full-time residence on their respective reservations.

Throughout the early 1870s Apache raiding and warfare declined, and they maintained a more settled existence than neighboring tribes. During this period the Apache were regarded as having been more cooperative and obedient than other tribes on the reservation. Agents viewed them more favorably, stating in 1872 that they were "better disposed than their associates . . . if they can be removed from the evil influences of the Kiowas and Comanches they will do well." The following year agents again commented: "The Apaches were very attentive, working themselves with the hoe, and that they have remained quiet; they seem very anxious to settle down and become farmers." [8] In contrast to the Kiowa and Comanche, who persisted in raiding and warfare activities, favorable characterizations of Apache behavior continued throughout the early 1870s, perhaps in part due to the group's notably smaller size. Consequently no Apache leaders were imprisoned at Ft. Marion, Florida.

As Foster and McCollough (n.d.: 15) note, by 1875 all three tribes were confined to the KCA reservation: 120 Apaches resided on the Cheyenne and Arapaho reservation, while 444 resided on the Kiowa, Comanche, and Apache reservation. "Some" Apache remained on "the Cheyenne and Arapaho reservation throughout the reservation period, and . . . an unspecified number, most of whom had married with Cheyennes and Arapahos, were transferred to the Cheyenne and Arapaho rolls" (Foster and McCollough n.d.: 15). Throughout the 1880s Apaches suffered from an insufficient food supply and in 1891–1892 were hit particularly hard by several epidemics. Significant numbers of Apache converted to Peyotism (later known as the Native American Church) after 1890 and to the Ghost Dance from 1890 to 1917. Under the Oklahoma Indian Welfare Act (OIWA) the Apache established their own tribal government in 1936, but did not adopt an OIWA constitution. After 1966 the Apache were able to establish their own tribal government; since receiving a federal land claims settlement in 1974 over the disputed Jerome Agreement of 1892, the Apache Business Committee has been able to provide tribal members with social services and has undertaken some economic development projects. In 1987 the Apache tribal government lowered tribal enrollment to one-eighth degree Apache blood.

Population

While prereservation Plains Apache bands were undoubtedly larger than those of later declining, yet reliable, reservation era enumerations, estimates are dubious. The Apache probably remained relatively small throughout the last two hundred years. Most scholars (Mooney 1898; McAllister 1935; Brant 1969) estimate that they probably never exceeded six hundred people; however, other sources indicate that while they remained relatively small, they were at one time larger.[9]

The varying estimates that follow are reported in Foster and McCollough (n.d., 20–22). These include Abraham Nasatir's (1930:531) four small Pado or Toguibaco bands; Lewis and Clark's 1804 estimate of 300 to 400 Cataka and 120 to 200 in the Dotane band (Moulton 1987:423–425); 375 Cataka and 200 Dotane or Dotami in 1820 (Morse 1822:366); 80 to 100 families of "Lipans of the Plains" (Ruiz 1972:8) associated with the Arapaho, which may have been only an Apache band; and Dodge's (1836:25) estimate of 1,200 "Appachees of the Plains" in 1835. The annual reports of the Upper Arkansas agent recorded the following population estimates: fifty lodges in 1850, forty lodges or 320 people in 1855, sixty lodges or 415 people in 1861, and forty lodges in 1862, which reportedly accounted for a total population of 160 to 200 people in 1865. Eighty-six lodges containing 516 Apache were recorded at the Medicine Lodge Treaty in 1867, which is the most reliable prereservation count, yet may not have included all Naishan bands. On the KCA reservation 288 Apache were reported in 1869 and 200 in 1871. Approximately 120 Apache remained at the Cheyenne and Arapaho agency during the early 1870s. Twelve bands consisting of 602 Apache were enumerated in 1874, which may have included some who were absent from the reservation or residing with the Cheyenne and Arapaho. In 1875, 344 Apaches were recorded on the KCA reservation, with 180 absent (Foster and McCollough n.d.:22). Population estimates before circa 1880 are suspect at best, due to intermarriage, epidemics, and various portions of the tribe residing with or near the Cheyenne and Arapaho from 1867 to 1874 following the Medicine Lodge Treaty. Later, more reliable, enumerations are recorded in Indian agency records, including 332 in 1880, 241 in 1892, 226 in 1895, and 173 in 1900.

As Foster and McCollough point out (n.d.:22–23), despite the questionable reliability of early estimates, the Apache have always been a small Plains population that, like most Native American populations, consistently declined throughout the eighteenth century and after allotments for various reasons. Disease played a major role in significant population loss (Ewers 1973:108–109, cited in Foster and McCollough). The Apache population declined in part due to smallpox epidemics in 1816, 1839–1840, and 1861–1862; cholera in 1849; measles and fever in 1877; and whooping cough and malaria in 1882; it declined from 325 people in 1891 to 241 in 1892 following an epidemic of whooping cough, measles, pneumonia, and influenza. Malnutrition during the reservation period and membership transfers through intermarriage with Cheyenne and Arapaho or with Kiowa and Comanche and relocation to their rolls may also explain population declines. Foster and McCollough (n.d.: 22) go on to summarize population increases in the twentieth century. The Apache population reached a nadir of 139 in 1910, then began to recover. The population rose to 184 in 1930 (Swanton 1952: 296), 400 in 1951 (Brant 1951: 148), 1,001 by 1984, and (after reducing the blood quantum to one-eighth in 1987) 1,342 in 1992. Currently the Naishan Apache reside near the towns of Fort Cobb, Apache, Boone, and Anadarko, Oklahoma.

Apache Ethnography

Apache and Kiowa tribal history maintains that the Apache were already associated with the Kiowa in Montana when both were allied with the Crow and Sarsi prior to migrating south from the northern Plains. In addition, genealogies collected by James Mooney indicate frequent Apache and Kiowa intermarriage extending well into the 1700s, when both tribes were allied with, residing near, and intermarrying with the Crow and Sarsi in Montana.[10] The Apache received little early ethnological attention. James Mooney (1898: 245–253) performed limited fieldwork among the Apache, publishing only a portion of his collected materials and very few data of consequence. Although he documented and recognized their Athabascan origins and the incorrectness of the attributed name "Kiowa-Apache" and noted that their known history extended nearly seventy years before that of the associated Kiowa, he unfortunately dismissed the Apache for further ethnological inquiry as he viewed them as "practically a part of the Kiowa in everything but language" (Mooney 1898: 248). Following Mooney, almost all modern information concerning Apache ethnology comes from the work of J. Gilbert McAllister (1935, 1937), who performed ten months of fieldwork on Apache social organization in 1933–1934; Charles Brant, who conducted fieldwork in 1948–1949 (1951, 1969); and William Bittle (1962, 1971), who led several ethnographic field schools among the Apache during the 1960s and 1970s.

Although historical and ethnographic sources generally neglect the Apache and focus on the Kiowa, Comanche, and Cheyenne, sources indicate that the Apache pursued a mode of existence similar to that of their Southern Plains neighbors. By the time the Apache migrated onto the Southern Plains they followed a "typical" Plains equestrian lifestyle involving bison, horses, and tipis, although they differed in Athabascan language and in some mythology. Frequently thought of as politically and culturally affiliated with the Kiowa, the Apache were also allied at various times with the Cheyenne, Arapaho, and Comanche during portions of the nineteenth century, but were in fact autonomous, spending much of their annual cycle separately. Their relationship with the Kiowa during the nineteenth century was probably longer and more intense than with any other group, as demonstrated by numerous cultural similarities.[11] Yet throughout this period the Apache maintained their own identity as a separate ethnic group, due to several factors. Linguistically, the Athabascan Apache are quite distinct from other neighboring Southern Plains tribes. Contrary to Bittle's (1962:153) assertion that communication between the Apache and Kiowa depended upon sign language, several Apache and Kiowa elders have indicated that many Apache learned to speak at least some Kiowa, although few Kiowa reciprocated.[12] While Comanche served in the past as a *lingua franca*, many Southern Plains peoples in the past were multilingual in local native languages.

Although the Apache intermarried with surrounding tribes, tribal censuses and family genealogies indicate that they did not intermarry with Euro-American and Hispanic populations to the degree neighboring Southern Plains tribes did. The 1900 Apache tribal census shows a high percentage of Apache descent with greatest intermarriage with Kiowa, Arapaho, and Mexican populations, a few Mescalero Apache, very few Cheyenne, and no Comanche at this time. Captives did not play as large a role among the Apache as among the neighboring Comanche and Kiowa. Whereas Kiowa and Comanche captured, enculturated, and intermarried with significant numbers of Hispanic, Anglo, and Native American captives of both sexes, Apache captives consisted largely of women from other tribes, as males and Anglo captives were rarely taken alive.[13] Although informally enforced, this semiendogamy appears to have been followed by the majority into the early reservation era (1875–1900), producing a tight kin network in which all Apache were in some way related.

Intermarriage has continually increased, and family genealogies indicate current intermarriage with individuals from at least thirty-nine non-Apache populations including Anglo, African American, Hispanic, Asian, and other Native American tribes. Close kin bonds formed an important role in Apache social organization; as McAllister (1937:165) notes, "The whole tribe was bound into one large kinship unit, and however distant or even fictitious these ties may have been, they were, nevertheless, very real to the Kiowa-Apache" and (1937:99) "the Kiowa-Apache are like one large endogamous band, with a keen feeling of unity." The combination of preferential endogamy with the selective taking of captives in warfare may be an important factor in explaining the consistently smaller Apache population. In addition, a number of Apache women married Kiowa men and later enrolled as Kiowa, another factor keeping Apache numbers small.[14] As we shall see, this small population significantly affected the size, number, and vitality of Apache military societies.

APACHE SOCIAL ORGANIZATION AND SODALITIES
Kinship

The Apache kinship system is of the Matri-Hawaiian type, containing no generational merging (McAllister 1935; Murdock 1949:228–229). Merging does occur with same-sex consanguineal kin at each generational level, except for separate terms used in the parental generation for the mother's brother (including father's sister's husband) and father's sister (including mother's brother's wife). Terms for same- and opposite-sex siblings include parallel and cross cousins respectively in one's own generation. Real and classificatory children of same-sex siblings are distinguished from those of real and classificatory opposite-sex siblings in one's children's generation. Older and younger siblings, real and classificatory, are distinguished from one another. This system differs from that of the Lipan Apache in only one aspect: the Lipan do not utilize reciprocal terms for members of the grandparental and grandchild generations. The Apache definition of incest was narrower than among the Kiowa and Comanche and permitted marriage between some consanguineal kin (McAllister 1937:145–146). Gift exchange between the two families was common in arranged marriages and elopements. The levirate and sororate were also common in remarriage.

Social Organization

At least four levels of prereservation Apache social organization are known: (1) extended family (*kustcrae*), (2) local or residence band (*gonka*), (3) division (composite *gonka*), and (4) the entire Apache community; the second and third probably refer to smaller and larger *gonka*, which frequently changed in size and composition depending upon season and focused activities. The core social unit was the extended domestic family or *kustcrae*, a small group of nuclear family–based tipis, with residence determined in part by kinship relations with a preference for matrilocal residence. Multiple *kustcrae* formed a larger group known as a *gonka*, which resembled a residence band and varied in size according to the popularity of the current leader. Multiple *gonka* formed divisions like supraband structures which were probably named groups. Although band membership was voluntary, it tended to follow family lines, as ownership of tribal bundles did. During the nineteenth century all *gonka* or the entire Naishan community came together as a political bandlike component in the annual Kiowa (or other tribal) Sun Dance; after this the Apache divided again into several *gonka*, whose membership fluctuated according to changing inter-*kustcrae* relations (McAllister 1935).[15] Although there is no indication that the Apache held their own Sun Dance, Apache participation in the other tribal Sun Dances, in men's societies, in intermarriage, and in other social activities suggests that the Apache valued such occasions for social, religious, and economic interaction. Apache participation in Kiowa, Arapaho, and Cheyenne Sun dances was not annual; it varied according to which of their closest allies was currently conducting a ceremony. Like other tribes, the Apache had a council of elders (*dah-ko-luth-chee*, council) for consensus-based decision-making and camp criers (*gon-kah-zhee-ghah-dah-veth-chee*, talking through the camp) for communication purposes.[16]

While the number of prereservation Apache bands (*gonka*) has not been established, at least three major bands existed, each containing a tribal medicine bundle. A fourth residence band is indicated by the fact that one tribal medicine bundle was split and formed into two to facilitate the needs of Apache not in proximity to the other three (McAllister 1965:212–213). According to Foster and McCollough (n.d.:15), during the early reservation period Apache bands fragmented into smaller domestic units, usually in the form of extended families, which moved about the reservation area between annuity and ration days, and "in 1875 the Kiowa Agency recognized twelve Apache [beef] bands for ration distribution," which increased to fifteen by 1885.

By the 1890s these units had begun to cluster in five geographic areas as rations were distributed to domestic units rather than bands (Foster and McCollough n.d.:15–16). I have identified at least five Apache communities that continued earlier band formations or developed sometime between entering the KCA reservation (1875) and 1890. Four of the five "bands" were known by ethnonyms referring to their physical surroundings: (1) Washita Apache (along the Washita River near present-day Fort Cobb, Oklahoma), (2) Cache Creek Apache (along Cache Creek near present-day Boone, Oklahoma), (3) Pecan Grove Apache (along Cache Creek, near present-day Alden, Oklahoma), (4) Kichai Hills Apache (along Apache Creek in the Kichai Hills, near present-day Cement, Oklahoma), and (5) Daveko's family residing along the Washita River (just north of present day Anadarko, Oklahoma).[17] By 1900 the Kichai Hills group had relocated around Apache, Oklahoma, where they took allotments and were absorbed into the Cache Creek or Boone Apache. Daveko, who died in 1898, had no direct descendants. His brother's family resided in the Cache Creek area.[18] Whether formal band reference titles were used prior to the reservation period or whether bands were referred to by the current band leader remains unclear. The Apache first took allotments in 1901, tending to choose lands closer to Kiowa than Comanche communities. From 1901 to 1903 and in 1908 they took 150 allotments of 160 acres each throughout some twenty-one townships in southwestern Oklahoma.

From these five reservation-period communities two major Apache residence areas formed, the Cache Creek or South area containing the Chalepah family, and the Washita River or North area containing the Tselee or Redbone family. These two residential clusters formed the primary social identities that have characterized the Apache sociopolitical community and military societies from allotments to the present.

Sodalities

A series of cultural institutions, in the form of sodalities, also acted as integrational factors. McAllister viewed the Apache as a tightly integrated group in which kinship terminology and behavior were closely associated and attributed their cultural survival to a tight social structure that combined elements of horizontal and vertical organization. The Apache bilateral kinship system linked every tribal member, however tenuously, to all others and to membership in the military societies. Apache kinship and political and religious organizations linked individuals along primarily vertical lines of descent. Vertical groupings of social organization, including links formed through band chiefs, tribal religious bundles, heraldic tipis, and shield societies, all of which involved descent patterns, provided cohesion among members of the same extended family. As McAllister (1935 : 149–150) notes:

> In contrast to the dancing societies which cut across the tribe were the political and religious groups which tended to follow family lines. It has already been noticed that political groups were merely clusters of individuals about an important "chief," and that the leader's relatives formed the nucleus of his following. If he proved himself to be capable his following increased, but fell away as soon as his reputation declined. These were not, then, fixed segments, except in so far as a man's family remained

loyal to him for his immediate family group would tend to support him throughout life. These groups may or may not have had a continuity in time. More important groupings were those pertaining to the three (now four) worship bundles. These were the most important factors establishing a unity in time. These sacred objects very definitely belonged to families and were usually inherited in the male line. The bundles were respected by all Apaches, but certain taboos might be observed only by the owner's family. One of the bundles was considered more important and was deeply venerated by all members of the tribe, thus tending toward integrating the whole group.

Like tribal medicine bundles throughout the Plains, the Apache bundles and their tipis provided protection for those in danger (as a form of holy ground) from fellow tribal members, were used by their owners to mediate disputes, and were sought out by individuals and families needing spiritual and medical aid. In addition, the primary bundle served as a ceremonial focus for the tribe during annual periods of bundle opening and renewal when the entire Apache tribal history was recited from a pictographic calendar contained in the bundle during an all-night ceremony.[19] Although less is known about the ownership of heraldic painted tipis and Apache shield societies, these small groups of related men provided another form of integration, usually through the further integration of small groups of male consanguineal relatives. Acquisition of *tijje* (supernatural power or "medicine") through visions was closely associated with ownership of shields. McAllister (1935:18–22) reports one shield society, the Red Shields, yet his consultants indicate there may have been more.

In contrast to forms of vertical integration, a series of warrior or military societies also contributed to Apache tribal unity through horizontal integration. It is these organizations on which military ideology, ethos, and an *esprit de corps* were focused; their traditional roles of honoring the warrior and maintaining symbols associated with a prereservation warrior culture have continued to the present day. Regarding the integrative role of Apache military societies, McAllister (1935:148–149) states:

> The only clearly defined segments among these Apaches are the adult dancing societies, composed of all important and prominent men or women. All families were represented and bound into a sort of brotherhood or sisterhood. Thus, these groups cut across family lines and unified the tribe as a whole. It has already been noted how the children's society, the Rabbits, acted as an integrating agent, bringing all the Apache youngsters together, not only giving unity to an age group, but giving the chil-

dren a feeling of intimacy with the most important ritual of the tribe, and thereby establishing a continuity in time.

The Apache state that the society meetings might occur at any time, but were more frequent in the spring and summer. From what is known of other Plains tribes and especially of Apache culture, it would have been difficult for societies to meet except when the whole tribe was together. The tribe was usually divided into several bands, and the members of the dancing groups were scattered during the winter months. After the Apache entered the reservation, meetings could have been held at any time, the conditions remembered by present elders. The last Sun Dance held by the Kiowa and Apache was in 1887, but even before that time it had ceased to be an annual affair. It was at the Sun Dance that the entire Apache tribe aggregated and Apache tribal integration was affirmed through common rites. Apache military societies interacted and participated with Kiowa societies during Kiowa Sun Dances. Based on the phenomenon of chapter organizations in Plains military societies, it is reasonable to expect that the Apache interacted with the societies of other Plains groups during alliances, as with the Arapaho in the late 1860s and early 1870s.

APACHE MILITARY SOCIETIES

Clark (1982:355) first mentioned Apache military societies in 1885: "1st, Big Horse; 2d, Raven; 3d, Swift Fox." McAllister (1935:92–95, 107–114) later listed the Katsowe, Manatidie, Klintidie, and the Izuwe, a women's society. Society synonymy is established by comparing society names and characteristics in Clark (1885), McAllister (1935, 1937), Bittle (1962), and my own fieldwork.[20]

Membership and Organization

At first glance Apache societies appear to have been age-graded, with the children belonging to the Rabbits, middle-aged men predominantly to the Manatidie, and older men to the Klintidie. The mention of the Swift Fox by Clark (1982:322) and Bittle's *gxa'd'idi'e'* ([*gxa'tidie*] Arm Clan–People) indicate additional Apache men's societies; however, their content and relations to the others are unknown. The few references in Bittle's fieldnotes concerning the *gxa'd'idi'e'* demonstrate that practically all knowledge of this group was gone. Apache societies were organized on a coordinate or non-age-graded basis, yet they possessed qualities of de facto age-grading in that there were loose generational divisions that coincided with society membership. While boys belonged to the Katsowe, they usually outgrew or lost interest in the society by their teen years, when they began to accompany raiding and war parties. From around age twenty to thirty, young men frequently concentrated their efforts on activities that, while physically demanding, also brought a period of general freedom and license. By age thirty most young men were married, and promising or outstanding warriors were solicited for membership in one of the adult men's societies (McAllister 1937:144). Young men became Manatidie Society members around age thirty, and older, more mature warriors belonged to the Klintidie. While a pattern of increased age appears to correlate with progression in the societies, there was no set graded order; thus, members could be taken from the Katsowe to the Klintidie society, from the Klintidie to the Manatidie, or, although rarely, remain Rabbits (McAllister 1935:113–114, 1937:149). While they are less documented than the Kiowa societies, the association of age with progression through the Apache men's societies suggests that they were loosely ranked in terms of social rank that was influenced by the interconnected factors of age, increasing martial participation, wealth, and status. While it is possible that the Apache were influenced by the lengthy interactions with the Arapaho, who had age-graded societies, it is presently impossible to attribute a direct age-grading process to the Apache without further knowledge of the status, position, and membership characteristics of the other, largely undocumented Apache men's societies. The presence of de facto age-grading among the Kiowa associated with age, social and war status, and increased wealth weighs against a direct influence from Arapaho age-grading. As with Kiowa societies, military society membership focusing upon martial values formed a significant stage in most prereservation Apache men's lives.

While there are no clear indications, population estimates and similarities to Kiowa and Cheyenne military societies suggest that the Apache were organized similarly, practicing cross-band or pantribal membership. Comparison of Apache population estimates with those for each society shows that there simply were not enough adults for band or divisionally based societies. While a man's society position was not hereditary, a woman's position in the Izuwe was, being passed on to a female relative (McAllister 1935: 113–114, 1937:149).

Society Partners

In the nineteenth century the relationship between biological brothers formed one of the strongest social bonds in Apache kinship. This bond

TABLE 4 Apache Military Society Synonymy

Source	Society Name					
	1	2	3	4	5	6
Clark 1885 (1982)	—	Raven	Big Horse	Swift Fox	—	—
McAllister 1935	Rabbit	Manatidie	Klintidie	?gxa'd'idi'e'	Izuwe	—
Bittle 1949–1964 (WB)	K'a'.lcu'we'. Rabbit Clan	Ma'na't'idi'e' Blackfoot	Kli'ndi'di'e' Horsemen	Arm Clan Arm People	Izuwe	Da'ba'.s'a's War dance
A. Chalepah H. Klinekole (1994)	Katsowe (Rabbit)	Manatidie (Mana People) (Blackfeet)	Klintidie (Horse People) (Horsemen)	+/?*	+/?*	Dahvashsahgootas (Pawnee or War Dance)

*Note: +/? = presence of a society known, but name unknown.

involved the occasional practice of the levirate, sharing of wives, and avoidance of in-laws, as well as the admonition to remain with a brother in battle and, if necessary, to sacrifice one's life. The strength of the social bond known as "friendship" (honorary, fictive, or non-kin-based kinship) carried similar weight between society partners or brothers in Apache military societies. In the Manatidie and Klintidie members were organized in pairs of society partners or friends. This selection of partners might evolve after a man was taken into the society, but a friendship usually existed prior to entry, and good friends might be taken in together to become ceremonial "friends." New partners were acquired if the relationship was not amicable (McAllister 1937:123–125).

Although society partners never addressed one another by sibling terms, they were obligated to each other exactly as consanguineal brothers were. The intimate behavior between "friends" was considered to be as intimate as blood relationships among the Apache. Since a "friend's" relatives were classified as one's own, acquiring a society partner brought an entire new set of classificatory relatives. These relatives took on consanguineal kin terms, whereby the children of "friends" became siblings and were thus prohibited from marriage (McAllister 1937:125, 145). Although data are lacking, it is likely that all members of the same society were regarded collectively as "brothers" and thus their families were all linked as classificatory relatives, a common Plains military society trait. A similar quality can be observed in contemporary *Manatidie* performances. The effect of society "brothers" on possible marriage partners is unknown, due to the lack of society membership rosters and sufficient genealogies. However, given the small Apache population, the prohibition against marriage between relatives of fellow society members in this sort of classificatory kinship would have ruled out significant numbers of potential spouses and was therefore probably not as defined as in some groups. Although societies were most active during the Sun Dance, they affected social relations throughout the year. The non-blood-kin relations between society members as "brothers" provided kin, social, and economic ties that linked segments of an individual society residing within a residence band throughout the year. While nonblood relations undoubtedly promoted integration in cooperative socioeconomic efforts involving subsistence, trading, and warfare, they deterred intracommunity marriages, so that exogamy may have been culturally preferred in this system.

This relationship apparently had far-reaching ties; McAllister (1937:125) reported a legal case involving inheritance which resulted from the practice of society partner kinship and the classificatory manner of grouping relatives. In one case an individual claimed equal inheritance rights to the property of his grandfather's Manatidie partner, thus recognizing this individual as his grandfather's actual brother and himself as a legitimate descendant. Such relationships were reported to have been legally sanctioned earlier, but the agency refused to recognize this claim. Although I have found no indications that current Apache recognize or maintain this form of social relations, these military society–based relations formed one of the strongest and most far-reaching prereservation integrative social structures.

Apache Military Society Functions

Apache military society functions focused upon providing police and military service, charitable economic aid, and collective labor service. Both the Manatidie and Klintidie policed bison hunts. As in many other Plains groups, if an individual guilty of breaking hunt laws was whipped and took it without fighting back, he would later be given gifts and forgiven. If he fought back, the police had the authority to kill him if needed. If he resisted and was not killed, no gifts were later given (Brant 1969:113–114). There seems to have been some flexibility in Apache concepts of hunt restrictions; Brant's (1969:113) Apache consultant stated that "if anyone really needed to go hunt, he had to give a smoke to them [the police] and get permission to go." Brant (1969:113–114) and the 1935 Kiowa Santa Fe fieldnotes indicate that the Apache frequently participated in the Kiowa Sun Dance and in the preparations.[21] Upon nearing the final encampment site after the four movements, the Manatidie, and probably the other Apache societies as well, began their society songs. Later the Manatidie helped cut and drag brush for the construction of the Kiowa Sun Dance lodge, while the women (probably the Izuwe Society) brought in sand and dirt for the floor. This information correlates with the Kiowa practice (Meadows 1995) in which the military societies began their regular meetings and dances during the progression to the Sun Dance encampment, continuing into the Brush Dragging and construction and sand hauling of the Sun Dance lodge. Thus, it is clear that the Apache and Kiowa societies were actively functioning at the same time, in the same encampment, sometimes cooperatively. The following descriptions of Apache societies are largely based on McAllister's works (1935, 1937), supplemented by William Bittle's fieldnotes between 1949 and 1964, archival sources, and my own fieldwork (1989–1997) in order to obtain the most thorough description of past and current Apache societies.[22]

THE KATSOWE OR RABBIT SOCIETY

The *Katsowe* or Rabbit Society was the last of the Apache societies to cease functioning in the twentieth century and was the society about which most was known during McAllister's fieldwork (McAllister 1937: 139–143). Membership included children of both sexes ranging in age from newborns to teenagers, at which time they were either inducted into another society or, becoming involved in adult affairs, lost interest. No formal initiation procedures existed; newborn children were brought to dances to dance and to benefit from the associated worship and prayers as soon as possible.

Meetings resulted from a pledge made by the parent of a sick child in return for his or her recovery or for the future welfare of their children. "If my child gets well, I will call the Rabbits together." There were no set meeting times for the group, although summer was most common, as it facilitated larger tribal aggregations which included the keeper of the primary Apache religious bundle. The family sponsoring the event informed the bundle keeper of their pledge the day before a feast and prepared a large meal. The next day the bundle keeper announced the dance and invited all the Rabbits to a large tipi erected by the sponsoring family. The tipi cover was rolled up, allowing the parents and visitors, who remained outside, to view the children seated inside. The bundle keeper sat on the west side of the tipi with the honored child positioned just in front of him. Placing his hands on the child's shoulders, the man proceeded with lengthy and repetitious prayers for the child's health and longevity.

Next the children began dancing in a circular formation in imitation of Rabbits, by hopping up and down with knees bent and hands cupped above their ears resembling rabbit ears. The bundle keeper was assisted by two middle-aged men who sang and drummed. An older boy was selected to serve as the "bull," although in some cases an adult was chosen. In one instance, Apache Sam Klinkole, one of the four Apache bundle keepers, served in this position.[23] As badges of office, this individual carried a whip and a knife, which was stuck into the ground in front of his position in the tipi. The bull encouraged the children to dance and could whip recalcitrant dancers or at the end of a dance could cut either their shirt sleeves or their bangs. As a youth, Louise Saddleblanket (born in 1893) once saw the dress sleeves cut off a girl who was reluctant to dance at a Rabbit Dance.[24] Brant (1969: 57) reports a similar case which may have been the same individual. Punished individuals could not resist, because all the Rabbits would jump upon them and tear their clothing. Such actions were intended to shame an individual into proper behavior and involved no real physical harm. At this first level in the series of Apache military societies, youths were encouraged to emulate the martial ideology and actions of their elders, such as counting coups in battle and later reciting them, which would form an important part in their adult life as warriors and in their social status. Dances might be stopped by youths imitating their elders' war deeds through the recitation of their own coups. Upon walking up to the drum and hitting it, a youth would recite, "Wait now, I'm going to tell you a story. Way down there I kill a rabbit [he hits the drum]; over there I kill a bird [he hits the drum]; over there I pick up a turtle [drum]. There is my witness" (McAllister 1937:140). Thus, the emphasis on counting and reciting war deeds with independent verification by witnesses was taught at an early age.

During the dancing and feasting, joking and occasional obscenity prevailed. Children made fun of the bundle keeper, who sometimes, pretending to be asleep, was aroused with sticks and made to dance. The bundle keeper always danced facing west, with his back to the group. Wearing only a loincloth, he would expose his buttocks and sing a Rabbit song, "When rabbit runs to the creek, you see his white buttocks," embarrassing the women and visitors, while delighting the children into laughter. Interspersed with rest periods, the dancing continued until around noon. Then a large dish of food was brought in and prayed over, to ensure that the food would promote the children's health and longevity. On the first passing of food, each member took only four spoonfuls, after which members ate as much as they could, competing between sides. The bundle keeper announced the loser, entitling the winners to maul the defeated and producing a general melee, after which the children ran out of the tipi, ending the activities.

During Katsowe Society gatherings, pauses in the dancing were often used to conduct naming ceremonies for Apache children. Several current elders received their personal Indian names at Rabbit Dances from prominent elders such as Apache John, who was the whipman for the Manatidie Society. The curing of children who were bedwetters also took place at society meetings. These children were brought forward and placed in front of the singers, who sang while the children danced and fanned them with feather fans. The parents of each child supplied a cottontail tied to a long string, which was tied around the child's waist with the tail against the skin of the child's backside, after loosening the clothing. After four days and nights the tail was removed, and a child's bedwetting problems were reportedly cured.[25]

Membership in the Rabbit Society fulfilled a number of socializing functions during the formative years of Apache children, as they became familiar with each other and developed close relationships with those individuals they would be intimately associated with as adults. For Apache boys, the introduction to martially oriented practices prepared them for a lifestyle emphasizing and honoring the warrior and his martial abilities. Encouragement of self-expression led to evaluations of individual abilities and character by adults and within peer groups. Social discipline was taught through respect for established social institutions such as the head bundle keeper of the tribe, the structure of the Katsowe Society, and obeying leadership as represented by the "bull." Thus, the martial ideologies and ethos which would form such a significant part of later adult life in hunting, raiding, warfare, and participating in the men's and women's societies were taught at an early age.

The man who inherited the head tribal religious bundle automatically became the Rabbit Society leader. In order to inherit the bundle the man must have proven himself a chief, and the acquisition of the bundle added greatly to his prestige. Upon acquiring the bundle the keeper was required to become virtually sacred, no longer being able to do wrong, to act mean, to lose his temper, to be stingy, or to criticize anyone. McAllister (1935:14) reports that the Apache regarded Rabbit Society gatherings as a "worship; like going to church." Although the bundle itself had no direct association with the society, the bundle keeper was the Rabbits' permanent leader and, as the most respected individual in tribal religion, was intimately involved with the children. His semiobscene behavior during dances demonstrated his relationship to the group, who, not yet being of age, were to be tolerated, but it would have been inappropriate for adults. His presence thereby provided a role model demonstrating the differences between proper and improper social behavior. The existence of such sanctioned obscene actions in association with the sacredness of the Rabbit Society dances reflects the importance of the learning process in youth development.

McAllister (1937:142) states that forming close relationships between members of relative age groups and association with the head bundle keeper were among the most important integrating forces for the tribe as a whole. This again suggests the formation of informal, de facto, generational age-grades. As in accounts of elders in neighboring tribes, some Apaches have compared the Katsowe to the Boy Scouts as a training organization. In sum, the Katsowe provided youths with a feeling of unity and importance while enculturating them into the larger social system and the roles they would fulfill in later years. It emphasized many of the cooperative qualities upon which prereservation life depended. The relationship of the society to the larger social system was one of advance training, preparing individuals with the martial ideology and ethos needed to survive in a warrior-based culture through introduction to a children's military society (with an emphasis on martial activities, esteem for veterans, society meetings with distinct rituals and symbols, coup recitations, leadership offices), while instilling the various integrative social relationships (kinship, respect for secular and religious authority, cooperation in work) needed to maintain the larger social system.

Brant's (1969:39, 56–57) consultant reported his first attendance at a Rabbit Dance as a boy in 1885 or 1886 and the last Apache Rabbit Dance about 1915. Katsowe Society dances continued only occasionally into the 1930s, including many of the functions such as naming ceremonies and prayers for the children's longevity. By World War II Katsowe Society functions had ceased. From the late 1960s to the mid-1970s Apache Rabbit dances were revived and regularly held as part of the morning program of the one, and later two, Apache Manatidie Society encampments; after several years they again ceased. Since the cessation of Rabbit Society dances, the various socialization functions for children, although now qualitatively different from earlier periods, have taken the form of various games and sporting contests sponsored at current Manatidie encampments. Elders and ethnographic materials indicate little difference between the Apache Rabbit dances and those currently held at the annual Kiowa Gourd Clan Society dances, which some Apache occasionally attend.

MANATIDIE: THE BLACKFEET SOCIETY

The Manatidie is presently the only surviving prereservation Apache society. It is most commonly known today as the Apache Blackfeet or Blackfoot Society. Apache oral tradition maintains that the society name originated during a battle in which an Apache man captured a staff from another tribe. According to one account of this event, a member of the opposing force shouted out a word which sounded to the Apache like *Manatidie*, resembling the term for a tribal name. Although the Apache have another term for the Blackfeet tribe, the name "Blackfeet" has remained for the society; however, the exact translation and etymology of the name *Manatidie* is no longer known. According to elder Apache consultants, *mana* is a word for another tribe (implying some unknown northern tribe from which elders insist it originated), while *tidie* denotes "people" or "group" and is used as a suffix, denoting society names.[26] Late prereservation–era membership included twenty to fifty males who were organized in pairs through nonblood society kinship. Society partners painted and dressed alike; sat, danced, and fought together; provided aid to each other; and in general viewed each other as best friends. This fictive kinship extended to all relatives of one's society partner and, if similar to society partners in other tribes, may have prohibited marriage between families of society "brothers" (McAllister 1935:108–109).

To the Manatidie fell the duty of policing camp movements and communal hunts. Failure to abide by tribal law resulted in a whipping, destruction of property, or worse if resisted. As was typical in many Plains tribes, if the punishment was accepted congenially, the society might replace the offender's property through gifts or sponsor a dance in honor of the man. One of Brant's informants thought that some individuals might have broken the rules intentionally as an economic investment, knowing that they would receive more property and horses than they lost, following an unresisted beating administered by the police. The Manatidie policed Apache attending the Kiowa Sun Dance (Brant 1969:113–114), but were under the jurisdiction of the Kiowa Tʼáimé Keeper and appointed policing society. The Kiowa data indicate that the Apache and any visitors were under their jurisdiction during the Sun Dance, just as any visiting tribe was at another tribe's Sun Dance. The Manatidie are also reported to have functioned actively in the tribal decisionmaking processes, although the extent to which they were involved is unknown. Contests were sometimes held within the society or against members of the Klintidie, with the two societies interacting amicably. The Manatidie have continued to play the role of a "charitable organization" from which people in need can seek aid. Throughout the history of the Manatidie, this has been one of their greatest functions and a symbol of their sense of continuity with the past (McAllister 1935:111).

The Apache literature suggests an integral relationship between the Manatidie and raiding and warfare ventures. Brant (1969:8) states that the Manatidie "was a dance for adult males which was concerned with warfare and raiding." McAllister (1935:111) reports that the Manatidie did not fight, raid, or hunt as a group; however, he also states (1935:109) that "meetings were held at any time of the year, usually before raiding or war parties set out." Bittle (1979:40) points out that members of outgoing raiding parties usually gathered to sing the night before setting out on a raid. Did the society act as a collective fighting force, or did it simply represent the majority of an outgoing raiding party? Since the Manatidie contained fifty or more members and thus the majority of the adult Apache male fighting force, it was the largest Apache sodality; references indicate that combat experience was a prerequisite for membership. These accounts all suggest that such preparations for raids could have been Manatidie oriented.[27] As Plains revenge raids generally followed Sun Dances and as practically any Apache raiding party could have been numerically dominated by members of the largest society, the Manatidie, it is likely that society meetings served to prepare for raiding expeditions. Even if the entire society did not fight, raid, or hunt together, at least some members probably worked cooperatively with each other in economic ventures, because the society's membership included most adult men and because of their fictive relations. Thus, society membership was advantageous economically in that collective society-based ventures netted more ensured returns. The organization of these societies provided a larger collective basis for pooling resources and providing aid to those in need, including fellow members. As Levy (n.d.a) found among the Kiowa, Apache societies probably also financed fellow members for raiding and war ventures and thus served as a credit union for members of similar socioeconomic status. These activities further integrated sodality and community members socially.

Meetings could occur year round, but were usually held before the departure of raiding or war parties; although they were open to the public, announcements were kept secret as long as possible by the four staff owners. Meetings were held inside a tipi with the sides rolled up or inside specially constructed windbreaks. Individuals sometimes sponsored feasts based on a previous vow or honored a relative. All members were required to attend society meetings or else be heckled for "marrying their mother-in-laws" as an explanation for their absence.

According to one consultant, if a staff owner or whipman died, the society postponed all meetings until the next spring. The whipman and staff owners performed the funeral for deceased society members.[28] The society was also required to smoke, to mourn, and to pray with the relatives of the deceased before obligations to the family were concluded (Opler and Bittle 1962: 386–387). When the members of the society wished to hold their next meeting, they sent someone to notify the deceased's relatives of their plans (McAllister 1935:109). The messenger sought the family's permission to hold their functions and to enjoy their activities and encouraged the family to cease their mourning. Upon obtaining the family's permission, the society collected gifts from each family's camp, displaying them in a pile. On the night of the dance the society proceeded with its drum to the camp of the deceased's family, singing as a group. The collected gifts were redistributed among the deceased's family. A pipe was given to the father or another male relative, who smoked and prayed with it. When the pipe was returned, the society members told the relative that they were all going to cry with him for the last time. They removed and burned the relative's old clothing and all wept together for a short period. When the relative arose and accepted the new set of clothes provided by the society, he stated that he felt better and was glad to be with all the members again. The society concluded the matter by striking the drum four times.

Similar procedures were performed not only for members, but also upon the death of any member's relatives.[29] Failure to do so entitled the relatives to stop the society's proceedings. In one case, a male relative of the deceased entered a Manatidie Society meeting and stopped the dance by destroying the drum and other property with a knife. Afterward the society took a horse to the father and mourned with the family, who then gave the society permission to resume the dance on the following day. Today a feast, cedaring (prayerful incensing with cedar smoke), and a "hitting of the drum" are still commonly held for the family of a deceased member, prior to the society's next function.[30]

Manatidie dress included special paint, short buckskin skirts of spotted fawn skin, and a long buckskin or bison hide trailer which was painted red and dragged on the ground. A turkey beard roach made from turkey "whiskers," a red deer tail, and eagle feathers were attached to the scalp lock, securing the trailer (McAllister 1935:109–111).[31] McAllister (1935:109–110) indicates that any member, once painted and dressed for a meeting, could have intercourse with any women he encountered who did not avoid him. Later he stated that Manatidie members had no "privileged license with the wives of the other groups as is sometimes found on the Plains," implying that this license was restricted to wives of fellow society members (McAllister 1935:111). One elder Apache stated that he was told this license applied among only the four staff owners, the whipman, and their wives, who were always returned after the ceremony ended.[32] During this period, a member was prohibited from showing jealousy toward anyone around his wife, as this was believed to cause bad luck.[33]

At one regular spring meeting, the members gathered at a tipi where the four staffs, the most prominent and central martial symbols of the society, were ritually rewrapped with buck sinew and otter hides, which were painted yellow on the inside. The repairs were held at a specified member's camp, accompanied by singing. Special songs, which the elders state are no longer known, were sung during the rewrapping, and prayers were offered. In the morning each otter hide was cut into strips as a song was sung. When the hides were prepared the members sat and smoked. At noon the society was served a meal. In the afternoon the group continued working on the staffs and singing. The staffs were then rewrapped, eagle feathers were tied on, and a metal point was tied to the base of each shaft. The entire procedure, of which we have only a partial description, took two days of preparation and must have included much ritual.[34]

Following the renewal of the staffs, members of the society sang and danced through the camp toward the arena, which suggests that the ceremony was conducted upon arriving at the final location for the Sun Dance. Blunt arrows were shot into the air; there was no protest if they accidentally hit someone. Any dog crossing the society's procession was considered taboo and was killed and later eaten inside a special tipi. Although the exact reason for this custom has been lost in Apache oral history, the taboo still exists among several KCA military societies. Brant (1969: 113) states:

> On the four day trip to the place of the Sun Dance, if a dog crossed the path of the Manatidie, they would shoot it and drag it to the Sun Dance place. Then the women would cook it, and all of them had to eat some, whether they liked it or not. Just before the Manatidie reached the Sun Dance place, they would start to shoot arrows into the air and dance and sing. If an arrow accidentally came down and killed or hurt someone, nobody did anything about it. If the Manatidie brought in a dog that crossed their path, they all went into a special tipi where they ate it. Then the Manatidie did their part of the work to prepare for the Sun Dance. They helped cut down brush and bring it in. The women brought in sand and dirt to fix up the Sun Dance place. Upon entering a meeting tipi or dance circle, members sat on the north and south sides, proceeding clockwise once inside. The staff owners probably sat on the west side, and the whipman by the door. In leaving all proceeded clockwise, those on the north were followed by those on the south.

According to McAllister (1935), the society maintained four types of dances and numerous songs, which were accompanied by eight hand drums. One type of dance is referred to today on the Southern Plains as a Shuffle Dance, in which members hop from one foot to the other or shuffle in place in time to music, while extending the lifted leg forward, making a slight kicking motion. Another form of dance, although referred to by an Apache consultant as "a round dance," resembles a Reverse Dance. The society began dancing inside a lodge, moving out into the open and proceeding in a circular clockwise procession. In recognition of the military ethos, an elder warrior with combat experience danced in a counterclockwise direction. This veteran carried a gun which was periodically fired during the dance to the cries and ululations of all present. Apache women frequently gaveaway on behalf of their male relatives during this song. While this is the only known description of such a dance among the Apache and it is no longer performed, it closely resembles the warfare-based Xàkóigácùngà (Turn Around or Reverse Dance) of the Kiowa Tòkógàut and Áljóyìgàu Societies (Meadows 1991, 1995) and further illustrates many of the similarities in Southern Plains dance forms. The origin of this dance among the Apache is unknown. Dancing was also performed clockwise except by the Bull, who proceeded one cardinal direction at a time counterclockwise, beginning in the east, from which position he supervised the dancing. No one was permitted to touch the four staff owners or to walk in front of them during dances, as they were regarded as martially high-ranking individuals (McAllister 1935 : 107–109).[35]

The women played a role in upholding the Apache martial ethos and recognizing and honoring male success in warfare: Scalp Dances were held during rest breaks in *Manatidie* Society Dances. Sets of five or six Scalp Dance Songs would be played for the women to dance to while the men rested and smoked. Warriors gave their lances and other weapons with scalps and other war trophies tied to them to the women to dance with. Lines of five to ten women, each carrying some form of war trophy, danced side by side in a horizontal formation toward the drum, periodically reversing back and forth across the arena as the tempo of the music changed. Women accompanied their husbands to society functions, sitting outside the tipi behind their husbands, where they sang and danced, and interacted little with the men during the dancing (McAllister 1935 : 107–109).[36]

Offices

The Manatidie Society contained seven recognized offices symbolic of elevated martial ability: four staff bearers, one whipman or Bull, and two *bajraye* or assistants to the other five (McAllister 1935 : 108). These officers and their insignia have continued to the present as the principal symbols of nineteenth-century Manatidie Society and Apache martial ethos. The staff owners and whipman were respected leaders of the tribe and were considered to have knowledge, wisdom, and courage, admired by members of the tribe. The four staffs, called *chah-chey-chu-zhey* (literally stomach openers or gutters) from their use in warfare as lances, play a central role in the society's history and ceremony to the present day. Each staff was associated with a rope or sash which was used in battle to stake oneself down. According to Apache and Kiowa oral tradition, the four staffs were acquired one by one in warfare with other tribes, after which the society was developed.[37]

Society Staffs

The martial origins and ethos associated with these staffs are exemplified in an account of one staff's acquisition recorded during my fieldwork in 1991. The Apache once met another tribe. A medicine man from the other tribe went to the center of the area between the two groups to demonstrate his bravery. Sticking his staff in the ground, he formed a bundle of his possessions and lay down. Taking out his bow and an arrow, he placed the bow string in his mouth and drummed on it with the arrow. After singing, he signed to the Apache, "Come on, let's fight. Try to kill me." The Apache asked for a volunteer to meet the challenge, stating that a man could make a name for himself if he went out there. One young man from a poor and undistinguished family volunteered. The other man was still singing out in the center, periodically stopping to yell and say in sign language, "I'm going to kill you." The young Apache man said, "I'll try." His grandparents told him if he desired to go he could, but asked if he knew what he was up against: "If you don't kill him, he's going to kill you."

The young Apache man removed his shirt and began to walk around the north side of the medicine man, continuing to harangue him. The Apache rubbed an arrow and his bow, touched the ground, rubbed his bow again, and gestured toward the man, who yelled defiantly at him. The Apache man moved his bow and arrow in a circular motion before him then shot the arrow upward. It descended, landing between the man's left arm and chest. He continued to the east side, where the medicine man turned to watch him. Repeating the same process, he shot a second arrow, which landed between the man's right arm and chest. He continued to the south side as the medicine man lay there with his leg over his other knee, singing. The third arrow landed between the man's legs, whereupon he shouted at the Apache, "I'm going to kill you."

The young man proceeded to the west side; both men continued to watch each other, as the medicine man sat singing. The Apache man took out his best arrow and, repeating the same process, shot it upward. Suddenly a loud sound was heard; the medicine man rolled over and the arrow was seen sticking out of his chest, buried to the fletchings. Capturing his staff, the Apache man also took his knife and scalped him. Years later when the two tribes had made peace, the other tribe inquired as to who had killed their man. The Apache man, then old, arose and said, "I did," recounting how he had performed the deed. The other tribe filled a pipe and handed it to him. Smoking the pipe, he stated, "I killed your dog," to which they replied, "Good, it is good that you killed him"; the tribe had feared him because he was a powerful medicine man suspected of witchcraft.[38] All four Manatidie Society staffs and the whip were captured through similar war exploits by the Apache.

The position of staff owner, which was held for life, involved the development and expression of a martial ethos to the extreme. The staff owner was obliged to stake himself down in the most dangerous battle position with the rope or sash that accompanied each staff.[39] The four staffs included two crook-shaped and two forked or Y-shaped lances. These were decorated with eagle, roadrunner, or goose feathers, which were removed from the staffs and stored when not in use. The two forked staffs reportedly contained feathers which stuck out from the tips.[40] When the end of the staff was pointed at an enemy in warfare, the owner was required to use it. The staffs could not touch the ground unless placed on a row of bison chips or stuck into the ground through one. This may relate to the widespread Plains practice of a returning scout sticking a lance through bison chips, which mandated that he give a truthful report. Accidentally dropping a staff necessitated the aid of a combat warrior; after reciting a personal battle coup, he returned it to the whipman, who, in turn, returned it to its owner and admonished him to take better care in handling it.

Visibly demonstrating qualities of a martial ethos, dancing with the staffs was considered analogous to using them in battle; once a staff was picked up the owner could not stop until his purpose, either dancing or fighting, had been accomplished. This ideology is continued by the Chalepah family in current *Manatidie* dances, as dancers must hold the staffs throughout the entire society dance. During breaks in the dancing the staff holders may rest the end of the staffs upon modernized bison chip bags or on their foot, but never on the ground. The four staff owners symbolized ideals of Apache bravery and martial status. As Alfred Chalepah described, "Those men with staffs were like generals. High up position, they were warriors."[41]

The staffs were ranked, perhaps by the order in which they were acquired, were inherited through male lines, and were thus intimately connected to four particular families. While chronologies of the staff owners are incomplete, two of the original captors of the staffs were named by Rose Chalepah Chaletsin in 1964 as One Man Who Went to War on His Horse and Speared One of His Enemies.[42] The name of another captor of a lance, *Chatzupah* (Gut Necklace), was provided by one elder Apache consultant.[43] One lance is reported to have been captured from the Pawnee. The last four staff owners from the nineteenth century and the staffs they maintained are shown in Table 5.

The staff of Kosope was inherited from his brother Captain (born in 1816), who was better known as White Man, who inherited it from another of his brothers. This staff is believed to have been captured from the Blackfeet tribe. White Man reportedly had the staff taken away from him for having ridden upon a Sioux (unspecified) enemy and turned away, failing to use the staff. It is said to have been given to another Apache, who finally

TABLE 5   Reservation-Era Apache Staff Keepers

Name	Lifespan	Type of Staff
1. Captain Kosope	1868–11/23/1937	curved
2. Joshua Kaudlekaule	ca. 1860–ca. 1930	forked
3. Taho	1857–1941	forked
4. Archilta	1860–1923	curved

killed the enemy. However, the staff apparently reverted to the family; after the death of White Man, his brother Kosope assumed the name "Captain," inherited his brother's staff, and was henceforth commonly known as Captain Kosope.[44] The staff of Joshua Kaudlekaule, who was also known as *Ida'.ye'ci'sa'but* (He Cut Up a Man on the Warpath), was believed to have been captured by him while he was a young man, but because of his age was in fact more likely inherited.[45] The origins of the staff kept by Taho are unknown; it is possible that it descended from his father, Iron Shirt, a prominent tribal leader.[46] The fourth staff was passed from a grandfather or great-grandfather to Tse-long (Long Lock or Long Hair), to a son or grandson, then to the latter's brother Archilta, who passed it on to his son-in-law Chaletsin or Apache Ben, who then left it to his last wife, Rose Chalepah Chaletsin, upon his death in 1956. This was the last of the staffs made for dances circa 1910 and unfortunately was destroyed in a house fire in 1981.

Despite this loss and the renewal of the staffs, the ideology and symbolism associated with staffs (acquisition in battle, bravery, willingness to use them in battle, protection of the people, and leadership exhibited by the owners) continued, as demonstrated in the ethnographic accounts of reservation and postreservation generations. The use of the Manatidie staffs as symbols for a variety of associated cultural elements reappears in later twentieth-century revivals.[47]

The four Manatidie staff owners were formerly organized in pairs, with the owners of each set or type of staff acting as society partners and dressing alike. The staff owners planted their staffs in front of them during meetings, with the curved-staff owners sitting on the north side and the forked-staff owners on the south side. All four staff owners wore hairplate draggers with a yellow bison calf tail attached to the end, which most likely symbolized the past use of no-retreat sashes which accompanied the staffs.[48] According to McAllister (1935:110), these staffs were never destroyed, but were passed on to a brother, son, or grandson, which included a wide range of male individuals in the classificatory sense. However, Apache elders indicate that upon the death of an owner his staff was broken and was buried with its owner, along with his other equipment, which one elder stated "represented the end of his duty as a warrior." Thus, being a society staff owner entailed obligatory military duties regarding the care, maintenance, and use of a staff and behavior exemplary of a martial ideology. A male relative of the previous owner was then selected by the remaining three owners. Leaders sought to initiate a person from the same family and of the same character as the deceased: the best warrior in the family and someone that people felt would have the courage to use the staff, who would become a leader, and upon whom they could depend. When a satisfactory replacement had been chosen, a new staff was made and a "routine" was performed to initiate the new keeper. The society sought the permission of the family and "hit the drum" to show respect to the family and to enable their future functions to continue.[49] Of the last four staff owners born in the prereservation era, three had no male successors; some of the staffs were cared for by women. Archilta chose his son-in-law Chaletsin or Apache Ben to inherit his staff, prior to his death in 1923. Much of the knowledge used to revive the society in 1959–1960 came from Apache Ben before his death in 1956 and from his surviving wife, Rose Chalepah Chaletsin, and her son Alfred Chalepah. As Alfred Chalepah described, "Like this Blackfeet society, it stopped way, way back there. The identity almost went. Who owns this? I just happened to be around where the men was called [named publicly] who owns this and who owns that, and how the routine, how it is put together. I put all of that on this, on this kind [tape recorder] and on a [video] camera."[50] Staff owners selected new members, sent the *bajraye* on errands, and decided when dances were to be held.

The Whipman

Possessing the ultimate martial symbol of authority, the Manatidie Society whipman carried a serrated wooden whip (*klin-deh-sah-sey* or *klin-bey-sah-sey*) with a red fox pelt for a wrist loop as his badge of office and was known as the Boss of the Whip or *Klin-deh-sah-sey-yhep-shpoon-lay*.[51] The whipman conducted the society's activities, holding authority over all, and was reportedly the only one with the power to induct new members. He is said to have practiced contrary behavior like that in the Klintidie Society. During Manatidie dances the whipman prevented children or dogs from running into the arena and was the only individual allowed to go between the society staffs and the drum. When any article of dress was dropped by a dancer, members regarded it as an enemy and danced around it, feigning an attack.

The whipman had a combat veteran retrieve the article and, after reciting a war deed (*daht-tah-kah*), returned it to its owner, who was admonished to secure his dress better in the future.

Descriptions indicate that the whipman carried a bow and arrows along with the whip and its attached red fox skin and is therefore likely to have been the man who led the society's processions into the arena, while scouting for and shooting any stray dogs.[52] There are references to a long knife (probably a sword), which was captured from a group of Anglo soldiers and was perhaps once owned by a member or used in the society's functions.[53] A long stick said to represent a knife that was previously used in combat and carried by a *bazaye* in the Manatidie in 1960 (Bittle 1962:158) most likely symbolized this sword.

The Manatidie whip was originally captured from another tribe by an Apache man whose name is no longer remembered. It was inherited by his great-grandson Rolling Pony (*Daisxate* or *Dahaishque*), who later served as an agency policeman and is remembered to have danced with the whip in a Manatidie dance in 1908, shortly before his death that same year. Having no surviving children and not wishing the whip to be destroyed, his wife passed it on to his two nephews, *Ba-i-zodeh* (Good for Him or Lucky Man), also known as Big Tom, and his brother *Gonkoncheyhastayyah* (Man over His Camp or Man Guarding His Camp), who is better known as Apache John, the last recognized Apache tribal chief. After serving as whipman, Big Tom, then in declining health, passed it on to his brother Apache John before his death. Relatives displayed photographs of Apache John holding the society whip, which, according to one individual, bore a depiction of two horses facing each other. A similar pattern is depicted on the current society whip kept by the Chalepah family. After the death of his wife, Apache John came to live with Rose Chalepah Chaletsin's family; her son Alfred Chalepah helped care for Apache John after he became blind and learned much of the old culture from him. Upon the death of Apache John in 1927, his land and possessions, including the Manatidie whip, were willed to Alfred Chalepah, who was Apache John's wife's sister's grandson and now lives on his allotment. In June 1993 Alfred Chalepah formally passed the whip and position as whipman to his son Alonzo Chalepah at the Annual Chalepah Apache Blackfeet Society dance.

Since the division of the revived Apache Blackfeet Society in 1963, both societies have used numerous individuals as their temporary whip and thus the position often varies from dance to dance. Nevertheless, the whipman continues to direct the ceremony and the traditional forms of respect symbolized in holding control over the arena are still associated with the position.

SUCCESSION OF THE MANATIDIE SOCIETY WHIP

1. Captured by an unknown Apache man from an enemy tribe.

2. Passed to a great-grandson Dahaishque, Rolling Pony, sometimes identified as Roan Pony or Grey Horse, who died circa 1908.

3. Passed to Big Tom (1855–January 24, 1920); Ba-i-zodeh, Good for Him, a nephew of Rolling Pony).

4. Passed to Apache John (1849–1927; aka Gonkoncheyhastayyah, Man over His Camp, a nephew of Roan Pony and brother of Big Tom).

5. Passed to Alfred Chalepah in 1927 (a grandson of Apache John's wife's sister).

6. On June 20, 1993, Alfred Chalepah formally passed his leadership position and society whip to his son Alonzo Chalepah during a public speech at the Chalepah Annual Blackfeet Society encampment, west of Fort Cobb, Oklahoma.[54]

Like the succession of staff keepers, that of the *Manatidie* whip demonstrates that the organizational significance of authority was maintained in individual families.

The Bajraye

The last office in the Manatidie was the two *bajraye*. According to McAllister (1935:107), "Two of the leaders, the Bajraye," ran errands and messages for the four staff owners, tended the meeting fire, brought water and tobacco, and spied on members' wives during all-night meetings. During some dances they led the staff owners, of whom they were not "afraid." These members also captured new initiates by sneaking up on them; when caught, they could not refuse membership. Although membership was considered an honor, men frequently avoided induction because of the lengthy dances and dangerous responsibilities associated with membership, typical of many Plains societies. The office of *bajraye* is not recognized by contemporary elders and is not maintained in either of the current Manatidie Societies. Bittle's (1962:158) description of the two "Bulls" employed in the early 1960s reflects the post-1959 changes in duties and regalia of a past single whipman to two modern positions of what his consultants called the "janitor" of the dance or *bazaye*. This term is used for the whelp of a litter, which may be McAllister's *bacaye*. One of Bittle's consultants even stated that the *bazaye* belonged to the Klintidie. Although the distinctions are difficult to distinguish now and McAllister's descriptions were contested by Bittle's consultants, the time of McAllister's work and the age of his consultants, the last of the members from the prereservation era, give credence to his accounts.

The current position of whipman in the society reflects a combination of the duties of the past positions of whipman and *bajraye*. The Apache *bajraye* closely resemble a cross between the Kiowa positions of the adult whipmen (áljóqî) and the youth servant members (áujòqî or íjéqî), although they appear to have been adults in the Manatidie. The presence of only one whipman in the Apache Manatidie may explain this combination of duties. Among many Plains societies, the families of newly inducted members feasted the society and gave presents to the leaders in honor of their relative (McAllister 1935:107–108).

In summary, the Manatidie was the largest Apache military sodality. It contained the majority of warriors, served as the focus for warfare and raiding activities, affected tribal decisionmaking processes, and performed numerous community services (hunt and camp police, charity, etc.). The society exhibited many of the core elements associated with Apache martial ideology, which were represented and conveyed through society symbols.

KLINTIDIE: THE HORSEMEN'S SOCIETY

The Klintidie (Horse People or Horsemen's Society, from *klin*, horse, and *tidie*, people or society) was a small contrary society, containing many of the characteristics common to the Plains "Dog Soldier" complex, including contrary behavior, sashes, and staking oneself down in battle. There were ten to sixteen individuals, who were the oldest and bravest men of the tribe. Members were paired and, if they did not get along amicably, could change partners, as it was believed that partners should be like blood brothers (McAllister 1935:111; Newcomb 1970:20). Similar to the Kiowa Qóichégàu, the Klintidie also contained older men who were lifetime members, but who had "retired." These elders no longer had any active obligations in warfare, but continued to function as advisory members of the society concerning music, dance, and ceremonial aspects of the organization.[55]

Four individuals known as "Dogs" and a fifth individual known as the "Owl Man" or "Ghost Man" served as leaders. Each of the four Dog members wore a distinguishing red or black sash over his left shoulder, which passed under his right arm and trailed onto the ground. The red and black sashes could also be worn by an owner's society partner. Each member also wore a headdress of split owl feathers, and some wore clusters of owl feathers attached to their shoulders. Members carried rattles of deer hooves, and eagle bone whistles were blown while dancing or when a member became angry. The whistles were blown for relief, as members were prohibited from expressing anger under any circumstances (McAllister 1935:112, 1970:45).

The society had several contrary characteristics typical of the larger Plains "Dog Soldier" complex, including the use of backward speech in both battle and dances. Thus, if commanded to retreat, the Klintidie were required to charge. If ordered to remain, a member responded, *Aho, aho* (thank you, thank you) and then retreated. As contraries, the society represented the utmost in Apache martial bravery. Joe Blackbear described such bravery in battle, which also suggests that the society was on a journey as a unit:

> One time the Klintidie were eating. When they started out again, some other Indians attacked them. They began to run. No one spoke to him, so the man with that rope stopped, dismounted, and let his horse run off. He put the rope and arrow on the ground. The leader of the enemy group charged past him, but he sidestepped and shot him with an arrow. Then one of the Klintidie came up and said, "Stay right there." So he jumped onto that man's horse and rode away with him.[56]

In battle, Klintidie members were expected to release their mounts, slapping them to make them run away. Sash wearers were required to stake themselves down by planting an arrow through the end of their sash and remain there until another person pulled the arrow out and commanded them to remain. If the sound or mimicry of an owl was heard in battle, all society members were irrevocably required to hold their ground, regardless of circumstances (Brant 1969:47). McAllister (1937:150) received the impression from elders in 1934 that requiring a man to stand his ground in battle, even though he might be killed, was "expecting too much." He believed that this change was a recent development due to the impact of Euro-American firearms, against which a man's bravery and physical prowess had little chance. Contrary behavior was required only during warfare-related activities and not in everyday camp life.[57] Despite the honor associated with membership and the seriousness of these duties, likely candidates often ran away from camp during meetings to prevent induction (McAllister 1935: 111–112). There are Apache accounts in which parents even sent their sons out of the camp to hunt, to swim, to visit other camps, and so forth, to prevent their induction by the society during the four-day society meetings.[58] According to one consultant, membership was not voluntary, and initiations were uncomfortable.[59] Initiations occurred after two members of the society caught a prospective member and escorted him back to the society meeting. Despite attempts to escape induction, it is said to have been only a matter of time until the Klintidie found you.

Differing from what is known concerning other Southern Plains contrary societies, the Klintidie were associated with worship, expressed through smoking and praying during their meetings. Dances and prayers were held for general illness as well as for epidemics. As one of McAllister's (1935:113) consultants related, "They usually prayed to the medicine bundles which had been given them by their fathers. They prayed to everything: trees, grasses, water, anything that our father made. They worshiped with this dance." Connected with the religious quality of the Klintidie was a special relation with the owl, which was often viewed as having malevolent associations. The Apache saw the owl as a spirit or ghost which could bring facial distortion or more serious illness if seen. The presence of an owl represented the return of a deceased's spirit to haunt the living. The hooting of an owl or its imitation by someone after an all-night meeting required another day of dancing and if heard in battle required the society members to stand their ground.

According to McAllister, one of the most important Klintidie members was known as the "Owl or Ghost Man." He was supposed to be able to understand and to interpret the mysteries and sounds of the owl, which were used for prophecy in a number of Plains tribes, especially for predicting the outcome of war ventures. The feathers were worn to acquire supernatural power, which was to bring "good luck" by protecting the wearer from sickness, poison, and death.[60] While regularly praying for the health and happiness of all, this individual was known to disrobe during ceremonies and to have license with any woman, unless she commanded him in the contrary to do so. During meetings the Owl Man, wrapped in a blanket, could expose himself to members and, upon shaking out his breechclout, indicate that the society would dance for four days and nights (McAllister 1935:113). McAllister (1937:155) interpreted this behavior from the Emile Durkheim and A. R. Radcliffe-Brown perspectives as "perhaps another instance of the sacred's being set apart and made awesome by shocking or antisocial conduct." Brant (1951:55), however, viewed it as an institutionalized outlet for repression produced by a lifestyle based upon the social interactions of a close primary group.

Only two of the last Klintidie members are known today. One was an Apache man referred to by his Kiowa name as *Wdlkwwn* (possibly Áulkáuàun, Poor, Pitiful Hair), who was very old in 1867. The other was Old Man Chewing, one of the four Klintidie sash owners and the father of Daveko,

Saddleblanket, Lot of Bows, and White Shirt (McAllister 1965:213, 1970: 45–46).[61] The four Klintidie sash owners or Dogs and the Owl Man, the four Manatidie staff owners and whipman, and the four tribal medicine bundle owners may have represented a standard number of officers, but this cannot be confirmed without information on other Apache societies which is no longer available.

Meetings, which were probably centered around the preparatory period for the Sun Dance, lasted from one to four days. Wives attended the meetings of their husbands, which were generally held inside a tipi. Meetings were announced several days in advance; as was common among Southern Plains communities, tardiness or absence resulted in the taunt of "marrying or sleeping with your mother-in-law" by fellow members (McAllister 1935: 111–112). The lyrics of only one Klintidie Society song are known to have been recorded. Joe Blackbear provided the following song, which reflects the elevated levels of bravery typical of other Plains "Dog Soldier" societies, in 1949: "I know I am going to get killed. But my bed place will always be back there."[62]

Although the Klintidie performed counterclockwise round dances, it is unknown if these resemble contemporary round dances. Some elders stated that the "hop" step now danced in the Manatidie came from the Klintidie. Little knowledge of the Klintidie remained by the time of McAllister's fieldwork; it has now almost totally disappeared, with elders remembering only generalities regarding the society. Musically, the society has neared extinction. Because songs on the Southern Plains frequently outlive their associated societies, it is often possible to record military society song texts several generations after the cessation of a society. However, the cultural erosion of the Klintidie was demonstrated by John Beatty (1974:6), who was unable to recover a single Klintidie song in its entirety during his survey of Apache music. Elders still occasionally speak of the group as the "top warriors" or "bravest of the brave" among the Apache. While little knowledge remains concerning the Klintidie, the society name continues to symbolize the highest ideals of Apache martial ideology.

THE SWIFT FOX SOCIETY

There are indications that at least one and possibly two other Apache men's societies existed in prereservation times. My eldest Apache consultant knew of the existence of a fourth Apache men's society, but was reluctant to speak of it. Although the organization's names have been lost, one current elder was told by his grandfather Kosope that the organization had something to do with adultery and was abolished because of this. My eldest consultant, Alfred Chalepah, stated: "There were four societies. . . . This third one, I heard a little bit, but I let it go. I didn't want to talk about this other one because it wasn't decent. . . . It was a man's, man's [men] only. It belongs to a high ranked society of men." [63] While this may be associated with earlier forms of the Manatidie, Klintidie, and Izuwe (McAllister 1935:113, 1937: 111), it may refer to the Swift Fox organization listed by Clark (1982:355). Although Clark was unable to provide a complete list of Apache societies, his inclusion of the Swift Fox is nevertheless important in showing the existence of another military sodality.

DAHVASHSAHGOOTAS (PAWNEE DANCE): THE APACHE WAR DANCE SOCIETY

Like the Kiowa Óhòmò Society received from the Cheyenne and the Comanche War Dance Society acquired from the Ponca, a version of the widely diffused Grass, Omaha, or War Dance also spread to the Apache in the latter nineteenth century. The War Dance was given to the Apache by a contingent of Pawnee who came to visit on Daha Creek sometime prior to 1900 and is said to have formally established peace between the two tribes. The lack of any mention of this society by Clark (1982:355) in 1885 may suggest that its acquisition came later. The Apache War Dance Society continued to gain in popularity well into the 1930s. The Pawnee, who according to the Apache received the dance from the Ponca, also provided a drum and a set of wooden drum-holding sticks with it; the Apache gave a number of horses in return for the dance, which signified peace between the two tribes. The dance is thus known as the *Dahvashsahgootas* (Pawnee Dance). The dance was originally viewed as a male warriors' dance and was performed by prereservation period veterans. Only traces of the society's structure and ceremonial organization could be obtained from archival sources and contemporary elders. [64]

The number of officers in the society is unclear. Like the other Apache men's societies, the War Dance Society contained a whipman position. Accounts indicate that there were originally two whipmen. One of the whipmen, Frank Taho, who inherited the position through his family line, would arise at the beginning of songs and dance down the line of seated dancers, each of whom would rise as he passed and begin to dance behind him. At the end of each song, after the dancers were seated, the tail of each song was danced only by the whipmen. There are indications that the War Dance Society, like the Manatidie and Klintidie Societies, may have had four leaders, but this remains unclear. Apache Jay and Captain Kosope are known to have served as drum keepers, although this office is thought to have been a post-1900 development. Four princess positions were maintained in the society by Jeanette Berry Mopope, Suzie Redbone Wetselline, Ivy Mowatt, and Rose Chalepah. Dressed in their finest clothing, they sat near the drum and danced along the inside edges of the arena. According to one War Dance Society member whose mother was a princess, the rule about resigning their positions upon marrying and having children did not apply; he recalled seeing his mother as one of the society princesses when he was a small boy. There are also indications of informal society partners, as some members always sat and danced together as "buddies." Initiation procedures are unclear; however, members' families frequently gave-away in honor of their relative at the annual Apache War Dances.[65]

Resembling the War Dance of other societies, the Apache War Dance contained a starting song in which members danced through openings on each side of the arena, a Chief's Song during which the head tribal chief alone danced, a Giveaway Song and Dance, and a Quitting Song. The Starting Song was the same as that used by the Kiowa Óhòmò Society today. Elders do not recall the presence of any whistle men or Horse Stealing Songs or Dances in the Apache War Dance. Apache War Dance Society songs were largely Apache in style. Elders do not remember the use of Pawnee or Ponca songs, but suggest that they might have been used previously. Several Apache have been members of the Kiowa Óhòmò Society, and a few Apache personal songs are still sung in that society's dances.[66]

Dances were held for three to four days during annual summer dance encampments, usually around the Fourth of July, and dancing was limited to daytime hours. Between circa 1890 to 1920 these annual War Dance Society encampments may have functioned as a surrogate for earlier tribal-level communal gatherings with the decline of the other Apache men's societies in the late nineteenth century and the end of the Kiowa Sun Dance in 1890. Combat veterans were publicly acknowledged through their role in retrieving any part of a dancer's outfit which had been dropped. A veteran returned the dropped object after dancing around it and reciting a personal war deed. These annual encampments were held at a number of individual allotments, including those of Apache Jay, Captain Kosope, and Apache Jim Wetselline. My oldest consultants recall that the style of War Dancing was originally a "straight War Dance," and members wore predominantly old-style Apache buckskin clothing. In the 1920s the choreography and dress styles associated with the "Fancy War Dance" began to supplant the earlier style of dance and dress. My oldest Apache consultant recalled first seeing Fancy Dance bustles in 1922, attributing the spread of the Fancy Dance and new dress styles to Chester Lefthand (Southern Arapaho) and

Steve Mopope (Kiowa), who had introduced the style in the local area by 1917. Bustles from this period were smaller, had two spikes and two trailers extending down from them, and were less decorated overall than today. Women's Scalp and Round Dances were included in War Dance programs, being performed periodically while the male dancers took rest breaks. Elders recall that the War Dance was not danced every weekend, as it is today, but only in the summer.[67]

As with neighboring tribes, the rise of the War Dance attracted the outside interests of Anglos, who frequently hired tribes to dance as entertainment for various Anglo holidays and celebrations. Brant's Apache consultant (1969:60, 83, 101) reports being paid for Fourth of July dancing exhibitions as early as 1893 and 1894. Alfred Chalepah recalled traveling in a party of 125–150 Apache and Kiowa to dance inside large canvas show tents at the city park for the Waco centennial in 1914. Participation of Apache and other neighboring servicemen in World War I created a need to revitalize the traditional wartime martial relations. In response, a number of combined Apache War and Scalp Dances were held in which women performed Scalp and Victory Dances with captured German helmets and uniform parts. After a brief period of intensity (1917–1919), such martially focused celebrations soon declined, as War Dancing and powwows continued. In 1921 a large contingent of Ponca attended the Apache War Dance, where they performed a Brush Dance for the Apache, giving them many gifts and presenting a drum to Apache Jay, Apache Jim Wetselline, Captain Kosope, and Apache Ben Chaletsin. The Apache reciprocated by feeding the Ponca then dancing for them and giving-away to them.[68]

Despite being the most recently acquired military society, the Apache War Dance began to lose its importance as a society with the deaths of elder members. While the original members were mostly of veteran status, the cessation of warfare led of necessity to the induction of nonveterans as time progressed. According to one consultant, most Apache men belonged to the society circa 1920. As Ray Blackbear stated, "This organization lasted until the late '20s, then all those old members died out, seemed like they took it with them. . . . Epidemics during World War I killed lots of those old members."[69] In the 1930s the rise of contest dancing and social powwows began to lure dancers into performing more frequently in social and nonsociety or nonceremonial contexts and outside the tribal community. Many elders are remembered for voicing protests against contests, which they felt jeopardized their beliefs regarding the dance. As one of my consultants emphatically stated, "In the 1920s there was no money in it [the War Dance; i.e., no contests]. This dance belonged to men that fought."[70]

Even with few remaining veterans by the 1920s, the dance was still associated with honoring veterans and the military ideology of the original society ethos. The influences of World War II briefly revived the frequency of Apache War Dancing as a tribal community, but not as a society, with the sponsoring of numerous powwows for outgoing and incoming veterans by the Apache Service Club. Dances continued to be held until 1957, when efforts began to concentrate upon meetings for planning and preparing the revival of the Manatidie Society.[71] While formal society War Dances are no longer held by the Apache today, many men and women continue to dance at an occasional Apache dance, and in the more frequent powwows of neighboring tribes, in which War Dancing generally occurs as the evening portion of dance programs. These occasions almost always follow an afternoon performance of the Manatidie and are primarily limited to the larger annual Apache functions. A number of Apache dancers participate in War Dances of neighboring tribes. While the Kiowa and Comanche have been able to maintain formal War Dance societies and more numerous powwows to the present, the Apache have not, possibly due to factors of population size, economy, and competition in developing a following.

Although acquired relatively late, the Apache War Dance was adapted to and reflected the preexisting Apache martial ideology found in earlier military societies. As an alternative continuation of military society traditions, the War Dance was viewed as a veterans' dance, and combat veterans were honored and performed integral functions in the society. In addition, Scalp Dances, the traditional manner for women to honor returning and successful warriors, were incorporated into the new society's performances. Although many of the original traditions had declined by the late 1920s, the prereservation ideology associated with warfare and the role of veterans has been maintained by later generations born during the reservation era.

THE IZUWE

The Izuwe, the only known Apache women's society, was practically unknown to McAllister's eldest informants in 1934 and remains so today. William Bittle's fieldnotes indicate that the oldest tribal members were still reluctant to discuss the Izuwe.[72] While several current Apache elders acknowledge the existence of a women's society, none could produce a name for the group or any information concerning the society during interviews. Most of McAllister's information was obtained from Taho (1857–1941), whose mother was a member. The Izuwe derived their name from a musical accompaniment performed by rubbing a dried buffalo hide with an object which produced a washboard sound, "zuh, zuh, zuh." Membership included approximately twenty of the oldest women and one old man; however, the secrecy surrounding the organization resulted in little surviving information. Hereditary membership existed in that positions were passed on to female relatives. Deaths of members resulted in the replacement by a daughter, niece, or sister of the former member. Replacements were reportedly not required to feast the society or to give presents, as they were in some other Plains women's organizations. Meetings were sponsored by a successful man who had asked the women to pray for his success before leaving on a war party. Upon returning, he erected a tipi, filled a pipe, and held it while the women successively smoked it and prayed for him again.

Dances were held upon the return of a successful war party in a tipi containing a partition near the door, thereby preventing others from looking in on the meeting. The one male member of the society was an old man who sat on the west side, where he sang and drummed from underneath a blanket. Thus, no males knew the entire ritual. The women wore feathers resembling horns on the sides of their head and red face paint with black markings; they danced but did not sing (McAllister 1935:114–115).

Taho and Apache Stephen were once peeping in on a meeting when commanded, "Coyotes, come in." Once inside, one woman exclaimed, "Our enemy has come." The old man prayed for them and ensured them of a long life. For Taho, the blessing assuredly worked, as he lived to the age of eighty-four and was the oldest member of the tribe at his death. While the women danced, they began to peck the boys and to caw like crows until the boys got away and ran out (McAllister 1935:115).[73]

Although the society was not connected with the Sun Dance, members bit any anatomical war trophies brought home by the men during Scalp Dances, which suggests that they had a role in the performance of traditional women's dances held to honor returning warriors. Little is known about the Izuwe, but they were said to be associated with religion and were asked to pray for the sick (McAllister 1935:115). The functions and descriptions of the Apache Izuwe closely resemble accounts of the Kiowa Sétchǫhyòp (Bear Old Women) and Xálìchǫhyòp (Calf Old Women) Societies, which were directly associated with ensuring the success of male war power.[74]

A REANALYSIS OF APACHE MILITARY SOCIETIES

Following McAllister's initial work, very few data regarding Apache military societies have been collected. Apache societies are only briefly mentioned in the works of Charles Brant (1949:60–61, 1951:51–56, 112–113, 121, 1953:196–197). His data and interpretations derive almost totally from McAllister's (1937) work, which contained little analysis of the Apache societies. Furthermore Brant's (1951:112–113) own comments on Apache military societies illustrate a poor understanding of both Plains and Apache sodalities:

> There were but four of these and they were not strictly age-graded as with Plains peoples, among whom age-grading is an important feature. Moreover, the attitude of the Kiowa Apache towards these societies — the reluctance to assume the obligations of membership, the fear of the *Klintidie*, whose exploits imposed risk of life and limb upon the members — certainly does not indicate a Plains outlook. Again the available evidence indicates that these societies became part of Kiowa Apache culture very late, that they never became well integrated and were among the first features to break down and disappear under the initial impact of white contact.

Brant (1949:60–61) also states: "It should be pointed out that Kiowa-Apache ceremonialism was a weakly developed imitation of dancing societies, lacking both the number of societies found commonly in the Plains and the fixed age-graded sequence." He maintains (1953:196–197) that the Apache groups were weak compared to those of the Kiowa in terms of numbers of societies, participation, and interest and reiterates McAllister's (1935:17) lamentations concerning the lack of data available on Apache shield societies, which "were not, or at least appear not to have been very important among the Apache." Brant (1949:60) indicates that the rapid decline of Apache military societies following Anglo contact strongly suggests that they were superficial, recently acquired organizations that were not basic or well integrated in Apache tradition.

Although Brant's theoretical interest lay in assessing the Apache adaptation to a Plains economy, technology, and ceremonialism while measuring the retention of Apachean characteristics such as language, kinship, folklore, and culture, his arguments concerning societies are weak and erroneous in several aspects. First, as only five of over thirty Plains tribes contained formally age-graded societies, this is hardly grounds for singling the Apache out as unusual. Brant's view suggests that the Apache were "not in vogue" because they lacked formal age-graded societies. Second, as the Apache population has always been small, why should we expect a large number of men's societies, when the population could not have supported them? If the Apache had possessed several more societies, as Brant suggests they should have, then numerically larger groups such as the Cheyenne and Comanche, who had fewer military societies than the Kiowa, should have had more.

The level of interest and participation in the Apache Manatidie Society may have been higher than for similar organizations in other tribes. Two types of meetings must be considered: (1) formal meetings held during the Sun Dance, containing ceremonial rituals and including all members, and (2) less formal meetings including some members for raiding purposes. If McAllister's (1937:151) statement that "meetings were held at any time of the year, usually before raiding and hunting parties set out," is accurate, as Bittle's fieldnotes support, then groups of Manatidie members perhaps served as a preparatory focus or core for Apache raiding activities and perhaps met more frequently than societies of neighboring Southern Plains tribes, who generally congregated as a whole only during Sun Dances. This frequency was undoubtedly influenced and facilitated by the small Apache population, enabling significantly larger portions of the tribe to gather more often than with larger tribes. Although Brant could not have foreseen the revival of Southern Plains military societies in the late 1950s, genealogical data on the acquisition of the Manatidie staffs and whip also argue against a late acquisition of Apache societies.

That Apache sodalities declined rapidly after intense Anglo contact should not be surprising, as the already small Apache population declined rapidly from 332 in 1880 to 139 by 1910. With a decreasing population, the few adult males were hard pressed to maintain larger organizations such as the Manatidie, let alone the Klintidie. The 1892 Apache tribal census lists only 57 males over the age of eighteen, 45 by 1900, and 38 by 1905, some of whom were elderly and in poor health; this is clearly too few to maintain a set of men's societies. The rapid decline of the Klintidie, reflected in the absence of a single surviving member in 1934 and the scarcity of collectible data, is even less surprising given the decline of warfare (as a means for membership and to achieve male forms of honor), Sun Dances, and the policing of hunts and large composite camps among Plains peoples. A similar situation is found with the Qóichégàu Society of the Kiowa, among whom societies were definitely a well-established part of the cultural composition. The last Qóichégàu Society meeting occurred in 1878; only two apprentice members or Colts, from whom most of the existing data were recovered, were living in 1935.[75] Because the Kiowa Qóichégàu Society required war honors to be considered for admission, it quickly died out with the cessation of active warfare. With numerous correlations between the two chapter contrary societies, why should we expect anything less of the Apache Klintidie?

Furthermore, Brant (1949:60) misinterpreted McAllister's (1937:150, 153) comments that Apache males were reluctant to join the Manatidie and Klintidie because membership in these societies was arduous and dangerous and potential candidates often ran way from camp during meeting times to prevent forced induction. Nearly identical recruitment methods and claims of avoidance are found among the Kiowa societies (Meadows 1991, 1995). The Kiowa data indicate that, whether members wanted to join or not, modesty was required upon receiving the honor of induction into a men's society: the candidate must appear, at least superficially, to resist induction. Manatidie membership brought honor and recognition, which further increased with admission into the Klintidie. The same rise in status occurred with progression in Kiowa military societies. With the Apache maintaining the widespread Plains emphasis on warfare and honor, membership, although perhaps dangerous, would have been beneficial to the status of an Apache male. It is unlikely that a society would desire cowardly individuals; after all, this was a Plains culture which placed a great emphasis on bravery and warfare, promoted through a set of military societies (McAllister 1937: 150). Brant may have been elaborating on McAllister's (1937:150) footnote indicating that after the introduction of firearms physical prowess and hand-to-hand combat were more disadvantageous for Apaches and that for leaders "to stand their ground even though they might be killed was expecting too much." While Brant views this practice as shirking the responsibility of membership, the modesty displayed during the induction process and the technological impact of guns on warfare perhaps better explain the cultural changes. In sum, Brant's analysis does not account for several historical factors which clearly affected Apache military societies. These data show that nineteenth-century Apache societies closely resembled larger Plains patterns in function, organization, behavior, ritual, and material culture.

THE DECLINE OF THE APACHE SOCIETIES

I have already mentioned the more general factors which led to the decline of the Apache societies, including a small and declining population, the loss of acquisition and use of supernatural power, and the cessation of prereservation warfare. McAllister (1935:14) states that upon the cessation of active warfare the Manatidie and Klintidie continued for only a short period as "honorary groups," as did reservation-era societies among neighboring tribes. Compared with the neighboring Kiowa and Comanche, Apache raiding and warfare had declined in the early 1870s. A few opportunities for largely non-combat-based scouting existed during the Red River War

(1874–1875), during which several Apache including Black Bear, Soontay, Nokozis (Brant 1969:66–69), Pacer, Daha, Apache John, and Big Tom briefly served as scouts for the United States Army, received uniforms, and encouraged remaining Kiowa, Apache, and Comanche to come onto the reservation. According to membership rosters, no Naishan Apache served in Troop L at Fort Sill from 1892 to 1897.[76] The position of agency police (post-1880) provided a few men such as Rolling Pony (a Manatidie whipman) and Apache Ben Chaletsin (the recipient of Archilta's Manatidie staff) with the opportunity to achieve and to maintain some forms of martial status, albeit through changing, warrior-related traditions. The cessation of the Kiowa Sun Dance in 1890 clearly accelerated the decline of Apache military societies, which were most closely linked to this ceremony. The Apache were briefly associated with the Cheyenne and Arapaho (1867–1874) following the Medicine Lodge Treaty, and contingents of Apache attended Southern Cheyenne and Arapaho Sun Dances from the 1880s into the 1930s. The degree of interaction during this period is unknown; participation did not include the entire Apache tribe, and there are no available post-1890 indications of Apache military society participation at Cheyenne and Arapaho Sun Dances. The reservation period (1875–1900) is typical of initial encounters with forced assimilation and acculturation. The events of this period reflect both Victor Turner's (1968:22) discussion of the collapse of traditional systems and their associated symbols and Wilbur Jacobs's (1987) model of an "era of depopulation and despondence" in which populations are beset with numerous problems following contact and defeat by a colonizing power. Thus, while the knowledge and symbols associated with Apache military societies remained, they were being passed on to fewer individuals and were becoming inactive.

The frequency of Manatidie Dances following 1890, the date of the last Kiowa Sun Dance, is unclear, but as in neighboring tribes they may have totally ceased. By the early 1900s Apache military society dances began to be held only in association with special events. With occasional Katsowe and Manatidie dances, only the recently acquired War Dance Society functioned annually. The last regular dances of the Manatidie occurred in 1902, ca. 1907 to 1910, 1919 to 1922, and 1927.

Rose Chaletsin attended a Manatidie dance around 1908, at which the staffs, kept by their individual owners, were renewed. At this dance a tipi was put up; the four staff owners brought their staffs and placed two on each side of the lodge. After entering and being seated, the men smoked and prayed for a while. Singing occurred before dinner was served. At some point in the meeting the sides of the tipi were raised to increase the available room and probably for greater ventilation. Dances were held inside the lodge, with the drum and singers situated on the west side and the dancers on the north and south sides. After the men had danced for a while, meat, bread, fruits, and other foods prepared by the members' families were brought into the lodge in four large pots. The staffs were kept outside during meals. Standing to the east, they prayed over the food and buried a portion of it at their feet as an offering. All food was required to be consumed; it could neither be left nor be taken out of the lodge. If a member could not finish his portion, he could give it to another, but was required to provide a present for the service. After dinner the pans were removed and the drum was struck four times. A prayer was given by Apache John, who sang four songs. The society then moved outside the tipi to continue dancing. Beginning with those on the north side, the men took the drum and exited in a clockwise fashion. The drum was placed to the west and supported by wooden holding sticks. Members sat on the ground on blue and red blankets, a popular style prior to the rise of the Native American Church, but now widespread. Members arose to dance in front of their seats, while only the staff owners were permitted to dance with the staffs. Women rose and danced where they had been sitting.[77]

In 1918 a dance was held on the allotment of Captain Kosope, a Manatidie staff owner, to celebrate the end of World War I. Several Scalp Dances were held following World War I and probably also occurred at this celebration. Frank Methvin, an Apache World War I veteran who had been shot in the arm, was honored at this celebration and named Wounded Arm. Although Methvin was the only Apache combat veteran in that war, his return provided the traditional occasion for holding both Manatidie and Scalp Dances.[78]

Around this time an Apache Flag Song was composed based upon an older song which some Apache say may have been a Scalp Dance song. In 1927 Captain Kosope, a noted singer, song composer, and Manatidie staff owner, composed new words which were used in an old Manatidie song because the original version reportedly resembled the Kiowa flag song (which is also based upon an old Scalp Dance song). This version is now the Apache flag song.

Our flag got saved.
Our young men got saved.
That is why we sleep good at night.[79]

Another Manatidie dance was performed by seven Apache at the Diedrick's Lake Powwow in 1922, during which several Southern Plains tribes performed military society dances as part of the program. Alfred Chalepah remembered participating in the dance and wearing "hairplate draggers with plumes, attached to braided locks of hair with pieces of broomweed."[80] The organization of the ceremony differed greatly from that recorded by McAllister in 1934 (1935:152) and Bittle in 1960 (1962). At this dance the two curved-staff owners were on the north, while the two forked-staff owners were located on the south. The whipman was situated to the east, with the drum to the west. Each dancer proceeded into the arena two or three steps from where they were seated and danced in place. This description corresponds well with statements that all four staffs were not previously located together, that only the owners danced with the staffs, and that each pair of staff owners dressed alike, differing from the other pair. In light of McAllister's (1935) brief descriptions, this account is probably the best record of the actual choreography of the dance itself prior to its revival in 1959–1960. Although society dances had declined and were infrequently held, their associated martial symbols and the knowledge of their derivation from an earlier warrior heritage remained alive in society activities.

In the early 1920s Manatidie members attended Kiowa Tôkôgàut (Black Legs) Society dances held on the allotment of Jack Sankadota, near Stecker, Oklahoma. While some Apache today claim that the Kiowa picked up their dance and began performing it, one elder Apache who attended this dance stated that the Apache were specifically invited to this dance "to give a demonstration" of their Manatidie dance, which only lasted around thirty minutes. At this time women were still not allowed to dance inside the arena. Both Apache and Kiowa elders recall seeing some of the Manatidie staff owners present at these dances, including Captain Kosope, Archilta, and Taho, who had their staffs planted near where the Apache contingent was gathered singing.[81] Although some of the staff owners were too old to dance, the fictive kinship of society partners was maintained at this time by relatives of the staff owners' dancing together in their place.[82] There are also indications that each tribe had its own society dances, which in some instances were performed together (Meadows 1991:93–102, 1995:82–83). Occasional Manatidie dances are reported between 1907 and 1922, and one elder in 1964 indicated that the Apache had inducted four or five Kiowa into the Manatidie at this time. One Kiowa youth was led around the drum and arena by the whipman as part of his induction in 1919.[83] These early-twentieth-century patterns of military society activity reflect both continuations and perhaps intensified revivals resembling Bruce Ryan's (1969) period of "syncretic integration" and Jacobs's (1987) "contra-acculturation" stage in which individuals tend to revive their culture in modified form with a renewed appreciation of their rituals, in part as an adaptive strategy to avoid cultural extinction. The revival of various types of dances following World War I may also have influenced this increase. There are rumors that a small Manatidie dance was held at the end of World War II, and one performance at the American Indian Exposition at Anadarko may have occurred in the mid- to late 1940s.[84]

Apache elders attribute the decline of the older men's societies to several factors, including a lack of warfare and the means to achieve war-related honors, the rise of the Native American Church, War Dancing, powwows, the deaths of knowledgeable elders, and the numerous strict rules associated with membership. As Alfred Chalepah stated concerning the rise of the Native American Church, "The big leaders took to it, and when the older ones that were interested in it [the Manatidie], that carried it, died out, it just faded away." As we shall see, this was only the beginning of a long relationship between the Manatidie Society and the Apache Native American Church.

As in neighboring tribes, the rise of the Ghost Dance and of the modern "Fancy" War Dance diverted membership from the older military societies. Acquiring the Ghost Dance from the Kiowa, who held Ghost Dances from 1890 to 1917, the Apache held their own Ghost Dance from 1890 to 1892 near Hatchetville, Oklahoma, as well as participating in Kiowa dances. Brant (1951:145) reports Apache participation in Ghost Dances until 1910 and in regularly held Ghost Dance meetings and singing practices throughout the year (Brant 1969:42–43). Although Christian churches began missionizing during the prereservation period, the majority of conversions occurred after allotment. Methodist, Baptist, and Dutch sects were established in five locations and attracted the majority of the Apache Christian church membership (Brant 1951:169–175). After allotment, many Apache began to attend annual summer and winter encampments including either Christian church activities such as camp meetings or traditional dances held by Apache and neighboring tribes. Christian conversions accelerated after allotment, and camp meetings were frequently held, while traditional and new forms of dancing were held on the allotments of older tribal and military society members. The Fourth of July, Armistice Day, and Christmas were primary occasions for Apache community gatherings up to World War II. A large collective camp, involving many Apache families and including hand games, dancing, singing, and other traditional cultural forms, was held throughout much of the year at Henry Archilta's near Boone, Oklahoma.[85] Both forms constituted active social gatherings for Christian and non-Christian followings. As an alternative form of military society traditions, the Apache War Dance acquired from the Pawnee in the late nineteenth century continued to grow in popularity into the 1930s.[86] Rose Chalepah recalled a shortage of available dancers for the Manatidie during this time due to the increased popularity of War Dancing.[87]

The popularity of the dress and dance style combined with the increase in dancing "competitions" for money also hastened the decline of the older warrior organizations, as Indians were being commissioned to dance at Anglo fairs and social events as entertainment. As early as 1894 a number of Apache were hired to perform in a two-day engagement at Chickasha, Oklahoma, for the Fourth of July celebration (Brant 1969:83, 101). Dances in the Cache, Boone, and Washita communities continued during the first two decades of the twentieth century, and I recorded at least thirteen regularly used Apache dance grounds. However, the growth of War Dancing and powwows was by no means left unchallenged by the Indian Agency.

In attempting to suppress Indian cultural activities, agents frequently threatened to withhold annuity payments, the principal form of Indian income between 1890 and 1920, to force compliance with agency decisions. Although they are less frequently mentioned in the agency reports than their Kiowa and Comanche neighbors, similar policies were instigated against the Apache. In August 1916 Agent Stinchecum reported to Commissioner Sells that two Gift Dances had been planned that summer, one by the Apache and another by the Kiowa. When John Whiteman (a Comanche who was simultaneously a traditional tribal leader, peyote priest, and tribal policeman), the sponsor of the Apache dance, heard of Stinchecum's threat to withhold annuity payments, he canceled the dance. A visiting contingent of Cheyenne arrived to find the dance site unoccupied and were forced to return to their agency. As described in Chapter 3 for the Kiowa, several Apache were included in the lists of individuals who had their four percent annuity payments withheld until they signed affidavits which the agency compiled in January, May, and July 1916.[88] Apache elders state that the numerous agency attempts to suppress dancing, peyote, the Ghost Dance, and giveaways affected all KCA communities similarly.

By the late 1920s many of the older Apache in the War Dance Society had died.[89] The cessation of warfare left no way for younger men to achieve the status which was the basis of the military societies and was necessary for maintaining certain society offices. Throughout the 1930s to the late 1950s the Apache continued to participate in the increasingly popular War Dances, contest powwows, Christian church activities, and the Native American Church, which flourished in their area. During World War II over forty Apache men served in the armed forces, with several serving in combat or as POWs. Traditional concepts of power and protection in warfare continued in the form of the Native American Church. Meetings were held for many outgoing veterans, for whom prayers were offered. Many veterans carried protective medicine in the form of a peyote button worn around the neck in a small leather bag. The increase of Apache in active military service, from a total Apache population of only around 400 (Wright 1951: 178), created new veterans, who were supported and respected by the elders. It was this renewed status as veterans that would eventually play a dominant part in reviving the Apache Manatidie.

The formation of the Apache Service Club, a women's support group formed of female relatives of servicemen, provided the tribe with a support organization. This organization held fundraising activities such as raffles, box suppers, and powwows to raise money for veterans in service as well as to help needy families at home. As in the revival of other women's societies among neighboring tribes, Apache Service Club members wore club insignia in the form of a red blanket containing the name of their veteran relatives, their rank and organization, and the club name. Songs similar to the War Mothers' songs of neighboring tribes were composed for Apache veterans and contained martial themes of veterans' bravery and their prolonged absence. Continuing earlier women's traditions of honoring veterans, celebration dances were held for departing and returning servicemen, but ceased soon after the war ended.[90] Although the acknowledgment of their warrior heritage received a boost, the years immediately following World War II focused upon readjusting to community life and political and economic changes. While the symbols associated with their earlier military societies and heritage were again largely inactive, what they represented—a warrior ideology emphasizing the veteran—was by no means forgotten.

REVIVAL OF THE MANATIDIE SOCIETY: REESTABLISHING APACHE IDENTITY

By the 1950s a growing concern among the Apache with maintaining a distinct ethnic identity, combined with a large-scale reacquisition of veteran status, led to the revival of the Apache Manatidie Society in 1959 (Bittle 1962).[91] With the continued cultural lumping of the Naishan Apache with the Kiowa, the use of the name "Kiowa-Apache," and confusion with the nearby Fort Sill Apache, many non-Indians did not acknowledge the distinctions between these tribes. The Apache abhor this ethnic lumping because it denies them recognition as an autonomous ethnic entity, which they clearly deserve based on their linguistic and cultural background.

Because the Apache are numerically smaller than the neighboring Kiowa and Comanche, they have not attracted as much recognition through tourism and historical accounts and thus were less known among Indians and non-Indians as well. As a small tribe the Apache were not able to support as many organizations or to sponsor the frequent integrative powwows of larger neighboring tribes. All prereservation tribal-level Apache ceremonies had lapsed. While the Apache Native American Church, Christian church activities, naming and funeral ceremonies, and many smaller Apache cultural activities continued, these affected smaller groups and not the entire tribal population. Larger neighboring tribes frequently sponsored dances, numerous women's societies from World War II continued to function, and the neighboring Kiowa had recently revived two of their old military societies as the Kiowa Gourd Clan and Kiowa Black Legs Society in 1957–1958. By 1959 the Apaches were interested in reviving their Manatidie Society because of a conscious concern that the Apache were not known and as a means of asserting and maintaining their distinct cultural and ethnic identity. That the recently revived military societies of neighboring groups influenced and in part led to the growing Apache concern for identity and the revival of the *Manatidie* Society is not as important as that a growing Apache awareness for ethnic identity had developed.[92]

It was the rebirth of the Manatidie which gave the Apache a communal sense of tribal identity and a traditional cultural forum for integrating and maintaining past and present values and ritual symbols associated with military service and traditional prereservation life. The revival of the Manatidie society provided the Apache tribe with a vehicle for enculturation that other existing social forms had not achieved. With the return of numerous World War II and Korean War veterans, an improved postwar economy, and a growing rise in the revival of Indian dancing and culture, the Apache were ready for change.

The revival of the Manatidie reflects several anthropological processes. Because Manatidie Society rituals and most of the society songs had stopped in the 1920s, the revival of the society was a clear acknowledgment of a conscious revitalization movement, which Wallace (1956) defines as an attempt to revive past or currently threatened cultural traditions to produce a more satisfying culture. The revival of the Manatidie reflects a second level of Jacobs's (1987) revival or "counter-acculturation" stage and James Slotkin's (1975) nativistic nationalism. The Manatidie revival also reflects Joseph Jorgensen's (1972) and David Aberle's (1982) "transformative" social movements because the improvements sought occurred during the actors' lifetime. Apache today indicate that it was the elders of the 1950s, individuals born after the era of prereservation warfare who had continued traditional concepts of Apache martial ideology, who initiated the revival of the society, which was then taken up by the younger people. Apache elders began to meet to collect songs and recollections of what they knew and had observed about the society as a basis for reviving it. Dr. William Bittle, then of the University of Oklahoma, was contacted to help the tribe gather ethnological data to aid in reconstructing the society's ceremony. A number of benefits were held throughout 1959 to raise funds for a Manatidie dance in the summer of 1960.

The account of the revival and the society's first dance was extensively recorded by Bittle, who described the revived Manatidie as "a rather remarkable fusion of ethnographic description and modern Kiowa-Apache creativity," combining both anthropological accounts and the recollections of tribal elders (Bittle 1962 : 156). The Apache were simply practicing good ethnohistory for their own purposes. Although ethnographic descriptions were used, the accounts of elders were given weight where current recollections did not agree with those collected by McAllister. McAllister's accounts, collected from the last original members and officers, suggest a greater correlation with prereservation practices. Although differences between the performance of the Manatidie as described by McAllister, Bittle, and other eyewitnesses of earlier dances are easily identified, the 1960 revival nevertheless produced a distinctively Apache ceremony.

The initial reception of the society by the Apache and neighboring tribes was good, and the society was soon receiving requests and invitations to perform for other tribes. One of the early tenets of the society was to perform whenever asked to, which has been maintained as much as possible to the present. The revived society had "consolidated" (Nettl 1978, 1985) numerous social forms and functions, as reflected by the inclusion of Brush and Rabbit Dances, invocational prayers, flag raisings and lowerings, Sunday morning Christian prayer services, bow and arrow competitions, games for children and adults, and evening powwows containing various social dances. The original intent of the society was to induct only Apache veterans as members. The great popularity and success of the Manatidie, as well as its relatively small enrollment and few veterans, soon led this requirement to be dropped as nonveterans and non-Apache members requested membership and were inducted. While some Apache supported this extension of membership, others, who felt the dance should be kept within the tribe, voiced strong opposition. Although a martial ethos was still closely associated with the society and visible in its ceremonial, regalia, oral history, and the recognition of veterans, the more integrative role and social attributes entailed in this broader membership altered the society's focus solely on

veterans and a martial ethos. Eventually a separate veterans' association developed from the original Manatidie base through fission.

Division of the Revived Manatidie Society

On November 27, 1961, the Manatidie Society was officially chartered with
a certificate of incorporation from the secretary of the state of Oklahoma
as the "Kiowa-Apache Blackfoot Society (Manatidie)." The Blackfoot or
Blackfeet (both names are commonly used today) Society functioned with
increasing popularity as a single unit until the summer of 1963, when, in its
fourth year, underlying factionalism within the tribe and the society flared
into open disagreement, splitting the society into two groups. The two
societies were renamed the Chalepah Apache Blackfeet Society and the
Redbone Apache Blackfeet Society, each claiming that it was maintaining
and preserving the traditions and functions of the original society. The
Chalepah Society maintained the set of staffs used in the original 1959 revival, while the Redbone Society constructed a new set of staffs which were
dedicated at a dance in Sterling, Oklahoma.[93] Since then, each group has
developed its own set of headsmen, singers, dancers, and members and its
own following. Each group also holds its own benefits and annual dances,
which differ slightly in details of ceremonial performance.

The reasons behind the fission of the revived society are lengthy and
highly disputed. It is one of the best-documented events in Native American
factionalism: William Bittle, who was conducting fieldwork during and after the initial split, collected over three hundred pages of fieldnotes regarding the fission. Briefly, there are several primary factors. One involved ongoing dissent between the two major divisions of Apache, the northern or
Washita Apache and the southern or Boone and Cache Creek Apache, which
may have been preallotment in origin. Factionalism has existed for some
time; members of the southern group have stated that "no chiefs were allotted among the Washita group" and that "the Washita Apache do not speak
Apache right. They sound like Lipans." The Washita group is often described as more progressive, wealthier, better educated, and more assimilated. In contrast, the Boone Apache have been stereotyped as more traditional, less progressive, less assimilated, poorer, and, as some Apache have
described, "more backwards."[94]

Another historical factor was a court battle between the Redbone (Washita area) and Chalepah (Cache Creek area) families over the inheritance of
Apache John's allotment near Alden, Oklahoma, following his death in 1927.

While the dispute centered upon which side cared for and supported Apache John (who had gone blind) during his last years, the Chalepahs were eventually awarded the estate by the Indian Bureau agency.[95] In addition, Bittle (1971:32) reports two Apache Native American Church chapters, which he believes may reflect a long-standing tribal division along which the two Manatidie Society groups split in 1963. My Apache consultants and Kenneth Beals (1967:15–20) report that the peyote ceremony was first introduced by Dayugal (a Mescalero or Lipan Apache) to four Apache men: Saddle Blanket, Archilta, Daveko, and Apache John, who became the first four peyote chiefs in the tribe.[96] Beals (1967:20) indicates the presence of factionalism early on, stating that "the four chiefs were divided, with the shaman Daveko representing the conservative faction; and the remaining chiefs, particularly Old Man Archilta, being responsible for the elimination of shamanism and the incorporation of God and Jesus into the cult." The relationship of control in the early Apache Native American Church and the basis of power in the Manatidie were clearly centered around the Boone and Cache Creek Apache, as Saddle Blanket, Archilta (a Manatidie staff keeper), and Taho (a Manatidie staff keeper) were all Cache Creek or Boone Apache, while Big Tom and Apache John (post-1908 Manatidie whipmen) were from the Pecan Grove Apache. In contrast, one Manatidie staff keeper, Kaudlekaule, was from the Washita Apache, while Daveko's family resided in relative isolation north of the Washita River. As some of these individuals were not society leaders at the start of Apache Peyotism in the 1870s (Stewart 1987:84), it is difficult to assume cause and effect on this basis.

In some Plains populations many of the prominent military society leaders (staff and sash owners) were also medicine bundle keepers. For the Apache, such correlations are inhibited by a lack of knowledge of society membership lists and office succession. Available genealogies for the Apache tribal bundle keepers correlate in one case: Old Man Chewing, a Klintidie sash owner, was a bundle keeper who passed his medicine on to his son Saddle Blanket. Likewise, Apache John, who was a bundle keeper and one of the first four Apache peyote leaders, later became the Manatidie whipman. Although insufficient data inhibit further correlations, this suggests that, as in other Plains populations, bundles were owned by many of the prominent warrior families, such as Old Man Black Bear, who was another keeper. Apache tribal bundle keepers initially did not accept Peyotism, and a bundle keeper was not supposed to partake of peyote. Klinkole, for example, gave up peyote to become a bundle keeper, while the sons of two other bundle keepers did not accept the inheritance of tribal medicine bundles held by their fathers, because of their participation in Peyotism. These views soon declined as some bundle keepers such as Saddle Blanket became active Peyotists.[97]

It is thus likely that the influence of the first peyote leaders among the Apache spread within the tribe. Daveko's influence apparently lay primarily with the Cache Creek Apache as he had no direct descendants at the time of his death in 1898; his nephew Sam Klinkole was the recipient of his painted tipi, teachings, and medicine. The influence of the other three peyote chiefs was clearly strongest in the Cache Creek or Boone area, thus reflecting domination of the Native American Church by the southern Apache communities.[98]

Subsequent to the revival of the society in 1959–1960, there are clear indications of a struggle for both political and financial control, as well as for the maintenance of tradition versus the introduction of innovations in the Apache Native American Church. Several contemporary Apache have likewise indicated this division to me. The last Manatidie dance held prior to the split of the society in 1963 was at Sadie Nestell's, during which arguments concerning food concession proceeds developed. Following this there were arguments over which Apache would travel to perform a dance for the Ute Tribe in Colorado. Just prior to their departure, a death occurred in one of the prominent families involved. The others were asked not to go at this time, but went ahead; a number of calamities befell these individuals, including hearing an owl (an omen of death and/or bad luck), dropping the Manatidie staffs, and legal problems involving some arrests.[99] The division of the society into two independent family and community-based organizations soon followed.

Bittle (1971:32) describes the problems surrounding the society at the time of the division:

> During the winter of 1959–60, the so-called Blackfoot Dancing Society was revived by them and this gave, for a period of time, a new cogency and sense of identity to the tribe. The confusion between the Kiowa Apache and the Kiowa, rampant even in the town of Anadarko, and infuriating to the Kiowa Apache, was resolved in part, and the Kiowa Apache joined the other tribes in Oklahoma in having a unique performance which could constitute a central core for their summer powwow. During the mid-1960s, however, factionalism produced a split in the Blackfoot Society, and from that time until the present, two such societies are in operation, each claiming historical authenticity, and both competing with one another for members and invitations to perform.

This has, in essence, tended to "de-Apachify" the Blackfoot Society, since both groups have inducted members from other tribes in order to assure that there are sufficient dancers, drummers, and singers to effect a performance. In both societies at present, there are many fewer Kiowa Apache than non-Kiowa Apache, and whatever integrating function the society had briefly has terminated.

One elderly Apache analogized the breakup of the society to the old Kiowa story of how two chiefs fought over a killed animal, which resulted in the tribe splitting in two, one going north and the other going south.[100]

In hindsight, Bittle's analysis was clearly premature, but accurate at the time. It is important to realize that the Manatidie Society was revived in a period of considerable uncertainty about the continuation of the joint KCA government as a result of the Termination movement, the Relocation program, and the series of attempts to break the KCA up into separate tribal governments. Numerous meetings and discussions concerning the formation of a separate Apache tribal government were held during 1962 and 1963. The factionalism occurred at a time when a formal vote was first passed to break the KCA government up. The two predominant families involved in the factions in turn prepared for a power struggle to form and control the new Apache tribe, a struggle that continued from the Apache's formal separation from the joint KCA tribal government until 1969, when the Apache tribal constitution and government were officially installed. Following the split of the Manatidie, it is difficult to surmise whether the societies served as organizations around which factions formed or factions served as organizations around which societies formed. It appears that a reciprocal influence existed between the faction and society for both sides. Thus, the society was revived to bring about tribal solidarity, but instead resulted in the formation of two societies that reflected a long-standing community division. The fission of the Manatidie Society demonstrates that as sodalities military societies are not immune to kin- and community-based factions.

Following the split of the Manatidie into two groups, there was reportedly a period of around seven years during which each side had little interaction with the other. This period of separatism came during and just after the Apache left the joint KCA government and established their own tribal government, suggesting that, despite internal factionalism, the larger cohesive tribal needs of self-government superseded the smaller segmental community and society-based disputes by providing a means to renew tribal integration through the acquisition of an independent tribal government.

Following the fission into two societies, a segment from the Redbone Society reportedly split to form the Apache Veterans Association (AVA), suggesting that that society no longer sufficiently met veterans' concerns. The AVA continues to sponsor annual Veteran's Day celebrations at the tribal complex in Anadarko, Oklahoma. Since these events, both groups have slowly begun to work together more, while still maintaining their own separate dances. Most of the elders directly involved in the split of the society are now deceased. Recently there have been suggestions to merge the two societies, but no steps have been taken to do so. As their descendants have assumed society leadership, the two groups, while maintaining their independent organizations, have continually increased their mutual support. Today the group sponsoring a function nominally dictates the dance style; however, in all of the dances I have attended over the last six years, members of both groups attended and helped with the functions and singing of the other society's dances, but might or might not dance. Membership in both societies today is open to all Apache, with small boys frequently taking part, although they are not allowed to dance with the staffs. Non-Apache membership is common in the Redbone Society, while the Chalepah Society is more conservative in this aspect.[101]

THE CURRENT MANATIDIE CEREMONY

The Manatidie is a martial celebration by a culture with a long warrior tradition which is still actively acknowledged and honored. The society dance is viewed by most Apache as a serious martial ceremonial and not as a powwow or social dance. Elements of an earlier Apache martial ethos are evidenced today through ceremonial song, dance, regalia, society staffs and whips, oral history, and the honoring of past and present veterans. As Alfred Chalepah emphatically states, "This dance is not religious. It is a straight ceremony, a victorious dance. The society stands for warriors. It is a victorious dance to show off our trophies and the ability of [our] warriors. It is not worshiped, but highly respected for those men that captured those staffs. Those that started the society were men of all men—real men."[102]

Although the Manatidie ceremony of both Apache groups is quite similar overall, some differences exist. The following description of the society ceremonial combines literature sources (Bittle 1962; Beatty 1974) and my personal observations of both societies' dances over an eight-year period. Both groups currently use the same dance ground for their annual encampment and dance (the Chalepah group on Father's Day weekend in June and the Redbone group on the first weekend in August, which are the two largest annual Apache gatherings). Both groups also use the Apache tribal complex in Anadarko, Oklahoma, for most of their local benefits throughout the year. The male dancers line up on the west side of a square dance arena and the female dancers are situated on the north side. The "whip" is located on the south side of the arena. All face one or two large rawhide basslike drums in the center of the arena, around which the male singers sit, with the female singers to the east and behind the row of men. The singers typically dress in Western-style Anglo clothing, although items of Indian jewelry and women's shawls are always present in varying degrees. Both sexes participate in singing, with the men always starting the songs.

At least five men are required to perform the dance, four to dance with the staffs and a whipman, emphasizing the traditional martial leadership offices of the society. The male dancers wear varieties of Straight War Dance clothing consisting of moccasins, leggings, breechclout, cloth shirt, hairplates or fur draggers, and either roaches or otter fur turbans. Although there is no indication of any female society members prior to the 1959 revival, both societies currently maintain a society princess, who is in her teens, unmarried and without any children. The women who dance usually wear knee-length Apache leggings, feathered fans, beaded purses, and hairpipe breastplates and frequently wear the red and blue cloth "Victory Dresses" common among the Southern Plains tribes. The Apache clearly have a concept of appropriate Manatidie attire and its differentiation from other Southern Plains tribes. Red and black fabric in the clothing and otter fur turbans as headdresses are particularly common. Red cloth draggers extending from the back of the neck downward are said by some to represent the no-retreat sashes associated with the martial behavior of the Manatidie and Klintidie Societies of the past.

While initiations of new members were frequently held during the early years of the revival, individuals have indicated that no such initiations have been held for the last twenty years, as new dancers often simply join informally today. The dance itself contains four major forms in five parts: (1) the four Opening Songs, (2) the dance proper, which is divided into (3) the Smoke Song, (4) another portion of the dance proper, and (5) the four closing songs. Differences between the two groups can be found in all four segments of the performance. To differentiate between the two Blackfeet groups, I will use "group I" for the Chalepah group and "group II" for the Redbone group, after Beatty's (1974) study.

During the four opening songs, the group I dancers carry the staffs and advance in single file from the west to each cardinal direction consecutively, advancing to the north during the first song and ending up on the west during the fourth song. The whipman always remains one cardinal direction clockwise behind the processional. Thus, at the end of the fourth song, the dancers are again at the west and the whipman at the south, where they remain until the closing of the dance. Group II begins the opening at the same cardinal positions, the dancers to the west and the whipman on the south. The staffs remain in a set of wooden stands, while group II remains in place during the first three songs. At the beginning of the fourth song, the northernmost or head dancer leads the dancers in a clockwise procession around the arena. Upon returning to the west side of the arena, the first four men move forward, remove the staffs from the holders, and begin dancing with them. While proceeding around the drum, the singers strike the side or frame of the drum, then shift to an increased drumming on the actual drum head and vigorous singing when the staff owners approach the staffs. According to one elder, the four Opening Songs are believed to be associated with the previous story of how one of the *Manatidie* staffs was acquired in battle, as the dancers, like the Apache man in the story, proceeded to each cardinal direction for one song, during the fight.[103]

One of the major differences between the two societies is their handling of the staffs, which are regarded as ceremonial objects of great martial and historical importance. This is most evident in the second part of the ceremonial, the dance proper. In group I the dancers hold the staffs throughout the entire performance. As in the past, the staffs are not permitted to touch the ground. During breaks in the ceremony the staffs are placed on the foot of the dancer, held in the curve of the dancer's arm, or upon small bags containing dried bison chips located near the men's bench, with the mouth of the bags facing west. Although the staffs now lack the sharp metal points of earlier times, they are still treated with great respect. While the individuals who act as the four staff handlers may vary from one dance to another, this never changes once the dance has begun. In group II the staffs are replaced in wooden stands located between the dancers and the drum for each song. Before picking the staffs up each time, the dancers come forward and caress the staffs by running their hands down the shaft and smoothing the feathers. They then pick them up and dance with them, often shaking them vigorously as if they were actual lances. At the end of the song the staff holders await a signal from the whipman before returning the lances to their holders and resmoothing them. In group I the whipman carries a serrated wooden whip, with designs painted on both sides. In group II the whipman has been observed carrying only a wing fan and no whip or in some instances a bow and arrows. Periodically, the whipman signals another set of four men to move forward and dance with the staffs. After advancing eastward in the arena toward the staffs, the remaining dancers move together to close the hole created by the advancing dancers.

Construction of the staffs also differs between the groups. In group I two curved and two forked staffs are used, while group II utilizes two curved and two straight staffs. Both groups, however, position the curved staffs in the number one and four positions and maintain the order of the staffs during the dancing. The handling of the staffs has been a long-term disagreement between the two sides. Each side treats the staffs with care and respect and follows a number of rules associated with their use. Group I handles the staffs very cautiously, in an almost reverent manner. Group II caresses the staffs and at least some members I have observed appear to be speaking or praying to the staffs as they fan them, before and after they handle them. However, group II dances with the staffs in a much more vigorous fashion, including stabbing motions as with a lance. Some group I members feel that this is excessive, and one elder stated that such movement "does not demonstrate the respect owed to the staffs." As one elderly Apache related to me, "The dance with the staffs should be dignified . . . [it should be] only fancy on the battlefield where he has the right to do so."[104]

The third part of the performance is known as the Smoke Song, which is said to be newer than the four Opening and four Closing Songs, but is nevertheless an old addition to the ceremony. Before this song, no one is supposed to smoke and the dancers are not allowed to drink any liquid. The major difference here between the two groups is the order in which the individuals are watered during the break. While the dancers and singers rest, speeches and historical accounts are often recited over the public address system. Until around 1935 Scalp and Victory Dances were performed by elderly women during rest breaks in Manatidie and War Dances.[105] These dances have not been revived in current Manatidie Society dances, and the women's role is confined to dancing in place along the north side of the arena arbor. Today elders state that, while the actual Smoke Song used to be sung and is recorded on tape, a substitute song is currently used. Following the Smoke Song, the fourth segment of the ceremonial, consisting of more sets of regular dances, is held, which often includes specials and giveaways for various purposes.

The fifth and last portion of the dance consists of the four Closing Songs. Group I remains in place during these last songs, exiting after the fourth song, while group II circles the arena on the fourth song, just as with the four Opening Songs. During this song female dancers in group II follow the men during their processional and dance the last portion of the song behind them on the west side.

Four different forms of dancing are contained in the current ceremonial, based on Beatty (1974) and my observations of both societies. The first three, the Basic, Shuffle, and Hop steps, are used by both groups. The fourth variation or Processional step is practiced only by group II. The Basic step is a knee-bend and heel-drop step, with an accented beat when the dancer drops to his heels, followed by an unaccented beat in which the dancer bends at the knees and rises on his toes. A faster variation involves a double-time step in which every beat is accented, in some cases producing a small jump on every second beat. Another variation commonly seen in the Manatidie dances involves a knee-bend, heel-drop movement of one foot, with the toe-heel step, commonly found in War Dancing, with the other foot. Consultants indicate that in the initial revival in 1960 society members used to dance in time with one another, performing a single choreographed dance. It is common to see at least three dance forms being performed during the same song, with the older members performing the appropriate forms as dictated in the initial revival, while greater variation is exhibited by younger members, some of whom have not been instructed in the proper choreography, according to the elders.

The Shuffle Dance (*Chey-shjo-goo-tas*) step involves an alternating movement in which one foot is lifted and extended in the air as if kicking forward, while the other remains on the ground, supporting the body weight. The dancer continues to hop from one foot to another, while extending the raised foot. Group I dances this step in place, while group II has a tendency to move back and forth at intervals. The Shuffle Dance is only occasionally performed today. The Hop step is performed the same as the Shuffle, except that the foot is not brought forward, but in a more upward direction, and the beat is slower than that used in the Shuffle. I have not seen this form performed by either society. The Processional step is used only by group II, during the two songs in which the dancers proceed in a circuit around the drum. Some Apache have stated that the Hop step belonged to the Klintidie Society but was included in the revived Manatidie out of respect for the Klintidie. McAllister noted that the Manatidie contained four forms of dance steps that would probably have included the Processional, Basic, Shuffle, and Reverse Dances, as similar forms in other Southern Plains tribes suggest. While some blending between the two societies is indicated in the current Manatidie, the contents cannot be fully differentiated.

Manatidie music originally contained songs with words, vocables, and combinations of the two which originated with and acclaimed the deeds of past warriors. Beatty (1974: 16, 37, 58–61) reports that although the Apache music is predominantly Plains in style, it contains strong Athabascan and

Basin traits in several categories of songs, including the last Opening Song and the last two Closing Songs of the Manatidie ceremony, as well as several newly composed Manatidie and Peyotism songs. Although many other categories of songs, with which comparisons could be made, are no longer known, only a few Manatidie songs indicate a southwestern origin. There are also indications of diffusion, contemporary revisions of old existing songs, and new songs acquired through increased mobility to other regions. Thus, Apache music still maintains Athabascan and a few southwestern traits, while having developed in a Southern Plains style. During Beatty's (1974:15) study of Apache music, he noted that there were only two active song composers, both of whom were composing Manatidie songs. Today consultants stated that the only regularly used Manatidie song containing Apache words was composed by Ray Black Bear after the 1959–1960 revival: "No matter where you are at, my mind is with you" (I am thinking of you).[106]

During my fieldwork I heard no songs containing texts. Manatidie songs are the same as those used by the Kiowa Black Legs and the Comanche Tuhwi Societies and continue to spawn arguments concerning ownership due to lack of recognition of prereservation and reservation-era intertribal military society interaction. While Manatidie songs containing Apache words have for all intents and purposes ceased with the decline of fluent speakers, the songs remain important symbolic representations of past feats performed by earlier society members. Even when the exact history of particular songs is no longer known, it is recognized that every song once had an associated history, frequently derived from a warfare context, and thus songs continue to symbolize and to convey past martial traditions. As one elder described for the current Manatidie Society:

> We respect those people when we dance with that [the staffs and whip]. They dance to those songs which are composed by the men that had this culture, that made these songs. . . . These songs were made, they were composed, they got meanings. . . . All these songs have got history to it. Through them, something that's in it. Sometimes that song come [*sic*] to them like they know it and they sing them and they say well this is the way I felt and this is the way the story goes. That song means that. So that every song has got history to it, could be made before or after the battle. . . .[107]

Continuity with the prereservation warrior ideology and many of its constituent elements is maintained through song, although in a modified form. In addition to choreography, much of the warrior ideology associated with the Klintidie has been transferred and integrated into the current Manatidie and is now virtually indistinguishable. While the Klintidie remains a symbolic representation of the Apache prereservation warrior ethos, the Manatidie continues to serve as a syncretic vehicle of Apache martial ideology and identity. It has combined elements of Manatidie and Klintidie Societies, continuing to honor the role of the warrior and reflect pride in a lengthy martial heritage and ideology.

Manatidie Society Benefit Dances

Continuing its prereservation role as a charitable organization which individuals could approach for aid, the Manatidie continues as a service organization. Today this is done primarily by performing the Manatidie ceremonial at benefit dances. The influence of the revival of the Manatidie upon the Apache Native American Church (NAC) is significant. While the initial rise of the Native American Church was a factor in the decline of the Manatidie, the relationship reversed following the 1959 revival. Tom Hill and Kenneth Beals (1966:7) report a decline in Apache NAC attendance in the early 1960s as high as 50 percent in some instances, resulting from the Manatidie's revival and its increasing attractiveness as a social event.

Three other factors contributed to the rapid rise of the revived Manatidie Society as a popular and integrating social force among the Apache: (1) the declining social importance of the NAC, (2) the increasing fusion of Western and Christian elements, and (3) the increasing importance of the NAC as a vehicle of pan-Indianism. The following summaries of these events are derived from Hill and Beals (1966:23) and Beals (1967, 1971:86–88), who chronicle Apache Peyotism from 1850 to 1971. First, Apache NAC meetings declined due to the rise of the Manatidie Society, which is most active in the summer months and which replaced Peyotism by serving the same end. Second, the NAC has been supplanted by increases in Western curing methods and missionizing by Christian churches, which altered the potential level of participation. The reduction of tribal agencies of social control by Western political and legal systems has also led to a decline, thereby eradicating forms of postmeeting advice and moral persuasion associated with the NAC. Third, the recruitment of younger Apache for membership was dramatically affected by Relocation Act programs, which primarily involved younger age groups. There has also been a decline among younger Apache in attending NAC meetings and in learning the Apache language, which is necessary for singing and praying during NAC meetings. Teaching of youths, which stressed individual action and was formally based upon observation and participation, is now difficult for members in distant areas and has led to a

decline of the NAC institution. As an intertribal organization, the NAC unified against outside Western pressure groups, which led to greater intertribal participation and promoted the NAC as an important vehicle of pan-
Indianism.

At a time when the Apache were actively seeking an expressive form of
tribal identity, Manatidie Society dances quickly supplanted the Apache
NAC as the single most important institution fostering tribal identity (Bittle
1962), which reversed the role of the NAC in leading to the decline of the
men's societies earlier in the century. Continuing its charitable role, the
Manatidie has also supported the NAC to the present by dancing at benefits
which raise money for the Apache NAC Chapter. These funds are then used
by a contingent of Apache to travel to the Laredo, Texas, area to gather the
next year's supply of peyote.

As a charitable organization, the Manatidie still provides services to the
Apache Tribe and to other tribes by performing the society's ceremonial at
benefit dances. While the Apache Service Club once performed such fundraising and charitable functions, its decline left the Apache without an active
supporting sodality to integrate large numbers for these activities. Today
benefits are usually co-hosted by other Apache organizations such as the
Apache Veterans Association or intertribal organizations to finance a common goal. The Chalepah and Redbone Societies both hold an annual encampment and dance, and throughout the year each society performs for
various causes. On the whole, the Redbone Society performs more frequently (sometimes as often as two or three weekends per month), is numerically larger, and attracts the largest following; however, both societies
struggle to maintain enough dancers for performances. I have attended
Manatidie Society dances for birthday recognitions, princess inductions and
retirements, medical benefits for organ transplants, dedications, naming
ceremonies, memorial dances, and general fundraising for various causes, in
addition to its fundraising for the Apache NAC.

This broadened level of interaction, participation, and alliance with
various Apache and non-Apache organizations reflects the development of
"consolidation" of the varied functions now performed by the revived Manatidie, as described by Bruno Nettl (1978:132, 1985:26) and Eric Lassiter
(1992, 1995). The Manatidie now serves a greater range of functions and,
while still focusing upon a martial ideology, now has a broader, less specific
cultural significance (Lassiter 1992, 1995); it has evolved from a select fraternal sodality to a broader, multipurpose tribal sodality, which serves as
an adaptive strategy to ensure cultural and ethnic survival. Other cultural
forms have been incorporated into society programs, including communal

gatherings, camping, feasting, prayers, recitation of oral history, speeches, games, giveaways, memorial services, and naming ceremonies. Accordingly, opinions vary concerning the role of the current societies. Such diverse changes are reflected in the comment of one elder Apache woman who, while acknowledging the continuity of the veterans' tradition, described the contemporary Manatidie as a service organization: "Blackfeet, it's like a service club, it's not sacred like it used to be, with our ancestors, but it's used to help one another, anytime. Anytime someone needs help with something." Another Apache woman emphatically stated, "It's not merely a social club. The Blackfeet is still an active, functioning warrior society."[108] Although it is not totally so in membership, it is clearly so in Apache ideology and ethos.

Prior to an event, a family or interest group asks the society to perform at a function. The frequency of society performances is often criticized by both Apache and non-Apache, who state that "performing so frequently makes the dance a show" and "is abusing it, not properly respecting it." The frequent participation of intertribal members and intertribal co-hosting reflect not only the limits of a smaller population to support two organizations, but, more importantly, the ability to increase alliances, followings, and support to ensure cultural continuity through the integration of external ethnic entities.

The Manatidie has unquestionably become the single most important social and economic tool in contemporary Apache culture. Today practically every Apache dance or social event of any size includes a performance of the Manatidie as the afternoon program, during which raffled items are sold outside the dance arena. The evening program usually consists of Gourd or social and War Dancing, during which raffles, blanket dances, and other fundraising events take place. Even though the Apache acknowledge that the Gourd Dance is a recently (post-1920) adopted tradition from the neighboring Kiowa, which increased significantly following the revival of Gourd Dancing by the Kiowa in 1957, it often serves as the evening program for a dance. At many nonsummer Apache dances I have attended, the evening program is composed of an "all–Gourd Dance program," as there are not enough dressed dancers to hold a War Dance. Because the Manatidie is truly the last prereservation Apache ceremony on a tribal level, it has in a sense become the primary billing to attract people to Apache social functions. In discussing the economic role of the Manatidie, one elder stated that many tribes "use their culture as a drawing card" to attract people and resources to social events.

Afternoon performances of society dances across the Southern Plains frequently involve participation of other tribes, which maintains a series of long-lasting friendships among families, tribes, and various sodalities. William Bittle's lists of annual individual family encampments at Manatidie dances in the early 1960s demonstrate a significant number of Kiowa and some Comanche families who have regularly camped and participated in the society's functions.[109] Today the Manatidie are frequently asked to perform at or to co-host Cheyenne or Comanche functions, where they provide a similar service for the family, society, or interest group sponsoring the event. These visits are later reciprocated by an invitation to, for example, a Comanche Gourd Dance group to co-host an Apache dance. Continuing another prereservation tradition, both Apache Manatidie Societies perform mourning rituals including cedarings upon the death of a member or for families that have recently lost a relative. Reflecting further consolidation of functions and the socially integrative role of the Manatidie, cedaring, which was formerly a more family-oriented activity, was taken up by societies sometime in the early 1970s and brings a greater number of people together. Although both societies perform cedarings, the Redbone Society provides these services more frequently than the Chalepah Society, perhaps because of its larger size.

Regardless of the purpose behind a Manatidie performance, the recognition of the connection to the past—in its martial origins, the meanings (sense of community, maintenance of ethnicity, and social, cultural, and economic functions) associated with specific symbols (staffs, whip, songs, dances, the society), and the appropriate respect for these items—has not been lost. The utmost respect is invested in the treatment of the staffs and whip. Elders addressing the crowd regularly mention the acquisition of the staffs in combat, the traditional concepts of bravery associated with their origins, and the lengthy existence of the society. Outgoing and incoming servicemen are regularly honored and a "special" (a song, speech, and giveaway) is regularly held for them. Occasionally combat experiences are recited by veterans to retrieve a fallen object from a dancer. Deceased veterans' flags are frequently flown over the annual weekend encampments. Elderly veterans and POWs are frequently honored at dances. Based on data from the 1960s, Bittle (1979:34) states that the exploits of past Apache warriors "are today even relatively well known by the younger members of the group." Continued recognition of veterans and the inclusion of varied associated symbols, from staffs and the whip to military uniforms and the American flag, have been eloquently syncretized in the Apache form of honoring and recognizing present servicemen, as well as the tribe's past military history.

Although the society and its symbols have changed, these changes involve the peripheral aspects of the society more than the core ideology and ethos of its traditional organization and functions. The Manatidie demonstrates significant continuity in function and content, including the integrative role of sodalities over kin-based levels of social organization and the ongoing emphasis on the veteran and associated martial symbols in Apache culture. Representative of this blending is the recognition of veterans by service rosters and pictures in the annual Manatidie dance programs, which also provide the martial history and origins of the society.[110] During the Persian Gulf War several dances and celebrations including Manatidie performances were held for returning and departing servicemen. As in neighboring tribal communities, the level of enthusiasm associated with such performances escalated throughout the community daily with continuing news of the war. This heightened intensity, as demonstrated by the widespread participation in prayer meetings, parades, dances, and rallies, elevated military themes from ideology to ethos. The importance of veterans and their accomplishments indicates that a strong martial ideology remains among contemporary Apache. The ability of old symbols to take on new meanings that reinforce traditional understandings and make cultural innovations acceptable reflects both the function of military societies as adaptable enculturative units and the ability to interpret new social realities in ways that are culturally acceptable as well as adaptable, such as the syncretism involved in blending aspects of traditional military societies with contemporary United States military service. Thus, the peripheral structure of the Manatidie Society has changed more than the core values, organization, functions, and ideology.

As the degree of knowledge about older cultural forms changes, respect for them is clearly being passed on, at least to those who attend or participate in society activities. However, direct participation is sometimes relatively small; the societies, although drawing significant crowds, often have difficulty in getting the minimum five dancers needed for a performance. Yet, with its associated symbols, the society provides the single existing tribal-level ceremony which strengthens and maintains Apache cultural identity.

Conclusion

The Apache ethnography (McAllister 1935, 1937; Bittle 1962) provides a clear example of how a larger seasonally dispersed sociopolitical entity was linked together through the combination of a widely extended bilateral kinship system and a series of sodalities. While sodality ties were more intensely expressed through meetings involving shared ritual symbols held during the

Sun Dance, non-blood-kin relations of society "brothers" provided kin, so-cial, and economic ties that linked segments of an individual society residing within a residence band throughout the year. Bittle's (1979) comments re-garding raiding behavior suggest these ties as well. Supporting these hori-zontal ties were vertical links such as "band chiefs," tribal religious bundles, small shield societies composed of bilateral kin groupings, and heraldic tipis, which integrated extended family groupings within the tribe.

These links were progressively weakened by forced assimilation, under-mining of traditional leaders' power, population losses, the loss of opportu-nities for martial achievement and expressions, and various adjustments to reservation and postreservation life. As a result, many of the traditional integrative social forms (including military societies) rapidly declined or were significantly altered. Opportunities to express these cultural forms and achievement and recognition of the warrior role became extremely limited and were attained by fewer and fewer individuals. Although the Apache are numerically smaller than most of their neighboring tribes and have fewer veterans as a whole, the importance of the concept of honoring the veteran in Apache culture has not ceased for individuals or for the tribe as a whole. The large-scale reacquisition of veteran status during World War II com-bined with conscious attempts to preserve and to maintain tribal identity spurred the Manatidie revival.

The symbolic role of the society is significant because it links contem-porary Apache with their past, while adapting to the present and preparing for the future. The society revived traditional warrior symbols through the staffs, whip, songs, and dances that were uniquely Manatidie, and thus Apache. While many of the symbols have changed (such as society dress and paint) and new symbols have been adopted (such as the U.S. flag and mili-tary insignia), many of the core elements of the *Manatidie*, such as its em-phasis on honoring veterans, providing aid, and integrating the tribe, have remained. Although the meaning and form of symbols do change through time, they can provide both continuity and adaptation in evolving. The oral history, speeches, program publications, honoring and send-offs for veter-ans, performances of the society, and statements quoted here convey how the Apache feel about their societies. These sources demonstrate that the two current Blackfeet Societies maintain many of the traditional concepts associated with the Manatidie Society, with veterans, and with the assertion of Apache ethnic identity.

Revival of what was once the largest and farthest-reaching sodality within the tribe allowed for a return to broadly integrated functions or "consoli-dation" (Nettl 1978, 1985) of tribal cultural, economic, social, and ceremonial aspects. The military society and its associated symbols provided the enculturative arena for the inclusion and continuity of other cultural forms. As a revitalization movement, the Manatidie has revived past or currently threatened cultural traditions and, despite change and consolidation, provides Apache identity and integration as a distinct ethnic group.

The role of the Manatidie as a symbol of Apache identity permeates many socioeconomic spheres of contemporary Apache tribal life. The basis of the tribal flag song is derived from the society, while the depiction of a single dancer holding a curved Manatidie staff or, more commonly, of four costumed dancers and four Manatidie staffs has served as the official logo of the Apache tribe. Manatidie designs are currently found on the coffee mugs, T-shirts, jackets, and other items sold at the Apache tribal store, on the Redbone Apache tribal dance grounds sign, on the dance shawls of the women's Apache Service Club, on Apache tribal certificates of achievement given at annual education banquets, on official tribal stationery, and on tribal license plates. Recently a new design containing a tipi with two Manatidie staffs on each side of it and a sun above it has been placed on the Apache Tribe of Oklahoma tribal flag, Housing Authority emblem, tribal stationery, and other items. The Manatidie design is growing in popularity as an official Apache tribal symbol, and it can be said that today the Manatidie is a large part of what it means to be Apache.

The importance of the integrational role of the two current Apache Blackfeet Societies for the Apache Tribe of Oklahoma cannot be overstated. With only six fluent speakers remaining, the Apache language does not truly hold the tribe together. Likewise, with the cessation of tribal bundle ceremonies, the Sun Dance, and other societies and the increase of intermarriage, many earlier integrating forces are less significant than they once were. The relative inactivity of the other Apache dance sodalities, the Apache Gourd Clan, Apache Veterans Association, and the Apache Service Club also results in larger followings and responsibilities for the two Blackfeet Societies. Besides providing a living example of their "traditional" culture and a sense of pride and distinct identity, the two societies hold great importance for the Apache people in the political and economic spheres. Perhaps because of the small size of the tribe, they lack the numerous descendants' groups found in larger neighboring tribes that provide a reaffirmation of consanguineal relations or vertical integration, which is often publicly expressed through the sponsoring of an annual powwow or family reunion. The limits of a smaller population and resource base further necessitate and facilitate the integrational and economic roles of the two Apache Blackfeet or Manatidie societies. The two current societies are clearly the largest and farthest-reaching sodalities in the Apache Tribe, which enables them to provide services and aid to a greater number of individuals on a regular basis. As nearly every Apache family has at least some members associated with one of the two Manatidie societies, all Apache are to some degree connected to the societies and concerned with their continuation. With the consolidation of varied cultural practices, the Manatidie, as an adaptive unit of social organization, functions as a vehicle of Apache enculturation; military society symbols form a core through which varied cultural forms are continued.

The importance of the continuing role of veterans and the Manatidie for contemporary Apache in nearly all social, political, cultural, and economic arenas can be demonstrated through several comments gathered during my fieldwork. They reflect the deep symbolic levels of martial and ethnic continuity which elements of the society convey, as well as the moral aspects, which can be considered sacred. One elder referred to the society's importance in continuing Apache tradition and a sense of past identity, including martial themes:

> We don't worship that Blackfeet, but we got respect for it because these men were brave enough to capture these staffs. Now we look at these people that were brave, courage, and knowledge, and respect, proud. They have all that possession. They are that kind of person. We respect these people when we dance with that. They dance to those songs which is [sic] composed by the men that had this culture, that made these songs. . . . They were composed. They got meanings. . . . All these songs have got history to it, through them, something that's in it. Of course I weak, I'm forgetful. But still I try to hang on to the way my tribe lived at one time, our self respect. . . . The longer I talk about my culture, the closer, more sincere, it makes me feel.[111]

Another elder commented on the seriousness associated with the performance of the society: "We try to keep it close to the older days, but much has changed or been adopted. But still, we respect it, we don't like to mess around when we are having that ceremony."[112] Finally, a middle-aged individual who is diligently training to follow in his father's footsteps as a tribal historian commented on the crucial role of the Manatidie for future Apache integration and identity: "I don't know where we would be without it. If we didn't have the Blackfeet Society, I'm not sure there would be an Apache Tribe today. It's really what's holding us together."[113]

Despite some continuing factionalism, the two Manatidie still integrate the Apache population, providing a basis for a distinct identity and an arena for continuing other enculturative forms. Both societies provide a greater range of functions (through consolidation) that have a broader cultural significance than those of earlier manifestations of the society. The Manatidie is focused upon a number of symbols based upon an earlier martial ideology, which reflect significant functional and symbolic continuity through time, while acting as an adaptive form of social organization according to traditional Apache ideology. There is indeed a continually growing renewal of interest in the society among Apache. In the 1995 American Indian Exposition opening day parade, the Redbone Apache Blackfeet Society tribal float contained the society whipman with a bow and arrows and another member with a staff, dancing to society songs. Epitomizing the importance of the two existing Blackfeet Societies for the Apache Tribe of Oklahoma and Apache identity, the banner on the float stated simply, "Searching for Your Identity? Try Tradition."

5 COMANCHE MILITARY SOCIETIES

Anthropologists beginning with Wissler (1914, 1927) have often labeled the Comanche anomalous compared with other Plains Indian communities because they are said to have lacked such traits as men's military societies, the Sun Dance, and forms of social organization alleged to have been "typical" of other nineteenth-century Plains populations. This chapter reconstructs Comanche military societies and their organization, functions, and associated symbols, to test whether the Comanche were actually atypical of the Plains area, based on a critical reanalysis of Comanche ethnographic sources and contemporary fieldwork. The chapter demonstrates the existence of Comanche military societies and aggregative ceremonies in the nineteenth century, assesses their similarity to surrounding Plains communities, discusses their theoretical importance, and demonstrates continuity of traditional military societies and symbols in contemporary Comanche culture.[1]

The distribution, membership, leadership positions, fictive kinship, and aggregative roles of Comanche men's societies are discussed here, as well as their functional roles in the hunt, march, and Sun Dance and similarities between Comanche, Shoshone, and other Southern Plains military societies. Because the Comanche and Shoshone are related and maintained contact well into the nineteenth century (Wallace and Hoebel 1952:6; Kavanagh 1996:245), I include a comparison of Shoshone societies with Comanche societies and those of other Southern Plains tribes. The chapter includes a discussion of Comanche military society ceremonials and brief histories of individual sodalities and their associated symbols. While they were a rather late historical development in comparison with more northern neighboring populations, Comanche military societies did in fact share many characteristics with other Southern Plains tribal military societies, including fictive kinship, coercive and police functions, supervision of communal hunting, preparatory functions for integrative sociopolitical ceremonials, distinct insignia, officer positions, and the fostering of a warrior ideology. My results counter the idea that the Comanche were anomalous;

Comanche societies and their Sun Dance differed from other Plains groups largely in the degree of integration and evolutionary stage of development rather than in their actual content. Melburne Thurman (1980), Thomas Kavanagh (1986, 1996), Morris Wade Foster (1991), and Michael Davis (1996) have argued against the idea of a supposed Comanche anomaly in other areas of social and cultural organization. I examine Comanche military sodality structures, concluding with a discussion of the importance of strong pan-tribal sodalities for tribal formation as argued by Elman Service (1962) in relation to Comanche social organization and the contemporary military sodality roles.

THE COMANCHE

The Comanche are a number of Numic- or Shoshonean-speaking peoples currently located in southwestern Oklahoma. As the easternmost Shoshone speakers, they are related to the present-day Shoshone of Fort Hall Reservation in Idaho. They refer to themselves as *Numunuu* or *Numina*, Our People. The name "Comanche" is probably derived from the Ute name for the Comanche, *kumanchi* "stranger, different," although Opler (1943:156) lists the Ute *komantsia*, as meaning "anyone who wants to fight all the time." Oral and archival accounts support a Comanche separation from the Shoshone and southern migration during the mid- to late seventeenth and early eighteenth centuries (Shimkin 1940; Schlesier 1972:103). Numerous linguistic studies (Shimkin 1940; Hulkrantz 1968; Wright 1977) suggest a recent separation (circa A.D. 1500) prior to European contact in the early 1700s, while David Shaul (1986) argues for a much older separation.

The seminal role played by the Comanche in the military and political development of Texas, New Mexico, and Mexico from 1706 to 1875 was enormously significant. I will examine this period only briefly, because it has been discussed by several authors (Twitchell 1914; Hackett 1923–1937; Thomas 1932, 1935, 1940, 1941; Richardson 1933; Winfrey and Day 1966; Loomis and Nasatir 1967; Simmons 1967; John 1975, 1984, 1985; Thurman 1980; Kavanagh 1986, 1996, n.d.a; Foster 1991:38–52). Although other tribes probably knew of them earlier, accounts of the Comanche date to at least 1706 (Thomas 1935:61; Hackett 1923–1937:3:382). During the first quarter of the eighteenth century Comanche-Spanish relations "alternated between peace and hostilities" (Kavanagh 1996, n.d.a:2). After acquiring French guns, the Comanche displaced the Apache, driving them back into the Southwest and gaining control of trade routes between Santa Fe and the Plains. Mutually beneficial trade with the Spanish fluctuated throughout the

1730s, often ending in violence; it later ceased. By the 1740s the Comanche had made French trade contacts from Illinois and Louisiana. This resulted in the Spanish reopening Comanche trade to ensure a buffer zone against competing European powers lasting into the 1760s (Hackett 1923–1937:3: 382; Thomas 1935:61, 1940:11; Kavanagh n.d.a:2).

Peace with the Spanish was reestablished, as Comanche leaders signed a treaty at San Antonio in 1785 (Faulk 1964:64) and Santa Fe in 1786 (Thomas 1932:305). Despite minor disruptions and depredations against each other, generally advantageous relations followed for some time. Comanche-Spanish relations in Texas were less stable, but improved with the establishment of Mexican independence, as the Comanche signed treaties in 1822 and 1828. The activities of Anglo-American horse traders, present as early as 1791 (Loomis and Nasatir 1967:205), created a larger demand for horses than the Comanche could meet; as a result they focused their efforts toward raiding Spanish ranches in Texas and farther south in Mexico. Meanwhile, Americans were attempting to persuade the Comanche to end their Spanish alliances during the first quarter of the nineteenth century. With the opening of the Santa Fe Trail in 1821, Americans tried to keep the Comanche away from the route (Kavanagh n.d.a:3–5).

During the late 1700s and early 1800s the Comanche competed with other encroaching tribes such as the Kiowa, Pawnee, and Cheyenne for control of access to Spanish trade on the Texas–New Mexico frontier. Comanche resistance involved a number of fights, including several with the Kiowa in 1801–1806. Peace with the Kiowa (and probably with the Plains Apache, who were already allied with the Kiowa) was finally made in 1806, cemented by the marriage and postmarital residence of the Kiowa chief El Ronco and the daughter of the principal Yamparika chief, Somiquaso (John 1985; Loomis and Nasatir 1967:450; cited in Kavanagh n.d.a:5). By the late 1820s the Cheyenne and Arapaho had gained control of the upper Arkansas River region and, aided by Bent's Fort, were aggressively expanding southward (Hyde 1968:58–82). The Kiowa, Comanche, and Apache, supplied with guns by the Choteaus, prominent traders of French descent, fought a series of battles with the Cheyenne and Arapaho along the Canadian River and upper Texas panhandle (Mooney 1898:271–276). Peace was declared in 1840, after which the five loosely unified Southern Plains tribes focused their efforts against encroaching eastern tribes and Euro-Americans.

Raiding into Mexico did not involve large numbers of Comanche until well into the late 1820s. Raiding increased from the 1820s through the early 1850s, when it coincided with the peak of demand for horses during the California Gold Rush (Foreman 1939:163 and Smith 1970:62, cited in

Kavanagh n.d.a: 5–6). After the Texas Revolution in 1836 most Texans refused to acknowledge Comanche territorial claims; however, a truce and trading with some of the bands closest to Texan settlements occurred in 1838 (Winfrey and Day 1966: 1: 52). Continual raiding by some Comanche led to blame of all Comanche. Texans' attempts to hold hostage (for recent depredations) a visiting party of Comanche who had entered San Antonio on March 19, 1840, for peace discussions and trade resulted in the killing of thirty-five and the capture of twenty-seven Comanche. Although this constituted a betrayal that was never totally forgiven, a treaty concluded in the fall of 1844 led to relative peace for the next decade (Winfrey and Day 1966: 1: 228, 2: 114; Kavanagh 1996: 262–264).

American expansionism proved to be the final stage of Comanche independence. Even prior to the annexation of Texas by the United States, Americans concluded treaties indicating the U.S. authority over Texas. The Yamparika agreed at Fort Atkinson in 1853 to the establishment of military posts and a right of way along the Arkansas River, in return for an $18,000 annual annuity. Despite occasional incidents, travelers along the Santa Fe Trail were largely unhindered by Comanche. In 1854 a reservation for the Peneteka was established on the Clear Fork of the Brazos River in present-day Throckmorton County, Texas, but this did not stop northern Comanche raids into Texas. Pressures from land speculators in part resulted in the removal of some 1,500 Texas Indians, including 384 Peneteka Comanche, to the newly formed Wichita Agency along the Washita River at Fort Cobb, Indian Territory (Kavanagh n.d.a: 7–8, 1996).

During the Civil War both the United States and Confederate governments made formal treaties or informal agreements with the Comanche; in 1863 several Southern Plains leaders who were taken to Washington to reaffirm their treaties and accept annual annuities of $25,000 agreed to stay away from the Santa Fe Trail (Richardson 1933: 280, cited in Kavanagh n.d.a: 8). The Comanche and Kiowa were declared "hostile" in 1863 after a series of attacks along the Santa Fe Trail, resulting in a retaliatory attack upon them by Lt. Col. Christopher "Kit" Carson on November 19, 1864. Throughout the Civil War, the Quahada developed a lucrative cattle trade with New Mexico ranchers for stolen Texas cattle. In October 1865 Yamparika and Kiowa leaders signed a treaty on the Little Arkansas River, establishing much of the Texas panhandle as reservation lands. In October 1867 this treaty was revised at Medicine Lodge Creek, Kansas, decreasing the size of their reservation; it was signed mostly by Yamparika, being refused by the Quahada and other Comanche. As some Comanche entered the reservation, others, such as the Quahada, who continued to pursue a trade in cattle, did not. Capt. George B. McClellan's attack on a Quahada camp on September 29, 1872, was designed to stop this; after he captured 124 women and children, many Comanche temporarily moved to the Fort Sill vicinity, exchanging Anglo captives for their relatives. Many left the following spring after the Comanche captives were returned (Kavanagh n.d.a:7–9, 1996: 410–432).

While some Comanche, especially the Yamparika, continued to participate in the lucrative bison hide trade and were guaranteed sole hunting rights to their lands, Anglo hunters could not resist the potential high profits to be gained by slaughtering the bison herds south of the Arkansas River. By the spring of 1874 a group of bison hunters had established a base at Bent's old adobe post on the Canadian River in Texas. The Comanche met for a major political meeting to discuss this economic threat, during which the Quahada shaman Isatai proclaimed that he had the ability to be bulletproof and supply unlimited amounts of ammunition. Under his influence, several hundred Comanche, Kiowa, and Cheyenne attacked the hunters' post on June 27, 1874. After losses of several men at Adobe Walls, the attack was called off, people lost faith in Isatai, and the Indian forces scattered (Kavanagh 1996:435–453). By 1875 the Quahada were consistently harried by patrols and scouts and, with the rapidly diminishing bison herds, surrendered at Fort Sill by June.

Although the Comanche traveled and raided far afield, their core territory lay between the foothills of the Rocky Mountains in New Mexico and central Colorado on the west, the Arkansas River to the north, the cross timbers of central Oklahoma and Texas on the east, and the Rio Grande to the south. Within the Southern Plains existed several alliances of Comanche bands representing larger divisional gatherings with specific territorial ranges. During the eighteenth century there were two main Comanche divisions, the Yamparika and the Cuchanec or Cuchanica, later known as the Kotsoteka, who were frequently referred to as Eastern and Western Cuchanec. The eight known Kotsoteka bands in 1786 had diminished to two by the 1870s (Thomas 1932:321). A third division, the Jupe, Hupe, or Yupe (Timber People), are mentioned in Spanish records, but these ethnonyms disappear by 1820, probably merging with the Yamparika, possibly as the Ditsakana band (Mooney 1912a:393; Kavanagh 1996:478–485).

Comanche social organization changed dramatically during the nineteenth century as warfare, depopulation, and the collapsing Spanish empire brought changes. By the mid-1800s the Kotsoteka had fissioned, forming two new divisions. By the 1830s the Eastern Kotsoteka in Texas were known as the "Hois" or Timber Comanche and by 1846 were known as the Peneteka (Honey Eaters). The Western Kotsoteka in New Mexico, along with Comanche of other divisions, had begun to reorganize, being known by the 1860s as the Kwahada Detsakana (Antelope Sewers) and later as the Quaradachoko or Kwahada Coko (Antelope Skinners). By the late 1860s their name was simply Kwahada or Quahada (Antelope). The Tenewa (Downstream People) formed as a splinter group of Yamparika, Taovaya, Wichita, and others along the middle Red River, led by El Sordo in about 1810. They are first mentioned by David Burnet (1954:121) in 1818. The Nokoni (Wanderers or To Go Somewhere and Return) are first mentioned in 1846 (Butler and Lewis 1846), and in García-Rejón's 1865 vocabulary. The origins and political histories of the Nokoni, located along the upper reaches of the Red River and the head waters of the Pease River, are unclear (Kavanagh 1989:101, 1996:478–485, n.d.a). Between 1850 and 1875 Comanche social organization consisted of numerous (seventeen to thirty-seven) bands representing five major divisional groupings: the Peneteka (Honey Eaters), Kotsoteka (Buffalo Eaters), Nokoni (Wanderers), Yamparika (Root Eaters), and Quahada (Antelopes). This system was in flux, as Kavanagh (1986, 1989, 1996) has identified at least thirty-seven local band leaders from six divisions and others of undesignated band affiliation between 1869 and 1874.[2]

The Comanche tribe was never a single political unit (Kardiner 1945: 54; Wallace and Hoebel 1952; Kavanagh 1980, 1986, 1989, 1996, n.d.c; Thurman 1980, 1982, 1987). Prereservation Comanche social organization included four levels of sociopolitical integration: "the nuclear family, the extended family, the residential local band, and the political division" (Kavanagh 1996:41). The simple family included a man, one or more wives, and various dependents such as children, parents, or parents-in-law. The bilateral extended family or *numunahkahni* (residents of a household) formed the basic social unit. Local bands were composed of one or more extended families and attached but unrelated nuclear families and individuals, which have been referred to as *rancherías* or subsistence bands, ranging in size from forty-five to two hundred people in the early reservation period. These bands formed around a core extended family whose leader was the local band headsman, who attracted and maintained peripheral families and individuals in the band through his own ability and skill in hunting, military prowess, judicious marriages, and politics (Kavanagh 1986:49). Band membership frequently changed due to seasonal subsistence strategies, decline in confidence in a band leader, and individual disputes, which frequently led to fission and formation of new bands. The headsman possessed the authority to impose physical sanctions on troublemakers and was succeeded by the most able individual, who was not necessarily his son. A headsman's position was based upon his ability to attract and hold a following through control of access to strategic resources obtained through trade, warfare and raiding, or European political gifts.

Prudence in the redistribution of captured war booty often determined the basis for political power as "a reputation for fairness in dividing the spoils enhanced the prestige of a war leader and gained him followers" (Hoebel 1940:25), showing the importance placed upon generosity in Plains ideology. A number of smaller residence band leaders sometimes looked to a greater band leader for guidance and support, thus forming a multiresidence band following. When these abilities were compromised a leader could rapidly loose his following, which then began to follow a new leader, took up residence in another band, or fissioned, forming new bands.

For Comanche men, the means to social status was largely through a war record. Like many other Plains populations, male youths underwent considerable physical, psychological, and martial training during their youth and adolescent years (Wallace and Hoebel 1952; Kavanagh 1986, n.d.b). To be a *tekniwop* or *tekwuniwapi* (literally "brave" or "hero," a warrior) was the Comanche ideal. All *paraivo* (leaders, headsmen, or chiefs) were *tekniwop*; however, there was no formal separation between civil and military spheres of action. Thus, as there were no formal terms for "peace" and "war" chief, distinctions were expressed through prefixal modifiers such as *uhda paraivo* (literally "good leader or chief," a civil leader or chief) or *wauhau paraivo* (literally "enemy chief" or war leader or chief). A *maiheemeeahnuh paraivo* (from *maihee*, war; *mieeah*, to go; *nuh*, people) was a war leader or war chief. The term *paraivo* also held connotations of agent or representative, covering both direct authoritarian and passive representational roles, and was used primarily for political relations with nonkin concerning relative power. Differences depended upon circumstances, including assessments of differential political and military power (Kavanagh 1986, 1996:36–39, n.d.a).[3]

Eighteenth-century warfare tactics ranged from small raids to large coordinated attacks with hide-armored, full-body shield-carrying horsemen used as shock troops (Lummis 1898:77; Thomas 1940:26; Secoy 1953; Loomis and Nasatir 1967:363). The introduction of firearms and increasing availability of horses shifted these tactics to quicker strikes by smaller parties. Horse and cattle stealing for consumption and trade became important components in the Comanche domestic and political economy.

The maximal level of Comanche political organization was the division, which included tribal-like divisional alliances of local bands linked through ties of kinship and men's societies or "tribes" in the strict structural sense as implied by Service (1962; see Richardson 1933:317; Kavanagh 1980, 1986,

1996; Thurman 1980, 1982, 1987). As Stanton Tefft (1961) hypothesized, the Comanche began to adapt to a Plains economy focusing on hunting, warfare, and raiding after separating from the Northern Shoshone. This resulted in changes from a bilocal to a more patrilocal form of residence and from a bicentered to a more patricenter-based division of labor. Yet descent, kin terminology, and private ownership systems remained largely unchanged. Bilateral descent and bilocal kinship with occasional sororal polygyny were practiced. As marriage with any recognized consanguineal relative was prohibited, which was sometimes applied to all members of a local residence band regardless of relationship, marriage was normally band exogamous, but intradivisional (Hoebel 1940:12; Kavanagh 1989:101). While these four levels of sociopolitical integration are recognized analytically, their boundaries were often fluid (Kavanagh 1989:100).

The Comanche have a longer documented existence on the Plains than any other population typically considered "Plains Indians." During the eighteenth century the Comanche had assumed many of what were later considered typical Plains traits, such as the horse-buffalo-tipi complex. Prior to completely entering a reservation in 1874–1875, the Comanche were the largest Southern Plains population. As such they held significant roles in trade and horse acquisition. Comanche was widely used as a *lingua franca* for Southern Plains trade. Today there are nearly 9,000 enrolled Comanche, about half of whom reside on allotted lands in and around Apache, Fletcher, Cyril, Lawton, Geronimo, Walters, Faxon, Cache, and Indiahoma, Oklahoma. Other Comanche reside in larger urban centers such as Oklahoma City, Tulsa, Dallas, and Denver and in California.

THE COMANCHE ANOMALY

While all Comanche divisions were linguistically related, their level of social organization (whether or not they were a "tribe") has formed a major debate in Plains ethnography. Beginning with Wissler (1914, 1927), the Comanche have been characterized as anomalous compared with other Plains tribes. The characterization of the Comanche as atypical was based largely on the absence of "typical" traits as defined by Wissler (1914, 1927), who himself included the Comanche as one of the "most typical Plains tribes." While the Comanche shared similar technological traits with other Plains tribes, such as an equestrian-based bison subsistence and items of material culture such as the tipi, shield, and travois, their political organization was argued to be anomalous compared with other Plains tribes. Five characteristics deemed typical of Plains communities and ecologically adaptive to Plains life (Oliver 1962) are alleged to be lacking among the Comanche: (1) tribal political structures, (2) authoritative leaders, (3) a tribal council, (4) men's sodalities with periodic police functions, and (5) annual solidifying communal ceremonies such as the Sun Dance. In other Plains tribes such institutions functioned to maintain tribal integration in a number of ways. This chapter focuses on three of these allegedly absent components: military societies, their role in tribal political structures, and their association with tribally aggregative ceremonies and ethnic continuity.

Theories of Comanche Ethnography

As outlined by Kavanagh (1986:19–41, 1996:6–8), three theoretical approaches—cultural, historical, and ecological—have been offered to explain the Comanche situation. The historical proponents, using largely diffusionist arguments (Kroeber 1939:80; Hoebel 1940, 1954:129; Lowie 1954; Eggan 1980), argued that the unique features of Comanche social organization resulted from the addition of Plains features to a Basin culture, which, they contended, explained the peculiarities of Comanche forms of the policed hunt, military societies, and levels of tribal integration. The argument of a late arrival on the Plains frequently has been used to explain their lack of "typical" forms of social organization found elsewhere on the Plains. As Wallace and Hoebel (1952:22) stated, "The Comanche band was strikingly similar in organization to the aboriginal Shoshone groups of the Great Basin in the days preceding white contact." Other scholars have suggested that the Comanche may have exploited the Plains for a considerable time prior to European contact (Shimkin 1940; Kavanagh 1986, 1996; Shaul 1986).

Two cultural explanations have also been offered. First, Symmes Oliver's (1962:74) criteria for "typical Plains tribes" indicated that since the more highly structured Plains populations had been agriculturalists before migrating onto the Plains, Shoshone and Comanche hunting and gathering origins resulted in structurally less complex sociopolitical forms. This argument is invalid, as the Shoshone developed both sodalities and a Sun Dance (Shimkin 1953, 1980; Lowie 1963; Tefft 1965). Others proposed that the recent arrival of the Comanche on the Plains meant there was not adequate time for them to "completely shed their Shoshone heritage" or borrow "typical" Plains traits (Hoebel 1940, 1954:129; Oliver 1962:74). However, as the Comanche were on the Plains longer than other communities that met Oliver's Plains criteria, such as the Cheyenne, this argument does not hold up. Second, Tefft (1960a, 1960b, 1965), unlike Kroeber, proposed a cultural-ecological argument whereby significant differences existed between Comanche and Shoshone and between these two and other Basin peoples. He argued that the Wind River Shoshone exhibited more "typical" Plains traits than the Comanche, whose borrowing was inhibited by their remote geographical location and because the Comanche placed "such a high value on individual freedom, that government was held to a minimum" (Tefft 1960b: 109–110).

Ecological arguments (Kroeber 1939:80; Wallace and Hoebel 1952:61, 235; Colson 1954; Oliver 1962:73–74; Wilson 1963) were variants of niche theory and claimed that, if numerous other Plains groups developed similar institutions in response to a shared ecological situation, then the Comanche must not have shared a similar situation since they lacked these institutions. These proponents claimed that the Southern Plains was a richer ecological niche than other areas of the Plains and therefore did not require the development of social institutions such as military societies. However, the exact criteria for this assessment and its applicability in other Plains ecological zones have not been demonstrated. Elizabeth Colson (1954) argued that climatic differences reflected in larger bison herds and milder winters on the Southern Plains permitted larger permanent local units than were found on the Northern Plains. This in turn removed the need for large groups to assemble during the summer, so hunting remained a primarily uniband activity and formal policing was unnecessary. She failed to provide data to support this proposition, however.

Oliver (1962:72–76) rejected this theory, demonstrating that bison were not available on the Southern Plains in large quantities in certain areas and at certain times of the year. Though adopting an ecological analysis, he took a middle position, citing influences from historical, cultural, and ecological theories in explaining the Comanche situation. He offered four key ecological points in attempting to explain the Comanche anomaly. First, the Comanche were a widely scattered people, some of whom were more involved in the acquisition of horses than in full-time bison subsistence. This suggests that only some Comanche were "True Plains" communities in light of Oliver's criteria. To bring a large population (he claimed nearly twenty thousand) together in one encampment for any length of time would have posed serious problems of food, firewood, and pasture. Second, they were so involved in the acquisition and ownership of horses that they verged on being pastoralists. Third, the ecology of the Comanche residential area differed from that of other Plains groups as well as differing between areas of Comanche divisions, which may account for some of their anomalous social organization. Fourth, the Comanche retained elements of the Shoshone background because of the allegedly abundant Southern Plains environment, which explains their cultural differences from other Plains tribes. More recently, William R. Brown Jr. (1987) and Douglas Bamforth (1988) have argued that the Southern Plains had a lower carrying capacity than other areas of the Plains, permitting only a dispersed form of social organization. However, the reliability of 1890s (Brown 1987) and more contemporary data (Bamforth 1988) in modeling earlier ecology is unclear.

Fred Eggan (1980) has offered a combined historical-ecological explanation, arguing that, as all Shoshone speakers were organized in "family band[s]" the Comanche anomaly was the result of changes in their Shoshone culture during migration onto the plains. Melburne Thurman (1980, 1982, 1987) and Daniel Gelo (1987, 1988) have recently championed opposing positions over whether reevaluating the Comanche anomaly is necessary. Thurman supports a reevaluation, arguing that the Comanche had a number of traits similar to other Plains groups, including well-established suprabands and forms of social organization similar to those of other Plains groups. He therefore does not view the Comanche as anomalous and, in disputing Wallace and Hoebel's analysis, supports an ecological model. Gelo argues against a reevaluation, maintaining that the Comanche were indeed anomalous, lacking many of the strongly developed forms of social organization found in other Plains groups.

To date, Kavanagh (1986:19–41, 1996, n.d.b, n.d.d) and Davis (1996) have provided the most in-depth discussions of problems encountered in the Comanche anomaly, combining ethnographic fieldwork with ethnohistorical research.[4] But current literature only partially addresses the issue of the Comanche anomaly. As Kavanagh (1980:46–59, 1996) discusses, the problems not only involve paradigmatic counterinstance (as defined by Kuhn 1962), but require a reexamination of the data upon which the anomaly was based.[5] As Kavanagh (1986, 1996) points out, these data have never been fully explored and call for a critical reanalysis. Indeed most of the problems in understanding Comanche political history as outlined by Kavanagh (1996) result from the confusion of distinct ethnonyms and political histories emerging from temporal and differential resource availability, geographical locations, and internal and external political relations. A review of the 1933 Santa Fe Laboratory of Anthropology fieldnotes on the Comanche men's societies and Sun Dance, as well as other archival, published, and oral sources, does not support the existence of the anomaly even though these are the same data upon which most Comanche ethnography and the reputed anomaly are based. The problems with the Santa Fe investigations in 1933,

from which the stereotyping of Comanche military societies was largely derived through Wallace and Hoebel (1952), are evident. These ethnographers were undoubtedly influenced by Lowie's works emphasizing the role
of military societies as stepping stones toward a state-level hierarchy of organized coercive power and authority.

A review of the surviving three-fifths of the 1933 field school notes reveals a noticeable lack of attention to ethnographic descriptions of Comanche military societies. While we can only speculate as to the reasons for this,
the view that Comanche societies were not presumed to have had coercive
powers on the same level as the Cheyenne may have affected this level of
inquiry. In addition, the fact that the 1933 Comanche consultants were considerably fewer and younger than the 1935 Kiowa consultants, who provided
important data concerning military societies, may hold significance. Thus,
the interviewers may have considered Comanche societies more as dance
societies and therefore did not fully pursue their role in basic social organization. Yet such topics are frequently alluded to in the Santa Fe materials,
indicating that the arguments for the absence of Comanche tribal political
structures, authoritative leaders, a tribal council, men's societies with periodic police functions, and annual integrating communal ceremonies such as
the Sun Dance are unfounded and that these features indeed existed in the
nineteenth century if not earlier.

SOURCES FOR COMANCHE MILITARY SOCIETIES

Compared with other Southern Plains populations, sources for Comanche
military societies are few, brief, and problematic; however, they suggest that
most Comanche military societies were formed at a relatively late date (after
circa 1810). I present these sources chronologically, highlighting their contributions and associated problems. Like other Plains communities, the
Comanche maintained several types of men's and women's sodalities, including shield, medicine, and military or soldier societies during the nineteenth
century as well as various forms of more social dances. Noel Loomis and
Abraham Nasatir (1967:277) mention a party of Taovaya and Wichita
which traveled to visit and dance with the Comanche in January 1787. Although dances are frequently mentioned in early Spanish accounts, particularly those held prior to the departure of war parties and "Scalp" and other
forms of Victory Dances following the return of a war party, they do not
indicate the presence of military societies.

The earliest known source is A. B. Thomas's (1929; 1932:324–325, 385)
translation and interpretation of a 1786 Spanish document, depicting a con-

tingent of allied Comanche under Ecueracapa who fought a modestly successful campaign against the Apache.[6] According to Thomas (1932:324), the *tarja* or tally sheet was sent in blank form by Governor Don Juan Bautista de Anza to Ecueracapa in the summer of 1786 so that "there might be indicated on it by means of lines and signs the chiefs who might be set out on the campaign, in the expedition under his command, against the Apaches, the number of men which each detachment be composed, and the successes that might be achieved." The document was returned by Ecueracapa's son Ohamaquea or Oxamaquea, commonly known as Yellow Hand (Hulkrantz 1968). The tally sheet includes five detachments: an advance party under Cuetaninaveni with 31 men, Ecueracapa with 114 men, Sabambipit with 88 men, Encagive with 50 men, and Piaquegipe with 64 men, a total of 347 men plus the 5 leaders. Each named leader carried a crooked lance (*patso'ikowe kwitubi*) held point down except Ecueracapa, who carried a sword which he had received from de Anza.

The depictions were explained to de Anza by Oxamaquea. Kavanagh (1986:58) maintains that only Kotsoteka participated in this battle. This appears to be correct, although the information contained in the *Noticia* (Thomas 1929, 1932) indicates that the five leaders and their groups include members of the Kotsoteka, Yupe, and Yamparika divisions and that these divisions were present during the Apache campaign between May 13 and July 15 and in the Santa Fe and Pecos Pueblo area until July 14, where the Comanche-Spanish peace was celebrated (Thomas 1929, 1932:324–329; Hoebel 1940:38; Simmons 1967:12–14). Clarification is obtained by comparing the names of the five battle leaders, who all appear to have been Kotsoteka, with those of the five camp leaders contained in the *Noticia*, which included members of all three Comanche divisions attending the Santa Fe and Pecos celebrations.

Thomas (1932:385) suggests that the presence of a sword indicates the existence of military societies: "The Spanish *sable*, for sword, technically signifying a weapon in Spanish military orders, appears to indicate that the New Mexican Spaniards recognize the formal organization of the Comanche in military societies." Thomas (1929:291–292) suggests that military societies are indicated by their "standing in a very definite position with regard to each group," the presence of five groups, each with a distinct leader carrying a lance or sword, which he compares to Clark's 1885 (1982) and Lowie's (1915a) lists of five Comanche bands (divisions) and societies, and the fact that the number five is a well-known number among Basin Shoshone. He further contends that the two forms of lances depicted in the drawing, straight and curved, a widespread insignia of Plains military societies, also support the presence of military societies, as most Plains societies were known to have had only two grades of leaders.

There are several problems with Thomas's assumptions and conclusions which do not support the presence of Comanche military societies. First, Ohamaquea's translations to de Anza do not indicate that these groups were in fact military societies. As Hoebel (1940:39) has pointed out, these formations are more representative of band leaders or headsmen and their supporting male constituency, as indicated by the mention of women and children (Thomas 1929:295). Second, Thomas's (1929:292) belief that the five groups depicted in 1786 may correspond to the later known five divisions of historic times implies that all Comanche were present and negates the recognition of changes in Comanche band and divisional social organization from 1786 to circa 1850. However, as Ecueracapa and Cuetaninaveni were known Kotsoteka leaders, and as only Kotsoteka are believed to have participated in the campaign (Kavanagh 1986:58), this seems unlikely. It is also unlikely that the Kotsoteka had five military societies at this time, as the only known Kotsoteka society as of 1829, reported by Ruiz to Berlandier (1969: 70–75, 117–118; 1972), was the Lobos. Third, the numbers of the five groups, ranging from 31 to 114, are simply too small to have been individual societies in relation to estimates of the entire Comanche population at this time. Fourth, Thomas's assumption concerning the presence of curved lances carried by the group leaders is unsupported. Furthermore, individuals indicated by an "f" in the drawing, numbering three, nine, nine, five, and five per group, respectively, are too numerous and inconsistent to represent society assistant leaders. Later Comanche societies are known to have had one or two whipmen per society, who appear to have been the society heads because no division between leaders and whipmen exists in the available documentation, as is commonly found in other Plains military societies. The men depicted by the "f" symbols in the de Anza Tally Sheet more likely represent chiefs or prominent headsmen of their respective residence bands, possibly wearing bonnets or other significant forms of insignia or possibly even personal (but not society) curved lances; they were organized by residence or divisional bands and not by societies. When analyzed in light of what is known of Comanche and other Plains military societies, the de Anza Tally Sheet does not indicate Comanche military societies (Hoebel 1940:38–39).

These groups may reflect Spanish military influences on existing Comanche band and divisional military structures. A considerable number of early accounts of Comanche raiding, warfare, and political activities exist (Twitchell 1914; Hackett 1923–1937; Thomas 1932, 1935, 1940, 1941;

Winfrey and Day 1966; Loomis and Nasatir 1967; Simmons 1967; John 1975, 1984, 1985; Kavanagh 1986, 1996; Foster 1991). Review of these largely early-eighteenth-century accounts clearly demonstrates that while the Comanche carried out large-scale and well-organized military ventures against numerous enemies, there is no indication of any Comanche organizations resembling other documented Plains military societies. Between 1750 and 1785 several factors had evolved which may have led to changes in Comanche military structure and tactics and may have made de Anza's offer of peace in 1786 more congenial. Comanche raids into Puebloan and New Mexico communities had proved so disastrous that the area was to some degree impoverished, providing little impetus for further large-scale raiding concentrations. The smallpox epidemic of 1780–1781 considerably weakened the Comanche population. As the Comanche continued to migrate southeastward, their attention focused more on the settlements of Texas, Coahuila, and Chihuahua than on New Mexico. Finally, the enticements of trade, annual gifts to allied Indian leaders, and Spanish military officer titles may have induced some Comanche leaders to ally with the Spanish again.

Marc Simmons (1967:15–16) offers evidence which suggests that the Comanche were directly influenced by their interactions with the Spanish military forces in New Mexico. During the several decades of friendly and unfriendly contact with the Spanish in New Mexico during the 1700s, the Comanche undoubtedly made observations on the Spanish military system and tactics. The Comanche are known to have defeated Mexican troops more than once in pitched battles on the plains of Durango (Simmons 1967: 16). Following the death of the Comanche leader Cuerno Verde (Green Horn) in 1779, the Comanche, at the suggestion of Governor de Anza, selected Ecueracapa (Leather Jacket) to serve as a head chief with authority to speak for the entire tribe. The Spaniards in turn bestowed on Ecueracapa the title of "General of the Comanche Nation" and provided an annual distribution of gifts (Simmons 1967:13). Comanche leaders continued to be referred to as captains and generals. After peace was made between the Comanche and the Spanish in 1785–1786, annual gifts were made to the "captains" and "Indian leaders of the Comanches," which appear to be the formalization of Spanish military titles bestowed on prominent Comanche war leaders, as proof of Spanish intentions. Large contingents of Comanche frequently accompanied Spanish expeditions against the Apache and Pawnee (Simmons 1967:23, 29). Comanche parties commonly entered Spanish settlements organized under their own "generals" and "captains," frequently wearing articles of Spanish military apparel and insignia. Such political and prestige gifts were often given by Spanish authorities in Santa Fe (Simmons

1967:15–34) and later by Anglo-Americans (Kavanagh 1996) in negotiating and cementing political alliances with Comanche populations. "Prestige gifts included medals, flags, swords, and uniforms" (1996:479), and "prestige gifts of canes, flags, medals, and uniforms went exclusively to divisional principal chiefs" (Kavanagh 1996:377). In 1856 Agent Miller (Miller 1856) on the Arkansas River wanted "18 coats and pantaloons . . . ornamented with the military buttons and lace which will serve as a mark of distinction for the head chief." Political gifts among the Comanche are well documented from at least 1739 to 1873, and even earlier for the Apache (Kavanagh 1996). The Comanche adapted several elements of the Spanish military system, tactics, and martial symbolism for their own purposes.

These data suggest that Comanche military societies were a relatively late, nineteenth-century development. While detailed ethnographic descriptions are generally lacking and it is possible that eyewitnesses may not have recognized the presence of societies or their incipient stage of growth, rather than their actual absence, the lack of references to any societies or to any recognizable society names, regalia, dances, or associated behavior further suggests their absence. Thomas (1932) contains multiple references to both groups and portions of groups who chose to stand their ground and remain in a fight or to flee in retreat. Neither is indicative of military or contrary societies, and this may suggest the presence of regular raiding and warfare parties, as societies generally acted as units and not segments.

Two particularly well-documented accounts from the early 1800s (John 1984:348; Noyes 1993:159–163) suggest the absence of sodality policelike organizations with coercive police functions among two, and possibly three, Comanche divisions in the early 1800s. In 1802 several Comanche leaders successfully prevented a raid on Texas and Coahuila in revenge for a series of killings which had occurred between Comanche, Lipan, Spanish, and residents of San Antonio; however, a Comanche revenge party in search of the Lipan returned with several Texan horses. The leader Izayat returned the horses to San Antonio in an effort to cease further actions which might break alliances between the Spanish and Comanche. That fall, when a number of Comanche chiefs were discussing treaty enforcement, a Kotsoteka leader named Chihuahua offered to form a tribal (police) force to curb the actions of wayward tribesmen and ensure Comanche compliance in their treaties with the Spanish. The next year Chihuahua led two hundred Comanche to council with Governor Juan Bautista de Elguézabal in San Antonio. At that council Chihuahua brought thirty warriors to serve in a policelike fashion and requested that they receive Spanish uniforms (Elguézabal

1802).[7] Chihuahua and Izayat also requested the posting of Spanish troops in the eastern part of the Comanchería, which was not Yamparika, but Eastern Cuchanec (Kotsoteka) and later Peneteka territory, to assist in maintaining peace. However, Spanish policy prohibited the posting of troops with any tribe. Governor Elguézabal could only promise to supply the uniforms when he received further shipments of supplies and outfitted the thirty warriors in 1804 (John 1984:351–352). Occasional depredations by both sides continued.

In 1806 depredations by Comanche against Spaniards resulted in a dispatch from Governor Cordero through the Cuchanec (Kotsoteka) indicating that "there were no signs of action by Chihuahua's thirty policemen" and that "the ineffectiveness of their uniformed police was deplorable, and improved control was essential" (John 1984:354). This resulted in the election of a principal chief Sargento, later known as Chief Cordero after the Texas governor, for the "eastern Comanches," as had existed among the Western Kotsoteka and Yamparika for several years. As Eastern Comanche were known to have included Eastern Cuchanec or Kotsoteka (from whom the later Peneteka split) at this time, this lack of police organization in the form of military sodalities suggests that military societies were also initially lacking among the later Peneteka. In 1810 (John 1984:360–361) Yamparica and Eastern and Western Cuchanec depredations against the Lipan and the Spanish communities of San Marcos and Laredo resulted in a combined effort of Comanche and Spanish troops to recover property and identify the raid leaders. To emphasize the importance of upholding treaty relations, "Governor Salcedo uniformed Cordero's forty warriors to underscore the official import of their mission" (John 1984:360–361).

Traditional concepts of legal control at this time revolved around public consensus and the persuasive abilities of prominent chiefs to make an individual's actions conform for the benefit of the group. When compared with what is known of military societies in other Plains populations, these accounts suggest that for at least the Yamparika and the Cuchanec or Kotsoteka (and probably the latter's descendants, the Hois and Peneteka), Comanche military societies with coercive police functions were lacking as of 1802–1810. Had there been military societies, it is plausible to assume that as the largest form of male sodality they would have held some level of police authority or related coercive powers or were at least the most likely group to hold sufficient power to assume such forms of authority. The approach to the Spanish military to organize and uniform such a force for police actions further suggests the lack of such organizations, which would

most likely have had their own insignia and regalia. Thus, the heavy interaction with and influence of the Spanish military may be one possible factor in the origin and development of Comanche military societies.

Clear documentation of Comanche military societies does not appear until the 1820s. Thurman (1980:7) reports an uncited 1820 document that
indicates the presence of a Wolf Society whose members wore untanned
wolfskin straps and were prohibited from fleeing in desperate situations;
however, this is unavailable for review. Accounts of named Comanche military sodalitylike actions such as the Na'wapina'r were observed in the 1820s
to 1840s (Neighbors 1852 : 132; Burnet 1954 : 131; Berlandier 1969 : 73–74).

Los Lobos: The Wolves Society

Although the society's origins are unknown, we are indebted to Ruiz's 1824
account to Berlandier (1969:70–75, 117–118), which provides the only
known eyewitness account of the Los Lobos (Wolves Society), a society of
contrary warriors among the Texas Comanche (Eastern Kotsoteka);

> The Wolves (lobos) are very rare because of the rigorous duties they must
> take upon themselves. This military institution, which is basically noth-
> ing but an association or society of elite fighting men, very much re-
> sembles that of the Kites and the Yanktons, peoples of the United States
> of North America. Among them the bravest and most enterprising men
> over thirty or thirty-five years take a sacred oath never to flee from dan-
> ger, nor to fly before an enemy. Among the Comanches the Wolves must
> stand and conquer or die, unless their leader orders them to withdraw,
> no matter how great the enemy forces may be, and no matter whether
> their fellow warriors have taken flight. They dress like other braves on
> the warpath, distinguished from them only by the long strap of untanned
> wolf skin they trail behind them, and from which they derive their name.
> So long as the war lasts, and particularly when the enemy has been
> sighted, they ride apart from the main body of troops, forming the van
> or rear guard, or riding the flanks, as circumstances may dictate. These
> Wolves enjoy great privileges among their own people. They are treated
> with the greatest respect, and when they enter a village they knock down
> everything that strikes their fancy without anyone's daring to complain.
> When they return victorious from a campaign the old men, the women,
> and the children run out to meet them; impromptu dances are begun to
> which only the unmarried girls are invited, with orders to comply with
> every desire of the victorious warriors. But if, on the other hand, one of

these same Wolves has committed an act of cowardice, he is covered with infamy forever. The chiefs goad the women to insult him, to taunt him with being nothing more than a woman like themselves. Women and children run to break and burn his tents and belongings and to destroy everything belonging to the man who has played the coward. If a Wolf should be killed in battle, and his brother Wolves escape from the slaughter instead of standing and dying, they must wander alone in the deserts or go to some other tribe where there is no relation of the dead, since any such would relentlessly slay them the moment they relaxed their vigilance. Often the very women who were so eager to offer their favors as rewards for the Wolves' mighty deeds try to kill them as the only way to slake the fury and disgust they have aroused.

In volunteering to serve on raiding and revenge parties, the Wolves sang their "war chant" while keeping time to a pebble-filled gourd shaken in one hand. In the other hand was held the weapon of their choice for the particular battle, which was used on foot or on horseback. If no weapon was brought, it signified that the warrior would only stand and sing in the most dangerous part of the battle. Comanche warriors who did not belong to the Wolves were not prevented from retreating in battle. During the "little war" (Berlandier 1969:74–75), which is Lowie's (1915a) Na'wapina'r, the wolves ended the preparatory dancing by forming a column separate from the other fighters, which advanced at a trot, indicating their obligation not to turn about.

Berlandier's (1969:74–75) descriptions of the Wolves' functions resemble those of the Shoshone Yellow Brows and other Plains "Dog Soldier" societies, but their position reflects the duties performed by the Shoshone Big Horses. It is interesting to note that while the earliest description of a Comanche warrior society comes from Ruiz (Berlandier 1969:74–75), only the Wolves are listed, but they are absent in later ethnographic accounts (Ten Kate 1885a; Lowie 1915a). Why are the Wolves absent in the later listings of Comanche societies? Perhaps the society was exterminated in battle, became defunct, or changed into a presently unrecognizable form. The formation of the Peneteka and Quahada divisions from the Kotsoteka by the mid-1800s (Kavanagh 1989:101, 1996:479–482), with which the Wolves were associated, suggests one possible factor in their decline. The presence of the "pebble-filled gourds" and singing in battle, sometimes with no martial resistance, resemble the later Pukutsi, who were individual contrary warriors. No further discussion of contrary characteristics was noted for the Wolves, so we can only speculate as to the fate of the Wolves Society.

For the Utes Lowie (1915a:823) states that "the Dog company (*sari tsi + u*) is the only institution comparable to the Plains societies." Descriptions of their roles in scouting and announcing approaching enemies, forming a rear guard during camp movements, slit wolfskin sashes, and Dog behavior suggest that they were a contrary or Dog Soldier–like Plains society. As Lowie (1915a:823) reported, the Ute Dog Society "existed before my informant's time, in the days before the Utes had guns." While we lack corroborating data, it is possible that the Comanche Lobos and the Ute Dog Society had historical connections, as the two tribes interacted heavily until at least 1726 (Wallace and Hoebel 1952:5). Despite little documentation concerning the Lobos, their ideology and functions exemplify the highest ideals associated with a martial ideology and ethos.

Later Sources

Neither David Burnet (1954:117, 121), who spent over one year "with or in the vicinity of the Comanches of Texas" during 1818–1819 and should have made ample observations of the majority of at least one division's annual cycle, nor Robert Neighbors (1852) mentions any group resembling a military society. Although it is highly unlikely, Burnet (Winfrey and Day 1966:3:86) further stated, "I could never discover that they had any songs, legends, or other mementos, to perpetuate the fetes of arms, or other illustrious deeds of their progenitors. . . ." By this time the Comanche were in close contact with the Kiowa, Apache, Cheyenne, and Arapaho, who all had well-developed military society complexes by 1800. As reflected in numerous well-documented accounts of joint Comanche-Kiowa camps and raiding parties, at least some Yamparika or Northern Comanche were allied with the Kiowa and Apache by no later than 1806 and with the Cheyenne and Arapaho by 1840 (John 1984, 1985; Kavanagh 1996:146, 272), frequented subsequent Kiowa and Cheyenne Sun Dances (Mooney 1898; Linton 1935), and had a long association with Spanish military units; they were undeniably aware of and in contact with the military organizations of other groups, which may have stimulated development. In light of Boon's (1982:102) analysis of Lowie (1920), suggesting that "such 'sodalities' reveal a tribe's capacity to sample alternate social forms, without necessarily adopting them as the central components of its social machine. Each tribal population appears almost to toy with patterns that are fundamental to its neighbors," it is feasible that the Comanche may have begun to adopt formal military societies' structures from their Southern Plains neighbors following these developments.

Accounts of other named Comanche military societies are not common until around the 1870s (Ten Kate 1885a; Nye 1962:180; Attocknie 1965; Kavanagh 1996). Later sources from the third quarter of the nineteenth century clearly indicate the presence of widespread Comanche military societies. One of the best indications of Comanche perceptions of soldier formations was recorded in 1873 (Campbell 1926–1928:639; Nye 1937:177), when Tokomi told Governor Edmund J. Davis of Texas, "Tell that old man I am Black Horse, a soldier chief. He may take me if he can but he may have a little trouble doing it." Hoebel (1940:33) identifies Black Horse (and possibly his father) as a Big Horse Society member; "I might make many errors and fall down many times," said Black Horse on taking up the insignia of the Big Horse. "I shall take my father's road and maybe I'll come out a somebody."

In 1885 Clark (1982:355) recorded the names of Comanche soldier societies which he called "bands," noting that they differed primarily in their dances prior to marshaling a war party. The Dutch ethnographer H. F. C. Ten Kate (1885a:128) also recorded the names of several social and military society dances, including:

> la danse des corbeaux (*tebwi-niskera*), la danse du taureau de bison (*tasse-wou-niskera*), la danse des renards (*wautcheah-niskera*), la danse du dindon (*wako-niskera*), la petite danse du cheval (*tiddiapohk-niskera*), et la grande danse du cheval (*pibiapohk-niskera*), la danse du cercle (*otchi-niskera*), la danse de la gourde (*otrewa-niskera*), la danse de guerre (*naouteke-niskera*), la danse du scalp (*woth ou wos tabe-niskera*), et une danse d'amour (*nisir-niskera*).

The French text and associated Comanche terms indicate the presence of the Raven, Bison, Fox, Turkey Cock, Little Horse, Big Horse, Circle, Gourd, War, Scalp, and Love Dances. Of these the Raven, Fox, Little Horse, and Big Horse Dances are easily recognizable ethnonyms which correlate to known Comanche military societies recorded by Lowie (1915a), the 1933 Santa Fe Field School (Kavanagh n.d.b), and my own fieldwork.

The first primary description of Comanche military societies is from Lowie's (1915a:809–812) brief fieldwork in 1912; after spending only a week, he unexplainably found the Comanche "less than ideal informants." Lowie's four-page account was the lengthiest account of Comanche societies. As with his material on Kiowa military societies (Lowie 1916b), Lowie missed a golden opportunity to record what must now be reconstructed from fragmentary and sometimes contradictory sources. Lowie provided minimal discussions and did not connect the names of specific dances with particular societies; although he noted that certain societies were associated with certain divisions, he sometimes appears to be unsure of his own data (Lowie 1915a:810). Edward Curtis (1930:187, 229) denies the existence of Comanche soldier societies, while R. N. Richardson (1933:36) states that "there is some evidence to indicate the existence of military societies among the Comanches, but there is not much information on the subject." This statement is important, for the lack of recorded ethnography led to the presumed absence of men's societies, which in turn forms a major component in the "Comanche anomaly."

While I have found no evidence of any formally organized or named Comanche women's military sodalities, Comanche women did make martial contributions. Oral and written sources indicate that they actively fought in the defense of their own villages, occasionally accompanied and fought with raiding parties (Ewers 1997:197), held active roles in Scalp and Victory Dances, and performed active roles in teaching young men, and presumably women, fighting skills. The lack of recorded ethnography undoubtedly obscures the full depth of Comanche women's martial contributions.

Compared with many Plains populations, no serious, in-depth ethnological examination of Comanche culture was undertaken until the Santa Fe Anthropological Field School in 1933. Their fieldnotes contain brief but vital descriptions of Comanche societies that, with supplementary sources, permit the best available reconstruction of prereservation Comanche military societies. Yet these notes lack detailed data regarding many of the basic functional, social, and ceremonial aspects of the societies, which suggests that their importance was qualitatively different than in many other Plains populations or that the associated knowledge had declined significantly during the lifetime of the 1933 consultants (post-1870). Another problem has been the ongoing lack of theoretical focus and inquiry in interpersonal studies in anthropology. Focusing on only the larger structural functions, the 1933 Santa Fe party did not look at the actual Comanche gatherings to determine their sociology or the extent of everyday relations in conjunction with larger-level social forms. Had they inquired into Comanche and military society social structure in light of everyday activities, relationships, and involvement, we would have a more accurate and complete depiction of the extent of these social relations.

While this fieldwork contains perhaps the richest source of Comanche ethnology, its limits must be recognized. First, this inquiry was conducted nearly sixty years after the Comanche were confined to their final reservation in 1875. Great changes in Comanche social organization had already occurred prior to their final surrender in 1875; portions of some bands, such as the Peneteka, had already entered a reservation-based economy years earlier and numerous residence and band formations had occurred. More importantly, most data concerning the role and functions of Comanche societies were obtained from a limited number of consultants. Nearly all accounts of Comanche societies policing communal hunts, for example, came from *Naiya* (Slope). Similarly, the oral history describing the relation of Comanche societies to larger Comanche social organization and society dances was obtained primarily from Post Oak Jim, who contributed nearly one-fifth of the 1933 Santa Fe data, and Howard White Wolf. As Post Oak Jim was sixty-four years old in 1933 and thus only six to seven years old when the Comanche entered the reservation in 1875, his accounts must be used cautiously. In his defense, however, the accounts of several similar-aged Kiowa in the 1935 Santa Fe notes contain highly accurate data concerning Kiowa military societies. Some of the other 1933 Comanche consultants did not agree with Post Oak Jim's accounts on some issues; Hoebel described him as "a willing and self-regarding informant, but not reliable on all aspects" (Kavanagh n.d.b: 14). Whether these disagreements resulted from legitimate historical discrepancies in data or from more personal motivations such as jealousy or disdain at cooperating with the field party cannot be ascertained at this time. These data must be examined, albeit cautiously. Yet the accounts of Comanche military societies by Ten Kate (1885a), Clark (1982), Hugh L. Scott (HLS-2), Lowie (1915a), eight fellow 1933 Comanche consultants, and Attocknie (in Kavanagh 1996:49–50) give credence to Post Oak Jim's accounts.

Wallace and Hoebel's (1952) characterizations of Comanche military societies were based largely on Post Oak Jim's accounts. These views and the confusion surrounding Comanche societies have been echoed in later literature and further inhibit the acquisition of a more accurate and complete picture of these organizations. Hoebel (1940) mentioned military societies, citing earlier authors, but provided no in-depth discussion. While remaining unsure of the existence of the societies in Comanche culture, he referred to traits that are typical of Plains military society functions. Wallace and Hoebel (1952:33–34) argued that the horse-bison-tipi complex made the Comanche typical, but debated whether the Comanche possessed cultural features such as military societies and the Sun Dance. They used a number of descriptive terms in referring to Comanche men's military sodalities, including "soldier band," military club," "military fraternity," "dance group," "military society," "military police," "military society police," "fighting societies," and "semi-military fraternities" (1952:33, 56, 224, 235, 272–274, 370).

The various terms reflect Wallace and Hoebel's inability to determine the presence and extent of the private and civil functions of Comanche societies, as well as their assessment of these organizations. Thus, Wallace and Hoebel (1952:272) stated: "Military fraternities did not become a developed and integrated part of Comanche culture to the extent that they did among other tribes of the plains. Most of the Comanche warrior groups appear to have been informal organizations compounded of mutual friendship and interests, and they were not continuous or permanent." They continued (1952:224):

> The warriors of most of the Plains tribes were organized into a series of fighting societies or military fraternities. These organizations were secondary arms of the tribal government or, at least, they functioned as strong pressure groups. The Comanches, however, in keeping with their lack of internal segmentation, possessed only the slightest trace of military fraternities. Informants explained that their societies were something like a combination of our present-day army regiment and lodge organization. Their dearth of historical data and the paucity of material, combined with the lack of information on the part of contemporary Comanches, indicates that the associations were not a developed and integrated part of Comanche culture.

Lowie (1953:124) challenged Wallace and Hoebel's (1952) theory that a Shoshone background explained the weakly developed military societies, emphasizing that Comanche military organizations "were not *police* societies":

> Actually the Comanche did have military fraternities and their concomitants even if they "did not become a developed and integrated part of Comanche culture" (p272 et seq.). What holds true is that they were less formal and functioned discontinuously, yet some of the most characteristic concomitants of the system appeared among the Comanche, though not necessarily in the same context as elsewhere.

He cited Comanche examples of insignia for obligatory battle behavior, combat recklessness by the *Pukutsi* (Contraries), and warfare ideology analogous to several other Plains groups (Lowie 1953). As we shall see, Lowie was correct in this portion of his analysis. Finally Lowie suggested that the Comanche phenomenon was explained by "a highly selective borrowing process" which was not limited solely to material culture (Lowie 1953:124). To determine the criteria for adaptation, Lowie suggested a more in-depth comparative study of the Shoshone and Ute.

Oliver (1962) drew largely upon the works of Wallace and Hoebel (1952), Hoebel (1940, 1954), and Richardson (1933) for his assessment of the Comanche, but did not refer to Lowie (1915a) or Clark (1982). This portion of his work is largely a literature review that contributed analysis, but few new data. Oliver (1962:22–24, 71–76) maintained that the Comanche were anomalous among "True Plains" tribes because they had a simple level of social organization and lacked tribal congregations, the policed hunt, and a Sun Dance, yet he contradicted himself in stating that Comanche societies were both absent and weakly developed. Thurman (1980, 1982) discussed the inaccuracy of these sources while providing a proposed synonymy of Comanche society names from ethnographic sources. He also mentioned problems associated with past Comanche ethnography. Gelo (1986:34) stated that "the military societies common to other Plains tribes, which evolved to regulate communal buffalo hunts but often assumed police duties throughout the year, were virtually absent among the Comanches." Having conducted fieldwork in the early 1980s, Gelo (1986:34, 182, 1987, 1988: 540) later acknowledged the presence of Comanche sodalities, providing contemporary data on one of several current societies (1986:218–226).

While Kavanagh (1980, 1986, 1996, n.d.b:31–40, n.d.d), Thurman (1982), and Davis (1996) have provided compelling reassessments of the Comanche debate, I seek to establish the origins and basis of Comanche men's societies and to explain their role in the larger levels of Comanche social organization. Like Kavanagh, I argue that the assertion that the Comanche were anomalous and the associated confusion concerning the existence and organization of these sodalities are largely the result of inadequate research of available material, specifically, the failure to perform any in-depth field-work concerning the sodalities and the failure to review and compare these data with data for neighboring Southern Plains populations. The relatively late development and less integrated position of these societies in nine-teenth-century Comanche culture are also factors. Previous debates have centered solely upon the alleged presence or absence of Comanche military societies and the extent of their coercive powers, without fully investigating the available data or, more importantly, comparing them with similar data for other Southern Plains tribes before drawing conclusions about these organizations.

EVIDENCE FOR NINETEENTH-CENTURY COMANCHE MILITARY SOCIETIES

Origins

The existence of Comanche military societies in the nineteenth century can be established through a critical and in-depth historical analysis of oral and archival sources. Data relating to the origins of Comanche military societies are extremely sparse, which inhibits a clear picture of their development and suggests that these organizations were nineteenth-century acquisitions. Julian Steward (1938) and Abram Kardiner (1945) indicated that the Western Shoshone periodically gathered in small groups for dances and socialization, but had no associations. While the origins of Shoshone military societies is unclear, it is likely that they arose following the division from the Comanche, as the Comanche Yellow Hand is known to have transmitted the Sun Dance to the Shoshone around 1800 (Shimkin 1953, 1986). It is also likely that the Comanche transmitted military societies to the Shoshone. Lowie's data on the Ute (1915a:823), with whom the Comanche closely interacted until 1726 (Wallace and Hoebel 1952:5), indicate that the Ute had only one organization which resembled Plains societies. As the Ute lacked a strong tradition of military societies, it is unlikely that they influenced the Comanche regarding the acquisition of military societies. Berlandier's (1969:70–75, 117–118) 1829 account of the Los Lobos Society is the first clear description of a Comanche society; further data indicating the origins or presence of other Comanche societies are lacking until Ten Kate's (1885a) account.

The Comanche Gourd Dance

While several mythological stories involving ponies, turtles, and other animals exist for the origins of the Comanche Gourd Dance, archival and Comanche oral history accounts provide greater insights into the origins of these dance groups, especially when compared with Kiowa and Cheyenne historical accounts. Numerous Comanche, Kiowa, and Cheyenne sources indicate that the Gourd Dance associated with the Comanche Big and Little Horses Societies of the later Quahada division was acquired in 1837 during a battle with the Cheyenne. By the late 1820s the Comanche, Kiowa, and Apache were being forced southward from the upper Arkansas River region by the rapidly encroaching Cheyenne and Arapaho. The ensuing period of conflict was most likely aggravated by the competition for trade created by the presence of the William Bent family along the upper reaches of the Arkansas River in present-day Colorado and Texas (Hyde 1968) and the Chouteaus along the lower reaches in south-central Oklahoma (Foreman 1926: 238). Acquiring firearms from the Chouteaus, the KCA defended against these movements in a series of battles along the Canadian River Valley in western Oklahoma and northeastern Texas, which culminated in the 1837 annihilation of an attacking party of Cheyenne Bow String Society members by combined Comanche, Kiowa, and Apache forces and the defensive battle on Wolf Creek in 1838. Following Pierre Chouteau's death in the winter of 1839, efforts behind the trade war appear to have lessened; the Southern Plains tribes now turned their attention toward rapidly increasing pressures resulting from population reduction through diseases and migrational and technological pressures from the Osage, Pawnee, Delaware, Sauk and Fox, and other groups who were expanding westward. In 1840 a lasting peace was made between the five allied Southern Plains tribes, which was never broken. In addition, pressures for trade acquisition declined as the Bents soon thereafter obtained a license to trade with the Comanche (Lecompte 1972: 278; Kavanagh 1996:248).[8]

According to Ed Yellowfish, the dance known today as the Gourd Dance was obtained from the Cheyenne. A Comanche met up with a Cheyenne scout, then each returned to his own group. When the Comanche party journeyed out from their camp to find the Cheyenne man, they found a party of Cheyenne located in a set of earthworks typical of the form constructed in numerous Plains battles for defensive purposes. As Mr. Yellowfish narrated,

> And they came to this place by the fork in the river, Comanches came up there and there were the Cheyennes like they were dug in, you know kind of waiting for them if they was going to have an encounter there, they was waiting. When they came up on them the Cheyenne warriors were dancing this dance. They didn't have a rattle or a gourd like we see now or have heard about, they were using I believe arrows, two together some way so that they would make a rattle sound. I think this was kept alive for some time until either the use of that went away because the people who believed in it perhaps took the tradition with them as they passed on.[9]

Haddon Nauni described the events surrounding a similar battle between these two groups: "Well this group that went over there they said after they travel a while, they went over a hill and there those Cheyennes were, like soldiers, they had a trench or something, and they were dancing. They had these arrows, they were dancing with. . . ."[10]

These accounts suggest a link to the events surrounding a battle in 1837, in which a party of forty-eight Cheyenne Bow String Society members were killed after being located near a combined encampment of Comanche, Kiowa, and Apache who were preparing to hold a Sun Dance (Mooney 1898: 271–272, 1907:377; Grinnell 1983:45–62; Hyde 1968).[11] According to Joe Attocknie (Kavanagh 1996:244), the Comanche named the battle *Yu'a-hora-kahni* (Robe-dig a hole-house) or the Robe Entrenchments, after the robe-draped entrenchments dug by the Cheyenne. The allied KCA were also to-gether when the Cheyenne and some Arapaho attacked their camp on Wolf Creek in retaliation the following year. Kavanagh (1986:192) reports that contemporary Comanche have indicated to him that during one of these episodes, probably the former (1837), the Comanche "captured the rights" to the Gourd Dance from the Cheyenne Bow String Society.

As Joe Attocknie stated, "The organization was a warrior group for the younger fighting men in the tribe."[12] The accounts of Post Oak Jim, Joe Attocknie, John Woosypity (Howard 1976), Haddon Nauni, and Ed Yellow-fish indicate that originally arrows and later rattles were used in the Coman-che Gourd Dance, which correlates with Cheyenne accounts I have col-lected of Bow String Society ceremonials.[13] I have also obtained substantial evidence from Kiowa pictographic calendars, fieldnotes, and interviews which indicates that the Kiowa also acquired the Gourd Dance during the same battle and organized their Jáifègàu Society in the winter of 1838–1839.[14] Shoshone societies lacked any form of dancing similar to Gourd Dancing, which further suggests that the Comanche obtained the dance af-ter migrating southward. Although there is no documentation as to when the Comanche formally formed a Gourd Dancing sodality, ethnohistorical records and oral history indicate that Kiowa and Comanche both partici-pated in the same battle and obtained the dance at the same time. After this event there is virtually no mention of the Little Horses until the 1933 Santa Fe notes, which indicate that the society served as march and camp police en route to the Adobe Walls Fight in 1874.[15]

Tuepukunʉʉ: The Little Horses

Tuepukunʉʉ (Little Horses or Little Horse People) is translated from *tue* (little), *puku* (horse), and *nʉʉ* (plural, people), but is commonly known today as the Little Ponies. Ethnographically, little has been recorded for the Little Horses society. Lowie (1915a:811) reports that the Little Horses wore buffalo-skin sashes lacking the typical slit found elsewhere and used rawhide rattles, decorated with yellow-hammer (flicker) feathers. Post Oak Jim in-dicated that the organization was run by a single leader carrying a club, who held control over the others as "they are his horses."[16] If the leader wanted a particular man to enter, he had the announcer or crier (who also con-ducted business for the leader) call for him. If a man who was physically able refused to dance, the leader went after him. Absent members were publicly shamed by the society leader, who struck the drum and called for the indi-vidual to recite some of his alleged indiscretions, such as having intimacies with an old woman. Upon the start of the music, members arose, advanced into the arena, and began to dance. No particular formation was practiced; members were simply a large group dancing individually. Women were not invited by the men, but did participate and could dance beside a man if they wished. Individuals who admired a friend's dancing often honored a fellow member by giving him a gift and dancing beside him, usually accompanied by the family of the recipient in appreciation. This behavior is very suggestive of behavior between society partners. Punishment for recalcitrant dancers followed patterns found in other Comanche societies, in which the whipman could strike the dancers. Of particular interest is the mention that no feast was associated with the dance; this may be an error, as feasts were one of the primary social activities associated with Plains military societies. Dances were generally held during the late afternoon and at night, when it was cooler. Post Oak Jim commented that a tent was put up if the weather was cold, which may indicate that the dance was performed in nonsummer months, implying that society functions occurred at times not connected with a Sun Dance or other large summer aggregation. The ability to gather at such times would have been facilitated by the Comanche form of divisional-based social organization.

According to Post Oak Jim, originally only two or three men, organized by the whipman, danced with rattles in accompaniment to the music.[17] Members held arrows in their hands while dancing. Post Oak Jim stated that rattles were originally made from the dried scrotum of a bison, which was filled with dirt and molded in shape until dried, then emptied, filled with pebbles or large trade beads, and attached to a handle made from a bison tail. This form is typical of rattles in many Plains populations and of those that a Cheyenne Bow String Society member described to me.[18] Gourds and baking powder tins were later adopted for use as rattles after the Comanche entered the reservation.[19]

John Woosypity (Howard 1976:244) stated that "older people had told him that formerly dancers in the Gourd Dance wore a quiver of arrows on their backs and held a single arrow in their right hands instead of the rattle presently carried. The knee-flexing, up-and-down motion of the dance caused the arrows in the quiver to rattle, providing the rhythmic accompaniment presently achieved by shaking 'gourds.'" One Comanche consultant also described this previous style of dancing and said that when Little Pony members became older they became Big Horse Society members, which is supported by the existence of these two societies among the Quahada.[20] Wakini noted that the Big Horses did not dance alone; as both the Big and Little Horse Societies were Quahada societies, danced at Na'wapina'r festivals (Lowie 1915a:810–812), and had a similar form of Gourd Dance choreography, it is possible that both societies danced together on a regular basis.

Pibiapukunᵾᵾ: The Big Horses Society

One of the least known Comanche societies was the Big Horses or Big Horse People. The name *Pibiapukunᵾᵾ* (Big Horses) is formed from *pibia* (large or big, plural), *puku* (horse), and *nᵾᵾ* (plural, people). According to Lowie (1915a:809–812), the only political function of the Big Horse Society was policing or guiding tribal movements and establishing peace with other tribes. Lowie's (1912) interview with Wakini states (Kavanagh 1996:48–49):

> Big Horses used dew claw rattles. Very few Big Horses. Appointed in traveling by leader of people while marching. These Big Horses acted as guides of march. Another badge consisted of neck skin of buffalo worn as a sash, near knee. They have [nothing?] to do with buffalo hunt. . . .
>
> Big Horses had little different song from other songs. Never danced by themselves.
>
> Big Horses took *ekwipca* (red body paint [red rock] and painted bodies down to waist and had rattle, shook them.
>
> Took hawk and sparrow hawk feathers tied to back of head so they would flutter as they moved. BH remained in office every time people were on march as long as they pleased. No function outside of marching. [Wakini] saw them in action himself.
>
> BH were never young men. [Wakini] never saw more that [*sic*] 20. Main function was to make peace with another tribe.

Lowie (1915a:812) later published a condensed account of this material:

> Wakiní said that the Big Horses numbered about twenty and were always mature men. They had a distinctive song, but never danced by themselves. They painted their bodies red, down to the waist, and tied hawk and sparrowhawk feathers to the back of the head, so that these would flutter as their wearers moved. They carried dewclaw rattles and wore a sash made from a part of a buffalo taken from its neck.

Members are said to have danced like the Ravens (*Tuhwi*), but used gourd rattles, which suggests that they performed some type of Gourd Dancing in which members danced up and down in place, rising on their toes.[21] Lowie (1915a:811) also noted, "I was only able to learn that the Horses and Little Horses wore buffalo-skin sashes that lacked the typical slit found elsewhere, and used rawhide rattles, decorated with yellow-hammer [flicker] feathers; the Horses also had spears, trimmed with eagle feathers." Kavanagh (n.d.c, n.d.d : 28) translates the name of these lances as *woinutsik nahaikorohko* (spear decorated with a ruff of crow feathers). Itovits reported in 1933 that the Horse dance was his favorite as a child; after the group's leader *Wuraohapitu* (Yellow Bear) taught him the songs and dances as a child, he joined when he grew up.[22] Howard White Wolf reported membership of the Big Horses at sixty to seventy men, with officers.[23] According to Post Oak Jim, the Horse Dance Society contained two whipmen: Chebatah, a Lipan Apache, and the other a Comanche "scout" (probably a Fort Sill scout). Post Oak Jim stated in 1933 that "the Horse Dance has disappeared."[24] Hoebel (1940 : 33) indicated that the Big Horses, like the Crow Tassel Wearers, may have been focused upon warfare and the acquisition of status, which suggests differential age, social status, and societal cooperation in economic raiding and warfare ventures.

Because a more comprehensive account of this society was not recorded and the society has not been maintained, little information was obtained in literature searches or in recent interviews. Elder Comanche consultants all acknowledged the society's existence as a prereservation and Quahada division–based military society. Further interviews produced only indications that the society danced an ancestral form of what is today known as the Gourd Dance and was composed of older men than those in the Little Ponies Society.[25] Consultants indicated that Little Pony members, upon growing older, commonly became Big Horses members.[26] The society is best remembered and often spoken of in terms of age distinction (viewed for all intents and purposes as a loosely divisional based age-grade), in opposition to the Little Horses.

The Buffalo Dance

The Buffalo Dance was a warfare-related, society, and socially oriented dance which was performed by several Comanche divisions and is performed by some Gourd Dancing societies today. As recorded by the 1933 Santa Fe party:

> It was given the night before a war party. Men and women dance up by stages from opposite sides. After they progress a few minutes the music stops. Then the drums beat fast and the dancers and singers whoop; then the dancers relax and the dance continues. After several such shifts, after reaching the center, it is over, and they turn and dance back towards their

places. The leader carries a coup club and can make people dance with it. Four men dancers out front. One carries a gun and shoots it occasionally. Eight drummers and singers, including women, follow close behind the dancers. A row of women in costume, some wearing war bonnets and carrying spears. They dance slowly into the dance circle. The man with the club is on the horse. When in the center of the dance circle, the leader raises his hand and counts coup on his club with the dancers standing around him. There were then four more songs and they disband.[27]

The Buffalo Dance is known as the *Aanʉhka* (Horn Dance) or the *Ta'siwoonʉhka* (Bison Dance). According to contemporary elders, the dancers mimic the loping of bison by rocking or bouncing up and down in place while keeping their feet together and slightly shifting from one side to another. When the music changes tempo, they take a series of steps in a fashion similar to the Trot Dance, but lower and smaller, and the music for the Buffalo Dance is faster than that of the Trot Dance. On the last step of the dance, the dancers and singers would shout out *ta'siwoo*, an old Comanche word for bison. Elders indicate that the Buffalo Dance was performed at the end of Gourd Dancing and later in this century during powwows, in which it was followed by a Snake Dance. Today the Buffalo Dance is infrequently performed as the concluding session of Gourd Dances, usually only at the larger annual dances.[28]

The Tuhwi or Tuuwinʉʉ Society

Comanche accounts of the origin of the Tuhwi vary greatly. Gelo's (1986: 219) Comanche consultant reports a battlefield origin: "There was a warrior who was wounded and abandoned. He lay there; he was dead. And after a long while he heard a voice telling him to do a certain dance and use a kind of medicine—a root or herb. He opened his eyes and there was a crow dancing up and down on his belly. You can see crows do this. And he was cured, and returned to his tribe. And he had crow medicine." Gelo (1986:220) notes that several variations of this myth are given, including an entire group of warriors who receive the medicine, four crows appearing to aid the Indian(s), and in some versions a man who is instructed to caw like a crow.

Comanche elders most frequently stated that a unit of United States Cavalry soldiers were defeated by a group of Yamparika Comanche in a battle, in which several black-handled sabers were captured, some of which have reportedly been handed down in some families.[29] The presence of European sabers among the Comanche has a long history in itself. Sabers were frequently given as a status item by European powers concluding treaties with prominent Comanche leaders and were also sought as trade items by the Comanche, who refashioned the blades into lance points (Kavanagh 1996). Stanley Noyes makes several references of gifts of sabers by the French in 1723 (1993:18–19), their possession by Comanche in 1751 (1993:9), and the gift of a saber by De Anza to Ecueracapa in 1786 (1993:80–81). Berlandier witnessed the Comanche trading for sword blades in Béxar in 1828–1829. In one instance One-Eyed Chief (aka El Tuerto) demanded to be given a sword that had already been presented to the Yamparika chief Big Star by the trader James, in return for letting the Anglos remain alive (Noyes 1993:171, 197).

Despite the lengthy presence of sabers among various Comanche divisions, early sources suggest that they were primarily political prestige gifts bestowed on divisional principal chiefs (Kavanagh 1996:377, 479). Comanche accounts state that the sabers associated with the Tuhwi Society were acquired in combat. Based on Comanche accounts and a review of Randy Stephan's (1978) compilations of United States Cavalry dress and arms, the acquisition of these "black" sabers most likely occurred between 1861 and 1872. Although current elders indicate the swords were "black-handled," it is unclear whether earlier Comanche emphasized the black sword handles, grips, knots, or belts. In 1861 the U.S. light cavalry saber was introduced, replacing the heavier 1840 "wrist-breaker" model. While the 1840 model contained buff, gold, and black knots, brass scabbards, and silver grips, the 1861 model contained a black handle and saber knot. The scabbards for officers' 1861 model sabers were "blue-ironed," while those for regulars were "browned" (Stephan 1978:20, 70–76, 123). By circa 1855 the First Regiment U.S. Cavalry was issued all black saber belts and accessories (Stephan 1978:34–36), which, combined with leftover supplies from the Civil War, formed the basis for post–Civil War cavalry dress. Descriptions of the 1861 model sabers, which were issued until a newer model appeared in 1872, closely match those of Comanche accounts of "black-handled" swords.

Unfortunately, it is not clearly known if the Tuhwi existed prior to the acquisition of these war trophies; although some Comanche publicly state that the society existed in the early 1700s, there is no verifiable documentation supporting this claim, nor any evidence of known Yamparika societies in the early 1800s.[30] Based on these data it is possible to suggest two possibilities: (1) that the Yamparika Tuhwi Society was a rather late (post-1860), short-lived historical development, probably influenced by the increasing interaction of the Yamparika with the Kiowa, Apache, and Cheyenne in the early to mid-1800s or (2) that the acquisition of sabers, which may have occurred between 1861 and 1872, was an addition to the history of an earlier (post-1810) warrior sodality without any precise documented origins.

Nineteenth-century documentation for the Tuhwi Society is extremely sparse. Howard White Wolf and Howard Chekovi provided brief descriptions for the Santa Fe Field School in 1933. According to both consultants, the *Tuhwi* or Raven Dancers were composed of sixty to seventy men with officers and belonged to the *Yapainᵾᵾ* (Yamparika) division. All archival sources as well as all current elders I interviewed emphatically state that the Tuhwi was strictly a Yamparika society. The society used a special dressing tipi in preparation for dances which were held outside. Howard White Wolf reported that the society sometimes combined two or three tipis to construct a large lodge for dances. Dancers gathered and, upon the leader's arrival, began to drum and sing. The headsman of the regiment carried a serrated whip with a gray fox tail attached. The leader rode a painted horse which had its tail tied with red cloth and an eagle feather. Members swore an oath to stay together in battle and fight side by side.[31]

Lowie (1915a:810–811) first described the Tuhwi:

> The Crow Dance was generally regarded by my informants as the exclusive property of the Yápairèka band. The performers marched through the entire camp, two abreast, with an officer on either side, armed with a heavy war club with a wrist loop of swift-fox skin, decorated with tassels. The officers deputized certain men to act as guards during the procession. The best dancers took the lead. After having proceeded some distance, they halted to form the arc of a circle. Then the dance began. At first possibly only one couple would advance, then the others followed. The dancers imitated the motions of a crow. The managers would stop the dance after a while and tell about the war that was to follow the na'wapina'r or make some other announcement of general interest, at the same time going through some motions while the drummers were beating their drums. There was a strict rule, that no dog must run ahead of the performers lest it be shot; so women would bid their children take care of any dogs they prized. Sometimes, however, a man who specially liked his dog might be asked to sacrifice it on this occasion. This taboo may have been common to several groups of dancers, but dogs were especially offensive to those of the Crow division.

The *Tuhwi* or *Tuuwinᵾᵾ* is commonly referred to by two names, the Black Knives and the Black Crow, which are both used among contemporary Comanche today. While most individuals maintain that Black Knives is the correct name of the society, both names played an integral part in the society's origins and beliefs; the distinctions are clarified through oral history. The literal translation of the society name is *Tuhwi*, "Black Knife," or *Tuuwinuu*, "Black Knife People." The name is derived from *tuu* (black), *wihi* (knife), and *nuu* (plural, people). However, the term also denotes crow, probably in reference to the crow's black bill. The society members are also called Crows or Ravens from their black feathered emblems. Crows were also known as *hai* or *haiht*, an archaic and echoic word as in the Comanche version (*Haihtsicht*, aka Heidsicki) of the name of the Kiowa leader Crow Lance (Càuáufîtâu or Ga-a-pi-tan). Gelo (1986:220) notes that the use of *tuhwi* for both black knife and crow invokes a double-edged metaphor, as black knife has clear martial connotations, while crow connotes scavenging battle fields.

As Gelo (1986) notes, Comanche refer to at least three species of carrion eaters with the same term, the common crow (*Corvus brachyrynchus*), the common raven (*Corvus corax*), and the white-necked raven (*Corvus cryptoleucus*). The association between crows and warfare is common throughout the world, as H. A. Tyler (1979:209) states: "War associations follow crows and ravens all around the world, because they eat dead things." Although Plains symbolism varies considerably, the color black was widely associated with war and death, such as the black face painting of returning members of revenge raids (Lowie 1963:106, 1983:225; Grinnell 1972:2:40–41; Mooney 1898:291; Wallace and Hoebel 1952:84, 269); thus, crows may be associated with war and death because of their color and behavior. Despite this association, crows and their power are viewed as beneficial to humans; crow feathers are used with cedar by Comanche eagle doctors in doctoring, in repelling ghosts, and as protective amulets on doors and babies' bedposts, and crows are the natural enemies of owls, which can be ghosts (Jones 1972: 48–49; Wallace and Hoebel 1952:160; Gelo 1986). Crow power is sometimes analogized to eagle power in Comanche oral history, and the wearer of a *haimudya* (crow basal rosette) headdress was worthy of the same respect as the wearer of an eagle feather bonnet (Gelo 1986:221).

In the Comanche language, *tuuwihi* (black knife) is used to describe the black-handled sabers acquired in battle. One elder consultant gave the term *tuuwiiyu* (black awl) as a synonym for black sabers. Some Comanche have indicated that awls (*wiiyu*), knives (*nahuu'*), and sabers are for the same purpose: making holes. Thus the term *tuhwihi* (Black [awls, knives, sabers]) was apparently applied to the captured sabers. Similarly *tuuwikaa* is the name for the common black crow. If shortened, either term can become *Tuwhi*.[32]

According to Ed Yellowfish, the common crow was an ally of the Comanche and served as a watchdog. As nothing can sneak up on a crow without it sounding an alarm, *aw'h aw'h*, no one could sneak up on the Tuhwi. In recognition of the crow's awareness of its surroundings and enemies, and help in combat, the Tuhwi Society honors the crow through dance and by using its call.[33] Crows are perceived as wary, deliberate, and intelligent birds, so warriors could clearly benefit from the power gained through emulating their behavior. Furthermore, crows post a sentinel when feeding (Robbins et al. 1983:212; Gelo 1986) and join en masse to attack threatening hawks and owls. As mentioned in one Tuhwi Society origin myth, crows and ravens hop when alighting upon their prey and are one of the few North American species of perching birds that walk. Thus, society members assumed these tactical principles and behaviors upon receiving crow medicine (Gelo 1986: 221–222).[34]

Lastly, it is interesting to note Mooney's observation (1896:1044–1045) that the name *Wï'dyu* (*Wiiyu̲*) or awl was formerly used to refer to the Yamparika or Yapai division, which the Shoshone used to refer to all Comanche. Elders indicate that because the Yapai were the northernmost division of the Comanche, they interacted more with their Shoshone relatives. Kavanagh (n.d.c) indicates that the Tuhwi were also called the Crow, from their crow feather emblems. Thus, both *Tuuwihi̲* and *Tuuwikaa* have important relations to the origins of the society's name, which is generally accepted to be *Tuuwihi̲* (Black Knives, in reference to sabers), given in shortened form as *Tuhwi* or *Tuuwi*.

Gelo (1986:3–8, 218–226) provides an interesting discussion of the role of the Tuhwi and their association with the crow in terms of Comanche mythology, belief, and ritual in paradigmatic (vertical) and sytagmatic (horizontal) relationships. However, this discussion must be used cautiously.[35] As the Tuhwi were pledged to defend against tribal attacks, their choice of the crow as a mascot is symbolic of its wary, defensive nature. Indeed crows gather in mass to attack and drive off owls, which are predatory, nocturnal birds with a haunting call that are associated with negative things such as ghosts, disease, and enemies. On the contrary, crows are "martial" birds which are frequently seen scavenging on battlefields. Thus, as Gelo (1986) explains, the symbology of the relationship can be expressed as:

crow   —   thwarts   —   owl
soldier   —   thwarts   —   enemy

This paradigm centers on the belief that crows and soldiers are similar, as are owls and enemies. The paradigm is further expressed by the natural enmity between crow and owl, as crows and soldiers are viewed as defenders.

In terms of structural formulas or diagrams, paradigmatic relationships are vertical, while sytagmatic ones are horizontal (Gelo 1986: 3–5, 8); thus, animal behavior serves as a model for human behavior and a basis for paradigmatic unity.

Because corvines are polysemous and symbolic intermediates between eagles and owls, and between life and death, they have curative and life-preserving powers like the eagle, although the eagle remains preeminent. Crows are opposed to owls in curative aspects and in representing a desirable death in battle, rather than an undesirable one from illness, possibly from witchcraft or ghost sickness. Gelo (1986: 221) expresses this relationship as:

(+) Eagle   (+)   Crow (−)   Owl (−)
life   life noble death   ignoble death

That the Tuhwi functioned as a unit in warfare and had a strong martial ideology is clear. Howard White Wolf's statement in 1933 that Tuhwi members swore to remain together and fight in battle reflects a strong sense of societal identity and martial ethos.[36] Dana Chibitty, born in 1897, described a Tuhwi dance she saw as a child. The dance was inside a tipi in which all members sat. When the singing began, all arose and cawed like a crow. Whenever a dog ran in front of them they were required to kill it.[37] Hoebel (1940: 17, 119) states that Comanche did not kill dogs because of their affinity with the Comanche trickster Coyote, due to which they are believed to possess some form of power. To kill a dog was believed to bring ill-fortune, especially to one's children. The relationship between this belief and the Yamparika division Tuhwi taboo is unknown; however, a taboo associated with dogs exists in several other Southern Plains military societies.

Wotsianoka (The Swift Fox or Fox Whip Society) or Wotsianɯɯ (Fox People)

The Wotsia, Wontsi, or Woxtsia, is the least known of the Comanche societies. Although the society's origins are unknown, it was reportedly a pre-reservation Peneteka and Nokoni society. Lowie (1915a) lists this group as the Swift Fox Society, but notes that another consultant indicated that it referred to a form of swift (flying bird). Post Oak Jim provides the only description of any length concerning this society. The dance was held prior to the Sun Dance or other major events, in a large arbor constructed to represent an eagle's nest. Women whose noses had been cut off as punishment for adultery were prohibited from entering the dance. The dancers appear to have held some taboo about this, as they would scatter upon the approach of such a woman, after which the leader with his club reportedly had a difficult time rounding them up. The *Woxtsia* or *Wotsianoka* (Fox Dance) was similar to the Horse Dance, as members would "jump up and down"; the exact choreography (and whether gourds were used) is unknown.[38] Kavanagh (1996:48) suggests that the society's name is *Waa'ne* (Fox). One contemporary elder indicated that this society was composed of younger men, gave the name of this sodality as *Wot-see-ah*, and independently confirmed the earlier ethnography concerning their taboo toward women whose noses had been cut off.[39]

O-hah-koo-hee-ma: The Wearers of Yellow Headgear (Yellow Roaches, known today as the Comanche War Dance Society)

Received from the Ponca, the Comanche War Dance of the Quahada represents a late-nineteenth-century diffused segment of the Grass Dance. According to Comanche accounts, the dance was acquired following a three day battle between the Comanche and Ponca which had stalemated. On the fourth day the two groups met and made peace, during which a number of gifts were exchanged. The Comanche gave the Ponca a number of horses; the Ponca reciprocated by giving the Comanche their Man Dance, a drum, and four songs.[40]

Known today as the Comanche War Dance Society (CWDS), the society was originally known as the *O-hah-koo-hee-ma* (Wearers of Yellow Headgear or Yellow Roaches), which refers to the wearing of the *eh-kah-koo-yah* or roach headdress, from *eh-kah* (red) and *koo-yah* (on top of the head), and the yellow (*o-hah*) painted roach feathers worn by members. The War Dance is known among the Comanches as the *Noyonuhka* (Testicles Dance).[41] Some elders indicate an association of the War Dance with the Big Horses, a Quahada Society which performed an ancestral form of today's Gourd Dance. It is not known if the War Dance was originally performed by the Big Horses, from which the O-hah-koo-hee-ma may later have developed, or if the O-hah-koo-hee-ma were organized independently as a Quahada division society, after receiving the War Dance from the Ponca. If the society's origins lay in a battle context, then it is likely that the Big Horses or perhaps a number of their members may have been involved in the acquisition and rise of the War Dance among the Comanche because both the Big Horses and the War Dance were primarily associated with the Quahada. Although the name of the society is not contained in the ethnographic literature, the O-hah-koo-hee-ma may have branched off from the Big Horses, as many younger men who did not have war honors soon came to dominate the rising Grass Dance societies of many other Plains tribes. That the majority of early members resided in the Cache and Indiahoma area also points to the society's origin in the Quahada division and the likelihood that at least some original members previously may have been Big Horses.

The Pukutsi (Contraries)

As in many Plains societies, a small number of individual Comanche assumed the role of contraries. There is no indication that the Pukutsi ever formed a contrary sodality as other Plains groups did, but they functioned as individual contraries. Their focus on warfare and their similarity to the Wolves Society merit their inclusion. The Comanche name for these individuals, *Pukutsi*, means contrary or stubborn in behavior or doing exactly the opposite of what is asked or expected of one. Unfortunately, there are only a few references to these individuals and their behavior. Frank Moetah stated:

> Any man brave enough and with the desire could become a *Pukutsi* on making up his mind. He could never retreat in a raid. With a bow in one hand and his rattle in the other he would take his position and sing until victory or death. Should he give way after the fight is done, the other warriors would taunt him in an attempt to egg him into overt action so they could kill him. He carried a rattle made from a buffalo scrotum. He would go through the camp singing no matter what else might be going on. He was never molested because he was so recklessly brave, no matter what his action.[42]

As Frank Chekovi stated, "The *Pukutsi* were called 'doing things backward.' He was a warrior who unrolled a red strip from his belt then shot an arrow into the end. Then he couldn't retreat unless a friend pulled it out." Post Oak Jim added, "The *Pukutsi* was a warrior who carried a roll of cloth under his armpit, fastened to his shoulder. In battle he would unroll the sash and shoot an arrow into the end. Thereafter he couldn't retreat unless a friend pulled the arrow out. Also he did everything backward. There was no vision before doing it."[43]

Mrs. Birdsong described similar battle characteristics for a group she referred to as the "Comanche Legion of Death":

> Certain dauntless men. When [they] would meet an enemy [they] would drive a stake into the ground (their picket stake for their horse)—and tie

themselves to it. If they retreated, they would be killed by members of the society. Some warriors had hooked sticks for this (stake pin) with a long spear-point at the bottom, decorated with two pairs of eagle feathers. Legion of Death membership usually ran in families, tho[ugh there were] no regulations regarding such. Children of Legion of Death members usually became members themselves, but [it was] not compulsory. Used a rope, a brand new rope to tie themselves secure to the stake. Must never turn themselves lose. Would carry [the] rope draped over [their] shoulder—just as beads in [a/the] picture.[44]

A favorite story still told by contemporary Comanche involves the escapades of a Pukutsi. The following account from *Hekiyani* was collected by the 1933 Santa Fe Laboratory of Anthropology party:

Hekiyani knew only one. He went around the camp with a rattle, singing. He went into a tipi with a pot boiling over a fire and shot some arrows into the fire, and helped himself to what's in the pot, ate it, and went to another tipi. He's sure always to do just what you don't want him to do. He wasn't brave, but wasn't afraid to do anything. A *Pukutsi* was going through camp singing as usual. An old woman stopped him and said, "*Pukutsi*, I want you to kill me a buffalo for my saddle; I have no boys to do it for me." He went and was gone for a long time. Finally he came back at night with a Pawnee's skin, with the feet and hands on it; he hung it standing on her arbor. He told the old lady her hide was on her arbor. She got up early and found it and was frightened. A man told her she shouldn't ask a *Pukutsi* to do such a job; he was afraid of nothing. She said she didn't ask him to bring her an enemy. But the old lady jumped and sang, she had an enemy scalp, which she kept.[45]

The divisional membership and account of Hekiyani indicates that Pukutsi were present among the Yamparika.[46] While other divisional distributions are unknown, acknowledgment of the Pukutsi by members of various divisions suggests that such contraries existed in several divisions. The Pukutsi were possibly individual continuations of the Kotsoteka Wolves Society, as the Kotsoteka are known to have splintered around the mid-1800s to form the Peneteka and Quahada (Kavanagh 1989:101). While ample ethnographic statements indicate the existence of the Pukutsi as contrary warriors, the term is often used in a different context by younger Comanche today. Although most individuals asked discussed the role of the Pukutsi as a contrary, the term is often used today as a joking word for elderly men or children who are considered to be stubborn or hard-headed, in the context of being "no good." While *Pukutsi* does translate as "contrary" or "stubborn," the original context was the warfare-related contrary behavior of these individuals, and it is this association that most elder Comanche acknowledge. Although the Pukutsi remain only in story, they symbolize the epitome of Comanche bravery in warfare, which is still respected and continues to hold importance for current Comanche identity and concepts of a warrior ideology and ethos.

The Crow Tassel Wearers

Although the Crow Tassel Wearers appear to have been a short-lived and relatively small group, they personified the fullest definition of the term "military society." They were a group of men who collectively and incessantly pursued warfare. Hoebel (1940: 31) states that there were never more than two to four such members per generation; however, these numbers appear too small to have operated in warfare for the lengthy periods attributed to them. Members were reportedly men who had no surviving families or who descended from lineages with strong warrior traditions to uphold. For orphans, who had little to lose and everything to gain, the road to warfare brought either death or great prestige, while others sought to uphold their family's reputation as warriors. They fought and raided as a group with a strong obligation of loyalty to one another. Their distinguishing insignia was a tassel worn in their hair and on their shoulder and a special form of bonnet constructed of fine feathers clipped short except for one larger feather with scalloped edges.

As Hoebel notes, they pursued warfare so singlemindedly that they were not a part of the larger society during the duration of their membership and thus had little social impact. If they met an outgoing party when they were returning to camp, they were required to accompany it, thus contributing to their lengthy absences from Comanche society. They were free to disband at any time and at the end of a successful career are said to have became leading men in their communities due to their high level of prestige (Hoebel 1940: 33–34; Kavanagh n.d.b). Hoebel (1940: 31–32) describes how the society disbanded. Although I cannot determine their divisional distribution, the Crow Tassels are perhaps best viewed as an extremely small society that focused upon the martial (warfare and raiding) and not the social (singing and dancing) aspects of Plains military societies. Based on Hoebel's discussion of Jeannette Mirsky's data, the Crow Tassels probably represent a short-lived medicine group (with a military emphasis somewhat resembling a shield society, although no associated society shields are known) rather than a major soldier sodality.[47] Like the Pukutsi, the Crow Tassel Wearers reflect the martial ideology of other Comanche military societies.

Compared to Northern Plains data, documented Comanche military societies appear to have been relatively late historical developments. In comparison with temporally comparable Southern Plains studies among the Kiowa in 1935, the Apache in 1934, and the Cheyenne in 1935–1936, the lack of data and few references to Comanche military societies in the 1933 Santa Fe fieldnotes also suggest that they were a relatively late acquisition which did not perform as great an integrative role as among other Plains groups.

COMANCHE MILITARY SOCIETY SYNONYMY

Table 6 demonstrates a proposed synonymy of Comanche military societies and divisional groupings. An obvious question arises regarding the identification of societal and dance ethnonyms: which names refer to social groups (sodalities), which refer to dances, and which dances are associated with specific military societies? Some scholars have stated in conversations that they consider "Gourd" to be a "dance" and "Little Ponies" to be a "society," distinguishing between the names of choreographies (dances) and social organizations (sodalities). I contend that analysis of names, traits, and ethnographic descriptions clearly distinguishes among dances which are sodality based (Tuhwi-Crow-Raven, Big Horse, Little Horse, Fox–Swift Fox), general Comanche dances (Buffalo, War, Love, Drum, etc.), and those affiliated with specific warrior groups such as the Pukutsi and Crow Tassel, which were much smaller martial-oriented warrior groupings.

In reviewing ethnographic descriptions of Comanche societies, because the names of many Plains military society dances refer to the society which performs them, I believe that synonyms for Comanche societies and dances are discernible. Analogous names are clearly present when comparing Lowie's (1915a) listings of Comanche societies to divisional associations. With the exception of the Yamparika Tuhwi, most sources do not provide divisional associations. Following Lowie's list of Comanche military societies, Thurman (1980:7) has compiled a substantial list of probable associations between Comanche military societies and tribal divisions from historical sources. To this I have added those mentioned in Kavanagh (n.d.b) as well as two lists of "Soldier Bands" provided by Quanah Parker and *Cabaya*, Comanche interviewed by H. L. Scott in 1892, and my own fieldwork.[48] Although Scott did not collect divisional associations for societies, the lists he obtained from Quanah and Cabaya are important ethnographic statements

TABLE 6 Comanche Military Society Synonymy and Divisional Distribution

Sources	Yamparika	Quahada	Quahada	Peneteka	Kotsoteka & Nokoni Los Lobos/Wolf	All Divisions
Berlandier (1969)	Crow	Little Horse	Big Horse	Fox	—	Buffalo
Lowie (1915a)	Crow	Colt	Horse	Swift Fox	—	Buffalo
		Suggested Correlations				
Clark (1885) [1982]	Raven Crow	Gourd Little Horse	Gourd Big Horse	Swift Fox Fox	Afraid of Nothing	Buffalo Bull
Ten Kate (1885a)	Corbeaux Tebwi	Petite Cheval Tiddiapohk	Grand Cheval Pibiapohk	Renard Wautcheah	—	Buffalo Bull
Kavanagh 1986, 1996	Tuwinɨɨ Tuwekane	Tuapukunɨɨ Tuepokene	Pibiapukunɨɨ Piveapokune	Waa?ne? Wotsine	—	Buffalo
Kavanagh n.d. b	Black Knife People/Crow	Little Ponies	Big Horses	Fox People	—	—
Cabaya 1982 (HLS-2)	Black Leggins	Rattle	Rattle	—	—	Buffalo
Quanah 1892 (HLS-2)	Black Leggins Crow	Little Horse	Big Horse	Fox Whip	—	Buffalo
Meadows 1995	Tuwinɨɨ or Tuhwi Black Knives or Crow	Tuapukunɨɨ Little Horses	Pibiapukunɨɨ Big Horses	Wotsia Fox	—	Buffalo Aanɨhka or Ta'siwoonɨhka

Dances—Assumed to be at least interdivisional if not possibly panComanche: Drum, Turkey Cock, War, Love, *Pukutsi* or Contrary, Crow Tassel.

by native informants who were unquestionably knowledgeable concerning prereservation Comanche culture. As Cabaya related to Scott:

> The Comanches have soldier bands who are common to all Comanches and when they went to war a man took a pipe around to the different bands—it didn't take long to go from the Yaparikas to the Peneteckas in Texas & from there to the Quahadas at the head of Red River then when we came together the soldiers had their own dance[;] each company might have men from every Comanche band in it. 1. Black Leggins 2. Rattle 3. Rattle 4. Walk Around 5. War Club 6. War Bonnet. Six soldiers in all. The bull dance can be borrowed by any soldier co[mpany], the Kiowas the same.[49]

Scott also wrote: "Quanah gave the name of the soldier bands as follows: 1. Black Leggins 2. Big Horse 3. Little Horse 4. Fox Whip 5. Crow. The Bull dance is used by any soldier band also among the Kiowas. The Bull dance is used in the same way."[50] Despite lacking associated distributions, these society names correlate well with those from other sources.

SOCIETY MEMBERSHIP, DISTRIBUTION, AND ORGANIZATION

While the existence of nineteenth-century Comanche military societies has been demonstrated, the question of their distribution and organizational basis remains. Scholars have speculated whether society membership was unidivisional or cross-divisional. Most contemporary scholars (Kavanagh 1980: 64, 1986: 51; Thurman 1980: 7, 1982; Gelo 1988: 540) have suggested that Comanche societies operated on the divisional level, with each tribal division having its own societies, although no substantial data for this characterization have been presented. Scott suggests that excluding the Yamparika's Tuwhi Society, a society might "include men from every band."[51] Portions of the 1933 Santa Fe Comanche fieldnotes vaguely mention society distribution.[52]

   The question then is whether Comanche societies were unidivisional or pandivisional (pan-Comanche) or whether more than one society could exist per division, but not in all divisions. The solution lies in clarifying the descriptive terminology used in the ethnographic sources. As Kavanagh (1980, 1986, 1996) has stressed, a review of Comanche terminology illustrates some of the problems associated with the origins of the Comanche anomaly. To determine the basis for organizational distribution, it is crucial to provide identification, context, and assessment for statements in various ethnographic sources. The difficulties in distinguishing among groups, bands, bunches, regiments, companies, divisions, and tribes have led to incorrect assessments in the literature. The problem is that descriptions do not clarify whether they refer to a group of bands which together form a single division such as the Yamparika or whether the "bands" are in fact divisions such as the Yamparika and Quahada, which in turn form a larger Comanche ethnicity or nation. The following data demonstrate that Comanche men's societies were in fact primarily unidivisional, with each tribal division, composed of a fluctuating number of bands, maintaining one or more military sodalities, but that Comanche societies were in no way pandivisional or pan-Comanche in the usual tribal sense. While a Fox Society existed in both the Peneteka and Nokoni divisions and the Quahada division contained the Little Horses and Big Horses societies, the majority of Comanche societies were unidivisional, and none existed in all Comanche divisions.

Lowie's ambiguous writing style produced difficulties in determining how Comanche societies were organized in relation to tribal divisions. He indicated that dances were at least preferentially associated with specific bands (divisions) such as the Quahada, Yamparika, and Peneteka, although he stated that one of his informants denied such association. Wallace and Hoebel (1952:274) note that the Comanche societies "seem to have been limited to the northern bands," which reflects Plains diffusion but is also misleading.

Society Distribution

Cabaya told Scott that soldier bands were common to all Comanche, that a pipe was taken to the different divisions prior to setting out on war ventures, and that during dances each "soldier group" had its own dance that might include men from every Comanche band.[53] Does his statement mean that all Comanche divisions had their own societies and were thus important as distinct political groupings? In stating that soldier bands were common to all Comanche, was Cabaya describing multidivisional membership or simply saying that all bands were associated with some military society? In saying that each society held dances in which members of all bands participated, was he referring to all the bands that made up a division or to all the divisions that made up a larger pan-Comanche ethnicity? I suggest that he was referring to the presence of at least one society per Comanche division, whose membership was drawn from all of the bands of a single division, but he was ambiguous in his descriptive terminology.

Foster (1991:182) reports that his Comanche consultants suggest that sodality membership did cross-cut divisional or supraband boundaries, which contradicts some older ethnographic accounts. He indicates that current Comanche report a traditional strategy whereby a family maintains at least one member in each dance society, confirming a more restricted interpretation of Comanche divisional functions. However, this phenomenon is influenced by the geographical concentration of Comanche following the reservation period, as there are adequate earlier data to the contrary.

Although a pan-Comanche membership pattern exists today, a closer review of ethnographic sources indicates that not all prereservation-era societies were found in every Comanche division. In comparing societies to companies of soldiers, Lowie (1915a:809) makes an odd statement: "If nothing unusual happened, a man would remain true to the division he had first chosen, but there was no special bond of friendship between members of the same company." Here the terms "division" and "company" are both used in reference to sodality. This implies that individuals could choose from more than one society "division." If only one society per division existed, then changing societies would require a change in band and divisional residency as well. If multiple societies existed within one tribal division, as with the Quahada Little Horses and Big Horses, then shifting between societies could be possible, although this situation is ethnographically unconfirmed. The part of Lowie's statement regarding the level of camaraderie within these men's organizations is also puzzling. While members of Kiowa societies occasionally changed society membership during their lifetime, Cheyenne members rarely did. Most societies enjoyed high levels of camaraderie and friendship, and numerous forms of social and economic cooperation in the form of nonblood kinship as society partners and fraternal brothers. Wallace and Hoebel (1952:272, 274) report a number of social and economic functions performed by societies which contradict Lowie's assessment. "Members are somewhat like brothers. They went on the warpath together and helped bury and mourn a dead fellow member." They state that a man leading a revenge party could usually rely on the support of his society, although other warriors were welcomed, and when a leader acquired a party in which his society's members were the majority, the War Dance was referred to by that society's name.

Numerous Comanche band and divisional names (Kavanagh 1996, n.d.b; Thurman 1980) indicate that the Comanche, like most Plains tribes, experienced a continual growth, decline, and reorganization of bands and divisional composition which was accelerated by external European-induced influences. Nineteenth-century Comanches frequently moved from one division and one local or residence band to another for various purposes. It is logical to assume that a man would have been allowed to participate in the society of the division of his residence, as exclusionary practices would have been counterproductive to larger level social integration. Thus, it is likely that Comanche societies held long-term identification for their members.

In contrast, Wallace and Hoebel (1952:272) suggest that society membership held only short-term identity: "Most of the Comanche warrior groups appear to have been informal organizations compounded of mutual friendship and interests, and they were not continuous and permanent." This statement suggests the presence of social and economic cooperation, although the frequency and duration of their activities would be ecologically and seasonally influenced. Post Oak Jim indicated similar social relations between fellow medicine society members: "All Eagle Medicine Men had friendly feelings toward each other; they were bound together by their common source of power."[54]

It is likely that the social bonds surrounding society membership functioned as sources of long-term identity as long as larger elements of Comanche social organization endured, even when societies were not actively meeting or raiding, for two reasons. First, societies were specific to particular Comanche divisions; second, because the majority of men would have belonged to the society of their divisional residence, they were tied to one another fictively through their society membership. Fellow society members would have interacted with one another throughout the year, whether their society was collectively active or not. Comanche societies are known to have functioned at least periodically as societal-based cooperative raiding parties (Lowie 1915a:810; Wallace and Hoebel 1952:274). Male solidarity was clearly an economic necessity in the Comanche raiding- and warfare-based economy, with the strongest ties being between brothers. While residence band and divisional groupings of men frequently cooperated in military activities, the adoption of distinct symbols and associated elements of military societies probably strengthened the level of *communitas* between members of each grouping in relation to their opportunistic exploitation in raiding and warfare. As members of the same Comanche society are still considered "brothers," this social bond promoted integration. Yet the frequently changing social organization of Comanche residence bands due to changes in band leaders, warfare, differential relations with external populations, diseases, depopulation, and initial lack of military sodalities may have partially undermined this sense of community, in comparison with neighboring tribes.

Wallace and Hoebel (1952:274) mention a number of traits common among other Southern Plains military societies. A prospective male frequently joined the society of his father or brother but was not obliged to and, having announced his choice, was inducted upon the society's approval. Rivalry between societies for rising warriors with a reputation for bravery is said to have existed and "sometimes the pipe was forced into their mouth," another common practice across the Plains, obligating the smoker to join the recruiting society. The rivalry for membership again suggests either a multidivisional membership or a change in divisional residence, as no competition could occur if there were only one men's society per division.

Unidivisional Societies

Several statements suggest that Comanche societies were indeed linked to particular band groupings or divisions. Most data on the relationship of Comanche societies to Comanche social organization were obtained from Post Oak Jim and must be cautiously examined due to the lack of other available data. As Post Oak Jim commented:

> Each honorable man had his bunch. A group was named after its leader. In the dances they would call the leader's name, and tell him to "round up his horses," and come forward and tell his brave deeds. The announcer would call the names of persons present and call on them to come out and tell brave deeds; (he says "the people's eyes are on you; don't be afraid of them,") "only the eyes of people are on you, you won't be hurt." He called on the most notable to be honored.[55]

Other statements made by Post Oak Jim likewise imply that individual societies belonged to different divisions: "Each band had different dances"; "Each band dances its own way"; and, perhaps referring to a relatively late post-1870 situation, "When people came together in a tribal gathering, each band had its own dancers, and put on its one part of the show at the center of the encampment." He further stated: "At the Sun Dance, each band danced one day, one from the east, one from the west, north and south; each danced their own way."[56] As there were clearly more known Comanche bands than known military societies or days associated with a Sun Dance during the third quarter of the nineteenth century, this statement must refer to divisions or to various non-society-oriented dances which various residence bands held. Post Oak Jim makes several pertinent points: (1) that there was some form of at least multiband or divisional if not multidivisional (but probably not pantribal) gatherings, which (with military and economic changes and population losses) changed toward more pantribal gatherings in late prereservation times such as the 1874 Sun Dance; (2) that each division was apparently composed of a number of bands and perhaps assigned to designated camping locations; (3) that societies maintained different dances and their own membership; and (4) that military society membership appears not to have been cross-divisional or pantribal.[57]

According to Howard White Wolf, "A man could belong to one 'regiment' only. All the men of a band belonged to its regiment and could not switch band affiliation."[58] While the first statement resembles the situation in other Plains tribal military societies, the second does not, because men in some other Plains tribes often changed society affiliation throughout their lives. If accurate, this suggests that the Comanche used their divisional organization as a basis for their military societies instead of a residence-band-level distribution as found among the Plains Cree. Two Quahada division men's societies existed, with young men belonging to the Little Horses and joining the Big Horses later in life, while the Swift Fox Society was found in the Peneteka and Nokoni divisions. From 1850 to 1875 at least seventeen Comanche bands forming five tribal divisions existed. Since band membership frequently fluctuated, residence bands were not a feasible basis for the four or five known military societies, which must have been linked primarily to the larger divisions, since there were clearly fewer societies than bands.

Thurman (1980:6) discusses the problems associated with determining the extent and quantity of Comanche bands and tribal divisions. Listings of Comanche bands and divisions have ranged from Padillo in 1820 and Berlandier in 1829, who listed three, to higher lists of three, six, seven, and eight, by Burnet in 1819, Butler and Lewis in 1847, Ten Kate in 1885, and Pike in 1861, respectively (Thurman 1980:6), and five active and eight "practically extinct" bands by Mooney (1896:1044–1045). At least seventeen divisional and band names were collected by the Santa Fe party in 1933. Kavanagh reports at least thirty-seven local band leaders from six divisions, and others of undesignated band affiliation between 1869 and 1874.[59] While some lists mix band and divisional ethnonyms, the identification of those clearly known multilocal band divisions provides about seven divisions, all of which did not exist at the same time, and four society names, including one society which was attributed to two groups or divisions. These estimates of Comanche bands also exceed the number of known Comanche military societies, which suggests that societies were indeed multiband or divisional oriented and not specific to an individual local residence band, although those contained in more than one division may reflect diffusion.

However, it is important to remember that Comanche band and divisional groupings changed dynamically over time (1700–1875) due to a number of factors including warfare, disease, intermarriage, social relations, treaties and alliances, and the constant rise and fall of prominent band and war leaders. Among the Comanche the residence leader or headsman was the key to maintaining a band. When a band fragmented, the members rapidly regrouped under a new leader or switched residence to another band. New Comanche residence bands are known to have constantly formed and dissipated as groups depended upon the charisma of their leaders to attract and hold a following (Wallace and Hoebel 1952:23, 210–212; Kavanagh 1986, 1996). Comanche band leaders' role in maintaining social organization was far stronger than the integrative roles of military societies or of society leaders who were residence band leaders, as found among other tribes. Thus, the frequently irregular band residence was too unstable to have served as a long-term basis for sodalities.

It is also important to recognize that all Comanche bands and divisions were not conducting the same relations with one another or with external groups. Various Comanche had different relations with the numerous intradivisional and interdivisional Comanche, with other tribes, and with French, Spanish, American, and Texan interest groups. Numerous examples demonstrate that a number of Comanche residence bands or various divisions held alliances with a particular configuration of tribes or European governments while other Comanche did not (Thomas 1932; Winfrey and Day 1966:5:173, 185–186, 200; John 1984, 1985). For example, only the Yamparika signed the 1853 Fort Atkinson Treaty with the Kiowa and Naishan Apache and the Quahada and Kotsoteka did not sign the 1867 Medicine Lodge Treaty due to other commitments that week (Kavanagh 1996:411–412). While larger interdivisional segments of Comanche did sometimes act cooperatively in conducting treaties and warfare and in trade fairs, the entire pan-Comanche population was not a single political entity (Thomas 1929, 1932; Wallace and Hoebel 1952; John 1984:346, 353; Kavanagh 1996).

Various Comanche groups were likewise following different subsistence pursuits, such as the Peneteka, who, probably because of the reduction of local bison herds (Davis 1996:121–122), had assumed a horse-trading and later reservation-based economy by the mid-1850s, while the Quahada remained on the Staked Plains until finally surrendering in 1875. The Quahada are in some ways analogous to the Cheyenne Dog Soldiers, as many Comanche who were more resistant to surrendering and accepting a reservation existence gravitated to join this division. A major difference was that Quahada military society functions were developing toward but had not yet reached the coercive level of authority held by the Cheyenne Dog Soldiers. Remaining nomadic bands, such as the Quahada, were more active in warfare and raiding and are likely to have retained military societies longer than reservation-based bands such as the Peneteka, who, having surrendered earlier, had less incentive for maintaining such organizations. Recognition of the emergence of reservation and nonreservation bands, changes and origins of bands and divisions, and their geographical relocation is important in considering their potential for adapting and maintaining military societies.

Bands and divisions contained some distinct differences in alliances, food, dress, dances, and other cultural forms (Wallace and Hoebel 1952; Kardiner 1945:54). Although less frequent than in local residence bands, changes in divisional orientation and membership and identity occurred throughout the nineteenth century. Yet did this changing orientation and membership in larger social institutions (bands and divisions) affect military society identity? Regarding social organization, Wallace and Hoebel (1952:24) state: "Cultural differences persisted, although it was mandatory upon an individual to follow the customs of the group with which he lived in order to be socially accepted by his new associates, and this despite the frequent exchange of band allegiance and the inter-band marriages." Because of their territorial and geographic proximity, residence bands contained more frequent marriage and kin ties to one another and affected the intensity of interaction on a number of levels, including divisional social occasions. Local residence band changes probably would not have resulted in any significant changes, as residence bands of the same division would have contained the same military society.

Changes to a residence band in another division should have resulted in the adaptation of the new residents to the military society of that division, which may or may not have been the same society depending on the division. A member moving from the Peneteka to the Nokoni would have (according to Lowie's 1915a military society distributions) been a Swift Fox Society member in each division. However, Quanah was originally a Nokoni and would theoretically have become a Swift Fox Society member upon remaining in that division. Yet his presence as a Little Pony among the Quahada suggests that changes in society membership coincided with changes in divisional residence. The formation of a new division such as the Quahada could have had different consequences, for which conclusive data are lacking. One can speculate that the society of a newly formed division might take the form of the society maintained by the largest or most influential segment of the newly formed division or that some degree of syncretism between two or more societies may have occurred.

Accounts of the march to Adobe Walls in 1874 include the names, divisions, and societal associations of prominent Comanche men, which in turn correlate with the divisional and societal distributions collected from numerous ethnographic sources. Included were Quanah and Yellowfish, who were Quahada and Little Horse Society members, and Attocknie, who was a Yamparika and a Tuhwi Society member (Kavanagh n.d.d: 38).[60] Quanah's account of this event to Scott also indicates divisional-based societies. After describing how he had offered a pipe to the Quahada and Nokoni for support in the raid, he stated: "Have big dance tonight. Big Horse dance here; Little Horse dance over there, Fox Quirt dance over there. . . ."[61] The first two dances are Quahada dances, while the last is a known Nokoni and Peneteka divisional dance. Although some Yamparika participated in the Adobe Walls fight, there is no mention of them or the Tuwhi Society, which suggests that they may not have been present at this dance.

In listing divisional names, Howard White Wolf again stated that each regiment had different dances. For the *Yapainʉʉ* (Yamparika), he states, "These same companies or regiments gave other dances also, for example the Crow and other dances."[62] This suggests that each division performed its own military society dances as well as other dances of a more social and pan-Comanche nature, such as the Buffalo, Scalp, and Shake Down Dances. The position of military societies also supports the idea that Comanche divisions were important political groupings. While multidivisional councils under a head chief were occasionally formed and recognized, divisions were not consistently on the same side in political decisions such as war and peace, suggesting that the division was the highest level of regular and effective political organization. The coercive role of any society appears to have been normally limited to the divisional level, unlike those of neighboring Southern Plains tribes.

Linguistic data also suggest that Comanche societies were division based. Several Plains tribes have a collective reference term for their tribal military societies, such as the Blackfeet *Ixkonnokatsiyiks* or All Comrades (Wissler 1913:365; Ewers 1988:105), the Kiowa Yàpfàhêgàu (Temporary Police, Soldiers), the Cheyenne *Nutqio* or Warriors (Mooney 1898:229, 1907:412), the Arapaho *Běni'něna* or Warriors (Mooney 1896:986), and the Lakota *Oko'lakićiye* (Friends Together), of which the *Aki'ćita* (Guards, Police) were one type (Densmore 1992:284, 313; Walker 1982:28, 32–34). While Comanche have a word for Anglo soldiers (*eksahpahnah*, literally "red stomach high up," in reference to the red waist sashes worn by military officers), elderly Comanche and society leaders stated that no single reference term for all Comanche military societies exists.[63] The closest similarity is the term *Nʉhkanʉmʉ* or *Nʉhknʉm* (literally Dance Comanche), which is used to differentiate between *Puharaivonʉʉ* (Christian Church People) and *Wokwetʉhkatʉʉ* (Peyote People); however, these distinctions developed during the reservation period.[64] My consultants all indicated that the Tuhwi was a Yapai dance and that the Little Horses, Big Horses, and War Dance were

Quahada-based dances. One consultant specifically indicated that the Wo-tsia dance belonged to the Nokoni. Elders also indicate that most Nokoni, Peneteka, and Kotsoteka dances were dropped long ago, and little is known of them today.[65] By examining the various ethnohistorical sources the previously fragmented sources become complementary and offer an explanation for the relationship between Comanche military societies and larger elements of social organization.

In view of these data, I suggest that Comanche societies, although in some cases present in two divisions (the Peneteka and Nokoni Swift Fox Society) or with more than one men's society per division (Quahada Little and Big Horses and the later War Dance Society), were clearly associated with a limited range of specific divisions and were not pan-Comanche in prereservation times. This suggests that the division, and not the pan-Comanche community, was the highest level of Comanche political organization, which in turn supports the contention of Richardson (1933:317), Thurman (1987:554), Kavanagh (1996, n.d.a, n.d.d), and Davis (1996) that Comanche social organization should be viewed as several politically independent tribes (tribal divisions) rather than as divisions of a single pan-Comanche tribe.

SOCIETY LEADERSHIP AND ORGANIZATION

The exact organizational arrangement of Comanche military society officers is unclear. However the owner of a *pianʉpai* (big whip) or whipman (*tuh-a-pai-yah*, literally: He is carrying a whip) appears to have been the central leader and may have combined the positions of society leaders and whipmen found in other Plains military societies. Whipmen were probably *maimiana paraivo* (war chief) or a leader who held war honors and was regarded as a *tekniwop* (warrior, hero, combat veteran). These individuals were considered the bravest warriors in the "band" (society) and carried large, flat, wooden clubs with serrated edges, fox pelt handles, and leather lashes as insignia of their bravery, obligating them not to retreat in battle. Two whipmen existed in both the Big Horses and Tuhwi Societies, and there are numerous references to each "band" having one or two club bearers or whipmen who carried a *pianʉpai* or Big Whip. Carved upon Penaro's whip were scalp symbols representing the owner's victims (Wallace and Hoebel 1952:271). Whipmen participated in society dances, standing on each side of the dancers. Personal battle coups were recited during breaks in the dancing, upon which the whipman might swear to the sun that his testimony was truthful, with consequences of a potential supernatural sanction for lying. A whipman was required to tell the truth about his battle exploits lest he be shamed by a contradicting witness or die soon as supernatural punishment for lying. During dances, society members sat in a line, rising together to dance. Recalcitrant dancers were struck by the whipman and instructed to participate and were required to provide a good reason for not dancing. As in the case of hunting infractions, if a man could recite a greater war deed than the whipman, he was released; otherwise he was fined and forced to dance.[66]

White Wolf described this principle in 1933. A man refusing to dance had his shirt torn off and was struck by the whipman. He stated that he was a poor dancer and told of a battle in which he had killed several men, saying that if the leader could boast of more brave deeds he would dance as best he could. Unable to better the deed, the leader was thus shamed and backed down. Men also used this practice to leave a dance early. If they could out-recite the leader, he had to dance.[67]

Although recalcitrant dancers were known to be whipped, Kwasia stated: "An onlooker who saw the coach coming for him will usually hop to get in before he is struck."[68] Whipmen could strike dancers, but they could not keep them from participating in dances. Whipmen held control over the other dancers, who could not refuse their wishes, perhaps in part because of their reputation as great warriors. As was typical of other Plains military societies, Post Oak Jim indicated that a club owner's authority to whip individuals and enforce order was limited solely to dance and thus society occasions.[69] Naiya illustrated the jurisdiction of whipmen, which can be inferred to distinguish two forms of dances: "There were two kinds of dance, one is on the return from a raid" (such as the Scalp, Victory, or Shake Down Dances), the "other is when men are whipped" (society dances).[70]

According to Howard White Wolf, whenever a society leader was killed, nominations for a replacement were made by members of that society.[71] Post Oak Jim indicated that the tribal leaders made the selection.[72] In either case, the results were similar; the war records of all those named for candidacy were compared and the man holding the best war record was chosen as the successor. Reportedly, if a *paraivo* (chief or headsman) held enough honors he could also become a club bearer. A deceased man's club was hung in a tree to deteriorate or, like a shield, was placed in a stream of water to wash away. Successors are said to have made whips designed after those of their predecessor, which suggests societal stylistic patterns. Sometimes, a vacancy was not filled for some time due to lack of a qualified man. Because a man could not assume the rights to the position by himself or be so bold as to seek the position, a worthy candidate had to be found. This description resembles those of anthropologist Ralph Linton (1935:423), in which every

Comanche band had a War Whip Bearer who was the most important warrior in the band. Some of the known nineteenth-century whipmen, *Esahabbit* (Milky Way), *Paruakuhma* (He Bear), and White Horse, were all prominent tribal leaders. Contemporary elders recall Chebatah, a Lipan Apache who later permanently lived with the Comanche, serving as a whipman in the 1920s. Following his death he was succeeded by his brother Penaro, who inherited the whip.[73] Each society also apparently had an official crier who made announcements for the society leader.

In 1933 Linton was adopted by the Comanche at a Brush Dance in Walters, Oklahoma. Upon reading his World War I service record, he was named Red Buffalo, in memory of the buffalo who had so much power that he had thrown the Comanche "witch" up to the moon with a toss of his horns, where she can still be seen. The last *pianɨpai* (big whip) was then presented to Linton by Penaro or Pine-dapoi who announced that he "was relinquishing it to a younger and greater warrior" (Kavanagh n.d.d: 29; Wallace and Hoebel 1952:272).[74] While the motivations for this act beyond honoring can only be speculated upon, it is possible that the elder society members believed that the society and the means for Comanche to achieve a war record comparable to the past were no longer available.

MILITARY SOCIETY KINSHIP

Non-blood-based (fictive) kinship in the form of "society brothers" was one of the primary distinguishing features of nineteenth-century Plains military society organization. Contrary to Lowie's conflicting statements (1915a: 809–811), close social ties between members of the same Comanche men's society and especially between pairs of members or "partners" within the same society existed (Neighbors 1852:131; Berlandier 1969:73–74, 117; Gladwin 1948; Kavanagh 1996:40). Through this practice a man gained a "brother" or "friend who was even closer to him than a real brother" (Kardiner 1945:57). This institution is well documented in archival sources as well as by current tribal elders.[75] In 1824 Ruiz (Berlandier 1969:73–74, 117) observed "war dances" or a "little war" held during preparations for a multidivisional revenge raid. During the dances, Ruiz noted men dressed in their finest clothing marching in double file order, which suggests the presence of society partners. Lowie (1915a:810–811) referred to this relationship in his description of both a Tuhwi Society dance and men preparing to leave on a revenge raid. Naiya, Post Oak Jim, and Herman Asenap all reported such relationships in 1933.[76] Two friends who were very close would call each other "brother," often forming relationships for life, typically after one individual saved the life of another or when two men went on several war expeditions together, whereby the relationship grew until it was "official" and publicly recognized (Gladwin 1948:91). As Post Oak Jim put it, "A *tebitsi nahaitsna* was a 'true friend'" and "true friends were closer than actual brothers, especially in time of battle. . . . So long as there was any life left in a fallen warrior, his brother couldn't desert him in battle."[77] Although not consanguineally related, society brothers were often closer than biological brothers, exactly the basis for most Plains military society relationships.

Hoebel (1939:448) states: "The institution of formal friendship among men also entails the use of the brother terminology. The friend (Comanche *haits*) staked the status of his 'brother' in the relationship system of his comrade's family, thereby taking over all the privileges and restrictions which go with the new status." As the acceptance and maintenance of fictive kinship and behavior practiced between the two men and their family members demonstrates, society partners were viewed as consanguineal relatives. Comanche society partners addressed each other's families exactly as their own family and observed all avoidance relations and taboos associated with one's own biological sisters, including the prohibition against marrying or even talking about each other's sisters. Thomas Gladwin (1948:91) reports that brothers were constant companions sharing everything, including their "women friends."[78]

Thus, "brothers" referred to each other's wives as "our wife" or "our sweetheart," while others referred to the wife of one "brother" through a dual possessive form. Hoebel (1940:20) reports that when "peace" chiefs went to war, they sometimes left their wife under the protection of their partner, who was authorized to help her carry out his instructions. This situation seems unusual, however, in that partners were reported always to have been together whenever one set out on a war journey. Aside from economic cooperation in raiding, partners also shared payments collected for *nanʉwokʉ* (payment of damages) or fines collected by a cuckold and were thus considered "husbands" in adultery cases. Society brothers exhibited strong levels of joking with each other, frequently talking roughly to one another and about their partner to others, which was considered inappropriate between consanguineal brothers.[79]

Society brothers frequently went on raids together and were alleged never to desert each other in battle. Naiya told of one Comanche horse raiding venture in which the owners of the stolen horses pursued the Comanche. In the ensuing fight one brother was surrounded by the enemy after having his horse shot out from under him. Another member of the retreating party saw what happened and told the man's "brother," who immediately turned back to his partner's aid. Both were killed; when the returning party reported the fate of the two friends to their parents, they were saddened, but proud of their "sons."[80] Society brothers were expected to stand together through thick and thin. Failure to do so brought disgrace, and riding past one's partner without aiding him was grounds for terminating the relationship. Occasionally, if relationships were not amicable, new partners or "brothers" were sought as replacements.

Members were sometimes separated in battle and one partner was killed. After his death, the father regarded the surviving partner as an adopted son. Upon returning from the battle, the surviving partner said, "The horse has come," indicating the death of the man's son, and then related where the battle took place and how his "brother" was killed. The name of the father of the deceased was called aloud so he could feel satisfied that his son had died bravely. The surviving partner's family then came and mourned just as if the deceased were one of their own biological sons.[81] Hoebel (1940:121, 124) reported two cases in which the surviving partner inherited property upon the death of his "best friend" and, in one case, reportedly had the rights to first claim on the deceased's property.

By the time Gladwin (1948:91) collected data on Comanche kin behavior in 1940, the practice of "brothers" had lapsed among all but a few individuals. Ed Yellowfish stated that "friends danced together" in the 1930s, and in contemporary Comanche societies men still occasionally "take another man for a brother," after which their relationship is like that of biological brothers, with the pair dancing together and generally acting as "close friends."[82] Although less prominent today, fictive kinship was an important element in Comanche military societies and continues to the present. I can attest that there is an observable *esprit de corps* in current Comanche societies from my own membership in the Comanche Little Ponies, in which members still address one another as "brother." Fictive kinship among Comanche societies was similar to that among the Kiowa, Apache, and Cheyenne societies (McAllister 1935, 1937; Meadows 1995).[83]

COMANCHE MILITARY SOCIETY FUNCTIONS
Communal Hunt Police

Policing of communal bison hunts, one of the most common Plains military society functions, is frequently argued to have been absent among the Comanche in support of claims denying the existence of military societies.

However, ethnographic accounts indicate that some semblance of hunting laws did exist. Burnet (Winfrey and Day 1966:5:87) observed in 1818–1819: "They have no established game laws, but they regard the ingress of strangers and hunters with a jealousy that is sometimes fatal to the intruders. This seldom occurs unless the destruction can be consummated with impunity." The 1933 Santa Fe notes demonstrate that a form of policed hunt did exist among the Comanche, but different than in other Plains groups.[84]

Group hunts normally occurred in late summer or early fall when the bison were fat, their robes were good, and there were fewest flies to contend with while processing the meat and hides. The Comanche communal hunt began with scouts who were sent out to locate a herd. Hunters were admonished to stay together, and the hunt was then policed by men under the direction of a chief, who was presumably a war leader with special hunting skills. As in other Plains groups, this unit formed a line between the hunters and their quarry, preventing anyone from taking an unfair hunting advantage. Once the chase began, each individual hunted independently, identifying the quarry by individual arrow markings. Whether the hunt leader was appointed formally or through general consensus is unknown (Hoebel 1940:16; Wallace and Hoebel 1952:59).[85] As Naiya commented, prior to the actual hunting, "watchers" were posted: "They always tried to watch when they neared the bison to prevent pre-killing; they especially watched doubtful characters if they were known. The chief appointed watchers. There was no regular police."[86] Whether the "watchers" were simply the populace as a whole, a group of temporarily selected individuals as practiced among many village tribes, or designated positions is unclear, and what constituted "regular police" was not specified.

Unlike those in neighboring Plains tribes, Comanche military societies did not play a major role in policing the hunt, although some men apparently served as temporary police, which was common among many eastern village-based Plains tribes. Comanche hunt leaders may have appointed members of their own military society to serve as "watchers" because the leader would have had more familiarity with, influence over, and perhaps confidence in his fellow society brothers than in nonmembers. This method would not necessarily have required an entire men's society; as men of a residence band would primarily have belonged to the same society, their cooperation included a societal presence, whether formal or not.

Naiya reported one case of premature hunting in which a man had preceded a group of hunters who were awaiting daylight. The hunter had killed several animals, planning to skin them later. When the hunting party discovered the animals the only punishment was the destruction of the man's quarry, by cutting the animals' hides and insides and rubbing dirt into the meat, making it unfit for consumption (Hoebel: 1940:82).[87] In yet another case, a Comanche living among the Cheyenne was caught hunting alone and had his property destroyed by the Cheyenne Dog Soldiers Society. The individual pleaded that hunting alone was not considered a crime among his people and that he did not realize that the Cheyenne felt differently about it (Hoebel 1940:82). Thus, the Comanche recognized the problems associated with premature hunting, but apparently took only informal coercive measures to prevent it when particular individuals were suspected. Lowie (1915a:812) reported that the only punishment for overzealous actions during the hunt was to rebuke the guilty party verbally. While there was no physical punishment, the guilty party assuredly had to deal with the hunt leader, who was a man of great social standing. A reputation from such incidents undoubtedly plagued an individual and prompted improvement in his behavior. Both Lowie and Naiya's descriptions closely resemble Shoshone hunting sanctions. Punishment for hunting infractions was not corporally oriented, but focused on shaming the individual into cooperating for the benefit of the larger community. Hoebel's (1940:176) statement that "Comanche law expressed individualism checked at critical points by social use of other individuals" aptly applies here.

While Hoebel (1940) argued that Comanche sodalities lacked the typical police functions of other Plains military societies, other data contest this characterization. Comanche military societies attempted to force reservation leaders and bands to attend the 1874 Sun Dance and to resist Anglo-American policies (Kavanagh 1986:174–175). Comanche tribal historian Joe Attocknie (Kavanagh 1986:52–53, 174–175, 1996:49–51, n.d.d:37–38) provided an account of a Comanche society policing the march to Adobe Walls in 1874.[88] In one instance Nohkahnsuh, a noted daring older warrior, left the main party to kill a bison. Upon seeing him, the Little Horse warriors came to confiscate the meat. As the Little Horses began to cut the bundles of butchered meat from Nohkahnsuh's pack horses, he raised his hand and proclaimed (Kavanagh 1996:49; n.d.d:37–38): "Wait you young warriors, wait! Way up north, on the Cimarron River, I met an enemy Osage tribesman, before witnesses I scalped this enemy Osage while he was still alive, unharmed and watching me. I left him alive after I took off his scalp so he could live to tell about it. Now then, if any of you young warriors can tell of your own battle act that can better mine, you can take my meat." After a period of silence, the Little Horses could not provide a more prestigious coup recitation and quietly withdrew. As in Shoshone policing regulations for communal hunts, a guilty party could outrecite an adversary in battle coups and go unpunished.

Camp and March Police

Asserting that Comanche societies had police functions similar to those in other Plains populations is difficult. The tumultuous events of the early 1870s were in a particular historical context which occurred under more restricted geographical constraints and increasing conflicts from encroaching Anglo-American pressures. Because this rapidly evolving political and military situation does not reflect prior events for the earlier Comanche community, they imply, but cannot necessarily be assumed to reflect, earlier society police functions.

There are also indications that Comanche societies served as camp police like the Cheyenne and Kiowa societies, in some cases controlling departures from encampments. In one such instance in 1874 attempts were made to prevent anyone from leaving to return to the agency (Haworth 1874:219; Kavanagh 1986:52–53, 1996:48–51). After gathering in the encampment prior to the Adobe Walls fight, some groups, not desiring to fight, prepared to return to the agency. The Little Horse Society served as march police to ensure that no members of the party reneged on their obligation to fight by returning home. When Mahseet, a Peneteka headsman, stated, "I am too old for this," and prepared to leave the war party to return home with his family, the Little Horses whipped him and confiscated his horses. Later when the Peneteka chief Asahabbit intervened and demanded the return of Mahseet's horses, he too was whipped by *Pahvotaivo* (White Man). Attocknie (Kavanagh 1996:50) indicated that members of other bands and societies were "in no position to help Mahseet." Eventually the war party leader and Little Horse Society member Quanah intervened, stopped the quirting, and allowed Asahabbit to take his horses (Kavanagh 1986:52–53, 1996:48–51). In this instance, the Little Horses clearly had coercive powers in the interests of the entire party that extended to the members of other divisions (and thus other societies) and the sanctioned authority to implement these powers prior to the event. These examples demonstrate that Comanche societies did function to some degree in policing communal bison hunts, and at least for the events surrounding the pan-Comanche Sun Dance and aggregation of 1874, tribal movements, and encampments. However, the lack of early examples of coercive authority suggests that these functions were weakly developed or were being adapted during a period of crisis nearing the 1870s, cut short by the beginning of the reservation era.

Societal Warfare and Raiding

Accounts of early Comanche history indicate that Comanche bands and divisions were effective fighting and raiding units and most Comanche scholars have suggested that military societies functioned similarly (Thurman 1980, 1982; Gelo 1987, 1988).[89] In 1933 Howard White Wolf indicated that fellow society members in the Tuhwi Society swore to remain together and fight in battle.[90] As noted among other Plains populations, Comanche societies once cooperated in warfare and raiding ventures as individual societies. Wallace and Hoebel's statements (1952:274) that "members are somewhat like brothers; they went on the warpath together" and that a man leading a revenge party could usually rely on the support of his society further imply sodality-based ventures. The association of Comanche societies with particular tribal divisions suggests their importance in warfare and economic ventures, although membership on at least some revenge raids was multi-divisional. In addition to the unique circumstances surrounding the more pan-Comanche–based raid on Adobe Walls during the summer of 1874, other earlier examples exist (Thomas 1932; Winfrey and Day 1966; etc.). With division-based societies, society membership and kinship ties would have promoted economic cooperation. Therefore Comanche military societies were probably organized on the basis of repeated patterns in focused activity group formations which were usually intradivisional, cross-cutting regional residence band boundaries, but which could expand to include interdivisional efforts for larger military undertakings. Given the presence of other documented characteristics such as the localized nature of societies and the fictive kinship found in numerous Plains societies, it is likely that Comanche societies were once cooperative warfare and economic units.

Similar evidence exists for Cheyenne (Bowstring and Kit Fox) and Kiowa (Cáuitémgòp) military societies, although the former were not division based, while the membership basis for the latter is unknown. Membership in raiding parties of these tribes later changed to intersocietal or interband membership because of severe losses suffered by single societies in battle.[91] Another little-known factor in the functional roles of the Comanche organizations involves the change from a hunting to a war-based economy. Foster (1991:39) argues that raiding and trade, especially in horses, became a prominent feature of Comanche subsistence by circa 1750. Thomas (1932) contains descriptions of events suggesting that raiding, particularly of the Puebloan groups, was used during periods of economic shortages such as times of natural drought when grass and bison were in short supply. If Richardson (1933), Kardiner (1945), and Hagan (1976) are correct that Comanche warfare and raiding had increased by the 1850s to the point that warfare had begun to rival hunting as a subsistence base, then the Comanche appear to have adopted a "predatory economy" as Kavanagh (1980:68) suggests. Such economic changes explain the lack of ethnographic emphasis placed upon the policing of the communal hunt and hence the primary association of societies with the Na'wapina'r ceremony.

As a horse-based economy grew, smaller raiding parties were necessary for success, which precluded some activities by larger segments of divisions and thus significant portions of an entire military society. While warfare and raiding activities intensified, the number of men needed for such undertakings decreased, particularly in raiding for horses. However, examples of particularly popular leaders dominating a number of residence bands are known (John 1975; Kavanagh 1986; Foster 1991). While many descriptions of Comanche raiding and warfare activities exist, there are no indications of society-based actions. Wallace and Hoebel (1952:250–251) state that raiding and military activity focused on revenge motives and was an individual enterprise and not an extension of residence or divisional memberships, which also suggests the efforts of local residence bands and not a divisional or societal role in such activities. As such actions were normally limited to men in close proximity to one another, they would include primarily men of the same residence band or division, and thus fellow society members.

Comanche Military Society Dances and Warfare

As one of the more visible activities, dances provided the setting for many of the military society social functions. Wallace and Hoebel (1952:274) report many standard Plains military society characteristics for Comanche dances, such as coup recitations, distinctive society-specific insignia, dress, and songs, and military society–sponsored social dances: "When a group sponsored a dance, none but members could attend, except by invitation. Social events were sponsored with dances during the day or evening, but more frequently in the evening. Dances occurred more often immediately preceding the departure or following the return of a war party or at the time of the communal hunt. Both men and women took part in the social dances." There is also a reference to members themselves prompting dances, which may refer to larger divisionally aggregative society meetings.

As Post Oak Jim put it, "When the young men wanted to dance, they took it up with the chief, who then had the crier tell of the forthcoming dance by calling the men he wanted to dance."[92] Confirmation of Post Oak Jim's account is unavailable, and whether this refers to social or society dances is unclear.

Comanche in the nineteenth century clearly distinguished between dance groups and warrior groups. As Post Oak Jim stated in 1933, "Dancing clubs were organized with the leader handling all the business. There were no clubs or societies in the old days." Four days later he stated: "If a stranger came along and was asked to join a warrior's group, he couldn't refuse." This suggests that such sodalities were viewed in native terminology more as "warriors' groups" than as the Anglo-based term "societies." The warrior then appeared before the people and recited his brave deeds to qualify for membership. If the warrior killed an enemy without witnesses he had to swear by the Sun and Earth. If a warrior's deed was witnessed in battle others were called in to testify on the matter.[93] The reference to a "stranger" may simply mean an individual who was not a current society member. Discrepancies in Post Oak Jim's statements may reflect how he categorized the activity with which a dance was associated. Thus, if held in preparation for a war raid, it might be viewed as a society or "warrior group" function, whereas a dance held for a primarily social function might be viewed as a "social" or dance club. These accounts may also reflect the reservation era and early twentieth century, with which he was familiar.

While raiding activities often included small parties from a limited residential and thus usually a divisional area, revenge raids among many Plains populations generally involved large aggregations of multiple residence bands or larger divisions and among some groups such as the Kiowa, Cheyenne, and Comanche (at least in 1824 and 1874) were often formed in large communal encampments following large integrative ceremonies. Multiple accounts indicate multiband- or multidivisional-based revenge raids for the Comanche. According to Lowie (1915a:810), most Comanche society dances occurred during a festival known as *Na'wapina'r*, which is clearly Berlandier's (1969:73–74) "little war" and Burnet's (1954:131) "militant parade." Neighbors (1852:132) wrote: "When a chieftain wishes to go to war, he declares his intentions, and the preliminaries are discussed as a war dance." Winfrey and Day (1966:3:214) record this event as a "war dance prior to going on war expeditions. This routine is gone through with several days, until sufficient volunteers are collected."

One of Kavanagh's consultants translated *Na'wapina'r* as "stirring up," which appears to fit the descriptions of a preparatory ceremony during which warriors raised their spirits prior to setting out on a war venture.[94] The translation of the Kiowa Gúdáugá (Stirring Up [Emotions] Songs), commonly called "War Journeys" and later transformed into today's "49" songs, is nearly identical in content and suggests a broader pattern.[95] Such instances suggest the elevation of a military society–based martial ideology to an ethos. The Na'wapina'r was essentially a preparatory encampment for a revenge raid, during which a man wishing to avenge the death or injury of a friend or relative by an enemy announced his intentions and a location for a general encampment. Those issuing the announcement for such a raid formed a preliminary encampment, awaiting other interested contingents; in some cases, the entire aggregation lasted two to three months. Smaller tipis were used during collective revenge journeys, and a number of women often accompanied the men to assist in caring for the herds, cooking, and transporting captured property (Berlandier 1969:72). These events in- cluded multiple processions led by war chiefs, war speeches, and military society dances (Berlandier 1969:70–75; Lowie 1915a). The growing body of warriors camped a short distance from the main encampment where they danced at night; warriors periodically rode through the main camp singing and boasting of their prowess. As Berlandier (1969:72–73) describes:

> When another rancheria arrives, the captain and the warriors of the tribe, bedecked with feathers and covered with their war ornaments, mount their horses and form two lines, in which formation they make a tour of the camps of those who have already arrived, singing as they go. They promise to distinguish themselves in the coming war and to supply all possible succor to those who are exposed to too great danger. The host tribe replies to this visit with a ceremony of the same sort, and this scene is repeated at the camp of each tribe that has come to join the plain- tiffs on the warpath. These meetings sometimes take place one or two hundred leagues distant from the enemy. They are sometimes major events, lasting two or three months, so as to give everyone a chance to get there, and meanwhile the most complete harmony prevails among all the tribes. . . . On the morning of the day set aside for this practice war the warriors don their war costumes and, some on foot and others on horseback, march in double file and amidst the captains and the great warriors, and in the rear guard the women and children, all wearing their choicest finery. In this order, and to the sound of their drums, whistles, and pebble-filled gourds blending with their war chant, they parade through the encampment. The old men who once enjoyed such reputa- tions as warriors mount horses too but stay outside the ranks to boast of

the brilliant deeds of their youth and to exhort the young fighters to die rather than allow themselves to be taken by the enemy. Then they urge the unmarried girls to satisfy all the desires of those warriors who distinguish themselves in battle, and not to forget to heap scorn and opprobrium on those who show cowardice. The homilies are delivered with such fervor and energy that they inspire almost all who are present. When this ceremony is over they remain silent until sundown.

Berlandier (1969:74–75) describes the final preparations prior to embarking:

As soon as twilight steals across the sky a remarkable thing happens. These natives, who never go to attack their enemies by night, except on a raid for plunder, launch their *little war*. Only the men may take part. They light a great bonfire and all gather about it standing in war regalia, forming a great circle some 30 feet in diameter, leaving a gap on the side toward the enemy dwelling. Through this come the warriors and the chiefs, armed only with their bows and lances. At a little distance you can see in the shadows several platoons of savages representing a little army with a center and separate wings. Before the whole thing begins the bravest of the warriors recount, in a loud voice, the glorious deeds they have done, producing visual proof of their stories, and in the end beg their comrades at arms to promise that if, during this campaign, they should stray from the fine career they have begun, they will kill them, firing at them as if they were the enemy. When the various speeches are over the right wing breaks off from the rest and comes into the circle to stand around the bonfire. The men who comprise it begin to dance and sing the war chant. The others pretend to attack those who are around the fire, and fire their weapons at will. Those who come closest to the circle of warriors prove their valor and their desire to distinguish themselves in battle. This scene lasts from eight to ten minutes and is enlivened by the crack of their firearms and the exhortations of the chiefs who cheer them on to demonstrate their courage. When the firing and the dancing stop, all together give a horrible, piercing cry, which seems to voice their thirst for vengeance. At this same moment the dancers seize their own loaded guns and open fire above the heads of the chief, who is usually somewhere in the direction of the enemy, then return to their former places. The chief, who until then has been inspecting the forces outside the circle, rides into it at full gallop, straight up to the fire, whose flames, whipped by the desert winds, light this scene at once wild and impressive. There he thanks the warriors for the courage and coolness they have shown and

gives them proof of his gratitude. He adds that he hopes the other warriors will be as brave and then withdraws to allow the left wing to play
the same role. After they have done their duty, the center and three or
four scouts especially chosen for the honor perform their dance and
withdraw. The Wolves wind up the little war, forming a column that does
not march with any of the fighters, and, as if in battle, advance at a trot
so as never to turn about. The *mitote* is then over and everyone retires to
rest until morning.[96]

Such elaborate preparations were made only for larger collective cam-
paigns and not for the more frequent and smaller raiding parties. During the
period of aggregation, a council of chiefs and elders met to "decide who is
to guard the camp, and they wait for the *Pouhahantes* or the medicine men
to give them helpful inspiration for attaining the purpose they have set
themselves in for this war." Scouts were sent out in search of the enemy;
upon their reconnaissance, final decisions were made, and then reported to
each "tribe" by their camp criers. The plaintiff had the sole ability to pro-
long the venture if he felt sufficient revenge had not been dealt to the enemy.
Further reprisals occurred: "when the time stipulated for the war has passed
and the tribes which have fought separately are back again in the rallying
place from which they started, and where each one recounts what has occurred" (Berlandier 1969:73–75).

It is likely that Comanche societies regularly held such meetings and
dances at the Na'wapina'r, which appears to have been a multidivisional
or more partially pan-Comanche (portions of multiple divisions) effort.
Lowie's (1915a:811) statement that "on the night before setting out the
tribesmen assembled, coming in pairs toward the front and in single file
behind," suggests the presence of military societies in which partners are
said always to have gone to battle together. Although Burnet (1954:131–
133) does not specifically mention military societies, he reports spring and
fall multidivisional raids as early as 1818–1819 that were clearly accompanied by similar preparatory ceremonies focused on fostering martial spirit
and ethos prior to setting out:

> The day previous to starting for war, the party militant parade through
> the village mounted and accoutered, and bedaubed with paints, in their
> most gallant and frightful style. They march or rather gallop in a line of
> single file, and have very few revolutions; but they contrive to give diver-
> sity and effect to their maneuvers, by frequent hideous yells, and antic
> gesticulations, which, combined with their wild and savage costume, give

to the exhibition, if not a dreadful, at least a superlatively ludicrous appearance. . . .

Berlandier (1969:73–74, 117) also reported Ruiz's observations of interdivisional raids in 1824. Ruiz "was present at a gathering of Comanches, Chariticas, Yamparikas, and other allied people who were going to war against the Osages, their sworn enemies," at which "war dances" prior to their departure occurred. During a parade in the preparatory ceremonies, warriors dressed in their finest clothing marched in double file, again suggestive of society partners.

Lowie (1915a) provided similar accounts of gatherings, which he stated could last "several weeks." During the preparatory period various dances alternated, including the Buffalo Dance, the Crow Dance (Tuhwi) and the Horses (Big Horses) and Little Horses Dances. Quanah Parker related an account to Hugh L. Scott (Thomas 1932:373; Nye 1962:180) in which he enlisted a revenge party prior to the Adobe Walls fight in 1874, by taking a pipe around to different groups including the Quahada and Nokoni divisions, as well as to the Kiowa and Cheyenne. In one passage Quanah described several Comanche military society dances occurring within the same composite encampment.[97] The night prior to their departure the warriors danced with their wives or girl friends. The Na'wapina'r and the war party's departure were supposed to occur only after dark to prevent bad luck. One group that violated this admonition never returned and thereafter served as a reminder to all (Wallace and Hoebel 1952:252–253). Upon meeting, the sponsor recruited members for the revenge party by passing a pipe around.

Military society dances at multidivisional Comanche encampments resemble those of other tribes held during the preparatory phase of large, lengthy aggregations and focused upon fostering a martial ethos prior to setting out toward an enemy. While some warfare ventures were undertaken by a single division, other examples of large cooperative interdivisional Comanche participation in treaties, trading fairs, and warfare between the 1780s and 1870s exist, usually based upon the reputation of a particularly esteemed leader (Thomas 1932; Burnet 1954; Hagan 1976; Winfrey and Day 1966; Berlandier 1969:73–74, 117; John 1984; Kavanagh 1996). These examples negate the allegation that Comanche lacked large aggregative and ceremonial occasions. While the Sun Dance diffused to the Shoshone through the Comanche following their separation and southern migration, the relationship of Comanche societies to their Sun Dance and the relationship between Shoshone and Comanche military societies are less well known.

Comanche Military Societies and the Sun Dance

Many primary Plains military society functions involved supplying the manpower for the preparatory aspects of large tribally integrative communal ceremonies such as the Sun Dance. It is clear that the Comanche had large ceremonials associated with divisional gatherings. Part of the problem is that there were unquestionably major Comanche ceremonial occasions at which divisions ritually expressed their *communitas*, such as the Beaver Ceremony, the Eagle Dance, the Na'wapina'r, and some form of Sun Dance (Lowie 1915a; Wallace and Hoebel 1952:175; Shimkin 1953; Berlandier 1969; Thurman 1982; Foster 1991:66, 183; Davis 1996:112–114; Kavanagh 1996:52–53). Whether the Comanche had Sun Dances has been long debated, and their alleged absence is frequently used to support contentions that the Comanche were indeed anomalous (Wissler 1914, 1927; Wallace and Hoebel 1952:33). Like the Comanche military societies, the Comanche Sun Dance has been misunderstood, largely because of its early cessation, lack of documentation, and continued comparison to a select number of Northern Plains–based traits which are considered to be "typical" Sun Dance traits.

Comanche refer to the "Sun Dance" as *piakne nʉhkana* (big house dance), or *nʉʉkado* (our Sun Dance) from the Kiowa name Qấujó (often spelled Kado) for the ceremony, while Ten Kate (1885a:127) gives *pikani niskera* or "big house dance." Descriptions indicating the presence of a Sun Dance–like ceremony among the Comanche are given by Curtis (1930:184), Linton (1935), McAllister (1949:83), Ten Kate (1885a:127–128), and the 1933 Santa Fe Laboratory of Anthropology Field School Notes. Many sources allege that the Comanche held only one such dance in 1874, prior to the Adobe Walls campaign (Linton 1935; Wallace and Hoebel 1952:319–320; Hagan 1976:105). However, there are clear indications that, while not held annually, such large integrating ceremonies were held periodically, as exemplified by the lengthy multidivisional aggregations associated with the Na'wapina'r. Linton (1935:420) states that several such ceremonies were held at "irregular intervals," the last of which occurred on July 29, 1878, and was marked by the total eclipse of the sun. Comanche tribal historian Joe Attocknie listed the leaders and locations of six Sun Dances, including one led by a woman.[98] There is a specific reference to a Comanche Sun Dance in an oral tradition recorded by McAllister (1949:83). Ten Kate (1885b:394) reported the preparations for a dance in 1883 which were aborted due to the inability to obtain a bison hide for the center pole. There are also several references indicating that the Comanche attended other

Southern Plains Sun Dances, particularly those of the Kiowa and Cheyenne as early as 1837 (Mooney 1898:271–272, 322; Linton 1935:427; Thurman 1980:8; Kavanagh 1996:426, 445).[99] Similar to that of other Plains groups, the Comanche Sun Dance was not held annually; scanty data concerning the timing, regularity, rituals, and most importantly the political activities associated with the ceremony have distorted its presence and content (Linton 1935).[100]

Part of the problem in classifying and comparing the Comanche Sun Dance is clarifying what we mean by a "Sun Dance." If we are referring to Spier's (1921b) precise criteria then the Comanche comparison may be weak. If we examine the event as a large integrative tribal-oriented ceremony containing many of the primary sociopolitical features and functions of similar Plains ceremonies, then the Comanche are similar, despite the scanty amount of surviving knowledge. That Comanche culture allegedly did not include classic Plains-style Sun Dances or classic men's societies becomes problematic only because of the anthropological belief that these institutions were social, technical, and ecological necessities for Plains life. If these institutions are viewed as part of a historical combination of social and political relations, they are not problematic in the same way. If the Sun Dance and men's societies are seen as diffusions, then they are processes that occurred in a particular time and set of circumstances, and that period becomes a necessary factor in understanding those processes of growth and expansion. We know that the Comanche held ceremonial occasions at which divisions ritually expressed a sense of community. What the exact formation of the aggregation resembling the Plains Sun Dance was for the Comanche is now virtually unrecoverable, and to call it a Sun Dance in comparison with other Plains populations creates more problems. The anthropological concept of the Sun Dance as a unitary construction is faulty because so much emphasis is placed upon knowledge of the full range of possible variations and alternative forms. Therefore we cannot accurately evaluate the alleged variation in the Comanche ceremonies. Thurman (1982:578, 1987) has suggested that the Comanche Buffalo Festival may also have functioned as a large tribally integrating ceremony; Lowie (1915a) believed that each society performed its own dances at the festival. Unfortunately, too little is presently known about the Comanche Buffalo Festival for an in-depth comparison. The Beaver Lodge ceremony may have functioned similarly.

Descriptions of the Comanche Sun Dance show several similarities to the Kiowa version in both the preparatory and ceremonial stages (Shimkin 1953, 1986:327), including several ritual parts, animal calling ceremonies, masked ritual clowns, mock battles and buffalo hunts, curing and foretelling, public announcements, and the demonstration and transfer of ritual power (Linton 1935; Kavanagh n.d.b, n.d.d). Scholars have suggested that the Sun Dance and military societies were adaptations borrowed from the neighboring Kiowa and Cheyenne, which the Comanche name *nekado* (*nuukado*, our Sun Dance) derived from the Kiowa name for the Sun Dance (Qáujó), suggests. As most descriptions of Comanche Sun Dances come from Post Oak Jim, who was nine years of age at the last Comanche Sun Dance, they are probably influenced by subsequent visits to later Kiowa and Cheyenne dances, which are impossible to disentangle at this date. Corroborating Shimkin's findings, Linton (1935:427) states that his older Comanche consultants "were familiar with the Kiowa Sun Dance and considered their own as very much the same." However, an important point concerning Comanche military societies is the regularity of Comanche Sun Dances or other division-level integrative ceremonies, as division-specific military societies would have been integrally linked to division-specific preparatory rituals for such ceremonies. The frequency of divisional integrative ceremonies serves as one indication of the frequency of military society functions. Post Oak Jim indicated that Sun Dances were not necessarily held every year, perhaps because they had no hereditary sponsor.[101] By at least 1860, the ceremony occurred irregularly and the entire tribe probably did not participate (Linton 1935). It is therefore likely that the duties of Comanche societies were not as regular or as structured as those found among neighboring groups. While the 1874 Comanche Sun Dance was reportedly pan-Comanche, this should be viewed as the effect of a unique set of late prereservation circumstances involving decreased population and accelerated political and military pressures (Thomas 1932:373).[102]

Shimkin (1953, 1986) offers further evidence that the Comanche were well acquainted with the Sun Dance. His Shoshone consultants indicated that the dance was acquired around the year 1800 from Yellow Hand (a son of the principal Kotsoteka chief Ecueracapa), who was well acquainted with both the Kiowa Sun Dance and Spanish Christianity, having attended school in Spanish Mexico. Yellow Hand later resided among the Eastern Shoshone and led the Sun Dance (Shimkin 1953:417). Several traits associated with the Sun Dance were also adapted by the Eastern Shoshone and are absent among more Northern Shoshone groups. If we accept that the classic Sun Dance diffused from an upper Missouri River–based center, then it is likely that the Comanche, who were remotely located from this distributional center, did not receive the Sun Dance and military society complexes until later than most other Plains tribes. This in turn points to the assumed lack of development and low density of overlapping traits found in the Comanche forms.

Lowie (1919:393–398) reported a number of Shoshone Sun Dance traits resembling brush dragging and mock battles found in other Plains tribes. As in other Plains military societies, all the men donned war dress. One "company" of men located and marked trees by leaning poles up against them (Lowie 1919:397). Two men of the other company "scout[ed]" for the enemy, then returned singing and calling aloud, suggesting the presence of the two known Shoshone men's societies. If this follows the pattern in other Southern Plains military societies, the elder Logs would have been the group marking and defending the timber while the younger Yellow Foreheads Society assumed the offensive role.

After reciting their observations over a pile of bison chips, the second company attacked the first company in a "sham battle," forcing it to retreat into the timber. A coup was then counted on every marked tree. The victors sang as they dragged the poles into their encampment. Men broke off tree branches, which were dragged in to cover the enclosure, while women rode double with them in the brush dragging. A feast was held on the last day of the Sun Dance which was raided by the Yellow Brows Society. Lowie reported that the ceremony had changed and expeditions by two "companies" of men, who were formerly accompanied by women, went in search of materials to construct the lodge. One company acquired rafter materials while the other obtained the center and wall posts in a pattern similar to societal activities in constructing the Sun Dance lodge in the military societies of many Plains tribes (Lowie 1919:399).

Comanche and Shoshone military societies augmented chiefly power and formerly had few independent roles other than warfare and the bison hunt. In contrast, Arapaho societies served as expressions of a comprehensive social ordering based upon a progressive access to ritual knowledge and political influence. Cheyenne, Kiowa, and Apache societies were more highly integrated in political and judicial functions. Shimkin (1953:430–431) attributed the lack of prescribed functions and participation of Shoshone men's societies in the Sun Dance to their egalitarian background, a lack of formal hereditary leadership, and the Sun Dance's loose connection to the overall Shoshone social structure. He maintained that Shoshone men's societies and band chiefs had no real role in the Sun Dance aside from coup recitations, which is common in some Southern Plains tribes, where their duties were generally limited to the preparatory phases of the ceremony. However, Shimkin (1953:424, 431–432) did note the presence of society events and initiations during the Sun Dance, allowing personal achievement to be advertised through society dances, songs, paint, and dress, all widespread features of Plains military societies. As Lowie (1919) demonstrated, Shoshone societies were undoubtedly associated with the preparatory aspects of the Sun Dance and were probably associated with more functions than are presently recorded. A review of Lowie's and Shimkin's works suggests that Shoshone societies were previously associated with many preparational and martial-related or symbolic aspects of the Shoshone Sun Dance. By circa 1900 these associations had shifted from society roles to functions performed by aging warriors.

Although Linton (1935) does not directly mention Comanche military societies, and elsewhere flatly denies their existence, several of his descriptions suggest their presence and serve as a basis for several inferences.[103] First, the gathering and movement of numerous bands toward a final encampment location provided an opportune time for holding society meetings. Four preparatory days of lodge construction also offered opportunities for meetings. Because military society meetings generally occurred before and during these gatherings in other Plains groups, it is likely that the Comanche military societies' meetings did as well. Two references indicate that this was the practice. Post Oak Jim stated that the Fox Dance was held prior to "some big event, as, for example, the Sun Dance, etc. It was held just at the start of the Sun Dance."[104] Howard White Wolf stated that large oval tipis were used for society dances, with up to five or six such lodges combined into a single structure to facilitate large dances.[105]

Brush dragging or *puhinoo* (carrying of the limbs/boughs) performed by groups of men and women who joked and sang is also noted. Crowns of brush (*puhinona*) were worn for shade. Groups of men (probably societies) transported the materials, stopping to rest and sing four times. Brush dragging continued into the 1930s and was recently revived by the Comanche Little Ponies Society at the second annual Comanche Nation Fair in 1993.[106] Unlike the neighboring Kiowa, who focused their sham or mock battle upon the center pole prior to cutting, the Comanche performed theirs after the lodge was constructed, but included "scouting" by a combat veteran from a society. There are also indications of society dances or parades when all the "bands" assembled before their tipis and began a procession toward the Sun Dance lodge. Carrying a long flat club notched along one edge, a "War Whip bearer" drove the people, forcing all to dance. During the procession "each band did its favorite dance and sang a song of its own," then the War Whip Bearer "quenched the people's thirst" by reciting coups, after which the people began another song. Four halts occurred during the procession to the central lodge (Linton 1935).[107] In this instance I interpret "band" to mean division and thus imply sodality, as the terms "band" and "clan" are still commonly used by modern Comanche consultants when speaking about military societies and in some cases divisions.[108]

It is evident from these descriptions that the Comanche had many of the same opportunities as other Plains populations for meetings and functions of military societies. Why then are there so few references to the societies? Linton (1935:420) suggests that the Sun Dance was falling into disuse between 1858 and 1878, "due perhaps to the harassed life which the tribe had led during the preceding twenty years." Regardless of the causes of the Sun Dance's decline, its termination assuredly weakened the military societies as many of its regular functions centered upon large ceremonial gatherings. Among the Kiowa, Apache, and Cheyenne, military society functions and associated knowledge rapidly decreased with the decline of the Sun Dance (Meadows 1995). As Linton argues (1935:427), a wide variety of details concerning Comanche Sun Dance descriptions suggest that the Comanche had not had the dance long enough for a completely integrated form to develop. Shimkin's (1953, 1986) works dispute this argument, as the dance was well known and had diffused from the Comanche to the Shoshone by circa 1800–1820. If the Comanche were attempting to adapt to a Sun Dance pattern similar to that of neighboring populations, the presence of military societies would have been beneficial given what we know about other groups. If the Comanche Sun Dance resembled that of other groups, Comanche societies should have had a stronger, more integrated role, which may be distorted by the available documentation. Various Comanche Sun Dance descriptions may reflect influences from a number of neighboring tribes or divisional differences in procedure, suggesting that various Comanche individuals or groups were influenced by different forms of the dance and its leaders. Even Curtis (1930:184) states: "In this ceremony they used songs borrowed from other tribes. The customary Sun-dance lodge was not built; they employed instead a large tipi made by using broadly extended poles and overlaying them with several lodge covers." Except for allegations associated with their Shoshone origins and less integrated military societies, little information concerning Comanche sodalities has survived. Nevertheless, the previous data demonstrate the presence of Comanche military societies and a general similarity to other Plains populations in distribution, organization, and functions. Examining the relationship between Comanche and Shoshone societies is necessary for purposes of comparison.

SHOSHONE MILITARY SOCIETIES

Based on the previous data, the Comanche did not have military societies prior to separating from the Shoshone.[109] It should not be surprising that these societies were less structurally developed and integrated than those of other Plains tribes, given their late development (post-1810) in a tremendously dynamic and rapidly changing culture. That Comanche societies were less integrated has traditionally been viewed as resulting from their Shoshone origins and the less complex Great Basin system. However, factors of late development, in part the result of the Shoshone proximity to the Northern Plains source of diffusion, are perhaps more logical explanations for the developmental level of prereservation Comanche military societies.

Part of this confusion stems from Hoebel's use of Julian H. Steward's *Basin Plateau Aboriginal Sociopolitical Groups* (1938), which was limited to the Western Shoshone. Among the Shoshone, military societies were limited to the Eastern Shoshone, who were divided into two groups: the Buffalo Eaters (also known as the Sage Brush People) and the Mountain Sheep Eaters (also known as the Mountaineers), who later became collectively known as the Wind River Shoshone (Lowie 1909:216, 1920:283, 1924; Shimkin 1986: 308). Unlike their western relatives, these Shoshone maintained an intermontane and Plains–based existence, with social organization featuring primary groups based on bonds of kin and friendship and secondary band- to tribal-level groups maintained by stable, effective leadership in migration, hunting, and war. The *tēkwahïn* (a chief or middle-aged man of military and shamanistic distinction who gave orders affecting tribal marches and collective hunts and gave counsel on matters of joint decision) had various assistants and control of the two "military-police societies." In the tribe and, to an extent, in each band the conduct of chieftainship was thus aided by the two military societies. Shimkin's consultants indicated that society officers and tribal chiefs were distinct offices and that society members did not become chiefs. Close lifelong friendships between men, often entailing mutual support in warfare, were common in Shoshone society and suggest the institution of society brothers found among military societies of other Plains groups.

Origins for Shoshone military societies are uncertain. David Thompson's account of circa 1735 (Tyrrell 1916:327–332) includes a Shoshone assemblage of over 300 warriors, conducting formal battle (*nazu'nza*) with champions (*na'zohïmp*) backed by a line of shield-bearing warriors armed with bows, arrows, and clubs. However, military societies can only be inferred at this time. Lowie (1915a) provides the first formal account of Shoshone societies. By the time of Shimkin's fieldwork in 1937–1938, Shoshone societies had been defunct for more than sixty years. As Shimkin (n.d.:35) describes, "Warfare was a great concern to all my older informants, five of who had been in combat. Yet they already were participants in the tactics of the 1870s, when some features such as war honors were still active but the warrior societies had all but gone. Data on the Yellow Brows were entirely hearsay. . . ."

Two sodalities, the Yellow Noses, commonly translated as Yellow Foreheads (Lowie 1915a) or Yellow Brows (*Ohamupe*) according to Shimkin (1986, 1992), and the Logs (*Wopine*, translated as Box People by one of Shimkin's consultants), helped to reinforce the tribal leadership structure and performed some of the functions typical of Plains Indian military societies (Lowie 1915a:813–816). While competing to count coup and composing songs about each other, Shoshone societies were largely complementary, lacking many of the competitive aspects characteristic of Crow military societies. During camp movements and communal bison hunts, the two societies served as *ti'rakone* (policemen). The Yellow Noses were sometimes referred to as "herders," from their role in restraining impatient hunters wishing to rush a herd (Davis 1996:111). Tribal movements were led by the younger Yellow Brows, who formed a vanguard while the elder Logs formed a rear guard. Shoshone societies also served to police crime and civil disturbances.

Ohamupe

The Yellow Brows were identified by a short "cockscomb" hair style that contained a square bang plastered with yellow clay. Members cut off all their hair except that on the "tip of the head," painting the rest of their heads yellow as well. The Yellow Brows consisted of one hundred to one hundred and fifty men (twenty to thirty according to Lowie 1915a:813), with the bravest serving as officers. The Yellow Brows maintained several "contrary" warrior characteristics in their induction, battle behavior, and daily speech patterns. Membership seems to have been voluntary: when members asked a man to join, an affirmative answer meant he did not wish to join, while a negative reply indicated his desire to join, whereupon the members sat him down and cut and painted his hair to the society specifications. One of Shimkin's consultants indicated that "the club was made up from all the bands," and membership was for life. Elder members could remain as less active members but had to find replacements. A fixed number of membership positions existed.

The Yellow Brows were composed of men generally considered braver than those in the Logs. When an enemy was seen, the members stopped, gathered together, and began to sing and dance before fighting. Yellow Brow chiefs were distinguished by fringes on their shirtsleeves and leggings. In battle, officers carried seven-foot-long curved staffs that were painted, wrapped with strips of otter fur, and adorned with eagle feather pendants. Some of these staffs had an attached knife blade tip. These staffs were used to pull fleeing enemies from their horses and as nonretreat staffs to stake oneself down in battle. As one of Shimkin's consultants described, "Whenever an enemy is getting the best of the people, the chief will stick this into the ground and stay there. The *Ohamupe* will see him, come back and save him. Just the chiefs and sub-chiefs did this. These lances may be painted blue or red." Whenever a society chief died, the people prepared the body and interred it in the cliffs. He was succeeded by a subchief. In addition to serving as a vanguard for tribal movements, they also served as scouts.

One of Shimkin's consultants described the Yellow Brows as a men's club associated with war and dancing. As Shimkin notes, "The Yellow Brows prepared for battle with a special dance that brought man and horse into sacred ecstasy, the Big Horse Dance (*Piapongonikar*)." The Big Horse Dance was in preparation for war and was strictly a men's dance. It was described as a "war dance, with war equipment, dance boss [whipman] . . . and [they] get all their war clothes on." The ceremonial counting of coups was held at Big Horse Dances, for which the giving away of gifts was required. In the Big Horse Dance "they jumped like a horse, in a kind of circle" and "hop up and down in place." This dance was also called the Scare Dance (*Tiániboo*). "They stomp way up and down. Some led horses, others on foot." A fire was kept in the center of the dance, which was approached and left four times. One of Shimkin's consultants described the evening dances:

> Men come up on horseback, they dismount, and rush at the fire leading their horses, stomping heavily. They yell, mount their horses and gallop off again. They have guns in their hands. Their short bangs are painted yellow. They come in from all sides, then go away again. They return four times. The singers know the songs. Not in war clothes, but painted red. There are four songs for the dance. Members danced "up and down, dancing like chiefs, singing" in groups [clusters].

Dances were announced by a crier early on the morning of the day they were to be held. Both daytime and nighttime dances were held. Daytime dances took place in a large tipilike enclosure made of hides, in which the dancers formed a circle, with both ends meeting near the entrance. The society chiefs and singers sat opposite the entrance (probably on the west side). Women raised the bottom of the hide enclosure to eye level, sitting outside the lodge as spectators and joining in the singing, but were not allowed to dance. Accounts state that no rattles were used, but that four to six drummers used "tambourine drums" (possibly hand-held drums). Sometimes four "dance bosses" were among them. Although the society contained special songs, no prayers were associated with society activities, as "it was a social affair." Killers (veterans who had killed an enemy) had their faces painted (*Náruk'wičë*) and would yell *Yi!* Following Big Horse Dances, a feast of bison tongues, dried meat, choke cherries, and various cherry and root soups prepared by the members' wives was served to visitors from other bands, prominent guests, and the society members. Dances were held in the summer and winter. By the 1870s the Yellow Brows had ceased to function. In 1908 the society was briefly reorganized by some older members, but did not last long.

Wopine

In contrast to the Yellow Brows, little information exists concerning the Big Logs. The Logs were middle-aged men who acted as rear guards for camp movements and scouted for enemies approaching from the rear. They parted their hair in the middle and wore two fur-wrapped braids. Because all were honored for their military deeds, they were entitled to blacken their faces with paint and to be "Black Faced Ones" (*Nárukaviuse*). Whenever a horse lost its pack or travois, members fixed it. According to Shimkin's consultants, the Big Horse Dance and songs were associated with both societies. A system of society chiefs, subleaders, and other characteristics is suggested by the data.

According to Lowie (1915a), the Yellow Brows were of higher social status than the Logs, who were in some ways subordinate to them, the Logs being directed by the Yellow Brows to serve as scouts in locating bison herds. The Yellow Brows maintained control of communal bison hunts, enforcing their directions with persuasion and scolding (Lowie 1915a, 1920:283; Shimkin 1986:311, 319). The two societies always watched each other, each having its own dances. Shimkin notes that both societies presented some honors for war deeds that allowed the wearing of black face paint, although this was most prevalent among the Logs. It is unknown if this differed between the two societies.

Beyond the general Plains military society functions and the loosely structured political position of military societies, there is little similarity between Comanche and Shoshone societies. The Comanche Big Horses and Shoshone Logs resemble each other, as both regulated travel during camp movements. Three points suggest a lack of cultural similarity and detailed diffusion between the Comanche and Shoshone. First, the late acquisition of Comanche societies suggests that the Comanche Big Horses did not originate among the Shoshone. Second, the absence of rattles in the Sho-shone Big Horse Dance (of the Yellow Brows and Logs) suggests that the Comanche Little and Big Horses Societies (which emphasized the use of rattles in their choreography) did not completely diffuse to the Shoshone. Third, the quantity and the variety of Comanche societies and dances, contrasted with the Big Horse Dance of both Shoshone societies, suggest significant differences. Unfortunately, there are too few descriptions of ma-terial culture and ceremonial composition to assess further similarities. Co-manche parallels for the Shoshone Yellow Brows are even more difficult to determine. The closest parallel is with Lowie's (1915a) Afraid of Nothing Society, which is most likely the Comanche Lobos or Wolves Society, as the Pukutsi were individual contraries.

During communal hunts, both Shoshone societies cooperatively re-strained individuals attempting to gain an advantage over others. The Yellow Brows performed most of these duties because of their advance guard posi-tion and perhaps their younger age, while the Logs enforced the majority of laws and were known to have brought stampeders back, whipping their horses over the heads. While the Yellow Brows took the front position dur-ing hunts and defended against attacks, the Logs guarded against rear attacks and were entrusted with protecting the women. The Logs also directed set-ting up camp, prevented stragglers from falling behind, repaired broken lodge poles for those on the march, and were generally a service organiza-tion for those in need.

Shoshone punishment of offenders during communal hunts differed greatly from that of other Plains tribes. Whereas other Plains groups often meted out physical punishment to the offender, which, if not resisted, was generally repaid in the form of property, Shoshone policing focused upon persuading and admonishing individuals into socially acceptable behavior. Physical punishment was reportedly limited to an individual's private prop-erty, such as a man's horse or game, never involving the individual or his tipi. If game had been acquired prematurely, the police destroyed the hides of the animals but did not assault the hunter, as they had no authority to do so. While there are no known cases of hunters resisting police, it is interesting to note that one Shoshone informant believed that, had a man resisted the police, they would have disfigured the hunter's horse by, for example, cut-ting its ears off. Police "shame[d] the rider" into appropriate behavior by striking the face of the overzealous hunter's horse. Shoshone societies con-trolled social behavior by exercising police functions. Although they might encourage, exhort, and exert pressure upon the guilty party, they were not authorized to use force against an individual. Alliances with other Plateau groups were commonly made during communal fall hunts to ensure defensive strength against possible attacks from the Crow or Blackfeet. Although a hunt leader chose a number of middle-aged men to act as temporary hunt police, no other functions were performed at the end of the hunt (Hoebel 1940:141–142).

Hoebel (1940:142) incorrectly states that, although the Shoshone organized police units for communal hunts, they had no associations. Aside from the previously discussed functions, several characteristics among the Shoshone demonstrate the presence of military societies whose functions strongly resemble those of Comanche and other Plains societies. Membership in Shoshone societies involved neither purchase nor a specific age qualification; however, there was a preference for joining a society containing one's relatives or friends. Membership in the Yellow Brows was supposed to be for life or until retirement, yet men were also free to leave one society and join the other. Although the extent to which they did this has not been determined, Shimkin states that fictive kinship between members of Shoshone men's societies as well as between women played important roles in Shoshone social organization. Men planning to die in battle commonly went in pairs unarmed except for rattles or flutes (hence they were called *wiyagait* or criers or wailers); they sang constantly and rode upon the same horse when going to war. Because of their position, criers were considered to be the living dead. If they succeeded in killing the enemy barehanded or with their rattles, they returned to the living, apparently relieved of their suicidal requirements. These characteristics resemble the social bonds characterizing society partners.[110] That the Yellow Brows contained two headsmen is typical of other Plains military societies and also suggests society partners. Shimkin states (1953:429) that the two men's societies and blood brotherhood relations were the sole permanent forms of social organization beyond the family. Each society also maintained distinctive hairstyles as insignia.

Although both societies performed the same dance and songs, they often observed each other's dances. Dances commonly occurred before communal bison hunts and when meeting to discuss camp movements and were similar to the society meetings and dances held prior to communal bison hunts that preceded the Sun Dances of many Plains tribes. Society dances were typically held during the afternoon hours in tipis, with the singers sitting in the rear, the dancers in front of them, and the women, who helped in the singing, around the outside of the lodge. Among the Lehmi Shoshone "Big Horses" (Logs), the headsmen used quirts to make all members rise and dance. Although this description most likely refers to the Hot or Wolf Dance (the Shoshone version of the Grass Dance), the adaptation of "dance bosses" or whipmen reflects a military society. Following the actual dance, coup recitations and feasts concluded the meetings (Lowie 1915a:813–816), illustrating numerous common Plains military society traits.

Like Comanche societies, the Shoshone organizations were less integratively organized than many of the Plains military societies. Both, however, contained many of the organizational and social features associated with these institutions, such as police coercion, coup recitations, preparatory functions in the Sun Dance, fictive kinship, societal insignia, whipmen, and dances. Supporting evidence of continued interaction between the two populations comes from several sources. John Bell (1957) and Auguste Chouteau (1838) report continued Comanche-Shoshone relations in 1820 and 1838. Dorman Winfrey and James Day (1966:2:82) report some two hundred Snakes (Shoshone) residing with northern Comanche in 1844. Clark (1982: 119) and contemporary Comanche elders indicate Comanche and Shoshone intermarriage and residence of some Shoshone among the Comanche in the 1880s.[111] Mooney (1896:1043–1044) reports continuing residence, visitation, and communication between the two tribes into the 1890s.

While not conclusive, available data suggest the possibility that, like the Sun Dance, Shoshone military societies either were adopted from the Comanche following their separation and migration to the Plains or were derived from a neighboring Northern Plains tribe. The relatively weak development of societies among the Shoshone suggests a Great Basin and Comanche influence. How the Comanche adapted to their new ecological and social environments in the south may provide the answer. The fact that the Comanche introduced the Sun Dance to the Shoshone following their division gives weight to the likelihood that they also may have diffused military societies to the Eastern Shoshone, as military societies did not exist among other Western Shoshone populations. Many Shoshone society functions focused upon the preparatory period for the Sun Dance, acquired circa 1800, which also suggests their late development. In light of Shimkin's work and comparison of Comanche military societies with those of neighboring tribes, it appears that the position and functions of Comanche and Shoshone societies were influenced by their late acquisition and less extensive integration in the larger Shoshone social structure and not necessarily determined by Shoshone social organization itself.

THE RELATIONSHIP OF MILITARY SOCIETIES TO COMANCHE SOCIAL ORGANIZATION AND CULTURE

Having overturned prior interpretations of Comanche and Shoshone military societies and demonstrated similarities to other Plains military societies, I will now turn to the theoretical implications of the level of differences and their significance. While the Comanche differed from neighboring Southern Plains tribes, my reconstruction of Comanche military societies counters the idea that they were "anomalous." Comanche social organization in relation to the existence of "tribal" structures has been discussed by Kavanagh (1980:3–5, 51–69, 1986, 1996, n.d.a, n.d.b), Thurman (1980, 1982, 1987), and John (1984). Linguistically and sociologically, nineteenth-century Comanche were generally similar; however, despite numerous cases of interdivisional cooperation in warfare and raiding, there was no pan-Comanche tribe as a single integrated political entity (Wallace and Hoebel 1952:22): "the tribe consisted of a people which shared a common way of life. But that way of life did not include political institutions or social mechanisms by which they could act as a tribal unit."

Most recently, Kavanagh (1980, 1986, 1989, n.d.a, n.d.d), Thurman (1980, 1987:554), and Davis (1996) have all suggested that the eighteenth- and nineteenth-century Comanche did not constitute a single political entity and that there was no single Comanche tribe, but this does not imply that there was no larger sociopolitical significance or that there was only a band-level Comanche political organization. They assert that because the division, composed of numerous local residential groups (bands) and linked by sodalities, was the maximal level of Comanche sociopolitical organization, divisions should be analyzed as tribal in structure and that there were in fact several Comanche tribes which have previously been labeled divisions ethnographically. This is supported by the four levels of Comanche sociopolitical structure: the nuclear family, extended family, local residential band, and political division, which were horizontally linked by small-scale medicine and larger-scale military sodalities on a divisional level. The realization that Comanche sociopolitical organization probably fluctuated throughout the nineteenth century due to numerous native and non-Indian influences begins to place Comanche culture in a clearer focus.

The requirement of pantribal sodalities for the classification of a tribal level of social organization as defined by Service (1962:113–115) is problematic. The assignment of all Comanche to the category of "tribe" is based on the assumption that they had pantribal sodalities. However, my research counters this assertion and reaffirms and expands Kavanagh's and Thurman's conclusions, as nineteenth-century Comanche military societies were divisional and not pan-Comanche. Neither ethnographic sources nor the large estimates of Comanche population support the existence of pan-Comanche military sodalities. While sodalities were present and functioning, they were not at the level of organization associated with the analytical term "tribe" as defined by Service (1962) or by Fried (1968, 1975).

It has been the undifferentiated usage of the terms "band," "division," and "tribe" in reference to the entire range of Comanche social organization that has primarily led to views of their "anomalous" social organization. The problem is that the term "tribe" refers both to a structure created by local residential units which are cross-cut by sodalities and to the maximal socio-cultural-political unit. In this view, the very existence of Comanche sodalities created tribes out of the residential units that they linked. However, they did not link the entire pan-Comanche populace, as demonstrated by different sodalities and relations with various external native and European populations, thus creating several division-based Comanche tribes such as the Yamparika, Quahada, etc. The Comanche division is demonstrated to have been the highest level of consistent sociopolitical integration during the nineteenth century, as it contained divisional military sodalities which functioned in at least incipient stages of tribal organization during summer camps, in communal hunts, and in the office of a temporary division chief. Similarly the pantribally integrative functions of the military societies focused upon the Na'wapina'r Ceremony (which could be multidivisional and thus more pan-Comanche or multi-Comanche tribal in composition), rather than across a wider range of tribal (pan-Comanche) activities.

There are several problems associated with assigning a tribal status that includes all Comanche. First, while Sun Dances may have been multidivisional, it is unlikely that the entire Comanche ethnic population gathered for such lengthy periods. Several other known Plains tribes, the Lakota, Blackfeet-Piegan-Blood, Cree, and Northern and Southern Cheyenne, and Pawnee, did not have unified pantribal military societies, and thus the Comanche should not be singled out as unusual. The Lakota held divisional gatherings with separate Sun Dances and military society complexes, many of which were analogous. Likewise, the Blackfeet maintained three distinct groups (the Blackfeet, Blood, and Piegan) who, despite sharing the same language and exhibiting only minor ceremonial differences, each maintained separate polities, head chiefs, Sun Dances, and sodalities (Wissler 1913; Ewers 1988:5). The Northern and Southern Cheyenne populations maintained separate Sun Dances and military society complexes, while the Plains Cree maintained uniband-based military societies. Thus, no single unified leadership of joint institutions occurred in these populations, which reinforces the need to recognize broader levels of variation in Plains social organization.

Second, environmental limitations, especially adequate pasture, were another problem for a totally pan-Comanche "tribal" aggregation during the height of their recorded population. Third, some scholars have suggested that as the Comanche were living in different environmental ranges, they were not all pursuing identical modes of subsistence, which in Oliver's (1962) viewpoint would have produced differing forms of social organization. While the initial movement southward was most likely influenced by the acquisition of horses, differential relations with various European powers produced varying subsistence and social organization, as demonstrated by the Comanche divisions (Kavanagh 1996). Kavanagh's works suggest that the Comanche were adapting to a different set of ecological circumstances, namely, Anglos and trade. Different subsistence and economic bases due to variation in emphasizing horse acquisition and trading, bison hunting, raiding, and warfare and different periods of entering a reservation economy also indicate Comanche divisional distinctions.

While these divisional features suggest incipient stages of tribal structure on the divisional level as defined by Service (1962), any pan-Comanche "tribal" structure was never very strong, as reflected by the office of division chief and the political autonomy of individual division-tribes and the frequently changing composition of residence bands. As Kavanagh (1980:6) suggests, and my findings reinforce, it is more likely that the territorial divisions developed incipient "tribelike" structures which did not encompass the entire pan-Comanche ethnic or linguistic population, but remained division-based, perhaps owing to an increasing reliance on warfare and raiding, which was generally division-based. If the political relationship between a leader and his supporters formed a stronger basis for integrating the Comanche than the military societies, as Post Oak Jim implied in 1933 and Kavanagh suggests, then the less integrated position of Comanche societies in comparison to other Plains organizations becomes clearer.[112]

N. D. Humphrey (1941) argues that the "single unifying feature" of Plains men's societies was not political, military, or ceremonial, but social integration. While Comanche men's societies functioned in all these categories, the social factor was indeed stronger than the other categories but weaker when compared with neighboring tribes, again reflecting an incipient stage of military society growth among the Comanche. Comanche societies should not be considered simply dance groups. Lowie (1948:395) and Service (1962:22) have argued that any sodality and "non-residential social group" can operate to integrate the entities of a social aggregate. Comanche military societies did integrate members into coordinate units but on a smaller (divisional tribal based) or incipient scale than the conventional level of truly pan-tribal Kiowa and Cheyenne social organizations.

The reason for the link between the distribution of military sodalities and tribal-level divisions is of anthropological significance. For the Comanche, this organizational difference arises from both ecological and cultural factors. Based on available data, a late development of military sodalities (post-1810) is clearly a factor. The dynamic socioeconomic position held by the Comanche from circa 1700 to 1870 placed them in a location in which they were constantly competing with a host of different European and native interest groups for access to and control of geography and resources. The development of military societies could have aided in adjusting to a dynamically changing Plains lifestyle and adapting to the Comanche alliances with neighboring Kiowa, Apache, Cheyenne, and Arapaho. As Boon (1982:102) points out, "sodalities reveal a tribe's capacity to sample alternate social forms, without necessarily adopting them as the central components of its social machine." The fact that different Comanche divisions were pursuing varying subsistence strategies in an extremely large and ecologically varied range is one factor preventing a truly pantribal system. Interaction was most frequent among divisional residence bands in closer proximity to one another. The Peneteka were reservation based by 1855–1859, while others did not enter such subsistence conditions until the mid-1870s.[113] Population is another cause; it was most likely ecologically impossible to keep such a large pan-Comanche population together, as occasional bison shortages are mentioned as early as the 1780s. While tribes are political and not necessarily residential organizations, the periodic reinvigoration of *communitas* is affected by the conditions of the period as well as the time of the year. Clearly the Lakota divisions could not maintain a single set of tribally integrative ceremonies and men's societies. Why then should we expect the Comanche to do so? Determining at what point a Plains population would no longer be able to function in a single aggregation in relation to social and ecological factors would answer this question more precisely.

Shoshone origins and social organization could have affected the degree and speed with which the Comanche adopted Plains sociocultural and ideological traits, as reflected by the similarly weak position of Shoshone forms of large social organization, sodalities, and martial-oriented headsmen (Steward 1938; Kardiner 1945). Gelo (1986, 1993:78) has recently discussed the presence of elements of Comanche myth and ritual which are more characteristic of the Basin than the Plains. Steward (1938) and Lowie (1909:216) stated that there were no Northern Shoshone (which suggests proto-Comanche as well) clubs or associations, yet we know that the Lobos Society was fully organized and functioning by 1824 (Berlandier 1969:70–75, 117–118). Again, it appears that the Comanche obtained military societies after separating and migrating southward from the Shoshone and after allying and being influenced by the Kiowa, Naishan Apache, and later Cheyenne. If Stanton Tefft's (1961) contention that adaptation to a Plains economy focusing on hunting, warfare, and raiding resulted in changes from a bilocal to a more patrilocal form of residence and from a bicentered to a more patricenter-based division of labor for the Comanche is true, then men's societies would have become more important as the primary initial division of labor shifted toward patricentrality in a growing economy featuring raiding, warfare, and hunting. A Plains adaptation also resulted in an increased integration of larger segments of the population for lengthier periods than Shoshone culture permitted. Thus, increasingly male-dominated economic, subsistence, and social forms (men's sodalities) should not be surprising.

Citing several cultural, economic, and psychodynamic examples, Kardiner (1945:82) suggests that "the traits of the Comanche were only extensions of the older culture and not a fresh start." Contemporary scholars generally dislike the idea that Shoshone origins in any way determined later forms of Comanche social organization, because it implies that Shoshone forms of social organization continued to determine Comanche social forms long after they separated from the Shoshone by no later than 1690–1700. Yet we cannot completely disregard the possibility of any such relationship. Tefft (1965) argues in partial support of this stance, stating that, as the productive system differed little from that of other Plains tribes, it alone did not explain their cultural difference. He maintains that "specific ecological and cultural factors influencing each tribe within its particular Plains niche" must be examined to explain cultural diversity and that "the presence or absence of pan-tribal organizations is as much a consequence of unique historical contacts influencing the ideological subsystem of each tribe as it is due to ecologic pressures or residue values carried over from the past life." That is, "external cultural and ecological relationships may operate to support or undermine political values" (Tefft 1965:169).

Shoshone economic and social organization did affect the development of larger cultural forms in at least two ways. First, having an initial form of economic and social organization that inhibited concentrations of larger numbers and thus the ability to maintain associations produced a cultural background lacking any large associations or men's societies. This is not to say that the Comanche could not have adapted such organizations, as large Comanche camps are frequently reported by the mid-1700s. The large numbers of warriors among the Comanche, the largest Southern Plains population, possibly negated the need for formally organized societies, although their role in enhancing *communitas* would undeniably have been advantageous. Second, formal military society development was at least initially inhibited by (1) the somewhat geographically remote position of the Shoshone and Comanche in relation to the Plains development and (2) the diffusion of technological and social forms (i.e., the date of intensified contact with populations with strong sodality traditions such as the Kiowa and Apache [post-1806] and Cheyenne and Arapaho [post-1840], preventing their acquisition until later than among other tribes). Regarding the diffusional distribution of the Plains men's societies and Sun Dance complex, I believe that the cultural background and geographically remote position of the Shoshone and later Comanche did affect the date of acquisition and length of development of these cultural elements, as more eastern tribes contained temporary police forces and numerous forms of social, religious, and ceremonial sodalities prior to migrating and adapting a Plains lifestyle. Increased interaction with the Spanish military and the formation of Comanche police in 1802–1810 also suggest a Spanish influence on the development of already large groups of Comanche warriors into distinct formally organized and named fighting units.

Our incomplete knowledge of Plains variation in these forms of social organization has also hindered our understanding of the Comanche forms of these institutions. Apparently the sodalities most responsible for holding together Comanche tribes were the political aggregations involving a leader and supporters, rather than the men's soldier societies.[114] These problems in data, terminology, and fieldwork undoubtedly led to Hoebel's (1940:39) confusion: "The tenuousness of the historical data and the paucity of material recorded by Lowie, when combined with the ignorance of present-day Comanches on the subject of military societies, all indicate that the societies were not a developed and integrated part of Comanche culture. Therefore they could not have played an important role in social control and government."

I suggest that the Comanche of the nineteenth century were exhibiting an evolutionary stage of pandivisional tribal sodality building and growth, which was prematurely inhibited prior to reaching fruition due to the collapse of the Comanche and larger Plains economy and reduced population through disease and military domination by the United States. Had the Comanche been allowed more time to evolve, a truly pan-Comanche level of integration might have developed, providing us with a very different interpretation of their social organization and military societies today.

COMANCHE MILITARY SOCIETIES IN REVIEW

The existence of Comanche military societies and their role in the preparatory aspects of the Na'wapina'r and Sun Dance during the nineteenth century counter the alleged "Comanche anomaly." Despite limited data, the functions and organization of Comanche military societies have been shown to have been generally similar to those of neighboring Southern Plains tribes. Shoshone sodalities also show a close correlation with Comanche and other Plains military societies. Comanche societies performed roles in the policing of the hunt, camp, and march, in the preparatory functions in the Sun Dance, and in fictive kinship and economic aid. They appear to have combined the position of society leaders and whipmen observed in other tribes and to have lacked any form of female society members or male youth members functioning as servants. Distinct regalia, songs, and dances containing coup recitations and leadership positions such as whipmen follow the larger Plains pattern. The Big Horses, Little Ponies, Tuhwi, and Comanche War Dance societies are all derived from warfare contexts. An *esprit de corps* and distinct expression of martial ideology and ability played a large role in society functions as found elsewhere on the Plains. Later revived Comanche military societies contain many of these elements in syncretic form, symbolic of an earlier period. If Comanche data were comparable in quantity to those for the Kiowa and Cheyenne, further clarification and expansion would be possible. These similarities have increased following the marked rise in joint residence, interaction, intermarriage, and generally shared post-1875 historical experiences.

Wallace and Hoebel's (1952:224, 272) characterizations of Comanche societies must be rethought in view of the revised functional and organizational attributes of these sodalities. Comanche military societies differed from other Plains military societies foremost in that membership was division based and not pan-Comanche, as among neighboring pantribally based tribes. The alleged absence of a leadership structure, large tribally integrative ceremonies, and pantribal sodalities (some of which were multidivisional or multi-Comanche-tribal but not pan-Comanche) that is cited in support of the Comanche anomaly has been shown to be incorrect, being based largely on a lack of in-depth ethnographic attention, confusion in terminology for levels of social organization, and inadequate use of available archival data. Future research should establish further similarities, on a less integrated level, between the Comanche and other Plains tribes of the nineteenth century and provide new insights into Comanche social organization.

Upon military subjugation of the Comanche by the United States, the less integrated position of military societies in Comanche culture and the apparent political integration based on a reliance on residence band leaders and supporters rather than men's societies and society leaders resulted in a more rapid decline of the military societies than among neighboring tribes which contained stronger military society traditions with more integrative functions. Because Comanche societies were of a more recent acquisition and were not functionally integrated as widely or deeply as among other Plains populations, they declined more quickly upon the cessation of their dependent or associated activities than in other Plains populations. This resulted in less surviving knowledge and documentation than for neighboring tribes, which has previously been used to support the anomalous characterization. I hope these data will begin to clarify some of the misconceptions about the Comanche, showing that, while they were indeed distinct compared to many other Plains populations, differences can be found between nearly all tribes in various aspects and knowledge of the extent of variation in Plains Indian social organization is still incomplete. The differences between the military societies of Comanche and other Southern Plains groups were more in the degree of utilization, intensity, integration, and interaction—in their stage of evolution—than in the total absence of a particular cultural institution.

THE DECLINE AND REBIRTH OF COMANCHE MILITARY SOCIETIES

Divisional organizations did not survive after the Comanche entered the reservation in 1874–1875, and several had begun to disintegrate between 1849 and 1874 (Kavanagh 1989: 105; Foster 1991). The confiscation of war-related shields and weapons by the government, the loss of many forms of war power, and the decreased access to warfare and related forms of supernatural power greatly inhibited the traditional warrior role. Some Comanche reportedly threw away shields, warfare power–related items, and traditional forms of religion upon entering the reservation. Other items were confiscated by the military at Fort Sill. Initial cultural decline (including military societies and associated ritual symbols) due to initially rapid social change correlates with Turner's (1968) and Jacobs's (1987) stages of conquest and acculturation, associated with the decline of many cultural forms and their symbols.

At the beginning of the reservation period (1855–1875) Comanche military societies likewise fell into disuse as effective social groups. As societies were organized on repeated patterns of focused activity that cross-cut residence bands, confinement to a reservation negated this function. All data indicate a decline of society activities beginning in the waning days of warfare with the United States. The circumstances upon which these organizations were based were no longer viable in Comanche culture at this time; they were living a harried existence, and their military power was decreasing in resistance to United States military forces, encroaching bison hunters, and a continually increasing migratory Anglo population. Ceremonial dances and their associated ritual symbols declined because their role in the preparation of hunting and raiding parties was no longer necessary due to decreasing bison herds, reservation confinement, and prohibited warfare. The geographical concentration of all Comanche on a reservation furthermore undermined the necessity, usefulness, and function of maintaining autonomous residence bands and tribal divisions (division-based tribes). Whereas division and societies previously included cooperation and participation of numerous social groups across a wide geographical area, all Comanche were now in relatively constant and close proximity to one another and, because of population losses, constituted a relatively small group. By 1881 local residence bands were beginning to lose cohesion (Kavanagh 1989:105). Participation of social groups now centered upon gatherings of reorganized reservation communities, as there is little evidence for the use of divisions for any form of social organization after circa 1875. Similar instances have been found in the reformation of prereservation Kiowa bands into later reservation communities.[115]

The reservation period correlates with Jacobs's (1987) stage of "depopulation and despondence," as reservation existence was beset with a series of social, medical, and cultural reverses which furthered the decline of earlier cultural forms. In the early reservation years Comanche social gatherings became limited mainly to ration days and, after 1885, to semiannual grass payments prior to the emergence and growth of Peyotism. A series of community-based encampments emerged, occurring around the Christian winter holidays of Christmas and New Year. Recognizable summer encampments were reported as early as 1906 and had become focused around traditional dances by 1911 (Foster 1991). Both Comanche elders and those in neighboring tribes have frequently pointed out that large numbers of Comanche converted to Christianity very early in comparison with some neighboring tribes. Comanche consultants indicate that there were clearly strong Christian missionization pressures, as well as religion-based threats, against nearly all cultural forms, including dancing, which resulted in the loss of many earlier dances and songs. Many current Comanche elders cite Christianity as the major cause for the loss of traditional cultural forms.[116] During the first third of the twentieth century, many Comanche traveled from one summer "picnic" encampment to another, enabling them to visit relatives and friends in a number of communities. The performance of traditional military society dances was limited to older males, all of whom would probably have been society members prior to entering the reservation. As Tennyson Echawaudah related (Foster 1991:123), "They'd camp different places. Mostly, just the elders took part [that is, danced]. Just a few selected men, maybe five or six. They respected what they did."

A number of other new social and religious factors also began to supplant older traditional society dances. The growth of Peyotism and the subsequent formation of the Native American Church and, to a lesser degree, the Ghost Dance attracted large numbers of Comanche participants, focusing their attention away from the older traditional warrior society dances and religious forms. The rise of social War Dancing through the diffusion of the Plains Grass (War or Omaha) Dance became an alluring element which attracted many younger individuals away from the older society dances. The Indian Pioneer papers contain numerous references to Comanche dances and powwows occurring around the turn of the century, but do not allude to their content or form.[117] While a few of these may have been warrior society dances, the extremely high frequency suggests the growth of social War Dancing in the form of the burgeoning "War Dance" or "powwow." Multiple consultants indicated that dances during the 1920s and 1930s were focused primarily on War Dancing and various forms of social dances such as 49 Dances. Older military society dances such as Gourd Dancing occurred only infrequently.[118]

Efforts were made during this time to revive older Comanche warrior dances, which reflect Jacobs's (1987) "contra-acculturation" stage, Ryan's (1969) "syncretic integration," and Slotkin's (1975) "opposition to accommodation," including nativistic nationalism (see Kracht 1989). At least three causes for the short-lived revival of traditional Comanche dances in the early 1900s are known. First, the Comanche became concerned about reviving traditional rituals which had been abandoned between 1875 and 1900. Second, Comanche were sometimes hired by Anglos to dance at local civic celebrations and perform in local Fourth of July parades. Local entrepreneurs seeking profits from tourism often sought out Quanah Parker to recruit Comanche participants for such events. In 1903 and 1908 Parker hosted powwows near his home near Cache, Oklahoma, which attracted thousands of Indian and non-Indian visitors. These events included speeches, Indian dancing, mock Indian attacks on a train, stagecoach robberies, and rodeo events. Parker also led several contingents of Comanche to perform dances and reenactments at various festivals in Texas (Hagan 1993:102–103). Third, other Comanche also requested the performance of traditional dances by surviving military society members for intracommunity activities.

These revivalist efforts did not fully reach fruition; while other elements of Comanche culture such as the Native American Church and the War

Dance continued to grow, the older dance forms ceased to be performed by the mid-1920s. The most significant factor underlying this phenomenon is that younger Comanche were restricted, if not actually prohibited, from actively participating in the traditional military society dances of elder males at this time (ca. 1920), possibly due to a lack of veteran status. Several individuals have indicated that only the elders were allowed to participate in the older warrior society dances. Another factor was the reluctance of older generations to pass on older warrior traditions, including dances, to the younger generations. As one elder indicated, "The old people said, Why celebrate, you're done whipped. Why celebrate your defeat . . . why celebrate your own end. In the old days you could celebrate your victories . . . they quit everything and Christianity took over."[119] Lee Motei's observations (Howard 1976:244–245) of Little Horse Society Dances during his childhood (ca. 1910–1920) indicate participation by only adults and "old men." Tennyson Echawaudah's comments that only a few elders danced also point to the exclusion of younger generations (Foster 1991:123).

Many of today's elders were often away at various Indian boarding schools and consider this another cause for the lack of learning and maintaining older cultural forms. Concerning traditional culture and forms of power, Levy (1958:39–40) indicates that generational gaps regarding knowledge and admittance did evolve:

> But in the period from 1900 through 1920 the young men were not only frustrated but were also confronted with the White system which seemed more powerful. As a result they went through a period of not believing in the traditional forms of power. They refused to learn when the old men offered to teach and the old men often refused to teach before they died because they distrusted the ways of the younger generation.

Upon reaching middle age, this generation of Comanche, who would later represent many of those responsible for cultural revivals including military societies, came to value traditional culture and older forms of power. Some cultural forms, however, had been irretrievably lost. In Comanche, Kiowa, and Apache societies, I have found similar indications regarding a reluctance by elders to pass on traditions and ceremonial objects for fear that the younger generations "wouldn't use them right, wouldn't respect and uphold them," as one elder put it.

Although a few Comanche volunteered and served as scouts in Troop-L at Fort Sill from 1892 to 1897, which provided a form of martial-related social status, there were no actual combat encounters during this tenure. With participation by at least thirty-one Comanche in World War I, outgoing and returning veterans provided a link, albeit weak, to the military societies, dancing, and the honoring of warriors. Some Comanche servicemen were sent off to war at Apache, Oklahoma, to the accompaniment of Tuhwi Society songs but without dances (Kavanagh n.d.c). Although many former society symbols were inactive at this time, the society songs and send-off or farewell gatherings demonstrate the continued connection to the earlier prereservation warrior ideology and the use of the Tuhwi Society symbols as a vehicle to convey these traditional ideologies in a syncretic form. Honor dances were held for outgoing and returning veterans by surviving military society members, who performed traditional warrior songs and sponsored celebration dances to honor the returning men as warriors. Although these men were considered warriors and were publicly honored, the celebrations were short lived following their return; while Scalp, Victory, and War Dances were held, no known military society dances were held. The Parker-Iseeo Post briefly served as a veterans' association for World War I veterans; however, little is known concerning its tenure. As in other tribes, there were not enough World War I veterans to sustain a complete revival of any of the men's traditional warrior societies. Society dances continued to decline, as the last Comanche "Gourd Dances" are reported to have occurred around 1924–1925.[120]

With the small numbers of World War I veterans and their impact on the diminishing warrior societies, other social forms rose in popularity. Social dance forms such as the "49" and Fancy War Dancing grew during the teens and 1920s onward, providing the younger crowd with more active participation in the gatherings. While these activities were increasing, the actual gatherings were still not focused on them. The exclusion of younger males from participation in traditional society dances also resulted in a generational gap in Comanche military society knowledge. Agents were concerned about the maintenance of Comanche traditions, periodic encampments which took people away from their homes and farming, and the giveaway, which they viewed as undermining the Comanche's respect for private property. As with the Kiowa and Apache, the agency superintendent attempted to curtail Comanche dances in 1917, by withholding annuity payments for those who were listed as participating in dances the previous year.[121] Despite these economic sanctions, the Comanche continued to hold summer dances.

These events correlate with Jacobs's (1987) stage of "contra-acculturation": after a period of depopulation and despondence, stabilization is followed by a revival of cultural forms in modified and syncretic form. Turner's (1968:22) observations that, once the initially rapid social change has slowed and stabilized, traditional rituals infused with new symbols are re-vived are also relevant. The reemergence of Comanche social activities and dances in the early 1900s reflects this stage of restabilization, syncretic ref-ormation, and growth.

By the mid-1930s most elder military society members with veteran status were deceased; as elders indicated, much of the knowledge associated with the older culture, including the military societies and dances, went with them. There are also indications that the economic situation during the 1920s and 1930s limited the acquisition of money and goods needed for holding dances and giveaways. The World War I veterans came to hold dominant roles in dancing by the late 1930s, largely in the form of the pow-wow. The large-scale return to veteran status for the Comanche would not come until World War II and the Korean War. During World War II many Comanches served in the Forty-fifth or "Thunderbird" Division. Several Comanche veterans brought home "war trophies" such as captured flags and banners, which were thrown to the ground and danced on by tribal elders. Elder Comanche acknowledged the return of veteran status through the ser-vice record of the younger generation in World War II. Forrest Kassanavoid described the reaction of tribal elders to Comanche participation in World War II and their return to veteran or warrior status: "Yah, they did that. Cause for a long period of time see, no one ever went off to war. So when we came back we were, you know, *maiheemeeah*, they call it. *Maiheemeeah*, that means someone who had gone into combat. You know and that's what they looked at us as, *maiheemeeah*, someone who had been in combat." [122] Seventeen Comanche men were selectively recruited into the Fourth Signal Company, Fourth Infantry Division, to use the Comanche language as the basis for developing a signal code in World War II. Since 1989 surviving Comanche Code Talkers have been honored at several Comanche events for their service (Meadows n.d.a).

Veterans of both World War II and Korea were welcomed home with Victory Dance celebrations, during which time Scalp, Victory, and social dances increased dramatically in number and frequency. The 1946 celebra-tion south of Walters, Oklahoma, for returning World War II veterans and the 1952 celebration at Walters for Korean War veterans have continued in the form of the "Comanche Homecoming." Serving as an annual opportu-nity for all Comanche to come together, this July homecoming clearly ex-presses Comanche identity; currently the program focuses on Comanche military society dances. [123]

World War II and the Korean War provided a second period of social and now economic stabilization, which facilitated further cultural revival in syncretic form. With Comanche involvement in World War II, veterans and other tribal members started to establish connections between dancing and the military societies and the impact of the war on the Comanche community. The powwow began to be used as a form of public gathering to honor incoming and outgoing Comanche servicemen, symbolic of the honoring of outgoing and returning warrior groups by nineteenth-century Comanche in the form of the Na'wapina'r prior to leaving and the *Wutanuhka* (Dance of Purification or Scalp Dance) and *Nah-o-kee-nuhka* (Dance of Joy; i.e., Victory Dance) upon returning. The decline in movements of servicemen following World War II led to fewer occasions for gatherings such as honor dances.

The cultural and ethnic threats posed by the post–World War II era Termination and Relocations Act policies also made the Comanche conscious of the need to express ethnic identity. Postwar increases in economic resources and transportation facilitated an increased number of social powwows, resulting in the emergence of various types of dances in the forms of homecomings, descendants' powwows, and honor and benefit dances. The initial reemergence of Comanche men's societies and associated symbols (dance, song, regalia, ideology) was exclusively in veterans' organizations aided by the auxiliary women's Comanche War Mothers.

CONTEMPORARY COMANCHE SOCIETIES

With the growth of Comanche powwows and dance activities, the revival of the Kiowa Gourd Dance in 1957 led to the larger growth of Southern Plains Gourd Dancing and the revival of other military societies. While many Comanche became active Gourd dancers, no Comanche Gourd Dance societies were formally organized until the early 1970s. Elder consultants indicate that the Comanche increasingly began to participate in the widespread Gourd Dance revivals of neighboring tribes throughout Oklahoma from 1957 to the late 1960s, prior to reviving any of their own societies. In addition, the larger social movement focusing on Indian identity during the 1960s and 1970s is also frequently mentioned by Comanche as making them more aware of themselves as Indians and as Comanche and of the need to express that identity visibly and culturally. This newly emphasized recognition of Indian identity served as another crucial factor in the revival of earlier Comanche societies and dance forms. Although participating in many of the larger dances, social activities, and powwows which had been ongoing since World War II, the Comanche had not yet revived any of their own societies. The AIVA (American Indian Veterans Association) was an attempt to form a national all-Indian, intertribal veterans' organization following World War II. The organization endured intermittently for a few years before splintering into more tribally specific interest groups.

From 1970 to 1976 five Comanche men's societies were formed or revived. Dancing societies became a renewed social arena for continuing and reinforcing Comanche identity through the enculturation of traditional sociocultural forms, while further supporting existing dancing and social activities associated with powwows. The Comanche War Dance Society was reactivated in 1970, while the Comanche Indian Veterans Association (CIVA) was formed after the division of the AIVA, sometime in the very early 1970s. A Comanche Gourd Clan publication dated May 1971 indicates that they at least briefly preceded the 1972 Little Pony revival.[124] The Tuhwi was revived in 1976. The Little Ponies and Tuhwi are known prereservation societies which claim a traditional and sometimes lineal base to their ancestral organizations. The Comanche War Dance Society represents the diffusion of the Grass Dance during the later nineteenth century. The CIVA and Comanche Gourd Clan are more recent societies, continuing the earlier tradition of Comanche Gourd Dancing and maintaining many general Comanche traditions, but maintain no direct association with named prereservation Comanche societies. Despite being revived after lengthy temporal absences, these societies continue to maintain a number of past functions, symbols, and individual characteristics. A review of their structure and activities demonstrates the continuity of their integrative and enculturative roles.

Tuepukunʉʉ: The Little Horses

The Little Horses Society continued holding functions into the early twentieth century. Although the regularity of their activities is unknown, they were probably limited to annual summertime encampments as with most societies at this time. Lee Motei indicated to James Howard (1976:245) that during Little Pony Society dances in his childhood (ca. 1910–1920) the old men dancing shook their rattles up and down during the first four songs then changed to a side to side motion as the singers began to pick up the tempo of the singing. Dancers remained in a stationary line and did not progress around the arena as is sometimes done today. A whipman made all dancers arise and dance, and membership was limited solely to adults; children were not allowed to participate. During breaks in the dancing, elders occasionally recited battle experiences. Elders have indicated that the last Comanche Gourd Dances were held in 1924–1925. Witnesses of these dances indicate that societal ties were still observed, as "friends" and members of the same society danced together.

Now officially known as the Little Ponies, the Tuepukunʉʉ were revived in 1972, forming a constitution on April 9 of that year. Elders I spoke with showed acknowledgment and awareness of participation in the ongoing larger Southern Plains Gourd Dance revival with the conscious intention of reviving and preserving Comanche traditions. According to Ed Yellowfish, a group of thirteen older men who were predominantly Peyotists and World War II veterans observed several younger Vietnam veterans watching a Comanche dance and felt that they should be honored and should be taking part:

> Seemed like they should be able to take part because most of these were veterans, they needed to be recognized or honored if you will. They might have been honored when they first got back from overseas, something like that, or from the service and that either because of interest or whatever that honor wasn't given to them until maybe something else happened. So it was like a vehicle, also like an identity like I said earlier for us [to] try to have something like this so that our young men could take part in these social things that were developed, Indian dances, mainly the Gourd Dance because it was becoming so popular. So in 1972 we formed this organization. There were thirteen of us.[125]

Knowing that the original society contained "medicine" in the past, the members decided to revive only the social part of the society, without the associated medicine power, yet still remain respectful toward the dance. As one elder stated, the society decided to exclude the society's medicine "because we knew that different ones of the older people had medicine, ways, customs that we didn't know anything about."[126] The Little Ponies constitution clearly identifies many of the current themes among Southern Plains tribes in the 1970s, including Indian awareness and a concern for maintaining traditional cultural forms, ethnicity, and tribal distinctiveness, that reflect a revitalization movement as defined by Wallace (1956).

The revival of the society as a symbol in itself and as a set of associated symbols served to fulfill many cultural needs during the 1960s and 1970s, a time of great social unrest and reassertion of ethnic awareness in America. As the Preamble of the Little Ponies charter says, "We dedicate ourselves to the preservation of Comanche Indian history, language, traditions, and lore to the best of our ability." In addition, Article II of the Little Pony Constitution states:

The purpose of this organization shall be: To propagate the history of the Little Pony Group known heretofore as Teh-da Puku Nu, according to investigative compilation of all available information, projecting the name Teh-da Puku Nu, as Comanche, into the front of the public mind with pride and dignity, preserving and enriching the historical significance of the Comanche tribe; encouraging and perpetuating all known traditions, language, art, and music of our tribe. . . .[127]

Thus, the society, which formerly focused on a select group of prereservation warriors, now had a broader, less specific cultural significance. Reflecting Bruno Nettl's (1978, 1985) principle of consolidation, the society had not become less culturally significant, only broader in the variety of associated functions and uses. While the martial origins and emphasis on recognizing veterans and the society as a warriors' group continue, the society has changed from a more specific (warrior sodality) significance to a more generalized cultural (Comanche) emphasis. The adaptability of the society has served to provide an arena of enculturation for future Comanche by serving to teach various aspects of Comanche culture.

Funds were raised through a series of benefit dances, bingo games, raffles, and concessions. A women's auxiliary was formed and aided in the society's development by making clothing for the dancers and items for fundraising. The Little Ponies continued to thrive as an active Gourd Dance society, frequently sponsoring or co-hosting dances throughout Oklahoma and abroad, while holding an annual dance every April in Apache, Oklahoma. Monthly business meetings were held to organize for events and provide communication and fellowship. The Little Ponies adopted the use of the red and blue shoulder blanket, similar to the dress of the larger Gourd Dance revivals, on which veterans frequently displayed their military insignia, a white waist sheet, the mescal bean and metal bead bandoleers, and a rattle and fan. A circular image containing four horses running counterclockwise in a circle, in the form of a beaded medallion or metal tie-tack or blanket pin, was adopted as the society insignia and worn on blankets and bandoleers. Some members attached chess knights to the tops of their rattle, symbolizing a Little Pony. Following a series of deaths and illnesses of several society officers and prominent members, including many of the thirteen founding members, the society became inactive in 1985. After a dormancy of nearly eight years, the Little Ponies were revived in April 1993 and soon began actively seeking and initiating new members and co-hosting throughout southwestern Oklahoma. Since 1993 the society has increasingly revived its interaction in the Southern Plains powwow community and has reestablished a new set of co-hosting relationships with other tribes, societies, and powwow groups.

As in most current societies, there are several syncretic aspects which should be mentioned. Society dress contains influences from the Native American Church in the form of blankets, jewelry, fans, and rattles, as is typical of Southern Plains Gourd Dancing. Elders I have spoken to state that there are no longer any Comanche Gourd Dance songs with Comanche lyrics that are sung, and I did not hear any during my fieldwork. It is not unusual at any dance to have a group of singers and drummers composed of members of various tribes, and songs with Kiowa words sung by both Comanche and Kiowa are frequent at Little Pony and other society dances. The Little Pony "club" song, for example, was given to the society in 1972 by Leonard Cozad, a Kiowa. Yet, despite syncretic forms, the society remains a distinctly Comanche-based social group.[128]

Since their revival in 1972 and reactivation in 1993, the Little Ponies have maintained a number of Comanche traditions, including fictive kinship. A society princess who is regarded as a sister to all the members is elected on a yearly basis and serves as an ambassador of goodwill. Although this is more publicly expressed by some members than by others, all male members are regarded as brothers, and all their families are related through membership in the society. Several society members continually address one another as "brother" upon meeting, and I have seen this familiarity extended to guests dancing with the society. Thus, the society in a sense forms a larger, horizontally linked family based on society membership. A number of Little Ponies customs regarding death are still followed. Following the 1972 revival all activities were stopped for one month upon the death of a member, during which time the society helped the family of the deceased with gifts of food and money. If any event has already been planned prior to the death, the society members ask the family for permission to hold the event; otherwise they will cancel it. Cedarings are still held upon a member's death. Upon the recent death of one member, the society asked the family if they wanted the Little Ponies to postpone their co-hosting activities for a period. The family thanked the society, but instructed it to continue its activities, having paid respect to the deceased and the family. Prior to dancing, all members present at the next dance were cedared and prayed for and those absent from that dance were likewise taken care of at the next society event they attended. Similar cedarings followed for the death of any member or relative of a member and his family.

Recently, the Little Ponies have participated in parades and Brush

Dances and host the afternoon sessions of Gourd Dancing at the annual Comanche Nation Fair. The Little Ponies revived the Comanche Brush Dance at the second annual Comanche Nation Fair in October 1993. At the 1994 Comanche Nation Fair Brush Dance, male and female dancers carried small tree limbs. Led by an elder on horseback, the society Gourd Danced, followed by female auxiliaries and a group of singers carrying a drum. The male dancers shook their rattles in time to society songs, as all marched in processional style, periodically stopping to dance in place. A gradual processional of four songs' duration was made toward the arena. Afterward an afternoon session of Gourd Dancing was held. The society has begun holding its own annual dance in May and continues to hold benefit dances and co-host with other local Gourd Dancing organizations throughout the year.

The Little Ponies reflect the flexibility of a sodality to retain the history and symbols of the past while adapting to the needs of contemporary culture. While the martial origins and emphasis as a warrior group are still emphasized in society meetings and in public speeches at society dances, the society has adapted to provide an arena for continuing numerous forms of Comanche enculturation (music, dance, language, oral history, religious cedaring, mourning customs, kinship, sodality identity, economic cooperation). The ability to integrate past and present to ensure the maintenance of Comanche culture for the future is reflected by the program (AICS 1994) from a recent Gourd Dance which the Little Ponies Society co-hosted:

> The Little Ponies began as a group of accomplished young men, mainly warriors and medicine men. They would celebrate their war victories or initiation of new members by dancing. Today, the society encourages younger and older men to join to learn about Comanche culture and history. They remember the songs of the Gourd Dance that represents the warriors riding together as a brotherhood and as a society.[129]

The Tuwinʉʉ or Tuhwi

Although few pre–World War I data on the society have emerged, Herwanna Becker Barnard (1941:49) states that "one secret order known to old-timers is the Black Crow Lodge," indicating that Comanche elders in the 1940s still retained knowledge of the society prior to its revival in 1976. Tuhwi songs, but not dances, were performed for departing and returning World War I veterans near Apache, Oklahoma, near the allotments of many Yamparika.[130] In the past, the Tuhwi Society and its members had an especially strong medicine associated with the crow, which was taken seriously.

While knowledgeable elders who probably had the authority to revive the society were still living following the conclusion of World War I, it is not known why they chose not to revive the dance. Fear of this strong medicine was given as the primary reason why the dance had not been performed since 1919, when, elders indicated, it last occurred.[131]

In 1975 the Comanche tribe received $27,000 in funding to prepare cultural demonstrations for the 1976 Bicentennial Festival of American Folklife in Washington, D.C. As a part of the Comanche cultural program, the Tuhwi Society was revived largely through the efforts of Joe Attocknie (a descendant of past Yapai Division and Tuhwi Society members), assisted by Brownie Sovo and others. These individuals taught the songs, dances, call, and customs of the society to over fifty members who performed the dance between June 7 and 11 at the 1976 festival. In recognition of the society's traditional emphasis on a martial ideology, the dance was revived to honor all Comanche veterans as well as all Native American veterans. While all prereservation members were reportedly veterans, this requirement was waived in 1976 in the interests of preserving the dance. Veterans are especially welcomed and honored; however, membership is now open to all Comanche, many of whom are not veterans. As one current society whipman, June Sovo, stressed, "It doesn't belong to me or anyone else, it belongs to all Comanches." Once a member, "you're tagged," and respectable behavior is expected of you inside as well as outside the dance arena and society functions.[132] In addition to a martial ideology, a social ethic is associated with and symbolized by society membership.

Since being revived in 1976, the Tuhwi is performed on an average of one to three times annually. Gelo (1986:218) reports that is was "recreated" in 1981, which may indicate full reactivation at that time. Performances are held for what are considered "serious occasions," which center upon honoring past veterans and returning servicemen. For example, on November 11, 1989, the Tuhwi danced at the Oklahoma State Capitol building in honor of the surviving Comanche and Choctaw Code Talkers of World War II, who were honored by the State of Oklahoma and the French government. In 1991 the Tuhwi danced for the returning Desert Storm veterans at the Comanche tribal complex. Since 1992 the society has danced in honor of all Comanche veterans and the remaining Comanche Code Talkers at the annual Comanche Nation Tribal Fair held on the Fort Sill Military Base each fall. Recently, the society has begun to hold annual performances at a Texas festival.

In 1977 Comanche traveled to Ignacio, Colorado, and performed the

Tuhwi for the Ute tribe. This event reenacted an 1870 attempt by the Comanche and Ute tribes to make peace, which ended in battle when someone
unexpectedly fired a shot, leading everyone to scatter. The reenactment included armed guards placed around the camp symbolic of the earlier meeting and the smoking of a pipe, an exchange of bison-hide scrolls, and hand-
shakes which concluded a peace agreement after nearly two hundred years
of hostility over hunting rights (O'Brien 1989:236).[133] In keeping with their
military ties of the past, the Tuhwi usually perform on Armed Forces Day
in May each year. The most regular performance of the society is at the
annual July "Comanche Homecoming," held at Walters, Oklahoma.

Unlike other dance clubs, the Tuhwi generally hold no benefit dances
and only occasionally perform outside of the current Comanche home area.
Occasionally a request for a dance performance in Texas has been made and
granted. Small collections of money for food and gasoline are sometimes
offered by the group asking the society to dance, but are generally small
amounts and are not the basis for dancing. Dances are usually kept within
the Comanche tribal area, to facilitate the participation of larger numbers of
dancers, and are arranged when an individual requests the group to dance in
honor of someone. Thus, the society performs as a service organization by
honoring veterans, while upholding and maintaining elements of Comanche
culture. The Tuhwi dance is regarded as an honor dance which is performed
only for the benefit of and out of respect for past and present warriors.[134]

The night before a Tuhwi dance, members and their families meet at a
leader's house where a cedaring is held, along with prayers. At a dance the
society members meet inside a tipi, where they dress and prepare for the
dance. The society dress code includes what is considered "traditional Comanche men's clothing": buckskin leggings, moccasins, black aprons, red
breechclouts, bone breastplates, and bonnets, roaches, or horned headdresses. Weapons such as shields, lances, guns, or a bow and arrows are also
carried, with other dress items being optional. Some members wear crow
feathers appended from their hair. Presently there are around twenty-five
active members who dance, with older members frequently attending to
sing. Dances I observed between 1989 and 1996 averaged eleven male dancers. An elder is selected to lead a blessing and prayers are offered inside the
tipi. Dancers again "smoke" or incense their clothing in cedar smoke inside
the tipi. Additional prayers are offered for anyone who needs a physical or
psychological blessing. Prayers are also "asked for any mistakes which might
happen," such as dropping an item of dancing equipment. When this occurs
during a dance an elder can "tell a story" or recite a military deed (coup),

after which the dance can continue. The seriousness of the dance is then stressed to the dancers, which is said to be greatly appreciated by the elders.[135]

While most members are not veterans, the dance still stresses and recognizes the role of the warrior in Comanche culture by honoring past and present Comanche tradition and veteran service and is performed in the military spirit that made the Comanche one of the most formidable powers in the history of the Southern Plains. During the opening song of the performance, the names of deceased veterans are frequently read aloud, with dedication of that day's dance to their honor and memory. Even though few dancers are veterans, the society recognizes veterans at several points throughout the program, calling them out to dance along the perimeter of the arena, as well as verbally emphasizing the role and characterization of the Comanche as "Lords of the Southern Plains" or even as "Lords of the Plains." As the dance begins, the emcee calls for silence, explains the history of the dance, and admonishes individuals to restrain their dogs from entering the area. In speaking of "the revival of the Tuhwi," the emcee at the 1993 Walters Homecoming performance demonstrated the society's emphasis on recognizing its martial origins:

> Today the *Tuhwi* is danced in honor of our veterans and especially of our Comanche warriors [the names of several deceased Comanche veterans are read aloud]. . . . The *Tuhwi* or Black Knife has been handed down from days past, when our Comanche ancestors roamed free across the Plains. This dance is only danced to honor warriors returning from a victorious battle and it was performed by only the most feared warriors in the Comanche tribe.
>
> . . . the *Tuhwi* or Black Knife dance is also danced to inspire the spirit of war. It is in no way a healing or medicine dance. . . . It is a dance for the brave and fearless who proudly depend upon their own personal ability. . . .[136]

There are several offices or positions in the contemporary Tuhwi Society: the Dog Man, two whipmen, four women, and the regular members. These women are the only women allowed to have physical contact with the male dancers and are responsible for attending to the men's needs during performances. Being sisters or wives of members, they serve as personal valets to the male dancers. Originally each member reportedly had a female relative who saw to his needs during society dances.

Performances of the Tuhwi vary slightly from one dance to the next but follow a general pattern. When the Tuhwi prepare to dance, the camp crier announces the dance to the camp, instructing people to tie up their dogs. The group processional into the dance arena is a slow forward toe-heel step, which is led by the Dog Man, followed by the two whipmen, the four or more women members, the regular members, women dressed in *Tekwuniwapi Kwasu* ("Women's Warrior Dresses" or red and blue taffeta Victory Dresses), and the singers carrying in and playing the drum while singing. Today these dresses are worn by Comanche women primarily at Tuhwi and Veterans' Day functions.[137] In some performances the dancers are situated around the arena toward which the officers proceed, picking up the members as they complete their processional around the arena. This formation is said to symbolize past whipmen proceeding through the encampment, gathering men from the various camps. The Dog Man is situated twenty to thirty feet ahead of the other members, dancing low to the ground with a strung bow and notched arrow and "looking for any dogs" that might cross the society's path. Following the Dog Man are the two whipmen, who always carry large, serrated whips which can be used to whip the dancers if they are not dancing hard enough or correctly. The whipmen also wear long hair plates (long leather strips with attached silver plates) secured to the back of the head through a braided portion of hair commonly known as the scalp-lock. In the past, these hair plates are said to have hung on the ground and were staked down in battle, similar to sashes used by numerous contrary societies across the Plains. Having had an active role in dancing, June and Gene Sovo were chosen for this position in 1976. According to one consultant, the two whipmen were always biological twins, as are the Sovos, but it is likely that society partners may have fulfilled this office in prereservation times. This custom was also maintained, as society "brothers" would always "fight together in battle until death or victory." During one dance the two whipmen danced with sabers drawn from their scabbards.[138]

Behind the whipmen are the four women attendants. These women are said always to have been a set of sisters and today are three biological sisters of the whipmen and a fourth cousin (classificatory sister) through the adoption of the whipmen as sons by the late Joe Attocknie. During the processional to the dance arena, these women each carry one of the two whip ropes and the two hair plates worn by the two whipmen. According to one consultant, when the group which originally captured the black sabers returned to camp, they began a dance. Two women who had been on the war party had been shot and, unable to walk, were led on horseback by holding onto the ends of the two leaders' hair plates.[139] The Dog Man first enters the arena, when the four women drop the whip and hair plate ends. After the whipmen drag these a short distance (approximately fifteen feet), the women pick up the hair plate ends and hold them until the men start to dance to the second song, after which the whips and hair plates are released and dragged throughout the dance. After the second song, the men proceed to designated seats in the circular dance arena. Only members are allowed inside the arena during the dance, and intruders can be whipped by the whipmen. Female relatives of members frequently dance in place behind members, outside the men's portion of the arena.

The Tuhwi style of dance is very physically demanding. Members assume a crouched position from which they hop up and down and from side to side, while maintaining the crouched position. During the beginning of each song, one member at a time hops out three to four steps, cawing like a crow, and stops, remaining crouched and scouting the horizon, then returns to his seat. The last ones to do so are the whipmen, who continue the motion, after which all the other members join in, in unison. This dance style mimics the "false starts" of the crow, which is respected by the society. The crow can frequently be observed making brief up and down starts off the ground before taking off in full flight. During dances, the members periodically "caw" out loud like crows, *aw'h*, *aw'h*. An average song lasts three to five minutes, but may be extended if the whipmen "feel the spirit, feel good," and signal the head singer, who sits facing them. The lower the dancers crouch while dancing, the harder and longer the singers continue. As the dancing progresses, some of the members can be observed changing their dance style to a less rigorous toe-heel step. A single water break and rest is usually taken during the middle of the dance. At one dance I videotaped, a special song was sung, during which all remained seated; afterward the seated dancers were given water and a rest break. During these rest breaks the emcee often recites historical information about the society while the four female dancers attend to the needs of the male dancers. These women frequently fan the men with feather fans, adjust and smooth their hair, and serve them water. Comanche *Tuhwi* Society songs are the same as those used by the Kiowa Black Legs and the Apache Blackfeet Societies and are vigorously contested among the three tribes. None of the *Tuhwi* songs I recorded during my fieldwork contained any lyrics, and I was unable to find any Comanche elders who knew any *Tuhwi* Society song texts. With a sufficient number of fluent speakers who are also singers, and when compared with neighboring populations, this suggests a later, diffused development.[140]

Occasionally special individuals or groups are invited to enter the arena and dance with the society. At the 1993 Walters Homecoming the Comanche Little Ponies (having recently reorganized after a hiatus of several years) and all veterans were invited to dance one song. The veterans generally dance along the perimeter of the arena with lances or other weapons loaned to them by the dressed performers, which they return to the dancers at the end of the song. The remaining Comanche Code Talkers are frequently recognized during the middle of *Tuhwi* Society dances. Later in the program women are invited to perform the *Wᵾtanᵾhka* or Purification Dance (popularly referred to as the Scalp Dance by Anglos), during which women dance in honor of their male relatives with the men's lances and other martial items. This dance was originally performed when warriors returning from a war journey followed the custom of bathing in a nearby stream and being cedared by a spiritual leader prior to reentering the camp. At this time women came from the camp, took the men's lances and any war trophies, and returned to the camp, where the dance was begun. The dance is performed in a straight line, and at certain times the dancers reverse and return toward the direction from which they came. Several women frequently dance together in a line throughout the dance.[141]

The four women in the Tuhwi dance perform in the center of the arena while all other women dance around the circle of seated male society members. Several of these dances contain a uniquely accentuated beat, with a series of forward shuffling steps interspersed with periodic pauses in their forward motion. Following this portion of the program is the *Nah-o-kee-nᵾhka* (Dance of Joy) or Victory Dance, during which the Comanche War Mothers and other women select honorees out of the crowd and dance in a single-file formation around the arena. Veterans are frequently invited to participate in this portion of the program. Although some elders indicate that this dance was previously often performed in a counterclockwise direction, most are clockwise today, being led with the left foot and raising the right foot in a stepping motion. Comanche women and men, non-Indians, and even visitors are frequently asked to participate at this time. The audience is often asked to stand as the Tuhwi perform their concluding dance. The last dance has no false starts; the Dog Man, whipmen, the four women who pick up the whipmen's hair plate draggers and whip ends during the processional around the arena, and the regular members exit in the same order in which they entered.[142]

Despite changes, the Tuhwi remains a distinctly Comanche Society that is now open to all Comanche, including nonveterans. The society has continued its martial emphasis by performing in honor of veterans and acknowledging the martial ideology associated with its origins, history, and symbols. In doing so, it has evolved into a broader-based entity, which serves as a principal component of large-scale pan-Comanche integrative gatherings and as an arena for cultural continuity.

The revival of the Tuhwi has generated some controversy in the Comanche community, especially among older, conservative tribal members. One common objection is that the members who participate in the society are "boys" and are not "warriors" or "veterans." [143] Some elders have stated that it is bold and even insolent or disrespectful for nonveterans to recreate a warrior society dance, even if such performances are held to honor and recognize older decorated veterans. [144] One frequent objection in past years is that members of the tribe die every time the society performs. Some assert that four deaths follow every dance, a belief consistent with the mythological account of four crows reviving the lost warrior and the general concept that deaths come in fours. Although the latter belief also exists among the neighboring Kiowa, no correlation with any men's societies is known. Gelo (1986:225) reports that three Comanche died during the weeks the Tuhwi dance was performed in the summer of 1983; while no one was willing to attribute these deaths directly to the Tuhwi, some were willing to speculate that the dance "might have something to do with it." However, there is no indication that this belief has any temporal or mythic precedent, nor could anyone explain why a society would be revived if such a serious side effect were known to be associated with it. [145] Gelo (1986:225) reports that many elders at the 1983 Comanche Homecoming disliked the revival and that one singer stated that no one at the drum really knew the songs and they were singing them incorrectly.

As Gelo (1986:225–226) points out, the powwow is an arena for partisan conflict, and much of the discontent surrounding the Tuhwi revival results from intratribal politics. As the society revival coincided with the Oklahoma oil boom, around 1980, tensions between bands and families were exacerbated by increased oil production on Comanche lands. Although some Comanche oppose the current society because it is largely controlled by a single family (the Sovos), opponents of the society have not challenged it directly (Gelo 1986:226). As Gelo (1986:226) notes, the discord about the society may be seen as a continuation of traditional attitudes that is not solely the result of economic conditions or reaction against revivalism. Gelo (1986:226) states that the society is problematic because it is unable to offer the benefits which traditionally counterbalanced its antisocial status—that is, the members are not warriors or veterans and "they no longer insure the survival of tribal members in the natural world, merely the survival of tribal identity in the intertribal milieu." Yet the maintenance of tribal identity is one of the most important functions to be performed in contemporary Indian communities in light of past and present issues of Termination, sovereignty, and cultural and religious freedom.

More recently, control of the Tuhwi Society by the Sovo family, increasing performances of Tuhwi dances in Oklahoma and Texas, and allegations of payment for performances have led to increased controversy in the Comanche community. In 1995 an independent Tuhwi ceremonial was performed by fifteen male Comanche Little Ponies members and six Comanche women of the Little Ponies Auxiliary to celebrate the birthday of Doc Tate Nevaquaya, a Little Pony member and noted artist and flute player. A second performance by this group was also held in 1995 at the Fall Festival in Oklahoma City. Whether internal or external, factions and the development of splinter groups in Southern Plains military societies are nothing new. All KCA societies have experienced an attempted or successful fission or an independent development of a similar society. How these developments will unfold and their effect on future Comanche Tuhwi ceremonials remains to be seen.

However, despite controversy, there is no indication that the society will discontinue. The dance is gaining acceptance among the Comanche and is becoming a regular part of the Comanche Homecoming and Comanche Nation Fair programs. Membership has slowly but steadily increased. There is a more casual, relaxed presentation of the society over the past several years, which appears to be taking on a somewhat more secular tone as it increases in popularity.[146]

The Comanche War Dance Society (CWDS)

Although little is known of the society's reservation-era activities, elders indicate that the dance continued until around 1919. While intertribal powwows continued to grow in popularity during the early twentieth century, the society ceased functioning.[147] When Forrest Kassanavoid, Melvin Kerchee Sr., and Bernard Kahrahrah decided to revive their War Dance Society in 1970, many Comanche in the Cache and Indiahoma area were approached for support. The Comanche also invited the Ponca, who came to dance with them. Following the revival, a new drum was later presented to the Comanche by Lamont Brown of the Ponca. The current CWDS is led by four committeemen, one of whom is known as the "head committeeman." These leaders are in charge of the society, run the dances, and, as the dance originated among the Quahada, have traditionally been selected from families in the Cache-Indiahoma area. As of 1992 the four headsmen were Melvin Kerchee Sr., Billy Komacheet, Bernard Kahrahrah, and Forrest Kassanavoid. The practice of maintaining all-Comanche headsmen was continued from 1970 until October 1993, when two of the Comanche headsmen retired and were replaced as officers by Anglo hobbyists by one of the remaining Comanche headsmen. The CWDS has allowed non-Indian participation as associate members since 1970 (which some Comanche analogize to the past tradition of taking in non-Indian captives who were enculturated as Comanche). However, some Comanche have expressed their disagreement with the induction of non-Indians as society headsmen to me.

Four Tail Dancers dance the end or tail portions of each song. Originally the society maintained only one whipman; however, after 1970 two additional whipmen were added due to the increase in the size of the society. Today two whipmen (Melvin Kerchee Jr. and Richard Martinez) are seated inside the arena near the entrance. These two men are dressed out and are in charge of the arena during dancing. A third whipman (Douglas Komacheet), who does not dress out, is stationed outside the arena and usually carries a whip and a feather fan. His duties include making sure that the water boy has adequate water for the dancers, seeing that items are raffled, and policing the outside arena for any disturbances. There are also three water boys, one for each side of the arena and one for the drum.[148]

The current Comanche War Dance is held twice a year, on the second weekend of April and October, usually in Cache or Lawton, Oklahoma. Maintaining their long-term intertribal relations, the Comanche always invite the Ponca to dance at each dance, which is reciprocated at each of the two annual Ponca dances. Invitations are also extended to a number of Anglo hobbyist groups, including the Ace Man Dance (Massachusetts), Lone Star War Dance (Texas), White Bear (Illinois), and a number of other hobbyist organizations from Texas and California. Often hobbyist dancers outnumber the Indians participating in the dancing.

Individuals wishing to join usually approach the committee for permission. Later prospective members are brought in; after purification, the committeemen perform a "roaching ceremony," during which they tie the dancer's headdress on him and lead him around the arena, instructing him on the traditions and importance of the dance. The initiate's family then dance with him in the arena, after which they have a brief giveaway (usually four gifts) for him. New members are later expected to have a full giveaway or to provide a complete meal for the dance to pay for their seat. If a member acquires a position in the society he will hold another giveaway for the honor associated with serving in this position. In a tradition derived from the Ponca War Dance, the head committeeman and the two whipmen inside the arena have a giveaway at each (twice annual) dance for the duration of their office. The head committeeman's giveaway is generally held during the afternoon dance session, while the whipmen's giveaways are held in the evening sessions.[149]

The CWDS sing predominantly Ponca songs with Ponca lyrics, although some vocable or nonlyric songs are Comanche. No Comanche songs containing lyrics are currently sung by the society. While members sing Ponca songs, several society elders stated that few can completely understand the Ponca words, know the historical stories behind the songs, or can fully translate them.[150] As the dance was obtained from the Ponca, the CWDS follows a Ponca style of "straight dancing" and etiquette. While elders state that earlier members may have worn some feathered bustles, there is no known history of the use of feathered dancing bustles in the CWDS, and they have not been used since the 1970 revival. The use of "straight dance" clothing predominates, following the pattern of northeastern Plains War Dancing of the Ponca, Osage, Oto, and Pawnee. The majority of the Comanche participating dress in straight dance clothes of Ponca style, although distinct Comanche elements such as beadwork, leggings, otter caps, and metal jewelry are present. Anglo hobbyists who dance with the CWDS generally wear straight dance clothes in the style of the Comanche and Southern Plains or of the Prairie tribes such as the Ponca or Osage.

The dance style of the CWDS is that of a formal War Dance society, with dancers proceeding in a clockwise direction around the arena. Each of the two annual formal War Dances is held as a two-day weekend dance, with afternoon and evening sessions of dancing on Saturday and Sunday. In a formal War Dance, having once entered the arena, dancers may not leave until the session of dancing is completed. The four headsmen are seated on the west side of the arena, the whipmen on each side of the arena entrance on the east side. The whipman to the left of the headsmen begins to dance counterclockwise (toward the north side of the arena), while the other whipman, the headsmen, and all male dancers begin dancing clockwise. When the two whipmen meet on the west side, the whipman dancing counterclockwise reverses his direction and all continue in a clockwise direction. The same procedure is used when watering the dancers during rest breaks. The third whipman remains on the outside in regular clothing to assist in any matters outside of the arena. All male dancers are permitted to dance each song; however, they must take their seats immediately following the main portion of the song, as only the society whipmen or appointed representatives of guest societies dance the "tail" portion of each song. Regular dancers may dance this part of a song, but must give-away (usually a small amount of money) to someone outside the arena at the end of the song.

Dancers are also restricted from drinking other than when being "watered" by the society, and some dancers refuse drinks offered by outsiders during the dance.[151] A set of Ponca Trot Dance songs is played in the evening dance program.

One of the tenets of the Big Horse Society and especially of the *Ohaku'ema* Society was functioning as a service organization which provided for the needy. This has been maintained by the CWDS to the present day. At both annual formal War Dances, the CWDS continues to give food baskets to elders, orphans, widows, and disabled individuals. The society also redistributed goods and money to families throughout a period of great political and economic strain when the Comanche Tribal Government formally ceased to function, having been temporarily shut down by the United States Government from late 1979 to mid-1981. At this time many of the Comanche tribal services and programs were either cut or temporarily relocated in the jurisdiction of other distant agencies. Further hardships were created when the jobs of many Comanche were cut after the tribe officially ceased to function. The CWDS decided to assist people financially through the redistribution of excess funds which the society had managed to accumulate; the motivation for this came from within the society itself. Applications to receive funds were submitted to the CWDS committee, who met, reviewed the applications, and decided upon a recipient. On an average, the committee was able to help one family every other month during this period from the society funds. While on a relatively small scale, the aid provided by the CWDS was important for two reasons. First, it provided help to some Comanche families until elections could be held, the Comanche tribal government reorganized, and the associated tribal jobs and social services programs returned to the tribal administration. Second, this process followed a form of redistribution performed in the context of Comanche tradition through one of its sodalities—that is, it represented Comanche taking care of Comanche during a period of economic stress in a traditional form.[152]

Although the CWDS does not contain as many martial themes as other Comanche societies, veterans are still honored and recognized. Furthermore, Comanche traditions involving dance, song, kinship, generosity, cooperation, and other forms are maintained in the society's activities. Thus, like the Tuhwi and Little Ponies, the CWDS also serves as an arena for furthering Comanche enculturation on a number of levels. With the retirement of two society headsmen in 1992 and a factional power struggle within the society, one former officer revived a Big Horses Society in the spring of 1995. While this society was originally a Gourd Dancing society, its current activities are focused upon War Dancing and are said to differ little from those of the CWDS.

The Comanche War Scouts

Although of recent formation, the Comanche War Scouts focus on military service for membership and efforts in recognizing and honoring all Comanche veterans. The Comanche War Scouts were organized in February 1990. The founding members were Melvin Kerchee Jr., Charlie Kerchee, Larry McCurtain, and Adolph Paukei, all of whom are direct descendants of members of Troop L, Seventh Cavalry Indian Scouts who were based at Fort Sill from June 30, 1891, to May 31, 1897. The name "War Scouts" was chosen to honor the original Indian scouts at the fort, who were primarily Kiowa, Comanche, and Fort Sill Apache. Because there were sixteen Comanche scouts, the group decided to limit membership to sixteen members.[153] Two runners (errand boys) and a princess, whose terms expire upon graduation from high school, are also included. As a nonprofit, state-chartered group, the War Scouts focus on upholding and teaching Comanche traditions, honoring and respecting elders, paying homage to veterans, and representing the Comanche People in an honorable and dignified manner.[154] Although the group's origins are based upon descent from Troop L scouts, the founding members drew upon the analogy of intertribal alliances of the past in opening up membership to include members of several other tribes as well as one non-Indian. All of these members have reputable service records, some including decorations for combat valor, being wounded in action, and having been held as prisoners of war (POWs).[155]

The War Scouts are a War Dancing society and frequently participate in gatherings, dances, powwows, funerals, parades, and other special occasions. With other Comanche societies and veterans' associations, the War Scouts participate in sponsoring and co-hosting a number of benefit activities throughout the year. Collectively, the members have served in all four branches of the United States military. Thus, they function as a veteran-based service group. Since November 1993 the group has raised funds to erect a fitting monument to honor Comanche veterans who were killed in action (KIA), remain missing in action (MIA), or were taken as prisoners of war while serving in the U.S. armed forces. The monument includes a granite marker with a bronze plaque containing each honoree's military accomplishments, with a sixteen-foot flagpole behind each marker. The POW-MIA or service flags of these individuals are flown on the poles, which are lighted for night display and changed annually during Veterans' Day observations. Currently thirteen individuals have been identified for inclusion in the monument, which is known as the Comanche Circle of Honor. Although Circle of Honor honorees are not required to be enrolled Comanche, all are required to be at least part Comanche. Present honorees include Bruce Klinkole, Myers Wahnee, Doc Pewewardy, and Inman Cloyd Gooday (World War II POWs); Melvin Myers, Eli Hosetosavit, Thomas Chockpoyah, Henry Kosechata, and Henry Conwoop (World War II KIA); Meech Tahsequah (Korea MIA); Dennis Karty (Korea POW); and Russell Eugene Pesewonit and Robert Carlos Pahcheka (Vietnam KIA).[156]

Contemporary Comanche Society Characteristics

While many modern dance organizations and societies do not feel that a direct claim or use of the name of an ancestral society is necessary, it is important at least to acknowledge this difference in discussing such organizations. Kavanagh (1980:98–99) initially categorized the *Tuhwi* differently from the other four societies because it performs "only on special occasions and therefore has no part in the general pow-wows." The frequency of performance and the level of integration with powwows are not the sole distinguishing criteria, as most prereservation Plains societies did not perform dances year-round and many contemporary military societies perform in a nonpowwow context. In his categorization of "ritual" versus "secular" Gourd Dancing, or of "recreations" of old-time societies versus "new" organizations which utilize Gourd Dancing, Kavanagh (1980:102, 113–114) confuses intertribal differences and similarities in military society dances. Having worked with all three tribes and in light of my knowledge of most Southern Plains military societies, I offer clarification concerning this criterion. Kavanagh includes the Kiowa Tia-Piah (Jáifègàu), Kiowa Black Legs (Tǫ́kǫ́gàut), and Apache Manatidie Societies as "ritual versions" of Gourd Dancing, while the "secular version" is found in many tribes who never traditionally had the dance. These groups, he contends, all "utilize a form of the Gourd Dance, but with an attention to ritual that is not present in" secular Gourd Dancing. First, the Kiowa Black Legs and Apache Manatidie Societies are not Gourd Dancing groups and have never had Gourd Dancing or any form of gourd instrument in their regalia. Both societies have four different styles of dance and song and have distinct names for each type of dance (Meadows 1995). Most Gourd Dancing societies use only one form of dance step and, depending upon the performers, the Buffalo Dance as a concluding dance (Meadows 1995). The Kiowa had two Gourd Dancing societies, while Apache state that they never originally had any society using Gourd Dancing, but adopted it from the Kiowa strictly as a social dance in the early 1900s (Meadows 1995). Kavanagh has since revised his characterizations of such groups; however, his general point about the political messages which could be sent via the "ritual" versus the "secular" dances remains valid.[157]

As shown earlier, "chapter organizations" or military societies exhibiting similarities in dances, songs, regalia, taboos, and ceremony existed among several Southern Plains tribes, as shown by the similar "Dog Soldiers" throughout much of the Plains. These similar societies did participate together in intertribal society dances held during each other's prereservation Sun Dances. Thus, the Kiowa Black Legs, Apache Manatidie, and Comanche Tuhwi have numerous similarities, as do the Comanche Little Ponies and Big Horses, the Kiowa Jáifègàu and Chèjánmàu, and the Cheyenne Bow Strings. Kavanagh's (1980, 1982) classification of ritual Gourd Dancing is largely based upon choreography. Although a form of dance steps resembling what is today considered Gourd Dancing (bobbing in place during the chorus of a song and taking several small steps during the refrain) still exists among nearly all Southern Plains tribes, tribal linguistic terminology and classification schemes for different dance steps provide clarification. While other tribes used a similar step, no gourd was used in many of these societies and the dance was therefore not emically viewed as Gourd Dancing. A classification of "ritual" and "secular" societies based on a group's relationship to earlier tribal societies, dance paraphernalia, and a review of all dance types and terminology, and not solely on the presence or absence of Gourd Dancing, is perhaps preferable.

Membership in Comanche societies since their revivals in the 1970s is truly pan-Comanche or pantribal, in that the Comanche have been geographically concentrated since entering the reservation in 1875 and divisional groupings currently hold little political importance. Whereas the Little Ponies and War Dance were formerly Quahada division societies and the Tuhwi a Yamparika division society, their modern manifestations are spoken of by contemporary Comanche as "Comanche societies." Some Comanche speak of a strategy in which a family attempts to have at least one member in each dance society. Contemporary Comanche societies are generally organized around a committee (chair, vice-chair, secretary, treasurer, etc.) or a set of "headsmen," although the Tuhwi and the War Dance Society still maintain a number of traditional offices. Several Comanche Gourd Dancing Societies exist; this is clearly beneficial in that they integrate significant portions of the tribal community, which are in turn often further integrated through the continual co-hosting of two similar societies. The dates of most society's larger events do not overlap or create serious competition and provide integrative events throughout the calendar year. This organizational basis promotes further social and economic cooperation with limited competition for resources and followings, while promoting Comanche enculturation.

Several of the societies and Gourd Dance clubs maintain a princess (*Tananaivi*, Our Young Lady), and members in two societies have indicated that she was considered a sister to all the members until she married. As both archival sources and elders indicate, the four women in the Tuhwi Society appear to have been the only prereservation positions analogous to society "princesses" found in neighboring tribes. Elders indicate that contemporary Comanche princesses developed from elections of Indian Fair tribal queens in the 1930s. Although there are no indications that male youth members or errand boys ever existed in prereservation Comanche societies, one younger man in the recently formed Comanche War Scouts organization publicly inducted a youth in such a position.

Prereservation Comanche military societies continue to affect current Comanche culture, as demonstrated by the fact that military society dances or outgrowths of these forms still constitute the majority of Comanche dance and military activities. Of these, Gourd and War Dancing represent the core of most dances throughout the year. In 1991 the Comanche forty-fifth annual armed forces celebration contained Memorial and Flag Songs, a processional by the Vietnam Era Veterans honor guard, recognition of the Comanche Code Talkers, and performances of veterans' honor dances by the Tuhwi, Gourd Dancing hosted by the Comanche Indian Veterans Association (CIVA), and formal War Dancing (tail dancing) sponsored by the Comanche War Dance Society. Society dances continue to constitute the major social forms at the larger tribal aggregations such as the Comanche Homecoming in July and the Comanche Nation Fair in October (since 1992). Afternoon sessions of Gourd Dancing followed by performances of the Tuhwi and an evening session of War Dance, all society-based forms of dancing, make up the general program of the Comanche Homecoming. The increasingly popular Comanche Nation Fair contains a similar program of society-based dances, in addition to other social activities such as hand games, hymn singing, and horse races. Thus, society-based activities still constitute the core of many forms of public gatherings, which also involve other cultural activities.

There is no doubt that modern manifestations of traditional military ideology and societies are still important in contemporary Comanche culture.

As Kavanagh (1980) discusses, they serve a number of pantribal and integrative social functions and have allowed the Comanche to become more and more integrated as Comanche, since the geographically enforced proximity of their divisional groupings in a reservation context. Activities thus continually provide social and cultural integration for all Comanche interested in participating. Economic redistribution continues to function through the maintenance of giving-away and fundraising in various benefit activities and dances. Elders have expressed the view that dance societies are particularly important for their assistance to society and tribal members and for the preservation of culture through dance, music, values, and material culture. Some feel that this priority has shifted, as everyone in the past was intimately familiar with the culture, and the societies have taken on an important role in reducing the impact of Christianity in terminating traditional Comanche culture, which is still the goal of some Nazarene, Mennonite, and Baptist sects.

Contemporary Comanche military society dances are replete with martial-based ideology and symbols which serve to reinforce traditional Comanche concepts of honoring veterans and their past heritage. Tribal and societal identification and maintenance of ethnicity are fostered through the use of culturally distinct dance societies, which exhibit unique symbol systems of Comanche and individual society identification through song, dance, dress, insignia, and customs, many of which continue to exhibit historical connections to nineteenth-century warrior themes. There are various levels of symbols and meaning for each society. Although all current Comanche organizations are pan-Comanche in membership, many are still associated with particular prereservation divisions. I have frequently heard the Comanche refer to the Little Ponies as a "Quahada society" and the Tuhwi as a "Yapai society," continuing to elaborate on various attributes of each respective society and division. Thus, a name alone can be symbolic of a whole range of data, history, behavioral forms, and traditions—all that a society consists of and stands for.

The Tuhwi Society is replete with symbols (songs, dances, sabers, whips, women's Victory Dresses, distinct behavior, and ethos) that focus on a prereservation Comanche warrior ideology. This maintenance is still important, as reflected by the participation of different generations. From my observations of Comanche powwows, society dances, and tribal events, this maintenance of a martial ideology and identity (modeled from the mid- to late 1800s) is more visible at Tuhwi Society functions than in any other Comanche society, as reflected in the quality and quantity of both the verbal (speeches, references, conversations, etc.) and nonverbal (regalia, insignia, dances, attendance, behavior) expressions and symbols used to convey information about the society. Other behavioral (expectations), kinship, economic (cooperation), and cultural (singing, dancing, cedaring, prayer) elements are also contained within and symbolized by the society and its ritual and nonritual symbols. Thus, the Tuhwi Society serves as a distinct enculturative tool for Tuhwi as well as general Comanche culture.

The Comanche Little Ponies Society contains a whole series of generally similar yet distinct symbols. Membership has allowed me to observe many of the more subtle elements of the society's composition than an external view would have permitted. On the surface the society is viewed as a revival of the nineteenth-century Little Horses Society, which is most frequently described by Comanche (society members as well as nonmembers) as having been composed of young Quahada men who were younger than the Big Horses, were warriors, and fought and protected their tribe. Today such attributes as society insignia, the giveaway, participation as a co-host, dance rattles, or more complex forms such as historical accounts may be brought to mind simply by the name "Little Ponies."

While this military ideology and the connection to the past are frequently acknowledged in public speeches, there are deeper symbolic levels which the society promotes, which also reflect the society's adaptive qualities as an enculturative arena through time. These principles and how they are symbolized through speech, action, or objects are not as easily observed and in many cases are not directly spoken of, but are often understood by the members and those closely associated with the society and are symbolized by the society as a whole. While the Little Ponies Society is now a Comanche society and not just a Quahada society, it has developed into an enculturative arena for all Comanche. The maintenance of Comanche culture—often focusing upon generosity, cooperation, kinship, aid to others, language, and society and tribal history through society activities (dances, giveaways, work projects, benefits, meetings, visiting and eating)—has become a principal emphasis of the society. Thus, these societies have "consolidated" or broadened their functions to become important enculturative tools for continuing Comanche culture on a more general level, based upon a symbol system originating from their earlier military societies. Such complex elements of societal composition may be symbolized by something as simple as the name ("We are *Tuepukunuu*"), regalia or insignia bearing a horse, or more intricate forms such as expectations of appropriate behavior: "That is the Little Pony way of doing things."[158]

These principles, activities, behavior, meanings, and history become symbolized on a number of levels. For example an object such as a Tuhwi saber can be seen as a symbol of the society or as a martial symbol of the society's warrior origins. The society name can convey a whole host of related abstractions beyond the literal content of the name, such as regalia, dances, functions, ancestral members, divisional association, history and development, and social, ritual, and kin behavior. Although there is always a core of somewhat overlapping and shared symbols, the extent to which they are symbolic often varies depending upon an individual's knowledge and reaction to a symbol. Yet all of these symbolic levels return to two central themes: (1) a military or warrior ideology originating from the past and (2) the ongoing role of these societies as adaptive units of social organization which serve as enculturative tools in furthering ethnic identity and cultural maintenance.

Other cultural traditions are linked to a society context. While many family cedarings are still held throughout Comanche country, most public cedarings are generally associated with men's dance society activities, and not with regular dances or powwows. Some elders stated that, although there is still a "brotherhood" quality associated with membership in a society, these bonds are not as tight as they once were due to changes in the type of lifestyle, as reflected in the results of benefit activities. Like residence communities (Kavanagh 1989), contemporary Comanche men's societies do not always exhibit a strong political cohesiveness. While more family-based segments of societies in some cases function together politically, it is not uncommon to see societal factions or society members voting differently even when a fellow member is running in an election. One elder male attributed this to the fact that politics were traditionally more residence band based than division based, and not society based.

Some elders consider the Tuhwi, the Little Ponies, and the War Dance Society more traditional organizations with "tradition"-oriented members, while the Gourd Clan, CIVA, Oklahoma Intertribal Club, and the Comanche Homecoming groups are seen as less traditional groups with more "progressive" members. Several individuals have pointed out that society functions also serve private interests as public forums for seeking, earning, and exhibiting a number of personal social accolades, including recognition of one's status based on descent from an important ancestor or recognition for leading in or sponsoring social functions (generosity).

Despite numerous innovations, traditional Comanche forms of honoring warriors have continued from their lengthy prereservation military history to contemporary military service, as demonstrated by the large receptions held to honor and recognize returning Desert Storm veterans in 1991. As World War II Comanche Code Talker Charles Chibitty stated, "Veterans are still honored a lot. They try to include all the veterans, Desert Storm, Vietnam, and everybody. That's one of the things they hold high in the tribe."[159] Numerous cedarings, prayer meetings, and patriotic rallies were held during Operation Desert Storm for the eighteen Comanche serving overseas. The celebration for the returning Desert Storm veterans was held at the tribal complex, and the cooperative efforts of several of the larger Comanche dance organizations and men's societies made it a truly tribally oriented collective effort. Veterans of all conflicts were recognized with songs, dances, and prayers.

Tribal, martial, and societal pride is becoming increasingly visible, as symbolized by numerous secular and ritual forms. Many younger Comanche can be seen sporting colorful T-shirts, caps, jackets, and other miscellaneous items such as key chains, water bottles, and license plates with a picture of a mounted warrior on a colorful background and the creed "Comanche Nation." Powwow flyers (advertisements), T-shirts, and other items bearing the same design often bear the slogan "Lords of the Southern Plains." One member of the *Tuhwi* Society recently carried a dance shield with this design painted on it, but without the words, in a society dance. Although the slogan "Lords of the Southern Plains" derives from the 1952 Wallace and Hoebel ethnography, *The Comanches: Lords of the South Plains*, the associated image and its constituent symbols of the Comanche as dominant warriors of the Southern Plains are proudly embraced by many contemporary Comanche. Similarly, the Comanche Little Pony members have their society name and logo on several items, including bumper stickers, beaded medallions, T-shirts, and vests. Each society contains a number of distinct but generally similar symbols and functions as a larger symbol in itself. The consciousness of the earlier Comanche warrior tradition and the associated symbols (songs, dances, dress, societal kinship, respect and honoring of veterans, cedaring, *communitas*, cooperation) continue to the present day and remain a necessary, vital, and adaptive part of contemporary Comanche culture. Many of these cultural elements are promoted through the enculturative functions of contemporary Comanche military and dance societies.

6 COMPARISON AND CONCLUSIONS

This chapter summarizes the larger patterns in the development of military societies through the four designated periods: prereservation (pre-1875), reservation (1875–1900), postreservation (1900–1945), and post–World War II or contemporary (post-1945). It concludes with a discussion of the importance of these sodalities for social organization, the role of martial symbols as enculturative agents, and future prospects of these organizations for Southern Plains Indian communities.

PRERESERVATION (PRE-1875)

Data ranging from 1680 (Hennepin 1698:280; Abel 1939:187) to 1803–1804 (Abel 1939:116, 245; Thwaites 1904:1:130) suggest that the idea of men's societies existed among some western woodlands groups prior to full migration onto the Plains. While detailed accounts of prehorse-era society functions are lacking, available data indicate a role in maintaining social control. Policing of periodic bison hunting excursions was also likely in the prehorse era, as an adaptation to new larger communal hunting of bison in an open Plains environment which required large-scale group coordination that differed from forested woodlands hunting techniques. Such methods were maintained by posthorse-era Prairie-Plains groups well into the 1800s and later adapted by the Eastern Shoshone venturing onto the western Plains to hunt bison. By the early 1800s military societies are recorded throughout the Plains. While it is presently impossible to derive the precise origin of many of the older Southern Plains societies, data suggest that most were acquired while residing in the Northern Plains prior to migrating southward or at least diffused from this direction (Lowie 1916a). Some of the earliest accounts of Sioux (Thwaites 1904:1:130), Kiowa (Meadows 1995:64), Comanche (Berlandier 1969:70–75, 117–118), and other tribal military societies (Wissler 1916a) suggest that contrary societies were one of the earliest, most widespread forms, and possibly the original type of Plains military society.

Prereservation military societies performed several economic, martial, social, and political functions that were vitally important to the integration and maintenance of their respective Plains communities. The policing of the bison hunt was clearly one of the most significant and earliest-documented economic functions. Were societies necessary for the ecological adaptation of Plains bison hunting or simply useful for various sociointegrational purposes? It could be argued that, while they were not the only possible form of adaptation (as demonstrated by various forms of civil and hunt police used by sedentary village horticulturalists), they were functionally necessary and were certainly the more logical adaptation for posthorse mobile hunters and gatherers lacking clan-based organization. The increased documentation and distribution of posthorse-era military societies suggest that they were a functional necessity for many Plains groups who maintained several military sodalities. Groups such as the Shoshone developed two military sodalities for occasional bison hunting and camp moves out onto the Plains, also reflecting the military sodality's importance and functional necessity for a Plains adaptation. Military societies ensured greater equality during communal hunts, but this was from the vantage point of maintaining the status quo, as hunters from wealthier families with better horses retained clear advantages. Yet greater equality appears in civil matters, as cases involving the punishment of one's own high-status relatives are recorded (Richardson 1940; Llewellyn and Hoebel 1941). In some aspects societies provided psychological insurance, while in others they ensured actual equality. Increased military sodality functions suggest that the ecological impacts on tribal subsistence strategies and social integration developing in the posthorse post-Plains migration period created new adaptations. Societies developed and expanded to meet some of these needs.

Francis Haines's (1976) assertion that Plains men's societies became more important as warfare increased is reasonable, despite the scarcity of early accounts. "Unafraid Of" (commonly called Dog Soldier) Societies appear to have been one of the earliest documented and most widespread forms of Plains societies (Lowie 1916a:889, Wissler 1916b). The role of military societies as collective raiding and warfare units should not be discounted despite limited documentation, as sources clearly indicate that some Kiowa, Comanche, Apache, Cheyenne (Grinnell 1983), Pawnee (Murie 1914:573), Lakota (Wissler 1912:93; Lowie 1916a:898), and Crow (Lowie 1983) military societies once engaged in individual society raiding and warfare activities. Accounts of the Kiowa Cáuitémgòp, Comanche Los Lobos, and Cheyenne Bow String Society indicate that unisocietal ventures were common prior to circa 1840. Such ventures later ceased due to extermination or significant losses of entire societies that made tactical errors in battle and increased horses, guns, and military posts, resulting in outgoing parties of mixed membership or multisociety membership. Tribal histories indicate the prior existence of additional Plains societies and that the content of individual tribal military society systems periodically changed with the addition and cessation of individual societies. The introduction of the horse and firearms led to the decline of large groups of warriors in most activities except larger-level revenge raids (Secoy 1953). As smaller parties were advantageous for nocturnal horse raiding and as firearms increased the martial power of individuals, large raiding parties were generally neither necessary nor desirable. Numerous Anglo military posts were established by the 1850s (Nye 1937), forming several links across the Southern Plains. Increasing cavalry patrols made travel by large parties more difficult without detection. Yet despite these changes, societies still served as the primary arena for celebrating collective martial successes and continued their socially integrative roles.

In Plains Indian social organization, military societies were the largest forms of sodalities, and the role of these organizations has been grossly overshadowed and underexamined. As sodalities, military societies solidified social organization on numerous levels, performed a number of integrative functions that residential family groups could not, and served the needs of the community above the interests of particular lineages. These included the policing of the Sun Dance encampment, tribal movements, and communal bison hunts. Although powerful residence and tribal bands often focused on a primary family containing a band leader and a large, supportive kin base centered around several male relatives, the role of military societies was significant. As the largest form of sodality, military societies included the largest and farthest-reaching political, social, military, and economic segments of a tribe, affecting not only the members but their interconnected families as well. Many Plains military societies functioned as economic aid groups to those in need, such as the Apache Manatidie (McAllister 1935), the Arikara Straight Head and Buffalo Societies (Lowie 1915c:661–662), the Ponca men's Helocka and women's Nodan Society (Skinner 1915b: 784–785, 790), and societies among the Hidatsa (Bowers 1992:210) and Iowa and Cree (Skinner 1915a:523, 1915c:691). Economic redistribution was also a common function among the Ponca, Kiowa, and Comanche War Dance societies. Socially, societies provided a whole series of dances, feasts, and activities, many of which completed the necessary preparations for tribally integrative religious ceremonies. It is from these Plains military society ceremonial origins that today's contemporary Plains-based powwow descends.

The widespread institution of society brothers through nonblood kinship formed an ingeniously integrative force by linking two sets of previously unrelated families into a horizontally based nonblood kin grouping that was considered to be as close as biological siblings. This arrangement formed cooperative economic alliances on larger levels (between the families of two partners) that were further linked (between the members and families of each society) through the principle of all society members being "brothers." Thus, all families of a society's membership constituted another, larger set of relatives. These relationships resulted in many interpersonal relations derived from society membership throughout the annual cycle. Similar Iroquois nonblood kinship relations (Snow 1994:73) suggest the widespread existence of such social institutions. Patricia Albers (1993) discusses how widespread and formalized friendships and fictive kinship through adopted sibling or parent-child relationships were integrally linked to Plains trade, the diffusion of religious and military sodality rituals, and the activation of social labor in the deployment of resources within and across interethnic boundaries. She notes (1993:121) "the convergence of the Plains nomads' kinship systems along generation relationships in military sodalities and under other situations promoting joint collaboration across tribal boundaries." Fictive kinship and intermarriage increased the formation of chains of social connections affecting the production and exchange of specialized goods. Dominant residence band leaders in many Plains populations were often military society leaders, who brought a much greater extended supportive kin base due to their influence in their fraternal brotherhood.

As most males were vertically linked to some form of a large extended kin base, the linking of society brothers expanded this connection by linking two previously unconnected and larger vertical kin bases horizontally. The principal of cross-band membership in men's societies and the kin relations with and obligations to fellow society "brothers" in other bands provided an economic support group for fellow members and the tribe as a whole through charitable society functions. This horizontally based nonconsanguineal kin group functioned somewhat like a clan-based system found in other tribes, in that societies provided aid and performed a range of duties, based upon the circumstances and kin (including military society kin) relations. Plains military sodality systems may have been an adaptation for groups lacking clan-based social organization, as these sodalities were most developed among those groups. Because fellow society members were obligated to help one another during periods of difficulty and any war-related or natural catastrophe generally affected an entire residence band, the fraternal link of a men's sodality ensured a greater resource base. A smaller set of consanguineal brothers located in the same residence band would be more likely to have been affected by the same calamity. As such, military societies were often characterized and functioned as charitable aid groups, reinforcing the strong Plains emphasis on pity, generosity, and charitable aid.

The legal and coercive powers of military societies were significant; societies had the authority and power to check and balance the interests of vertically integrated kin-based segments, for the interests of the whole, through the horizontally linked sodality. Societies enforced the decisions of tribal councils and religious leaders at the most crucial periods of greatest sociopolitical integration. Mishkin (1940), Richardson (1940), and Llewellyn and Hoebel (1941) provide numerous examples of societies exercising these roles, which they were able to do because of their organizational basis and because they were communally vested with both the necessary power and authority. Societies were not consanguineally based, so they promoted social stability and tribal solidarity.

Data concerning the Kiowa and Apache societies and other Plains populations (Cheyenne, Ponca, Iowa, Crow) point to the existence of a general widespread form of de facto age-grading in those populations previously considered to have ungraded or coordinate societies (Meadows n.d.b). Widespread characteristics involving children and adult societies, differential assignment of duties, varied forms of intersocietal rivalry, and association of general age differences with individual war rank, wealth and social status, order in society parades, and general social grading in relation to society membership and ranking all point toward this conclusion.

As martially oriented groups, military societies epitomized the very essence of a warrior ideology through the ritual symbols expressed in ceremonies and culturally sanctioned behavior and goals which they publicly embraced, exhibited, and fostered. While a martial ideology is only one element of the social content of many Plains groups, this ideology was elevated when needed to become ethos, as reflected by the enthusiastic spirit in War Journey gatherings, military society dances, coup recitations, and warfare contexts. In cultures which elevated the warrior as the ideal role model for an adult male to emulate, military societies provided the collective and ever present model. In turn, societies constituted a major arena for economic redistribution through the individual and family giving-away of resources captured on raids and in battle, to demonstrate the ability of a leader to provide for his following, to demonstrate generosity, to increase social status, and to honor and recognize military deeds. Individually, societies functioned as social clubs, but more importantly as an arena for the display and advertisement of martial prowess, which was a primary means for social mobility. This sometimes included heated competition between societies (the Crow Foxes and Lumpwoods) to outdo one another in feats of war, hunting, and romance (Lowie 1983; McGinnis 1990:166).

A whole host of cultural items including duties, songs, dances, coup recitations, insignia, social ranking, and oral history functioned (1) as symbols of a shared martial ideology and (2) as components of a larger symbol, the individual military society, which (3) reflected yet another symbolic level, the culture itself. Although military societies were largely secular, their role in fostering and promoting martial ability and in recognizing martial achievement was a crucial part of their respective cultures and was inseparably linked with many tribal cultural and religious systems centering around the acquisition of supernatural and sometimes warfare-related power. In some ways, warfare and religious systems supported and sanctioned each other.

Most prereservation Plains military societies may be defined as (1) not priesthood, moietylike, or clan or town oriented, (2) not temporarily appointed on a nonsodality basis, (3) voluntary in membership with the exception of some contrary societies, (4) containing cross-band membership, (5) either age-graded or coordinately organized, (6) having a group name which is generally associated with some aspect of their dress, dance, duty, or associated group ideology, (7) conducting limited meetings in conjunction with tribal aggregations, (8) sometimes (but not always) engaging in warfare as a collective unit (prior to circa 1850), and (9) focusing on warfare and individual deeds including coup recitations and performances celebrating and enhancing martial activities, as opposed to doctoring and shield societies focusing upon specific forms of war power and healing. It is the last criterion, the visible promotion of a common central theme in the form of a warrior tradition or a warrior ideology, which at specific times can be argued to be an ethos, which holds a distinguishing and dominant part in the organization, functions, and history of these organizations.

THE RESERVATION PERIOD, 1875–1900: CHANGES AND FACTORS OF DECLINE

Why did the vast majority of Southern Plains military societies cease to function in the late nineteenth century? There are various causes, some of which influenced some tribes at an earlier date and to a stronger degree than others, but all of which had significant impact. Immediately following the

Civil War, the United States increased efforts to subdue all remaining autonomous Plains tribes, because they were no longer needed to supply horses through trade and because of Anglo desires to complete western expansion and Manifest Destiny. The systematic slaughter of bison by Anglo hunters and fur takers in the 1870s eliminated the core of the native subsistence base, inducing starvation and a growing reliance on annuity rations. The early 1870s were an extremely tumultuous period for Southern Plains peoples. Following starvation and economic collapse, Southern Plains tribes were finally relocated onto reservations in 1875 after a series of raids and skirmishes dubbed the Red River War. With reservation confinement and declining bison herds, tribes were reduced to relying on annuity rations and occasional longhorn cattle, which were often inadequate in amount, late in arrival, and unfit for human consumption. The end of warfare considerably weakened the role and importance of Plains military societies in fostering military spirit and recounting martial exploits, a primary method for enhancing one's social status within the community. The end of warfare immediately affected societies requiring combat deeds for membership. Many of the so-called Dog Soldier societies (such as the Kiowa Qóichégàu and Apache Klintidie) soon ended, as it was impossible for new recruits to acquire combat deeds and thus eligibility. The Cheyenne Dog Soldiers remained intact longer, due to the unusual circumstances whereby their membership had encompassed much of the tribal population by the 1870s.

Many societies which continued to meet and hold dances became more commemorative, honorific, hereditary, and socially based, as men's war records became frozen in time. While the ideals, ritual symbols, and ceremonies associated with the older military societies were still largely intact, the means upon which they were based were no longer available. As a result, younger men born too late to have engaged in combat were initiated as members. As Kiowa military society membership lists reflect, some societies either dropped combat requirements or focused upon inducting individuals from socially prominent families, many of whom were descendants of earlier members, out of necessity. Arapaho age-graded societies also lowered age requirements for membership drastically during the reservation period (Lowie 1916a:971).

Population decline from diseases and warfare also affected the vitality of military societies. Sudden population declines made it numerically impossible for smaller tribes like the Naishan Apache to sustain such organizations. The ongoing depopulation of Southern Plains tribes from 1875 to 1920 would have left nearly every family in a frequent if not continual state of mourning, and the widespread practice of not dancing until the next Sun

Dance (up to a year's duration) undoubtedly weakened participation. While most Southern Plains societies continued to meet during the early reservation years, many of their functions were severely curtailed in comparison to those of the past. With confinement to reservations and no available Southern Plains bison by 1879, the previously significant duties surrounding the policing of tribal hunts were gone. The economic base of the Southern Plains tribes had collapsed with the systematic slaughter of the bison by Anglos, and tribes were attempting to regroup in terms of both subsistence and social organization. Tribal communities were struggling through a difficult period in which adjustment to an annuity-based subsistence did not readily facilitate the continuation of older social forms, including large aggregations and tribal leadership structures (continually undermined by government policies and Indian agents), which often required large amounts of resources for feeding, entertaining, and giving-away.

The suppression of tribal-level integrative religious ceremonies like the Sun Dance by government and Christian missionaries led to a further decline of more social forms. Engaging in agency-prohibited activities, such as the attempted Kiowa Sun Dance of 1890, resulted in threats and rumors of United States military intervention, compelling obedience. With the cessation of the Sun Dance by 1890, Kiowa and Apache societies rapidly declined, as Comanche societies already had. Some Indian agents threatened to withhold rations for a variety of purposes, forcing accommodation to the agent's wishes (Buntin 1931:36, 39). Some agents later threatened to withhold Indian grass lease payments, the primary source of Indian income between 1890 to 1910, if they did not abandon traditional customs including dancing and giving-away. With the end of warfare, bison hunts, and the Sun Dance, societies lost their functional context. They no longer had any direct link to the central pandivisional or pantribal integrative religious ceremonies and their associated social duties and functions. With the end of the Sun Dance, societies no longer had a focus for their ceremonies. Missionizing by numerous Christian groups further sought to eradicate all native sociocultural forms. Many societies that ceased meeting at this time were never revived.

The prereservation and reservation periods reflect Jacobs's (1987) stages of (1) "congenial relations" in which exchange and trade give way to encroachment, overt hostility and warfare, and defeat, resulting in bewilderment and loss of respect for one's own culture; and (2) an "era of depopulation and despondence" in which native groups, beset with a host of various problems, experience the decline of many existing social structures, often developing a scorn for many indigenous customs. Turner's (1968:22) discussion of the decline of tribal religions and associated ritual symbols also applies. Yet, as Turner points out, these initial losses are followed by reconstructive periods which attempt to provide an adaptive counterstrategy to cultural and religious extinction. As the establishment of a new social order developed, it brought initial instability followed by social cohesion and the formation of new symbols. Once the period of initially rapid social change slowed and stabilized in the reservation period, traditional rituals infused with new symbols were revived (Turner 1968). Two such Southern Plains adaptations involved service as agency policemen and cavalry scouts.

Agency Police

The Indian agency police was formed in May 1878, primarily as an alternative to reliance on United States military forces and to relieve the anomalous conditions that existed on reservations due to an absence of laws applicable to native peoples (Hagan 1966:42, 154). For Anglos, native police forces expedited the acculturation process by undermining the traditional authority structure and discouraging cultural practices deemed undesirable by the agents. Indian police and court systems provided a reasonable solution to the problem of providing law and order on reservations and educated native peoples in elements considered vital by the encapsulating society. While agency policemen served as a bridge between two cultures, they also occupied in some respects a position in the native communities similar to those of the older soldier societies by administering social control, formerly through the chiefs and tribal councils and now through the Indian agents (Hagan 1966:162, 174).

Although insufficient pay was always an issue among agency police forces (Hagan 1966), the job provided a regular income. In addition to full rations, KCA agency police officers received ten dollars per month, while privates received five dollars (Buntin 1931:62). More importantly perhaps, the position provided a means of gaining status in a period of rapid changes, through the power and prestige associated with the position. Like later army scouts, agency policemen introduced new symbols of authority that were linked to older warrior traditions: uniforms and badges (distinct regalia) and the right to bear arms (military weapons) to ensure law and order (society-vested coercive authority) among the people (Buntin 1931:62).[1] Like scouting, police service allowed for the expression of more traditional warrior society roles, albeit in a modified form, as duties among the KCA were confined largely to reservation contexts and involved no active scouting or combat. Some policemen were involved in many crime-related cases in the early stages of the agency forces. One elder born in 1897 recounted that when he was a youth policemen did very little actual policing and, although on the police payroll, often performed maintenance or general labor at the agency and Indian schools.[2] As policemen gained in the embodiment of a growing extratribal power and the opportunity to exercise power and command respect, they evoked some relationship with traditional warrior and policing society duties and values and provided at least a constricted means of compensation in a period of rapid social change. Anthony McGinnis (1990 : 146) found similar developments among Northern Plains Indian policemen. Those KCA who served as United States marshals appear to have had similar experiences. Several KCA elders have stated to me that their ancestors were proud to serve as an agency policeman or U.S. marshal and "wear that badge."[3] While a limited number of positions were filled mainly by young men, they offered a means of choice and the acquisition of a new set of martial-related symbols that provided some link with their sense of a military past, which some obviously chose and found useful. Several Kiowa who belonged to high-status military societies and were cavalry scouts also served as agency policemen.[4]

Scouting in the United States Army

Scouting provided another means to retain some form of veteran status. While military combat was unavailable to the recently relocated Southern Plains tribes, some occupations provided a taste, albeit small, of the past. During the "Red River War" of 1874–1875 several KCA members served as scouts in persuading the "holdouts" of their tribes to surrender. Unlike the Pawnee in the Northern Plains and numerous southwestern Apachean groups, there was no combat service for the KCA scouts; resistance was ended quickly with a minimum use of scouts and no real combat. Limited scouting was performed by individuals to persuade remaining tribal members to surrender, which occurred uneventfully. A small contingent periodically served as scouts, primarily to carry messages to outposts, guard payrolls, and police for deserters and outlaws on the reservation.[5]

Further scouting by KCA individuals did not develop until 1891, some sixteen years after the end of active warfare and entering the reservation. In March 1891 the secretary of war authorized the enlistment of an Indian contingent for each cavalry and infantry regiment, which provided an opportunity for men to serve in a military fashion. Under Lieutenant Hugh L. Scott at Fort Sill, Oklahoma, Troop L of the Seventh Cavalry functioned from June 30, 1891, to May 31, 1897. L-Troop, as it was known, was composed largely of Kiowa, Fort Sill Apache, and a few Comanche. While these scouts resided with their families in tipis located at Fort Sill just north of the trading post, their duties included no combat action; they served primarily by policing the reservation for trespassers, land squatters, illegal cattlemen, timber thieves, and whiskey peddlers; leading hunting parties for visiting Anglo military dignitaries; and providing deer and turkey for the officers' holiday dinners. Scouting duties were not onerous, and much time was spent in camp playing the card game monte (Mooney 1898:223, 362; Nye 1962: 261–262).[6]

Yet scouting was beneficial for Southern Plains tribes. For the Plains as a whole, Thomas Dunlay (1982:201–207) has shown that there were definite advantages to be gained from cooperating with whites by scouting, including material gain, more favorable governmental and agency treatment, and the chance to adjust to a set of radically changing conditions in ways that were relatively easy and familiar. Although benefits varied, resistance or noncooperation would have produced less than was otherwise obtained. While scouting provided families with a reliable source of income during a period of poor living conditions, the position held some importance for individuals raised in prereservation cultures. The role of the KCA scouts was largely in a postconfinement, reservation context. Although the older men had had the opportunity to distinguish themselves and had their war exploits to recount, their war records were frozen. Newer generations had few traditional ways to gain status as men or warriors and thus little to look forward to according to traditional criteria.

Higher-ranking elder KCA warriors may have viewed full-time scouting with disdain, as those enrolled in L-Troop were largely younger men; their birthdates indicate that most had little or no battle experience. However, some scouts were well-known warriors with noted battle records such as Háunèmídâu (Unafraid of Danger), a son of the chief Jòhâusàn (Little Bluff Recess/Concavity, tribal chief from 1833 to 1866). Review of L-Troop, Kiowa agency police, and Kiowa military society membership rosters demonstrates that many younger society members, who were largely noncombat veterans, served as scouts and agency police.[7]

Having been forcibly stripped of the means to achieve status in the traditional manner, younger men were forced to adapt to an existence based on annuities and agriculture and thus had no traditional means for distinguishing themselves as warriors. Yet maintaining the use of scouts only inhibited the larger Anglo desires toward total native assimilation (Dunlay 1982). In retrospect, the continuation of mobile, horse-based, martial practices and ideology in scouting perpetuated the very processes which Anglo reformers and missionaries spouting acculturation were attempting to stop.

Scouting provided a new means of gaining status, and for the younger scouts, most of whom had limited prereservation warfare experiences, perhaps a means for gaining martial status. With the loss of all KCA Sun Dances and the decline of military societies by 1890, the presence of L-Troop between 1892 and 1897 came just when younger men were faced with being without an active means of acquiring, and even expressing, traditional male roles of martial ideology and status. As Dunlay summarizes (1982:207),

> scout service held an attraction for men who regarded war as their proper occupation and horses and weapons as the attributes of manhood. It was possible, at least for a time, to adjust to a new and trying situation, and a changing way of life, in a more acceptable fashion than that demanded by the Indian agents. The adjustment was less drastic, and partially on their own terms. The military, which had to regard organized violence as within the range of normal human activity, could accept aspirations and emotions that the humanitarians could not.

Scouting, albeit brief, undoubtedly helped to fill this void. Although it still subjected native peoples to Anglo authority and life in a culturally prejudiced manner, scouting provided a form of accommodation and adaptation that was more consistent with native ideology. In retrospect, scouting provided a choice that aided in their great adaptability to trying circumstances, although not always in the ways white reformers intended. This new means of gaining prestige was important for some, as evidenced by the fact that the descendants of L-Troop members still espouse great pride in their ancestors' service as scouts.[8] Michael Tate's (1977:115) assessment that the scouts probably conserved more than they destroyed also applies for the KCA, but in a more cultural context. Like police service, scouting reflects Turner's (1968:22) summation that the symbols associated with revivals are "hybridizations between old and new" ritual symbols which are often difficult to distinguish. In providing a temporary means of attaining respected martial-derived status, scouting produced syncretic changes by blending old symbols such as martially focused group formations, distinct dress and regalia, and societally vested coercive authority with newly acquired and symbolic forms of uniforms, functions, and agendas.

Because military society membership rosters exist only for the Kiowa, it is difficult to estimate the extent of the correlation between society membership and later service as scouts and agency police among the other Southern Plains tribes. However, such correlations exist: Rolling Pony, an Apache Manatidie Society whipman, later served as policeman. Review of the ages of Kiowa policemen who served between 1880 and 1895 indicates that most were born during the 1850s, had limited prereservation combat experience, and were middle-aged as policemen, the age group which normally contained the majority of vested coercive authority in prereservation times. While these included no earlier known (pre-1875) military society leaders, Sankadota, one of the last apprentice members of the Qóichégàu, was made head of police when the force was organized on October 1, 1880 (Buntin 1931:63; Corwin 1962:152), which suggests a possible connection between his socially upward military society status and his early position as chief of police. Thus, many younger prominent society members who would have become society leaders served in agency positions as scouts and police.

New Cultural Forms

During the reservation period, several new and growing religious forms also diverted interest away from older society functions. Several Kiowa "prophets" attempted in vain to revive the nearly exterminated bison herds during the 1880s, leaving the people in further dismay while attempting to adapt to their new existence (Mooney 1898:347–350, 356–357; Marriott 1945: 142–154; Nye 1962:268–270). By 1890 the Ghost Dance, Peyotism, and Christianity had each developed a significant following, varying in intensity among respective communities and tribes. In 1890 the Kiowa Ghost Dance provided initial encouragement, but it was denounced by Ahpeahtone (Áfîtàu, Wooden Lance), who had visited the Paiute Messiah Wovoka, temporarily abandoned, then later revived in altered form (Mooney 1896, 1898). The Kiowa Ghost Dance continued until 1917; according to eyewitness consultants, sacred prayers and limited numbers of trances continued to this time. Individual Kiowa communities also held monthly Ghost Dance singing practices and encampments.

Peyote, which had existed among the Naishan Apache since the 1870s, spread among the Comanche and Kiowa by 1885. Peyotism provided an "expressionistic" escape from many of the Anglo-induced pressures placed upon native peoples in the late 1800s (Ryan 1969). Gaining further popularity after the initial introduction of the Ghost Dance, Peyotism surpassed many traditional religious practices. As a new aggregative form with all-night ceremonies initially limited primarily to all-male participation, Peyotism provided an alternative socioreligious integrative form which, focusing on a pacifistic and expressionist emphasis, indirectly drew participation away from the older military society activities.[9]

Between 1880 and 1941 Christianity undoubtedly had the most detrimental effect on military society functions. Unlike other native religious forms, Christian missionaries explicitly mandated the cessation of nearly all native cultural practices. Although initial attempts by Quakers and Episco-palians were unsuccessful, missionizing by Baptists, Methodists, Catholics, Presbyterians, and later Pentecostals converted many KCA individuals and prominent leaders to Christianity (Kracht 1989:39). Methodist churches were reportedly more lenient toward dancing. Several Kiowa were expelled from the Saddle Mountain and Red Stone Baptist Churches for having at-tended dances.[10] Despite these numerous religious forms, great diversity ex-isted: John J. Methvin, the first Methodist missionary among the Kiowa, encountered great variation in beliefs held by Kiowa groups he encountered from 1887 to 1920 (Kracht 1989:39). Overall, Christianity led to the decline of dancing and traditional practices among large segments of tribes who converted. As Kiowa elder Atwater Onco recalled of his youth in the 1920s and 1930s:

> In a certain area [time] there, everything kind of died out and Christian-ity had pretty much a hold on everybody. . . . At the time I was growing as a little boy, like I said, Christianity was pretty strong among the Kio-was and the Native American Church. So far as like your Jáifè dancing, all these dances were kind of held down because of you know, everybody, their social life was around church oriented gatherings, Baptists and Methodists.[11]

This assimilationist strategy has continued among some Christian Indian families; however, recently many families have been rediscovering and par-taking in traditional dances and activities that their families had been sepa-rated from for decades. With the end of the Sun Dance and its associated roles and functions in the larger aggregative ceremonies, shield, men's and women's warrior, and tribal medicine societies all began to decline. Al-though some items were being physically cared for, their associated uses, knowledge, and beliefs were not being actively passed on. While elements continued in syncretic form as a part of the new religious forms, many older traditions were being surpassed by Peyotism and Christianity. Following Ryan's (1969) discussion of "syncretic integration," involving a pattern of adjustment during a coalescence of "alternative systems," Kracht (1989) has shown how traditional Kiowa and Christian religions were combined to produce a distinct entity. What other effects did this period of restabiliza-tion have upon the older military societies and dancing?

The Grass Dance

The rapid diffusion of the War-Omaha-Grass Dance in the late nineteenth century provided another impetus that led to the decline of older warrior societies. The Grass Dance was a diffused Omaha warrior society dance, which the KCA initially accepted as such and placed in the existing pattern of respective tribal military society complexes (Sun Dance duties, organizational roles, fictive kin partners). The end of the Kiowa Sun Dance in 1890 prevented the Óhòmò Society, acquired in 1884, from becoming fully involved in the more traditional society warfare and policing functions. This relationship was short-lived, and the Óhòmò Society soon came to dominate the older tribal societies.

Many earlier Omaha warfare requirements and ceremonies were omitted or altered according to individual tribal tastes as groups accepted, changed, and later passed the dance on to others. Lowie (1915a:833) notes similar changes among the Shoshone and Lakota; the latter are said to have heavily secularized the original Omaha version after 1865. The dynamic dress and dance styles quickly came into vogue for young men, many of whom quickly left the declining and "honorary" older societies to join various new "War Dance" societies. This process occurred across the Plains. As Lowie (1915c: 663–664) notes for the Arikara, "The Young Buffalo continued their dance for a time, but when the Grass Dance was introduced, many members left to join the new society"; "The Black Mouths decreased in numbers owing to the popularity of the Grass Dance." Pliny Earle Goddard (1914:470) demonstrates the rapid attraction of the burgeoning new society for younger Sarsi men ("Among the Sarci it was clearly a social organization, largely in the control of the younger members of the tribe"), as do James Murie (1914: 624) for the Pawnee and Regina Flannery (1947) for the Gros Ventre. Both the 1935 Santa Fe notes and Mooney's fieldnotes contain several individual histories demonstrating how Kiowa men left previous societies to join the Óhòmò Society.[12] It becomes clear that during the last decade of the nineteenth century the burgeoning War Dance Societies, with their new dress and dance styles, greatly attracted the younger generation of men and surpassed the declining older military societies. The adoption of War Dance Societies by the KCA suggests Ryan's (1969) concept of "syncretic integration": the large-scale acceptance of the War Dance represented more than a late diffusion of another form of military society; the War Dance Societies, being a syncretic product of numerous native "alternative systems," offered a cultural adaptation that was more attractive to native peoples, while remaining more conducive to the ongoing Anglo-induced changes. With numerous social changes and the establishment of a period of relative restabilization, the stage for further social change through cultural revivals was nearing.

We may characterize reservation-period (1875–1900) military societies as primarily declining forms of their earlier manifestations that, while still focusing upon the enculturative principles, ideology, and ethos of their pre-reservation antecedent forms, developed more toward informal hereditary and honorific societies, which celebrated past achievements while continuing many of the earlier social aspects. These groups in turn declined due to lack of access to warfare, opportunities for integrative ceremonies, competition with new socioreligious forms, loss of primary functions in integrative contexts, and the diffusion of the burgeoning Omaha-Grass-War Dancing Societies.

POSTRESERVATION: 1900–1941
Allotments

The formation of individual allotments, implemented by the 1887 Dawes Act and enacted between 1900 and 1912, further restructured KCA residence communities which had formed during the early reservation period. While the Kiowa received less than 500,000 acres in individual allotments, over two million acres were opened for non-Indian settlement on June 26, 1910. This produced a mosaic or checkerboarding of land held by Indians of different tribes, whites, blacks, and Hispanics. Like many Oklahoma Indians, the KCA have been in contact with and influenced by a number of non-Indian cultures since the turn of the century. Although some groups remained somewhat clustered together, allotments made community integration more difficult. Such agency disruptions of traditional family structures further altered prior community structures, and pressure to end polygynous marriages broke up families.[13] The early 1900s were economically difficult for most Oklahoma native peoples. Several elders commented that during the Dust Bowl and the Great Depression of the 1920s and 1930s they had few finances, little to eat, and even less that they could afford to give-away at dances.[14] Individuals often had to request permission from the agent to hold communal gatherings, which were often called "picnics." The agency withheld rations and annuity payments until affidavits were signed by blacklisted individuals promising not to dance or give-away. Nevertheless, many endured and continued to hold cultural activities on remote allotments, disguised as "picnics."

The growth of the War Dance resulted in a lack of interest in older society traditions among the younger generations; in some instances a shortage of willing participants to maintain the older society functions affected the Apache Manatidie. This trend occurred throughout the Plains. As Alfred Bowers (1992:211) describes for the Hidatsa, "In recent years, societies went together to purchase other dances such as the Grass and Night Grass dances brought to the tribe by the Sioux. This destroyed the age-grade character of the system and the societies quickly died out through failure of the younger men to continue the purchases." The rise in the late nineteenth century of the diffused Omaha, Grass, or War Dance later led to the emergence of more social and contest dancing—the evolution of the Plains "powwow." Although some Kiowa and Apache military societies had been revived and were conducting annual dances by 1908–1912, they were relatively small, annual community-based events that were struggling. They were attended by significant segments of the tribe, but participation focused upon particular communities and did not function on the same level of past pantribal integration. KCA military societies were clearly being surpassed by the increasing regularity of the burgeoning social powwow. For most Plains tribes, the War Dance evolved as the central form of dancing during the 1880–1910 period and dominated all dance forms by 1920.

World War I

The United States' entrance into World War I in 1917 provided the first opportunity for most Native Americans as a whole to regain veteran status since entering a reservation (1875 for the KCA). The native response to the war was a tremendous outburst of patriotism and national devotion. Native American participation in World War I included nearly 10,000 individuals in the United States Armed Forces by 1918, with 75 to 85 percent joining by voluntary enlistment (Haynie 1984: 7; Bernstein 1991: 22; Parman 1994: 60).[15] This significant turnout by Native Americans came at a time when some were still denied United States citizenship and the ability to share in the constitutional rights for which they were willing to fight and die.

Nearly 17,000 Indians served in World War I. Compared with the Indian population at the time, Indians volunteered and were inducted at a rate nearly twice as high as that of the rest of the American population (Holm 1996: 99). To represent this reacquisition of veteran status, servicemen were given heroes' farewell celebrations, frequently to the accompaniment of military society and War Journey songs and dances. Their returns in the winter of 1918–1919 were even greater occasions for celebration as large contingents met incoming servicemen at local train stations. Throughout the summer of 1919 numerous families sponsored traditional homecomings in the form of large community or tribal encampments, at which Scalp and Victory Dances and in some cases powwows of a social nature were held. The family of each returning veteran usually sponsored such a celebration.

In 1919 Commissioner of Indian Affairs Cato Sells complained that many
Indian veterans had returned from the war in France, where they had
"counted coup" in modern form, only to take part in Victory Dances, watch
as their sisters and mothers performed Scalp Dances, and be ritually
cleansed from the taint of combat by tribal medicine people.[16]

KCA elders indicate that during this period the reinvigorated tribal military ideology was elevated to an ethos in support of their young veterans, as
the community's attention and daily news focused upon the war. Because
they contained dancing, singing, and giving-away, veterans' celebrations
were still technically illegal and were disdained by Indian agents attempting
to eradicate them. However, the outpouring of celebration associated with
the war was so great that agents could not counter them. With their distinguished service records (Bernstein 1991:41) and a return to active martial
combat, the younger generations revived the traditional forms surrounding
the role of warriors and the culturally appropriate means of honoring them.

Similar celebrations occurred in neighboring Cheyenne and Arapaho
communities in western Oklahoma (Parman 1994:62–64). Newspapers reported a willingness to enter the military and a significant increase in ceremonies. Numerous Scalp and Victory Dances were reported weekly. A large
dance was held at Watonga, Oklahoma, shortly after the armistice.[17] One
veteran honored for his heroism was given a new name and the title of
chief.[18] Several Cheyenne veterans joined warrior societies after the war.
Once repulsed by stereotypes associated with scalping, local newspapers
gleefully reported stories of Indians returning home with German scalps.[19]
Indian and white relations were at least briefly improved as Anglos donated
food for the Armistice Day Dance in Watonga, Oklahoma, and were invited
to perform a Scalp Dance at a county fair. Likewise, some 2,000 people
attended the burial of Harvey Goodbear, a Cheyenne killed in France,
whose body was returned to Thomas, Oklahoma, in 1921. A few months
later, the founding veterans of the Thomas American Legion Post named
the post after Goodbear and a deceased Anglo veteran from Thomas.[20] The
increased ceremonialism among numerous Plains tribes following World
War I demonstrates that the war rekindled past traditions on a widespread
basis.

The celebrations and honorings were brief in tenure, but they were significant because they revived the symbols, ideology, ethos, and community
gatherings associated with traditional forms of honoring veterans. While
meaning continued largely intact, significant adaptations in form had occurred. Service in the war facilitated native reacquisition of martial status in
a form acceptable to both native communities and the larger Anglo society,

although the KCA had too few veterans to revive an entire set of warrior societies. The number of veterans was too limited to completely revive military societies, and thus society activities continued to be superseded by the growing War Dance societies and powwows.

Native participation in World War I led directly to three forms of legislation which aided later revival of cultural forms, including military societies, by removing governmental interference and pressures against indigenous cultural forms. The first involved the granting of optional citizenship to all World War I veterans in 1919, and later to all Native Americans without citizenship, through the Indian Citizenship Act of June 2, 1924. This produced a new awareness of Native American civil rights for Native Americans and non-Indians. Second, influenced by the 1928 Meriam Report, the 1934 Indian New Deal focused on reservation economic development, Indian land bases, the organization of tribes to manage their own affairs, and the establishment of civil and cultural rights. With this legislation it was now technically legal to hold dances, ceremonies, practice native religions, and speak native languages. The Indian New Deal officially reversed the forced assimilation practices of the last sixty-plus years, although by this time numerous ongoing acculturative agents continued through encapsulation alone. Third, the Wheeler-Howard Indian Reorganization Act of 1934 concerned strategies to implement these objectives, including the end of allotting of Indian lands, creating appropriations to purchase new lands, creating a revolving financial credit fund for loans for tribal land development, consolidating fractionalized allotted lands and the delivery of allotments back into tribal estate, liberalized requirements for entrance into the civil service, legitimization of Indian civil and criminal legal codes, and the empowerment of tribes to write constitutions establishing local self-government and economic cooperation. This in turn fostered greater awareness of political self-rule and organization, as well as identity. The KCA tribes did not accept the political provisions of the Oklahoma Indian Welfare Act (the 1936 version of the IRA for Oklahoma Indians).

By the 1920s most prereservation combat veterans were deceased, and those who lived into the late 1930s were generally too elderly and too few to maintain military society meetings and public performances. Although the knowledge associated with the older societies was retained by increasingly fewer people and became inactive, awareness of these organizations and what they meant to their respective cultural groups remained. With no new veterans between 1875 and 1917, there simply were not enough veterans for tribes to sustain the previous sets of warrior societies, and there was no way to gain combat veteran status. As a result some societies altered membership requirements, while others simply ceased to function. Among the KCA, some older warriors were reluctant to pass on associated knowledge and regalia and to allow younger nonveterans membership in the rapidly declining older societies. One result of this reluctance may have been the formation of the Parker-Iseeo American Legion Post, composed of Kiowa and Comanche World War I veterans. Installed on November 11, 1927, the post was short-lived due to financial problems. According to one elder Comanche consultant, a Comanche member allegedly absconded with the post's treasury. The increasingly popular War Dance may have been not only a cause for the decline of the older societies, but, in the eyes of the younger men, a more easily obtainable replacement. In addition to the popularity of the Fancy Dance and dress styles, many younger followers were attracted because the newer societies had dropped many of the associated ritual aspects and "strict rules" characteristic of older societies by the 1920s.

Efforts by tribal agents and legislation in the early twentieth century also inhibited the rights to cultural freedom of Southern Plains tribes. Passage of the 1924 Indian Citizenship Act still did not ensure cultural rights to native peoples, as Kiowa Agency efforts to stop dancing continued until 1931. Even with the Indian Reorganization Act of 1934, which "legalized" cultural and religious practices again, military societies remained largely dormant due to a scarcity of veterans and contention with Christianity, the Native American Church, and the growing War Dance. In the late 1930s and early 1940s War Dancing, social and contest-oriented powwows, Christian churches, and the Native American Church continued to prosper as prominent social and religious forms among Southern Plains tribes in southwestern Oklahoma. As the War Dance grew, it became more secular in form, with increasing pan-Indian influences. Only occasionally did elder members perform military society dances.

While Christianity and Peyotism stabilized during the early 1900s, Christianity taught that Peyotism and dancing were not acceptable to the "Jesus Road." As KCA communities turned to various religious forms seeking relief from sociocultural oppression, membership in the two forms of religion was not always mutually exclusive. Yet while new forms of religion (Peyotism and Christianity) gained ground in native communities, many older cultural forms declined.

We may characterize postreservation-period (1900–1941) military societies largely as further declining forms of earlier manifestations that, while still focusing upon many of the same enculturative principles (ideology, ethos, symbols, and respect for veterans) of their prereservation antecedent forms, continued as informal hereditary and honorific societies, which celebrated past achievements and preserved many earlier social aspects. The brief cultural revivals fueled by World War I enabled many of the traditions associated with song, dance, and honoring of veterans to live on among younger generations. However, military societies continued to decline due to the same factors as in the reservation period: a lack of large-scale access to warfare, lack of opportunities for traditional integrative ceremonies, competition with new socioreligious forms, loss of primary functions in integrative contexts, and the continued growth of War Dancing societies and social powwows. Native peoples suffered tremendously in terms of radical forced changes to their freedom, subsistence base, and cultural and religious practices, which were constantly threatened by Indian agents, missionaries, and congressional acts. As Native Americans were continually stripped of their lands and encroached upon by non-Indian settlers, their subsistence base was replaced by annuities, leasing, and forced participation in a capitalist economy. Based on theories of sociocultural causes of revitalization movements, cultural and religious syncretism (Wallace 1956; Ryan 1969; Jorgensen 1972; Slotkin 1975; Aberle 1982; Jacobs 1987; Kracht 1989), and the variety of ongoing sociocultural problems, the stage for social change through cultural revivals was set.

POST–WORLD WAR II: REVIVALS OF SOUTHERN PLAINS MILITARY SOCIETIES

While the role of Native American participation in World War II has been discussed by Tom Holm (1985, 1996), Donald Fixico (1986), and Alison Bernstein (1991), only Duane Hale (1992) has focused on the people of Oklahoma. For Native Americans collectively, the war marked perhaps the most influential turning point in the twentieth century. As a significant watershed, native participation in World War II, and to a lesser degree in the Korean War, concern for the Termination Act, and the roots of a developing Indian awareness movement were the most prominent causes behind the revival of Southern Plains military societies.

Prior to the attack on Pearl Harbor on December 7, 1941, 4,000 Native Americans were already in the armed forces. By the winter of 1942 over 10,000 had registered for the draft. During World War II over 25,000 Native Americans served in the United States Armed Forces, including several hundred women in the WACs and WAVEs. As a whole, Native Americans enlisted at a rate of one and a half times the number that were drafted, and Plains volunteers exceeded inductees by a ratio of two to one (Haynie 1984: 7; Bernstein 1991: 35, 39–41). The percentage of Native American participation in relation to their total population was higher than for any other American ethnic group represented, including Anglo-Americans (Collier 1942:29). Over one-third of all able-bodied men aged eighteen to fifty served, which was as high as 70 percent in some tribes. The Forty-fifth Infantry Division, a National Guard unit from Oklahoma and New Mexico, logged 511 days of combat in North Africa, Italy, and southern France and contained the greatest percentage of Native Americans of any army division, nearly one-fifth. Native American patriotism was unsurpassed, as reflected in the *Saturday Evening Post*, which stated, "We would not need the Selective Service if all volunteered like Indians," and by President Dwight D. Eisenhower, who said, "Never did I hear a complaint about the battle conduct of the Native American Indian."[21] Native American performance in World War II was rewarded with the highest praise and admiration. The service records of Native Americans during the war included over two hundred citations and medals, excluding Purple Hearts: seventy-one Air Medals, fifty-one Silver Crosses, forty-seven Bronze Stars, thirty-four Distinguished Flying Crosses, and two Congressional Medals of Honor (both by Oklahoma Native Americans in the Forty-fifth Infantry Division). Native Americans in the Army Air Corps received thirty Distinguished Flying Crosses (the highest honor in the Army Air Corps), seventy Air Medals, and one Distinguished Flying Cross (Bernstein 1991:53). During the war, 550 Native Americans were killed and 700 (or nearly one thirty-fifth) were wounded in action (Haynie 1984:7; Bernstein 1991:55, 61).

More important than any decorations they received for their heroism, individuals were able to regain traditional forms of male status as warriors, on their own terms and on a large scale. Veterans were once again seen as warriors by their respective tribes, and no greater traditional honor could be regained. Although modern weapons and tactics had been employed, nothing replaced their courage. Numerous swords, flags, weapons, and other items were captured in combat. The actions and symbols which defined martial status in prereservation times had been regained. World War II provided opportunities for men to fulfill their traditional roles as warriors in culturally approved forms that were acceptable in both tribal and Anglo views. It was this opportunity which most significantly revived tribal and individual concepts of warrior status and led to subsequent Southern Plains military society revivals.

Although they were intended in a positive way, stereotypical images of Native Americans were widely used throughout the news and motion picture media to boost public and military morale (Bernstein 1991; Holm 1993; Parman 1994) and later as signs of assimilation to support Termination policies. The mass media use of native stereotypes of "chiefs," "warriors," and generic "Indians" only further reinforced Anglo misconceptions of Native Americans and their associated cultural and martial ideologies and Native Americans' views of expected Anglo perceptions. With over 90 percent of all Native American veterans in the army, they were often in the most dangerous assignments and repeatedly encountered the enemy. Holm (1993, 1996) demonstrates how the stereotypical and even racist concepts of the "Indian Scout Syndrome" (that Native Americans allegedly possessed superhuman genetic abilities) resulted in their proportionately extraordinarily high use in dangerous assignments as scouts and point men. Yet, despite these inaccuracies, Anglos viewed the associated Native American stereotypes as positive.

A new outburst of patriotism on a scale far exceeding that of World War I swept throughout Indian communities, once again raising traditional concepts of martial support and ideology to an ethos. Numerous tribal and intertribal rallies, celebrations, tribute dances, benefit activities, and war bond rallies were held throughout tribal communities across the country (Hale 1992:414). The Kiowa staged a patriotic rally to which all Oklahoma Indians were invited (Hale 1992:414). In June 1942 the Kiowa, Comanche, Apache, Caddo, Wichita, Cheyenne, Arapaho, Pawnee, and Ponca danced in tribute to the thousands of enlisted Native American servicemen. The Lac Court Oreilles Chippewa held performances of their Medicine Dance, Chief Dance, and Dream Dance (Ritzenthaler 1943). The Northwest Coast Bella Coola also celebrated the Allied Victory over Germany (Kennedy and Bouchard 1990:338). The formation of several Native American War Mothers chapters (Kiowa, Comanche, Cheyenne, Oto-Missouri, Pawnee) and other women's veteran support groups (Kiowa, Apache, Cheyenne) during the war further enhanced and reinforced traditional women's roles in supporting Native American veterans (Gamble 1952a, 1952b; Anderson 1956; Schweitzer 1981, 1983). These women's organizations deserve mention because they continued to honor and reinforce traditional men's roles and status, furthered the awareness of Indian veterans at home and abroad, and preceded the later revival of men's societies. Many tribal ceremonies were held to bless and protect servicemen preparing to depart overseas. Accounts of these departures and returns of Southern Plains veterans during the war indicate that there was almost always some family sponsored going-away or homecoming powwow occurring. Nearly every veteran had some event "put on" for him by his relatives and one of the women's veteran auxiliary organizations, as a normal and traditional family responsibility in the honoring of a family warrior. As in World War I, continuity in ideology and meaning was accompanied by adaptations in form.[22] Similar events occurred throughout the country, as the Lakota held victory celebrations and ceremonies and composed new songs for outgoing and returning veterans. A 1947 Hunkpapa celebration included a mock battle against a "German" position, their surrender, counting coup on the enemy, and Scalp and Victory Dances (Howard 1951).

World War II also provided the impetus for a number of later social, economic, political, and legal changes. In the first large-scale exodus from reservation and traditional communities since the military defeat of their ancestors, Native Americans serving overseas and at home in the defense effort were introduced to other parts of the world. Servicemen and women visited major cities and were free to socialize and drink alcoholic beverages without fear of arrest such as they experienced at home. Throughout the war, men and women not already in the armed forces left tribal reservations and communities to seek work in urban locations. Nearly 50,000 Native Americans left their home areas between 1941 and 1945 to work in the expanded wartime industries. By 1945 over one-third or an estimated 150,000 Native Americans had gained a broader national or international exposure by directly participating in the military, industrial, and agricultural war efforts (Prucha 1984:2:1005–1006; Holm 1985:156; Fixico 1986:6). Native Americans also invested over $17,000,000 of restricted funds in war bonds and donated significant resources to the war effort including food, money, minerals, range land, forest, agricultural resources, economic investments, and reservation lands for military bases or Japanese relocation camps (Hale 1992:417–422).

Upon the return of veterans, awareness of citizenship rights and political astuteness increased dramatically as ethnic identity and native traditions intensified. Veterans became aware of veteran preference in federal jobs and the use of the GI Bill for educational loans. The NCAI (National Congress of American Indians), the first national, all-Indian political organization in the United States, was formed in 1944 to represent Native American and returning veterans' concerns and issues, by giving them a formally organized public voice on a national level. Increased community-based political activity began as returning veterans ran for various offices.

Readjustment to community-based life was difficult for many veterans. Native peoples had left their isolated reservations and tribal communities and had successfully interacted with other ethnic entities, which resulted in congressional actions aimed toward further assimilating more native peoples into mainstream American culture. With little postwar employment in local tribal areas, returning veterans only increased competition for limited employment. Having experienced life and better employment opportunities outside of their home communities, some suffered from alienation and re-adjustment problems. In frustration, many veterans turned to programs developed in the federal Relocation Act, moving to large urban areas as the only available means to find job training and employment. These programs affected nearly every tribe in the United States (Holm 1985:164) and scattered significant numbers of Native Americans across the country's larger urban centers. Like other rural peoples, Native Americans were affected by the growth of metropolitan areas at the expense of rural areas (Jorgensen 1971:85). As the work force was drained toward the fast developing urban cities, rural communities were left with decreasing economic and political power. Having endured lengthy historical periods in which they maintained little control over their own resources, Indian communities suffered further from lowered socioeconomic levels. This phenomenon of largely under-developed rural Indian communities, poverty, and political oppression is described by Joseph Jorgensen (1971:84–89; 1972:9–10) as "neo-colonial subjugation" and, like earlier religious revivals, led to subsequent wide-spread cultural revivals.

As Native American veterans were readjusting to civilian life and exploring new economic and political opportunities, they were soon faced with more immediate concerns of federally sponsored Termination Act policies. While no Southern Plains tribes were recommended for Termination as recorded in the 1954 House Report Number 2680 (Fixico 1986:203), all were examined for it. Several World War II and Korean War veterans indicated that concerns about Termination weighed heavily on their minds during the early 1950s.[23] As Native Americans encountered a host of postwar socioeconomic problems which now threatened federally recognized tribal existence, the recent widespread reacquisition of veteran status completed the stage for massive cultural reorganization and revival.

Several scholars have developed models which correlate with the postwar revivals encountered on the Southern Plains. Turner (1968:22) found that, once initial rapid social change slowed and stabilized, traditional rituals infused with new symbols were revived with hybridization between old and new symbols. Similarly, in Jacobs's (1987) "contra-acculturation" stage, revival of culture in modified form is combined with renewed appreciation of one's own arts, crafts, and rituals. Slotkin's (1975) model of how "national-istic" movements form when a dominant society exerts acculturative pressures on smaller encapsulated societies is similar, as is Ryan's (1969) "syncretic integration" involving adjustment patterns which occur during a coalescence of "alternative systems," in which traditional and innovative patterns and symbols fuse and appear as distinct entities. Prolonged discrimination eventually produces a renewed group unity and solidarity in response to resentment of subordinate status. When a group attempts to change its status in regard to the dominant group through a cultural means using syncretic cultural symbols created in opposition to the dominant group, nativistic nationalism occurs. The syncretic blending of vastly different religious systems is often followed by a widespread distribution of the new form, as occurred in the rapid revival and widespread diffusion of postwar military societies.

The Impact of World War II on Military Society Revivals

American Indian participation in World War II led to the revival of nearly defunct warrior societies, which were supported by "a strong warrior tradition," among certain Plains tribes (Holm 1985). Holm maintains that these tribal ideologies were "based on ideals of continuity and order": the Creator had placed them on earth for a special purpose and maintenance of social order depended upon social, economic, and ecological balance, which tradition and tribal equilibrium helped maintain. Such "strong warrior traditions" perpetuated these beliefs, as "the keepers of social philosophy and tribal ceremony were most often males who had counted coup on an enemy of the tribe and therefore on an enemy of tribal conceptions of order" (Holm 1985:159). Holm (1985) implies that being a warrior symbolized defending tribal beliefs and values against external opposition. Thus, enemies encountered overseas were similar to those encountered at home in the Bureau of Indian Affairs or in Congress, and the revival of traditional warrior symbols was a nativistic movement allowing individual tribes to reaffirm and espouse distinct tribal and cultural identity.

While many aspects are involved, the revival of Southern Plains military societies as a direct response to the varied and ongoing acculturative pressures follows Holm's (1985) model and the previously discussed acculturation models concerning the reaffirmation of ethnic identity. Yet whereas many revived or revitalized cultural forms are religious, these were secular. As many Native American religions formerly permeated all aspects of their respective cultures, such secular movements are important in examining the range of religion and revivals; major segments of Kiowa, Apache, and Comanche religion, medicine, and cultural practices were closely linked to warfare and hunting as integral elements of nineteenth-century society. As Howard (1976:256–257) notes for the revival of the Gourd Dance, sacred and secular aspects are often intertwined, "in that it is a deliberate, conscious, organized effort by members of Native American society to create a more satisfying culture. Like many recent movements of this type it is secular in nature, though a certain religious feeling has come to be attached to it by many of its adherents, whose behavior strongly resembles that of converts to a new religion."

Korea

Military service in Korea only reinforced the ongoing rise in patriotism, with some 29,700 Native Americans, including many World War II veterans, serving in the United States military. Levy (n.d.b) reports antagonisms among southwestern Native American World War II and Korean veterans: older veterans declined to recognize younger veterans' status because Korea was a "police action," which is essentially a native use of an Anglo criterion. Although World War II veterans clearly still hold the bulk of leadership positions and control most of the post–World War II revived KCA societies, I have not found any significant degree of this animosity. I suspect that whatever degree existed has faded for the most part, as many KCA were veterans of both wars and Korean War veterans are found in almost every group. While some Vietnam veterans have formed their own groups, many also belong to the older revived societies.

Prior to World War II, powwows among the KCA were largely limited to occasional family-sponsored dances, Fourth of July celebrations, the American Indian Exposition or "Indian Fair" in August, and November Armistice Day celebrations. Dances held for World War II veterans (1941–1946) declined, until the process was repeated for Korean War veterans (1950–1954). As a result of the numerous farewell celebrations and homecoming dances sponsored by families and the revived women's societies during World War II and Korea, the frequency of holding dances and "powwows" increased. Dances that included dancing, giveaways, food and craft booths, and benefit raffles began to be held throughout the year and in indoor community buildings during colder months. The frequency and attendance of powwows increased in the 1950s; numerous powwow "circuits" developed, based upon the sponsoring of annual dances held on regular dates by various tribes throughout Oklahoma. These dances served to diffuse pan-Indian traits and reinforce distinct Indian and tribal identity (Lurie 1971:450–451; Young 1981), which soon produced declines in the attendance at Native American Church and Christian church activities.

It is no surprise then that the revival of Southern Plains military societies accompanied the larger growth of dance and powwow revivals during the late 1940s and early 1950s, as they were formally revived shortly after the Korean War. Following Ryan's (1969) model of the spread of alternative systems containing syncretic integration, the initial revival of the Kiowa Gourd Clan in 1957 resulted in a series of subsequent military, veterans', and dancing society revivals throughout Oklahoma. While most Southern Plains societies were revived between 1957 to 1976, with several initially limited to veterans, the formation of new and less exclusive dancing sodalities and traditional dance forms based upon models of revived societies (War and Gourd Dancing) continues today.

With the return of such large numbers of Native American veterans, one might have anticipated heavy participation in Anglo veterans' associations such as the American Legion and VFW. Many Native American veterans joined local American Legion and VFW clubs soon after returning from service; however, some veterans found them unsatisfactory because they did not provide a comfortable social atmosphere and emphasized drinking alcoholic beverages. Many Indian veterans perceived discrimination regarding participation in legion or post activities and felt that they were treated as a minority when included in activities. Yet some veterans did not experience discrimination in American veterans' clubs, especially regarding the ability to purchase and consume alcohol, which was still prohibited in many Indian communities. As one elder Comanche veteran stated, "Many veterans joined simply to have a place to drink a cold beer without getting arrested. They didn't hassle you in the veterans' clubs, you weren't discriminated against." While these organizations satisfied some, other veterans felt they did not provide an adequate social basis. One veteran, however, found membership enjoyable despite the VFW's frequently featuring him as their "token Indian veteran."[24]

Overall, dissatisfaction with the inequality in Anglo veterans' associations left many veterans with a desire for social groups which would meet their needs: to recognize veterans according to their own cultural forms and to provide a social atmosphere in which they would be culturally comfortable. As Philleo Nash (1955:442) found, the ritual symbols in revitalization movement ceremonies often reveal the deprivation and destitution experienced by the participants and reflect the general attitudes of the populace and their chosen course of action. Southern Plains military society revivals reflect the recent large-scale acquisition of what had been denied for so long: access to and expression of traditional male roles through martial activities, the primary traditional means of achieving male status among many Plains tribes. The need for such a social group provided yet another factor which led to the revival of military societies. As Fowler (1982, 1987) found with the Arapaho and Gros Ventre, the revival of sociocultural forms (societies) provided the arena for expressing these values in a means acceptable to the people themselves, as well as reactivating numerous cultural forms in celebrating their long suppressed heritage. The revival of past or currently threatened cultural traditions, as well as the achievement of such improvements within the lifetime of the initial actors involved, correlates with Wallace's (1956) second form of revitalization movement and Jorgensen's (1972) and Aberle's (1982) transformative movements. In this case the cultural awakening and unity were achieved by a revival that, while originally loosely linked to traditional religious structures, was now of a more secular form. There were no formal attempts by Anglos to suppress these revivals, as the impeccable native service record in World War II which formed the basis for these revivals and reinvigorated past cultural heritage was beyond question.

Society revivals were well received by most tribal members and soon formed their own "circuit," with various societies holding annual dances at specific dates each year. Throughout the 1960s and 1970s the general rise in ethnic awareness, demands for equal rights, and growing social injustice occurring throughout the United States also reached Native American communities, which provided further incentives for maintaining distinct cultural identities in culturally acceptable forms according to their own criteria.

Vietnam

As in the Korean War, the participation of at least 42,000 Native Americans in the Vietnam War (Holm 1996:123) further reinforced existing revived military societies and their associated ideologies; the celebrations for outgoing and incoming servicemen, veteran recognition, and the maintenance of ethnic identity and a martial ideology and ethos continued. Representing 0.6 percent of the entire U.S. population and 1.4 percent of all U.S. troops in Southeast Asia, Native Americans disproportionately served in the military forces in Vietnam: approximately one out of four eligible men compared to one out of twelve in the general American public (Holm 1996:10–11, 123). Although an increased level of militancy was associated with some Native American Vietnam veterans (Holm 1993), Native American reactions to participation in Vietnam differed tremendously from those of the larger American society. While American troops were often verbally and physically assaulted upon returning home, Native American veterans were honored, respected, and praised by their home communities as warriors and as men and women who answered the government's call, regardless of the United States' inability to determine whether they were involved in "conflict," a "police action," an "operation," or a "war."

Holm (1996) has demonstrated four major patterns concerning Native American participation in Vietnam (as well as earlier wars), which correlate with my findings here. First, the reasons behind the wide-scale Native American enlistment in America's twentieth-century wars (often assumed by Anglo-Americans to be largely due to factors of assimilation, a desire to enter mainstream American society, and economic necessity) are primarily derived from native—and not Anglo-American—cultural influences and value systems. First, Native Americans joined for reasons of their own, largely based upon tribal and family traditions and values surrounding the role, social status, and physical and spiritual experiences of the veteran in many Native American populations (Holm 1996:19–22, 102, 117–128, 166–167). Second, a "warrior tradition" and "ethos" with its related rituals, values, and beliefs still exists and serves to sustain many veterans during military service (Holm 1996:167–168). Third, many groups have syncretized service in the American armed forces with several of their own warrior traditions, societies, customs, and value systems (Holm 1996:19, 101, 191). Fourth, a high correlation exists between veterans resolving their problems and participation in tribal rituals connected with warfare and/or ceremonies of healing. Traditional forms of healing and ritual cleansing for veterans are still valid and directly help in veterans' readjustment to society (Holm 1996). For many tribes veterans and military societies play a significant role in all these aspects.

Operation Desert Storm

While residing in the KCA area during Desert Storm, I had the opportunity to view both the mainstream Anglo-American and respective KCA tribal responses to the war. I was also able to see the existing KCA martial ideology expand to an ethos, as the KCA communities' central focus of attention turned toward the war and the tribal traditions associated with protecting, honoring, and supporting veterans. Numerous dances, celebrations, religious and prayer services, parades, and patriotic displays were held. New veterans' songs were composed, and several Desert Storm veterans were inducted into military societies upon returning. As with past wars, similar displays occurred throughout Oklahoma and U.S. Indian communities.[25]

A DIFFERENT KIND OF RECEPTION

Even brief observations of how Anglo-American and Native American communities respond to their veterans through time demonstrate that the reception is qualitatively different. While Anglo-Americans produce large-scale, intense receptions for some wars, they are brief and soon forgotten. Native Americans celebrate every veteran's return, individually and collectively, at the time of initial arrival as well as throughout the remainder of the veteran's life. Many KCA people stated to me that "Indian people uphold their veterans more than non-Indians." The Reverend David Paddlety, a Kiowa veteran of World War II, described the differences between Anglo and Native American levels of patriotism:

> The degree of patriotism is very remarkably different, I mean more intense. Whenever the person would be drafted into the army and go away to service, they always related that to the early days of like when the men went forth to battle. They were accorded the same kind of importance as they did when the Kiowa or any other tribe's members went out to battle. This is what they say then and they call it a war journey. And they would have war journey songs and sometimes those people would be singing war journey songs and they'd be standing there singing with tears in their eyes, whenever their loved one went or left. With every celebration, if it was for a particular person, they would call an honor celebration and the mother and the father with their children in the army would gather together and give emotional support to one another. It's quite a deal, especially for those that didn't come back.[26]

Despite the continual failure of the U.S. government to fulfill its treaty-based legal obligations to native communities, Native Americans continue to display patriotism and serve in the U.S. Armed Forces. Many Native Americans frequently and publicly state that they are proud to be Americans as well as members of their respective tribal nations. I am constantly asked by students and non-Indian visitors who are puzzled at the inclusion of the American flag and U.S. military insignia in contemporary Native American dances and cultural activities, "Why would they want to include the American flag or serve in the military after what has been done to them?" Many appear confused, with a mixed sense of guilt and irony. The following World War II veteran's statement sums up what many veterans of that era stated to me:

> They often ask us, "Why would you want to have the American flag out here [in the arena]? Why would you want to serve in the U.S. military after all that happened?" I tell them. We went through all that once. We're not going to go through it again. We have survived and we're still here. This land is still OUR home. When the war started [World War II]

we thought, if someone else was to take over this land, they might treat us worse than the Americans did, if that is possible. We didn't want to take that chance. So we were willing to fight to protect Our land and Our people first and foremost. I am a member of my tribe and the United States.[27]

As one Native American Special Forces veteran stated (Holm 1993:345):

I went to Vietnam, was wounded twice and won the Silver Star, not because I have any particular loyalty to the United States but because I have loyalty to my own people, my own tradition. We are pledged by a treaty to provide military assistance to the U.S. in times of war. I know that the U.S. has broken its part of the bargain with us, but we are more honorable than that. If we respond in kind, we are no better than they are. The point is, we are better than they; we honor our commitments, always have and always will. Even the ones which are inconvenient or unpleasant. So it was my obligation to do what I did, even though I didn't really want to.

The difference in reception is perhaps best demonstrated by the following contrast. As one Indian Vietnam veteran described his return to Holm (1996:187), "We fought a white man's war, you know, and the first thing that happened when I get back is that some white kid, a girl, at the L.A. airport spits on me." As an elder Kiowa World War II veteran stated on Veterans' Day in 1993, "Our men have always been treated by their Indian people as heroes. I have never, ever, heard of one Indian that spit on any of their boys when they come home from Vietnam."[28] Likewise, during the national "flag burning" debate of 1990, Kiowa families honored their veterans' military service amidst dozens of American flags. The emcee at the July 4 Kiowa Tia-Piah Society Dance repeatedly reminded all in attendance, "You'll never see an Indian burn the American flag" (Lassiter 1992:55). Such patriotism and graciousness in light of past U.S. governmental policy and treatment contains much wisdom and deserves recognition.

Several elders have stated that the rising impact of Indian awareness also directly and dynamically affected social and cultural revivals among Southern Plains tribes during the 1960s and 1970s. As one elder Comanche society leader stated,

I think more than that [the influx of new veterans from World War II], what really brought that on right after, . . . in the mid-50s, was the revival into Indian Awareness. When this came about, they started bringing back these old dances which had been dormant for so long, and I think with this, that's when they started having dances every weekend, you know, and all the tribes were really getting into it. I think this Indian awareness revival was the one that really brought back those old dances, the Gourd Dance, the formal War Dance for certain tribes, also the revival of the Tuhwi among the Comanches. I think that was what brought it back more than the returning veterans, I think this Indian awareness was what brought this on.[29]

In retrospect, this view is significant considering the relatively late development, less integrated prereservation position, and later post-1970 revivals of Comanche societies versus the earlier Kiowa and Apache (1957–1960) revivals, which elder Comanche veterans concede influenced their own revivals.

Why Military Societies?

Of all the possible cultural forms which could have been revived, why were military societies chosen? Other social and religious forms which might have provided significant large-scale integration such as the Sun Dance, Ghost Dance, and tribal bundle ceremonies could have been revived, but were not. The reasons are found in past cultural emphases, in the later adaptations to these past traditions, and in the unique historical circumstances at the time of the revivals. As Fowler (1987:4) notes, cultures "are to great extent products of the way they were in the past and of what has happened to them over time."

The most significant reason is the wide-scale participation in World War II, which led to the large-scale return of veteran status as the primary traditional form of male status and rank, the revival of many of the martial symbols associated with earlier tribal warrior traditions, and the revival of the women's societies which fostered and supported these developments. The honoring, ritual cleansing, and reintegration of soldiers into the home community were facilitated by the renewed practicality of the traditional cultural content of these societies. Yet other reasons existed. The unique political situation of the 1940s and 1950s also led to the revival of these organizations. The large-scale return of veterans combined with a growing acceptance by the larger Anglo population, the increase of more positive (even if stereotypical) images of Native Americans, increased civil rights, and the educational and employment opportunities for veterans resulted in a growing pride and ethnic awareness. In addition, the sudden concern for Relocation and, more importantly, Termination policies threatened the cessation of tribal and federal government relations and of distinct tribal ethnic identities which had only recently been reinvigorated to a greater degree than since entering the reservation era.

The continually growing powwow had become the largest and most frequently held form of social gathering following the Sun and Ghost Dances. While Christian church activities maintained significant followings, they were not an indigenous cultural form and had begun to decline somewhat by World War II. The powwow is particularly significant because it continued a traditional strong emphasis on song and dance as the focal points of social gatherings. While veteran status had declined in the early twentieth century, dancing had not. At the time of the revivals (from 1957 on) the powwow, as an adaptational outgrowth of the older military societies, constituted the largest ongoing traditional cultural form. With such a large-scale return of veterans, the lengthy KCA tradition of military societies, and a generally shared emphasis on a warrior culture, military societies were the most likely form to be revived. Not only did societies integrate and reinforce tribal ethnic identities, but they did so according to both past and present traditional sociocultural forms, honoring veterans through song and dance.

We can only speculate what might have happened had World War II and the large-scale native participation in it not occurred. Some elders feel that without the war there would have been no society revivals. As one elder Kiowa veteran of World War II and Korea stated:

> See, that's old Kiowa way you know. They call it Gúdàugà before they went on a war party. It was a social thing before they went out on war parties, and after they return from a war party, then they have these organizations honor the warriors with Scalp Dances, Victory Dances, and all that . . . World War II did revive a lot of that . . . World War II had a lot to do with your Jáifè and your Black Leggins. After World War II, that had a lot to do with it . . . I don't know if we had never had a war, I don't know if these dances would have ever come back. I don't know if we would have these dances today.[30]

Although Termination and Relocation policies might not have been implemented for some time, if another revitalization movement had occurred in response to the sociocultural circumstances of the 1950s, it might have been of a more religious form like the Ghost Dance of 1890. Because of World War II, the revival of KCA military sodalities provided functions and temporal links between contemporary veterans and a continuing tradition of honoring veterans through song and dance that other cultural forms could no longer provide. The Kiowa Sun Dance was integrally linked in a thanksgiving relationship with bison, which were no longer available in sufficient numbers, so the revival of the Sun Dance at this time would not have been directly linked to the current circumstances. Likewise, the Ghost Dance was not really relevant to the improved postwar socioeconomic and political situation. Military sodalities contained integrational qualities that were not based solely upon religion, but upon a more general cultural heritage, thus reaching both Christian and non-Christian segments.

Christianity and Military Societies

Powwows and military societies have not always been totally embraced by the Christian segments of Southern Plains tribes. Many individuals raised in families which converted to Christianity were taught that dancing and Indian cultural events were detrimental to their welfare and that, as Baptist and Methodist churches proselytized, one could not be a true Christian and continue attending Indian dances. Churches frequently blacklisted any congregation members caught attending dances and expelled them from the church. As Kracht (1989:975–976) reports for the Kiowa, I also found that some of the younger generations of several KCA families stayed away from such events until after their parents died, out of respect for them. The long-term result of the Christian prohibition against dancing and traditional cultural forms was that the Christian and non-Christian segments of the tribe lost contact with many of the cultural activities maintained by the other. Yet some exchange and knowledge on both sides clearly continued.

I have met several Christian KCA individuals who have never danced, attended a Native American Church meeting, or been to some of the major military society ceremonials. Likewise, some "traditionalists" have never been actively associated with any Christian churches, fellowships, and camp or prayer meetings. In time, many individuals began to participate in more than one form of religious belief and cultural activity. Some individuals participate in one, two, or all three of the "Dance," "Peyote," and "Christian" roads. More and more Christian Indians began to participate in more traditional events, especially dancing. Although some have found no difficulty in bridging the two worlds, others have remained adamant in not attending dances. Some families have been removed from dancing and dance-related cultural forms for several generations; as one woman stated to me at a society ceremonial, "They [Christian Indians] are just now discovering what the rest of us have been doing our entire lives. Now everyone wants to join. Where have they been all these years?"[31] While some Christian segments were not initially attracted to the revivals as quickly as some traditionalists, some Christian society members have held leadership positions since the first revivals. Presently, there are fewer and fewer families who do not at least attend powwows or society dances, and today societies often contain significant numbers of Christians.

SOUTHERN PLAINS MILITARY SOCIETIES:
SYMBOLS, FUNCTIONS, AND FUTURE PROSPECTS

Symbols

Geertz (1973:91) defines a symbol as "any object, act, event, quality, or relation which serves as a vehicle for a conception" or the symbol's meaning. A plethora of martial-derived symbols continue to function actively among Southern Plains military societies. The use of a comparative approach has provided a general sense of each group's ideology, ethos, and range of variation concerning sodality structures. Each society contains a multilevel and lengthy cosmology of ongoing symbolic meaning. Regalia, songs, dances, names, behavior, functions, and historical attributes represent varied parts of each sodality, with associated meanings conveyed through varied visual and verbal symbols. As a distinct entity, each society also constitutes a larger symbolic level that is in turn linked to larger levels of tribal and ethnic identity.

Yet the same symbols do not always convey the same meanings to all individuals. Factors of knowledge associated with a symbol, community of residence, individual family histories, personal interests, and participation often determine the extent of an individual's contact and familiarity with particular sociocultural forms. The interpretations of symbols and the meaning they convey vary. Some families have stronger ties to particular societies and symbols than others. Some individuals have never attended military society dances of their own tribe, which have been revived for over thirty years, while some are familiar with one society, but admit they know virtually nothing of another. Symbolic meaning can even vary within the same society: for example, the red capes of the Kiowa Black Leggings hold a qualitatively different meaning for the descendants of Gúlhèi̇̀, who captured the cape, than they do for nondescendant members. It is the generally shared heritage, cultural experiences, and their associated symbols which serve to connect enough of the symbolic meanings so that they hold some shared levels of significance and understanding for all. However, it is important to realize that such cultural values need only be held and actively participated in by one segment of a society to be present and acknowledged by the rest.

These revivals are also related to the growth of the contemporary pan-Indian "powwow," derived from older military societies. Numerous vestiges of nineteenth- and twentieth-century culture and religion are preserved through ritual symbols in contemporary Southern Plains military society ceremonials. Membership in contemporary societies provides current tribal members and veterans with considerable prestige in their communities by continuing the traditional emphasis placed on recognizing veterans. Members and societies are also reunited with "traditional" nineteenth-century symbols associated with war power and ideology (insignia, painted tipis, dances, songs, ritual, regalia, coup recitations). These societies also contain aspects which border upon ancestor worship; they are replete with symbols (regalia, oral history, speeches, and family songs) commemorating former ancestral heroes who held prominent positions in the society's history, whose deeds are continually recounted, praised, and cherished by societies and descendants. One World War I Comanche song contains lyrics about the German Kaiser. Several Kiowa songs contain lyrics specifically naming and describing the individual and collective warfare deeds of tribal warriors or societies. Society members often wear regalia symbolic of past and present warrior dress and captured combat trophies.

Contemporary society ceremonials also display a great deal of cultural and religious blending. While blending between nineteenth- and twentieth-century warrior symbols occurs (e.g., wearing contemporary army rank and insignia on nineteenth-century modeled dress regalia), the way in which this status is symbolized, expressed, and viewed reflects a native adaptation according to native, and not Anglo, choices and ideologies. Despite changes in the symbols used to illustrate veteran status, their role, along with the traditional practice of demonstrating rank and prowess at society events, continues. Such demonstrations may occur visually by wearing military insignia or verbally by recounting or having one's own battle experiences recited. Southern Plains military society revivals are characterized by the blending of nineteenth-century Christianity and Peyotism belief and symbol systems, which facilitated the revival and preservation of cultural elements. Syncretism of traditional tribal belief systems, Peyotism, and Christianity is conspicuous in society ceremonials, as activities relating to warfare, Christian and traditional prayers, peyote symbolism, flag raising and lowering observances, cedaring, and various types of songs and dances appear in a single performance. Both native and Christian etiquette emphasize fellowship and the sharing of food, especially in establishing social and kin ties with non-blood relatives.

Functions

Military societies continue to serve numerous functions for both individual tribal and intertribal populations in Oklahoma. Because of their integrative role as cultural arenas, social, cultural, and economic functions hold great importance for their respective societies in reintegrating and honoring returning veterans and in maintaining distinct ethnic identities. With the recent resurgence in ethnic awareness and expression, participation should increase in the future. Although a direct connection to the old societies is not deemed necessary by all dance societies (namely, many of the more recently revived Gourd and War Dance groups), the more "conservative military societies" which make direct claims to prereservation societies through name, functions, or ritual clearly acknowledge these links and, as leaders often described, "try to keep it as close as possible." The continuation of older cultural forms constitutes a large part of current society activities. Society functions including ceremonial songs, dances, and benefits are a key form of publicly maintaining numerous cultural elements on various levels of social organization, ethnic identity, and symbolic significance. Using numerous visual and verbal symbols, societies publicly maintain important segments of rapidly disappearing and unrecorded tribal histories. These sodalities thus represent some of the oldest existing forms of prereservation sociocultural organization.

By maintaining military and related cultural forms and providing an occasion for including other cultural forms, military society dances have become "arenas of enculturation." While public cultural events have always performed enculturative functions, the role of military societies is perhaps more important in ensuring distinct ethnic identity now because of their current ethnic position in a larger encapsulating culture. One elder Kiowa veteran's comments are reminiscent of cultural revitalizations aimed at maintaining ethnic identity in the face of Termination policies and the continual acculturative pressures of socioeconomic and political encapsulation:

> In my own thinking this culture . . . it's not meant to die out. It's not meant to die out. We've got to keep that culture alive. See, the traditions have died out, the language has died out. But we have to show that we're still Indian. We're still Kiowas or what other tribe, so we have to keep something. We can't just lose everything. So that's one reason I think that this culture and dancing all came back. . . . Somebody higher up than us led some individual to make sure we hold on to our culture.[32]

Because most larger Southern Plains public events focus upon military society performances or descendant manifestations of these dances, they also serve as arenas for the introduction of new cultural changes and forms in songs, dances, dress, giveaways, economics, and sign language performances of prayers and songs.

Language

Military societies continue as one of the oldest cultural events in which native languages are still used through songs containing lyrics, opening and closing prayers, cedaring and naming ceremonies, speeches, historical accounts, coup recitations, and conversation among elders. As the number of KCA speakers declines, the partial use of at least some native languages will continue for perhaps one more generation by the remaining elderly fluent speakers. Elders are frequently sought to provide prayers, blessings, and perform many social functions due to their ability to speak their language. Many songs contain lyrics which are frequently sung even by younger non-speakers, who are in some cases unfamiliar with the translation. Although numerous song composers still exist, fluent elders and singers have pointed out several recently composed songs that contain grammatical and semantic errors, reflecting the general decline in speaking fluency.[33] There are currently 6 Naishan Apache, less than 200 Comanche, and less than 400 Kiowa who are estimated to be truly fluent speakers. Because songs often survive their associated cultural manifestation (e.g., defunct Sun, Ghost, and society dances) song texts will probably outlive language and prayers, which require a greater command of fluency and grammar. In some instances songs have already begun to replace language as a symbolic link to traditional cultures and ethnic identity (Lassiter 1992, 1995). These patterns will most likely continue as the number of fluent speakers decreases.

Social Organization

For tribal integration, military societies continue to aggregate large segments of tribal populations and to focus the energies and resources of significant numbers behind a group of headsmen, in some ways resembling the followings of band headsmen and society leaders of the past. However, factionalism is common among the KCA and their military societies. Holding a position as a society leader or headsman brings great social and economic benefits in the form of social status, invitations to co-host at other groups' dances, and gifts of money, blankets, food, and other goods. Much of the factionalism in KCA societies is derived from internal competition for leadership. Recently one individual attempted to form a third Apache Manatidie Society and to take the leader of one of the two existing societies to court over the rights to the society staffs. The leaders of one Kiowa society had to reproach members for attempting to perform that society's ceremonial songs and dances out of state for payment. Finally, a past Comanche society leader with hereditary claims resigned from a society, which had been "usurped" by others, and is currently planning the formation of a similar society under a new name.

Despite ongoing and underlying factionalism, these organizations, large or small, still integrate varying portions of tribal or intertribal populations. Even in tribes where societies have factioned and split into similarly based organizations (such as the Kiowa Gourd Dance Societies and the Apache Manatidie or in tribes containing several independent groups, as with numerous Kiowa and Comanche War and Gourd Dance organizations), multiple organizations still play integrative roles that are more complementary than counterproductive to each other and their respective tribe. Although the institution of society partners is rarely found today, there is still an undeniable feeling of society brotherhood, societal community, and a society-based *esprit de corps* exhibited among society members. Members and their extended kin bases still frequently and cooperatively work together for society and larger beneficial causes. By drawing segments of a population together to support and maintain an organization, societies continue to enhance the maintenance of a sense of collective ethnic identity, tribal pride, history, and community.

Societies continue to provide horizontal integration through fictive kin ties and co-hosting arrangements that are larger and farther reaching than the vertical integration of descendants' groups which reaffirm consanguineal ties. Society events provide horizontal integration within and between tribes in two ways. By integrating family-based units to participate or support their kin members, societies help maintain a series of kin-based units in a single tribe as a sodality working toward the goals of a larger organization. This integration is often intertribal, thus strengthening intertribal relationships. The growing pattern of intertribal co-hosting continues to strengthen these relations, and some organizations essentially depend on the co-hosting of other intertribal organizations in order to hold their larger activities. Society functions also provide opportunities for families to gather, socialize, eat, and reinforce ethnic identity through fellowship and participation in their cultural heritage. Economically, these events provide social acknowledgment through honorings and giveaways, while redistributing resources on tribal and intertribal levels.

In many Southern Plains communities, military society events or offshoots from them featuring dancing have become the focal aspect of most communal and tribal-level social gatherings. As many individuals have been forced to relocate to distant urban areas out of economic necessity and are not in everyday physical proximity to their tribal community, society-based events have come to provide "homecoming" events for significant segments of tribal and increasingly intertribal populations. These sodalities have evolved and adapted to historical circumstances, taking on new roles while keeping certain traditional cultural forms alive. In assuming new functions, society dances and music are now used in new and broader ways. As a result of "the broadening functions and uses" of these dances (like the Gourd Dance) and music today, they now have a "broader, less specific, cultural significance" (Lassiter 1992:40), the process which Nettl (1978:132, 1985: 26) calls "consolidation." Although these groups have changed to satisfy contemporary needs, this does not imply more or less significance, only broader functions and uses. These changes have preserved musical forms which would otherwise have been lost; "as a store house of various musical traditions," songs hold great significance in maintaining and promoting tribal heritage and ethnicity, as demonstrated by Lassiter (1992:41) for the Kiowa Gourd Dance. These societies serve as native adaptations to contemporary life and economic demands which provide the opportunity for reinforcing and maintaining distinct tribal integration and ethnic identity.

The role of Southern Plains military societies in maintaining distinct tribal identities in an intertribal context is most concisely demonstrated by the parades held during the annual American Indian Exposition in August. Since the 1930s this week-long intertribal encampment has hosted dancing and other cultural performances and contests which draw regular contingents of over fifteen Oklahoma-based tribes as well as visitors from other tribes and numerous non-Indian tourists. In the opening day parade on August 7, 1995, I saw several military society–oriented floats and cultural performances, including a color guard by members of the Kiowa Black Leggings, Gourd and Rabbit Dances by the Kiowa Tia-Piah Society, a Gourd Dance performance by the Séttháidé (White Bear) Descendants, War Dancing by the Kiowa Ohoma Lodge Crow dancers, and an Apache float containing the Manatidie whipman and another member dancing to society songs. Indicative of the continuing importance of these societies, the banner on the Apache Manatidie Society float succinctly stated, "Searching for Your Identity? Try Tradition." The Comanche Little Ponies have also recently performed in exposition parades. Although tribal identities are also maintained at the exposition through the use of language, art, dress, and dwellings, society-based dances are clearly in the forefront of many current cultural performances.

That maintaining a distinct ethnic identity is still important for native peoples is clear in light of governmental attempts at Termination in the

1950s, increased ethnic awareness in the United States since the 1960s, and the failure of the "melting pot" theory, as evidenced by the continuity of numerous ethnic communities throughout the United States. For Southern Plains communities, military societies are an integral part of maintaining a distinct ethnic identity in order to continue to preserve the distinct relationship between individual tribes as sovereign entities and the United States government. For many people, direct participation in tribal community celebrations is a significant part of defining what it means to be a member of their respective tribe.

For the Apache, the two Manatidie Societies hold the only current ceremonies on a tribal level. As such they represent the core of any program (social dance, benefit dance, annual tribal encampment); other events (War and Gourd Dancing, princess inductions and farewells, naming ceremonies, birthday celebrations, honorings, giveaways, games and contests, etc.) are also included in the program. The Comanche Homecoming, originally started to honor returning World War II and Korean War veterans, and more recently the Comanche Nation Fair are the largest Comanche tribal gatherings and function similarly. In addition to various social and kinship-based integrative features of large tribal aggregations, the core activities during these tribal events focus upon traditional and modern military society–based dances. Performances by the Tuhwi Society, Gourd Dancing by the Little Ponies, Comanche Gourd Clan, and CIVA groups, women's Scalp and Victory Dances, and intertribal evening War Dances including the Comanche War Dance Society are the focus of daily afternoon and evening programs. These same individual society dances held throughout the year likewise provide these integrative qualities on other occasions.

Military society functions are likewise the largest tribal-level integrative gatherings currently held by the Kiowa. The annual Óhòmò Society's encampment in July and the twice annual encampments of the Black Legs draw significant followings which focus upon War Dancing and Black Legs Society dances, Gourd Dancing, and War Dancing, respectively. The Kiowa Gourd Clan, Tia-Piah Society of Carnegie, and Tia-Piah Society of Oklahoma all draw large numbers during their Fourth of July encampments, while the Kiowa Warrior Descendants provide a similar Labor Day weekend encampment. Sodalities reinforce and offer the opportunity for tribal integration and maintenance of ethnic identity.

Despite society "annuals," the majority of smaller social events held throughout the year are based upon forms of dancing originating from earlier military societies. Southern Plains dances, whatever their purpose, contain Gourd and or War Dance segments of the program. While some Gourd

Dance societies hold only a few set benefit dances throughout the year, others hold benefits or co-host for another society nearly every weekend. Although distinctions involve regalia, choreography, ceremony, functions, organization, and origin of names, consultants often differentiate a "society" from a "dance club" by frequency of performance. A "society" holds annual or limited performances, while a "dance group" or "dance club" performs and holds more frequent benefits.[34] The Gourd Dance segment of a program is usually co-hosted by one or more Gourd Dance societies, from one or more tribes. Although this is less frequent at smaller dances, War Dance segments of powwows are sometimes sponsored by a formal War Dance society. Each form of choreography, even when not sponsored by a recognized society or when held in a more social than ceremonial context (such as a benefit dance rather than an annual society ceremonial), is a derivation from earlier Gourd and War Dance societies. Today some individuals no longer recognize these historical associations.[35] Military societies also serve ceremonial functions and for some tribes have replaced many earlier integrative ceremonies such as the Sun Dance and tribal bundle ceremonies. The Apache Manatidie is the only existing tribal-level integrative ceremony of a prereservation origin. Cheyenne military societies retain an integral role in preparing and assisting in the performance of the Sun Dance and thus have not been elevated beyond their earlier roles, as with the KCA.

While often competing with other social events and interest groups for resources and followings, most society functions are scheduled so that they do not interfere with each other's primary ceremonials or with the larger annual powwows. An increasing number of annual powwows, especially those containing dancing and singing contests, sometimes lure members away from society ceremonials due to the opportunity for cash prizes. I witnessed one society struggle to produce enough singers for one weekend ceremonial after the majority of the drum (singing group) requested to be paid for singing at the ceremonial. After the society refused to "pay our own members for performing at our own ceremony," the singers went to sing at a powwow in Tulsa where they were paid. After a two- to three-year hiatus, they began to return as if nothing happened. Most society ceremonials do not include contests in the social dance portion of their programs, which are smaller than regular powwows. Most people at society ceremonials come to participate and watch the society and not the social dances. Some conservative elders have expressed their disdain for contests and large urban intertribal powwows because they are detrimental to maintaining tribal ceremonies and language. Thus, the dates of numerous smaller, regular nonsociety-oriented powwows and benefit dances held on nearly every weekend have begun to overlap with annual society ceremonials. Although less numerous than powwows, military societies and formal War Dances in Oklahoma compose their own "circuit" throughout the year, just as people speak of the regular "powwow circuit." There is a "society circuit" or schedule of tribal military society dances and encampments aside from other tribal homecoming encampments, annual and social powwows, and Gourd Dances.

Economics

As sodalities, societies are able to perform numerous integrative functions due to their strong economic role. Because they remain the largest form of Plains sodality in many Oklahoma tribes, military societies integrate significant portions of their respective tribes, resulting in a larger economic base from which to function. All current community events require a number of items such as advertisements, rental of a meeting facility, food, singers, a public address system, raffles, and many other necessary expenses. To ensure the survival and success of social events, fundraising has had to cover expenses.

Due to competition for resources and a following, some societies have opened membership to intertribal and even non-Indian participation. At some society meetings I attended, younger members openly expressed disdain for the inclusion of non-Indian membership. In two cases I observed, society elders quickly reprimanded the youths for their behavior; in one case an elder officer arose and stated that because of the current lack of tribal participation and support and the socioeconomic position of their tribe and the society "outside money . . . from non-Indian participation is necessary to ensure the existence of our society."[36] Dances now occur nearly every weekend of the year, providing the opportunity for holding more frequent integrative events than in the past. Thus, the frequency of society-sponsored or co-hosted dances and benefits reflects the important socially integrative and economic roles which societies play in their respective communities. Most social functions include one or more types of dancing (military society or descendant clubs), indicating the usefulness and necessity of these groups in holding communal gatherings and attracting and integrating a following. As economic adaptations, many societies are used as "drawing cards" for raising funds. As one elder Apache stated,

> I think we're all doing it now, we're all using our culture you know. The Kiowas they use Gourd Dance, and I think there is about three clubs that

War Dance. Comanches they Gourd dance . . . Apaches they use the Blackfeet. It's just something that's a way you know we can put something together, a way of [covering] expense. We wanted to do this and this is a way that we might be able to get people to come, and serve supper, and sell chances, and to add a little funds to what we're going to do you know, and use for expense. That's why they done it. . . . We're like other tribes.[37]

Societies also help to ensure the economic survival of one another to some degree. While the rise of the Apache Native American Church (NAC) and War Dance Society resulted in part in the decline of the Manatidie in the early 1900s, it later revived and today helps to ensure the vitality of the Apache NAC as well as numerous Apache interest groups through their performances at benefit dances. The well-developed practice of co-hosting each other's dances further ensures the longevity of groups by minimizing the overlapping of dances on the same date, while drawing supporters and resources from a greater range (all co-hosting groups), often on an intertribal level, to provide support for the host organization's activity. The co-hosting is then reciprocated at another group's dances; thus, the long-term result is an amicable relationship between similar organizations, which nets more proceeds, more supporters, and a tradition of interdependence for all groups involved in helping sustain one another's organizations and cultural activities.

Continuity and Change

Throughout the period from 1800 to 1997 Southern Plains military societies have shown both significant continuity and change in numerous social, functional, and symbolic forms. While a current trend in ethnohistory leans toward emphasizing cultural continuity over loss, it would be hypocritical not to admit that both have significantly occurred, as the previous tribal discussions demonstrate. Continuity can result from the persistence of particular customs and ideas or resistance to change; however, change does not necessarily represent cultural loss. Identity continues as new concepts emerge and as values and symbols are invented, discarded, and reinterpreted as they are adapted to new social realities. These changes occur because native groups adapt to a changing social world (Fowler 1987:4–10). As Fowler (1982) notes, it is important to recognize how native populations interpret and react to external relations; to overlook these processes distorts the process by which societies change.

Southern Plains military societies are but one cultural entity which reflects the interpretation of new social realities that are culturally adaptable to the people themselves, as well as being adaptive to the larger sociopolitical circumstances of the encapsulating Anglo society. While society meetings were once primarily midsummer tribal aggregations, they have been adapted to modern veteran and holiday dates. These dates are convenient for employment schedules, yet still achieve native cultural goals and functions in a culturally distinct and ongoing traditional means of maintaining, expressing, and honoring veterans. The addition of United States military insignia, flags, and procedure to traditional forms of regalia and ceremony also represents a syncretism of systems that symbolize and convey traditional ideologies. The revival of traditional military society symbols (warrior ideologies, staffs, whips, songs, dances, and regalia) revitalized traditional society and tribal martial values, relationships, and ethnic pride. The lengthy history of celebrating U.S. veterans' holidays, changes in the views of Indians as a result of their distinguished World War II service record, and the syncretic inclusion of contemporary U.S. military symbols were reassuring to non-Indians. As old symbols both revived old meanings and took on new ones, their newly hybridized forms reinforced traditional understandings and motivations while making adaptations culturally acceptable.[38]

While changes in social communities have necessitated changes in social relationships, beliefs, and symbols, these adaptations are derived from indigenous and not Anglo-imposed forms, and thus the role of native perception and response must be recognized. The varied responses found in KCA military society histories evidence the integrity of separate, yet similar cultural communities and not simply acculturation. Thus, accommodation and adaptation counter theories focusing solely on forced acculturation, and reinforce the view that native communities are constructed in their own terms and interaction continues to be organized and facilitated according to indigenous cultural forms (Fowler 1982).

SHARED SONGS—CONTESTED SOCIETIES

As Fowler (1987) demonstrates, a tribe's history and concepts for defining its own and other groups' identities are products of the history of interaction, generational gaps, and intertribal rivalries. Contested origins, ownership, history, innovations, and symbolism of cultural forms are common among tribes with a lengthy history of close interaction and generally similar cultures. Related but contested cultural forms are common among the Gros Ventre and Assiniboine (Fowler 1987), the Ponca and Osage, and the Cheyenne and Arapaho. The Kiowa, Comanche, and Naishan Apache are no exception to this.

These groups frequently differentiate themselves from one another. Despite prereservation alliances, cultural diffusion, intermarriage, and ongoing cooperation in powwows and elsewhere, the KCA continue to exhibit a love-hate relationship stemming from at least the early 1800s (Gelo 1986: 213–214). The Kiowa and Comanche ridicule the Apache for their small population and alleged dependency upon and total adoption of "Kiowa" or "Comanche" culture. Some Apache feel "ganged up on" by the larger tribes. Comanche often describe Kiowa as overly impressed with themselves, clannish, and aloof, while Kiowa often characterize Comanche as overly aggressive, obscene (in reference to Comanche joking styles and personal names), having had no "real" culture, and generally "no good." One Comanche man married to a Kiowa once jokingly told a story explaining that the reason why the Kiowa had so many more cultural forms than the Comanche (such as tribal bundles, men's societies, the Sun Dance, etc.) was that the Comanche were all around the Kiowa fighting off everyone else, enabling the Kiowa to stay in the middle and be "mystic." Kiowa are noted for lengthy speeches as well as frequent honorings and giveaways, especially when honoring veterans; other tribes frequently criticize them for being long-winded and ceremonious. Following a lengthy honoring of a deceased Kiowa veteran which included a flag ceremony and processional of weeping War Mothers, one Comanche man commented, "They're the only veterans in the world[, that is], they think they are," while another commented, "Comanches don't do that. You can't bring 'em back. We just find a good place to put [i.e., bury] them, and that's the end of it" (Gelo 1986:214).

Objectively, all three tribes continue to have vibrant, rich cultures which differ significantly from each other; cultural elements from each can be clearly shown to have diffused to the others. Consequently, much of this ethnocentric maintenance of self-identification and intertribal rivalry is carried over into claims about the origins of various dance forms and men's societies by the KCA and the neighboring Southern Cheyenne. Realistically, it is important to recognize that these societies, like all cultures and cultural forms, are in an ongoing stage of evolution and that rivalry is a part of this history and evolution. Although the absolute origins, duration, and diffusion of all Plains military societies are not known, invention, innovation, and diffusion continue with the decline of older societies and development of newer ones. Just as the Great Lakes Jingle Dress and Dance has been recently introduced and grown in popularity among Oklahoma tribes, other earlier dances and cultural forms—including prereservation military societies—have developed, diffused, been altered, declined, and reappeared in changed forms throughout time. To understand the present situation of such organizations completely, the complexity of each individual society history must be grasped. To achieve this, various resources, including early documents, published ethnography, and modern practice, must be examined. This study provides ethnographic and ethnohistorical data which aid in discussing the origins and diffusion of two major types of Southern Plains societies, the Southern Plains Gourd Dance and the Kiowa Black Legs, Apache Manatidie, and Comanche Tuhwi or Black Knives Societies. Multiple modern manifestations of these two types of societies share many of the same older (pre-1950s) songs, but differ significantly in dance, dress, and format.

A perfect example of such contested oral histories involves the Gourd Dance on the Southern Plains. Adequate data in the form of Anglo-documented historical accounts, native oral history, and native pictographic calendars demonstrate that the Kiowa and Comanche obtained the dance from the Cheyenne in 1837. However, the two respective versions today have greatly changed. Musically, there were probably greater differences in the rhythm and tempo of Cheyenne, Kiowa, and Comanche Gourd Dance songs early on; however, today the songs and dance are similar. It is apparent that the post-1957 revival of the dance is heavily Kiowa influenced for the following reasons. First, Apache elders indicate that the dance was never native to them and that they began dancing in small numbers with the Kiowa in the early 1900s. Second, Comanche, who did have documented prereservation Gourd Dance societies and songs with texts, state that the rhythm of the songs sung today does not lend itself to Comanche lyrics. The presence of numerous current Comanche Gourd Dance songs lacking words, with numerous fluent elder singers, suggests the use of another style, as it is not logical for a tribe with a lengthy history of varied song texts to compose songs which are not conducive to their language. Some Cheyenne have likewise stated that, although they had songs which formerly contained words, current songs are not conducive to the inclusion of Cheyenne lyrics, and Cheyenne Gourd dance songs I have collected contain no lyrics.[39] Only Kiowa Gourd Dance songs contain lyrics today; the songs are often sung with or without Kiowa lyrics by the Kiowa and other tribes. Many Kiowa singers sing at Comanche dances, and the Comanche Little Ponies' club song was composed and given to them by a Kiowa, when the society was revived in 1972.[40] Thus, while several tribes contained prereservation societies with various forms of the dance, the present form that was initially revived and diffused so rapidly was the Kiowa version of the dance.

Similarly, several factors explain the contested accounts of the revived Kiowa Black (Legs) Leggings (1958), the Apache Manatidie (1959–1960),

and the Comanche Tuhwi (1976). First, all three were in close prereservation contact with one another, and Kiowa and Apache societies participated together. Second, the reservation and postreservation communities in
which these societies remained active into the mid-1920s were all in relatively close proximity to one another. The Kiowa Black Legs were centered
around Stecker, Oklahoma, while the Apache Manatidie Society was located
in the adjacent communities of Apache, Boone, and Fort Cobb, Oklahoma.
The Kiowa Black Legs and Apache Manatidie Societies continued interacting and sometimes performed their respective society dances at the same
dance gathering into the 1920s. Evidence of continued interaction between
the Kiowa Black Legs and Apache Manatidie Societies after their revivals
in the late 1950s is found in a flier from the First Annual Mopope Powwow held at the home of Steve and Jeanette Mopope (August 6 to 8, 1965),
east of Fort Cobb, Oklahoma. The Saturday, August 7, program contained
a 2:00 P.M. "Kiowa Blackleggings Society–Ceremonial Dance," followed by
a 3:30 P.M. "Kiowa-Apache Blackfeet Society–Ceremonial Dance." Kiowa
and Apache women's societies also performed together, as the Kiowa War
Mothers, Kiowa Veterans Auxiliary, Carnegie Victory Club, and Kiowa-
Apache Service Club all participated in the processional activities of the program. Finally, the Comanche Tuhwi, a Yamparika society, was concentrated
among the northern or Yamparika Comanche, the division with the lengthiest alliance with the Kiowa and Apache (Kavanagh 1996), who were allotted
near Apache, Oklahoma. With their long historical association, continual
intermarriage, and proximity of the core membership within twenty miles
of each other, the similarity of their cultural manifestations should not come
as a surprise. Although the origins, ownership, and "rights" to these societies continue to be hotly contested among the KCA, a critical examination
of available sources, including early sources from native peoples themselves
(calendars and ethnographic interviews), offers a more complete explanation
that, while incorporating contemporary accounts, precedes current elders'
memory.

Conclusions

Methodologically, this work has adopted the approach associated with
"New Indian History," by emphasizing Indian to Indian relations through
time while also acknowledging and accounting for external non-Indian influences. The relationship between continuity and change and the recognition that all sociocultural forms undergo a series of multiple and varying
adaptations in their evolution are also acknowledged. To achieve this, a mul-

tifield approach combining archival sources, participant observation, and extensive interviewing was necessary. To reiterate Moore (1987:317), "any historian or ethnohistorian who raises issues that are within the experience of modern informants simply *cannot* be excused from the necessity of doing fieldwork." Only extensive, long-term, and frequent interaction permitted the elicitation of integral information and the connections between various segments of these three cultural systems. A comparative approach allowed a constant cross-checking and inquiry, which in turn produced better methods of inquiry and better and more complete results. It is hoped that this work serves as a demonstration of the possibilities for those interested in combining early documents, published ethnography, and modern practice (Moore 1987). Often one source of information from an elder or ethnographic fieldnotes in one tribe later prompted questions and facilitated answers in another community.

We may characterize post–World War II Southern Plains military societies as revivals of earlier manifestations which have continued with much of the same enculturative principle, ideology, and ethos of their antecedent forms. These contemporary groups now celebrate past and present achievements, continuing many of their earlier martial and social aspects. Although these societies still maintain informal hereditary and honorific elements, the reacquisition of veteran status on a large scale provided greater continuity with earlier forms, which permitted military society and powwow revivals to grow to large-scale integrative sociocultural events. Although many organizations no longer require veteran status for membership, many initial revivals did. The symbolic, social, and functional roles of these societies continued after unisocietal raiding parties had declined. It is these functions, centered around a shared martial ideology, ethos, and sense of historical community, which are of greater consequence through time for their respective communities than the actual participation in warfare as a distinct unit. As society events developed into major tribal community celebrations, numerous other new and revived sociocultural activities were introduced into their programs which have now become established traditions. Some societies have obviously diverged more from their ancestral namesakes than others. Yet society integrative and enculturative forms and their related dances have significantly increased to become the largest and most frequent sociocultural community activity. Through song and dance, these societies provide KCA communities with a connection between their past and present and will probably continue as one of the most primary and significant future sociocultural forms.

The vitality of Southern Plains military societies continues in the preservation and enculturation of the Kiowa, Comanche, and Apache tribes of Oklahoma. Because these tribes have an incredibly rich military history with strong warrior traditions which they never relinquished, even during periods of inactivity, they were able to revive them with the large-scale return of veteran status. As the largest forms of prereservation sodalities and aided by their nonkin basis, these societies have continually functioned as adaptive units of social organization for preserving and maintaining earlier traditions and a distinct ethnic identity. This strength in size and diversity allows military societies to continue as major arenas of cultural adaptation and enculturation. They facilitate the use of martial symbols to provide cultural continuity in adaptations of indigenous sociocultural forms, while providing a public arena for the continuity of both older cultural traditions and change.

Contemporary Southern Plains military societies perform numerous social, cultural, religious, economic, and political functions for their respective communities. Yet there is clearly a differential emphasis on functions in individual societies, as reflected by the economic, yet cultural role of the Apache Manatidie, the more cultural-ethnicity role of the Kiowa Gourd Clan and Comanche Little Ponies, and the veteran focus of the Kiowa Black Leggings. Because the functions and emphases of all societies overlap in similar forms and to varying degrees, it is not necessary to attempt to classify these organizations on the basis of their primary functions. Despite multiple active and inactive periods and the lengthy changes which these organizations underwent, distinct similarities between the roles these organizations performed in the prereservation era and today still exist. While numerous peripheral sodality elements have changed, many of the core functional and ideological elements which they contained at an earlier date continue today. Despite changes in both, there has been greater continuity in meaning than in form.

Anyone who has done fieldwork in Plains communities recognizes that there is great cultural variability in contemporary native communities and often "many different styles of Indian life" (Grobsmith 1981:44; Fowler 1987:4; Lassiter 1995:126) within a single community. Such variation in Southern Plains communities in Oklahoma is reflected by different "styles" of Indian life involving participation in one or more of the following: military societies, powwows, Christian churches, hymn singing, softball leagues, bingo, committees, tribal languages, the Native American Church, hand games, sweat lodges, tribal religious bundles, the Sun Dance, or dealing with everyday life from an Indian perspective. All of these constitute social, public activities which may be seen as arenas of enculturation, because all contain continuations of earlier forms, additions of new traditions, or manifestations that are distinctly native in style and that lead to cultural and ethnic maintenance. Thus, the KCA often speak of "peyote people," "powwow people," "hand game people," "bingo people," or "church people" or say, "They took care of it according to [the] Indian way." Participation in community events or "Indian doings" constitutes an important portion of everyday life and to some extent determines one's actual existence in the Indian world. Although some participate in several spheres and others in only one or two, only a few participate in all. Yet all are distinct parts of an interrelated world in which social participation remains integral to the maintenance of ethnicity and a sense of community. Participation, responsibilities, and interpersonal relationships are a never ending realm for members who choose to remain active in their tribal communities. Because contemporary Indian community life is so diverse and complex, it is no longer practical to speak of aggregates of individuals; one must speak of the different realms of cultural activities in which individuals participate.

It is important to recognize that military societies are but one arena of contemporary Southern Plains Indian life and thus not everyone (including some veterans) participates. Interest and participation are often influenced by individual and family cultural interests, upbringing, and religious background. Direct participation in community celebrations remains a large part of how these native peoples define what it means to be Kiowa, Comanche, or Apache. Participation in military society events is one arena for the definition and maintenance of ethnicity. The same situation exists for other arenas. However, these organizations constitute one of the lengthiest ongoing forms of social organization, which involves the majority of these three Southern Plains communities through direct participation in the various sodality activities or through the related powwow.

The views expressed here do not represent the opinions of all segments of the community. While many data were acquired from elders, society members, and fluent speakers, the input of younger people and nonmembers was essential and insightful. The views of younger generations naturally differed quantitatively and qualitatively from those of the elders, but they still expressed many of the earlier ideas associated with veterans, military societies, their associated ritual symbols, participation in community celebrations, and the maintenance of ethnic identity. It is important to realize that for ethnic maintenance, (1) only certain elements of a culture need be maintained, (2) participation of only a segment of a community is sufficient to keep a tradition alive and acknowledged by the rest, (3) cultures choose to retain what they feel is necessary or significant, and (4) these selections can serve as symbols or emblems of ethnic boundaries for the group itself.

Yet symbols of ethnicity do not have to be visible and material in orientation; they are often ideological forms such as language, behavior, concepts, values, attitudes, and emotions (Neely 1991).

Perhaps the most important aspect to recognize is that the ideology involved in recognizing and honoring the traditional role of the warrior through song and dance continues. Analogizing past and present, Martha Poolaw remembered the impact of World War II on the Kiowa community and the continued importance placed upon military service and honoring veterans:

> It's very important within the tribe that they do that . . . I do remember World War II and the things that were happening around us, and the people talking about so and so going overseas, that was a big thing . . . not only for their families but just within that tribe that went over. And I think the major thing was if they could come back, you know, intact. And so I think that, to me that is, what their main emphasis was, that they returned. You know, they went somewhere and they went to war and they came back. But then when I look at it, it's kind of like that in the old days you know, it was like it was a necessity I guess for them to go out sometimes and do that. A lot of times they all came back and sometimes somebody didn't come back. And so we've always lived that life and it carried over into modern times, because we got away from that old lifestyle, that old way of doing things [i.e., the Kiowa lifestyle has changed], but yet that was the same concept for them I think, and that's why they have carried it on.[41]

Integrally linked throughout these cultures, warrior and veteran ideologies permeate Southern Plains song, dance, art, regalia, sodalities, oral history, personal names, tribal insignia, and forms of economic redistribution (benefits and giveaways). Recently, both traditional warrior and more contemporary veteran symbols have been incorporated into tribal license plates. The Apache use the design of four Manatidie Society dancers and four society staffs on their tribal license plates. Comanche tribal license plates include a circular design with a silhouetted warrior mounted on a horse and carrying a lance in red against a yellow background. This portion faces a blue background with a rippled edge toward the center of the design, symbolic of the Plains sign language sign for the Shoshone and Comanche—the snake. In 1997 the Kiowa redesigned their license plates to include their tribal logo of an armed warrior mounted on a horse. In addition, both the Kiowa and Apache began issuing special numbered tribal veterans' license plates in 1997, such as "VET-15" or "VET-34."

Whether discussing the last battles their grandfathers fought against the United States and other tribes or service in Operation Desert Storm, native peoples frequently speak of military service as "fighting to protect our people and our land." Many veterans and elders spoke of military service as protecting "tribe and country," with tribe emphasized before country, illustrating continuing concepts of ethnic community. The change from tribal-based warfare to service in the larger United States Armed Forces has not weakened the intensity, courage, or devotion of native peoples' military service. Many native peoples still recognize the role of the warrior and are conscious of coming from a martial tradition. This is not to imply that the Kiowa, Comanche, and Apache are in any way militant-minded (the American Indian Movement [AIM] had little influence in Oklahoma and remains generally disapproved of in Southern Plains Indian communities) but that respect for the ongoing martial heritage in these cultural systems continues. This respect is reflected in conversations, in the songs which sustain the memory of the deeds of great warriors, and in the elders' accounts of their grandfathers' deeds in the 1870s and their own in later wars. Despite technological changes in warfare, nothing has replaced courage and Native American values associated with their own veterans. Whether they served stateside or as highly decorated combat veterans, Native American servicemen are continually welcomed home as heroes and frequently honored according to tribal traditions.

The widespread general acknowledgment of and respect for the concepts of a prereservation warrior-based culture and ideology have not been lost and are still espoused even by many of the younger generation. During my seven years of fieldwork, numerous individuals of all ages frequently pointed out or commented on the martial feats of their ancestors. Many KCA individuals asserted that Indian peoples honor their veterans to a greater degree and more frequently than most non-Indians do. As one Kiowa woman described:

I always thought they continued that [honoring veterans] because it was something they always did and a lot of the tribes . . . especially someone like our tribe, because you know we are a warrior society. All of their concept is built around them, so that's what they've always known and they've just brought it forward. And I'm sure it's going into the future. I think that's just a Kiowa concept of us, of a warrior society.[42]

Even some non-Indians have commented that Native Americans honor their veterans more than non-Indians do. An Anglo woman from Oklahoma who had lost a male friend serving in Vietnam mourned his death for years and never fully began the healing process. Only after returning to Oklahoma and attending Native American dances did she begin to recover, when she witnessed and realized the degree and frequency with which Indian peoples honored their veterans, something which, in her opinion, Anglo-Americans did not do.[43]

The effectiveness of native ceremonials and military societies in ritually cleansing and reintegrating veterans from World War I to Operation Desert Storm is significant (Holm 1996). Similar rituals are recorded for numerous other North American populations, including Hopi, Menominee, Caddo, Wichita, Cheyenne, Arapaho, Pawnee, Ponca, Lac Court Oreilles Chippewa, Oto-Missouri, Navajo Blessing and Enemy Way ceremonies, Cherokee Going to Water ceremonies (Holm 1996: 3, 187–188, 193), Delaware Big House ceremonies (Kehoe 1992: 271), Crow Sun Dances (Oswalt and Neely 1996: 226), and various forms of Scalp and Victory Dances. Because Native Americans have been able to nativize service in the U.S. military as a way of adapting to a changed sociocultural environment in ways that preserve their own traditions, they have established another means of reaffirming Indianness and have demonstrated a better rate of psychological healing than among non-Indian veterans because of the link to their cultural base and ideology (Holm 1993, 1996). According to Veterans' Administration and U.S. census records there are nearly 160,000 living Native American veterans, which constitutes nearly 10 percent of all living Native Americans. In percentages, three times as many Native Americans have been in the U.S. military as non-Indians during the twentieth century (Holm 1993: 345). With global military concerns and the continuing military service by native peoples today, there is no apparent shortage of veterans in the near future. Native American veterans have endured, and as long as native peoples are serving in uniform, there will be the need to honor and recognize their ideology and ethos in accordance with traditional forms.

As Atwater Onco, a Kiowa veteran of World War II and Korea concluded, "It's still in our blood you know, we still honor our veterans. It's still going on."[44]

NOTES

Archival Sources

Archival sources included in this work consist primarily of ethnographic field-notes, Kiowa Indian Agency Papers, Kiowa pictographic ledgerbooks, and oral history collections.

AGI Archivo General de Indias. Seville, Spain; microfilm copies, H. H. Bancroft Library, University of California, Berkeley, and Western History Collection, University of Oklahoma, Norman.

AGN Archivo General de la Nación. Mexico City; photographic copies, New Mexico Archives, University of New Mexico.

AM Alice Marriott papers. Western History Collections, University of Oklahoma, Norman.
> *Box 8:* The Sacred Spear of the Kiowa Indians manuscript.
> *Box 9:* small expanding folder, File C, Kiowa Field Notes; File D, Kiowa Dancing and Shield Societies fieldnotes.
> *Miscellaneous Folder:* Kiowa Dancing and Shield Societies manuscripts.

BA Béxar Archives of Spanish and Mexican Texas. University of Texas, Austin, microfilm edition.

DD Doris Duke Oral History Collection, Western History Collections, University of Oklahoma, Norman.
Kiowa
> T-246. Guy Quetone to Julia Jordan, 4/18/1968.
> T-637. Guy Quetone to Julia Jordan, 3/23/1971.
> T-214 and T-216. Domebo Calender.

Kiowa-Apache
> T-12. Alfred Chalepah to Julia Jordan.
> T-13. Alfred Chalepah to Julia Jordan.
> T-47. Alfred Chalepah to Julia Jordan, 8/9/1967.
> T-54. Ray Blackbear to Kenneth Beals, 6/15/1967.
> T-77-2. Alfred Chalepah to Susan Brandt, 6/15/1967.
> T-79. Louise Saddleblanket to William Bittle.
> T-121. Charles Tartsah to David Jones, 8/11/1967.
> T-223. Ray Blackbear to Julia Jordan, 2/10/1968.

Comanche
T-448. Joe Attocknie to Peggy Dycus, 6/17/1969.
T-117-1. Dana Chibitty to David Jones, 10/7/1967.
T-508. Francis Joseph Attocknie, 6/9/1969.

DSF Demitri Shimkin Fieldnotes. Collection No. 9942; Box 1, Folder 6; Box 18, Folders 9 and 10. American Heritage Center, University of Wyoming, Laramie. (Collection restrictions prohibit the citation of any of Shimkin's Shoshone consultants' names.)

FSL Ananthy Odlepaugh Ledgerbook, Fort Sill Museum Archives, Lawton, Oklahoma, MS:D-1049. This ledgerbook was reportedly by Cáulánàundáu̧ą or Cáulánàundáumà (Standing in the Footprints of Bison). Born in 1859, she was enrolled as Aun-au-dah-ah 1901 Family 334 and was the wife of Odlepaugh (Ôlpàu, Bison Bird). However, recent information (STP) indicates that the ledgerbook was actually compiled by Tonemah (Tónmàui, One Who Is Drinking Water) and later came into the custodianship of Mrs. Odlepaugh.

HLS-1 Hugh Scott Ledgerbooks (ca. 1882–1892), vols. 1 and 2, Fort Sill Museum Archives, Fort Sill Army Post, Lawton, Oklahoma.

HLS-2 Hugh Scott Papers (ca. 1882–1892), National Anthropological Archives, Smithsonian Institution, Washington, D.C.

HLS-3 Hugh Lennox Scott papers [Comanche Notes] (ca. 1898), National Anthropological Archives, Smithsonian Institution, Washington, D.C.

JM James Mooney Kiowa Fieldnotes, MS 2531, vols. 1, 6, 11. National Anthropological Archives, Smithsonian Institution, Washington, D.C.; Silverhorn Ledgerbook. James Mooney MS 2531, vol. 7, National Anthropological Archives, Smithsonian Institution.

KAF-NAA Kiowa Agency Files, National Anthropological Archives (NNA), Smithsonian Institution, Washington, D.C. The General Records of the Kiowa Agency, Anadarko, Oklahoma, from 1907 to 1939 provide important information regarding government and agency policies, correspondence, and attempts to suppress native cultures. These letters are arranged topically according to a decimal-subject classification system (see Hill 1981:46–57; Kracht 1989). Documents from the Kiowa Indian Agency Papers are listed by item number, year, and topic file number (such as 104547-1913-063). The principal topics of this collection include:

    062.   Feasts—Fiestas—Festivals.
    063.   Dances.
    066.   Forms of Government—Indian Judges.
    126.   Liquor Traffic—Cocaine—Drugs—Mescal.
    810.   Teaching and Training—School Curriculum.
    816.   Religious Training.
    816.2. Missions—Missionaries—Churches.
    820.   Pupils.

NARS-SFN National Archives and Record Service, Washington, D.C. 1935 Santa Fe Laboratory of Anthropology Field Notes—Kiowa. Weston La Barre,

William Bascom, Donald Collier, Bernard Mishkin, and Jane Richardson under the direction of Alexander Lesser. Weston La Barre papers, National Anthropological Archives, Smithsonian Institution, Washington, D.C.

STP   Scott Tonemah Papers. Courtesy of Mrs. Doris Tonemah and Anne Yeahquo. Copies in possession of the author.

WB   William Bittle Kiowa-Apache Fieldnotes, 1949–1964. Western History Collections, University of Oklahoma.

WHC   Western History Collections, University of Oklahoma. Letter from Ralph Linton to Alice Marriott, 3/25/1936. Box 8, Comanche Historical Notes Folder, Marriott Collection.

Oklahoma Newspapers

Arapaho Bee, 11/29/1918.
Calumet Chieftain, 3/27/1919.
Canadian Valley Record, 9/25/1919.
Kiowa Indian News, October 1994.
Sunday Oklahoman, 2/10/1991.
Thomas Tribune, 10/21/1921 and 1/12/1922.

1. Sodalities and Plains Indian Military Societies

1. Tabeau provides a rare account of a men's society controlling access to trade goods from competing European sources (Abel 1939:114–115, 120). He notes that Brulé military societies were not responsible for plundering the expedition's traders. Later, upon hearing of the generous distribution of British goods on the River St. Peter's, members of a men's society were instructed to close the trader's store and stood sentry until the owners lowered prices and provided a barrel of brandy.

2. See Victor Tixier's 1839–1840 account for the Osage in McDermott and Salvan (1940:210–217) and F. V. Hayden's 1859–1860 account (1863:281, 325–326) for the Cheyenne and Arapaho.

3. HLS-1:192, HLS-2:1–2.

4. In contrast to the pantribal membership of military societies, shield societies were much smaller sodalities, generally composed of limited units of bilateral kin, which were thus residential units according to Service (1962). Unlike members of later military societies, members of Kiowa shield societies were known to have fought and remained together in battle. Shield societies existed among the Kiowa, Apache, Cheyenne, Comanche, and other Plains populations (Thurman 1987: 553–554; Hoebel 1940; McAllister 1935, 1937; Bittle Papers; Marriott Papers, WHC).

5. Great variety is found in policing and societal functions among many of the eastern Plains and Prairie groups. Depending upon demographic variations, either a particular clan reserved the rights to perform policing duties or the village chief or a council of chiefs usually appointed a temporary leader and a group of individuals for the policing of the buffalo hunt. For the Osage, two joint civil

chiefs representing the two tribal moieties and particular clans (gens) appointed one man from each of the ten tribal clans to serve in this capacity, three of them serving in the position of police chiefs (Dorsey 1893–1894:80). Among the Iowa, the Elk clan (gens) provided soldiers or policemen, while among the Ponca the duty fell upon two particular clans. For the Pawnee, a chief's adjutant along with three appointed assistants regulated the buffalo hunt, while supervising one of four possible organizations selected by a priest (Dorsey and Murie 1940:113). As in other Eastern Woodland groups, public functions among the Winnebago were performed by a clan who held the responsibility for recruiting and supervising the camp police (Lowie 1943:69–70). While clan-based police might continue additional collective actions, the composition of other appointed interclan groups was more fluid than that of regular sodalities; they had no collective group functions upon the completion of the appointed hunting assignment. Despite the similarity of being vested with coercive powers, these units of social organization are not true military sodalities because they were kin based and held no other sodality functions beyond policing.

6. HLS-1:192, HLS-2:1–2.

7. The SFN 1935 Kiowa Notes, the Marriott fieldnotes at WHC, McAllister (1935, 1937), Bowers (1950, 1992), and other tribal ethnographies describe Plains women's roles in honoring and supporting male war activities and society functions, in addition to having their own societies which emphasize these functions.

8. Mails (1973) is essentially a condensed version of Wissler (1916b), which shows no indication of any original fieldwork. This work caters to the Anglo romanticization of the Plains Indian mounted warrior, regalia, and ceremony, but fails to investigate many of the more subtle, routine, everyday activities and relationships which military society membership encompassed, such as fictive brother pairings, kin relations, and economics. It is these less well known features that continue to function, while societies as composite entities were limited primarily to a few weeks' duration per year. This work also fails to mention any subsequent society activities or functions that continued into the reservation era and is thus a static portrayal.

9. I am also influenced by Eggan's (1950) work among six Pueblo groups, combining archival research with extended fieldwork in three pueblos and brief fieldwork in the remaining three. He used a historical explanation to establish the events which led to certain results and the comparative method to achieve insights into social organization in a controlled comparison of correlated phenomena.

10. Because of the constraints of funding, time, and political climate, only limited data for Southern Cheyenne societies are presented here. Thus, my research on Cheyenne societies serves primarily to supplement, clarify, and compare and contrast with KCA society patterns.

11. In exploring these societies, this study emphasizes efficient causality, or what an institution was being used for at the time of recorded ethnographic observations, more than original causality in relation to social organization. Data available for military societies before the introduction of horses are at present limited.

12. One of the most important facets of anthropology which North Americanists often underuse is the comparative method. Only through the comparative method can one escape particularism and accurately study the existence of a form

of related phenomena over a larger area. Only then is it possible to progress from hypothesis to testing, to verification, and finally to attempts to arrive at general sociological laws of human behavior, a fundamental goal of anthropology.

13. Regarding these criticisms, see Geertz (1973:147); Clifford and Marcus (1986); Morris (1987:316); Kracht (1989).

14. See Fowler (1982) concerning the structure, roles, symbols, political and cultural functions, and adaptive qualities of Arapaho age-grades to the present day.

15. Symbols, meaning, and their uses vary through time and among individuals. Because so much diversity often exists within even such a small group I do not feel that an absolutely rigid, codified "blueprint" of any group's ideology and ethos that is shared by an entire group's membership can be obtained. I do believe, however, that an understanding of a group's ideologies and ethos along with an understanding of the general range of variation existing at a given time can be obtained.

2. Yàpfàhêgàu: Kiowa Military Societies to 1875

1. This chapter focuses on Kiowa societies in the nineteenth century before the Kiowa were forced onto a reservation in 1875 and is written largely from data collected in 1935 and 1936 by two independent inquiries, the Santa Fe Laboratory of Anthropology and Alice Marriott. The Santa Fe Laboratory of Anthropology included five graduate students: William Bascom, Donald Collier, Jane Richardson Hanks, Weston La Barre, and Bernard Mishkin, under the direction of Dr. Alexander Lesser (*Daily Anadarko Democrat*, 8/29/1935). The party spent much of the summer of 1935 among the Kiowa. Alice Marriott collected ethnological materials in 1935–1936. The Santa Fe Party and Marriott interviewed many of the same elders on identical topics, which allows for good comparisons. Each also interviewed other elders, providing much complementary material. The birth and death dates of these individuals show that many of them experienced Kiowa culture before the beginning of the reservation era. All genealogical materials are from Kiowa tribal censuses obtained from Parker McKenzie, cemetery records of Kiowa tribal cemeteries, and my own fieldwork and interviews with family members. Where possible all special Kiowa phonetics in the main text are in the Parker P. McKenzie orthography. Note citations follow those names in the 1935 Santa Fe notes.

2. Kintadl to Richardson, 1935; Lone Bear to Collier, 7/6/1935; Horse to Bascom, 7/18/1935; Bert Geikamah to La Barre, 7/9/1935; Mary Buffalo to La Barre, 7/6/1935, SFN.

3. Horse to Bascom, 7/18/1925; Lone Bear to Collier, 7/11/1935, SFN.

4. Hwmpi to Bascom, 8/9/1935.

5. Charley Apekaum and HeapoBears to La Barre, 8/1/1935, SFN.

6. Ned Brace and Jimmy Queton to La Barre, 7/24/1935, SFN.

7. Charley Apekaum and Senkoi to La Barre, 7/22/1935; Ned Brace and White Fox to La Barre, 7/26/1935; White Fox to La Barre, 7/23/1935; Mary Buffalo to La Barre, 7/6 and 8/6/1935; Charley Apekaum and HeapoBears to La Barre, 8/15/1935, SFN.

8. Kintadl, Old Lady Horse, Hodltagudlma, Goutaha (Mrs. Blue Jay) to Richardson, 1935, SFN, pp. 576–586.

9. Kintadl, Old Lady Horse, Hodltagudlma, Sankadota, Mary Buffalo, Yellow Wolf, Gueton, HeapoBears to Richardson, Bascom, Collier, and La Barre, 1935, SFN, pp. 586–597.

10. Hodltagudlma, Mrs. Hokeah, Kintadl to Richardson and Collier, 1935, SFN, pp. 574–576. I have been unable to find any elders familiar with the name Pehodlma or to provide an accurate pronunciation of it.

11. In Kiowa there is a tendency for a change in pronunciation when the preceding syllable of a word or compound ends in *t* and the ensuing syllable begins in *f* (pronounced as a soft *p* in Kiowa). Thus, the *t* is changed in pronunciation to a stronger *p* and yàt, meaning temporary, becomes yàp in the compound form Yàpfàhêgàu. Parker McKenzie and Gus Palmer Sr. to author, 1992.

12. HLS-1:77–78. While stationed at Fort Sill in the 1890s, Captain Hugh Lennox Scott became proficient in Plains Indian Sign Language. During his years he recorded several hundred pages of cultural history from various Kiowa, Comanche, and Apache Indians, interviewing many of the same elders as James Mooney did. A significant number of Scott's ledgers were published by Nye (1962). When they are used cautiously in comparison with other published and unpublished sources I have found Scott's notes to be very complementary regarding dates, genealogical information, and cultural content.

13. Silverhorn to Mishkin, V-3, 7/1/35, Silverhorn to Mishkin, V-7, 8, 9, 7/2/1935, SFN, pp. 544–545; Old Man Horse to Bascom, XIV-2, 7/4/1935, SFN, p. 553; Bascom 1935, SFN, p. 556; Frizzlehead to Mishkin, VII-22, 7/30/1935, SFN, p. 555; HLS-1:1:192–193.

14. SFN 1935, HSL-1:192–193; Jack Doyeto to H. L. Scott, "History of the Chief Pe-a-vo-co," MS 4525, NAA; HLS-1:1:192–193.

15. Gumdw, Seko, Frizzlehead to Richardson 1935, SFN, pp. 1205–1206; Silverhorn to Mishkin, V-4, 7/1/35, SFN, p. 553.

16. Richardson, 1935, SFN, pp. 1234–1254.

17. Frizzlehead to Richardson, 1935, SFN, p. 1254.

18. Richardson, 1935, SFN, p. 1207; author's fieldnotes.

19. Gumdw, Seko, Guito to Richardson, 1935, SFN, pp. 1207–1208.

20. Although the word qájâi is often translated as "chief," it is a contraction of qấ-hî (man) and jái-dàum (brave) and thus literally means "brave man," referring to a warrior who held a war honor. The Comanche term *Tekwµniwapi* is similar. Gumdw, Guito to Richardson, 1935, SFN, pp. 1207–1208.

21. Ibid., p. 1208.

22. Seko to Richardson, 1935, SFN, p. 1233.

23. Lonebear to Richardson, VII-IIFF, VII-12, 1935, SFN, pp. 30, 608; Guito to Richardson, 1935, SFN, p. 1208.

24. HLS-1:1:193; Atah to Marriott, 2/1/1936, WHC. It should be noted that some Kiowa elders reject Mishkin's (1940) and Richardson's (1940) classifications of four levels of Kiowa social status. While all four terms are readily known by elders today, they usually only speak of ôdè (high status) and káuaùn (poor or pitiful) as general reference terms and not as designated social statuses. Kiowa elders state that there was no clearly stratified class system as in India. This system may have declined and changed to such a degree by circa 1880 that it was unrec-

ognizable to Kiowa born after 1870, as elders born around 1900 state that their parents did not acknowledge such a defined segmentation of society.

25. Frizzlehead, Guito to Richardson, 1935, SFN, p. 1195.

26. Guito, Seko to Richardson, 1935, SFN, pp. 1197–1198.

27. Guito, Kintadl to Richardson 1935, SFN, p. 1195; Kintadl to Richardson, VI-9, 1935, SFN, p. 76; Little Henry to La Barre, XXI-5, 8/13/1935, SFN, pp. 74–75; Lone Bear to Richardson, VII-22, 1935, SFN, p. 558.

28. Seko to Richardson, 1935, SFN, p. 1196; Tsoodle to La Barre, XXI-5, 8/13/1935, SFN, pp. 74–76.

29. Guito, Gumdw to Richardson, 1935, SFN, pp. 1197, 1200; Luther Samon to Bascom, XIX-1, 7/31/1935, SFN, p. 273; Horse to Richardson, 1935, SFN, p. 1237.

30. Tsoodle to La Barre, XXI-5, 8/13/1935, SFN, pp. 74–76.

31. Richardson, 1935, SFN, p. 1198; Little Henry to La Barre, XXI-5, 8/13/1935, SFN, pp. 74–76.

32. Ibid., pp. 1199–1200; 74–75; HeapoBears and Padalti to Richardson, 8/7/1935, SFN, p. 1262; Frizzlehead to Mishkin, VII-22, 7/30/1935, SFN, p. 636.

33. Frizzlehead, Seko, Gumdw, Guito to Richardson, 1935, SFN, pp. 1196–1197; Little Henry to La Barre, XXI-5, 8/13/1935, SFN, pp. 74–75; Lonebear to Richardson, VII-5, 1935, SFN, p. 384.

34. Richardson, 1935, SFN, p. 1201.

35. Seko to Richardson, 1935, SFN, p. 1196.

36. Frizzlehead, Seko, HeapoBears to Richardson, 1935, SFN, p. 1202.

37. Seko, HeapoBears, Frizzlehead to Richardson, 1935, SFN, p. 1202; Little Henry to La Barre, XXI-5, SFN, pp. 74–75.

38. Frizzlehead, Gumdw to Richardson, 1935, SFN, p. 1202; Little Henry to La Barre, 8/13/1935, SFN, p. 75; author's fieldnotes.

39. Frizzlehead to Richardson, 1935, SFN, p. 1253; Richardson, 1935, SFN, pp. 1202–1203.

40. SFN, pp. 1202–1204.

41. Frizzlehead, Lone Bear to Richardson, 1935, SFN, pp. 1217–1218; Richardson, 1935, SFN, p. 1218; Richardson, 1935, SFN, p. 1258; Luther Samon to Bascom, XIX-2, 7/31/1935, SFN, p. 267; Frank Givens to Marriott, 8/1/1935, WHC; White Fox to La Barre, XI-9, 10, 11, 7/26/1935, SFN, p. 548; Parker McKenzie to author, 4/30 and 6/16/1993; Gumdw to Richardson, 1935, SFN, p. 1217.

42. Ibid.

43. Ibid.

44. Gumdw, Frizzlehead to Richardson, 1935, SFN, p. 1213; Lone Bear to Richardson, VII-22, 1935, SFN, p. 558; White Fox to La Barre, XI-9, 10, 11, 7/26/1935, SFN, p. 548; Parker McKenzie to author, 4/30/1993.

45. Gumdw, Frizzlehead to Richardson, 1935, SFN, p. 1215; Parker McKenzie to author, 6/16/1993.

46. Yellow Wolf to Bascom, III-5, 7/2/1935, SFN, p. 552; Bert Geikaunmah and Mary Buffalo to La Barre, IV-5-6, 1935, SFN, p. 761; Frank Givens to Marriott, 8/1 and 8/2/1935, Atah to Marriott, 2/1/1936; Tso'odl to Marriott, 7/13/1936, WHC; author's fieldnotes.

47. Frizzlehead, Gumdw to Richardson, 1935, SFN, p. 1215; Frank Givens to

Marriott, 8/1 and 8/2/1935; Atah to Marriott, 2/1/1936; Tso'odl to Marriott, 7/13/1936, WHC.

48. Frizzlehead to Richardson, 1935, SFN, p. 1215; Bert Geikaunmah and Mary Buffalo to La Barre, IV-5-6, SFN, p. 761. The Arikara Fox Society similarly included two female youth members who were sisters to the society and were prevented from marrying any of the members or commoners; their society gave consent and gave-away at their weddings (Lowie 1915c:667).

49. Gumdw to Richardson, 1935, SFN, p. 1215; Tso'odl to Marriott, 7/13/1936, WHC.

50. Horse to Collier, 8/25/1935, SFN, p. 106; Bert Geikaunmah and Mary Buffalo to La Barre, IV-5-6, SFN, p. 761; White Fox to La Barre, XI-9, 10, 11, 7/26/1935, SFN, p. 548.

51. Atah to Marriott, 2/1/1936, WHC; Frank Givens to Marriott, 8/1/1935, WHC; Biatonma to Marriott, 7/16/1935, WHC.

52. Silverhorn to Mishkin, VII 7/2/1935, SFN, p. 555.

53. Seko, Gumdw, Guito to Richardson, 1935, SFN, p. 1206; Silverhorn to Mishkin, 7/2/1935, SFN, p. 41; Tso'odl to Marriott, 7/10/1936, WHC.

54. George Hunt to Mishkin, VIII-1, 7/31/1935, SFN, p. 555.

55. Gumdw, Frizzlehead to Richardson, 1935, SFN, pp. 1207–1208; George Hunt to Mishkin, VIII-1, 7/3/35, SFN, p. 555.

56. Yellow Wolf to Bascom, 11-5, 7/1/1935, SFN, p. 639; Mooney MS 2531 V.6:178.

57. Guito to Richardson, 1935, SFN, p. 1207; Little Henry to La Barre, XXI-5, 8/13/1935, SFN, p. 571; Frank Givens to Marriott, 8/1/1935, WHC.

58. Seko, Gumdw to Richardson, 1935, SFN, p. 1206.

59. Richardson, 1935, SFN, pp. 1212–1213.

60. Richardson, X-11, 8/5/1935, SFN, pp. 755–756.

61. Charley Apekaum, Frizzlehead to Collier, 7/25/1935, SFN, p. 120; Heapo-Bears to Richardson, X-11, 1935, SFN, p. 755. Bowers's (1992:185) Hidatsa work demonstrates a similar intertribal societal association among the Hidatsa, Mandan, and Arikara: "Collectively, each society addressed the same society of the other Hidatsa or the Mandan villages *irakúu* in Hidatsa or *kotomanaku* in Mandan, the kinship term for 'pal.'" Bowers (1992:212) elaborates on this intertribal military society relationship in describing the friend relationships between intertribal men's societies of similar form and those purchased from another village or tribe; this purchase and transfer was known as "taking in friends." In addition, these societal relationships resulted in the treatment of associate club members as "brothers," lodging during visits to others' villages or tribes, the extension of group assistance to similar men's societies in other villages, military aid in avenging blood feuds, the strengthening of village ties in the Knife River area, and contributing to extended peaceful relations between the Hidatsa and Mandan. Although many of these items are not specifically mentioned in archival sources, there are adequate data to suggest that these principles were also present and greatly enhanced by the presence and relationships between Southern Plains men's societies.

62. FSL.

63. Richardson, X-11, 8/5/1935, SFN, pp. 756, 1261; Kuiton to Mishkin, 8/16/ 1935, SFN, p. 280.

64. Gumdw to Richardson, 1935, SFN, p. 1213; Richardson, X-11, 8/5/1935, SFN, p. 756; White Horse and Monroe Horse to Richardson, 7/31 and 8/2/1935, SFN, p. 1294; Ray Blackbear (Kiowa-Apache) to William Bittle, 6/5/1963, WB.

65. Richardson, 1935, SFN, pp. 1208–1209.

66. Gumdw, Guito to Richardson, 1935, SFN, p. 1208; Tso'odl to Marriott, 7/16/1936, WHC; Biatonma to Marriott, 7/16/1935, WHC.

67. Ibid.

68. Hodltagudlma to Collier, I-26, 7/2/1935, SFN, p. 536; Gumdw to Richardson, 1935, SFN, pp. 1210–1211; Tsoodle to LaBarre, XXI-I, 8/13/1935, SFN, p. 569.

69. Gumdw to Richardson, 1935, SFN, pp. 1210–1211; White Fox to La Barre, XI-9, 10, 11, 7/26/1935, SFN, p. 548.

70. Seko, Gumdw to Richardson, 1935, SFN, p. 1211; White Fox to La Barre, XI-9, 10, 11, 7/26/1935, SFN, pp. 548–549; Tso'odl to Marriott, 7/13/1936, WHC.

71. White Fox to La Barre, XI-9, 10, 11, 7/26/1935, SFN, p. 548.

72. Tsoodle to Marriott, 7/10/1936, WHC.

73. Seko, Gumdw to Richardson, 1935, SFN, p. 1211; Tso'odl and Frank Givens to Marriott, 7/13 and 8/1–2/1936, WHC.

74. Guito to Richardson, 1935, SFN, p. 1211; Tso'odl to Marriott, 7/16/1936, WHC.

75. Frizzlehead, Gumdw to Richardson, 1935, SFN, p. 1212; White Fox to La Barre, XI-9, 10, 11, 7/26/1935, SFN, pp. 547–548; Lone Bear to Richardson, VII-22, and La Barre, 1a–5, 6/28/1935, SFN, pp. 558, 542.

76. Frizzlehead, Guito to Richardson, 1935, SFN, pp. 1210, 1212; White Fox to La Barre, XI-9, 10, 11, 7/26/1935, SFN, pp. 547–548.

77. Gumdw to Richardson, 1935, SFN, p. 1212; Guito to Richardson, 1935, SFN, p. 1210.

78. Ibid.

79. Seko to Richardson, 1935, SFN, p. 1212; White Fox to La Barre, XI-9, 10, 11, 7/26/1935, SFN, p. 549.

80. Guy Quetone, Horse to Collier, 8/25/35, SFN, p. 117; Guito, Gumdw, Seko to Richardson, 1935, SFN, p. 1210.

81. Gumdw, Seko to Richardson, 1935, SFN, p. 1211; Richardson, 1935, SFN, p. 1258; HeapoBears to Collier, XI-7, 1935, SFN, p. 658; Biatonma to Marriott, 7/16/1935, WHC; Tso'odl to Marriott, 7/10/1936, WHC: Frizzlehead and Yellow Wolf to Richardson, 1935, SFN, p. 1244. This term is also the address form for one's paternal grandmother. However, the reasons for the use of this term for retired society members are unclear.

82. Ibid.

83. Gumdw to Richardson, 1935, SFN, p. 1212.

84. Hodltagudlma to Collier, I-26, 7/2/1935, SFN, p. 536; HeapoBears to Richardson, 1935, SFN, p. 1220.

85. Hodltagudlma to Collier, I-26, 7/2/1935, SFN, p. 536; Charley Apekaum

and White Buffalo to Collier, III-4, 1935, SFN, p. 661. Some 1935 consultants confirmed the practice of an announcing society, while others denied it, attributing it to intratribal visiting in general.

86. HeapoBears to Collier, VI-7, 1935, SFN, p. 658; Charley Apekaum and White Buffalo to Collier, III-4, 1935, SFN, p. 661.

87. Frank Givens to Marriott, 7/16 and 8/2/1935, WHC.

88. Tso'odl to Marriott, 7/7/1936, WHC; Frizzlehead to Collier, V-11, 1935, SFN, p. 762.

89. Seko to Richardson, 1935, SFN, p. 1220; HeapoBears to La Barre, XIII-5, 7/30/1935, SFN, p. 560; Parker McKenzie to author, 5/13/1993.

90. Seko to Richardson, 1935, SFN, p. 1221; Kintadl to Richardson, VIII-2 and VIII-3–4, 7/22/1935, SFN, pp. 412–414; Parker McKenzie to author, 5/13/1993.

91. Seko to Richardson, 1935, SFN, p. 1220; Lone Bear to Richardson, VII-22, 1935, SFN, p. 559; Bert Geigaumah and Mary Buffalo to La Barre, IV-5–6, 1935, SFN, p. 761; Atah to Marriott, 2/1/1936, WHC; Sangko to Marriott, 8/5/1935, WHC; White Fox to La Barre, XI-9, 10, 11, 7/26/1935, SFN, p. 549.

92. Ibid., p. 1221; HeapoBears to La Barre, XVII-I, 8/7/1935, SFN, p. 151; Bert Geikomah and Mary Buffalo to La Barre, 1935, SFN, p. 760; Bascom, 1935, SFN, p. 762; Sangko to Marriott, 8/15/1935, WHC; Tso'odle to Marriott, 7/10/1936, WHC.

93. Seko to Richardson, 1935, SFN, p. 1221; Horse to Bascom, XI-3, 1935, SFN, pp. 762–763; Lone Bear to Richardson, 1935, SFN, p. 559.

94. Seko to Richardson, 1935, SFN, p. 1221; HeapoBears to Richardson, X-11, 1935, SFN, p. 755; Parker McKenzie to author, 5/13/1993.

95. Seko to Richardson, 1935, SFN, p. 1221; HeapoBears to Richardson, X-11, 1935, SFN, p. 755.

96. Seko to Richardson, 1935, SFN, p. 1221; HeapoBears to Richardson, X-11, 1935, SFN, p. 755; Parker McKenzie to author, 1994.

97. Seko to Richardson, 1935, SFN, pp. 1222–1223; Horse to Mishkin, 8/28/1935, SFN, p. 332.

98. Seko to Richardson, 1935, SFN, p. 1223; Parker McKenzie to author, 5/13/1993.

99. Lone Bear to Richardson, VII-12, 7/15/1935, SFN, p. 129; White Fox to La Barre, XI, 7/23/1935, SFN, p. 144, and XI-9, 10, 11, 7/26/1935, SFN, pp. 547–548; Mishkin, 1935, SFN, p. 295; Monroe and Horse to Bascom, XI-3, 1935, SFN, p. 762; Charley and Frizzlehead to Collier, V-11, 1935, and 7/25/1935, SFN, pp. 762, 118; Lone Bear to La Barre, 1a–5, 6/28/1935, SFN, p. 542.

100. HeapoBears to Richardson, 8/7/1935, SFN, pp. 1261–1262; Parker McKenzie to author, 6/16/1993; Lone Bear to Richardson, VII-12, 7/15/1935, SFN, p. 129; White Fox to La Barre, XI, 7/23/1935, SFN, p. 144, and XI-9, 10, 11, 7/26/1935, SFN, pp. 547–548; Mishkin, 1935, SFN, p. 295; Monroe and Horse to Bascom, XI-3, 1935, SFN, p. 762; Charley and Frizzlehead to Collier, V-11, 1935, and 7/25/1935, SFN, p. 762, 118; Lone Bear to La Barre, 1a–5, 6/28/1935, SFN, p. 542.

101. Ibid.; Richardson, 1935, SFN, pp. 1208–1209.

102. SFN, 1935; author's fieldnotes.

103. Collier, 1935, SFN, p. 668.

104. HeapoBears to Collier, VI-7, 1935, SFN, p. 667; Horse to Collier, IX-1, 8/6/1935, SFN, p. 671; Frizzlehead to Collier, V-6, 1935, SFN, p. 666; Monroe, Horse to Bascom, XI-I, 1935, SFN, p. 666; Mrs. Hokeah to Collier, IV-19, 1935, SFN, p. 672; Kuito and Ema'a to Mishkin, VII-24, 7/25/1935, SFN, p. 497; Horse, Paddlety to Richardson, 1935, SFN, p. 1309.

105. HeapoBears to Collier, VI-7, 1935, SFN, p. 667; Charley, Frizzlehead to Collier, 7/25/1935, SFN, p. 110; Gumdaw to Mishkin, VIII-7–8, 8/2/1935, SFN, pp. 502–504; HeapoBears and Kuito to Mishkin, and Collier, 8/2/1935, SFN, p. 504.

106. Hodltagudlma to Collier, I-23, 1935, SFN, p. 684; Little Henry to Bascom, XXI-2, 8/16/1935, SFN, p. 239; HeapoBears to La Barre, XIII-2–3, 1935, SFN, pp. 688–698.

107. HeapoBears to La Barre, XIII-2, 1935, SFN, p. 677.

108. HeapoBears to Richardson, X-11, 1935, SFN, p. 679; Horse to Bascom, XIV-1, 1935, SFN, p. 678; La Barre, IV-2, 1935, SFN, p. 674; White Buffalo and Horse to Collier, III-5, IX-13, 1935, SFN, pp. 671–672, 676.

109. HeapoBears to Richardson, X-11, 1935, SFN, pp. 679–680.

110. Ibid.; Horse to Bascom, XI-2, 1935, SFN, p. 683; Horse to Bascom, XIV-1, 1935, SFN, p. 671.

111. HeapoBears to Richardson, X-11, 1935, SFN, p. 682; Horse to Bascom, XI-2, 1935, SFN, p. 683; Horse to Collier, IX-14, 8/6/1935, SFN, p. 682.

112. HeapoBears to La Barre, XIII-2, 1935, SFN, p. 677; Hodltagudlma to Collier, I-24, 1935, SFN, p. 677; Mary Buffalo to La Barre, IV-4, 7/11/1935, SFN, p. 676.

113. La Barre, IV-6, 7, 1935, SFN, p. 759; Charley Apekaum and HeapoBears to La Barre, XIII-7, 1935, SFN, p. 689; Parker McKenzie to author, 9/15/1994.

114. Bert Geikomah, Mary Buffalo to La Barre, IV-3, 1935, SFN, p. 698; HeapoBears to La Barre, XIII-2–3, 1935, SFN, pp. 688–689; Collier, III-13, 1935, SFN, p. 745.

115. Frizzlehead to Collier, V-12, 1935, SFN, p. 697.

116. Bert Geikomah, Mary Buffalo to La Barre, IV-5, 1935, SFN, p. 700; Charley Apekaum and HeapoBears to La Barre, XIII-3, 1935, SFN, p. 700.

117. Frizzlehead to Collier, V-12, 1935, SFN, p. 697.

118. Horse to Collier, X-12, 8/13/35, SFN, pp. 757–758; Hodltagudlma to Collier, I-24, 1935, SFN, p. 784; Sangko to Marriott, 1/27/1936, WHC.

119. Sangko to Marriott, 8/5/1936, WHC.

120. Horse to Collier, X-12, 8/13/35, SFN, pp. 757–758; Hodltagudlma to Collier, I-24, 1935, SFN, p. 784.

121. Horse to Collier, X-12, 8/13/1935, SFN, pp. 757–758; Hodltagudlma to Collier, I-24, 1935, SFN, p. 784; Horse to Collier, X-12, 8/13/1935, and Horse to Bascom, XIV-1, 1935, SFN, pp. 757–758.

122. Bert Geikomah, Mary Buffalo to La Barre, IV-4, 1935, SFN, p. 760; Kintadl to Richardson, X-3, 1935, SFN, p. 259; Sangko to Marriott, 1/27/1936, WHC.

123. Sangko and Saioma to Marriott, 1/27/1936, WHC.

124. Kuito and George Hunt to Mishkin, 8/12/1935, SFN, p. 310; Horse to Collier, X-7, 8/15/1935, SFN, p. 222.

125. Bert Geikomah, Mary Buffalo to La Barre, IV-5, 1935, SFN, p. 700; Charley

Apekaum, Frizzlehead to Collier, V-12, 1935, SFN, p. 698; Horse to Bascom, 1935, SFN, p. 681.

126. Charley Apekaum, Frizzlehead to Collier, V-12, 1935, SFN, p. 698.

127. HeapoBears to Collier, VI-8, 8/2/1935, SFN, p. 745.

128. Gumdw to Richardson, 1935, SFN; Tso'odl to Marriott, 7/10/1936, WHC; Yellow Wolf to Bascom, 6/28/1935, SFN, p. 601; White Fox to La Barre, XI-9, 10, 11, 7/26/1935, SFN, p. 549; White Horse and Charley Apekaum to Richardson, 1935, SFN, p. 1293.

129. Silverhorn to Mishkin, V-3, 7/1/1935, SFN, p. 553; Old Man Horse to Bascom, XIV-2, 7/4/1935, SFN, p. 553.

130. Guito, Seko to Richardson, 1935, SFN, p. 1225; Frizzlehead to Mishkin, VII-22, 7/30/35, SFN, p. 555; Yellow Wolf to Bascom, I-4, I-6, 6/27–28/1935, SFN, pp. 601, 616; Kintadl to Richardson, 1935, SFN, p. 395; Peatomah to Marriott, 7/16/1935, WHC.

131. Little Henry to La Barre, XXI-1, 8/13/1935, SFN, p. 571.

132. Frizzlehead, Seko to Richardson, 1935, SFN, p. 1225; White Fox to La Barre, XI-9, 10, 11, 7/26/1935, SFN, p. 549.

133. Seko, Frizzlehead, Guito to Richardson, 1935, SFN, pp. 1225–1226; Kintadl to Richardson, VIII-3, July 22, 1935, SFN, pp. 408, 412; Donety and Jack Doyeto to H. L. Scott, "Story of Sheep Mountain," 1897, MS 4525, NAA; Kuito to Mishkin, VII-6; 7/23/1935, SFN, p. 556; Silverhorn to Mishkin, V-4, 5, 7/1/1935, SFN, p. 540; Horse to Collier, X-1, 8/13/1935, SFN, p. 219; Mary Buffalo to La Barre, XVI-3, 8/7/1935, SFN, pp. 226–227.

134. Kintadl to Richardson, VIII-3, 7/22/1935, SFN, p. 409.

135. Kintadl to Richardson, VIII-2, 7/22/1935, SFN, p. 413; author's fieldnotes.

136. Lone Bear to Collier, II-14, 7/11/1935, SFN, p. 410; Kintadl to Richardson, VIII-3, 7/22/1935, SFN, p. 410; author's fieldnotes.

137. Frizzlehead, Seko to Richardson, 1935, SFN, p. 1226; Frizzlehead, Guito to Richardson, 1935, SFN, p. 1230; Kintadl to Richardson, VIII-3, 7/22/1935, SFN, pp. 411–412.

138. Kuito to Mishkin, VII-6, 7/23/35, SFN, p. 556; Silverhorn to Mishkin, V-4, 5, 7/1/35, SFN, p. 540; Horse to Collier, X-1, 8/13/1935, SFN, p. 219; Mary Buffalo to La Barre, XVI-3, 8/7/1935, SFN, pp. 226–227; Jack Doyeto and Donety to H. L. Scott, MS 4525, NAA.

139. Frizzlehead to Richardson, 1935, SFN, p. 1226.

140. Guito to Richardson, 1935, SFN, p. 1226.

141. Richardson, 1935, SFN, p. 1228.

142. Richardson, 1935, SFN, p. 1228; Tso'odl to Marriott, 7/13/1936, WHC.

143. Little Henry to La Barre, XXI-1, 8/13/35, SFN, p. 568; Silverhorn to Mishkin, V-4, 5, 7/1/35, SFN, p. 541.

144. Silverhorn to Mishkin, V-4, 5, 7/1/35, SFN, p. 541.

145. Ibid., pp. 540–541.

146. La Barre, XVI-5, 8/7/1935, SFN, p. 563.

147. Richardson, 1935; Collier, III-13, 1935; Little Henry to Bascom, XXI-10, 8/16/1935, SFN, pp. 221, 745, 1229; Kuito and Ema'a to Mishkin, VII-24, 7/25/1935, SFN, p. 497; Kuito to Mishkin, MIII-3, 7/8/1935, SFN, p. 433; Silverhorn

to Mishkin, IV-4, 5, 7/1/1935, SFN, p. 570; Horse to Collier, IX-4, 8/6/1935, SFN, p. 248; HLS-1:77–78.

148. Seko, Guito to Richardson, 1935, SFN, p. 1229.

149. Ibid.; HeapoBears to Richardson, X-15, 1935, SFN, p. 525; HeapoBears and Kuito to Mishkin and Collier, 8/2/1935, SFN, p. 504.

150. HeapoBears to Collier, VI-8, 8/2/1935, SFN, p. 745; Frizzlehead and Charley to Collier, 1935, SFN, p. 110; Luther Samon to Mishkin, VIII-4, 7/31/1935, SFN, p. 501; JK/H to Mishkin, 8/20/1935, SFN, p. 325; Gumdw to Mishkin, VIII-7, 8, 8/2/1935, SFN, pp. 502–504; HeapoBears to Richardson, X-15, 1935, SFN, p. 525.

151. White Fox to La Barre, XI-8, 7/25/1935, SFN, pp. 539–540.

152. Ibid.; Richardson, 1935, SFN, pp. 1228–1230; Tsoodle to Marriott, 7/7/1935, WHC; Frank Givens to Mishkin, H-8, 8/21/1935, SFN, p. 288.

153. White Fox to La Barre, XI-8, 7/25/1935, SFN, pp. 539–540.

154. Ibid., p. 540; Jack Doyeto and Donety to H. L. Scott, MS 4525, NAA.

155. La Barre, XVI-5, 8/7/35, SFN, p. 563; Horse to Collier, IX-6, 8/6/1935, SFN, p. 201; L. Samon to Mishkin, VIII-5, 8/1/1935, SFN, p. 506; Kuito to Mishkin, VII-8, 7/23/1935, SFN, p. 166; Kintadl to Richardson, IV-4, 1935, SFN, p. 436.

156. Horse to Collier, IX-6 and X-1, 8/6 and 8/13/1935, SFN, pp. 201, 217–218; Horse to Collier, IX-14, 5/6/1935, SFN, p. 682.

157. Mishkin FG (Frank Givens/H8/22/3b), 1935, SFN, pp. 288, 291; Heapo-Bears to Collier, VI-13, 8/2/1935, SFN, p. 745.

158. Sengko to Marriott, 8/5/1935, WHC.

159. Kintadl to Richardson, 1935, SFN, pp. 393–394, 397.

160. Kintadl to Richardson, I-8, SFN, pp. 393, 397.

161. Mac Whitehorse was given his father's name (Whitehorse) by the older members of the Óhòmò Society when they chose him to succeed his father as the society bustle keeper; Mac Whitehorse to author.

162. James Mooney Fieldnotes, MS 2531(2):3, NAA. The Cáumáuqàudàl (Aiming Circle/Wheel) Game is given in abbreviated form as *Gam* in Mooney's fieldnotes.

163. Author's fieldnotes—Cheyenne.

3. The Decline and Revival of Kiowa Military Societies, 1875 to the Present

1. SFN, 1935; author's fieldnotes.

2. Ibid.

3. Ibid.

4. Troop-L File, Fort Sill Archives, Lawton, Okla.; Parker McKenzie to author.

5. Author's fieldnotes.

6. Charley Apekaum and Sengko to La Barre, 7/22/1935; Ned Brace and Whitefox to La Barre, 7/26/1935, SFN.

7. Author's fieldnotes.

8. Agent Hunt to Commissioner Hayt, 8/15/1878, Annual Report, Commis-

sioner of Indian Affairs (ARCIA) 1878:556 [1850]; Hunt to Hayt, 8/30/1879, ARCIA 1879:171 [1910].

9. Parker McKenzie to author. A group of Kiowa including McKenzie's grandparents were starving and were forced to kill a number of prairie dogs along this stream for food. This small branch starts near Rainey Mountain Church and flows north-northwestward between Mountain View and Gotebo, Oklahoma.

10. Old Man Horse to Mishkin, 8/20/1935, SFN.

11. Mrs. Hokeah to Collier, 1935, SFN.

12. Agent Myers to Commissioner Morgan, 8/27/1889, ARCIA 1889:190–191 [2725].

13. Commissioner T. J. Morgan to Kiowa Agency Agent C. E. Adams 7/24/1890, Department of Interior, Office of Indian Affairs, M.22313-1890.

14. Commissioner D. M. Browning to Acting Kiowa Agency Agent Capt. F. D. Baldwin, 8/4/1896, Department of the Interior, Office of Indian Affairs, Land, 29188-1896.

15. Little Henry to La Barre, XXI-1, 8/8/1935, SFN, pp. 568–569.

16. Seko to Richardson, 1935, SFN, p. 1244.

17. Ibid.; Frizzlehead to Richardson, 1935, SFN, p. 1220.

18. SFN, 1935.

19. Author's fieldnotes. However, the exact impacts of these factors cannot be accurately measured without further research.

20. Parker McKenzie to author; author's fieldnotes.

21. Author's fieldnotes.

22. Author's fieldnotes; Sells to Stinchecum, 7/11/1916, 72353-1915-063K; James Ahtone to Sells, 6/12/1916, 66449-1916-063K; Meritt to Ahtone, 6/27/1916, 66449-1916-063K; Ahtone to Sells, 7/8/1916, 66449-1916-063K; Meritt to Ahtone, 7/27/1916, 66449-1916-063K; Stinchecum to Indian Office, 7/26/1916; Western Union Telegram, 72353-1915-06K; Meritt to Stinchecum, 7/27/1916, 7293-1915-063K; Tennyson Berry to Congressman Scott Ferris, 8/16/1916; Western Union Telegram, 7293-1915-063K; Meritt to Ferris, 8/18/1916; Meritt to Berry, 8/18/1916, 7293-1915-063K; KAF-NAA; Kiowa Society membership lists in possession of the author.

23. Author's fieldnotes.

24. Frizzlehead to Richardson, 1935, SFN, p. 1218.

25. Francis Tsonetokoy, 12/8/1990, and Parker McKenzie 1991, 1994 to author. For a lengthier discussion of these events, refer to Kracht (1989:820–854).

26. Harry Domebo, Gus Palmer Sr., Mac Whitehorse, Parker McKenzie to author; author's fieldnotes.

27. Frizzlehead to Richardson, 1935, SFN, p. 1218.

28. Guy Quetone to Julia Jordan, 4/18/1968, DD:37:T246:9–11, 19–25, 3/23/1971, DD T-637:5.

29. Ananthy Odlepaugh Calendar, Fort Sill Museum Archives, Lawton, Oklahoma; Alice Soontay Domebo Calendar, WHC, University of Oklahoma, Western History Collections.

30. Gus Palmer Sr., Mac Whitehorse, Harry Domebo, Oscar Tsoodle, Alice Littleman to author.

31. In attempting to link the Kiowa Grass Dance experience to that of the Southern Cheyenne and Arapaho Crow Dance, Kracht (1989, 1994:329) contends that there was a direct link between the Ghost Dance and the Óhọ̀mò Society: "Since the Ghost Dance was associated with other traditional activities like dancing, it served as a vehicle to perpetuate the Grass Dance, a precursor of the War Dance." Although all of these dances are variants of the Omaha Dance, I contest this idea for three reasons. First, the Kiowa acquisition of the Óhọ̀mò Dance (1883–1884) preceded that of the Ghost Dance (1890) by some six years. Second, if the Ghost Dance served as a vehicle to perpetuate the Grass (War or Omaha) Dance it did so as a stimulus to perpetuate more "traditional" or old-time activities such as dancing in a general sense, possibly as conservative efforts against Anglo acculturative pressures. My eyewitnesses state that there were no Óhọ̀mò activities in or at the Ghost Dance in later (1910–1917) years and that at Ghost Dances they attended there was no other type of dancing except the actual Ghost Dance. As the Óhọ̀mò Society was burgeoning at this time, it had no immediate or competitive incentive to separate from the Ghost Dance (if it was ever associated with the Ghost Dance). Third, Kracht (personal communication, 1992) has not worked with the Óhọ̀mò Society leaders or interviewed any actual eyewitnesses of the Ghost Dance. I therefore do not believe that the Ghost Dance was linked with the Óhọ̀mò Society in light of society leaders, accounts of Ghost Dance eyewitnesses, and the larger pattern of Kiowa military society history discussed in this work. Parker McKenzie, Mac Whitehorse to author; Francis Tsonetokoy to author, 12/8/1990.

32. Parker McKenzie to author; Francis Tsonetokoy to author, 12/8/1990.

33. Vanessa Santos Jennings to author, 2/5/1994.

34. Francis Tsonetokoy to author; author's fieldnotes.

35. Parker McKenzie to author.

36. FSL 1 Ledgerbook.

37. Author's fieldnotes.

38. Weiser Tongkeamha and Mac Whitehorse to the author.

39. Weiser Tongkeamha to author, 2/2/1991.

40. Author's fieldnotes.

41. Author's fieldnotes.

42. Domebo Calendar, DD:38, T214–T216.

43. Domebo Calendar, drawings 89–106, DD:38, T214–T216.

44. Joyce Auchiah Daingkau, Weiser Tongkeamha to author.

45. Guy Quetone to Julia Jordan, 4/18/1968, DD:37:T246:23.

46. DD:T246:21. Boyd (1981:73) associates the wearing of black long underwear with the Tọ̀kọ́gàut at this time. However, this may be a confusion of the wearing of such dress by the increasingly popular "fancy" war dancers with bustles, such as those at the Craterville and Dietriech's Lake fairs.

47. Guy Quetone to Julia Jordan, 4/18/1968, DD:37:T246:9, 3/23/1971, DD:37:T637:4–11.

48. Guy Quetone to Julia Jordan, 3/23/1971, DD:37, T637:4–8. Doris Duke Collection, SFN, pp. 531, 1935; author's fieldnotes.

49. Harry Domebo to author, October 1989; author's fieldnotes.

50. Weiser Tongkeamha to author.
51. Laura Sankadota Tahlo to author, 7/1992; Harry Domebo to author; author's fieldnotes.
52. Weiser Tongkeamha to author, July 1990.
53. SFN, 1935.
54. Frizzlehead to Richardson, 1935, SFN, p. 1218.
55. Ananthy Odlepaugh Calendar, Fort Sill Museum Archives, Lawton, Oklahoma.
56. Ananthy Odlepaugh Ledgerbook, FSL.; Parker McKenzie to author, 1994; Francis Tsonetokoy to author, 1990.
57. Author's fieldnotes; Parker McKenzie, Francis Tsonetokoy, Atwater Onco to author.
58. Grace Tsonetokoy to author, 7/11/1991; author's fieldnotes.
59. FSL.
60. Grace Tsonetokoy to author, 7/11/1991; author's fieldnotes.
61. Marriott Papers, WHC; White Fox to La Barre, XI-9, 10, 11, 7/26/1935, SFN, p. 547; Lone Bear to La Barre, 1a–5, 6/28/1935, SFN, p. 542.
62. Tsoodle to Marriott, 7/10/1936, WHC.
63. "Kiowa Giveaway and Dance," Marriott Papers WHC.
64. Ibid.
65. Author's fieldnotes.
66. Stecker to Commissioner Valentine, 12/15/1909, 98759-1909-063K, KAF-NAA.
67. John Francis Jr., Acting Chief Clerk, to Stecker, 1/22/1910, 98759-1909-063K, KAF-NAA.
68. Stecker to Valentine, 1/25/1910, 98759-1909-063K, KAF-NAA.
69. Hauke to Stecker, 2/2/1910, 98759-1909-063K, KAF-NAA.
70. Stecker to Commissioner Sells, 7/25/1913, 98759-1909-063K (his emphasis), KAF-NAA; author's fieldnotes.
71. Author's fieldnotes; Parker McKenzie, miscellaneous papers in possession of the author; Stecker to Commissioner Sells, 7/25/1913, 98759-1909-063K, KAF-NAA.
72. Stecker to Commissioner Sells, 7/25/1913, 98759-1909-063K, KAF-NAA.
73. Hauke to Stecker, 8/29/1913, 91980-1913-063K, KAF-NAA.
74. Ah-pe-ah-to to Sells, 8/25/1913, 104547-1913-063K; Stecker to Sells, 6/26/1914, 9198-1913-063K, KAF-NAA.
75. Stecker to Sells, 6/26/1914, 9198-1913-063K, KAF-NAA.
76. Reverend Clouse to Stecker, 5/20/1914; Reverend Gassaway to Stecker, 5/27/1914, 91980-1913-063K; Reverend Treat to Stecker 6/6/1914, 91980-1913-063K; Reverend Andrés Martínez to Stecker 5/17/1914, 91980-1913-063K; Treat to Stecker, 6/6/1914, KAF-NAA.
77. Sells to Sit-ah-pa-tah, 7/6/1914, 91980-1913-063K; Sells to Stecker, 7/6/1914, 91980-1913-063K, KAF-NAA.
78. E. B. Meritt, Assistant Commissioner, to Stecker, 9/21/1914, 91980-1913-063K, KAF-NAA.
79. Ibid.
80. Stecker to Sells, 3/12/1914, 90918-1913-063K, KAF-NAA.

81. Stecker to Sells, 6/28/1915; Western Union Telegram, 72353-1915-063K; J. S. Rinefort to Red Buffalo, 6/23/1915, 72353-1915-063K, KAF-NAA.

82. Stinchecum to Sells, 7/1/1915, 72353-1915-063K, KAF-NAA.

83. Meritt to Sweeney, 7/1/1915, 72353-1915-063K, KAF-NAA.

84. Ibid.

85. Department of Interior "Memorandum," 7/2/1915, 72353-1915-063K, KAF-NAA.

86. First Assistant Secretary to Stinchecum, n.d., 72353-1915-063K, KAF-NAA.

87. Stinchecum to Sells, 8/1/1915, 72353-1915-063K, KAF-NAA.

88. Ibid.

89. Ibid.

90. Meritt to Stinchecum, 8/25/1915, 72353-1915-063K, KAF-NAA.

91. Ah-pe-ah-to to Sells, 8/31/1915, 91980-1913-063K, KAF-NAA.

92. Meritt to Saitahpetato, 9/13/1915, 91980-1913-063K, KAF-NAA.

93. Saitahpetato to Meritt, 11/15/1915, 91980-1913-063K, KAF-NAA.

94. Meritt to Saitahpetato, 12/9/1915, 91980-1913-063K, KAF-NAA.

95. Big Tree to Secretary Lane, 2/7 and 2/16/1916, 14842-1916-063K; Meritt to Big Tree, 2/21 and 3/16/1916, 14842-1916-063K, KAF-NAA.

96. Stinchecum to Sells, 4/26/1916, 72353-1915-063K, KAF-NAA.

97. Sells to Stinchecum, 7/11/1916, 72353-1915-063K, KAF-NAA.

98. James Ahtone to Sells, 6/12/1916, 66449-1916-063K; Meritt to Ahtone, 6/27/1916, 66449-1916-063K, KAF-NAA.

99. Ahtone to Sells, 7/8/1916, 66449-1916-063K, KAF-NAA.

100. Meritt to Ahtone, 7/27/1916, 66449-1916-063K, KAF-NAA.

101. Stinchecum to Indian Office, 7/26/1916; Western Union Telegram, 72353-1915-06K, KAF-NAA.

102. Meritt to Stinchecum, 7/27/1916, 7293-1915-063K, KAF-NAA.

103. Tennyson Berry to Congressman Scott Ferris, 8/16/1916; Western Union Telegram, 7293-1915-063K; Meritt to Ferris, 8/18/1916; Meritt to Berry 8/18/1916, 7293-1915-063K, KAF-NAA.

104. Stinchecum to Sells, 8/23/1916, 72353-1915-063K, KAF-NAA.

105. Author's fieldnotes. Several Christian and traditionalist Kiowa mentioned Saunkeah's role in blacklisting other Kiowa, some with clear disdain.

106. Stinchecum to Sells, 8/23/1916, 72353-1915-063K; Meritt to Berry, 9/9/1916, 72353-1915-063K, KAF-NAA.

107. Stinchecum to Sells, 12/4/1916, 72353-1915-063K, KAF-NAA.

108. Meritt to Stinchecum, 12/18/1916, 7293-1915-063K, KAF-NAA.

109. Stinchecum to Sells, 1/2/1917, 72353-1915-063K, KAF-NAA; author's fieldnotes.

110. Stinchecum to Sells, 1/2, 1/6, 5/31, and 7/6/1917, 72353-1915-063K, KAF-NAA. Kracht (1989:845) states that fifty-one signed.

111. Gus Palmer Sr., Mac Whitehorse, Parker McKenzie to author.

112. Parker McKenzie to author, 1991; Francis Tsonetokoy to author, 12/8/1990.

113. Author's fieldnotes.

114. Harry Domebo, Gus Palmer Sr., Mac Whitehorse, Parker McKenzie, Alice Littleman, Gertrude Yeahquo Hines to author. Kiowa veterans of World War I:

(1) (overseas in combat) Glen Whitefox, Herbert Dupoint, Joseph Gilbert Kauley; (2) (overseas noncombat) John Bosin, Casper Fritz Kauley, Norman Lon Ahpeahtone; (3) (stateside) Mark Keahbone, Homer Buffalo, Moses Poolaw, Charlie Apekaum, David Frizzlehead, David Poolaw, Frank Doyeto, Fred Quoetone. Steve Mopope was in stateside service and was medically discharged during the great outbreak of Spanish influenza.

115. Autobiography of a Kiowa Indian (La Barre n.d.: 38).

116. Author's fieldnotes; Luther Brace and Whitefox to La Barre, 7/18/1935, SFN; "History of the Dances" (cassette tape), Georgetta Palmer Brown and Joe Fish Dupoint, Ahtone Trading Post and Recording, Fort Cobb, Oklahoma.

117. Parker McKenzie to author.

118. Stinchecum to Commissioner Burke, 11/2/1921, 58849-1921-063K, KAF-NAA.

119. Stinchecum to Burke, 7/13/1921, 58849-1921-063K, KAF-NAA.

120. Morris Dayeto [Doyeto] to Meritt, 9/29/1921, 58849-1921-063K, KAF-NAA.

121. Ibid.; Stinchecum to Burke, 7/13/1921, 58849-1921-063K, KAF-NAA.

122. Stinchecum to Burke, 7/13/1921, 58849-1921-063K, KAF-NAA.

123. Burke to Stinchecum, 7/25 and 10/10/1921; Burke to Ha-to-go, 7/25/1921; Burke to Enoch Smokey and father, 7/25/1921, 58849-1921-063K; Stinchecum to Burke, 11/2/1921, 58849-1921-063K, KAF-NAA.

124. Ledgerbook, Fort Sill Museum Archives #D-1049, Lawton, Oklahoma; author's fieldnotes; Alfred Chalepah to author. Mr. Chalepah danced in the performance of this Apache Manatidie Society dance in 1922.

125. Oklahoma Historical Society (OHS-NAA): Reverend R. A. Blair to Commissioner Rhoades, Reverend D. H. Elliott to Rhoades, 6/16/1931; Elliott to Secretary Wilbur, 6/19/1931; Reverend P. Coleman to Rhoades and Wilbur 6/29/1931; Reverend J. Slater to Rhoades and Wilbur, 6/30/1931; Mrs. W. J. Jack to Rhoades, 7/15/1931; Reverend J. C. Mathews to Wilbur, 7/29/1931, 33833-1931-062K; Reverend R. C. Adams and Reverend H. F. Gilbert to Rhoades and Frank Smith, 5/22/1931, 33833-1931-062K, KAF-NAA.

126. Author's fieldnotes.

127. Reverend David Paddlety to author, 3/20/1993.

128. 1935, pp. 574–597, SFN.

129. Author's fieldnotes.

130. Ibid.

131. Ibid.

132. Bill Koomsa to author, 1/24/1995.

133. Author's fieldnotes.

134. Ibid.

135. Ibid.

136. Ibid.

137. David Paddlety to author, 3/20/1993.

138. Author's fieldnotes.

139. Gus Palmer Sr. to author.

140. Mac Whitehorse to author; Óhòmò Society meeting 1993.

141. Author's fieldnotes.

142. Ibid.
143. Ibid.
144. Jerrold Levy to author, 6/26/1990.
145. Kiowa Gourd Clan Ceremonials Booklet, 7/1–4/1976; author's fieldnotes.
146. Author's fieldnotes.
147. Ibid. Apparently, however, poor personal relations resulted in problems during Koomsa's vice-presidency and subsequent resignation. Some elders have indicated that Koomsa, the son of an influential and knowledgeable singer and Gourd Dancer, Bob Koomsa, was actually more familiar with the Gourd Dance traditions and thereby more qualified to actually lead the revival. In addition, some Kiowa state that Hainta's relationship as a son-in-law of Daugomah swayed a major portion of the vote in his favor, as many of the older men involved and consulted during the revival were relatives of Daugomah.
148. Author's fieldnotes, 1995.
149. Author's fieldnotes, Kiowa Gourd Clan, 7/4/1991.
150. Robert J. Stahl (Kracht 1994:334) has suggested that "Gourd Dance regalia was 'invented' by studying turn-of-the-century photographs of Kiowa, Comanche, and Plains Apache peyotists." I disagree, because the Kiowa still clearly distinguish between the two and many early-twentieth-century photographs of Kiowa Gourd Dancers lack shoulder blankets, red and blue blankets, and gourd rattles. While the dress styles of both have changed and are relatively similar, I do not find any clear basis for this diagnosis based on my own interviews with Kiowa, Comanche, and Apache elders.
151. Gus Palmer Sr. to author.
152. Author's fieldnotes.
153. Gus Palmer Sr. to author.
154. Gus Palmer Sr. to author. Lyndreth Palmer was the first Kiowa killed in action in twentieth-century warfare, on 12/14/1944. In June 1993 the Occitan Nation in Mountauban, France, presented Vanessa Santos Morgan, a relative of Lyndreth Palmer who was then visiting France, with several gifts in honor of him, including a clay plaque of France, a brass medal from the mayor of Mountauban, a red cloth bundle containing sage, and another containing a flicker feather and consecrated soil from France. These items were donated to the Kiowa Tribal Museum by Vanessa Morgan. A special Catholic Mass was held in France in memory of Lyndreth Palmer during this visit.
155. Author's fieldnotes; Gus Palmer Sr. to author.
156. Harris (1989:98) incorrectly states that Black Legs Society members wore red capes as part of their dress in the nineteenth century.
157. Author's fieldnotes.
158. Ibid.
159. Ibid.
160. In the past there were two of these curved staffs in the Kiowa tribe, one associated with the Tòkǫ́gàut Society and one associated with Se/osa of the Chèjánmàu Society. Yellow Wolf, who was once a pàubôn (curved lance) keeper in the Black Legs Society, remade and sold a pàubôn to Tǫ́càbáudài (Appeared from the Water), another Black Legs member, after the Qóichǫ́gàu became defunct.

161. Author's fieldnotes. Several elders indicated that songs from other societies had been brought into the modern Gourd Dance both due to their similarity and in order to keep them alive.

162. Author's fieldnotes.

163. White Fox to La Barre, XI-9, 10, 11, 7/26/1935, SFN, p. 549.

164. Author's fieldnotes, Kiowa Gourd Clan, 7/4/1993.

165. Author's fieldnotes.

166. While guests are always welcome as spectators, Kiowa opinions over the inclusion of non-Kiowa and especially of non-Indians in the Gourd Dance vary greatly. While some Kiowa wholeheartedly embrace the interest shown by outsiders, others are strongly opposed to it. Those Kiowa I have spoken with who were concerned about or opposed to such participation commonly complained about placing too much emphasis on protocol such as certain ways to walk around the drum, initiation rights and fees, and "trying too hard to be Indian." The use of Gourd Dancing organizations for personal profit through the holding of a leadership position was also criticized. Perhaps most offensive are (1) those individuals in a non-Indian organization claiming to have "the authority to do so and so" according to some sanctioned rights given to them by someone who allegedly had the authority to do so and (2) those who (not understanding change and adaptation, being frozen in a state of nineteenth-century romanticism) believe they are "experts" and try to tell the Kiowa, including the direct descendants of the original dancers, how to dance the Gourd Dance.

167. Author's fieldnotes.

168. The strength of Ellis's (1990) article lies in his discussion of the role of the Gourd Dance revival in broader native trends and its role as an agent of cultural reintegration. As a historical work, it definitely makes contributions to the knowledge of the Gourd Dance. However, there are several historical and ethnological inaccuracies, which are probably due to the academic tradition of historians concerning ethnographic fieldwork, knowledge of primary ethnological documentary sources, and familiarity with nineteenth-century military societies. Acquisition of these data and an ethnohistorical approach, I feel, would have clarified many points, thereby preventing Ellis's statement (1990:21) that "indeed, the tangled history of these early types of the dances makes it difficult to ascertain with any degree of certainty their precise role and function in the cultural life of the various tribes."

169. Author's fieldnotes—Cheyenne.

170. Author's fieldnotes—Comanche and Cheyenne.

171. Parker McKenzie, Gus Palmer Jr. to author; author's fieldnotes.

172. Author's fieldnotes.

173. Atwater Onco to author, 8/30/1994.

174. Author's fieldnotes.

175. Atwater Onco to author, 8/30/1994. This statement refers to the translation of Jáifègàu as "Unafraid of Death."

176. Author's fieldnotes; see also Lassiter (1992:44).

177. Bill Koomsa to author, 1/24/1995.

178. Billy Evans Horse to author, 1/24/1995.

179. Author's fieldnotes.

180. Ibid.
181. Ibid.; Eric Lassiter, personal communication, 1994.
182. Author's fieldnotes, 1995.
183. Author's fieldnotes.
184. The following description of the Black Legs Society and ceremonial is based on attending twenty-two ceremonial performances between 1989 and 1995, interviews with commander Gus Palmer Sr. and other officers and members, and residence with families closely associated with the society (see Meadows 1991).
185. Gus Palmer Sr. to author.
186. Ibid.
187. Ibid
188. Ibid.
189. Vanessa Jennings to author.
190. Charley Apekaum and White Buffalo to La Barre, 1935, SFN, p. 706; author's fieldnotes.
191. Author's fieldnotes; Gus Palmer Sr., Atwater Onco to author.
192. Gus Palmer Sr. to author.
193. Author's fieldnotes.
194. Ibid.
195. Gus Palmer Sr. to author.
196. Author's fieldnotes.
197. Author's fieldnotes.
198. Gus Palmer Sr. to the author; author's fieldnotes.
199. Martha Poolaw to author.
200. Author's fieldnotes.
201. My thanks to Eric Lassiter for providing me with an audio recording of this song.
202. Ibid.
203. "Saynday Was Coming Along . . ." program for the art exhibit at the Kiowa Tribal Complex, 1/18/1995.

4. Plains Apache Naishan Military Societies

1. Author's fieldnotes.
2. Author's fieldnotes. Concerning the varied names used for the Naishan Apache, Elizabeth A. H. John (1985: 395) surprisingly states: "Recently the group who have been labeled as the Kiowa Apaches for the last century have themselves rejected the term as misleading and confusing. Unfortunately, their remedy, incorporating themselves as the Apache Tribe of Oklahoma, only compounds confusion. Kataka Apaches might have been preferable for clear distinction and historical accuracy. From the era of this essay, Apaches del Norte has been selected as clearest in meaning." Foremost, it is not for anyone else to decide what the Apache choose to refer to themselves as. Second, while the name "Kataka" was once a current ethnonym, it is no longer a functional part of the contemporary Apache language and therefore should not be expected to be chosen as their own name. Concerning the various Apachean groups in Oklahoma and their relationship to other southwestern Apachean groups, there is more than adequate differ-

entiation in the general literature and it is Anglos, and not Indians, who have confusion differentiating the group.

3. James Mooney, Kiowa and Kiowa-Apache fieldnotes, 1993, NAA MS 2531.

4. Alfred Chalepah and Houston Klinekole to author.

5. Annual Reports of the Commissioner of Indian Affairs.

6. Alfred Chalepah to author, 1993.

7. Ibid.

8. Kiowa Agency reports, 1872.

9. Author's fieldnotes—Apache, Kiowa, and Comanche. There are clear indications that there were more Apache women and some men marrying and moving outside of the prereservation Apache community than non-Apache women and men marrying and shifting residing within the community (1900 Kiowa and Apache tribal censuses). Although Mooney's (MS:2531) fieldnotes indicate that social relations, prolonged visiting, and even partial residence during the Sun Dance and other portions of the year (some Kiowa were known to camp with their Apache in-laws during the Sun Dance, and descendants of such intermarriages often alternated visiting their different sets of relatives) were maintained between intermarried Kiowa and Apache, there was clearly a greater migration than emigration. There are, for example, more Apache women enrolled on the 1900 Kiowa tribal roll than Kiowa women enrolled on the 1900 Apache roll. This was no doubt affected by the numerically smaller Apache population, and Mooney's (MS: 2531) fieldnotes demonstrate Kiowa and Apache intermarriages well into the eighteenth century. Nevertheless, a core of the population was remaining Apache, while others were leaving the core, which suggests that there may have been problems in finding enough Apache females as marriage partners during some periods in the nineteenth century, which in turn facilitated an increase in the frequency of intermarriage, especially with Kiowa and Arapaho. While there are a great number of enrolled Kiowa and Apache tribal members on the 1900 census of mixed Apache and Kiowa descent, which shows a somewhat consistent pattern of intermarriage, this pattern increases again around 1900 when many Apache settled near Boone and Apache, Oklahoma, and continued intermarrying with Kiowa and Comanche residing near Stecker and Apache, Oklahoma. Several older enrolled Apache's Arapaho descent in 1900 can be linked to prereservation intermarriages with Arapaho, while many of the younger 1900 enrollees can be linked to Apache-Arapaho marriages in the late 1860s and early 1870s during a period of intense interaction between the two tribes.

10. James Mooney, Kiowa and Kiowa-Apache fieldnotes, NAA MS 2531, NAA; Ray Blackbear to William Bittle, 6/5/1963. All William Bittle interview citations are from WB.

11. While the Apache are most commonly associated with the Kiowa in Plains literature it is important to recognize their changing social relations, which included various periods of increasing and decreasing alliances with neighboring Plains populations. I believe that Apache relations with the Kiowa overshadow those with other populations because of the lengthy historical association which preceded the migration of the Apache and Kiowa onto the Southern Plains. My impression from ethnographic fieldwork, censuses, marriage and genealogy records, and cultural similarities is that, while the Apache maintained several chang-

ing relationships through the nineteenth century, the relationship with the Kiowa was of greater historical span and depth. Apache alliances with the Kiowa, Comanche, Cheyenne, and Arapaho during the mid-nineteenth century were always maintained yet continually shifted in degree and emphasis. These movements by the smaller Apache population may reflect opportunistic alliances of varied duration which were beneficial for the Apache as a smaller population. While the Apache always maintained their own ethnicity, their ability to interact intensely with a number of other distinct populations suggests that cultural adaptability was an important tool for cultural survival as a smaller population. The ability to change the intensities of ethnic affiliation with a number of other populations would have been beneficial in facilitating alliances with certain groups to adapt to the specific set of social circumstances at a given time. Bittle contends that the Apache's primary role in the Plains economy was as traders, and they appear to have moved away from trouble affecting trade at certain times. Hence the periods of varying emphasis on trading as brokers, warfare, peace with the United States in the late 1860s and early 1870s, and renewed alliances and increased intermarriage with Arapaho during this later time may reflect these strategies.

12. Author's fieldnotes—Kiowa and Apache.

13. Alfred Chalepah to author; 1900 Apache tribal census.

14. 1900 Kiowa tribal census.

15. Author's fieldnotes. Other Apachean groups are differentiated as Mescalero Apache, Jicarilla Apache, Lipan Apache, etc.

16. Alfred Chalepah to author.

17. Alfred Chalepah and Houston Klinekole to author.

18. Alfred Chalepah, 5/6/1992; Houston Klinekole, 6/23/1993, to author. Some elders attribute Daveko's lack of descendants to the "price of having been a sorcerer" (see McAllister 1970).

19. Alfred Chalepah to author.

20. Alfred Chalepah, Houston Klinekole to author.

21. 1935, SFN, pp. 120, 755–756, 1213, 1294.

22. I have been unable to locate McAllister's original fieldnotes to determine if any additional unpublished material regarding Apache military societies was collected.

23. Louise Saddleblanket, DD T-79-7.

24. Louise Saddleblanket, DD T-79-6.

25. Alfred Chalepah to author, 1992.

26. Alfred Chalepah, Houston Klinekole, Irene Poolaw to author, 1992.

27. Ray Black Bear, DD T-223:6.

28. Alfred Chalepah to author, 3/25/1993.

29. Rose Chalepah to William Bittle, 6/27/1961.

30. Sussagossa to William Bittle, 7/1/1961; Alfred Chalepah to author, 7/21/1995.

31. Rose Chalepah to William Bittle, 6/14 and 6/27/1961.

32. Author's fieldnotes.

33. DD T-223.

34. Rose Chalepah to William Bittle, 6/27/1961; Fred Bigman to William Bittle, 6/17/1963; Ray Black Bear to William Bittle, 6/8–9/1961.

35. Rose Chalepah to William Bittle, 6/27/1961; Alfred Chalepah to author, 7/21/1995.

36. Ray Blackbear and Rose Chalepah to William Bittle, 7/25/1961, 6/14/1961.

37. Alfred Chalepah to author, 4/1/1993. Although the Apache data are limited, the ropes or sashes were probably used in a fashion similar to that of most Plains military societies: staking oneself down in battle and standing one's ground until victory or until released by a fellow society member. Alice Marriott (WHC) collected several independent accounts in 1935 regarding the Kiowa Black Legs Society, which also maintained a curved, fur-wrapped staff. In addition, several Kiowa elders in 1935 mentioned the capture and use of similar staffs by Apache.

38. Alfred Chalepah to author, 9/19/1991.

39. Alfred Chalepah to author, 1992, 1993.

40. Ibid.

41. Alfred Chalepah to author, 9/18/1992.

42. Rose Chalepah to William Bittle, 6/11/1964.

43. Houston Klinekole to author. This was the grandfather of Alonzo Chalepah (ca. 1875–1943), who inherited his name *Chatzupah* or *Chaydlpah* (Gut Necklace).

44. Joe Black Bear to William Bittle, 3/18/1949.

45. Rose Chalepah to William Bittle, 6/10/1964.

46. Rose Chalepah to William Bittle, 6/11/1964; William Bittle, 1964.

47. Rose Chalepah to William Bittle, 6/10–12/1964; Alfred Chalepah and Houston Klinekole to author.

48. Alfred Chalepah to author.

49. Alfred Chalepah to author, 9/18/1992, 3/25/1993, 7/21/1995. This position was called bit-da-jhey by my eldest Apache consultant.

50. Some family members stated that Archilta chose his son-in-law Apache Ben Chaletsin as a successor for his staff because he lacked confidence that his own sons would care for the position and traditions correctly. I have found this hesitancy and fear in elders that the younger generation might not care for things "in the right manner" in several tribes, throughout the twentieth century. Author's fieldnotes.

51. Alfred Chalepah to author, 9/18/1992. The use of a red fox pelt as a wrist loop on the whip of military society whipmen is also found among several other Plains tribes. The whip was also supposed to contain some form of ball on the top of the end of the club; Ray Blackbear to William Bittle, 6/10/1961.

52. Rose Chalepah to William Bittle, 7/20/1961; Ray Black Bear to William Bittle, 6/8-9/1961; Alfred Chalepah to author, 4/1/1993.

53. Ray Black Bear to William Bittle, 6/10 and 6/14/1961.

54. William Bittle fieldnotes; author's fieldnotes. There is confusion between the use of the term *bazaye* for the whipmen by Bittle's consultants and the term *bajraye* for the two errand boys by McAllister (1935). However, it should be noted that current elders do not recall the position of these two individuals in the society. Likewise, there are a diagram and references in descriptions of a 1961 Manatidie performance by Apache consultants that state that there was one *li.ti'di'e'* serving as a whipman and two "Bulls" who stood on each side of the line of staffholders. Numerically, this does not agree with the positions described by McAllister and reflects a confusion in terminology. McAllister did not provide a

term for the whipman; however, as he worked with the last of the Apache male elders who were actual Manatidie members, his use of the term *bajraye* meaning assistants is followed here. In 1964 Rose Chalepah gave three terms which were said to have been used for the office of whipman: *nadizode, dindenadizo,* and *bazaye.* The last closely resembles the *bajraye* position described by McAllister. Rose Chalepah to William Bittle, 6/10–11/1964.

55. Ray Black Bear to William Bittle, 6/5/1963.

56. Joe Black Bear to William Bittle, 3/18/1949.

57. Louise Saddleblanket to William Bittle, DD T-79:9.

58. Joe Black Bear to William Bittle, 3/18/1949; Ray Black Bear to William Bittle, 6/3/1963.

59. Louise Saddleblanket to William Bittle, DD T-79:9. This account corresponds with descriptions of other Plains Dog Soldier Society initiations.

60. Ray Black Bear to William Bittle, 6/3/1963.

61. Houston Klinekole to author, 1993. After dancing for four days and nights without sleeping during a Klintidie meeting, Old Man Chewing received the design for a painted tipi in a dream. This design ensured longevity for its owner and allowed the tipi to withstand all storms. The tipi was thus a refuge for others and was inherited by his son Daveko and later by his stepson Klinekole or Apache Sam.

62. Frizzlehead to Richardson, 1935, SFN, p. 1237; Joe Black Bear to William Bittle, 3/18/1949.

63. Alfred Chalepah to author, 1993, 7/21/1995; William Bittle fieldnotes; Mike Davis to author, 2/13/1995.

64. Alfred Chalepah to author, 3/25 and 12/2/1993; Houston Klinekole to author, 6/30/1993; Rose Chalepah to William Bittle, 6/27/1961, 6/11/1964.

65. Alfred Chalepah to author, 3/25 and 12/2/1993; Houston Klinekole to author, 6/30/1993; Ray Blackbear to William Bittle, 6/5/1963.

66. Alfred Chalepah to author, 12/2/1993; Mac Whitehorse to author, 1993.

67. Alfred Chalepah to author, 3/25 and 12/2/1993; Houston Klinekole to author, 6/30/1993; Fred Bigman to William Bittle, 6/12/1963.

68. Alfred Chalepah to author, 3/25 and 12/2/1993; Houston Klinekole to author, 6/30/1993; Ray Blackbear to William Bittle, 7/25/1961.

69. Ray Blackbear to William Bittle, 6/5/1963.

70. Alfred Chalepah to author, 1993.

71. Alfred Chalepah to author, 3/25 and 12/2/1993; Houston Klinekole to author, 6/30/1993.

72. Rose Chalepah to William Bittle, 7/20/1961.

73. William Bittle fieldnotes, 3/18/1949. According to an account given by an Apache elder in 1949 who had obtained it directly from Taho, the women and the old man in the society all danced naked inside the lodge. The women threw Taho and Apache Stephen down and scratched at their heads. Afterward the women all went to the creek to bathe. Further descriptions of a sexual nature were included. See the original materials for further elaboration. These rituals undoubtedly had a significant purpose, possible symbolic ritual revenge, which is no longer known, as similar accounts exist in a number of other Plains Indian women's societies.

74. Author's fieldnotes.

75. Author's fieldnotes; SFN, pp. 755–756, 1261.

76. L-Troop membership rosters, Fort Sill Archives, Lawton, Oklahoma; Alfred Chalepah to author, 1995.

77. Rose Chalepah to William Bittle, 6/10–11/1964; Ray Black Bear to William Bittle, 6/10/1961.

78. Author's fieldnotes.

79. Alonzo Chalepah to author, 2/12/1997, phone conversation.

80. Alfred Chalepah to author, 1993; Rose Chalepah to William Bittle, 6/10/1964.

81. Alfred Chalepah to author, 3/25/1993; Houston Klinekole to author, 1993.

82. Alfred Chalepah to author, 3/25/1993.

83. Rose Chalepah to William Bittle, 6/11/1964.

84. Rose Chalepah to William Bittle, 6/11–12/1964.

85. Author's Kiowa fieldnotes.

86. Alfred Chalepah, Houston Klinekole to author.

87. Rose Chalepah to William Bittle, 6/27/1961, 6/11/1964; Alfred Chalepah to author, 1992, 1993.

88. Stinchecum to Sells 4/26 and 8/23/1916, 72353-1915-063K; Sells to Stinchecum, 7/11/1916, 72353-1915-063K; Stinchecum to Sells, 8/23/1916, 72353-1915-063K; Meritt to Berry 9/9/1916, 72353-1915-063K; Stinchecum to Sells, 12/4/1916, 72353-1915-063K; Meritt to Stinchecum, 12/18/1916, 7293-1915-063K; Stinchecum to Sells, 1/2, 1/6, 5/31, 7/6/1917, 72353-1915-063K; KAF-NAA; author's fieldnotes.

89. Alfred Chalepah, 12/2/1993, Houston Klinekole, 6/30/1993, to author.

90. Irene Chalepah Poolaw, 5/6/1992, Alfred Chalepah, 4/29/1992, to author.

91. Ray Black Bear to William Bittle, 6/5/1963; author's fieldnotes.

92. Alfred Chalepah, DD T-13:7.

93. "Kiowa-Apache Blackfoot Society (Manatidie)" certificate of incorporation, Office of the Secretary of State, State of Oklahoma, 11/27/1961, copy in possession of the author; author's fieldnotes; Houston Klinekole to author, 6/1993.

94. Author's fieldnotes; Mike Davis to author, 2/13/1995.

95. Kiowa Agency Files.

96. Alfred Chalepah, 4/21/1993, Houston Klinekole, 4/20/1993, 9/24/1993, to author.

97. Alfred Chalepah, 4/21/1993, Houston Klinekole, 4/20/1992, 9/24/1993, Irene Poolaw, 5/6/1992, to author.

98. Author's fieldnotes; Houston Klinekole to author, 9/24/1993.

99. Author's fieldnotes.

100. DD T-121, WHC.

101. Author's fieldnotes.

102. Author's fieldnotes; Alfred Chalepah to author, 3/25/1993.

103. Author's fieldnotes.

104. Ibid.

105. Ray Black Bear to Bittle, 6/14/1961.

106. Alfred Chalepah to author, 8/2/1992.

107. Ibid.

108. Author's fieldnotes.

109. William Bittle fieldnotes. The Manatidie often perform at descendants' organization dances, and Comanche do perform in Manatidie dances. In contrast to Kavanagh's (1980:114) assertion that Comanche did not participate in Manatidie Society dances, Bittle's fieldnotes show dancing and singing participation by numerous Kiowa and some Comanche families since the early 1960s. At some dances of the Redbone organization between 1990 and 1995, nearly half of the dancers were enrolled Comanche, many with no Apache descent.

110. Apache Blackfeet Society, ninth and eleventh annual dance booklets, 8/1–3/1969 and 8/6–8/1971, privately published.

111. Author's fieldnotes.

112. Ibid.

113. Ibid.

5. Comanche Military Societies

1. This chapter is respectfully dedicated to the late Edward Yellowfish and the late Forrest Kassanavoid. Both graciously shared their extensive knowledge of Comanche societies with me. Mr. Yellowfish was one of the original members of the 1972 Comanche Little Ponies revival and was responsible for my induction into the Comanche Little Ponies. Anyone who knew Ed knew of his soft humor, his dignified demeanor, and his great knowledge and respect for the Little Pony tradition and for the dance arena in general. I thank you for sharing your friendship and knowledge as a Little Pony brother. Mr. Kassanavoid was another extremely knowledgeable elder who served as a headsman of the Comanche War Dance Society for over twenty years and who loved to share his knowledge with anyone who was sincerely interested. *Uh-dah Haits!*

2. Tom Kavanagh, personal communication.

3. Author's fieldnotes; Forrest Kassanavoid, Charles Chibitty to author.

4. I am especially grateful to Tom Kavanagh, who has graciously shared personal and unpublished documentation on Comanche societies.

5. Kavanagh (personal communication, 5/5/1994) states that "it is a fine line as to whether I believe the 'problems encountered with the Comanche anomaly do not involve paradigmatic counter-instance.' Certainly not enough to throw out the entire Plains paradigm, but enough to raise questions about how it is applied." See Kavanagh (1986).

6. There are two versions of this drawing, one as recorded in the AGN and one as recorded in the AGI. The copy from the AGI (Thomas 1929:294, 1932:324) is the copy discussed here. The major differences are the position of the lances held by the group leaders, the presence (AGN) and absence (AGI) of an animal skin–like item beside the leader (B) in the second line or group, and the positions of certain alphabetical letters in correlation to their positions in the groups. Both are copies of an as yet undiscovered original, and it is not known which is the earlier copy. My thanks to Dr. Thomas Kavanagh for these two documents and personal communications concerning these documents. See also Kavanagh (1996:115).

7. The original statement from Elguézabal (1802) says, "la partida de treinta y dos gandules encogidos que han nombrados bajo las órdenes de Capt. Chihuahua

con el fin de que contengan a los que quieran hostiliaras [hostilizarios?]" (a party of thirty-two timid idlers serving under Capt. Chihuahua whose objective is to contain those who attempt hostilities against them). The term *encogidos* or "shrunken" literally implies "turned inward for protection." While the word "police" is John's (1984:351–352) addition, the use of the force to serve as a military or policelike unit to control Comanche who would be hostile is clear.

8. Author's fieldnotes. Sources vary as to who requested the truce.

9. Many of my arguments concerning Comanche societies are supplemented by additional ethnological descriptions concerning society origins, dress, dances, customs, etc., not presented in this work. Ed Yellowfish to Tom Kavanagh, 1979, transcript in possession of the author. Additional sources clarifying the origins and diffusion of the Gourd Dance on the Southern Plains include James Mooney, MS 2531:7:4–5, NAA; Mooney 1898; Grinnell 1983; Milton Toyebo and Yale Spottedbird to Boyce Timmons, DD T-651:13–16, 6/19/1971; Noyes 1993:278; author's fieldnotes—Kiowa, Cheyenne, and Comanche.

10. Haddon Nauni to Thomas Kavanagh (1979), transcript in possession of the author, courtesy of Dr. Kavanagh.

11. Mooney (1898:271–272) and Grinnell (1983:45–62) place the 1837 battle in the panhandle of Texas south of Fort Elliott, while Mooney (1907:377) later gives it as occurring in a southern tributary of the upper Washita River approximately twelve miles southwest of present-day Cheyenne, Oklahoma; Joe Attocknie, DD T-448; author's fieldnotes—Cheyenne.

12. Joe Attocknie, DD T-448.

13. Joe Attocknie, DD T-448; Post Oak Jim, 7/11/1933, SFN; Kavanagh n.d.b: 98; author's fieldnotes—Cheyenne and Comanche.

14. James Mooney, MS 2531:7:5; author's fieldnotes.

15. See SFN. Kavanagh n.d.b.:introduction.

16. Post Oak Jim, 7/11/1933, SFN; Kavanagh n.d.b:98.

17. Ibid.

18. Author's fieldnotes—Cheyenne.

19. Post Oak Jim, 7/11/1933, SFN; Kavanagh n.d.b:98.

20. Ed Yellowfish to author, 3/27/1992.

21. Howard White Wolf, 7/31/1933, SFN; Kavanagh n.d.b:195.

22. Itovits, 8/7/1933, SFN; Kavanagh n.d.b:235.

23. Howard White Wolf, 7/31/1933, SFN; Kavanagh n.d.b:195–197.

24. Post Oak Jim, 7/14/1933, SFN; Kavanagh n.d.b:127.

25. Author's fieldnotes.

26. Ed Yellowfish to author, 3/27/1992; author's fieldnotes.

27. Notes on Comanche Dance at Walters, Oklahoma, 1933, SFN; Kavanagh n.d.b:315.

28. Author's fieldnotes. Another term for Bison was *Num-ah-koot-soo* (Comanche Cow). One elder stated that the dance might be known by different names in different Comanche "clans" (divisions), as there was often more than one word for a single item, which has proven true in interviews in different Comanche communities.

29. Author's fieldnotes. Announcements read at Tuhwi Society performances

are somewhat inconsistent in that they give dates for the society's origin ranging from as early as 1700 to well into the nineteenth century.

30. Comanche Homecoming, Walters, Oklahoma, 7/17/1993.

31. Howard White Wolf, 7/31/1933, Frank Chekovi, 8/11/1933, SFN; Kavanagh n.d.b: 195–197, 249.

32. June Sovo, Ed Yellowfish, Forrest Kassanavoid to author.

33. Ed Yellowfish to author, 3/27/1992; author's fieldnotes.

34. Author's fieldnotes. Again Gelo (1986:221) seems to confuse distinctions between Crow Tassel Wearers and the Tuhwi Society, emphasizing Crow Tassel Wearers' limited members and antisocial behavior, in stating, "Recalling the behavior of the Crow soldiers, the corbines travel in small flocks and remain apart from all other species."

35. Gelo (1986:219, 222, 226) provides a discussion of the Tuhwi that, while containing several useful contributions to the society's history, contains several inaccuracies. Namely, he confuses the *Tuhwi* or Black Crow or Black Knife Society of the Yamparika division and the Crow Tassel Wearers, a small sodality of individuals who pursued warfare almost incessantly, which has not been associated with any specific Comanche divisional grouping. Hoebel's (1940:30–33) discussion, using Jeanette Mirsky's fieldnotes, is on the Crow Tassel Wearers and not on the Tuhwi Society. Gelo (1986:222, 226) focuses on analogizing the Crow Tassel Wearers' antisocial behavior and association with death to the Tuhwi in several instances. Yet he appears to distinguish the two groups (1986:222). Linguistic ethnonyms and a more thorough use of the ethnographic record (especially the 1933 Santa Fe notes) would perhaps have provided the necessary clarification.

36. Howard White Wolf, 7/31/1933, SFN; Kavanagh n.d.b: 197.

37. Dana Chibitty, DD T177-1. Several Comanche have reported the presence of a dog taboo among the Tuhwi Society.

38. Post Oak Jim, 7/17/1933, SFN; Kavanagh n.d.b: 135, 139; Carney Saupitty Sr. to author, 4/11/1994; author's fieldnotes. Some younger Comanche call this the Rabbit Dance; however, older Comanche, although unable to translate the name, state that *Wot-see-ah* is not one of the three Comanche names for the rabbit (*E-kah-nee-um*, *Tseek-quah*, or *Tah-voh-kee-nah*).

39. Carney Saupitty Sr. to author, 4/11/1994; author's fieldnotes.

40. Forrest Kassanavoid to author; author's fieldnotes—Ponca.

41. Author's fieldnotes. This by-name for the society refers to the scant clothing worn by early War Dancers. During one incident an individual's testicles dropped out of the side of his breechclout and, being exposed to all in attendance, resulted in this name for the dance.

42. Frank Moetah, 1933, SFN; Kavanagh n.d.b: 312.

43. Frank Chekovi, 8/10/1933, Post Oak Jim 7/26/1933, SFN; Kavanagh n.d.b: 247, 183.

44. Mrs. Birdsong, 10/30/1956, Comanche Misc. Files, Fort Sill Museum Archives, Lawton, Oklahoma. The Pukutsi were individual contraries, allegedly wayward youths. The members were dauntless in battle and would stand their ground until their rattles were taken from them by a middle-aged man following some conspicuous act of bravery, thereby relieving them of their battle obliga-

tions. They allegedly staked themselves down in battle and stood, bow in one hand and rattle in the other, neither fighting nor advancing, but singing until victory or death (SFN; Kavanagh n.d.b:247–248, 309–312).

45. Frank Chekovi gave a slightly different version of the same incident (8/10/1933, SFN; Kavanagh n.d.b:248): "A *Pukutsi* went through camp, entering tipis and singing. One old lady heard him and told him to get her a *dakwa* and make her a robe. He went on singing as though he didn't hear. That night he went on a war raid alone. Near an enemy camp he met and killed an Osage. He skinned him out, leaving the head, hands, and feet on, then he hurried back. People didn't hear him around camp, and wondered where he was. Finally they heard him coming singing. The woman came crawling out and reached up. She felt the hairless skin. She was scared, and called her husband. He brought a light and saw it was a human skin, and recognized the tribe from the hair dressing. Osages wore their hair clipped short and powdered with red in old days, maybe he had a crest down center [*sic*] of head; he looked terrifying." Hekiyani, 1933, SFN; Kavanagh n.d.b:309.

46. Hekiyani, 1933, SFN; Kavanagh n.d.b:10, 309.

47. Because Jeannette Mirsky's Comanche fieldnotes have not been located, the history and context of the Crow Tassel group cannot be more fully verified.

48. HLS-1:2:1–2.

49. Cabaya to H. L. Scott, HLS-1:2:2.

50. Quanah Parker to H. L. Scott, HLS-1:2:2.

51. HLS-1:2:11.

52. Kavanagh n.d.b.

53. Cabaya to H. L. Scott, HLS-1:2:2.

54. Post Oak Jim, 7/14/1933, SFN; Kavanagh n.d.b:127.

55. Post Oak Jim, 7/17/1933, SFN; Kavanagh n.d.b:140.

56. Post Oak Jim, 7/11–7/17/1933, SFN; Kavanagh n.d.b:99, 136.

57. Ibid.

58. Howard White Wolf, 7/31/1933, SFN; Kavanagh n.d.b:196.

59. Tom Kavanagh, personal communication, 1993.

60. Ed Yellowfish to author, 3/27/1992.

61. Quanah Parker to H. L. Scott, HLS-1:1:14–15.

62. Howard White Wolf, 7/31/1933, SFN; Kavanagh n.d.b:196.

63. Author's fieldnotes.

64. Ibid.

65. Ibid.

66. Post Oak Jim, 7/17/1933, Howard White Wolf, 7/31/1933, SFN; Kavanagh n.d.b:139, 195.

67. Post Oak Jim, 7/11/1933, Howard White Wolf, 7/31/1933, SFN; Kavanagh n.d.b:99, 195.

68. Kwasia, 7/5/1933, SFN; Kavanagh n.d.b:56.

69. Post Oak Jim, 7/17/1933, SFN; Kavanagh n.d.b:139–140.

70. Naiya, 7/6/1933, SFN; Kavanagh n.d.b:60.

71. Howard White Wolf, 7/31/1933, SFN; Kavanagh n.d.b:197.

72. Post Oak Jim, 7/11/1933, SFN; Kavanagh n.d.b:139–140.

73. Ed Yellowfish, 3/27/1992, and Forrest Kassanavoid to author.
74. Frank Chekovi, 8/10/1933, Kwasia, August 1933, Tunubeku 1933, SFN; Kavanagh n.d.b:247, 261, 297.
75. Author's fieldnotes.
76. Herman Asenap, 7/7/1933, Naiya, 7/27/1933, Post Oak Jim, 7/17–7/19/1933, SFN; Kavanagh n.d.b:80, 140, 154, 186.
77. Ibid. See also Kavanagh n.d.c.
78. Comanche today have told me how they teasingly tried to explain the importance of this aspect of Comanche tradition to their wives, but to no avail; author's fieldnotes.
79. Herman Asenap, 7/7/1933, Naiya, 7/27/1933, Post Oak Jim, 7/17–7/19/1933, SFN; Kavanagh n.d.b: 80, 140, 154, 186.
80. Naiya, 7/27/1933, SFN; Kavanagh n.d.b:186.
81. Herman Asenap, 7/7/1933, Naiya, 7/27/1933, Post Oak Jim, 7/17–7/19/1933, SFN; Kavanagh n.d.b:80, 140, 154, 186.
82. Ed Yellowfish to author, 3/27/1992.
83. Author's fieldnotes. Comparison of the characteristics of society partners among Kiowa, Comanche, and Apache military societies reveals great similarity.
84. Naiya, 7/7/1933, SFN; Kavanagh n.d.b:72–73. Had Davis (1996:122) seen the 1933 Santa Fe material he would have recognized the existence of Comanche policed hunts.
85. Ibid.
86. Naiya, 7/7/1933, SFN; Kavanagh n.d.b:72.
87. Naiya, 7/7/1933, SFN; Kavanagh n.d.b:72–73.
88. Ed Yellowfish to author, 3/27/1992.
89. Howard White Wolf, 7/31/1933, SFN; Kavanagh n.d.b:195–197.
90. Howard White Wolf, 7/31/1933, SFN; Kavanagh n.d.b:197.
91. Author's fieldnotes; John Moore to author, 1992.
92. Post Oak Jim, 7/11/1933, SFN; Kavanagh n.d.b:99.
93. Post Oak Jim, 7/13–7/17/1933, SFN; Kavanagh n.d.b:126, 140.
94. Joe Attocknie to Tom Kavanagh, personal communication.
95. Author's fieldnotes.
96. As Ewers (in Berlandier 1969:75) notes, "Spanish writers used the Aztec word 'mitote' to refer to an Indian dance or ceremony."
97. Quanah Parker to H. L. Scott, HLS-1:1:14–15.
98. Joe Attocknie, DD T-508.
99. 1935, SFN (Kiowa); author's fieldnotes.
100. See also the 1933 SFN; Kavanagh n.d.b.
101. Post Oak Jim, 7/17/1933, SFN; Kavanagh n.d.b:139.
102. Quanah Parker and Cabaya to H. L. Scott, HLS-1:1:1–2.
103. Ralph Linton to Alice Marriott, Marriott Papers, WHC.
104. Post Oak Jim, 7/17/1933, SFN; Kavanagh n.d.b:135.
105. Howard White Wolf, 7/31/1933, SFN; Kavanagh n.d.b:195.
106. Author's fieldnotes—Comanche.
107. Post Oak Jim, 7/17/1933, SFN; Kavanagh n.d.b:135–136.
108. Ed Yellowfish, 3/27/1992, and Forrest Kassanavoid to author.

109. Demitri Shimkin to author, 1992. While Lowie (1915a) stated that the "Big Horse" Society was a synonym for the Logs, Shimkin stated that no "Big Horse" society existed, but that this was the name of a Yellow Brow Society dance. Most data pertaining to Shoshone military societies come from personal communication with the late Demitri Shimkin and from review of his fieldnotes at the American Heritage Center at the University of Wyoming, Laramie. Because of collection restrictions prohibiting the citation of any Shoshone consultant names, I have listed below the nonpublished materials upon which the following discussion of Shoshone societies is based. However, it should be noted that Shimkin's consultants on Shoshone military societies and dances included several men and women elders born between the late 1840s and the 1870s and thus represent a well-sampled and reliable source of information. DSF, Box 1, Folder 6, Box 18, Folders 9 and 10.

110. Demitri Shimkin, personal communication, 1992; DSF, Box 1, Folder 6, Box 18, Folders 9 and 10.

111. Author's fieldnotes.

112. Tom Kavanagh, personal communication, 1994.

113. Author's fieldnotes.

114. Tom Kavanagh, personal communication, 1994.

115. Author's fieldnotes.

116. Matron's report for Cache District, July 1906, KAF; author's fieldnotes.

117. Indian Pioneer Papers, WHC. Based on the circumstances in surrounding tribal communities with whom the Comanche were interacting and participating, and in light of interviews with contemporary Comanche elders, it is feasible to assume that the vast majority of these dances focused upon social or War Dances.

118. Author's fieldnotes.

119. Ibid.

120. Ibid.

121. Open letter of 1/12/1917 to a number of Comanche, Business Committee file, Kiowa Agency—Fort Worth Archives; Stinchecum to Sells 4/26 and 8/23/1916, 72353-1915-063K; Sells to Stinchecum, 7/11/1916, 72353-1915-063K; Stinchecum to Sells, 8/23/1916, 72353-1915-063K; Meritt to Berry, 9/9/1916, 72353-1915-063K; Stinchecum to Sells, 12/4/1916, 72353-1915-063K; Meritt to Stinchecum, 12/18/1916, 7293-1915-063K; Stinchecum to Sells, 1/2, 1/6, 5/31, 7/6/1917, 72353-1915-063K, KAF-NAA; author's fieldnotes.

122. Forrest Kassanavoid to author, 7/12/1993.

123. Author's fieldnotes.

124. The Comanche Gourd Clan, Dallas–Ft. Worth Inter-Tribal Indian Association, Bulletin, May 1971.

125. Ed Yellowfish to Tom Kavanagh, 1979, transcript in possession of the author; Ed Yellowfish, Jack Codopony to author. The thirteen original members included Ed Yellowfish, Haddon Nauni, Ernest Micoby, William Poafpibitty, Robert Wallace, Doc Tate Nevaquaya, Jack Codopony, Leonard Riddles, Amos Pewonofkit, Carl Atauvich, Carl Tahah, Roy Wocmetooah. I have not yet identified the thirteenth member.

126. Ed Yellowfish to Tom Kavanagh, 1979, transcript courtesy of Thomas Kavanagh; author's fieldnotes.

127. Comanche Teh-da Puku Nu Constitution 1972, copy in possession of the author.

128. Ed Yellowfish to author, 3/27/1992.

129. American Indian Cultural Society Fall Gourd Dance Program, Norman, Oklahoma, October 1994.

130. Tom Kavanagh, personal communication, 1994.

131. Author's fieldnotes; recently there have been allegations by some Comanche that the Tuhwi medicine may have been associated with witchcraft, but these allegations have not been substantiated.

132. June Sovo to author, 3/3/1992.

133. Author's fieldnotes.

134. Ibid.

135. Ibid.

136. Author's fieldnotes; videotaped performance of the Comanche Tuhwi Society, Comanche Homecoming, Walters, Oklahoma, 7/17/1993.

137. According to one account I collected, a man who had been on a war party was known as a *Tekwɨniwapi* (literally "brave or courageous" but often translated as warrior), or *Mahimi'a'* (individuals who had been off to combat). Women who had accompanied a war party were known as *Tek-nee-whap-wai-ee-puh* (woman warrior) and as such were entitled to wear a *Tekwɨniwapikwasu* (Women's Warrior Dress), the red and blue cloth dresses.

138. Author's fieldnotes.

139. June Sovo, 3/3/1992, and Forrest Kassanavoid, 7/12/1993, to author.

140. Author's fieldnotes. When examined on video recordings, this song, used as a rest break, was the same as the Smoke Song in the Apache Manatidie Society. Alice Fletcher and Francis La Flesche (1911:486) note that the Omaha *Toka'lo* (a diffusion of the Dakota *Toka'la*) Society contained "no words to the songs," suggesting that the Dakota words were dropped upon being adopted by the Omaha. The lack of any Tuhwi Society song texts with over two hundred remaining fluent speakers suggests that at least parts of the Tuhwi were most likely diffused from the neighboring Kiowa and Apache societies.

141. Author's fieldnotes; Forrest Kassanavoid to author. The Comanche *Wɨta-nɨhka* or Purification Dance, from *wɨta* (purification) and *nɨhka* (dance), refers to the cleansing of the warrior upon returning and not to any scalps (*pah-peet-see-wee-nah*) that might have been taken. This form of dance is commonly called "Scalp Dance" by Anglos.

142. Author's fieldnotes. *Nah-o-kee-nɨhka* (Dance of Joy/Gladness) is the Comanche name for the Victory Dance, from *nah-o-kee* (gladness/joy) and *nɨhka* (dance). In addition to being performed at military society dances, the Nah-o-kee-nɨhka was performed at the Comanche tribal complex in 1981 when the Comanche Tribal Government was brought back. Older women stated that because their government was returned to them they would dance in joy.

143. Author's fieldnotes.

144. Ibid.

145. The belief that deaths occur in groups within a brief period is commonly espoused among the Kiowa. Indeed, during my six years of fieldwork with the Kiowa I observed several periods with no deaths of elders followed by the deaths of three or four elders within a brief period. Many Kiowa state that such deaths always occur in fours; although this clustering phenomenon is common, exceptions are also common. Some allegations of witchcraft have recently been made against the society by external factions for a variety of reasons, although these allegations cannot presently be substantiated.

146. Author's fieldnotes. Gelo (1986:226) supports these views.

147. Author's fieldnotes. Recently, some gourd dancers who are descendants of Ohaku'ema members have placed yellow horsehair in the tops of their rattles, although there is no known relationship between the two types of societies.

148. Forrest Kassanavoid to author.

149. Ibid.

150. Ibid.; author's fieldnotes.

151. Following a supper break at the Ponca dances, a set of Wolf Dances are performed by the women, similar in choreography to the women's Round Dance in proceeding in a circular and clockwise direction, while containing portions in which the dancers dance in place before proceeding; Marian and Forrest Kassanavoid to author.

152. Forrest Kassanavoid to author; author's fieldnotes.

153. *Lawton Constitution*, 3/2/1994:2a, 3/19/1994:1B, 4/25/1994:7a; author's fieldnotes. Lists of Comanche L-Troop members from the Fort Sill Museum Archives vary greatly as to the number of enlisted Comanche scouts.

154. *Lawton Constitution*, 3/2/1994:2a, 3/19/1994:1B, 4/25/1994:7a; author's fieldnotes.

155. *Lawton Constitution*, 3/2/1994:2a, 3/19/1994:1B, 4/25/1994:7a; author's fieldnotes. Other members include Gordon Whitewolf (Caddo-Comanche) as pipe keeper, Larry McCurtain (Kiowa) as quartermaster, Lanny Asepermy (Comanche-Kiowa) as camp crier, Jimmy Antelope (Apache-Cheyenne), Mike Blackstar (Comanche), Norman Keel Sr. (Pawnee-Otoe), Charlie Kerchee and Ernold Tate (Comanche), Richard Quoetone (Kiowa), Neil Wooster (Caddo), and Ed Briggs (non-Indian). Three men hold the title of *Esa Moneycut* (Wolf Scout): Carl Tahah and Samual Doc Pewewardy Jr. (Comanche) and Joe Toahty (Kiowa).

156. Ibid. Of these men, only Pewewardy and Gooday are living.

157. Author's fieldnotes.

158. Author's fieldnotes.

159. Charles Chibitty to author, 2/7/1995.

6. Comparison and Conclusions

1. In 1886 there were only five pistols for the twenty-eight agency policemen and no ammunition (Buntin 1931:96). Yet despite such shortages the symbolic role and significance of these positions should not be discounted.

2. Parker McKenzie to author, 3/5/1994. One Caddo policeman (Bob Thomas) worked as a janitor and mailman at the agency.

3. Author's fieldnotes.

4. Individuals such as I-see-o, E-mau-ta, Poolaw, Domat, Odle-paugh, and Wohaw are often listed under another of their Indian names in agency documents and can only be identified through familiarity with their multiple names.

5. The Kiowa scouts organized in 1875 by Laurie Tatum included Big Bow (sergeant), Gotebo (corporal), and Santiago (San-kei-ko), Goombi, Quot-sai, Tape-day-ah, Po-hau-ah, Tsa-lote, and Tsa-toke as privates (Parker McKenzie to author, 3/5/1994). Big Bow was the leader of the Áljóyìgàu Society. Nye (1962: 261) mentions the later additions of Eonah-pah (Unap), Set-maunte (Bear Paw), Pago-to-goodle (Lone Young Man), and Tsa'l-au-te. Pago-to-goodle was a Qóichégàu Society member, and the others had some combat experience.

6. Parker McKenzie to author, 3/5/1994; Membership Roster, L-Troop, Seventh Cavalry. Kiowa Misc. File, Fort Sill Archives, Lawton, Oklahoma.

7. Membership Roster, L-Troop, Seventh Cavalry. Kiowa Misc. File, Fort Sill Archives, Lawton, Oklahoma; Kiowa Military Membership Rosters—author's fieldnotes.

8. Author's fieldnotes—Kiowa, Comanche, Apache.

9. While their religion centers upon a solemn, dignified form of prayer, singing, and devout worship, Peyotists have continually been plagued by prejudice and misunderstanding, as evidenced by the many conferences and congressional inquiries concerning the legality of peyote use by Indians beginning in the early twentieth century. Several anthropologists, notably James Mooney, who played a seminal role in the establishment of the Native American Church in 1918, and later Weston La Barre and Omer C. Stewart, have defended peyote use for Native Americans (Stewart 1987; La Barre 1989; Moses 1984).

10. Author's fieldnotes.

11. Atwater Onco to author, 4/21/1995.

12. SFN, 1935; James Mooney, NAA MS 2531 (6).

13. Author's fieldnotes. Several elders I have spoken with who came from polygynous marriages indicate that agency and missionary efforts forced their father to give up one of his wives and their children and reside away from them.

14. Author's fieldnotes.

15. *Saturday Evening Post*, 11/7/1942:9.

16. *Annual Report of the Commissioner of Indian Affairs, 1919* (Washington, D.C.: U.S. Government Printing Office), p. 16.

17. *Arapaho Bee*, 11/29/1918; Parman (1994:62–64).

18. *Calumet Chieftain*, 3/27/1919, Parman (1994:62–64).

19. Author's fieldnotes; *Canadian Valley Record*, 9/25/1919; Parman (1994: 62–64).

20. *Thomas Tribune*, 10/21/1921 and 1/12/1922; Parman (1994:62–64).

21. *Indian's Friend*, January 1918; *Annual Report of the Commissioner of Indian Affairs, 1920* (Washington, D.C.: U.S. Government Printing Office), pp. 8–10.

22. Author's fieldnotes.

23. Ibid.

24. Ibid.

25. "Indian Rallies, Prayers, Support Troops in Gulf," *Sunday Oklahoman*, 2/10/1991.

26. Reverend David Paddlety to author, 3/20/1993.

27. Author's fieldnotes; see also Collier (1942).
28. Kiowa Victory Club Celebration, 11/11/1993; author's fieldnotes.
29. Forrest Kassanavoid to author.
30. Atwater Onco to author, 8/30/1994.
31. Author's fieldnotes.
32. Ibid.
33. Ibid.
34. Author's fieldnotes. Indeed, consultants state that a "society" can essentially secularize itself by performing too frequently and, as one individual said, by "getting too far away from its traditions."
35. It is not uncommon to find younger individuals who believe that the Fancy Dance was the original form of Plains War Dance, existing from time immemorial.
36. Author's fieldnotes.
37. Alfred Chalepah to author, 1994.
38. The adaptation of the Plains hand game to new social, temporal, and economic circumstances of the dominant society, while maintaining a distinct cultural structure and organization, serves as another example of the adaptability of Native American culture and communities; author's fieldnotes.
39. Author's fieldnotes.
40. Ed Yellowfish to author, 3/27/1992; author's fieldnotes—Comanche.
41. Martha Poolaw to author, 8/3/1995.
42. Ibid.
43. Author's fieldnotes.
44. Atwater Onco to author, 8/30/1994.

BIBLIOGRAPHY

Abel, Annie Heloise

1939   *Tabeau's Narrative of Loisel's Expedition to the Upper Missouri.* Norman: University of Oklahoma Press.

Aberle, David F.

1982   *The Peyote Religion among the Navajo.* Viking Fund Publications in Anthropology 42 (1966). Reprinted Chicago: University of Chicago Press.

AICS (American Indian Cultural Society)

1994   *The American Indian Cultural Society: Second Annual Intertribal Fall Gourd Dance.* Cleveland County Fairgrounds, Norman, Okla. (October 29).

Albers, Patricia C.

1993   "Symbiosis, Merger, and War: Contrasting Forms of Intertribal Relationship among Historic Plains Indians." In *The Political Economy of North American Indians,* ed. John H. Moore, pp. 94–132. Norman: University of Oklahoma Press.

Anderson, Robert

1956   "The Northern Cheyenne War Mothers." *Anthropological Quarterly* 29(3): 82–90.

Attocknie, Francis Joseph

1965   [Life Sketch of Ten Bears.] Manuscript in possession of Thomas Kavanagh.

Axtell, James

1979   "Ethnohistory: An Historian's Viewpoint." *Ethnohistory* 26:1–13.

Bailey, Garrick

1980   "Social Control on the Plains." In *Anthropology on the Great Plains,* ed. Margot Liberty and W. Raymond Wood, pp. 153–163. Lincoln: University of Nebraska Press.

Bamforth, Douglas

1988   *Ecology and Human Organization on the Great Plains.* New York: Plenum Press.

Bantista, Rudy

n.d.   *Twenty Fifth Aniversary—Kiowa Black Leggings Warrior Society.* Anadarko, Okla: Privately published.

Barnard, Herwanna Becker

1941   "The Comanche and His Literature: An Anthology of His Myths, Legends, Folktales, Oratory, Poems, and Song." M.A. thesis, University of Oklahoma, Norman.

Barney, Garold D.

1986   *Mormons, Indians, and the Ghost Dance Religion of 1890.* Lanham, Md.: University Press of America.

Battey, Thomas C.

1968   *The Life and Adventures of a Quaker among the Indians.* Williamstown, Mass.: Corner House Publications (originally published in 1876 in Boston).

Beals, Kenneth L.

1967   "The Dynamics of Kiowa Apache Peyotism." M.A. thesis, University of Oklahoma, Norman.

1971   "The Dynamics of Kiowa Apache Peyotism." *University of Oklahoma Papers in Anthropology* 12(1):35–89.

Beatty, John Joseph

1974   *Kiowa-Apache Music and Dance.* Museum of Anthropology, Ethnology Series 31. Greeley: University of Northern Colorado.

Bell, John R.

1957   *The Journal of Captain John R. Bell, Official Journalist for the Stephen H. Long Expedition to the Rocky Mountains, 1820.* Vol. 6 in Far West and the Rockies Historical Series 1820–1875, ed. Harlin M. Fuller and Leroy R. Hafen. Glendale, Calif.: Arthur H. Clark Co.

Berlandier, Jean Louis

1969   *The Indians of Texas in 1830.* Ed. J. C. Ewers. Washington, D.C.: Smithsonian Institution Press.

Bernstein, Alison R.

1991   *American Indians and World War II: Toward a New Era in Indian Affairs.* Norman: University of Oklahoma Press.

Berthrong, Donald J.

1976   *The Cheyenne and Arapaho Ordeal: Reservation and Agency Life in the Indian Territory, 1875–1907.* Norman: University of Oklahoma Press.

Biolsi, Thomas

1984   "Ecological and Cultural Factors in Plains Indian Warfare." In *Warfare, Culture, and Environment,* ed. R. Brian Ferguson, pp. 141–168. New York: Academic Press.

Bittle, William E.

1956   "The Position of the Kiowa Apache in the Apachean Group." Ph.D. diss., University of California at Los Angeles.

1962   "The Manatidie: A Focus for Kiowa Apache Tribal Identity." *Plains Anthropologist* 7(17): 152–163.

1963   "Kiowa-Apache." In Studies in the Athapascan Languages, ed. Harry Hoijer. *University of California Publications in Linguistics* 29: 76–101.

1971   "A Brief History of the Kiowa Apache." *Papers in Anthropology* (University of Oklahoma) 12(1): 1–34.

1979   "Kiowa Apache Raiding Behavior." *Papers in Anthropology* (University of Oklahoma) 20(2): 33–47.

Boon, James A.

1982   *Other Tribes, Other Scribes: Symbolic Anthropology in the Comparative Study of Cultures, Histories, Religions, and Texts.* Cambridge: Cambridge University Press.

Bowers, Alfred W.

1950   *Mandan Social and Ceremonial Organization.* Chicago: University of Chicago Press.

1992   *Hidatsa Social and Ceremonial Organization.* Lincoln: University of Nebraska Press. Originally published in 1963 as Bulletin 194 of the Smithsonian Institution, Bureau of American Ethnology, Washington, D.C.

Boyd, Maurice

1981   *Kiowa Voices, Vol. 1.: Ceremonial Dance, Ritual, and Song.* Fort Worth: Texas Christian University Press.

Brant, Charles S.

1949   "The Cultural Position of the Kiowa-Apache." *Southwest Journal of Anthropology* 5: 56–61.

1951   "The Kiowa Apache Indians: A Study in Ethnology and Acculturation." Ph.D. diss., Cornell University.

1953   "Kiowa Apache Culture History: Some Further Observations." *Southwest Journal of Anthropology* 9: 195–202.

1969   *Jim Whitewolf: The Life of a Kiowa Apache Indian.* New York: Dover Publications.

Brown, Kenneth, and Michael Roberts, eds.

1980   "Using Oral Sources: Vansina and Beyond." *Social Analysis* 4 (special issue).

Brown, William R., Jr.

1987   "Comanchería Demography." *Panhandle Plains Historical Review* 59: 1–17.

Bruner, Edward

1957   *Indian and White: Self-Image and Interaction in a Canadian Plains Community.* Palo Alto, Calif.: Stanford University Press.

Buntin, Martha Leota

1931   "History of the Kiowa, Comanche, and Wichita Indian Agency." M.A. thesis, University of Oklahoma, Norman.

Burnet, David G.

1954   "David G. Burnet's Letters Describing the Comanche Indians." Introduction by Ernest Wallace. *West Texas Historical Association Year Book* 30: 115–140.

Butler, Pierce, and M. B. Lewis

1846   Letter to W. Medil, dated August 8, 1846. Documents concerning Negotiation of Indian Treaties. *National Archives Microfilm Publication* T494, roll 4, frame 259.

Campbell, Charles E.

1926–1928   "Down among the Red Men." *Collections of the Kansas State Historical Society* 17: 623–691.

Chouteau, Auguste P.

1838   [Letter to C. A. Harris, June 28, 1838.] Letters received from the Western Superintendency. National Archives and Record Service Microfilm Pub. M234, 922: 353.

Clark, W. P.

1982   *The Indian Sign Language.* Lincoln: University of Nebraska Press. Orig. pub. L. R. Hamersley and Co., 1885.

Clifford, James

1986a   "On Ethnographic Allegory." In *Writing Culture: The Poetics and Politics of Ethnography*, ed. James Clifford and George E. Marcus, pp. 98–121. Berkeley: University of California Press.

1986b   "Partial Truths." In *Writing Culture: The Poetics and Politics of Ethnography*, ed. James Clifford and George E. Marcus, pp. 1–26. Berkeley: University of California Press.

Clifford, James, and George E. Marcus, eds.

1986 *Writing Culture: The Poetics and Politics of Ethnography.* School of American Research Advanced Seminar. Berkeley: University of California Press.

Colson, Elizabeth

1954 "Review of Wallace and Hoebel's *The Comanches, Lords of the South Plains.*" *Man,* first series 54:13–14.

Collier, Donald

1938 "Kiowa Social Integration." M.A. thesis, University of Chicago.

Collier, John

1942 "The Indian in a Wartime Nation." *Annals of the American Academy of Political and Social Science* 223 (September 1942):29.

Comanche Teh-da Puku Nu Society

1972 *Comanche Teh-da Puku Nu Society Constitution.* Lawton, Okla.: Privately published.

Cortés, José

1989 *Views from the Apache Frontier: Report on the Northern Provinces of New Spain.* Ed. Elizabeth A. H. John. Trans. John Wheat. Norman: University of Oklahoma Press.

Corwin, Hugh D.

1962 "Fifty Years with the Kiowa." Unpublished manuscript in possession of the author.

Curtis, Edward S.

1930 *The North American Indian.* Ed. Frederick W. Hodge. Vol. 19. Norwood, Mass.: Plympton Press.

Davis, Michael G.

1988 "The Cultural Preadaptation Hypothesis: A Test Case on the Southern Plains." Ph.D. diss., University of Oklahoma, Norman.

1996 *Ecology, Sociopolitical Organization, and Cultural Change on the Southern Plains.* Kirksville, Mo.: Thomas Jefferson University Press.

DeLaguna, Fredrica

1960 *The Story of a Tlingit Community.* Bureau of American Ethnology Bulletin 172. Washington, D.C.: Smithsonian Institution.

DeMallie, Raymond J.

1977 *The Unratified Treaty between the Kiowas, Comanches, and Apaches and the United States of 1863.* Washington, D.C.: Institute for the Development of Indian Law.

Densmore, Frances

1992   *Teton Sioux Music and Culture.* Lincoln: University of Nebraska Press. Originally published as *Teton Sioux Music,* Bulletin 61 of the Bureau of American Ethnology, Smithsonian Institution, 1918.

Dodge, Henry

1836   *Transmitting a Report of the Expedition of the Dragoons, under the Command of Colonel Henry Dodge, to the Rocky Mountains during the Summer of 1835.* House Doc., 24th Congress, 1st Session, no. 181. Washington, D.C.: Government Printing Office.

Dolgin, Janet L., David S. Kemnitzer, and David M. Schneider, eds.

1977   *Symbolic Anthropology: A Reader in the Study of Symbols and Meanings.* New York: Columbia University Press.

Dorsey, George A.

1905   *The Cheyenne: Ceremonial Organization.* Publication 99, vol. 9, no. 1. Chicago: Field Columbian Museum.

Dorsey, George A., and James R. Murie

1940   *Notes on Skidi Pawnee Society.* Anthropological Series 27. Chicago: Field Museum of Natural History.

Dorsey, James Owen

1893–1894   *Siouan Sociology.* Bureau of American Ethnology Fifteenth Annual Report. Washington, D.C.: Smithsonian Institution.

Dowd, Gregory

1992   *A Spirited Resistance: The Native American Struggle for Unity 1745–1815.* Baltimore: Johns Hopkins University Press.

Dunlay, Thomas W.

1982   *Wolves for the Blue Soldiers: Indian Scouts and Auxiliaries with the United States Army, 1860–90.* Lincoln: University of Nebraska Press.

Eggan, Fred

1950   *Social Organization of the Western Pueblos.* Chicago: University of Chicago Press.

1966   *The American Indian: Perspectives for the Study of Social Change.* Chicago: Aldine Publishing Co.

1980   "Shoshone Kinship Structures and Their Significance for Anthropological Theory." *Journal of the Steward Anthropological Society* 11:165–193.

Eisenstadt, Dr. S. N.

1954   "Plains Indian Age Groups: Some Comparative Notes." *Man* 3 (January): 6–8.

Elguézabal, Juan Bautista de

1802   [Letter to Pedro de Nava, Apr. 28, 1802.] Béxar Archives of Spanish and Mexican Texas. University of Texas, Austin, microfilm edition. BA 30: 498.

Ellis, Clyde

1990   "Truly Dancing Their Own Way": Modern Revival and Diffusion of the Gourd Dance." *American Indian Quarterly* 14(1): 19–33.

1993   "A Gathering of Life Itself": The Kiowa Gourd Dance." In *Native American Values: Survival and Renewal,* ed. Thomas E. Schirer and Susan M. Branstner, pp. 365–374. Sault Ste. Maríe, Mich.: Lake Superior State University Press.

Ewers, John C.

1997   "Women's Roles in Plains Indian Warfare." In *Plains Indian History and Culture: Essays on Continuity and Change.* Norman: University of Oklahoma Press.

Ewers, John C., ed.

1973   "The Influence of Epidemics on the Indian Populations and Cultures of Texas." *Plains Anthropologist* 18: 104–115.

1978   *Murals in the Round: Painted Tipis of the Kiowa and Kiowa-Apache.* Washington, D.C.: Smithsonian Institution.

1988   *The Blackfeet: Raiders on the Northwest Plains.* 8th ed. Norman: University of Oklahma Press.

Faulk, Odie B.

1964   *The Last Years of Spanish Texas, 1778–1821.* The Hague: Mouton.

Fenton, William

1952   "The Training of Historical Ethnologists in America." *American Anthropologist* 54: 328–339.

Fixico, Donald L.

1986   *Termination and Relocation: Federal Indian Policy 1945–1960.* Albuquerque: University of New Mexico Press.

Flannery, Regina

1947   "The Changing Form and Functions of the Gros Ventre Grass Dance." *Primitive Man* 20(3): 39–70.

Fletcher, Alice C., and Francis La Flesche

1911   *The Omaha Tribe.* Twenty-seventh Annual Report of the Bureau of American Ethnology (1905–1906). Washington, D.C.: Government Printing Office.

Foreman, Grant

1926   *Pioneer Days in the Early Southwest.* Cleveland: Arthur H. Clark Co.
1939   *Marcy and the Gold Seekers.* Norman: University of Oklahoma Press.

Foster, Morris Wade

1991   *Being Comanche: A Social History of an American Indian Community.* Tucson: University of Arizona Press.
1992   Introduction to *Rank and Warfare among the Plains Indians*, by Bernard Mishkin, pp. v–xv. Lincoln: University of Nebraska Press.

Foster, Morris Wade, and Martha McCollough

n.d.   "The Kiowa-Apache." Draft of chapter for upcoming *Smithsonian Handbook of North American Indians*, vol. 13, *Plains.* Copy in author's possession.

Fowler, Loretta

1982   *Arapahoe Politics, 1851–1978.* Lincoln: University of Nebraska Press.
1987   *Shared Symbols, Contested Meanings: Gros Ventre Culture and History 1778–1984.* Ithaca, N.Y.: Cornell University Press.

Frey, Rodney

1986   *The World of the Crow Indians: As Driftwood Lodges.* Norman: University of Oklahoma Press.

Fried, Morton

1968   "On the Concepts of Tribe and Tribal Society." In *Essays in the Problem of Tribe*, ed. June Helm. Proceedings of the 1967 Annual Spring Meeting of the American Ethnological Society. Seattle: University of Washington Press.
1975   *The Notion of Tribe.* Menlo Park, Calif.: Cummings Publishing Co.

Gamble, John I.

1952a   "Changing Patterns in Kiowa Indian Dances." In *Acculturation in the Americas: Proceedings and Selected Papers of the Twenty-ninth International Congress of Americanists*, ed. Sol Tax, pp. 94–104. Chicago: University of Chicago Press.
1952b   "Kiowa Dance Gatherings and Costumed Dancers." M.A. thesis, Washington University, St. Louis.

Garbarino, Merwyn S.

1983   *Sociocultural Theory in Anthropology: A Short History.* Prospect Heights, Ill.: Waveland Press.

García-Rejón, Manuel

1865   *Vocabulario del idioma Comanche.* Mexico City: Ignacio Cumplido.

Geertz, Clifford

1973   *The Interpretation of Culture.* New York: Basic Books.

1977   *Language and Art in the Navajo Universe.* Ed. Gary Witherspoon. Ann Arbor: University of Michigan Press.

Gelo, Daniel J.

1986   "Comanche Belief and Ritual." Ph.D Diss., Rutgers University.
1987   "On a New Interpretation of Comanche Social Organization." *Current Anthropology* 28(4):551–552.
1988   "Review of Wallace and Hoebl's *The Comanches: Lords of the South Plains.*" *Plains Anthropologist* 33(122):539–541.
1993   "The Comanches as Aboriginal Skeptics." *American Indian Quarterly* 17(1):69–82.

Gladwin, Thomas

1948   "Comanche Kin Behavior." *American Anthropologist* 50:73–94.

Goddard, Pliny Earle

1914   "Dancing Societies of the Sarsi Indians." *American Museum of Natural History, Anthropological Papers,* 9(5):461–474.

Goldstein, Kenneth

1972   "On the Application of the Concepts of Active and Inactive Traditions on the Study of Repertoire." In *Towards New Perspectives in Folklore,* ed. Américo Paredes and Richard Bauman, pp. 62–76. Austin: University of Texas Press.

Greene, Candace

1993   "Saynday Was Coming Along . . ." In *Smithsonian Institution Travelling Exhibition Service.* Washington, D.C.: Smithsonian Institution.

Grimes, Ronald L.

1976   *Symbol and Conquest: Public Ritual and Drama in Santa Fe, New Mexico.* Ithaca, N.Y.: Cornell University Press.

Grinnell, George Bird

1972   *The Cheyenne Indians: Their History and Ways of Life.* 2 vols. Lincoln: University of Nebraska Press (originally published 1923).
1983   *The Fighting Cheyennes.* 7th ed. Norman: University of Oklahoma Press.

Grobsmith, Elizabeth S.

1981   *Lakota of the Rosebud: A Contemporary Ethnography.* New York: Holt, Rinehart and Winston.

Gunnerson, James H., and Dolores A. Gunnerson

1960   "An Introduction to Plains Apache Archaeology—The Dismal River Aspect." *Bureau of American Ethnology, Bulletin* 173:131–260. Washington, D.C.: Government Printing Office.

1968   "Plains Apache Archaeology: A Review." *Plains Anthropologist* 13:167–189.

1971   "Apachean Culture: A Study in Unity and Diversity." In *Apachean Culture, History, and Ethnology,* ed. Keith H. Basso and Morris E. Opler, pp. 7–27. Anthropological Papers of the University of Arizona, 21. Tucson: University of Arizona Press.

1979   "Southern Athapascan Archaeology." In *Handbook of North American Indians,* gen. ed. William C. Sturtevant, vol. 9, pp. 162–169. Washington, D.C.: Smithsonian Institution Press.

Hackett, Charles Wilson, ed.

1923–1937   *Historical Documents Relating to New Mexico, Nueva Vizcaya and Approaches Thereto, to 1773.* Collected by Adolph F. A. Bandolier and Fanny R. Bandolier. 3 vols. Washington, D.C.: Carnegie Institution.

Hagan, William T.

1966   *Indian Police and Judges: Experiments in Acculturation and Control.* Lincoln: University of Nebraska Press.

1976   *United States–Comanche Relations: The Reservation Years.* New Haven: Yale University Press.

1990   *United States–Comanche Relations: The Reservation Years.* Norman: University of Oklahoma Press.

1993   *Quanah Parker, Comanche Chief.* Norman: University of Oklahoma Press.

Haines, Francis

1976   *The Plains Indians.* New York: Thomas Y. Crowell Co.

Hale, Duane K.

1992   "Uncle Sam's Warriors: American Indians in World War II." *Chronicles of Oklahoma* 69(4):408–429.

Hale, Kenneth, and David Harris

1979   "Historical Linguistics and Archaeology." In *Handbook of North American Indians,* gen. ed. William C. Sturtevant, vol. 9, pp. 170–177. Washington, D.C.: Smithsonian Institution.

Hanson, Jeffery R.

1988   "Age-set Theory and Plains Indian Age-grading: A Critical Review and Revision." *American Ethnologist,* 15(2):349–364.

Harris, Marvin

1968   *The Rise of Anthropological Theory: A History of Theories of Culture.* New York: Harper and Row Publishers.

Harris, Moira F.

1989   *Between Two Cultures: Kiowa Art from Fort Marion.* Pogo Press.

Haworth, J.

1874 "Annual Report, Agent, Kiowa and Comanche." *Annual Report of the Commissioner of Indian Affairs* (1874): 219–222.

Hayden, F. V.

1863 "Contributions to the Ethnography and Philology of the Indian Tribes of the Missouri Valley." *American Philosophical Society Transactions* n.s. 12: 274–339.

Haynie, Nancy Anne, ed.

1984 *Native Americans and the Military: Today and Yesterday.* Fort McPherson, Ga.: U.S. Army Forces Command Public Affairs, Command Information Branch.

Hennepin, Louis

1698 *A New Discovery of a Vast Country in America.* Ed. Reuben Gold Thwaites. Chicago: McClurg. Reprinted Chicago, 1903.

Herskovits, Melville J.

1958 *Acculturation: The Study of Culture Contact.* Gloucester, Mass.: Peter Smith Publishing.

Hertzberg, Hazel W.

1971 *The Search for an American Indian Identity: Modern Pan-Indian Movements.* Syracuse, N.Y.: Syracuse University Press.

Hill, Edward E.

1981 *Guide to Records in the National Archives of the United States Relating to American Indians.* Washington, D.C.: National Archives and Record Service, General Services Administration.

Hill, Tom, and Kenneth Beals

1966 "Some Notes on Kiowa Apache Peyotism with Special Reference to Ethics and Change." *University of Oklahoma Papers in Anthropology* (Norman) 7(1): 1–24.

Hoebel, E. Adamson

1936 "Associations and the State in the Plains." *American Anthropologist* 38: 433–438.

1939 "Comanche and Hekandika Shoshone Relationship Systems." *American Anthropologist* 41: 440–457.

1940 *The Political Organization and Law-Ways of the Comanche Indians.* Memoirs of the American Anthropological Association 54. Menasha, Wis.: American Anthropological Association.

1954 *The Law of Primitive Man: A Study in Comparative Legal Dynamics.* Cambridge, Mass.: Harvard University Press.

1978   *The Cheyennes: Indians of the Great Plains.* 2nd ed. New York: Holt, Rinehart and Winston.

Hoijer, Harry

1938   "The Southern Atapascan Languages." *American Anthropologist* 40(1): 75–87.
1962   "Linguistic Sub-groupings by Glottochronology and by the Comparative Method: The Athapascan Languages." *Lingua* 11:193–199.
1971   "The Position of the Apachean Languages in the Athapascan Stock." In *Apachean Culture, History, and Ethnology*, ed. Keith H. Basso and Morris E. Opler, pp. 3–6. Anthropological Papers of the University of Arizona 21. Tucson: University of Arizona Press.

Holm, Tom

1985   "Fighting a White Man's War: The Extent and Legacy of Indian Participation in World War II." In *The Plains Indians of the Twentieth Century*, ed. Peter Iverson, pp. 149–168. Norman: University of Oklahoma Press.
1993   "Patriots and Pawns: State Use of American Indians in the Military and the Process of Nativization in the United States." In *The State of Native America: Genocide, Colonization, and Resistance*, ed. Annette M. Jaimes, pp. 345–370. Boston: South End Press.
1996   *Strong Hearts, Wounded Souls: Native American Veterans of the Vietnam War.* Austin: University of Texas Press.

Howard, James H.

1951   "The Dakota Victory Dance World War II." *North Dakota History* 18(January):31–40.
1955   "The Pan-Indian Culture of Oklahoma." *Scientific Monthly* 18(5):215–220.
1965   *The Ponca Tribe.* Bureau of American Ethnology Bulletin 195. Washington, D.C.: Government Printing Office.
1976   "The Plains Gourd Dance as a Revitalization Movement." *American Ethnologist* 3(2):243–259.
1983   "Pan-Indianism in Native American Music and Dance." *Ethnomusicology* 27(1):71–82.

Hoxie, Fred

1984   *A Final Promise: The Campaign to Assimilate the Indians, 1880–1920.* Lincoln: University of Nebraska Press.

Hulkrantz, Ake

1968   "Shoshoni Indians on the Plains: An Appraisal of the Documentary Evidence." *Zeitschrift für Ethnologie* 93:49–72.

Humphrey, N. D.

1941   "A Characterization of Certain Plains Associations." *American Anthropologist* 43:428–436.

Hunter, David E., and Phillip Whitten, eds.

1976 "Sodalities." In *Encyclopedia of Anthropology*, p. 362. New York: Harper and Row Publishers.

Hyde, George E.

1968 *Life of George Bent: Written from His Letters.* Ed. Savoie Lottinville. Norman: University of Oklahoma Press.

Jacobs, Wilbur R.

1987 *Dispossessing the American Indian: Indians and Whites on the Colonial Frontier.* 2nd ed. New York: Charles Scribner's Sons.

James, Edwin, comp.

1823 *Account of an Expedition from Pittsburgh to the Rocky Mountains, Performed in the Year 1819 and 1820, by Order of the Hon. John C. Calhoun, Sec'y of War: Under the Command of Stephen H. Long.* 2 vols. Philadelphia: n.p.

John, Elizabeth A. H.

1975 *Storms Brewed in Other Men's Worlds.* College Station: Texas A & M University Press.

1984 "Nurturing the Peace: Spanish-Comanche Cooperation in the Early Nineteenth Century." *New Mexico Historical Review* 59: 345–369.

1985 "An Earlier Chapter of Kiowa History." *New Mexico Historical Review* 60: 379–397.

Jones, David E.

1972 *Sanapia: Comanche Medicine Woman.* Case Studies in Cultural Anthropology. Ed. George Spindler and Louise Spindler. New York: Holt, Rinehart and Winston.

Jorgensen, Joseph G.

1971 "Indians and the Metropolis." In *The American Indian in Urban Society*, pp. 66–113. Boston: Little, Brown and Co.

1972 *The Sun Dance Religion: Power for the Powerless.* Chicago: University of Chicago Press.

Jules-Rosette, Benetta

1979 *The New Religions of Africa.* Norwood, N.J.: Ablex Publishing Co.

Kappler, Charles J.

1973 *Indian Treaties, 1778–1883.* New York: Interland Publishers.

Kardiner, Abram

1945 *The Psychological Frontiers of Society.* New York: Columbia University Press.

Kavanagh, Thomas

1979 Ernest Mikecoby, Haddon Nauni, and Ed Yellowfish to Tom Kavanagh, July 1979. Unpublished interview; copy courtesy of Thomas Kavanagh.

1980 "Recent Socio-cultural Evolution of the Comanche Indians: A Model for Transformation and Articulation in Social Change." M.A. thesis, Washington University, St. Louis.

1982 "The Comanche Pow-wow: Pan-Indianism or Tribalism." *Haliksa'i* (University of New Mexico Anthropology Society, Albuquerque) 1:12–27.

1986 "Political Power and Political Organization: Comanche Politics 1786–1875." Ph.D. diss., University of New Mexico.

1989 "Comanche Population Organization and Reorganization 1869–1910: A Test of the Continuity Hypothesis." *Plains Anthropologist*, memoir 23: 99–111.

1996 *Comanche Political History: An Ethnohistorical Perspective 1706–1875.* Lincoln: University of Nebraska Press.

n.d.a "Comanche." Draft for chapter for upcoming *Smithsonian Handbook of North American Indians*, vol. 13, *Plains.* Copy in author's possession.

n.d.b *Comanche Sourcebook: Notes of the 1933 Santa Fe Laboratory of Anthropology Field Party Recorded by Waldo R. Wedel, E. Adamson Hoebel, and Gustav G. Carlson.* Courtesy of Dr. Thomas Kavanagh.

n.d.c Personal communication with the author.

n.d.d *Political Power and Political Organization: Comanche Politics 1786–1875.* Published as Kavanagh 1996.

Keesing, Roger M.

1986 "The Young Dick Attack: Oral and Documentary History on the Colonial Frontier." *Ethnohistory* 33:268–292.

Kehoe, Alice Beck

1989 *The Ghost Dance: Ethnohistory and Revitalization.* New York: Holt, Rinehart and Winston.

1992 *North American Indians: A Comprehensive Account.* 2nd ed. Englewood Cliffs, N.J.: Prentice Hall.

Kennedy, Dorothy I. D., and Randall T. Bouchard

1990 "Bella Coola." In *Handbook of North American Indians*, 7, *Northwest Coast*, vol. ed. Wayne Suttles, pp. 323–339. Washington, D.C.: Smithsonian Institution.

Kiowa Gourd Clan

1976 "Ceremonials Booklet July 1–4." N.p.: Privately published.

Kiowa Tia-Piah Society

1990 "Twenty-fourth Annual Celebration booklet, July 1–4." N.p.: Privately published.

Kracht, Benjamin R.

1989 "Kiowa Religion: An Ethnohistorical Analysis of Ritual Symbolism, 1832–1987." Ph.D. diss., Southern Methodist University, Dallas, Texas.

1992 "The Kiowa Ghost Dance, 1894–1916: An Unheralded Revitalization Movement." *Ethnohistory* 39(4):452–477.

1994 "Kiowa Powwows: Continuity in Ritual Practice." *American Indian Quarterly* 18(3):321–348.

Krech, Shepard, III

1991 "The State of Anthropology." *Annual Reviews of Anthropology* 20:345–375.

Kroeber, Alfred R.

1907 "The Ceremonial Organization of the Plains Indians of North America." *Congrès International des Américanistes,* 15th Session, Quebec.

1939 *Cultural and Natural Areas of North America.* Berkeley: University of California Press.

1983 *The Arapaho.* Lincoln: University of Nebraska Press.

Kuhn, Thomas

1962 *The Structure of Scientific Revolutions.* Chicago: University of Chicago Press.

La Barre, Weston

1935 Original 1935 Kiowa Fieldnotes. National Anthropological Archives, Smithsonian Institution.

1989 *The Peyote Cult.* 5th ed. Norman: University of Oklahoma Press.

n.d. "Autobiography of a Kiowa Indian." Copy in author's possession.

Lassiter, Eric

1992 "Rattles, Song, and Spirit: The Kiowa Gourd Dance." University of North Carolina, unpublished paper. Copy in possession of the author.

1993 "They Left Us These Songs . . . That's All We Got Now": The Significance of Music in the Kiowa Gourd Dance and Its Relation to Native American Cultural Continuity." In *Native American Values: Survival and Renewal,* ed. Thomas E. Schirer and Susan M. Branstner, pp. 375–384. Sault Ste. Marie, Mich.: Lake Superior State University Press.

1995 "Towards Understanding the Power of Kiowa Song: A Collaborative Exercise in Meaning." Ph.D. diss., University of North Carolina, Chapel Hill.

Lecompte, Janet

1972 "Bent, St. Vrain and Company among the Comanche and Kiowa." *Colorado Magazine* 49:273–293.

Lesser, Alexander

1978   *The Pawnee Ghost Dance Hand Game: Ghost Dance Revival and Ethnic Identity.* New York: Columbia University Press, 1933. Madison: Reprinted University of Wisconsin Press.

Levy, Jerrold E.

1958   "Kiowa and Comanche: A Report from the Field." *Anthropology Tomorrow* 6(2):30–44.

1959   "After Custer: Kiowa Political and Social Organization from the Reservation Period to the Present." Ph.D. diss., University of Chicago.

n.d.a   "Kiowa." Draft of chapter for upcoming *Smithsonian Handbook of North American Indians*, vol. 13, *Plains.* Copy in author's possession.

n.d.b   Personal correspondence with the author.

Liberty, Margot

1973   "The Urban Reservation." Ph.D. diss., Department of Anthropology, University of Minnesota.

Linton, Ralph

1935   "The Comanche Sun Dance." *American Anthropologist* 37:420–428.

1940   *Acculturation in Seven American Indian Tribes.* New York: Appleton Century.

Llewellyn, Karl N., and E. Adamson Hoebel

1941   *The Cheyenne Way: Conflict and Case Law in Primitive Jurisprudence.* Norman: University of Oklahoma Press.

Loomis, Noel M., and Abraham P. Nasatir

1967   *Pedro Vial and the Roads to Santa Fe.* Norman: University of Oklahoma Press.

Lowie, Robert H.

1909   "The Northern Shoshone." *Anthropological Papers of the American Museum of Natural History* 2(2):165–306.

1912   "Comanche Fieldnotes" (unpublished). Department of Anthropology Archives, American Museum of Natural History, New York.

1915a   "Dances and Societies of the Plains Shoshone." *American Museum of Natural History, Anthropological Papers* 9(10):803–837.

1915b   "Oral Tradition and History." *American Anthropologist* 17:597–599.

1915c   "Societies of the Arikara Indians." *American Museum of Natural History, Anthropological Papers* 9(8):643–678.

1916a   "Plains Indian Age-Societies: Historical and Comparative Summary." *American Museum of Natural History, Anthropological Papers* 9(8):877–986.

1916b   "Societies of the Kiowa." *American Museum of Natural History, Anthropological Papers* 9(11):837–853.

1917   "Oral Tradition and History." *Journal of American Folklore* 30:161–167.

1919   "Sun Dance of the Shoshoni, Ute and Hidatsa." *Anthropological Papers of the American Museum of Natural History* 16(5): 393–404.
1920   *Primitive Society*. New York: Liveright Publishing Co.
1924   "Notes on Shoshonean Ethnography." *Anthropological Papers of the American Museum of Natural History* 20(3): 185–314.
1927   *The Origin of the State*. New York: Harcourt, Brace and Co.
1943   "Property Rights and Coercive Powers of Plains Indian Military Societies. *Journal of Legal and Political Sociology* 1: 59–71.
1948   *Social Organization*. New York: Rinehart.
1953   "The Comanche, a Sample of Acculturation." *Sociologus* 3: 122–172.
1956   "Notes on The Kiowa Indians." *Tribus—The Journal of Ethnology and Its Related Sciences* (Linden Museum, Stuttgart, Germany) 4: 131–138.
1963   *Indians of the Plains*. Garden City, N.Y.: Natural History Press (originally published by McGraw-Hill Co., 1954).
1983   *The Crow Indians*. Lincoln: University of Nebraska Press (originally published in 1935).

Lummis, Charles Fletcher

1898   "Some Unpublished History: A New Mexico Episode in 1748." *Land of Sunshine* 8 (January): 75–78, 8 (February): 126–130.

Lurie, Nancy Oestreich

1961   "Ethnohistory: An Ethnological Point of View." *Ethnohistory* 8: 78–92.
1971   "The Contemporary American Indian Scene." In *North American Indians in Historical Perspective*, ed. Eleanor Burke Leacock and Nancy Oestreich Lurie, pp. 418–480. Prospect Heights, Ill.: Waveland Press.

MacLeod, William Christie

1937   "Police and Punishment among Native Americans of the Plains." *Journal of Criminal Law, Criminology, and Police Science* 28: 181–201.

Mails, Thomas E.

1973   *Dog Soldiers, Bear Men and Buffalo Women: A Study of the Societies and Cults of the Plains Indians*. Englewood Cliffs, N.J.: Prentice Hall.

Marcy, Randolph B.

1853   *Exploration of the Red River of Louisiana in the Year 1853*. Senate Ex. Doc., 32 Congress, 2nd Sess., no. 54. Washington, D.C.: Government Printing Office.

Margry, Pierre

1879   *Découvertes et établissements des français dans l'Ouest et dans le Sud de l'Amérique septentrionale 1614–1689: Mémoires et documents inédits*. Vol. 2. Paris: Maisonneuve et Cie, Libraires-Editeurs.

Marriott, Alice

1945   *The Ten Grandmothers*. Norman: University of Oklahoma Press.
1968   *Kiowa Years: A Study in Culture Impact*. New York: Macmillan.

Mayhall, Mildred P.

1962   *The Kiowas.* Norman: University of Oklahoma Press.

McAllister, J. Gilbert

1935   "Kiowa-Apache Social Organization." Ph.D. diss., University of Chicago.
1937   "Kiowa-Apache Social Organization." In *Social Anthropology of North American Indian Tribes,* ed. Fred Eggan, pp. 99–169. Chicago: University of Chicago Press.
1949   "Kiowa-Apache Tales." In *The Sky Is My Tipi,* ed. Mody C. Boatwright, pp. 1–141. Dallas: Texas Folklore Society; Austin: University of Texas Press.
1965   "The Four Quartz Rocks Medicine Bundle of the Kiowa-Apache." *Ethnology* 4(2) (April 1965): 210–224.
1970   *Daveko: Kiowa-Apache Medicine Man.* Bulletin of the Texas Memorial Museum 17. Austin: University of Texas.

McBeth, Sally J.

1983   *Ethnic Identity and the Boarding School Experience of West-Central Oklahoma American Indians.* Lanham, Md.: University Press of America.

McDermott, John Francis, ed., and Albert J. Salvan, trans.

1940   *Tixier's Travels on the Osage Prairies.* Norman: University of Oklahoma Press.

McGinnis, Anthony

1990   *Counting Coup and Cutting Horses: Intertribal Warfare on the Northern Plains 1738–1889.* Evergreen, Colo.: Cordillera Press.

Meadows, William C.

1991   "Tonkonga: An Ethnohistory of the Kiowa Black Legs Society." M.A. thesis, University of Oklahoma, Norman.
1995   "Remaining Veterans: A Symbolic and Comparative Ethnohistory of Southern Plains Indian Military Societies." Ph.D. diss., University of Oklahoma, Norman.
n.d.a   *Numurekwa'etuu—Comanche Speakers: The Comanche Code Talkers in World War II.* In press.
n.d.b   "A Reanalysis of Nineteenth-Century Plains Indian Military Societies: Definitions and Age-graded versus Non-age-graded Distinctions." Unpublished paper.

Methvin, Rev. J. J.

n.d.   *In the Limelight, or History of Anadarko [Caddo County] and Vicinity from the Earliest Days.* Anadarko, Okla.: N. T. Plummer Printing Co.
1927   *Andele, or the Mexican Kiowa Captive.* Louisville, Ky.: Pentecostal Herald Press.

Miller, Davis Humphreys

1985   *Ghost Dance.* New York: Duell, Sloan and Pearce, 1959. Reprinted Lincoln: University of Nebraska Press.

Miller, Joseph C., ed.

1980   *The African Past Speaks: Essays on Oral Tradition and History.* Folkestone: W Dawson.

Miller, Robert C.

1856   [Letter to A. J. Cummings, Nov. 29, 1856.] Records of the Central Superintendency. National Archives and Record Service Microfilm Pub. M856, 3:467.

Mishkin, Bernard

1940   *Rank and Warfare among the Plains Indians.* American Ethnological Society Monograph 3. New York: J. J. Augustin Publisher.

Mooney, James

1896   *The Ghost Dance Religion and the Sioux Outbreak of 1890.* Part 2, pp. 641–1110, of the Fourteenth Annual Report of the Bureau of American Ethnology, 1892–1893. Washington, D.C.: Smithsonian Institution Press.

1898   *Calendar History of the Kiowa Indians.* Seventeenth Annual Report of the Bureau of American Ethnology. Washington, D.C.: Smithsonian Institution Press.

1907   *The Cheyenne Indians.* American Anthropological Association, Memoirs 1. Reprinted New York: Kraus Reprint Corporation, 1964.

1912a   "Ditsakana." In *Handbook of American Indians North of Mexico*, ed. Frederick W. Hodge, p. 393. Bulletin 30. Washington, D.C.: Bureau of American Ethnology.

1912b   "Kiowa." In *Handbook of American Indians North of Mexico*, ed. Frederick W. Hodge, pp. 699–701. Bulletin 30. Washington, D.C.: Bureau of American Ethnology.

1912c   "Kiowa-Apache." In *Handbook of American Indians North of Mexico*, ed. Frederick W. Hodge, pp. 701–703. Bulletin 30. Washington, D.C.: Bureau of American Ethnology.

1912d   "Military Societies." In *Handbook of American Indians North of Mexico*, ed. Frederick W. Hodge, pp. 861–863. Bulletin 30. Washington, D.C.: Bureau of American Ethnology.

Moore, John Hartwell

1987   *The Cheyenne Nation: A Social and Demographic History.* Lincoln: University of Nebraska Press.

1992   Personal communication.

1996   *The Cheyenne.* Cambridge, Mass.: Blackwell Publishers.

Morris, Brian

1987   *Anthropological Studies of Religion: An Introductory Text.* Cambridge: Cambridge University Press.

Morse, Jedidiah

1822   *A Report to the Secretary of War of the United States, on Indian Affairs, Comprising a Narrative of a Tour Performed in the Summer of 1820.* New Haven, Conn.: S. Converse.

Moses, L. G.

1984   *The Indian Man: A Biography of James Mooney.* Urbana: University of Illinois Press.

Moulton, Gary E., ed.

1987   *The Journals of the Lewis and Clark Expedition.* Vol. 3. Lincoln: University of Nebraska Press.

Murdock, George Peter

1949   *Social Structure.* New York: Macmillan.

Murie, James R.

1914   "Pawnee Indian Societies." *American Museum of Natural History, Anthropological Papers* 9(7): 543–644.

Nasatir, Abraham

1930   "An Account of Spanish Louisiana, 1785." *Missouri Historical Review* 24(4): 521–536.

1952   *Before Lewis and Clark: Documents Illustrating the History of the Missouri, 1785–1804.* 2 vols. St. Louis: St. Louis Historical Documents Foundation.

Nash, Philleo

1955   "The Pace of Religious Revivalism in the Formation of the Intercultural Community on Klamath Reservation." In *Social Anthropology of North American Tribes,* pp. 347–442. Chicago: University of Chicago Press.

Neely, Sharlotte

1991   *Snowbird Cherokees: People of Persistence.* Athens: University of Georgia Press.

Neighbors, Robert S.

1852   "The Na-Uni or Comanches." In *Information Respecting the History, Conditions and Prospects of the Indian Tribes of the United States,* ed. H. R. Schoolcraft, vol. 2, pp. 125–134. Philadelphia: Lippincott, Grambo.

Nettl, Bruno

1978   "Some Aspects of the History of World Music in the Twentieth Century: Questions, Problems, Concepts." *Ethnomusicology* 22(1): 123–136.

1985   *The Western Impact on World Music.* New York: Schirmer Books.

1989   *Blackfoot Musical Thought: Comparative Perspectives.* Kent, Ohio: Kent State University Press.

Newcomb, W. W., Jr.

1970   "Summary of Kiowa-Apache History and Culture." In *Daveko: Kiowa-Apache Medicine Man* by J. Gilbert McAllister, pp. 1–28. Bulletin of the Texas Memorial Museum, 17. Austin: University of Texas.

Nichols, Roger

1988   "Something Old, Something New: Indians since World War II." In *The American Indian Experience: A Profile 1524 to the Present,* ed. Philip Weeks, pp. 292–313. Arlington, Ill.: Forum Press.

Northcutt, John Douglas

1973   "Leadership among the Kiowa 1833–1973." Master's thesis, University of Oklahoma, Norman.

Noyes, Stanley

1993   *Los Comanches: The Horse People, 1751–1845.* Albuquerque: University of New Mexico Press.

Nye, Colonel Wilbur S.

1937   *Carbine and Lance: The Story of Old Fort Sill.* Norman: University of Oklahoma Press.

1962   *Bad Medicine and Good: Tales of the Kiowas.* Norman: University of Oklahoma Press.

O'Brien, Sharon

1989   *American Indian Tribal Governments.* Norman: University of Oklahoma Press.

O'Crouley, Don Pedro Alonso

1972   *A Description of the Kingdom of New Spain, 1774.* Ed. and trans. Sean Galvin. San Francisco: John Howell Books.

Oliver, Symmes C.

1962   "Ecology and Cultural Continuity as Contributing Factors in the Social Organization of the Plains Indians." *University of California Publications in American Archaeology and Ethnology* 48(1):1–90.

Olson, James S., and Raymond Wilson

1984   *Native Americans in the Twentieth Century.* Urbana: University of Illinois Press.

Opler, Marvin K.

1943   "The Origins of Comanche and Ute." *American Anthropologist* 45:155–158.

Opler, Morris E., and William E. Bittle

1962   "The Death Practices and Eschatology of the Kiowa Apache." *Southwest Journal of Anthropology,* 17:383–394.

Ortner, Sherry B.

1973   "On Key Symbols." *American Anthropologist* 75(5):1338–1346.
1978   *Sherpas through Their Rituals.* Cambridge: Cambridge University Press.

Oswalt, Wendell H., and Sharlotte Neely

1996   *This Land Was Theirs.* Mountain View, Calif.: Mayfield Publishing Co.

Parman, Donald L.

1994   *Indians and the American West in the Twentieth Century.* Bloomington: Indiana University Press.

Parsons, Elsie Clews

1929   *Kiowa Tales.* Memoirs of the American Folk-Lore Society 22. New York: G. E. Stechert.

Pearson, Roger

1985   *Anthropological Glossary.* Malabar, Fla.: Robert E. Krieger Publishing Co.

Perrin du Lac, François Marie

1807   *Travels through the Two Louisianas, and among the Savage Nations of the Missouri.* London: Printed for R. Phillips by J. G. Barnard Publisher.

Perry, Richard J.

1991   *Western Apache Heritage: People of the Mountain Corridor.* Austin: University of Texas Press.

Poolaw, Newton

1981   "Revival of the Taipay Society." *Kiowa Indian News* (Carnegie, Oklahoma), April, p. 2.

Posada, Alonso de

1982   *Alonso de Posada Report, 1686: A Description of the Area of the Present Southern United States in the Late Seventeenth Century.* Ed. A. B. Thomas. Pensacola, Fla.: Perdido Bay Press.

Powers, William K.

1980   "Plains Indian Music and Dance." In *Anthropology of the Great Plains,* ed. W. Raymond Wood and Margot Liberty, pp. 212–229. Lincoln: University of Nebraska Press.
1990   *War Dance: Plains Indian Musical Performance.* Tucson: University of Arizona Press.

Provinse, John H.

1937 "The Underlying Sanctions of Plains Indian Culture." In *Social Anthropology of North American Indian Tribes*, ed. Fred Eggan, pp. 339–374. Chicago: University of Chicago Press.

Prucha, Francis P.

1984 *The Great Father: The United States Government and the American Indians.* 2 vols. Lincoln: University of Nebraska Press.

Rabinow, Paul

1986 "Representations Are Social Facts: Modernity and Post-Modernity in Anthropology." In *Writing Culture: The Poetics and Politics of Ethnography*, ed. James Clifford and George E. Marcus, pp. 234–261. Berkeley: University of California Press.

Ray, Verne F.

1974 *Ethnohistorical Analysis of Documents Relating to the Apache Indians of Texas.* New York: Garland Press.

Redfield, Robert, Ralph Linton, and Melville Herskovits

1936 "Memorandum for the Study of Acculturation." *American Anthropologist* 38:149–152.

Richardson, Jane

1940 *Law and Status among the Kiowa Indians.* Monograph 1. New York: American Ethnological Society.

n.d. Miscellaneous Notes on Kiowa Tonkonga Society. Copy in author's possession.

Richardson, R. N.

1933 *The Comanche Barrier to Southern Plains Settlement.* Glendale, Calif.: Arthur H. Clark Co.

Ritter, M. L.

1980 "The Conditions Favoring Age-set Organization." *Journal of Anthropological Research* 36:87–104.

Ritzenthaler, Robert

1943 "The Impact of the War on an Indian Community." *American Anthropologist* 45:325–326.

Rivera, Pedro de

1946 *Diario y derrotero de lo camionada, visto y observado en la visita que lo hizo a los presidios de la Nueva España septentrional.* Ed. Vito Allesio Robles. Mexico City: Secretaría de la Defensa Nacional.

Robbins, C. S., B. Brun, and H. S. Zim

1983   *Birds of North America.* New York: Golden.

Ruiz, José Francisco

1972   *Report on the Indians of Texas in 1828.* Ed. John C. Ewers. Trans. Georgette Dorn. New Haven: Yale University Press.

Ryan, Bruce

1969   *Social and Cultural Change.* New York: Ronald Press Co.

Schieffelin, Edward L.

1976   *The Sorrow of the Lonely and the Burning of the Dancers.* New York: St. Martin's Press.

Schlesier, Karl

1972   "Rethinking the Dismal River Aspect and the Plains Athabascans A.D. 1692–1768." *Plains Anthropologist* 17:101–133.

Schroeder, Alfred H.

1974   *A Study of the Apache Indians.* New York: Garland Press.

Schurtz, Heinrich

1902   *Altersklassen und Männerbunde.* Berlin, Germany: n.p.

Schweitzer, Marjorie M.

1981   "The Otoe-Missouria War Mothers: Women of Valor." *Moccasin Tracks* 7(1) (September):4–8.

1983   "The War Mothers: Reflections of Space and Time." *Papers in Anthropology* (University of Oklahoma Department of Anthropology) 24(2):157–171.

Scollon, Ron, and Suzanne Scollon

1979   *Linguistic Convergence: An Ethnography of Speaking at Ft. Chipewyan, Alberta.* New York: Academic Press.

1981   *Narrative, Literacy, and Face in Interethnic Communication.* Norwood, N.J.: Ablex.

Scott, Hugh Lennox

1911   "Notes on the Kado, or Sun Dance of the Kiowa." *American Anthropologist* 13(3):345–379.

Secoy, Frank Raymond

1953   *Changing Military Patterns of the Great Plains Indians: Seventeenth Century through Early Nineteenth Century.* Monographs of the American Ethnological Society, 21. Seattle: University of Washington Press.

Service, Elman R.

1962   *Primitive Social Organization: An Evolutionary Perspective.* New York: Random House.

Shaul, David L.

1986   "Linguistic Adaptation and the Great Basin." *American Antiquity* 51:415–416.

Shimkin, Demitri B.

1940   "Shoshone-Comanche Origins and Migrations." *Proceedings of the Sixth Pacific Scientific Conference*, vol. 4. Berkeley: University of California Press.

1947   "Wind River Shoshone Ethnogeography." *Anthropological Records* (University of California) 5(4):4.

1953   "The Wind River Shoshone Sun Dance." *Bureau of American Ethnology Bulletin* 151:397–484. Anthropological Papers 41. Washington, D.C.: Bureau of American Ethnology.

1980   "Comanche-Shoshoni Words of Acculturation 1786–1848." *Journal of the Steward Anthropological Society* 11(2):195–241.

1986   "Eastern Shoshone." In *Handbook of North American Indians*, vol. 11, *Great Basin*, ed. Warren L. d'Azevedo, pp. 308–335. Washington, D.C.: Smithsonian Institution.

1992   Personal communication to the author.

n.d.   "The Wind River Shoshone, Historic and Ethnographic Sketches." American Heritage Center, University of Wyoming, Laramie. Series III, Box 18, Folder 9. Collection No. 9942.

Simmons, Marc

1967   *Border Comanches: Seven Spanish Colonial Documents 1785–1819.* Translated, edited, and with an introduction by Marc Simmons. Santa Fe: Stagecoach Press.

Skinner, Alanson

1915a   "Political Organization, Cults, and Ceremonials of the Plains-Cree." *Anthropological Papers of the American Museum of Natural History* 11(9):513–542.

1915b   "Ponca Societies and Dances." *Anthropological Papers of the American Museum of Natural History* 11(9):777–801.

1915c   "Societies of the Iowa." *Anthropological Papers of the American Museum of Natural History* 11(9):679–740.

Slotkin, James S.

1975   *The Peyote Religion: A Study in Indian-White Relations.* New York: Octagon Books (originally published New York: Free Press, 1956).

Smith, Ralph A.

1959   "Account of the Journey of Bernard de la Harpe: Discovery Made by Him of Several Nations Situated in the West." *Southwestern Historical Quarterly* 62:246–259, 371–385, 525–541.

1970   "The Comanche Sun over Mexico." *West Texas Historical Association Year Book* 46:25–62.

Snow, Dean R.

1994   *The Iroquois.* The Peoples of America. Cambridge: Blackwell Publishing Co.

Spicer, Edward H.

1961   *Introduction in Perspectives in American Indian Culture Change.* Chicago: University of Chicago Press.

1971   "Persistent Cultural Systems: A Comparative Study of Identity Systems That Can Adapt to Contrasting Environments." *Science* 174:795–800.

Spier, Leslie

1921a   "Notes on the Kiowa Sun Dance." In Clark Wissler, ed., *Sun Dance of the Plains Indians,* pp. 433–450. American Museum of Natural History, Anthropological Papers, 16, pt. 6. New York: American Museum of Natural History.

1921b   "The Sun Dance of the Plains Indians: Its Development and Diffusion." *Anthropological Papers of the American Museum of Natural History* 16(7): 451–527.

Stephan, Randy

1978   *The Horse Soldier 1776–1943 — The United States Cavalryman: His Uniforms, Arms, Accoutrements, and Equipment,* vol. 2, *The Frontier, the Mexican War, the Civil War, the Indian Wars 1851–1880.* Norman: University of Oklahoma Press.

Steward, Julian H.

1938   *Basin and Plateau Aboriginal Sociopolitical Groups.* Bulletin 120, Bureau of American Ethnology. Washington, D.C.: Government Printing Office.

Stewart, Frank Henderson

1977   *Fundamentals of Age-group Systems.* New York: Academic Press.

Stewart, Omer C.

1987   *Peyote Religion: A History.* Norman: University of Oklahoma Press.

Sturtevant, William C.

1966   "Anthropology, History, and Ethnohistory." *Ethnohistory* 13:1–52.

Swanton, John R.

1952   "The Kiowa-Apache." In *The Indian Tribes of North America,* pp. 296–297. Bureau of American Ethnology Bulletin 145. Washington, D.C.: Government Printing Office.

Tate, Michael L.

1977   "John P. Clum and the Origins of an Apache Constabulary, 1874–77." *American Indian Quarterly* 3 (Summer).

Tefft, Stanton K.

1960a "Cultural Adaptation: The Case of the Comanche Indians." Ph.D. diss., University of Minnesota.
1960b "Sociopolitical Change in Two Migrant Tribes." *Proceedings of the Minnesota Academy of Sciences* 28: 103–111.
1961 "The Comanche Kinship System in Historical Perspective." *Plains Anthropologist* 6(14): 252–262.
1965 "From Band to Tribe on the Plains." *Plains Anthropologist* 10: 166–170.

Ten Kate, H. F. C.

1885a "Notes ethnographiques sur les Comanches." *Revue d'Ethnographie* 4: 120–136.
1885b *Reizen en Onderzoekingen in Noord-Amerika*. Leiden: E. J. Brill.

Thomas, Alfred B.

1929 "An Eighteenth Century Comanche Document." *American Anthropologist* 31: 289–298.
1932 *Forgotten Frontiers: A Study of the Spanish Indian Policy of Don Juan Bautista de Anza, Governor of New Mexico 1777–1787*. Norman: University of Oklahoma Press.
1935 *After Coronado: Spanish Exploration Northeast of New Mexico, 1696–1727*. Norman: University of Oklahoma Press.
1940 *The Plains Indians and New Mexico, 1751–1778*. Albuquerque: University of New Mexico Press.
1941 *Teodoro de Croix and the Northern Frontier of New Spain*. Norman: University of Oklahoma Press.

Thurman, Melburne D.

1980 "Comanche." In *Dictionary of Indian Tribes of Americas*, vol. 2, pp. 4–13. Newport Beach, Calif.: American Indian Publishers.
1982 "A New Interpretation of Comanche Social Organization." *Current Anthropology* 23: 578–579.
1987 "Reply to Gelo." *Current Anthropology* 28: 552–555.

Thwaites, Reuben Gold

1904 *Original Journals of the Lewis and Clark Expedition, 1804–06*. 8 vols. New York: Dodd and Mead.

Trigger, Bruce G.

1982 "Ethnohistory: Problems and Prospects." *Ethnohistory* 29: 1–19.
1986 "Ethnohistory: The Unfinished Edifice." *Ethnohistory* 33: 253–267.

Tsonetokoy, Dewey D.

1988 "The 1830s, Golden Age of Kiowas." In *Anadarko Daily News Visitors Guide*. Anadarko, Okla.: *Anadarko Daily News*.

Turner, Victor W.

1967   *The Forest of Symbols: Aspects of Ndembu Ritual.* Ithaca, N.Y.: Cornell University Press.

1968   *The Drums of Affliction: A Study of Religious Practices among the Ndembu of Zambia.* Oxford: Clarendon Press.

1977   "Symbols in African Ritual." In *Symbolic Anthropology: A Reader in the Study of Symbols and Meanings,* ed. Janet L. Dolgin, David S. Kemnitzer, and David M. Schneider, pp. 183–194. New York: Columbia University Press.

Twitchell, Ralph E., comp.

1914   *The Spanish Archives of New Mexico.* 2 vols. Cedar Rapids, Ia.: Torch Press.

Tyler, H. A.

1979   *Pueblo Birds and Myths.* Norman: University of Oklahoma Press.

Tyrrell, J. B., ed.

1916   *David Thompson's Narrative of His Explorations in Western America, 1784–1912.* Toronto: Champlain Society.

Vansina, Jan

1965   *Oral Tradition: A Study in Historical Methodology.* Chicago: Aldine Press.
1985   *Oral Traditions as History.* Madison: University of Wisconsin Press.

Voget, Fred W.

1956   "The American Indian in Transition, Reformation and Accommodation." *American Anthropologist* 58:249–263.

Walker, James R.

1982   *Lakota Society.* Ed. Raymond J. DeMallie. Lincoln: University of Nebraska Press.

Wallace, Anthony F. C.

1956   "Revitalization Movements." *American Anthropologist* 58:264–281.

Wallace, Ernest, and E. Adamson Hoebel

1952   *The Comanches: Lords of the South Plains.* Norman: University of Oklahoma Press.

Wedel, Mildred Mott, and Raymond J. DeMallie

1980   "The Ethnohistorical Approach in Plains Area Studies." In *Anthropology on the Great Plains,* ed. Margot Liberty and W. Raymond Wood, pp. 110–128. Lincoln: University of Nebraska Press.

Wheat, Carl I.

1957   *Mapping the Transmississippi West, 1540–1861.* 5 vols. San Francisco: Institute of Historical Cartography.

Wheeler-Voegelin, E.

1954 "An Ethnohistorian's Viewpoint." *Ethnohistory* 1:166–171.

1955–1956 "The Northern Paiute of Central Oregon: A Chapter in Treaty Making." *Ethnohistory* 2:95–132, 241–272; 3:1–10.

White, Richard

1991 *The Middle Ground: Indians, Empires, and Republics in the Great Lakes.* New York: Cambridge University Press.

Whyte, W. F.

1944 "Age-Grading of the Plains Indians." *Man* 44:68–72.

Wilhelm, Paul, Duke of Württemberg

1973 *Travels in North America, 1822–24.* Norman: University of Oklahoma Press.

Wilson, H. C.

1963 "An Inquiry into the Nature of Plains Indian Cultural Development." *Ethnology* 65:355–369.

Winfrey, Dorman H., and James M. Day

1966 *The Indian Papers of Texas and the Southwest, 1825–1916.* 5 vols. Austin: Pemberton Press.

Winick, Charles

1968 *Dictionary of Anthropology.* Totowa, N.J.: Littlefield, Adams and Co.

Wissler, Clark

1912 "Societies and Ceremonial Associations of the Oglala Division of the Teton-Dakota." *Anthropological Papers of the American Museum of Natural History* 11(1):1–100.

1913 "Societies and Dance Associations of the Blackfoot Indians." *Anthropological Papers of the American Museum of Natural History* 11(4):357–460.

1914 "The Influence of the Horse in the Development of Plains Culture." *American Anthropologist* 16(1):1–25.

1916a *Shamanistic and Dancing Societies.* Anthropological Papers 11. New York: American Museum of Natural History.

1927 *North American Indians of the Plains.* New York: American Museum of Natural History.

Wissler, Clark, ed.

1916 *Societies of the Plains Indians.* Anthropological Papers 11. New York: American Museum of Natural History.

Witherspoon, Gary

1977 *Language and Art in the Navajo Universe.* Ann Arbor: University of Michigan Press.

Wright, Gary A.

1977   "The Shoshonean Migration Problem." *Plains Anthropologist* 23:113–137.

Wright, Muriel H.

1946   "The American Indian Exposition in Oklahoma." *Chronicles of Oklahoma* 24(2):158–165.

1951   *A Guide to the Indian Tribes of Oklahoma.* Norman: University of Oklahoma Press.

Young, Gloria A.

1981   "Powwow Power: Perspectives on Historic and Contemporary Intertribalism." Ph.D. diss., Indiana University, Bloomington.

Young, Robert W.

1983   "Apachean Languages." In *Handbook of North American Indians*, gen. ed. William C. Sturtevant, vol. 10, pp. 393–400. Washington, D.C.: Smithsonian Institution.

INDEX

AIVA (American Indian Veterans Association), 344

allotments. *See* Kiowa Indian Agency

American Legion posts, 6; dissatisfaction with, 396. *See also* V.F.W. posts

anthropological theory: acculturation studies, 18–19; consolidation, 244, 250, 347; cultural revivals, 20–25, 226–227, 230, 339–343; culture change and syncretism, 20, 388–389; discussion, 15–30; ethnographic sources, 16–18; New and Old Indian History, 19, 418; religious focus on, 24; symbolic studies, 25–28

Apache John, 198, 210, 232, 233

Apache Manatidie or Blackfeet Society: account of, 200–212; bajraye, 211–212; benefit dances, 242–246; charitable aspect, 200–201, 242–246; charter of, 232; Chalepah Apache Blackfeet Society, 210, 232–239; current ceremony, 236–246, 410; dog taboo, 204; in early 1900s, 225–226; factionalism in, 235; frequent performances of, 243–246; and funeral rites, 202–203; and Native American Church, 227, 242–243; and raiding and warfare, 201–202; Redbone Apache Blackfeet Society, 232–239, 250; revival and division, 210, 229–236; Scalp Dances for, 205; similarities to other societies, 55, 204, 212, 220–223, 241, 416–417; staffs and keepers, 202–208; symbolic role of society, 245–250; whipman, 209–211

Apache military societies: account of, 177–250; bed wetting cure, 198; Blackfeet Society (*See* Apache Manatidie Society); decline of, 221–229; functions, 196; Izuwe Society, 219–220; Klintidie Society, 212–215; membership and organization, 192–193; naming ceremonies, 198; Rabbit Society, 197–200, 231; reanalysis of, 220–222; social organization of, 188–192; society partners in, 193, 195–196; and Sun Dance, 55, 192, 195, 196, 201, 204, 218, 224; Swift Fox Society, 215–216; synonymy of, 192, 194; War Dance Society, 216–219, 228; in warfare, 201–202, 213

Apache Veterans Association, 236, 248; Business Committee, 184; concern for ethnic identity, 229–231, 250; early cultural history, 177–186; enrollment quantum, 184; ethnography on, 186–188; ethnonyms, 177–182; Flag Song, 225; Gourd Clan, 248; Gourd Dance, 244; intermarriage, 180, 446 n.9; Kiowa ethnonyms, 35–36; language, 178, 187; medicine bundles, 180, 190–191, 197, 199, 233–234; medicine or supernatural power, 191; political autonomy of, 186–187; population, 184–186,